Praise for *Wooden*

"A meticulously researched and evenhanded assessment."
—*The New York Times Book Review*

"A clear-eyed look at a flawed but extraordinary man."
—*The Dallas Morning News*

"This is the first comprehensive biography about what made him into the man and hero he was."
—*New York Post*

"Seth Davis, the *Sports Illustrated* writer and CBS Sports analyst, is one of the country's most authoritative voices on college basketball. . . . *Wooden: A Coach's Life* [is] an exhaustively reported biography of the late, legendary UCLA coach."
—*Moment* magazine

"There was a definite mystique about Wooden. Seth Davis's book brings us both inside the curtains, and the mystique. . . . [*Wooden* is] a great book about both a man and an era."
—*Providence Journal*

"A comprehensive and crisply written biography of a legendary coach . . . John Wooden may well be the closest the sports world has had to a secular saint in the last half century [and he] has long stood as a giant in the world of college sports. In revealing the real man behind the legend, Davis has done honor to the legacy of a true gentleman."
—*Kirkus Reviews* (starred review)

"Genuinely exciting . . . A multidimensional, nearly cradle-to-grave portrait of a highly successful and revered coach and teacher [and] a history of the evolution of college basketball and profiles of many of its stars."
—*Booklist* (starred review)

"An unusually rich and illuminating portrait . . . In this hefty but well-paced account, *Sports Illustrated* scribe Davis provides entertaining play-by-play and color commentary on Wooden's dynasty-building, key games, and the grueling, authoritarian methods . . . he used to impart his innovative fast-break system."
—*Publishers Weekly*

"This is a superb biography, worthy of its subject. With deep research, clear writing, and objective thinking, Seth Davis has cut through the

mythology to present John Wooden and his UCLA dynasty in a fresh and compulsively readable way." —David Maraniss, author of
When Pride Still Mattered: A Life of Vince Lombardi

"*Wooden: A Coach's Life* is a truly remarkable achievement. Seth Davis has produced the most authoritative, comprehensive, and entertaining book ever written on John Wooden. He immerses us in every area of Wooden's life and provides a detailed and rich picture of this complicated and iconic man. I simply couldn't put it down. *Wooden* is a masterwork." —Jay Bilas, ESPN college basketball analyst and
author of *Toughness*

"Relentlessly researched and written with devastating detail and texture, Seth Davis has delivered the definitive biography on the most important figure in college basketball history. There are complexities in the simplicity of Wooden and his UCLA dynasty, and Davis peels back the myths to bring light to the truths. This is Wooden, in full."
—Adrian Wojnarowski, author of *The Miracle of St. Anthony* and Yahoo! Sports NBA columnist

"Who knew that John Wooden was a pool shark? That's just one of the many fascinating revelations in Seth Davis's insightful bio of the man who remains the gold standard for basketball coaches. No one needed humanizing more than the Wizard, and Seth figured out how to do it. Goodness gracious sakes alive (as Wooden would say), this is a terrific book." —Jack McCallum, author of the *New York Times* bestseller *Dream Team*

WOODEN

WOODEN

A Coach's Life

SETH DAVIS

ST. MARTIN'S GRIFFIN

NEW YORK

www.stmartins.com

Designed by Kelly S. Too

The Library of Congress has cataloged the Times Books edition as follows:

Davis, Seth.
    Wooden : a coach's life / Seth Davis. — First edition.
        p. cm.
    Includes bibliographical references and index.
    ISBN 978-0-8050-9280-6 (hardcover)
    ISBN 978-0-8050-9941-6 (e-book)
    1. Wooden, John, 1910–2010.   2. Basketball coaches—United States—Biography.
I. Title.
    GV884.W66D38 2014
    796.323092—dc23
    [B]

                                                                    2013020209

                    ISBN 978-1-250-06085-3 (trade paperback)

St. Martin's Griffin books may be purchased for educational, business, or promotional use. For information on bulk purchases, please contact the Macmillan Corporate and Premium Sales Department at 1-800-221-7945, extension 5442, or write to specialmarkets@macmillan.com.

First published in hardcover by Times Books, an imprint of Henry Holt and Company, LLC

First St. Martin's Griffin Edition: January 2015

10 9 8 7 6 5 4 3 2 1

For my teachers—

Zachary, Noah, and Gabriel

"I've always said I wish all my really good friends in coaching would win one national championship. And those I don't think highly of, I wish they would win several."

—JOHN WOODEN

CONTENTS

WOODEN

The Den

The first thing you noticed were the books. Big books, little books, picture books, children's books, art books, religious books, coaching books, sports books, fiction books, science books. Before I walked through the door, they were there to greet me in tall, neat piles in the front hallway. The books were stacked on floors, lined up on tables, piled on desks, jammed into bookcases. The apartment was barely two thousand square feet, yet it seemed that most of it was covered by something that could be read.

John Wooden was careful not to trip over the books as he made his way to his favorite easy chair in the den. Another dozen or so stood on the floor beside the chair, lined up as if on a shelf. The coffee table that sat in front of the television was likewise covered, a source of irritation for a man with a compulsive need for order. "Organization was one of my strengths for a long time, but now just look at that table with all that stuff on it," he said as he invited me to sit on the couch. I asked Wooden how many of the books in that room he had read. "Maybe half," he replied. "But I've browsed them all."

It was September 2006. Wooden was not quite ninety-six years old. Even at his advanced age, he was still a student of the world, eager to collect one more crumb of wisdom that he could dispense to the next friend, interviewer, former player, or stranger who came calling. Though his eyes were not as good as they used to be, and though he tired easily, this old widower still turned to books during those rare, quiet hours when he didn't have a visitor or the phone wasn't ringing. Besides keeping him company in the present, they also served as a tether to his past, a dog-eared monument to the person who influenced him more than any other: his father, Joshua Hugh Wooden.

Hugh, as he was known, loved reading, both to himself and to his children. Though he did not have any formal education past high school, he was so facile with the English language that when he did crossword puzzles, he invented ways to make them more challenging. "For instance, he'd do it in a spiral form until he'd end up putting the last letter right in the middle of it," said Billy Wooden, John's younger brother. After a hard day's work, Hugh loved nothing more than to sit down, crack open the Bible or another book, and read poetry to his four sons by the light of an oil lamp.

"I can just see my dad as I see you, if I close my eyes," Wooden said, doing just that. He channeled Hugh as he recited: *By the shores of Gitche Gumee, / by the shining Big-Sea-Water, / stood the wigwam of Noko-mis, / daughter of the moon Nokomis. . . .* Upon completing the verse by Longfellow, Wooden opened his eyes. "We had no electricity, no running water. He would read to us from the scriptures practically every night. For some reason, of all the poems he read, that's the only one I can just picture him doing."

When he laid down his books, however, Hugh did not have a lot to say. "He tried to get his ideas across, maybe not in so many words, but by action. He walked it," John said. Hugh didn't lecture his boys so much as he sprinkled seeds along their paths. When John graduated from the eighth grade, Hugh handed his son a small card upon which he had written his "Seven-Point Creed." John later carried that piece of paper in his wallet until it wore out, whereupon he rewrote Hugh's words on a fresh card. After he retired from coaching basketball at UCLA, John had the creed printed up on slick plastic cards and handed them out so others could plant Hugh's seeds into their wallets as well.

The first of the seven points paraphrased a line from *Hamlet*: "Be true to yourself." Number four read, "Drink deeply from good books." So John drank. As a young boy growing up in Indiana, he dove into the *Leather-stocking* tales and Tom Swift series. His favorite teachers at Martinsville High School were his English teachers. When he attended Purdue University, he became close with Martha Miller, an elderly librarian. Once, when he was coaching basketball at UCLA, Wooden was so taken by the enthusiasm evinced by a guest lecturer that he wandered into Powell Library to read more on the topic. He devoured Zane Grey's westerns and Leo Buscaglia's motivationals. Though his all-time favorite book was *The Robe* by Lloyd Douglas, his interest was truly piqued by books about his favorite historical figures—Winston Churchill, Mahatma Gandhi, Abraham Lincoln, Mother Teresa. He lost count of how many books on those last two he had received as gifts.

Then there were the poets. Dickens, Yeats, Tennyson, Poe, Byron, Shakespeare. Especially Shakespeare. In college, Wooden spent an entire semester studying *Macbeth*, followed by another semester just on *Hamlet*. His favorite sportswriter was Grantland Rice, who penned many of his columns in verse. Besides being the coauthor of nearly two dozen books, including four children's books, Wooden was himself a prolific amateur poet. An idea would strike him on his morning walk, and he would come home and scrawl some doggerel. He watched John Glenn orbit the Earth and Neil Armstrong walk on the moon, and he wrote poems about how those events made him feel. He set a goal of writing one hundred poems and assembling them in a compendium for his family. He structured the book into five tidy parts that reflected his love of balance: twenty poems each on family, faith, patriotism, nature, and fun. Even when he was well into his nineties, Wooden could still recite scores of poems from memory.

During the final years of his life, Wooden received countless visitors in that modest, book-strewn den. In between tales of championships won and players coached, as he recounted the fascinating twists and turns of his long life, Wooden would invariably bring the conversation back to the man who raised him. When he closed his eyes and recited Longfellow to me, his mind was transported back to the farm. But if it felt like a full-circle moment, it really wasn't. You can't circle back to a place you never left.

That, in essence, is the story of John Wooden's life, a quintessentially American tale that spans nearly a century. More than anyone else, he could appreciate how his story neatly divides into four balanced seasons. During the spring, our protagonist takes root on his family's spare midwestern farm. He alights as a young adult in a glamorous town by the Pacific, reaches prodigious heights of fame and glory in middle age, and derives warmth from relationships old and new that sustain him during a long, peaceful winter. Like so many great narratives, the accepted version, the one Wooden himself told, often diverged from fact, as the myth overtook the man. But when all the glorification is stripped away, the person at the center of our tale remains very much the same boy who was planted in the Indiana soil at the turn of the twentieth century. All those friends, interviewers, players, and strangers who came to that den the way I did, we all wanted to know the same thing: *How did you do it?* He could never make the answer clear enough, perhaps because it was too simple for a complicated time. Everyone wanted the old man's secrets, but he had no secrets, only seeds. For all the things that John Wooden accomplished—as a player, a coach, and most of all, a teacher—he never forgot his roots, or the man who planted them.

PART ONE

Spring

1

Hugh

John Robert Wooden enjoyed unparalleled success as a college basketball coach, and after he retired he built a veritable industry around his own personal definition of *success*. Yet the most lasting impression his father made on John was the manner in which he responded to a failure.

It happened in the summer of 1925, when John was fourteen years old. John, his parents, and his three brothers were living in the tiny town of Centerton, Indiana, on a sixty-acre farm they had inherited from the parents of John Wooden's mother, Roxie Anna. They grew wheat, corn, alfalfa, potatoes, watermelons, tomatoes, and timothy grass, which was used to feed cattle and horses. The town had few amenities—a water tower, a general store, a grade school—and the Woodens' life was not easy. But they never wanted for anything, so long as they were willing to work for it.

If they needed bread, Roxie baked it. If they wanted butter, Hugh churned it. If they needed water, they hand-pumped it from a well. When winter came and the kids got cold, their parents would heat up bricks on the stove and wrap them in warm towels. If they wanted to relieve themselves, they used the three-hole outhouse in the backyard. The family got eggs from their chickens and milk from their cows. They started off every morning with a hearty bowl of oatmeal. The house had just two bedrooms, so the brothers slept two to a bed. "We didn't have much money," Billy Wooden said. "Father worked for a dollar a day in the twenties, but ours was a happy family. We were always having company."

The setback came shortly after Hugh purchased about thirty hogs from a local farmer. Hogs were expensive, so he had to borrow money from a bank and put up his house as collateral. Hugh needed to inoculate the animals against cholera, but the vaccination serum he purchased turned out to be defective. All the hogs died. That, coupled with an untimely drought that killed off most of their crops, prompted the bank to foreclose on the farm. Just like that, Hugh Wooden's sole means for supporting his family was gone.

One of the handwritten lessons that Hugh passed to his four sons was what he called his "Two Sets of Threes": *Never lie, never cheat, never steal. Don't whine, don't complain, don't make excuses.* Here was the chance to walk what he talked. "Through it all, Dad never winced. He laid no blame on the merchant who had sold him the bad serum, didn't curse the weather, and had no hatred toward the banker," John would write decades later. "As instructive as it was to hear him recite the two sets of threes, seeing him abide by them as he lost the farm had a most powerful effect on me. That's where I came to see that what you do is more important than what you say you'll do."

Hugh's response was emblematic of the world in which John Wooden was raised. This was Depression-era Indiana, a time and place that valued masculine self-sufficiency. Feelings were demonstrated, not articulated. If Hugh ever embraced his sons or told them "I love you," John rarely spoke or wrote of it. Likewise, Wooden's parents were not physically affectionate with each other in front of their children. Johnny knew they were in love by the way they treated each other. They had married young—Hugh was twenty, Roxie was sixteen. John was their third child, born October 14, 1910, in Martinsville. (For most of his life, John claimed the town of Hall, Indiana, as his birthplace, but shortly before he died, a group of local researchers discovered he had been mistaken all those years.) When Johnny was born, Hugh was working as a buttermaker at a creamery in Martinsville. Three years later, the family moved to Hall, thirteen miles away, where Hugh worked on a small farm owned by a man named Cassius Ludlow. From there they moved to Monrovia, where he took a position as a rural mail carrier. Some of Johnny's favorite childhood memories involved riding with his dad on his horse-drawn carriage and helping him wash the buggy in a stream until it sparkled. When Johnny was six years old, his maternal grandfather passed away, leaving to his daughter the farm in Centerton. After the family lost that farm, nine years later they moved back to Martinsville, where Hugh and Roxie stayed for good.

By that time, the family had endured hardship far more painful than losing the farm. Johnny's older sister, Cordelia, died of diphtheria on January 5, 1913, at the age of three years and nine months. "Little Cordelia, as she was familiarly known, was a loving, bright and obedient child," read her obituary in the *Martinsville Democrat*. "She was greatly loved by all who knew her. Her last sickness was of short duration. She was confined to her bed with diphtheria which developed into pneumonia and paralysis of the heart. Her suffering was great, although she bore it with the patience of a lamb, always ready to take her medicine and do as she was told. She leaves a loving father, mother, two dear little brothers, four grandparents, and a host of relatives and friends to mourn their loss."

Three and a half months later, Roxie gave birth to another baby girl, who died during delivery. One can only imagine the wrenching anguish Roxie must have felt as she returned to the unremarkable cemetery in Centerton to bury her second daughter in four months. The plot would be marked with a gravestone that read, "INFANT."

The death of his sisters insured that John would grow up in a male-dominated household. In his later life, he wrote and spoke often about his father, but he seldom mentioned his mother. When he did, it was often in passing. "I think the person probably who had the most influence on me throughout were my mother and father, particularly my father," he said in one of his typical locutions. If Hugh was omnipresent in John's life story, Roxie was the quiet, sad shadow in the background. She was the skilled seamstress who stitched socks to create makeshift basketballs for her sons. The diligent maid who handwashed their clothes, mopped their floors, cooked their meals. The poor gal who walked on feet that were deformed from all those years of wearing shoes that didn't fit. "She was probably depressed," said Andy Hill, who played for Wooden at UCLA from 1970 to 1972 and became extremely close to him during the final decade of his life. "But in those days they didn't call it that. You just sucked it up." Wooden's daughter, Nan, added, "Daddy said her heart was broken."

Though the family didn't have much money, Hugh would sometimes take Roxie into Martinsville and splurge for dinner at Riley's Café. John often cited Hugh as an exemplar of the Reverend Theodore Hesburgh's credo that "the best thing a man can do for his children is love their mother." But without any sisters around, Roxie was the only feminine presence in Johnny's life, and she was not a strong one. That caused him to be intensely shy around girls. "John did not have an active social life as a kid," his younger brother, Danny, said. "He was concentrating on his school work and working and being with his family."

Hugh also embodied another of John's favorite credos: "There is nothing stronger than gentleness." Exhibit A was Hugh's interactions with animals. The Woodens had two mules on their farm, Jack and Kate, but Hugh, who, John said, was strong enough to bend a thick iron bar with his bare hands, refused to whip them. John loved to tell the story of the day he and his father came upon a man who was trying to retrieve two horses from a gravel pit. "The man was whipping them," John said. "My dad said, 'Let me take them.' The horses were frothing at the mouth. My dad just said to them, 'Get on your feet; let's go.' He gave one of the horses a light tap and then pulled them together. Somehow I never forgot that." John said his father had the same effect on other animals. "Dogs that would scare me, he'd pet 'em and they would wag their tails."

There was, however, one incident where Hugh was not so gentle. Johnny and his older brother, Maurice had been fooling around in a barn when Maurice grabbed a pitchfork and flipped a pile of manure at Johnny's face. Johnny lunged at Maurice in anger and cursed at him. Hugh had been standing nearby, but instead of reproaching Maurice for instigating the fight, he came down on Johnny for his foul language. Profanity was forbidden in the Wooden household—Hugh was a devout Christian, and John always claimed he never once heard him swear—and Hugh wanted to make sure Johnny understood the severity of his transgression. He whipped his boy with a switch.

It is odd that a man would refuse to beat an animal yet be willing to use a switch on his own son, but John didn't see the inconsistency. "It was the only time I remember him using it," he said of the switch. At any rate, Johnny learned his lesson. From then on, he, too, stayed away from profanity.

Above all else, Hugh imbued his sons with a core philosophy that would guide Johnny throughout his childhood, his marriage, and especially his playing and coaching careers. It was a gospel that would come to define John more than any other. "Dad tried to get across to us never try to be better than someone else. Learn from others and never cease trying to be the best you can be at whatever you're doing," he said. "Maybe that won't be better than someone else, but that's no problem. It will be better than somebody else, probably, but somebody else is going to be better than that. Don't worry about that. If you get yourself too engrossed in things over which you have no control, it's going to adversely affect the things over which you have control."

"I think I had it pretty good, learning from Dad," John added. "He told me to try to avoid peaks and valleys."

Later in life, when John wasn't quoting his father or telling parables about him, he was serving up Hugh's teachings in bite-sized portions. His own children began their mornings with a hearty bowl of oatmeal. If one of Wooden's basketball players uttered a profanity during practice, he was through for the day. Then there was the time after he retired when one of his former players at UCLA, Swen Nater, showed Wooden his new dog. "Do you hit him?" Wooden asked.

Yes, Nater confessed, sometimes he did.

"Don't," Wooden replied. "It never works."

Hugh's decision to move the family back to Martinsville after losing the farm turned out to be a smart one. The town was prospering due to bountiful artesian wells that had been dug there in the late nineteenth century. The water, which was full of minerals, had been accidentally discovered by prospectors who were searching for natural gas and oil. The liquid was said to have curative powers, even though it smelled rancid. Nearly a dozen sanitariums were built in and around Martinsville. These facilities were part spas, part hospitals, and they attracted people from all over the Midwest. The largest and most opulent of these resorts was the Home Lawn Sanitarium, which featured a dining room appointed with lush carpet and crystal chandeliers. Hugh found a job as a masseur at the Home Lawn. "I think that's why Daddy always has been such a generous tipper," Nan Wooden said. "A big part of Grandaddy's income was based on tips."

The move to Martinsville also exposed Hugh's sons to a growing local passion. It was a brand-new game called "basket ball," and though all the Wooden boys were quite good at it, Johnny was the best of them all.

Their first goal was an old tomato basket that hung on a hayloft inside their barn in Centerton. Hugh had popped the bottom out and tacked it up so that Johnny and his brothers could blow off steam. "He said there's always time for play. That's after the chores and the studies are done, of course," John said. Eventually, Hugh took a forge and replaced the basket with a real hoop made out of iron. Roxie made a ball by stuffing an old sock with rags and sewing it closed. Maurice was a good athlete—he later played football, baseball, and basketball for Franklin College—but even though his nickname was "Cat," Maurice was no match for Johnny's quickness and toughness.

At that time, the entire town of Centerton contained barely a hundred people, yet every Saturday and Sunday, the basketball court next to the grade school was teeming with kids. The court was not even paved; rather, it was made of sand and clay, a mixture chosen so it would dry quickly after it rained. The locals often referred to it as a "basketball diamond." In the wintertime, the kids often had to shovel snow off the court if they wanted to play. The school was just a few hundred yards up the road from the Woodens' house, and Hugh delighted in watching his boys play those weekend games. Hugh liked basketball, but his best sport was baseball, where he excelled as a pitcher. He even carved a diamond, *Field of Dreams*–like, amid the wheat and alfalfa on the family farm.

Centerton's school had three rooms for eight grades. The principal, who taught in the room for seventh- and eighth-graders, was a strapping young man named Earl Warriner. When Johnny was eleven years old, his dad allowed him to play basketball under Warriner's supervision. "Johnny says what helped him the most was the desire to play," Warriner said. "He wasn't a bully and neither was he a sissy. He had the grit to stay in there and fight." Wooden needed that grit to make up for his lack of size, but what really made him effective was his speed. "My trouble was trying to keep others up with him," Warriner said. "John was so much faster than everybody else, and he had his heart and soul in what he did."

Centerton's basketball team played a haphazard schedule of five or six games a year (weather permitting) against other schools in the area, including the junior high school team from Martinsville. The boys didn't have much by way of uniforms, just a bib to be worn on top of their overalls. "They were lucky if they had shoes," Warriner said. They played with a lopsided leather ball that often had to be unlaced and reinflated. Wooden later credited that ball, along with the lumpy court, with forcing him to develop into an expert dribbler.

However, it was baseball, not basketball, that was fast becoming Johnny's favorite sport. Though his diminutive stature prevented him from having much pop as a hitter, his quickness and agility made him an effective shortstop. "That little rat John," as Warriner called him, was still a teenager when he played for the town team alongside men who were in their twenties. "All he could do was get the ball over the infield, but he got more hits than anybody," Warriner said.

Young Johnny also fancied himself a bit of a practical joker. One day in winter, Warriner was feeling chilly while sitting in his office, so he went to the school's basement and asked a janitor named Hiram to turn up the heat. Hiram did as he was told, but the room was still freezing. They went back and forth several more times until Warriner checked the basement, where he discovered that the flue to his office had been shut.

Several months later, Warriner was walking around the school grounds and noticed that someone had written on the wall of an outdoor bathroom, "I turned off the furnace. Guess who?" Soon after, he was invited to dinner at the Woodens' house, where he revealed to the rascal that he knew his little secret. When Johnny asked Warriner how he found out, the principal replied, "John Bob, if you graded as many papers as I do, you'd know everybody's writing, too."

On the few occasions when Wooden was foolish enough to test Warriner, he paid a heavy price. Johnny was around nine years old when he and three of his classmates decided that they did not want to sing the national anthem at the morning assembly. So they pretended to sing it. The next day, Warriner called them out of the assembly, brought them into his office, and told them that if they didn't sing, they would get the business end of a paddle. They refused again, so Warriner brought them out and stung their behinds while all the other kids watched. One of the boys had worn two pairs of pants in anticipation of the punishment, but Warriner made him pull down the outer pair so he could properly feel his penance.

When Warriner's discipline combined one day with Johnny's love for basketball, the result was the ultimate life lesson. It happened when Wooden was in the eighth grade. Centerton was supposed to play a game against Hazelwood, but the game had been in doubt because of rain. The schools had called each other several times during the day to figure out whether they should play. They finally agreed to play when the skies cleared, but Wooden had not brought his game uniform to school. When Warriner asked him to go home and retrieve it during recess, Johnny refused, even though his house was right up the road. "I guess John wanted me to beg him to play," Warriner said.

Warriner told another player, named Freddy Gooch, that he would substitute for Wooden. Johnny was shocked. As soon as school was over, he raced home, got his uniform, and ran back to the school. He was there in plenty of time to warm up with his teammates, but when the game began, Warriner left him on the sideline. He stayed there during the entire contest, which Centerton lost. After the game was over, Warriner put his arm around Wooden's shoulder and said, "Johnny, we could have won with you in there, but winning just isn't that important."

It was a day the boy would never forget. "Johnny Wooden learned early in life he was not a necessary article," Wooden said during one of his frequent retellings of the incident. "It didn't make any difference how good I was in sports, business, or anything else. If I don't put out, I'm not worth a dime." He also learned that day that the bench was all the motivation a coach ever needed.

When Wooden graduated from the eighth grade, he faced the choice of going to Martinsville or Monrovia for high school. The Woodens were still a year away from losing the farm, and each town was the same distance from their home in Centerton. Martinsville, however, was a real hotbed for basketball. The school routinely drew huge crowds for games and had just won a state championship. The idea of making a living playing or teaching the sport wasn't remotely in Johnny's mind, but he did know that he loved playing and was very good at it. So he chose Martinsville. This was Indiana, after all. It was only natural that he would want to follow that bouncing ball.

2

The Artesians

On March 21, 1925, Dr. James Naismith arrived at the Indianapolis Exposition Building, where he had been invited by the Indiana High School Athletic Association to speak at the annual state championship game. There was, however, a problem at the door: the arena was full, and a security guard was not allowing anyone else inside. Naismith showed the man his ticket and his official's badge, but the guard wouldn't relent. Finally, a police captain approached and asked what was going on. When Naismith revealed his identity, the captain said, "Good Lord, man, why didn't you say so long ago?"

Naismith got a chuckle out of the mix-up. But what really tickled him was the spectacle that greeted him after the police captain showed him to his seat: a crowd of close to twenty thousand full-throated fans who were on hand to watch the sport Naismith had invented just thirty-four years before. That sight, Naismith wrote in his 1941 autobiography, *Basketball: Its Origin and Development*, "gave me a thrill that I shall not soon forget."

Thus did Naismith discover what those twenty thousand spectators already knew: basketball may have been conceived in Massachusetts, but it was born in Indiana.

"Basket ball," as it was still known, was part of an experiment that appealed to pious farm boys like Johnny Wooden. The organization that invented and proselytized the sport, the Young Men's Christian Association, or YMCA, advertised its mission as promoting a person's "mind, body and spirit." Wooden never had Naismith as a mentor per se, but the two were kindred spirits all the same. Like Wooden, Naismith grew up on a farm (in Ontario, Canada) where he learned the value of a hard day's work. He originally intended to become a minister, but upon graduating from the theological college at Montreal's McGill University,

Naismith decided he could have just as much impact through athletics as he could through the ministry. In 1890, he began formally studying at the YMCA's training school in Springfield, Massachusetts.

In those days, many religious scholars viewed athletics as a tool of the devil. A group of liberal Protestant ministers rebutted that way of thinking by launching a movement called "muscular Christianity." In the summer of 1891, the head of the Springfield YMCA's training school's physical education department, Dr. Luther Gulick, assigned Naismith the task of creating a new game that students could play indoors during the winter. Naismith used a phys ed class as his laboratory, but his first few attempts proved futile. Gymnastics was too boring, football and rugby were too rough, and there wasn't enough space in the gymnasium to play soccer or lacrosse.

Sitting in his office, Naismith tinkered with adapting a game he used to play as a boy in Canada called "Duck on a Rock," where points were scored by lofting small rocks so they would land on a bigger rock. But he was still concerned things would get too rough. That's when he experienced his eureka moment: *there should be a rule against running with the ball!* If the players couldn't run, they wouldn't be tackled. And if they weren't tackled, they wouldn't get hurt.

Excited by his breakthrough, Naismith sketched out thirteen rules using just 474 words. The rules did not include dribbling, so the players were stationary, and therefore safe. He then asked the building's superintendent to fetch him a pair of eighteen-inch boxes to use as goals. The superintendent didn't have any boxes, but he offered a couple of peach baskets instead. Naismith decided these would have to do.

The class consisted of eighteen students, and the first game featured nine men on each side. It was an instant hit. In the months that followed, Naismith continued to develop and modify his invention in the hope that other YMCAs and athletic clubs would adopt it in coming winters. He had two means of spreading the word. The first was the YMCA's official publication, *The Triangle*, which was delivered to clubs across the country. The second was the army of clergymen who came to study under Naismith at the training school in Springfield.

One such missionary was a Presbyterian minister named Nicolas McKay, who was the secretary of the YMCA in Crawfordsville, Indiana, sixty miles north of Martinsville. During the winter of 1892, Reverend McKay spent several months observing the new game and engaging in long talks with its inventor. He took his notes and a copy of Naismith's thirteen rules with him back to Crawfordsville, where he taught the game to his own students, including a pint-sized boy named Ward Lambert, who would later coach Johnny Wooden at Purdue University. Thus was a direct lineage established: Naismith to McKay to Lambert to Wooden.

The state of Indiana's first organized basketball game was played at the Crawfordsville YMCA on March 16, 1894. The next day's *Crawfordsville Journal* reported, "Basket ball is a new game, but if the interest taken in the contest last night between the teams of Crawfordsville and Lafayette is any criterion, it is bound to be popular." That was an understatement. As it turned out, the state provided the ideal platform for Naismith's game to lift off. Unlike neighboring Ohio, the Hoosier state did not have a bunch of urban manufacturing centers with schools that were big enough to field football teams. Rather, it was clustered with hundreds of small rural communities. The farming calendar was also not conducive to supporting football because autumn was harvest season. If people were going to look for entertainment, it had to be in winter—and indoors. Best of all, since basketball required only five men a side (as determined by a rule that was put in place in 1897), no school was too small to field a team. With high school teams popping up all over Indiana, the natural next step was a statewide tournament. The inaugural edition was held in 1911 at Indiana University in Bloomington, where Crawfordsville, fittingly, was crowned the first champion.

Martinsville was not going to be outdone by its neighbor. So in May 1923, the town set out on an ambitious project: to build the world's largest high school gymnasium. Thanks to the money spent by all those outsiders who came to visit Martinsville's gleaming spas, the town was able to complete its mission in swift fashion. On February 7, 1924, Martinsville unveiled its grandiose landmark in time for its first game against Shelbyville. On the morning of the game, the Martinsville *Daily Reporter* revealed that more than four thousand tickets had already been sold, and that 1,500 people from Shelbyville were planning to attend as well. Officially, the gym held 5,382 people, which was more than the entire population of the town. (That fact earned a mention in a popular, nationally syndicated column by Robert Ripley entitled "Believe It or Not.") Train lines that had been specially set up for the occasion brought spectators from neighboring burgs. Writers from Indianapolis, Vincennes, Frankfort, and Lafayette were on hand, as were a dozen or so local basketball coaches.

The occasion was so intoxicating that even the hometown Artesians' 47–41 loss couldn't dampen the enthusiasm. Under the headline "Gymnasium Dedication Was a Great Event," the next day's *Reporter* declared,

"The fact that this city now has a gymnasium that will take care of any crowd that wishes to witness a basket ball game overshadowed the feelings of regret because of the defeat. The big gym was packed to capacity, and the cheering throng, the music by the bands and the brilliant display of school colors presented a scene never to be forgotten by those who were present." Within a few years, dozens of communities across Indiana would build large high school gymnasiums of their own. From that point on, the sound of leather pounding wood would serve as the state's steady heartbeat.

By today's standards, a town of fewer than five thousand people is considered small, but back then the citizens of Martinsville justifiably thought of themselves as cosmopolitan and urbane, living as they did among the hustle and bustle of all those out-of-town visitors. Wooden was a small-town kid who seemed out of place when he arrived at Martinsville High School in the fall of 1924. "We Martinsville fellows were city slickers and he was a country boy," said Floyd Burns, a high school classmate. "John had on a drugstore outfit, snow white and clean, and we looked on him as a greenhorn. He was inexperienced, and he'd run faster than he could dribble and he'd lose the ball. But we all liked him and were amazed that he learned so quickly."

Since baseball was Johnny's favorite sport, he might have focused on that if Martinsville fielded a high school team, but it didn't. Nor did it have a football squad. Wooden lettered for two years in track—he finished sixth in the state in the 100-yard dash as a senior—but he devoted most of his energy to basketball. When that season came around, Wooden found himself under the tutelage of Glenn Curtis, known as the "Old Fox," who was emerging as one of the finest high school coaches in the state.

Curtis had already won two state championships, with Lebanon in 1918 and Martinsville in 1924. Like many coaches in those days, he deployed a plodding, ball-control offense that made it virtually impossible for opponents to recapture a lead once Curtis's teams seized it. This was aided by the rules that were in place at the time. After each made basket, the teams returned to center court for a jump ball. There was also no half-court line—that would not be added until 1932—and thus no ten-second counts or backcourt violations. And of course, the sport was decades away from implementing a shot clock. Thus, if a coach had guards who were reliable, quick dribblers, they could use the entire floor to avoid the defense and run out the clock.

Johnny did not hold the Old Fox in high esteem at first. His older brother, Cat, had been a member of Curtis's 1924 championship team, but Cat barely got into the games. Curtis appeared to confirm Johnny's fears early on while breaking up a fight between Wooden and one of his teammates. In Wooden's eyes, Curtis had unfairly backed up the other fellow. "You're not going to do to me what you did to my brother!" Johnny shouted. He flung off his jersey, his shorts, his shoes, and his socks, and he stormed off the floor in half-naked protest. He decided then and there to quit the team.

Curtis could have regarded Wooden as an intemperate fool and bade him good riddance. But he didn't. Instead, he spent the next two weeks trying to coax Wooden back on to the squad. Wooden resisted at first, but eventually he relented. He also never forgot his coach's graciousness in letting him back on the team, a lesson that Wooden would apply to his own players after he started coaching.

Wooden was fortunate to encounter early in his life a man who took his craft so seriously. Curtis systematically broke down the game into its smallest, simplest elements. His players worked for long stretches without using a basketball, and on his command they efficiently shuttled from drill to drill. A decade later, in 1936, Curtis started using a friend's movie camera to film games and instruct his teams. He was so impressed that he convinced the high school to purchase a camera so he could use it whenever he wanted. An official from the Eastman Kodak Company told the *Daily Reporter* that "no one has yet attempted to teach basketball through this medium."

Curtis was also renowned for delivering spine-tingling locker room speeches minutes before tip-off. That was one tactic that did not impress Wooden. Hugh had so emphatically pounded the importance of keeping an even keel that Johnny did not want his emotions to overtake him. However, once the games began, Wooden was struck by how Curtis regained his composure. On one occasion, when an opposing player took a cheap shot at Wooden, Curtis prevailed upon young Johnny not to retaliate. "They're trying to get you out of the game. Don't lose your temper," he told Wooden. Then he joked, "After the game is over, I'll take on the coach and you can take on the players."

Unlike his brother, Johnny was a starter on Curtis's team, and he led the Artesians to a sectional title in the 1926 Indiana state tournament.

The final rounds were to be played in Indianapolis at the Exposition Center, which was called the "cow barn" because twice a year it hosted livestock shows. Martinsville made it to the championship game—its third contest of the day—where it faced Marion High School. Marion's nickname was the "Giants," which was appropriate because the lineup featured the tallest player Wooden had ever seen: Charles "Stretch" Murphy, a six-foot-eight-inch center. The center-jump rule made having that kind of player an enormous asset. Wooden failed to score as Martinsville lost, 30–23.

Despite the disappointing finish, it was a terrific first season of varsity basketball for young Johnny. In the parlance of the day, he played the position of floor guard, which made him responsible for directing the offense much as a point guard does today. (A team's other guard at that time was typically called a back guard because he served as a de facto goalie, hanging back on defense to protect his team's basket.) As it turned out, Wooden's innate physical gifts were uniquely suited to this young sport. "I didn't have as much size as many, but I was quicker than most all, and that was my strength," he later recalled.

In addition, Wooden possessed a sturdy frame, thanks to all those years of physical labor on the farm. He also showed very little regard for his safety, which made him seem quicker because he was able to charge heedlessly toward the basket without slowing down to protect himself. "He could dribble with either hand, and when he'd drive for the basket, he'd go flying on the floor and into the end zone," one of his Martinsville teammates, Vinnie Bisesi, said. "He always had floor burns all over his legs, and he never was licked."

As a free throw shooter, Wooden was without peer. Using a two-handed, underhanded style, he could toss in shot after shot with ease. Quick as he was, he could stop on a dime and change direction, an essential skill for a game played in a confined space. He also had unusually large hands, which made him adept at dribbling quickly without losing control of the ball. "John could palm a basketball. I never could. Usually it takes a big man to do that," Billy Wooden said. Most of all, Johnny was in supreme condition—and he knew it. He stayed in constant motion so his defenders would eventually get tired.

Still, in the Wooden family, a game would always take a backseat to work. Since there was very little money, Johnny had to scrounge for whatever jobs he could find. He washed dishes, served meals, and cleaned the kitchen one day a week at the local Elks club. On weekends, he'd work as a box boy at a supermarket or the Collier Bros. Creamery. He canned tomatoes and peas at the Van Camp packing plant. He installed telephone poles, worked in an ice cream factory, laid gravel, dug sewers, and collected garbage. During the summers, he and his friends hitchhiked around the state looking for jobs. Sometimes, they would be away for weeks at a time.

Johnny and his buddies also liked to hang out at Wick's Candy Kitchen as well as a local pool hall, where he sharpened his billiard skills. Did Wooden also earn a few extra cents scamming the locals at pool? It's conceivable. He was, after all, not above a quick hustle. For example, when a carnival rode into town, he and Cat devised a plan to fleece the man working at the basketball shot. "They'd have these 'Shoot the free throw' contests," their brother Billy said. "They'd make an awkward pass. The fellow would persuade them to invest their money, and then they'd take their coat off and sink free shot after free shot. After they got prizes for everybody, finally the guy would try to get rid of them."

Wooden's classmate Floyd Burns recalled that Wooden developed a curious habit of keeping a toothpick in his mouth at all times—including when he played basketball. "It really could have been dangerous, but he always had a toothpick. Sometimes when we'd go into a store, he'd pick up the whole pack," Burns said. "He always wore his letter sweater and he'd carry the toothpicks inside the tucked-up part of the waist. And was he jealous of them. You'd have thought they were gold nuggets. John would always play [basketball] with a toothpick in his mouth, and I often heard a teacher say, 'John Robert, take that toothpick out of your mouth.'"

It was around this time that Wooden began to develop his fondness for phrases and aphorisms. "When he'd get hold of an expression, he'd use it all the time. And he loved to quote expressions he picked up from the classics, though they wouldn't always be exact," Burns said. "Many times we'd be walking out of the drugstore after having a Coke, and he'd stop, put his arm as if he were on the stage, and say, 'Varlot, insect, knave, back to the kitchen, the smell of the pots and pans is on ye.'"

Another favorite saying came from a newspaper cartoon called *Out at Our Place*. When one character asked his friend how he was doing, the friend would reply, "Pretty pert." Johnny copied it so often he answered to the nickname "Pert." That nickname appeared next to his basketball photograph in the Martinsville High yearbook for all three years he was a student there. Over the decades that followed, Wooden would tell people he got that nickname because it was short for "impertinent."

It was clear to his friends that Wooden had inherited his father's even temperament. One summer day when Wooden and his teammate Sally

Suddith were digging scwers, Suddith accidentally hit Wooden's finger with a hammer as they were putting up some boards to hold the dirt. Wooden dove on top of Suddith and started pounding him. Suddith assumed Wooden was irate, but after a few moments Johnny started laughing so hard he rolled on the ground. When Suddith asked if he was mad, Wooden replied, "Lord, no."

Curtis noticed this, too, and was not altogether pleased. He told Wooden that he would never win important games because he wasn't mean enough.

Martinsville in 1926 was a wonderful place and time to be a basketball star. Interest in the Artesians' games was so intense that homeroom teachers were assigned the task of finding tickets for students who couldn't afford them. On game night, the only gas station in town would close and put out a sign that read, "Be back after the game." (No need to say which game.) The only downside to all that attention was that it became difficult for the players to violate Curtis's 10:00 p.m. curfew. If one of them was in a movie theater, he might be visited by a flashlight-wielding usher saying it was time to go home.

In his junior year, Wooden paced the team in scoring and led the Artesians back to the cow barn for the 1927 championships. Over the course of two weeks, a field of 731 teams had been whittled down to 16, and the IHSAA removed hog and cattle stalls at the Exposition Center so they could squeeze in a few thousand more spectators for the final games. Wooden was the perfect floor guard to lead Curtis's ball-control offense. During the Saturday tripleheader, Wooden led Martinsville to a 26–14 win over Gary's Emerson High School in the morning and then put up 13 points in a 32–21 win over Connersville High School in the afternoon.

That earned the Artesians a date in the final for the second straight year. Their opponent, Muncie Central High School, was a much larger school, but the Bearcats learned early on that stopping their opponents' crafty little guard would not be easy. According to the *Daily Reporter*, Wooden took a pass off the opening tip-off in the title game and "dribbled under at lightning speed and scored a two point marker."

Down 4 points with four minutes to play, Muncie tried to ignite a rally, but Curtis countered with his patented stall. The tactic made for unexciting basketball, but it worked to perfection. Wooden tallied a game-high 10 points as Martinsville eked out a 26–23 win. Even by the standards of the era, it was not a pretty offensive game. Martinsville shot

9-for-42 from the field while Muncie shot just 8-for-33. Wooden was the second-leading scorer among the sixteen teams assembled in the cow barn that weekend. The *Muncie Star* reported the next day that the hometown Bearcats had suffered from a case of "too much Wooden." The article added, "The ever-fighting, plunging Wooden was as spectacular in the final victory as he had been throughout the earlier contests."

One of the officials for that 1927 championship game was Birch Bayh, who went on to sire a son (Birch Jr.) and grandson (Evan) who would represent Indiana in the United States Senate. Bayh officiated dozens of high school games in Indiana, and four decades later he still remembered the way Martinsville's whirling dervish dominated the games. "I've never seen another player give everything, regardless of what might happen to him, the way he did," Bayh said. "He would score by flying in from the side and use his bank shot. Many times he would slide on the floor and wind up under the bench. He spent a lot of time on the floor. I don't mean that he was awkward. He just gave everything. He held nothing back."

The young man's comportment made an even more lasting impression. "John was a complete gentleman," Bayh said. "I don't think I ever remember John showing any resentment to an official and I refereed a lot of his games. He never lost his temper and he never used bad language."

Needless to say, the victory over Muncie was big news back home. Hundreds of fans staged a parade and celebration the following Monday afternoon. The banner leading the procession read, "A team that won't be beat can't be beat—Martinsville High School." The mayor followed behind, as did packs of fans and students from every school in town. When the parade reached the town square, each member of the team got a chance to speak. Upon taking his turn, Wooden was asked how it felt to hit the floor so many times. "Wooden replied that it was not half so bad as it looked," the *Daily Reporter* wrote. The shy Wooden even flashed a rare smile for the team photo that was taken that day.

Each member of the Artesians' championship squad received a silver Hamilton pocket watch. (On the day Wooden died, that watch was still sitting in his Los Angeles condominium under a glass bell, ticking as well as it had more than eighty years before.) Several days later Wooden was selected all-state. Reporting the honor, the *Daily Reporter* said of Wooden: "Local people swell up like prideful toads at the mere mention of his name—and the greater the friendship, the bigger the swell."

Such praise could make a guy feel pretty pert.

3

Nell

She was, as he often described her, "the only girl I ever went with." She was also everything he wasn't. He was of Scottish and Dutch descent, cool and composed. She was red-blooded Irish. He was shy. She was outgoing. He avoided confrontation. She sought it out. She loved to socialize and go out on dates and was the life of the party. He hated parties. If he went at all, he'd mostly stand in the corner. She was hot-tempered, effusive, affectionate, feisty, and fun. If you crossed her—worse, if you disrespected him—she would let you know and wouldn't forget.

Also, she liked to dance. He didn't. On the rare occasions when he indulged her happy feet, she told him he looked like he was dribbling a basketball.

Nellie Riley was a year younger than Johnny Wooden. During his sophomore year at Martinsville High School, he noticed her in the hallways, but he never did anything about it. "Never met her or anything, but I saw her. I thought she was cute," he said. Nellie was best friends with a girl named Mary Schnaiter, the daughter of a well-to-do local businessman who owned a grain mill and building supply company. One day during the summer between Johnny's sophomore and junior years, Nellie joined Mary and her brother in the Schnaiters' family automobile, and the three of them took a drive out to Centerton. When they pulled up to the Woodens' farm, they saw Johnny in the distance plowing corn behind a mule. He was sweaty and caked with dirt. "I made a turn on this gravel road. They drove up to where I was turning. They motioned me over but I refused to go," Wooden recalled. "They kept trying but I refused. So they left. I didn't think anything about it."

Two months later, Johnny was coming out of his homeroom and was on his way to his first class. Nellie was waiting for him in the hallway. She walked right up to him and demanded to know why he had been so rude. "We made all these arrangements to go see you, and you didn't even come over to say hello," she said. He explained to her that he was dirty and didn't feel like socializing. "You all would have just made fun of me," he said.

Nellie replied, "I would never make fun of you."

They started spending time together almost immediately. Johnny would carry her books to school and take her on dates on the weekends. They spent evenings in her parents' living room playing songs like "Ramona" and "In a Little Spanish Town" on her parents' Victrola record player. There was a clandestine thrill to the relationship, because Glenn Curtis had a strict rule against his players dating during basketball season. This was a problem because the Rileys lived next door to Curtis, but Johnny still came around. "He was always polite and my parents liked him," Nell said, "but he was so bashful he could hardly hold his head up to say 'How do you do' to them."

Nellie did what she could to draw him out. She encouraged him to take a public speaking class. He did, but he didn't warm up to the teacher, Mabel Hinds, until she learned of Johnny's affection for poetry. Ms. Hinds got him to read aloud by assigning him Thomas Gray's "Elegy Written in a Country Churchyard." (*The boast of heraldry, the pomp of pow'r / And all that beauty, all that wealth e'er gave / Awaits alike th'inevitable hour / The paths of glory lead but to the grave.*") It would become Johnny's favorite poem.

Nellie was no stranger to basketball. When she was in grade school, she once made ten consecutive shots in a free throw contest. At Martinsville High, she fulfilled her fondness for music by joining the ukulele club, the dramatic club, the glee club, and operetta. Nellie's band instrument was the cornet, though Johnny teased her that she only held it to her lips and pretended to play. Playing in the band meant she had good seats for the games.

Once basketball season started, Johnny and Nellie developed a private pregame ritual. As he emerged from Curtis's huddle, he would find her in the stands, wink, and flash her the "okay" sign. They performed this ritual before every game he played and coached, right through his last at UCLA.

Johnny was a straight arrow, but Nellie had wandering eyes. This drove him to distraction. Even though Nellie professed devotion, she said she still wanted to have dates with other boys. Johnny was part sucker, part cuckold, tacitly granting Nellie permission to have her fun even though he had no interest in dating other girls himself.

On at least one occasion, she went too far. During the summer between John's junior and senior years of high school, Nell went on a date with a boy whom John didn't want her to see. John had been thinking about hitchhiking north to look for some fieldwork, so the day after Nellie mentioned the date, he expressed his displeasure by packing an extra pair of overalls and some belongings and hitting the road with a couple of buddies. The boys wore their letterman's sweaters because they knew it would make motorists more likely to stop.

Eventually, they made it to Lawrence, Kansas, where John asked the University of Kansas's forty-one-year-old basketball coach, Phog Allen, for help finding work. Allen got Wooden's crew a job pouring concrete for the new football stadium. The coach had ulterior motives. Allen knew full well about Wooden's basketball exploits, and he tried to convince him to move to Lawrence and eventually play for Kansas. Wooden declined and headed back to Martinsville, but he was still so angry with Nellie that he didn't even let her know he was home. "I didn't want to see her. She had to find out I was back," he said. Asked how she won him over, Wooden reached up his index finger and stroked his cheek, limning the tracks of her tears. "I'm ashamed," he said. "I have a bit of stubbornness in me, that's true. I admit that."

The couple grew even closer during Johnny's senior year—so close, in fact, that Curtis worried that Johnny would give up the chance to play basketball in college so he could stay in Martinsville and marry Nellie. Curtis warned Nellie's mother that she did not want her daughter to marry someone who would never make more than twenty-five dollars a week. Said Nell, "Mother thought to herself, if he ever makes twenty-five dollars a week, I'll be surprised." They were quite the item. The caption next to Wooden's senior picture in the *Artesian* that spring described him as "another person who lived in Centerton, but then it's not necessary to introduce 'John Bob,' especially to Nellie."

Though their personalities could not have been more different, they were soul mates in all the important ways. Wooden understood, at least subconsciously, that if he ended up with someone who was just like him, he would only retreat further into his shell, not quite distrusting the world but not fully embracing it, either. He needed a life partner who would challenge him. Someone who could ignite his passions, fight his battles, prod him, protect him, maybe even get him to dance once in a while. As a coach, Wooden would often tell his players that the two most important words in the English language were *love* and *balance*. Nellie Riley was the one person who gave him both.

Wooden was dedicated to his studies, so there was little doubt that he was going to college somewhere. The only question was whether his senior season would end with the Artesians claiming their second consecutive state championship.

The interest in the 1928 tournament was at an all-time high. The come-one, come-all field included a record 740 teams, and the finals would be played at Butler University's brand-new field house in Indianapolis. The arena had cost the school $1 million to build and had a capacity of fifteen thousand. The university originally planned to build a more modest venue, but the Indiana High School Athletic Association (IHSAA) convinced it to erect a bigger place so it could stage the state high school finals there. That was Indiana in 1928: basketball was a bigger deal to high schools than to colleges.

Once again, Martinsville won its sectional and regional tournaments to earn a berth in the sixteen-team pool that assembled in Indianapolis. By the time the big weekend arrived, Wooden was a statewide celebrity. A writer in Indianapolis dubbed him "the tumbling artist from Martinsville," adding that Wooden "is fast, he can dribble like a streak, he can guard, he can shoot long, he can twist 'em in as he flies under the basket."

After beating Rochester in the Friday night quarterfinal, Martinsville beat Washington on Saturday morning and Frankfort in the afternoon to earn a date with Muncie Central on Saturday night. The rematch of the previous year's finalists drew unprecedented attention. At WFBM radio in Indianapolis, a Dictaphone was set up in the studio to record the game announcers. It was just the second time a sporting event was being recorded by the station. (The first was the previous year's heavyweight championship boxing match between Jack Dempsey and Gene Tunney.) Back in Martinsville, a local telephone company manager provided a connection to the field house and set up loudspeakers at the offices of the *Daily Reporter*. Fans could also go to the Maxine Theater and follow the action on the electric scoreboard. Outside the Butler Fieldhouse, seven ticket scalpers were arrested for trying to sell tickets for as much as twenty-five dollars apiece. Inside, there was not a seat to be had.

The game was highly competitive, but it was also deflated by Curtis's somnambulant methods. The teams traded baskets in the early going and locked into a 4–4 tie. The next day's article in the *Indianapolis Star* generously characterized what ensued as "a spectacular defensive battle." The piece went on: "The Bearcats, whenever an opportunity was presented, attempted to use a fast-breaking attack but had limited success with this style of play." Martinsville led 9–8 at the half.

The Artesians scored three free throws after intermission to build a 4-point lead, but when that advantage was cut to 2 following a Muncie bucket, Curtis slammed on the brakes. During one five-minute stretch, both teams went scoreless. Heading into the final minute, Martinsville had a 12–11 lead and possession of the ball.

As the seconds ticked away, Charlie Secrist, the Muncie center, realized that Martinsville could win by stalling, so he called another time-out, knowing that his team would be assessed a technical foul because it didn't have any time-outs remaining. It was a clever strategy, because it meant that Muncie would have a chance to get the ball back via a center jump following Martinsville's free throw.

Wooden recognized this immediately. He told Curtis that he wanted to refuse the free throw and instead retain possession on an out-of-bounds play, an option that the rules allowed. Curtis, however, overruled Wooden and opted to shoot the technical. The strategy wasn't bad. He did, after all, have one of the finest free throw shooters in the state right there on his team.

Wooden stepped to the line with a chance to salt away the win. He flung the ball using his patented, two-handed, underhanded motion. It bounced off the rim.

With Martinsville still clinging to a 1-point lead, the teams returned to midcourt for the center jump. Muncie's plan was for Secrist, the tallest man on the floor, to tip the ball to himself (which was allowed under the rules) and then hurl it toward the basket while his teammates rushed to get the rebound. The play worked exactly as planned—almost. Secrist controlled the tip, waited a beat for his teammates to prepare for the rebound, and then he flung the ball underhanded toward the hoop. "It was the highest-arching shot I have ever seen," Wooden recalled. The ball sailed through the rafters, drifted downward . . . and splashed through "almost without disturbing the net," according to the *Star*. It was a total fluke, but it counted. The Muncie fans went wild as their Bearcats now owned a 13–12 lead.

The Artesians had about thirty seconds left to reverse their fortunes. This time, they won the center jump. Curtis knew the Muncie defenders would overplay Wooden, so he used his star as a decoy. Wooden dribbled around the backcourt and fired a pass to his center, George Eubank. The big man had a clear shot at the basket with no one around him, but he put too much spin on the ball and it slipped off the rim. As the official scorer fired his pistol to signal the end of the game, the Muncie fans rushed onto the court in what the Associated Press characterized as "an explosion of gaiety rivaling the Armistice signing." The Martinsville players, meanwhile, were inconsolable. "We just sat on the floor and cried," Sally Suddith said. "We were so close to two in a row."

Even in defeat, the Artesians won plaudits from their hometown paper. "Both Teams Played High Class Basketball from Whistle to Crack of Pistol," read one headline in the *Daily Reporter*. The accompanying article declared the game as "the greatest exhibition of real basketball ever staged in a state tourney." Even the writer from the *Muncie Press* called Wooden "flashy, hard hitting and sure shooting." Over the years, Wooden would often say that far more people told him they had attended that game than could fit inside the field house. Many of those people got their facts wrong, claiming that the final gun had gone off while Secrist's shot was airborne. They forgot that Martinsville still had one final possession. "They'll insist to me, 'I was there,' " Wooden said. "Well, I was there, too."

Wooden proffered a recollection of his own from that fateful evening in Indianapolis: he claimed to be the only one among his teammates who didn't cry. "I have never felt badly about that missed free throw," he said. Was that really true? Or did he just *want* it be true? It's difficult to imagine that a teenager who had just lost in such devastating fashion left the gym with dry eyes, much less without even feeling bad about it. Regardless, his point was a good one. Yes, Wooden had missed the pivotal free throw, but it wasn't for a lack of hard work or meticulous preparation. The ball just didn't go in. Secrist's did. In the end, Wooden knew he had given it his best shot, and that should have been enough.

As it turned out, the biggest impediment to Wooden's pursuit of higher education wasn't Nellie. It was baseball, his first love.

During the summer following his graduation from Martinsville High, Wooden spent several weeks in the town of Anderson working as a machine buffer. While he was there, he played shortstop for the town's baseball team and caught the eye of Donnie Bush, the veteran major league shortstop, who at the time was managing a minor league team in Indianapolis. Bush offered Wooden a pro contract. For a young man who never had much money, it was extremely tempting. In the end, though, Johnny turned it down, trusting his father's advice that the best way to achieve financial security was through education, not sports.

Needless to say, there were plenty of colleges interested in Wooden.

The place that made the most sense was Indiana University. The Hoosiers' basketball coach, Everett Dean, had built one of the finest programs in the nation, and Bloomington was only twenty miles south of Martinsville. Butler's Tony Hinkle and Notre Dame's George Keogan also wanted Wooden to come play for them, as did the coaches at Illinois, Kansas, Ohio State, and Wisconsin.

Wooden, however, was not going to let basketball dictate his decision. He aspired to be a civil engineer, and one of the few state universities that had a civil engineering program was Purdue. That school also had an excellent basketball team, and though Wooden had never visited the campus, several of his friends who were Purdue students recommended that he go there. As the summer of 1928 concluded, he decided to head for West Lafayette.

And what about the fiery little Irish girl with the turned-up nose? She would wait for him, of course. When Wooden left for college, Nellie remained behind in Martinsville, where she finished her senior year of high school and then went to work at the Home Lawn Sanitarium. Before he departed, he and Nellie had yet another awkward conversation about dating. He told her—again—that he preferred she not go out on dates but said he trusted her. Regardless, he promised he would not date any girls at Purdue. They also made a pact they would not have sex, not even with each other, until his four years at college were up. Upon his graduation, he would return to Martinsville, and together they would find a priest and get married. There was no proposal, no engagement ring, no getting down on one knee. They simply decided it would be so. Johnny Wooden possessed many virtues, but a flair for romance wasn't one of them.

4

Piggy

The world of college athletics that Johnny Wooden entered in the fall of 1928 was a far cry from the one that exists today. Instead of being coddled, canonized, and catered to, college athletes in Wooden's day were real-life amateurs who had to pay their own way. Purdue's basketball coach, Ward "Piggy" Lambert, helped his players get jobs to cover their $70-per-semester tuition costs, but that was pretty much the extent of his assistance. Wooden made ends meet by waiting on tables and cleaning dishes at the Beta Theta Pi fraternity house, where some of his friends from Martinsville were brothers.

Not surprisingly, Wooden's commitment to Beta's social life did not extend beyond his waiter duties. "I'm not a good fraternity man," he later said. "Even though I lived there, I lived there for my meals. I wasn't going to go through with the hazing and things of that sort. I was at odds with a lot of the people in the fraternity house because of my feelings about that." For Wooden, a wild night on the town was eating ice cream at the Purdue creamery or shooting pool at a local joint called Deac's. Wooden did imbibe some home brew on one occasion, but the beer made him so ill that he swore off alcohol for life.

Wooden made two significant discoveries early in his freshman year. The first was Purdue's policy to waive tuition costs for students who made the dean's list. Wooden would have made dean's list anyway, but that was a nice fringe benefit. At the same time, Wooden was disheartened to learn that in order to get his degree in civil engineering, he would be required to attend a special camp during the summers. That would be impossible because his family depended on the money he made in the summertime. Had he known of the requirement, Wooden said later, "I would have gone to Indiana. It would have been closer to Nellie, and I liked their basketball." But he was stuck at Purdue.

Around that time, Wooden developed a rapport with Dr. Herbert Creek, the head of Purdue's English department and a respected expert on Shakespeare. Dr. Creek reignited Wooden's love for the written word, instilled in him by his father. With civil engineering no longer a viable option, Wooden decided to major in English.

Waiting tables didn't cover all of Wooden's living costs, and his parents had no money to give him. So just as he had done in Martinsville, Johnny found outside work. "When you don't have much," he said, "you do." He helped the football team's trainer tape ankles for twenty-five cents an hour. He painted the stadium on weekends. He enlisted local high school players to sell programs before football games, splitting the revenue with his young salesmen and pocketing some additional money on advertising. "I'd do pretty well on the homecoming game," Wooden said. "I'd get over to the hotel the night before where most of the people come to homecoming would stay, and they'd be happy and celebrating despite the fact that it was the days of Prohibition."

Wooden's drive to earn extra money nearly cost him his college basketball career. At the end of his freshman year, he was invited to play an exhibition game for a semiprofessional team from South Bend that was competing in an Amateur Athletic Union (AAU) tournament. Wooden was offered a small stipend, even though accepting it would violate the rules governing amateur competition. One of the other players on the team was a Purdue football player named Joe Dellinger, who was allowed to play because he had already completed his senior season. Dellinger warned Wooden that he was taking a bad risk, but Wooden wouldn't listen. "I was really scared to think what Piggy Lambert would do to me, an upperclassman, if Wooden got in trouble," Dellinger said. "Lambert was just a little guy, about 125 to 130 pounds, but he was feisty and I was scared to death of him."

Wooden played the first half, but during halftime a spectator who recognized him from his high school days came into the locker room and threatened to notify Purdue if Wooden kept playing. Wooden told the other players to ignore him, but they eventually convinced the team's owner to leave him out of the second half. When Dellinger reminded Wooden of the incident many years later, Wooden chuckled and said, "That could easily have been my Alamo."

Since he was basically broke, Wooden did not get to see Nellie as often as they would have liked. She had a brother-in-law who owned a car, and once in a while he would drive her to West Lafayette. On other occasions, Johnny would hitchhike back to Martinsville. "There was no problem hitchhiking in those days. If there was room, anybody would pick you up no problem," Wooden said. "Times were hard. The bus might have been ten or fifteen cents. I didn't have it, and she didn't either."

Wooden was an intelligent, good-looking athlete, so naturally he turned some heads. He would have none of it. "He never brought a girl to any dance, but mostly stood off to the side and occasionally would dance with another fellow's girl," said Mary Dohn, a fellow student. "Everybody knew he was going with his high school girlfriend." Nellie, alas, was a different story. Not only did she continue to date other boys back home, but she would sometimes write Johnny letters detailing her active social life, which rankled him something awful. When he confronted her yet again during one of his visits, she told him that he was just going to have to trust that she was his girl and they would end up together.

Like all freshmen, Wooden was not eligible to compete with the Purdue varsity, so he looked to other sports. He spent two days during the fall of his freshman year practicing with Purdue's football team as a halfback until Lambert found out and ordered Wooden to stop. The following summer, Wooden played baseball for a team in Indianapolis, where he was working for the state's highway annex. During one at bat, he turned into a pitch that struck him hard in his right shoulder and damaged his rotator cuff. This was a major problem since Wooden's greatest asset was his arm. He explored the possibility of having corrective surgery, but once again, Lambert stepped in and said no. Thus did Wooden enter his sophomore year totally committed to playing basketball for Piggy Lambert, whether he liked it or not. He was only beginning to comprehend the myriad ways in which this fiery, exacting, brilliant little coach was starting to shape his life.

In John Wooden, Piggy Lambert saw a taller, younger version of himself. In Lambert, Wooden saw a male authority figure who could use basketball to nourish his mind, body, and spirit. At five foot ten, Wooden always thought of himself as small, but he fairly towered over his coach, who stood just five foot six and was sometimes referred to in the local newspaper as Purdue's "midget mentor."

Lambert was living proof that an indomitable spirit could overcome an elfin frame. Born in Deadwood, South Dakota, in 1888, he was two years old when his family moved to Crawfordsville. That's where Ward caught the basketball bug. As he bounced around the YMCA popping basketballs out of the coffee sacks that Reverend McKay hung from the rims, the older boys used to tease young Ward about the pigtails that flapped under his stocking cap. That's how he got the nickname "Piggy."

By the time he reached Crawfordsville High School, this little Piggy weighed all of 115 pounds. The school's coach, Reverend Ralph Jones, who would later coach for two seasons at Purdue, deemed him too small to play for the varsity. Still, Lambert was fast and determined, and he finally broke through at Wabash College in Crawfordsville, where Jones also coached basketball. Jones finally rewarded Lambert with a spot in Wabash's starting lineup as a sophomore. Lambert spent his last three years at Wabash as an accomplished three-sport star in basketball, baseball, and football.

Lambert was even more serious about his studies. After college, he earned a graduate degree in physics and chemistry at the University of Minnesota. But he could not resist that bouncing ball. He took over as coach at Indiana's Lebanon High School in 1911, and he was hired at Purdue six years later at the age of twenty-nine.

In West Lafayette, Lambert fashioned his teams in his own image. Basketball was very much a big man's game in those days. Not only could a taller player plant himself under the basket and score easily (this was long before the three-second violation), but he was also a great weapon for the center jump that was held after every made basket. Yet Lambert preferred players who were smaller and quicker, and he was determined to speed the game up. Sportswriters branded this strange style "fire-wagon basketball," but Lambert had another name for it. He called it the fast break.

It was not enough for Lambert's players to be quicker than their opponents. For his system to work, they also had to be in superior condition. The way he figured it, if his team was able to impose its fire-wagon style for an entire game, it would eventually wear out the opponent and seize control down the stretch. So he ran his guys ragged. "Our practices were hellish," said Charlie Caress, who played at Purdue from 1939 to 1942. Lambert placed so much emphasis on making his players run that he preferred not to stop practice to talk to his team as a group. When he wanted to correct something, he would pull individual players aside for brief chats. While other coaches let their boys go home during the Christmas holiday, Lambert insisted that they remain on campus so they could keep on running.

During his second season at Purdue, Lambert's Boilermakers set a new Big Ten record by scoring 35.6 points per game. According to *The Big Ten*, a voluminous history of the conference, one sportswriter who covered the league at the time "noted that offense was getting too much ahead of defense and predicted gloomily that basketball would soon be spoiled by 40-point games." Two years later, Purdue won its first undisputed Big Ten title, and over the next twenty-seven years, Lambert would claim ten more conference crowns and eventually earn enshrinement in the Basketball Hall of Fame.

His ethos dovetailed perfectly with Wooden's skill set, not to mention his farm-bred work ethic. "He was way ahead of his time in fast break basketball," Wooden said. "I tried to feel . . . that no one would be in better condition than I was. They may beat me on ability, but they'll never beat me on condition." When Lambert later referred to Wooden as the best-conditioned athlete he had coached, Wooden recognized it as the ultimate compliment.

No detail was too small to escape Piggy's discerning eye. For example, he was fixated on the condition of his players' feet. He ordered them to rub their feet twice a week with a solution of benzoin and tannic acid, which Lambert said would toughen up the skin. Instead of having his players wear one pair of thick wool socks as was customary, he told them to wear two—a cotton pair next to the feet to absorb sweat plus a medium-weight wool pair to reduce friction against their shoes. After they showered, he wanted his players to fan their feet, not towel them, and he reminded them to make sure they were dry between the toes.

Lambert was a stickler for routine. For an 8:00 p.m. tipoff, the players ate precisely at 1:15. The menu was always the same—fruit cocktail, medium-sized steak cooked medium well, peas, carrots, celery, green tea, and ice cream or custard cup for dessert. Then he wanted his players to take a short walk and lie down for a nap between 3:00 and 4:30. Outside of basketball, he said they should abide by what he called the "right rules of living." That meant no smoking, alcohol, overeating, or "irregular hours," even though Lambert himself was a smoker and inveterate poker player (and not a very good one at that).

When it came to teaching the game, everything Lambert did was predicated on speed. He preferred passing to dribbling because the ball moved faster. Whereas most teams tended to slowly walk the ball up the floor following an opponent's missed shot, Lambert drilled into his players the habit of immediately firing a long pass. "When you rebounded, your first look was down the floor," Caress said. "I don't know how many afternoons we practiced getting our hand behind the ball so that when we threw the ball the length of the floor, it wouldn't curve."

Lambert laid out all of these precepts in a textbook he wrote called

Practical Basketball. Published in 1932, it was one of the first technical volumes to be authored by a college coach, and for years it was considered to be a bible among Lambert's peers. The book was packed with intricate jargon that was supplemented by charts and photographs. (One photograph shows a crouched Johnny Wooden demonstrating a "low bounce dribble." The player is described as having "unusual speed.") Every facet of the game was broken down in the book, but what really came through was the author's unshakable faith in the gospel of up-tempo basketball. "The fast-break, with dependence upon the initiative of the players rather than upon set formations is, in my opinion, the ideal system, if the coach has the necessary material," Lambert wrote.

While Lambert had strict notions on the way the game should be played, his true genius lay in the broad freedom he gave his players to execute his vision. He figured it was his job as the head coach to get his guys into the best possible condition, teach them how to play—and then get out of their way. He had very few offensive plays, substituted infrequently, and rarely talked to his players about their opponent. This was another offshoot of the rules of the day, which forbade coaches from speaking to players during time-outs. (When the action stopped, the players simply huddled on the court.) Lambert often told his players that the team that commits more mistakes usually wins. "One of the dangers in teaching is overloading the players with knowledge," he wrote in *Practical Basketball.* "Most young players cannot absorb all of this knowledge, and there is more danger in overcoaching than in undercoaching."

Lambert whittled his philosophy down to three components: condition, skill, and team spirit. "He didn't have any complicated systems or anything of that sort," Wooden said. "He taught me the value of a controlled offense, but one that had freelance aspects to it. You build a base from where the offense would start, trying to get movement by design but not necessarily by a precise pattern. There was always somebody moving, in and out, crossing over, and then he would add little changes within that framework."

In other words, he was the polar opposite of Glenn Curtis, Wooden's coach at Martinsville High School. Whereas Curtis taught a deliberate offense and maintained an even keel, Lambert turned his horses loose and behaved frenetically on the sideline. "I've seen Piggy getting up, leading cheers, coaching, and officiating all at the same time," said Clyde Lyle, a college teammate of Wooden's. A veteran league official once complained that "it's an uncomfortable feeling to be calling them as you see 'em, knowing the little guy over there has never been wrong on a basketball

floor in his life." When Lambert retired in 1946 after having won 71 percent of his games and eleven league championships during his twenty-
nine-year tenure at Purdue, he admitted he was "anxious to be relieved of
the nervous strain and mental punishment that accompanies a head
coachship."

Lambert was tough on his players, but he generally took a positive
tack. This was yet another way in which Wooden saw Lambert as an
extension of Hugh. As Lambert wrote in *Practical Basketball*, "The coach
who continually tells his players they are rotten is sure to make them so."
Added Clyde Lyle, "He was a master psychologist. He had a tremendous
vocabulary and he didn't need a lot of profanity to let the players know
what he wanted."

With Wooden waiting in the wings as a freshman, the Boilermakers'
varsity posted an impressive 13–4 record and finished second in the Big
Ten. During one game that season, they set a new conference record by
scoring 64 points in a rout of the University of Chicago. Interest in the
team's exploits was so high that four of their home games were moved to
Jefferson High School, whose gym was nearly twice the capacity of Purdue's on-campus facility, Memorial Gymnasium. When the Boilermakers
did play at Memorial, the place was so jammed that some fans sat on steel
trusses above the floor. Lambert understood that basketball was a form
of entertainment, and the customers wanted running and scoring. They
would soon get their wish, thanks to the dynamic little player who was
ready to hop aboard Piggy's fire wagon and rip it into higher gear.

Lambert may have favored speed over size, but he was not ignorant to the
value of a big man. In the fall of 1926, two years before Wooden arrived
on campus as a freshman, a tall, skinny gift landed in Lambert's lap: Charles
"Stretch" Murphy, the six-foot-eight center from Marion whose team had
beaten Martinsville in the state final at the end of Wooden's sophomore
season. Most coaches who had big men on their roster planted them in
the middle and told them to stay there, but not Lambert. He resolved to
burnish Murphy's strength, quickness, and skill, just as he did with his
guards. The result was one of the first truly great big men the college
game had seen.

Murphy was quite the unfinished product at first. His weighed just
173 pounds, and his habit of flinging his elbows when cradling the ball
could be a menace to his teammates during practice. "He was a beanpole," Clyde Lyle said. "He was not clever at all, and most teams were

knocking him down by hitting him low because he didn't have much strength and didn't know how to keep his feet out for balance."

Still, Murphy was unusually coordinated for a player his size. Lambert installed him as a full-time starter his sophomore year, and the following season, Murphy set Big Ten records for scoring in a single game (26 points) as well as a season (143). When Wooden joined the varsity for Murphy's senior year in 1929, the two of them became a must-see tandem, although Wooden was not mentioned in the early stories that previewed the upcoming season. (The main local paper in West Lafayette, the *Journal and Courier*, referred to him that fall as "Jimmy Wooden.") After the Boilermakers opened the season with a 19-point drubbing of Washington University, the paper's beat writer, Gordon Graham, reported that Wooden "had proven himself capable" of handling college competition. The word was out.

The first big game Purdue played that season was a late December clash at Butler. It was such an important contest that Nellie decided to drive up from Martinsville to watch her Johnny play. Wooden bought her a comb, brush, and mirror set as a Christmas present, but he never made it to the game. As he was on his way to catch the train from West Lafayette to Indianapolis, Wooden flagged down a cleaner truck, and the driver invited him to hop on the rear bumper. It had just snowed in West Lafayette, and the roads were icy. As the truck carrying Wooden was stopped on a hill, another truck skidded from behind. Wooden saw the truck coming and grabbed the top of his own vehicle to swing his body, but he couldn't quite get his right leg out of the way, and it was pinned between the two trucks. His first concern was his gift to Nellie, which had been in his back pocket and was busted in the collision. Wooden was lucky his leg was not broken, but it was lacerated badly enough that he was laid up for days. It was the second straight year he spent Christmas in the hospital. (The year before he had come down with scarlet fever.) "Nellie and her sister and brother-in-law drove through bad weather," he lamented many years later. "I saw them at the hospital instead of at the game."

Without Wooden, Murphy was held to zero field goals against Butler, and Purdue lost, 36–29. The *Journal and Courier* noted that Wooden's absence was "keenly felt." Wooden also missed Purdue's next game, a win over Vanderbilt, but he rejoined the squad for its January 2 home game against Montana State. He wore a football pad on his injured thigh, but he was hurting so badly that he had to ask Lambert to take him out early in the second half. As a result, Purdue suffered its second loss of the season, 38–35.

To the degree that he paid attention to such things, that loss gave Wooden his first taste of the downside of high expectations. Graham's write-up of the Montana State game was scathing. "The Boilermakers, without a doubt, turned in one of the most disgusting exhibitions of basketball in the Memorial gymnasium last night that an Old Gold and Black team has ever been guilty of. Not ragged, just plain disgusting." Graham added that because of his accident, Wooden "lacked the stamina to hold the pace."

Once Wooden returned to form, the Boilermakers were off and running. Wooden was an ideal floor guard for Lambert's system. Not only was he an excellent passer who could direct the offense with aplomb, but he was also adept at quickly advancing the ball upcourt before the defense could get set. In later years, Murphy would refer to Wooden as "the Bob Cousy of our day." Gordon Graham recalled that when Wooden drove to the basket, "he often flew five or six rows into the stands, slid into the band instruments, open bleachers, and even brick walls. But he always bounced up and beat everyone else back on defense."

Wooden had all the playing time he wanted because Lambert hardly substituted. Back then, players were only permitted to reenter a game once. (Open substituting was added to the rules in 1944.) When the Boilermakers followed the Montana State loss with a slim 23–19 victory over Michigan, Wooden scored 7 of the team's final 14 points—an early example of how his dedication to conditioning paid off late in games. With Wooden and Murphy operating at high speed, the Boilermakers steamrolled through the rest of their opponents. They beat Northwestern, 39–22. They beat Loyola, 25–20 in overtime, to snap the Ramblers' thirty-four-game winning streak. Then, on February 2, they exploded for 60 points in a thrashing of Ohio State. Murphy scored 28 points in that game to break the conference single-game mark he had set the year before, while Wooden poured in a cool 17 of his own. Chicago coach Nels Norgren, whose squad lost to Purdue by 10 points on February 8, said, "You need to put two men on Murphy and two men on Wooden, and there are not many left to score baskets."

The fire wagon was running hot, thanks to this stellar, inside-outside tandem. It was just how Piggy envisioned it. "Lambert gave us considerable freedom in our play," Murphy said. "We attracted attention from the scouts, most of whom thought the kind of basketball we played was nuts.

We figured if we could hold our opponents to 25 or 30 points, we could beat them."

Wooden's performances weren't just effective. They were enthralling. This was a critical part of his basketball education. Most of the language in the *Journal and Courier*'s coverage was straightforward and anodyne, but references to Wooden were frequently embellished by colorful expressions. He was labeled the "Martinsville flash," "Purdue's electric dribbler," and "the fastest and cleverest little fellow we have ever seen on a court." His ability to beat the defense down the floor for uncontested layups was described as "his prize act." His "brilliant dribbling thrilled the crowd" in one game. In another, "the little Martinsville speedster got quite a hand from the overflow crowd for his spirited dashes."

After a win over Northwestern, Graham referred to Wooden as the "India Rubberman" in homage to his ability to bounce off the floor following his many hard falls. The nickname stuck, although in the decades that followed, many sportswriters mistakenly reported that Wooden's nickname had been the "Indiana" rubber man.

In between his falls and rubberlike bounces, Wooden developed some odd superstitions. One day he happened to tuck his locker key into the laces in his shoe, and he played so well that he decided to do that for every practice and every game. Moreover, his teammates, just like the guys he played with in Martinsville, were struck by a serene demeanor that belied Wooden's tenacity between the lines. "When I was a freshman and played against John in practice, I held him, pushed him, and shoved him, but I could never take the ball away from him," said Bob Hobbs, a Purdue teammate who was a year younger than Wooden. "After a workout, he'd come up and say, 'Nice practice, Bob.' He never held a grudge and you simply couldn't rattle the guy."

On March 3, 1930, Purdue clinched the Big Ten title by defeating Michigan, 44–28. It was the third time in five years that Lambert's team had won or shared conference honors. The only remaining items of suspense were whether the Boilermakers would go undefeated in league play, and whether Murphy would finish the season as the Big Ten's scoring champ. For most of the season, he had been locked in a tight race with Indiana center Branch McCracken, who was a close friend of Wooden's from childhood. (When Wooden lived in Centerton, his backyard and McCracken's backyard abutted each other.) Though Murphy ended up with the higher scoring average, McCracken took the overall title because Indiana played twelve conference games while Purdue played only ten, thus enabling McCracken to accumulate more points. However, Murphy got the last laugh by leading Purdue to the first perfect conference record in the Big Ten since Minnesota's in 1919.

The season culminated a week later when Wooden and Murphy were selected by the Associated Press to the Big Ten's five-man "all-star" team. They were joined by McCracken and two other centers. The AP called Wooden "a sophomore who promises to become an immortal of this league." It also noted that among the five all-stars, Wooden was "the only player who worked at guard all season to gain a job in his natural position. He is also the only man who will return next season."

Basketball fed Johnny Wooden's competitive appetite. It validated his devotion to hard work. The games were exciting. But the sport would not have held Wooden's regard if his mentors had tried to appeal to his baser instincts. As passionate as Piggy Lambert was about the intricacies of the game and the merits of the fast break, he was foremost a congregant in the Church of Naismith, where basketball had been conceived as a pathway to heaven. Wooden was raised in a home where the dominant male figure was to be paid proper respect without anyone questioning his authority. He gave Lambert the same kind of respect, and in later years when he became a coach, Wooden would demand the same from his own players.

The most indelible example of his deference to Lambert occurred during the spring of 1930, soon after Wooden's sophomore campaign was over. Lambert called Wooden into his office to report that a well-to-do doctor in town had offered to take care of Wooden's living expenses. When Lambert asked Wooden what he thought, Wooden replied that it sounded terrific.

Lambert persisted. How was Wooden going to pay the man back?

Now Johnny was confused. He responded that he didn't realize the doctor was expecting to be paid back.

Lambert told him he wasn't, but surely Johnny would *want* to pay him back, right? Of course, if he turned down the offer altogether, he wouldn't have to worry about it at all. He could finish up his last two years at Purdue and leave school without owing anyone a cent. Lambert told Wooden to think about it for a few days and then come back with his decision.

Even though Lambert didn't tell him what to do, Wooden understood what the coach wanted. Johnny returned a few days later and told Lambert he could tell this doctor fellow no thanks. "I knew you'd say that," Lambert replied. "When you walk out of here, your head will be up."

Lambert wasn't blind to Wooden's financial hardships. The coach had noticed that when the team traveled to places like Minnesota and Wisconsin, Johnny didn't have a coat to keep him warm. So Lambert told Wooden that this same doctor would buy him a thick coat, some decent clothes, and a pair of shoes. In return, Wooden would give the man his game tickets. Lambert promised that if Nellie or Wooden's family wanted to come to the games, he would get them in.

Thus did the ball that had bounced from Springfield to Crawfordsville to West Lafayette bounce again toward Johnny Wooden. With Lambert serving as his minister as well as his wagon driver, Wooden instinctively grabbed the ball and ran, sensing it was leading him to higher ground.

5

Johnny Wooden, All-American

The 1930–31 season was looked upon in West Lafayette as a rebuilding year. Three starters, including Stretch Murphy, had graduated from the team that ran the table in the Big Ten. Lambert named Wooden cocaptain alongside his fellow junior, forward Harry Kellar. The *Courier and Journal* noted that the new captains, both of whom were five foot ten, were "comparative midgets" next to the guys they replaced.

Wooden had attacked the rim with such verve as a sophomore that for his junior season, Lambert stationed football players along the baseline so they could catch Wooden before he careered into the bleachers. "The thing I remember the most is that he was so fast," said Bob King, who watched Wooden play in college and later became an assistant basketball coach at Purdue. "He ran into the stands and they threw him right back on the floor."

The young Boilermakers were not going to be able to ease into the season. Their first opponent was Notre Dame, which was squaring off against Purdue for the first time in seven years. With the game having been moved to Jefferson High to accommodate the heightened interest, Wooden rose to the occasion by scoring 21 points in a 34–22 rout. The *Indianapolis Star* reported that during the game, "Wooden was unstoppable on his speedy dribbles under the basket that usually ended with a seemingly impossible one-handed shot through the netting." After dispatching Washington University at home by 22 points, Purdue played a huge road game in late December at Pittsburgh, which had been tagged as the mythical national champions the year before. The *Courier and Journal* asserted that the Boilermakers needed to "defend the honor of Indiana, Big Ten and mid-western basketball." The paper also highlighted the opportunity for the Boilermakers to take their star performer on the road: "The majority of basketball critics rank Wooden as the most brilliant individual player the game has seen in years and the east's reaction to this 'India Rubber Man' will be interesting to say the least."

Alas, Wooden suffered yet another mishap in the days beforehand, when his hip got snagged on a loose floorboard during one of his frequent dives during practice. "It took a hunk of meat—and I mean *meat*—out of my hip," Wooden said. "It didn't hurt so much at the time. Things like that don't. But late that night I got in bad shape. I got a big kernel in the groin, so they took me to the hospital for that. They didn't have penicillin and things of that sort." For the third year in a row, he celebrated Christmas from a hospital bed.

Wooden accompanied the team to Pittsburgh for the game on December 30, but he was too sore to play for most of the game. With three minutes remaining in the second half and the Boilermakers trailing by 4 points, Lambert inserted Wooden into the contest. He immediately stole a pass and broke free for a layup to cut the margin to 2. About a minute later, Wooden missed a chance to tie the score when his outside shot rimmed out. Pittsburgh got the rebound and held on to the ball the rest of the way, dealing the Boilermakers a 24–22 loss.

As Wooden continued to delight crowds, Nellie attended as many games as she could, but she could never steady her nerves the way her beau could. During one intense game his junior year, she actually fainted in the stands and missed the end of the second half. Even as the Boilermakers lost four out of nine games beginning in January, Wooden developed a reputation as one of the finest guards in all of college basketball. His methods were as effective as they were uncomplicated. He simply worked harder than everyone else. "He was always moving," said Wooden's future assistant coach Ed Powell, who grew up in South Bend and attended several of his Purdue games. "He would be passing, cutting, dribbling, moving. Whoever guarded him would stay with him maybe for a quarter or two or three, but then, towards the end, John would get one or two steps away, just enough to score the winning basket. He didn't do anything differently towards the end than he did during the game, except that conditioning paid off."

Wooden and his teammates closed the season with five straight wins to finish second in the Big Ten with an 8–4 record. Lambert's young guns had matured quite a bit over the course of the season. Best of all, not a single starter or significant reserve was a senior. That meant the team was going to return intact for what was shaping up to be a very promising senior season for Johnny Wooden.

———

During the summer between his junior and senior years, Wooden was again offered the chance to play professional baseball, based largely on the potential he showed while playing semipro ball the previous summer. The Chicago Cubs and the Cincinnati Reds, who were either unaware of or unconcerned about his bum shoulder, offered Wooden contracts to join their farm system. Lambert had played some minor league baseball himself, so he knew what a grind it was. He also regarded the notion of playing sports for money as a corrupt enterprise. "You can't play in the dirt without getting dirty," he liked to say. He didn't tell Wooden explicitly not to play, but Wooden got the drift.

Wooden was more serious in contemplating an offer to be appointed to the U.S. Military Academy at West Point. The academy had the ability to recruit athletes from other schools and allow them to play for another four years. This time it was Nellie who shot down the idea. She had agreed to wait for him to finish at Purdue, but she did not want to wait any longer. She told Wooden that if he accepted, she would call off the marriage and join a convent.

So much for West Point.

After abandoning his initial plans to be a civil engineer, Wooden committed himself to become a high school English teacher. His plans took on another dimension at the start of his junior year when Purdue added a Physical Education department. The state of Indiana had just passed a law requiring teachers to have a Phys Ed degree in order to coach high school sports. Wooden hadn't given much thought to coaching, but with the new department in place, he loaded up on electives and got the extra degree. With an English degree, a Phys Ed degree, and a teacher's certificate, Wooden figured that he would always be able to find work in the state of Indiana.

As always, Wooden remained on the lookout for ways to make extra money. After Stretch Murphy graduated, he handed over to Wooden the rights to concession sales around Purdue football games. During his senior year, Wooden made a killing one weekend selling sandwiches, soft drinks, and cigarettes on the train that carried Purdue fans to the annual football game against the University of Chicago, which was coached by Amos Alonzo Stagg. Lambert had connected Wooden with a local butcher who provided him a couple of large hams. Wooden then brought the meat to the cook at the Beta house so they could grind it up and spread it on bread like butter. "We could make a lot more sandwiches that way," Wooden said. "I used to say I walked to Chicago and back because I was walking up and down the train all the way."

Most of the fans in West Lafayette knew Wooden for his exploits on the basketball court, but they learned of his equivalent talents in the classroom when the *Courier and Journal* published a story under the headline, "Johnny Wooden sets fast pace in class room." Purdue's registrar office had provided the newspaper with records indicating that Wooden had been on the school's Distinguished Student honor roll. Stating that Wooden "is generally recognized as the greatest dribbler of modern day basketball, and his alertness on defense has no equal," the article concluded: "Wooden is a senior in the school of physical condition, and intends to take up coaching as a profession after his graduation this June."

Wooden's final team at Purdue may have been long on experience, but it was short on stature. The Boilermakers were, in the words of their hometown newspaper, "a squad that depends more on speed and cleverness than physical power." They demonstrated as much by blitzing out of the gate with wins over Washington, Notre Dame, and Pittsburgh by a combined 45 points. By going on to score 51 points against both Montana State and Monmouth in Memorial Gym, the Boilermakers not only remained undefeated but pulled off the unusual feat of averaging more than a point per minute through their first five games. That was unheard of in 1931.

No matter how hard opposing coaches tried to collar the "Martinsville flash," Wooden's fully evolved skill and guile rendered their efforts useless. Notre Dame coach George Keogan went so far as to devise a "Wooden defense" specifically to contain his drives. Keogan assigned one player to guard Wooden up close while another shadowed him closer to the basket. "Finally John decided that going through our defense was playing it the hard way," Keogan later recalled. "What does he do? He started popping from out around the center, way back of the key."

For once, Wooden did not sustain a major injury in late December. However, his tonsils did flare up, and he had to have them removed during the semester break. That gave Wooden a clean sweep: four years at Purdue, four Christmases spent in a hospital.

On January 6, two days after the Boilermakers sprinted to a 49–30 win over Indiana, the Associated Press published a story describing the unique style with which Purdue was steamrolling its opponents. "Overwhelming offensive strength shown in pre-conference tilts and analysis of Coach Ward Lambert's veteran personnel are responsible for great optimism among Boilermaker fans on the eve of the twelve-game conference schedule," the story read. "[The players] are thoroughly fitted into the quick-breaking, free-shooting clever dribbling Lambert scheme. 'Fire department basketball,' they call it in Indiana, and the pellmell, headlong style of game seems to be coming back in vogue this season—with reservations—after giving way, for several seasons, to a slower, more methodical brand."

Wooden would not avoid the injury bug for long. A couple of days before the Big Ten opener against Illinois, he sliced the ring finger on his shooting hand while working in the Beta kitchen. Then, as he was riding to the game, the car driven by Lambert and carrying Wooden slid off the road and flipped. Fortunately, nobody was seriously injured, but Wooden suffered a badly bruised thigh. He still played against the Illini, but he had an obvious limp and was restricted by the heavy bandage on his shooting hand. He scored just 10 points as the Boilermakers lost, 28–21.

As it turned out, that would be the team's only hiccup. In its next outing, Purdue squeaked by Marquette, 26–23, after the final gun failed to go off when the scoreboard ticked down to zero. (Glen Harmeson, the freshman coach, had to rush onto the floor to inform the referee that the game was over.) Wooden was held in check for much of the following game against Ohio State, but when the contest went to overtime, he broke a 33–33 tie with a steal and quick assist to a teammate, a field goal of his own, and a free throw with a few seconds left, enabling the Boilermakers to prevail by 5. As the *Courier and Journal* reported, "Wooden had the faculty of delivering in the pinches." He added 15 points in a 15-point pasting of Northwestern and 17 in a 13-point win over Indiana. After watching Wooden increase his season scoring total to a league-leading 93 points against the Hoosiers, Illinois coach Craig Ruby, who was scouting the game, called Wooden "the greatest basketball player I ever saw in action."

Many of the victory margins would have been even greater had Lambert not emptied his bench once his team built huge leads. Oftentimes, he would leave Wooden as the only starter on the floor. "He had a way of stalling the game out by fantastic dribbling," said Wooden's younger teammate, William "Dutch" Fehring. "He would dribble from backcourt to frontcourt, and all around the court, and nobody could get that ball away."

Purdue would not have won in such dominating fashion had it been a one-man show. Still, everyone knew who the headliner was. On one train trip to a road game, Lambert took a blanket away from one of the reserves and gave it to his senior star. "Wooden's going to play tomorrow. All you're going to do is sit," Lambert said. Wooden was no longer an unbridled colt learning how to harness his talents. He was a seasoned veteran, and he had a bag full of tricks. "He had a very unusual thing he did. He would drive down to the foul circle, and he'd change directions, cause he's like a cat anyway. He would change directions and go either way and he could confuse everybody," said Kenneth Watson, a friend from Martinsville who watched many of Wooden's games at Purdue. Bob King added, "Wooden was somewhat of a folk hero here in Indiana. He was a tremendous competitor. He was a guy you had to kill, almost, to beat him."

In their penultimate game of the season, the Boilermakers again embarrassed Northwestern, their main challenger in the Big Ten race, by a score of 31–17 behind Wooden's 15 points. That clinched their second outright conference championship in three years. It was also the fourth time in seven years that Lambert's team had either won or shared the title. The only question to be settled in Wooden's finale against Chicago was whether he would score 15 points and break the Big Ten single-season scoring record of 147 set by his friend Branch McCracken two years before.

Wooden didn't score 15 points. He scored 21, leaving the new mark at 154 points. Purdue also established a league record for points scored in a season as the Boilermakers completed their campaign with a best-ever 17–1 record. At the time, there were no postseason tournaments or wire-service polls to determine an official national champion, but four years later, when the Los Angeles–based Helms Athletic Foundation retroactively selected national champions in college basketball dating back to 1901, it awarded Purdue the 1932 crown.

There was no question as to who should get most of the credit. An organization called the All-America Board of Basketball Coaches had convened for the first time that winter to vote on the five most outstanding college basketball players in the United States. The story that appeared in newspapers around the country was authored by a board member who knew Wooden all too well: Wisconsin coach Dr. Walter Meanwell. Though the board did not officially designate a national player of the year, Meanwell made clear who he thought belonged at the head of the class. "If the most brilliant amateur basketball player in the country was to be selected, the name of John Wooden outshines all others," Meanwell wrote.

Wooden was even more pleased a few months later when Purdue's president, Edward Elliott, presented him with the Big Ten's academic achievement medal. At the end of the first semester of Wooden's senior year, he ranked nineteenth in a student body of 4,675. He would forever cherish that honor. In his later years, that medal was one of the first pieces of memorabilia Wooden showed to visitors who came to see him in his condominium in Encino, California. "My teammates and my players helped me win every trophy I ever won, but this one I had to earn for myself," he said.

Wooden's exploits at Purdue were the stuff of legend. In 1943, when the Helms Foundation celebrated the first fifty years of organized American basketball by naming an all-time all-star team, it called Wooden "probably the greatest all-around guard of them all." In 1960, four years before he won his first NCAA (National Collegiate Athletic Association) championship as the coach at UCLA, Wooden was inducted into the Naismith Memorial Basketball Hall of Fame in Springfield, Massachusetts. To this day, he is one of just three men to be enshrined as a player and a coach. (The others are Lenny Wilkens and Bill Sharman.) When the Indiana Basketball Hall of Fame inducted Wooden in 1962, it was, in the words of the historian Ron Newlin, "because people remembered him thirty years prior as one of the greatest basketball players in the first seventy years of the game, not as a great coach."

Today, John Wooden is celebrated as the greatest coach the college game, and maybe any game, has ever known. But to folks of a certain era, he was Johnny Wooden, India Rubber Man, an electric flash who darted and dribbled his way around the court like no other, flinging his body to the floor and bouncing up. Nowhere were those images more indelible than in the Hoosier heartland. "Wooden to the kids of my era was what Bill Russell, Wilt Chamberlain, or Lew Alcindor is today," Tom Harmon, a former prominent high school player in Indiana whose brother played with Wooden at Purdue, said in 1968. "Johnny Wooden was king, the idol of every kid who had a basketball. In Indiana, that was every kid."

In 1932, there was not much pro ball to speak of outside of a few disparate leagues and barnstorming tours, but there was enough to keep Wooden busy through the spring and summer. He latched on with Stretch Murphy and several other former teammates in April to play a game in Chicago. Later in the spring, George Halas, the owner of the NFL's Chicago Bears, invited Wooden to play for the basketball team he owned, for a three-game play-off series. Halas paid Wooden $100 a game, which was a lot more than he ever made selling ham sandwiches.

Later that summer, Wooden received an even more lucrative offer from a barnstorming team called the New York Celtics, which had played in the American Basketball League before the ABL folded in 1931. The Celtics were willing to pay Wooden $5,000 for just one year. That was a lot of money for anybody during the Great Depression, much less someone who grew up as poor as Wooden did. However, when Wooden approached Lambert for his blessing, he was subjected to another Socratic grilling. "What did you come to college for?" Lambert asked.

To get an education, Wooden replied.

"Do you think you got it?"

Yes.

"Would you like to use it?"

Yes.

"So how would this be using it?"

Wooden turned the Celtics down. "He told me without telling me," he said of Lambert. "That was his way with so many things."

It's not that Wooden couldn't have used the money. Lord knows, he didn't have much. But he was bred to believe that there was something inherently unclean about using Naismith's game as a tool of avarice. That's not why the game was conceived, and it's not how Wooden was raised. Both his father and his coach believed the best path to a well-lived life was to get an education and use it. Wooden may have been itching to play ball and earn some dough, but the last thing he wanted to do was let either man down.

The best way for Johnny to honor both Hugh and Piggy was to become an English teacher and basketball coach. That, however, put Wooden in conflict with another cherished male role model, Dr. Creek, who suggested to Wooden that he remain at Purdue to study as a fellow in the English department. Lambert told Wooden that he could coach Purdue's freshman basketball team as well, but Creek was against that idea. "He wasn't much for athletics at all. He thought my thinking about going into teaching to become a coach was kind of foolish," Wooden said. Stuck between two mentors whom he greatly admired, Wooden preferred not to make the choice. He told Dr. Creek no thanks.

Wooden finally got an offer he could accept from a high school in Dayton, Kentucky. The barnstorming he did in the spring and summer of 1932 had left him with $909.05 deposited at the Martinsville First Bank and Trust. It was a nifty little sum, and Wooden planned to use that money to buy a new car. He had ordered a Plymouth for around $500, and the car was scheduled to be delivered in the first week of August. However, when Wooden went to the bank to take out his money, he found that First Bank and Trust had gone under. Wooden was completely wiped out. The only money he had to his name was the $2 bill his father had given him when he graduated from Centerton's grade school.

Wooden would never be the same after seeing his life savings disappear in a Martinsville flash. Like many people who lived through the Depression, he emerged from that experience with a deep-seated suspicion that nothing in life was totally safe, that even those entities with the word "trust" in their name can prove devastatingly unreliable. It imbued in Wooden a streak of insecurity that would forever be a part of his makeup.

After he lost his life savings, Wooden told Nellie he thought they should postpone the wedding, but the father of her good friend Mary Schnaiter said he would lend Wooden $200 to get him and Nellie through their first few weeks of married life. And so, on August 8, 1932, just a few days after the Martinsville bank went belly-up, Johnny Wooden and Nellie Riley were married at a small church in Indianapolis. Wooden's brother Cat drove up with his wife to stand as witnesses. After the ceremony, the newlyweds celebrated over dinner at the Bamboo Inn. As it happened, Wooden's favorite singing group, the Mills Brothers, were giving their first-ever performance in Indianapolis that evening at the Circle Theater. Johnny and Nellie, who had made their chastity vow four years before as high school sweethearts, took in the show, and prepared to begin their new life together.

The show dragged on for several hours. Many years later, Wooden had a chance to meet the Mills Brothers in Los Angeles. He told them that he and his new bride had watched the group play on their wedding night. "You guys sang so long, I thought you would never stop," Wooden teased. It may have been the closest he ever came to telling a dirty joke.

6

An English Teacher

There would be no time for a honeymoon. At the crack of dawn on August 9, 1932, the day after the wedding, John Wooden hopped the interurban railroad from Indianapolis to Martinsville to meet Piggy Lambert. The two of them then drove to Vincennes, Indiana, where Wooden assisted Lambert at a coaching clinic. Having just incurred a $200 debt, Wooden was happy to make a few bucks, but he and his new bride were still pretty much broke. A few days later, Nellie's sister, Audrey, and her husband, Ray, drove the newlyweds to Dayton, Kentucky, to Wooden's new job. Everything John and Nellie owned—which wasn't much—was piled into the back of the car. "We went down there with nothing, no place to stay or anything," Wooden said. When they arrived, the superintendent who hired Wooden, a fellow Purdue graduate named Olin W. Davis, brought Johnny and Nellie to their new apartment, on the top level of a duplex.

Dayton was a small hamlet across the Ohio River from Cincinnati. The high school had only about three hundred students, and the Wadsworth Watch Case Company and the Perry and Derrick paint factory were the only industries in town. The high school had a decent football program, but basketball lagged far behind. Wooden was hired to change that, which meant that the regular varsity coach, Willard Bass, was demoted to the girls' team.

Wooden had many responsibilities. On top of coaching football, basketball, track, and baseball, he was the athletic director and curriculum adviser for all physical education classes in grades one through twelve. He also taught five English classes a day. The only part that concerned him was coaching football. Martinsville High did not have a football team, and aside from the couple of days he practiced with the squad at Purdue, Wooden had no experience in the sport. Before he left Purdue, he spent some time picking the brain of Noble Kizer, the Boilermakers' football coach, as well as that of his assistant. It helped, but Wooden knew he was woefully unprepared. And there were few things Wooden disliked more than being unprepared.

The temperament that served Wooden so well as an athlete turned out to be in short supply when he had a whistle around his neck. It got the better of him one day in practice when he was giving a hard time to a big, rumbling lineman. The player got tired of hearing Wooden chastising him for his lack of effort, so he went right up to the head coach, who was several inches shorter, and dared Wooden to make him listen. "You're not man enough to do it," he said.

That was the wrong thing to say to Johnny Wooden.

It only took Wooden a few seconds to flatten the kid with his fists. Wooden suffered no repercussions for getting physical with a player—it was hardly unusual in those days—but it helped him realize the job was not for him, even though his team lost only one game. When the season ended, he asked the superintendent to relieve him of his football duties.

Basketball didn't go much better. Most of the students who came out for the team were football players moonlighting during the winter. Moreover, Wooden was asking them to execute a completely different style than the one they had been accustomed to under Bass. That meant a lot more running.

He conducted his practices with a firm hand. Sometimes he even carried a paddle in that hand, perhaps because he remembered how his grade school principal, Earl Warriner, had used the instrument to good effect the day Wooden and his friends refused to sing the national anthem. "We had some real loafers on our team," said Bill Smith, who was a captain of that first basketball team in Dayton. "He wanted us to go full blast up and down the court. He'd stand there with a paddle and speed 'em up." Charles Carmichael, a six-foot-two forward on that team, added, "If you missed an easy layup, he'd be right there to crack you. While he was doing it, the other guys would be standing there laughing at the guy getting paddled."

Wooden never used profanity with his players, and he rarely invoked his own pedigree. "He didn't say anything about his reputation as a player. He didn't boost himself at all to us," said Ben Stull, a sophomore on Wooden's first team. Then again, he didn't have to. When Wooden didn't like what his players were doing, he simply showed them what he wanted. Sometimes he would grab a couple of scrubs and challenge the starters to a scrimmage. "Fastest dribbler I've ever seen, bar none. Nobody could beat him to the basket," Smith said. During these workouts, Wooden would encourage the players to do whatever they wanted to stop him. "He wanted us to rough him up," one player said. "But if you got near him, you wound up on the floor. And we were all pretty good-sized guys, too."

"He was trying to teach the type of basketball that wouldn't be popular for thirty years," Smith said. "That's why we didn't win very many games. We just couldn't grasp his fast-breaking style."

As the years went on, Wooden would often wince as he reflected on this period of his life. "Having been a player of outstanding reputation, perhaps I expected too much," he said more than thirty years later. "The worst fault of a beginning coach is he expects too much and doesn't have enough patience."

At the end of one particularly heated game against Newport High School, the opposing coach, Lou Foster, accused Wooden of teaching "dirty basketball." Wooden, enraged, lunged at him. One eyewitness recalled decades later that as some players and bystanders restrained Wooden, the Dayton sheriff quipped, "Aww, turn him loose." The witness continued, "Johnny was so furious that it would have been the wrong thing to turn him loose. Foster would have been no match for him."

Wooden tried to encourage his players not to be concerned with winning and losing, but he got discouraged as the losses piled up. The most stinging defeat came when he took his team to play at Martinsville. "That was the first time I was ever in a big basketball court like that," Stull said. The local fans gave Wooden a glorious ovation. Then they cheered as Glenn Curtis led their Artesians to a 27–17 victory. Dayton finished the season with just 6 wins to 11 losses. It was the first losing basketball season of Wooden's life.

Despite the setbacks, the players couldn't help but appreciate Wooden's dedication. His office in the corner of the gymnasium was a hub of activity as students came by to shoot the breeze. "He was a very considerate man . . . and he'd treat you like a real person. He was such a good Christian man," Carmichael said. Wooden also made sure his players were home and resting the night before a game. "He laid down a set of rules and expected the guys to follow it. He used to walk the streets after 9 p.m. to see if any guys were out," said Bob Williams, who was a student manager. "You either produced for him or you didn't. It was as simple as that." Another former player, Howard Fahrubel, recalled that Wooden would host the players at his house the night before a game to be sure they weren't up late carousing. "He'd invite us for supper and we stayed the rest of the evening," Fahrubel said.

Wooden brought the same devotion to the classroom. Since he had to cover material within a week or two that he had studied for entire semesters at Purdue, he had to be thoroughly organized and prepared for each class. Students would long remember his meticulous, elegant penmanship. Though his reputation as a former collegiate basketball star overshadowed everything he did, Wooden thought of himself as an English teacher who happened to coach, not the other way around.

There was, however, one aspect to teaching that bothered him—the parents. Wooden noticed early on that they seemed overly concerned with their children's grades. To Wooden, this seemed counterproductive, immoral even. It reminded him of fans and sportswriters who judged a team's performance solely by the numbers on the scoreboard. Wooden knew from his playing experience that sometimes you can play very well and still lose; other times you can play poorly and win. To one student, a B is a great achievement; to another, it should be a disappointment. As an athlete, Wooden preferred to be judged solely on his effort. He wondered why parents weren't doing the same when it came to their own children.

As he ruminated on this problem, he thought foremost of his father, who had encouraged his four sons to be satisfied with their best effort even if it yielded an unsatisfying outcome. Wooden also reflected on an assignment he had once been given by his high school history teacher in Martinsville. The teacher had asked his students to come up with their own personal definition of *success*. Like most of his classmates, Wooden's answer centered on material gains, but now his definition was evolving.

While waiting to get his hair cut one day, Wooden came across a brief poem whose author was anonymous. It read: *"Before God's footstool to confess/A poor soul knelt and bowed his head/'I failed,' he wailed. The Master said,/'Thou did thy best, that is success.'"* Thus inspired, Wooden took another stab at his old teacher's assignment. The revised definition was a little clunky and verbose, but it was better than the one Wooden had proffered as a high school student: "Success is peace of mind which is a direct result of self-satisfaction in knowing you did your best to become the best that you are capable of becoming."

Finally, Wooden summoned the "ladder of success" that Glenn Curtis had presented to him when Wooden played for the Artesians. Wooden wanted to broaden that concept, so he settled on the idea of a pyramid. Thinking like the civil engineer he had originally aspired to become, he figured he would first need a pair of really strong cornerstones. From Curtis's ladder he selected "enthusiasm" and "industriousness." Building up from there, he took Lambert's three-part philosophy of condition, skill, and team spirit and laid them across the middle. Wooden plugged in additional elements in Curtis's ladder and added a few more of his own. It was a good first pass, but it would take more than a decade of tinkering for him to decide that his Pyramid of Success was complete.

After a year of implementing Lambert's fast-break system and running his players mercilessly in practice, Wooden's Dayton Greendevils enjoyed much more "success" in year two, posting a 15–3 record. The school's yearbook, the *Dayton Pilot*, observed: "Having only two regulars left from last season's squad, Johnny Wooden, our versatile coach, whipped into shape one of the best teams Dayton has sponsored in recent years." The Greendevils appeared poised for an even better season in year three. Not only were many of the players underclassmen, but a couple of the seniors were thinking about failing a few classes on purpose so they could stay and play another year. "Because of the Depression, there weren't any jobs for us anyway. So we figured there was nothing else to do but play ball," Smith said.

Wooden, however, was not long for Dayton. During the summer of 1934, Nellie had given birth to a daughter, Nancy Anne, in nearby Covington, and they ached to get back to Indiana. An opportunity to do just that presented itself shortly after the start of the 1934–35 academic year, when Wooden was offered a job in the South Bend school system. It was a chance to go to a bigger school in a bigger city for a little more money ($2,400). There was only one catch: the school already had a head basketball coach, so Wooden would be the assistant. Wooden didn't hesitate. He could be plenty happy just being an English teacher.

At South Bend's Central High School, Wooden was again wearing many hats. Besides teaching English and serving as athletic director, he also coached baseball and tennis. In addition, he was the school's comptroller, which was ironic since he was never very good with numbers. With so many responsibilities, Wooden did not plan to immediately get involved with the basketball team, but he spent the last four weeks of that first season working as an assistant to the head coach, Ralph Parmenter. Given Wooden's credentials as a player, his ascension to the head spot was inevitable. The shift occurred in the spring of 1936. That was a milestone year for the Wooden family, as Nellie gave birth to a son, Jim, that fall.

The town of South Bend was mad for basketball, but it was still a long way from Martinsville. The gymnasium was so small the basketball team could not even practice there. Instead the players trekked a couple of miles down the street to the YMCA, and the squad played its "home" games at various schools around town. While Wooden considered coaching to be secondary to his duties in the classroom, he understood that his superiors did not share that view. "I don't think South Bend knew whether I'd be a good English teacher or not. They hoped from my background that maybe I could be a pretty good basketball and baseball coach," he said. "I wanted to be a good English teacher. I wanted to be the best English teacher I could be, but they're not always looking for that." Wooden was so deft with language that when he took a job on the side as an editor for the Harper Grace publishing company, the executives there tried to hire him full-time.

It didn't take long for the folks in South Bend to realize just how stubborn their new head basketball coach could be. One of Wooden's primary team rules was that every player had to be on time. On the night of one of his first road games, several of Wooden's players, including the two cocaptains, were a few minutes late for the bus. Wooden climbed aboard and told the driver to leave without them. The players found their own way to the game, but Wooden left them on the bench.

Things did not get much better for the team as Wooden finished his first season as Central's coach with a record of 8 wins and 14 losses. This was apparently an unpleasant experience for him, because for most of his life he pretended it never happened. In the many interviews he gave and books he wrote over the decades, as well as in all of his officially distributed bios, Wooden always claimed that that first year in Dayton was the only losing record of his coaching career. It was a classic case of selective amnesia.

The benching of the tardy cocaptains was but a minor kerfuffle compared to the storm Wooden ignited during his second season as Central's head coach, in 1937–38. The Bears were scheduled to play their main rival in the Northern Indiana Conference, Mishawaka High School, on the same night that a big dance was being held at the high school by a club called The Smiters. Four of Wooden's players failed to show up for the game. The next day, Nell was looking through a newspaper and came upon a picture of the players at the dance. Wooden immediately booted them off the team.

One of those players, Bobby Osborne, happened to be the son of the assistant principal. The father insisted that Wooden reinstate Bobby and his three friends. The principal, P. D. Pointer, tried to intervene on the players' behalf, but Wooden told him that if he was forced to accept the boys back on the team, he would quit. Pointer backed off. "That made Wooden in South Bend," said Ed Powell, who arrived at Central in Wooden's second season and soon became one of his favorite players.

"It really shook up the town," said Eddie Ehlers, who at the time was an eighth grader and one of the better players in town. "One of the boys' mothers called my mother and told her Coach Wooden was a bad man and she shouldn't let me play for him. Thank goodness my mother said, 'I believe in my son, and he wants to play for Mr. Wooden.'"

Ehlers followed through on that desire once he reached high school. He also played baseball for Wooden, although the coach did not approach that task with the same degree of sobriety as he did basketball. "It was fun for him," Ehlers said. "It wasn't like basketball, where from the minute you walked out on the floor it was serious." When the players rode their bikes to baseball practice, they often stopped at a bakery along the way to buy five-cent pies. Wooden, who had a serious sweet tooth, would sit with them at the start of practice and devour the desserts. Still, the competitor in him came out during games, such as the day in 1939 when he sat his whole team down for fifteen minutes to express his displeasure at an umpire's missed call, and then resumed the game under protest. (The *South Band Tribune* reported that Wooden "registered vigorous disapproval" of the umpire's ruling. His protest was later denied.)

Wooden was just as stern while conducting his English classes. "It was always very orderly," Ehlers said. "Some of the coaches have class and it's an opportunity to goof off, but not with Coach Wooden." Ed Powell recalled that Wooden was a "stickler for good penmanship." Occasionally, Wooden would pass along a favorite poem to his players and ask them to commit it to memory. One he particularly liked was titled "Mr. Meant To":

> *Mr. Meant To has a comrade*
> *And his name is Didn't Do*
> *Have you ever chance to meet them?*
> *Did they ever call on you?*
> *These two fellows lived together*
> *In the house of Never Win*
> *And I am told that it is haunted*
> *By the ghost of Might Have Been*

Since Wooden learned most of what he knew about basketball from Piggy Lambert, it was only natural that he would implement many of

Lambert's ideas. That included enforcing the coach's "right rules of living" away from the court. "Three or four times a year, he would sit us down on the floor and talk to us about things other than basketball," said John Gassensmith, one of his former players. "How to behave, being good to the teachers. I remember he told us, after you eat dinner, congratulate your mother. Tell her what a good meal it was."

From the very beginning, Wooden put in place a strict smoking ban, making clear that a violation would result in dismissal. In one instance where he had caught a player smoking, the player repeatedly asked to return to the team, but Wooden refused. At the time, the player appeared to be headed for college, but after being kicked off the team, he never pursued his higher education. Though Wooden couldn't be sure things would have turned out differently if he had let the player return, he came to regret his inflexibility. "He quit school. Never went to college. I think he ended up a common laborer," Wooden said. "I'm not putting them down, but here's a player who was going to get a college education, to have a better chance, and it was because of my being perhaps too stubborn [that he didn't go]. But I saw no middle. It was either black or white. There was no gray area, and there is a gray area on many things. So that bothered me."

Wooden kept the no-smoking rule in place, but he subsequently dropped the specification of what the penalty would be. "Instead of saying if you smoke you're off the team, he said, 'There is to be no smoking. It will not be tolerated,'" said Jim Powers, who attended Central from 1939 to 1943. During Powers's senior year, Wooden briefly suspended one of his best players, Parson Howell, for smoking, but he allowed the other players to vote him back onto the team.

Ironically, Wooden was a smoker himself. He admitted as much to his players, but he also told them that he quit when practice began and didn't resume until the season was over. "He used this as an example to show that he could quit when he wanted to if he really put his mind to it," Powell said. Nell was also a heavy smoker, but unlike John, who eventually quit for good, she was never able to kick the habit.

Through it all, Johnny Wooden had no better friend, supporter, and defender than his Nellie. On every game night, she and John carried on the same pregame ritual they had begun back in Martinsville, with Wooden turning to the stands to make eye contact with his bride and then flashing her the "okay" sign right before tip-off. Nell had several more fainting incidents, but she never missed a game. There were no laundry facilities at the school, so John asked Nell if she would wash his players' sweaty uniforms, socks, and jock straps after each practice. She obliged, just as she did when he asked to invite his players to their house on Woodward Avenue. "She was almost my mother," Powers said. "She'd have those parties after the season was over. They knew I loved ice cream, so they'd get me a gallon of it beforehand."

Wooden was not a man of many hobbies, although he did spend time during the off-seasons playing some golf. During one memorable afternoon, he accomplished the rare feat of scoring a hole in one and a double eagle in the same round. (He kept that scorecard for the rest of his life.) That aside, Johnny, who was now in his late twenties and a married father of two, was still an introverted wallflower. As usual, it was up to Nell to provide balance. "He was very shy," Powell said. "His wife saw it, too. She knew it when he was speaking to people and would have his finger on his mouth." Wooden was combative during games, but away from the court it was Nell who was the loud one. One time Ehlers was riding in the backseat of the Woodens' car on the way home from a difficult loss against James Whitcomb Riley High School. The car was quiet until Nell spied a Riley player, in his purple letterman's sweater, walking down the street. The young man had an unfortunate pug nose. Nell rolled down the window, stuck her head out, and shouted, "You no-good little bulldog!" John grabbed her and pulled her back inside the car.

If there's one thing Wooden understood innately, it's that a teacher must set a righteous example if he wants his students to follow him. "You have to walk it," Wooden said. "You can't fool these kids. They know whether or not you really care about them." If he insisted that his players never smoked, then he wasn't going to smoke. If he said that they could never be late, then he could never be late. (He was there to greet them at the YMCA every morning at 6:00 a.m. so he could tape their ankles before practice.) And if he told them that they could not use profanity, he wasn't going to use any himself. Instead of cursing when he got mad, he adopted the habit of shouting "Gracious sakes alive!" If he was really ticked off, he would say "*Goodness* gracious sakes alive!" It was odd that a man with such affection for the English language would construct a phrase that made no sense, but there it was. When I asked Wooden where he came up with it, he replied, "I have no idea."

Wooden was a popular, respected basketball coach and English teacher, but there was little to augur that South Bend was witnessing some kind of legend in the making. To wit, when Wooden accepted an invitation to speak at a local banquet, here's how a local newspaper described the event: "Johnny Wooden, South Bend Central's basketball coach, will be the featured speaker at Elkhart High's sports banquet, although they had hoped to line up some prominent college coach."

Day by day, step by step, year by year, he perfected his craft. This wasn't just some English teacher chasing state championships in his spare time. This was a man who was laying the groundwork for a career that would dominate the sport of basketball.

Many of the tactics Wooden developed during his eight seasons as South Bend's head basketball coach were born of necessity. The facilities were so bad, and the gym time so limited, that he had no choice but to map out his practices in rigid detail. "We only had two hours, so he knew he had to get everything done," Powers said. "The practice had to be highly organized. You didn't have a moment to think about what you wanted to do."

The fixed schedule meant there was no time for frivolity. "He didn't take no foolishness," said Tom Taylor, who played at Central High from 1939 to 1943. "I found that out the first time he threw me out of practice. I was fooling around with another guy. He said, 'Go get your shower.' Then he'd coach you up later on. He didn't cuss, but he got it across to you."

Taylor was lucky that was all Wooden got across that day. The coach was far more incensed when he found out that his best player, Parson Howell, had been smoking. On the morning that Wooden learned of Howell's transgression, he marched upstairs to the auxiliary gym where Howell was shooting baskets and repeatedly kicked him in the rear end as the two of them walked down two flights of stairs. "He literally helped Parson down the stairs by booting him all the way," Powers said. Gassensmith recalled that when Wooden kicked someone, he could actually lift him off the ground. "I tell you, for a little guy he was powerful," Gassensmith said.

"Not everybody came out of their exposure to John Wooden and made the grade. He was very strict, and some people had a problem with that," said Stan Jacobs, another of his former South Bend players. "There were some failures, too, who were disappointments to him, who drank, who didn't stick to training rules, and who didn't get their academic work done and keep it up to par."

Like Piggy Lambert, Wooden immersed himself in the smallest details.

He refused to move on to the next fundamental until the players had mastered the one they were working on. It was all part of a grand design that extended well beyond a single practice. Once again, Wooden viewed a basketball season through the eyes of the engineer he nearly became. First, he had to set the foundation—a row of pipes here, a couple of gears there—and then he laid everything in place piece by piece. If a gear got stuck, he had to go back and apply a little more oil. Every drill, every practice built toward something, and Wooden was the only one who could see the full blueprint.

The season began with a focus on conditioning, footwork, and movement. "Everybody was in motion all the time. Everything was done at full pace," Powers said. When Wooden taught the players how to shoot, they had to learn the proper form first. The ball came later. Same thing with learning how to run an offense. "You just never had the ball in your hands," said Ed Powers, Jim's older brother. "You were always playing three on two, two on one, one on one, but you never shot the ball. It was just ballhandling. After you did that for two weeks, then you finally got to play basketball."

Wooden's education as a coach was bolstered in 1941, when Notre Dame, just across town in South Bend, hired Frank Leahy to be its football coach. Leahy jealously guarded his own practices—no writers or coaches were allowed—but he took a liking to Wooden and invited him to watch. Wooden considered himself organized, but he was floored by how efficient Leahy's workouts were. He ran a beautiful, well-designed engine. The players shuttled from drill to drill without missing a beat. The coaches also did very little talking, since each word that was spoken meant time standing idle. As a result of those visits, Wooden developed the habit of writing his practice plans on index cards so he could pull them out of his pocket without slowing down the action.

And slowing down was the last thing Wooden wanted his players to do. Lambert's fire-wagon style was more prevalent in Indiana than in any other part of the country, but for the most part, it was still the exception. Wooden thought it was particularly important that his South Bend teams be proficient at the fast break because they tended to be smaller than the teams they were playing. "The trick was to get all five guys thinking the way he thinks," Ed Powell said. "I used to wonder, what kind of coach would Coach Wooden be once he gets height?"

Also like Lambert, Wooden made sure his players took care of their feet. He taught them how to rub their feet with powder and wear two pairs of socks, and he had them wearing shoes that were one size too small. "I noticed that most players wear shoes that are too large," Wooden said. "Basketball is a game of quick movement—stop, start, turn, change of direction, change of pace. If there's that much sliding to the end of the toe, you're going to get some blisters. So I decided what size shoe you're going to wear. I want your toe right at the end of the shoe so that when you stop, there's not going to be any sliding back and forth. I think that's important."

In Wooden's eyes, blisters were about the worst enemy that could visit a basketball team. He was so concerned about them that he forbade his players to attend dances during the season. He even coached the way the players ate. "Wooden ordered the pregame meal, and even a manager had to eat the same dry roast beef and dry head lettuce and toast without butter he ordered," Jacobs said. "He was very concerned about nutrition, and he was very careful about food and what we ate. He had very strict training rules compared to other coaches of the day."

When the Bears ran their fast break, Wooden wanted the guard to stop at the foul line. When the guard fed the wings, Wooden wanted him to throw a bounce pass. Everything had to be precise. During one game, a Central player tried to catch and shoot a bounce pass that was thrown too low, but he lost his balance and the ball hit the underside of the rim. The Bears won the game, but Wooden had spied a deficiency that needed to be addressed. So at practice the following week, he devised a drill where he repeatedly rolled his players the ball as they ran full speed toward the basket. "There is no pass that is lower than a roll, so if you can handle a roll, you can handle anything," Powell said. "The next time there was a situation where the pass was low, we picked the ball up and put it in like nothing."

He wanted free throws to be shot two-handed and underhanded, just as he did. And in case his players doubted whether that form could be effective, Wooden was happy to demonstrate. "When I tell young coaches about the night after practice at the old South Bend YMCA that [Wooden] made 96 out of 100 free throws, they don't believe it," said Billy Bender, a former player. "When I tell them it was done shooting two-handed, they really don't believe it."

This was another of Wooden's assets as a teacher. Whatever he asked his players to do, he was able to do it far better himself. He showed how to get a rebound by grabbing the ball and sticking out his elbows. Sometimes he would show off by standing at midcourt sinking two-handed set shots. "He would demonstrate everything. There was nothing he couldn't do to perfection," Bob Dunbar said. Added Jim Powers, "He was a young buck. He could rebound better than we could, he could shoot better than we could, and he could dribble better than we could. He taught you by demonstrating. He didn't leave it to you to learn how to do things."

This came in especially handy when Wooden was displeased. One season, as the team was in the midst of a long winning streak, Wooden decided his boys were getting a little too cocky, so he set up a scrimmage with some other faculty members. "We couldn't stop him," Powell said. "I don't think he missed a shot the whole game. He had us faked out of our supporters. It was a humbling experience, but it brought us back down to earth."

He was, in short, a hard-to-please, detail-obsessed, hyper-organized taskmaster and control freak—which made it all the more jarring when he adopted a hands-off approach during games. Wooden believed it was his job to prepare his team to play. Once the game began, it was their job to show what they had learned. *Don't look over at the bench when the game starts*, he told them. *Just do what you've been taught to do.* "Practice was Mr. Wooden's domain. The game was the players' domain," Dunbar said. "He expected you to perform what you practiced all week. He made some adjustments, but you never saw him running up and down the sideline."

Wooden did not like calling time-outs. He saw them as a sign of weakness, and they only gave the other team a chance to rest. Likewise, if the opponent seized momentum, Wooden did not believe in making strategic adjustments. He would rather err on the side of consistency. "Back then, we used to think Wooden wasn't flexible enough," Powell said. "He couldn't change his style of coaching in the tougher, more demanding tournament games. He thought he could win just by having the better-conditioned teams. I think he learned later on that it took more than that."

Which is not to say Wooden was disengaged. For example, he could be brutal on referees. He may have mostly stayed in his chair, but he maintained a running dialogue with the officials. Jim Powers recalled a game that was officiated by a man named Pinkie Fink. When Wooden didn't like one of Fink's calls, he shouted, "Fink, you stink!" Oftentimes, Wooden let his assistant do the baiting, but there was no doubt who was giving the orders. "He was a lot more fiery than people knew," Ehlers said.

Wooden even had the bright idea to set up a regular game against a rival school coached by his older brother, Maurice. John later recalled that when his team won, Maurice "didn't speak to me for a year." After

South Bend won three straight, the brothers decided not to play again. "It was not a healthy situation," John said.

Above all, he was a fighter, quite literally if he was pushed enough. One person who found that out early on was Mishawaka coach Shelby Shake, who was a cousin of Glenn Curtis. During his eleven years at Mishawaka, Shake's teams won four sectional championships. He also had a flair for showmanship. He once dressed his players in warm-up pants with vertical stripes for a state tournament game, and for Mishawaka's home games, Shake introduced a contraption called the "Bask-O-Lite," where after each basket a red light mounted behind the rim would flash and the lights above the backboard would display the word "Goal." Like Wooden, Shake was an exponent of fire-wagon basketball, so when they squared off during Wooden's first season at Central, their teams put on a great show. Unfortunately for Shake, Central prevailed in both regular season meetings, the first time that had happened in thirteen years.

When the coaches went to shake hands following the Bears' second win, Shake muttered to Wooden, "How much did you pay those officials?" They exchanged a few tart words, and then Shake called him a liar.

That was the wrong thing to say to Johnny Wooden.

Wooden rushed at Shake and swung his fist. Immediately, players and a few fans moved in to separate them. One of Shake's players, a cocaptain named Art Van Tone, saw a boy wearing a Central letter sweater restraining Shake, so he intervened to protect his coach. According to the *South Bend Tribune*, Van Tone "dove into the pile and put on a flying block that knocked down more persons than any punches swung before since the dispute had opened." Wooden and his players eventually went to their locker room to cool off and change their clothes, but that did not dissipate the tension. "We had to have a police escort out of the building—the team and all—because there were people waiting for us," Ed Powell said. "I've never seen [Wooden] as upset as I did that night." Shake apologized for igniting the ruckus, but after the season, Arthur Trester, the secretary of the IHSAA, ordered Mishawaka to remove him as coach.

If Wooden was going to be a fighter, he would accept no less from his players. Eddie Ehlers found that out during a game against Goshen High School in 1941. On an exchange early in the first half, one of Goshen's players pinched Ehlers so hard on the leg that he was bleeding. Ehlers was furious. He showed Wooden the wound and was ready to retaliate, but Wooden told him to wait until the right time. Ehlers kept his composure until late in the second half. With Central holding a comfortable lead, Ehlers found himself being guarded on an inbounds pass by the player who had pinched him. Ehlers looked over at the bench and caught his coach's eye. Wooden nodded. "He was telling me to take care of him," Ehlers said. On the inbounds play, Ehlers faked in one direction, and when he shifted the other way, he punched the kid in the stomach as hard as he could. "I knew I hit him good because I could feel his backbone," Ehlers said.

The referees did not see the punch. After the next whistle, Wooden took Ehlers out of the game. The two never said a word about what happened, but as Ehlers sat down on the bench, Wooden touched him on the shoulder. "He handled it masterfully," Ehlers said. Told that his recollection contradicted the modern-day image of Wooden as a kindly old man, Ehlers replied, "He was anything but that. He was mean."

Not surprisingly, Wooden was at his most intense during the state tournament. During his fifth season, in 1940–41, the Bears were playing a tough state semifinal game against Jefferson High School in Lafayette. The team, and Ehlers in particular, had played a poor first half, and Wooden was eager to express his displeasure. But when they got to the locker room at intermission, the door was locked. They tried in vain for several minutes to find someone to unlock it. Finally, Wooden kicked it open. When the team got inside, he ripped them for the way they had played, Ehlers most of all. "I have never been chewed out like he chewed me out," Ehlers said. "I still don't know what I did to this day, but he raked me over the coals. It must have worked because we went out in the second half and beat them going away."

Wooden wanted to do for South Bend Central what Glenn Curtis did three times for Martinsville High School—win an Indiana high school state championship. But greater forces always intervened. Three times Wooden guided the Bears to a sectional championship, and twice they claimed a regional title, but he was never able to take them to the top. The most heartbreaking loss came right after the win over Jefferson in the 1941 regional final, when the Bears fell by one point to Froebel High School from Gary, Indiana. "I never saw Wooden so dejected in my life," Ed Powers said. "He was sick, because he thought he had a team that was going to go all the way. But we just weren't meant to be." Weeks later, Wooden's pain was still palpable. "I can recall at our banquet, he talked about how he was still really dejected," Ehlers said. "We were all depressed. We had a team that was good enough to win the championship."

Two years later, the 1943 tournament ended in similar fashion. Central had risen to the No. 1 ranking in the state during the season, and they faced another local rival, Elkhart High School, in the state tournament. Wooden's Bears entered the fourth quarter trailing by 16 points, but as usual they were the stronger, better-conditioned team down the stretch. They scored 17 points in the last stanza but fell 4 points short. "Those kids never quit," Wooden said softly in the locker room afterward. "You can't ask for anything much better than that rally in the last quarter."

His despair revealed an inner dichotomy that was at odds with the "thou didst thy best" image he tried to project. Wooden could talk all he wanted to his players about his definition of success, about how their only worry should be whether they were maximizing their potential, but his walk told them something else. He said so himself: you can't fool these kids. His players saw the deeper truth. This was one mean English teacher, and he wanted to win very badly.

7

The Kautskys

Besides teaching, coaching, mentoring, and occasionally feeding his players during his early years in South Bend, Wooden would from time to time invite them to watch him play professional basketball. It was a kick for his boys to see him in action. "I tell you, he was phenomenal," Ed Powell said. "He was very quick, although not very tall. But he could dribble—and I'm not exaggerating—down the floor faster than the rest of the players could run without the ball."

Just as he was the best collegian of his era, Wooden was among the most successful professional players in America in the 1930s. Problem was, professional basketball barely existed in America in the 1930s. The sport was mostly limited to a small group of franchises that barnstormed to each other's towns for exhibitions. Even for a player of Wooden's caliber, pro basketball was just a side gig, something that could feed his competitive desires while he made a few extra bucks.

Several professional teams were drawing sizable crowds in the Northeast, but Indiana, not surprisingly, was the hub of the Midwest. The visionary who tapped into that wellspring was Frank Kautsky, who owned a modest but profitable two-level grocery store on the south side of Indianapolis. A short, bald, cheerful man with a round face and a squeaky voice, Kautsky was a bundle of energy who fancied cigars and three-piece suits. He had played some semiprofessional baseball and sponsored his own baseball team in the 1920s, but after being introduced to basketball by a friend, he saw how much fun that game could be. More important, he saw how profitable it could be in his home state.

In 1930, he formed Kautsky A. C., which stood for Athletic Club. The team was generally called the Kautskys, and its owner displayed top-level talent before crowds that numbered in the hundreds. Though the Great Depression was wreaking havoc everywhere—forcing the nation's most popular pro circuit, the East Coast–based American Basketball League, to fold in 1931—Kautsky kept ticket prices low and never failed to pay his players what he promised. He carried a wad of cash in his pocket—his guys referred to it as his "big head of lettuce"—and if they had performed well, he'd slip them an extra five or ten bucks.

Kautsky loved the action, but during those first few years, he lost money. He understood that if pro basketball was ever going to turn a profit, he would need a real star. He got his chance in 1932, when Johnny Wooden finished his senior season at Purdue. Kautsky met with Wooden in Indianapolis and was able to convince him to play because, unlike the Celtics, the Kautskys would not require Wooden to give up teaching. Kautsky went out of his way to treat Wooden well, and in return, Wooden took a liking to him. "He was a very wonderful person," Wooden said. "It was very seldom that there wouldn't be a little extra in my envelope. He knew a little something about my eating habits, too. He knew I liked fruit salad, for example. I took a little rapping from some of the other players, but I got along with him very well. We had some wonderful times."

When the team hit the road, Kautsky plastered posters displaying Wooden's picture in advance of the games. "My dad always said [Wooden] could stop on a dime and give you five cents change," recalled Kautsky's son, Don. Kautsky signed up other prominent players, including Stretch Murphy, Branch McCracken, and Frank Baird, who had starred at Butler, but Wooden was the main attraction. Baird recalled a night when the Kautskys walked into a gymnasium in Pittsburgh packed with fans hoping to catch a glimpse of the India Rubber Man. "The first thing they asked us when we entered the court was, 'Which one was John Wooden?'" Baird said. "I don't know that John had ever played in Pittsburgh before, but he was certainly a drawing card there." Those fans would go home disappointed, as Wooden's teaching duties had kept him back in Dayton that night.

In that respect, Wooden was typical. "We played usually on Saturdays and Sundays because all the players, you see, were teaching or working somewhere else," Wooden told the author Todd Gould. "We had a loosely knit league. There were no commissioners, and each team got their own officials." The players also had to bring their own gear and provide for their transportation. "Sometimes I drove all night, went home, got a shower, put on a clean shirt, and went right to school," Wooden said. "I often worked on my lesson plans as I traveled. I don't think my teaching suffered because of it, but it wasn't easy."

Always on the hunt for prime competition, Kautsky linked up in 1932 with a businessman in Akron, Ohio, who worked for the Firestone Tire and Rubber Company. Together they set up a circuit featuring the best teams from their respective states. They called themselves the National Basketball League. One game drew more than four thousand fans, who saw Wooden score 21 points in a 1-point loss, but there were not enough such nights to sustain their efforts. The NBL disbanded after just one year.

Kautsky was unbowed. He could see that Indiana basketball fans were willing to embrace his product if he gave them something compelling to watch. So he continued to scavenge for opponents. The most popular draws were the three titans from the East Coast: the Original Celtics, the Harlem Globetrotters, and the best of them all, the Harlem Renaissance, who were known more commonly as the Rens. During the 1932–33 season, the Rens won 120 games and lost 8. Kautsky invited them to Indiana several times that season. It was not unusual for high school teams in Indiana to have black players, but the notion of entire teams comprised only of blacks was new to this part of the country. Whatever their attitudes on race, the people in Indiana loved entertaining, team-oriented basketball. Many of the games featuring the Rens drew upward of fifteen thousand fans into Butler Fieldhouse.

The first time Wooden faced off against the Rens in the Fieldhouse, he was held to just 7 points in a 34–28 loss. As a fan of the game himself, he was spellbound by the Rens' talent, their grace, and most of all, their exquisite teamwork. He often said it was the best team he ever saw. "I'd have to be careful I didn't stop playing and start watching them," Wooden confessed.

The next day's *Indianapolis News* paid similar tribute. "Great! That sums up the marvelous passing, ball handling, teamwork and basket scoring ability of the New York Renaissance colored quintet, which Sunday afternoon defeated the Kautskys 34–28 in one of the greatest, if not the greatest, exhibitions of basketball ever seen in this city," the story read. "Even Johnny Wooden's clever dribbling was lost as [Rens guard] Clarence Jenkins policed the Kautsky star throughout the contest."

The Kautskys weren't too shabby themselves. They prevailed over the Rens in a rematch later that season, and they also defeated the Celtics 37–29 at the Armory in downtown Indianapolis before another standing-room-only crowd. The *Indianapolis News* boasted that Wooden and the local boys had given the Celtics a "neat lesson in basketball," but the game was marred by an ugly fight between Kautsky guard Clarence "Big Chris" Christopher and the Celtics' Nat Hickey. The *News* reported that "Hickey tried to put Chris in the bleachers" but that Christopher was "smiling. After all, Chris takes it all in good fun. The fans expect him to be rough."

The scene was all too common. Pro basketball at the time was far different than the game Wooden had played at Purdue. The fans who attended college games were usually middle- and upper-class folks, graduates of the colleges that were playing or local citizens eager to take in the purity of competition. Pro ball, however, attracted a less-educated, blue-collar fan who wanted to feel a little civic pride. Those fans liked their basketball rough, and the teams obliged them. One of the more prominent barnstorming squads of the 1930s was an all-Jewish team from Philadelphia run by a man named Eddie Gottlieb, who promised "a fight in every game, guaranteed." Butler Fieldhouse was always filled whenever Gottlieb's team came to play against Kautsky's.

Wooden was never a fan of excessive roughness—like Piggy Lambert, he believed that basketball should be a finesse game—but he was never one to back down from a fight, either. One confrontation turned comical. Wooden had been playing against the Celtics when he was tripped by their center Joe Lapchick, the best big man of his era. (He would go on to coach for many years for St. John's University and the New York Knicks.) "I went down hard and I came up fightin' mad," Wooden said. "I went after him but I couldn't get him. . . . He had his long arms out and he had me by the shirt and I was swinging wildly but I'm not getting anywhere. It finally got funny and we both laughed."

Wooden's decision to move from Dayton to South Bend Central in the fall of 1934 lengthened his commute to Indianapolis, but since he was not the school's head basketball coach in his first year, he was able to make it to most of the games. "Wooden used to be gone two or three days a week," Ed Powers said. "He taught his classes, but he would leave at least a couple days a week, maybe three times, at two thirty in the afternoon when the next to last class would be over. He would go to Fort Wayne or Hammond or Indianapolis and he played ball. Then he could come back that night and the next morning he would be teaching."

With Wooden spearheading Kautsky's fire wagon, the team averaged nearly 40 points per game during the 1934–35 season, leading the local press to nickname them the "speed merchants." In one game against the Celtics, they scored 63 points. They were so well received that in November 1935 Kautsky reached out to his erstwhile partner from Akron to form yet another new league, the Midwest Basketball Conference. Their most popular events were doubleheaders at the Armory that also featured the Rens or the Celtics. Wooden was the league's leading scorer during the

1934–35 season, but the highlight was his incredible streak of 134 consecutive free throws. When he sank the one hundredth—underhanded, naturally—Kautsky came out of the stands and handed him a crisp $100 bill. "I was pretty excited, but my wife was really excited. She came down out of the stands and grabbed that $100 rather quickly," Wooden quipped. The Kautskys ended the 1934–35 season with a 9–3 record, but they faltered in the league championship game, where they lost to a less-heralded team from Chicago.

The Midwest Basketball Conference gained a foothold that would last several years. As the games continued to draw respectable crowds, the league wasn't just building on the popularity of professional basketball. It was helping to change the way the game was played.

The main dilemma basketball faced at the college, professional, and international levels was the prevalence of delay tactics that were bringing games to a standstill. In an effort to speed things up, the NCAA's rules committee added a center line in 1932 and required that the offensive team bring the ball past that line within ten seconds. The Midwest Basketball Conference took a more dramatic step in 1935 when, following a trend that was overtaking professional basketball, it decided to give the home team the option of eliminating the center jump after made free throws. Three years later, both the league and the NCAA eliminated the center jump altogether (except at the start of each half or quarter), a move that had already been made in international play. This was arguably the most significant rule change the sport ever adopted, before or since.

The center jump had long been a contentious issue among basketball's cognoscenti. The strongest voice opposing its elimination belonged to James Naismith, but by this time, his influence was on the wane. Naismith had been appointed as an original member of NCAA's rules committee when it was formed in 1909, but he disengaged from the sport he invented while traveling abroad for several years following World War I. In 1924, Naismith returned to the States and was named honorary chairman of the rules committee for life, but as the title suggests, that was mostly a symbolic position.

Naismith viewed the center jump as akin to a kickoff in football. He worried that its elimination would allow too much scoring, and the fans would grow bored. "One of the reasons I am sorry to see the center jump relegated to a subordinate place is that it takes from the game one of the large elements of suspense—something desirable in any sport," Naismith wrote in his memoir. "Which, do you think, appeals to the spectator the more: the actual dropping of the ball through the basket, or the suspense—the seconds when one wonders if the ball is going in?"

Wooden's only disappointment was that Naismith hadn't lost the argument sooner. "I'd have loved to play [more years] without the center jump," he said. "I would have been a far more effective player because my strength was my speed and quickness."

Despite his diminishing influence, Naismith remained a revered figure around the world. His pinnacle came in the summer of 1936, when he traveled to Berlin, Germany, to see basketball played in the Olympic Games for the very first time. Upon returning to the States, Naismith resumed his duties as athletic director and professor emeritus at the University of Kansas, where he had coached the basketball team from 1898 to 1907. When Wooden traveled to Kansas for a coaching clinic, he had the pleasure of shaking hands with the man who invented basketball. "He was a very gentle, nice person. I liked him," Wooden said. "It was a brief meeting—a moment in time." By the time Naismith died in 1939 of a brain hemorrhage at the age of seventy-eight, an estimated 20 million people around the world were playing his game.

Wooden played as many games as he could, but he never fully embraced life as a professional athlete. Besides the taxing commutes and rough play, the enterprise lacked competitive integrity. That was evident one night in Detroit, where the Kautskys had held a double-digit lead throughout the second half, only to wonder why the game was not ending. The players checked with the official timer (there was no scoreboard), who informed them that there were still two minutes remaining. So they played some more and checked with the timer, who once again reported that there were two minutes left. "We finally got the idea, so we went back to the center jump, and each time they'd throw the ball up, we'd stand and not move," Wooden recalled with a chuckle. "When they made the basket that put them ahead, why, the game was over."

Toward the end of the 1936–37 season, Wooden was invited to play an exhibition game against the Celtics for a new team based in the town of Whiting. The team's owner was a flamboyant young automobile dealer named Ed Ciesar, and though the team lost by 20 points, Ciesar got Wooden to agree to a one-year contract. "It was big news when Wooden signed. I remember the newspapers making a big splash of it," said Joe Sotak, another player on that squad. For the 1937–38 season, Kautsky and the other owners decided to change their name back to the National Basketball

League (even though all the teams were located in the Midwest) and eliminated the center jump after every made basket. Ciesar had stocked his team with celebrity players like Wooden, and he called them the All-Americans. Their most exciting game that year came against league-leading Oshkosh. The contest was held in a brand-new, six-thousand-seat, $600,000 civic center in Hammond. With the All-Americans trailing by 2 points, Wooden banked in a layup in the final seconds to send the game into overtime. Then he sealed the win with a steal and a free throw in double overtime.

Ciesar was a good businessman, but he was no Frank Kautsky when it came to dealing with players. Wooden found that out after he and a team-mate drove through a nasty blizzard to make it to a game in Pittsburgh. It was a scary trip, with their car spinning full circle several times, but they made it there by halftime. When Ciesar handed out checks to the players later that night, Wooden and his friend noticed that they were being paid half the usual amount. When Wooden asked why, Ciesar said it was because they had only played one half. Wooden protested that they had risked their lives just to make it to the arena, but Ciesar wouldn't budge.

Though they were supposed to play a game the following afternoon, Wooden told Ciesar that he and his buddy were going back to Indiana. "He was very upset," Wooden recalled. "He told us that we couldn't just go home. We had another game to play. I protested that if he was going to treat us this way, we were leaving. He eventually gave us our money, but he raised an awful fuss. We agreed to play the next game, but we quit right after that." Wooden finished out the season with the Kautskys, but all those years of diving to the floor were taking their toll. He gave up playing for good in 1939.

The National Basketball League went unchallenged until after World War II, when the Basketball Association of America was launched on the East Coast. After several years of cannibalizing each other in the hunt for the best players, the NBL and BAA decided to merge in 1949 to create a comprehensive pro league, the National Basketball Association. Wooden never played a game in the new league, but he had no regrets about quitting when he did. He had a good family, a good job, lots of good memories. Wooden had done much to push high school and college basketball to new heights. The pros would have to ascend without him.

After World War II broke out, Wooden could have avoided being drafted because he was a married father and high school teacher, but eventually duty compelled him to enlist in the navy, a little more than a year after the bombing of Pearl Harbor. Regrettably, duty did not compel him to inform his wife beforehand. Nell hit the roof when he broke the news. "It was probably the major disagreement that my dear wife and I had in all our years," Wooden said.

He was one of dozens of teachers and coaches in the South Bend school system who enlisted or were drafted into the armed services. They were all promised they could have their jobs when (and if) they returned. Wooden had no sea or air training, but the navy saw value in him as a high school coach and former college athlete. Uncle Sam wanted him to get young navy flyers into fighting shape.

The navy staged many of its training sites on college campuses. On April 22, 1943, Lieutenant (junior grade) John Wooden began his first assignment at the University of North Carolina in Chapel Hill. He and the other cadets were put through a thirty-day program that prepared them to enter the Naval Air Corps' V-5 physical fitness program. After completing his stint there, Wooden was sent to preflight school at the University of Iowa, where he received his first deployment orders. On what Nell later called "the saddest day of my life," Wooden learned he was going to serve as a fitness officer aboard the USS *Franklin*, an aircraft carrier stationed in the South Pacific.

Shortly before setting off for the *Franklin*, Wooden returned to South Bend for a brief leave so he could spend a couple of days with his family and tidy up his affairs. As he was driving back to Iowa City, he felt a sharp pain in his abdomen. When he arrived, he went straight to a doctor, who diagnosed appendicitis. At the time, the navy had a rule requiring at least thirty days to pass between the time a serviceman had surgery and the day he reported for duty on a ship. Wooden's deployment was therefore postponed.

As it turned out, Wooden knew well the man who replaced him aboard the *Franklin*. He was Freddy Stalcup, a former Purdue football player who was Wooden's fraternity brother in Beta Theta Pi. Several months later, Wooden received a piece of news that left him dumbstruck: Stalcup was working a gun position aboard the *Franklin* when the ship was struck by a Japanese kamikaze pilot. He was killed along with dozens of other men on board. Had Wooden's appendix not become inflamed, he could very well have lost his life that day.

The close call only fed Nell's ominous feelings about her husband's decision to enlist. Her children were young, but they picked up on her anxiety. "When Dad had to go into the service, I was very unsettled,"

Nan said. "I remember I had bad dreams. Mother worried a lot about it and I think it rubbed off on me."

After resuming his work at the Iowa preflight school in the summer of 1943, Wooden awaited his next deployment orders. The navy decided it was too hot to ask the cadets to play basketball in the University of Iowa's Field House, so they assigned Wooden to be a boxing coach. The cadets would typically spend the morning running, swimming, playing soccer, and otherwise developing their physical stamina, followed by an afternoon cramming in ground school. Then they would have dinner and meet Lieutenant Wooden for boxing class. "He explained all the techniques to us, how to protect your head and all that stuff," said Ed Orme, a former high school basketball player from Southport, Indiana, who was a flight student that summer. "He was a quiet motivator. As I look back, I can see why guys would really play their hearts out for him. He had that ability to get on you when you needed it, but he also had the ability to have a lot of fun with you."

Wooden was transferred three more times—first to flight preparation school at Williams College in Williamstown, Massachusetts; then to a radar training station on St. Simons Island off the coast of Georgia, where he stayed for eighteen months; and finally in the winter of 1945 to Chicago, where he worked as an underway watch officer on the USS *Sable*, an aircraft carrier anchored in Lake Michigan. Wooden brought Nell and the kids with him to the first two stops, but he did not want them living in Chicago, so they returned to South Bend. It was the longest he would ever live apart from them.

Along the way, Wooden played some basketball with his shipmates, but he suffered a nasty injury when another player accidentally pushed him into a steel post, rupturing a disc in his lower back. The injury would trouble Wooden the rest of his life, forcing him to wear a brace for long stretches and putting him through several hospitalizations. It also caused him to walk with a slight stoop that grew more pronounced as he got older.

During this extended period away from South Bend, Wooden had an epiphany. He received many letters from his basketball players, yet he hardly corresponded with his English students. He realized that even though he liked to think of himself as an English teacher, he was having a far greater impact as a coach. "I loved to teach English, but you get closer to those under your supervision in sports, I believe, than you do in just the classroom," he said. "I can name almost all of the basketball players who played for me, even going back in high school, but I can't begin to name all of the English students I had."

Wooden never got the hang of life on a ship, failing to grasp even the most basic aspects of navy life. "I often teased him. He'd say things like, 'We parked a boat.' I'd say, 'You don't park a boat,'" Ed Powell said. Fortunately, Japan surrendered while Wooden was still anchored on Lake Michigan, and he was honorably discharged as a full lieutenant in January 1946. He had managed to serve for two and a half years without leaving the country. Asked many years later about his experiences in the navy, Wooden replied, "I don't know how we ever won the war."

Having done his duty, Wooden was ready to return to civilian life in South Bend. It looked like it was going to be a happy existence, but the reality turned out to be different. For starters, the family to whom Wooden had leased his home had stopped making their rent payments. The bank that held his mortgage wanted to charge Wooden for the past-due amount, but he didn't have the money. As a result, he lost the house. His return to coaching at Central High also caused a painful split with his temporary replacement, Charlie Stewart, who had previously worked as Wooden's assistant. According to Jim Powers, Stewart was "incensed" that Wooden had reclaimed his job, and the two of them never spoke again. "It was a bitter experience," Ed Powell said.

Wooden took over for Stewart for the second game of the season, and he piloted the Bears to a 16–10 record. It was not an easy situation, but at least he had his old job back. That was not the case for many of his fellow coaches who returned from the war. The school system declined to rehire several of them, and Wooden couldn't help but notice that the ones who were shoved aside had been replaced by men whose teams won a greater percentage of their games. "I was a little disenchanted," he said.

He put the word out that he wanted to work elsewhere. Not surprisingly, he had plenty of suitors, including the athletic director at Williams College, who had gotten to know Wooden while he was stationed there. But Wooden liked being a high school teacher and coach, so when he was contacted about vacancies in Kokomo and Marion, two Indiana schools with proud traditions and immense gymnasiums, he thought hard about which one he would want to take.

Around that time, he received a surprise phone call from the president of Indiana State Teachers College in Terre Haute. Wooden's former high school coach, Glenn Curtis, an Indiana State alumnus, had been the coach there for eight years, but he was leaving to take over the Detroit

Falcons in the Basketball Association of America. Curtis had recommended Wooden to be his successor. The president called Wooden and offered him the job over the phone.

Wooden had turned down college jobs before, but since this one was in his home state, he figured he might as well take a flyer. It ended up being an immense life decision, but it did not feel that way at the time. "I talked it over with Nellie, and I said, 'Why not? We'll try it. If things work out and I want to continue this and I can do well, maybe I'll get a chance in the Big Ten,'" Wooden said. "I figured if it didn't work out, I've got a lifetime teacher's license and degree. I'll always have a job and won't go hungry." So he piled his wife and two kids back into his car and headed for Terre Haute. It was time to give this coaching thing the old college try.

8

The Hurryin' Sycamores

The new head basketball coach at Indiana State Teachers College stood on the baseline next to Bobby Royer, a sophomore forward from Bowling Green, Kentucky, who was the quickest player on the team. Both of them held a basketball. "Let's race," the coach said. "See who can get the ball to the other end of the court the fastest."

With his teammates looking on, Royer took off dribbling. He made it just a few steps before the coach fired a pass to another player waiting at the far end of the court. Race over.

"Let's try again," the coach said. Once again, Royer took off dribbling. Once again, he was no match for the pass.

Johnny Wooden, still channeling Piggy Lambert, had made his point. "We pass instead of dribbling," he told his team, "because that's the fastest way to get the ball down the court."

Since that philosophy was the direct opposite of the plodding system preferred by Glenn Curtis, it was not easy for the new coach to impart it. In fact, there was much about the job that was not easy for Wooden at first. Not only was the program stocked with returning players from Curtis's last team, which had won twenty-one games and lost seven, but hundreds of young men had returned to the school from military service to resume their education. On the first day of tryouts in the fall of 1946, Wooden, who also served as Indiana State's athletic director and baseball coach, was greeted by 187 men. This was astounding considering there were just over 1,000 male students in the entire school.

They scrimmaged for a full week across two courts. There were no officials—the players called their own fouls—and Wooden sat in the bleachers evaluating them without interruption. Each day, Wooden would post a new, shorter list of players who had passed the previous day's examination. It was not a pleasant task. "I always felt in teaching, one of the most difficult things I had to do was cutting the squad," Wooden said. "You have a lot of players come out, they all want to play, and you can only take so many. That's hard." The returning players were not well suited to Wooden's fire-wagon style. By the time tryouts were through, Wooden's team included fourteen freshmen and one sophomore, many of whom had played for him in South Bend.

This did not go over well, especially since so many of Curtis's players had grown up in Terre Haute. One of the few local boys whom Wooden kept was Duane Klueh, a wiry, agile, six-foot-five freshman center. "A lot of the locals were really disturbed with Coach Wooden when he came," Klueh said. "The team had been very successful the year before, and a lot of servicemen came back. Then all these guys from South Bend came to town. Some parents went to the sports editor to complain."

Besides coaching and teaching English, Wooden was also pursuing a master's degree in education at Indiana State. He taught a course in coaching, and he made his Pyramid of Success part of the curriculum. In the years since Wooden was in Dayton, Kentucky, he had continued to rework his pyramid in small, significant ways. He kept the blocks in the same order, but he introduced phrases that explained their meaning, and he frequently massaged those words. ("Industriousness: There is no substitute for work. Worthwhile things come from hard work and careful planning. . . . Confidence: Respect without fear. Confident not cocky. May come from faith in yourself in knowing that you are prepared.") Wooden also divined a clever way to introduce even more concepts—not by replacing the blocks but by spackling these fresh ideas into the gaps along the edges. The left slope imparted, from bottom to top: Ambition, Adaptability, Resourcefulness, and Fight. Climbing the right side were Sincerity, Honesty, Reliability, and Integrity. Finally, the two most important ideas were grafted together at top, right above Competitive greatness: Faith and Patience. After fourteen years of tinkering, Wooden decided his pyramid was complete. He would not spend much time discussing it with his players, but he hung a framed copy on his office wall, where he could meditate on its neatly stacked lessons for the rest of his working days.

Wooden's pursuit of his master's degree also required him to write a thesis. He wanted to submit a paper on the question of why high school students were reluctant to study poetry—he had been accumulating material on the subject for several years—but his department chairman preferred that Wooden write about basketball. So he compiled a study examining the effects of the elimination of the center jump rule. "It's

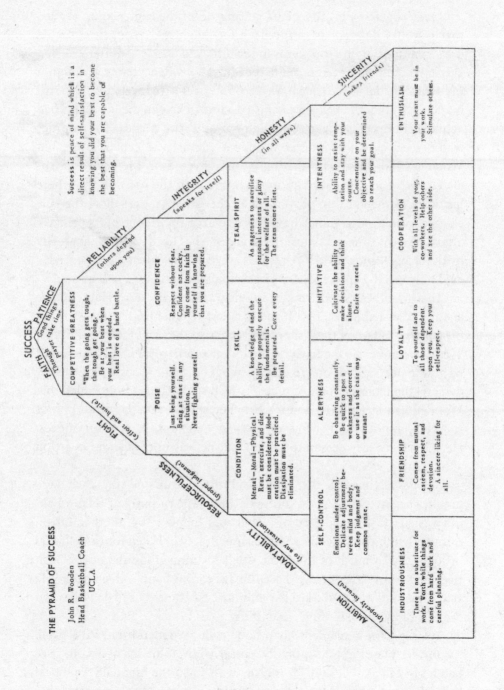

THE PYRAMID OF SUCCESS

John R. Wooden
Head Basketball Coach
UCLA

Success is peace of mind which is a direct result of self-satisfaction in knowing you did your best to become the best that you are capable of becoming.

SUCCESS

FAITH — Through prayer.
PATIENCE — Good things take time.

RELIABILITY (others depend upon you)
INTEGRITY (speaks for itself)
HONESTY (in all ways)
SINCERITY (makes friends)

COMPETITIVE GREATNESS
"When the going gets tough, the tough get going." Be at your best when your best is needed. Real love of a hard battle.

POISE
Just being yourself. Being at ease in any situation. Never fighting yourself.

CONFIDENCE
Respect without fear. Confident not cocky. May come from faith in yourself in knowing that you are prepared.

TEAM SPIRIT
An eagerness to sacrifice personal interests or glory for the welfare of all. The team comes first.

INTENTNESS
Ability to resist temptation and stay with your course. Concentrate on your objective and be determined to reach your goal.

ENTHUSIASM
Your heart must be in your work. Stimulate others.

FIGHT (effort and hustle)

CONDITION
Mental — Moral — Physical. Rest, exercise, and diet must be considered. Moderation must be practiced. Dissipation must be eliminated.

SKILL
A knowledge of and the ability to properly execute the fundamentals. Be prepared. Cover every detail.

INITIATIVE
Cultivate the ability to make decisions and think alone. Desire to excel.

COOPERATION
With all levels of your co-workers. Help others and see the other side.

RESOURCEFULNESS (proper judgment)

SELF-CONTROL
Emotions under control. Delicate adjustment between mind and body. Keep judgment and common sense.

ALERTNESS
Be observing constantly. Be quick to spot a weakness and correct it or use it as the case may warrant.

FRIENDSHIP
Comes from mutual esteem, respect, and devotion. A sincere liking for all.

LOYALTY
To yourself and to all those dependent upon you. Keep your self-respect.

ADAPTABILITY (to any situation)

INDUSTRIOUSNESS
There is no substitute for work. Worth while things come from hard work and careful planning.

AMBITION (properly focused)

amazing to me the thesis would be accepted, to tell you the truth, but it was," he said.

Many coaches who advocated getting rid of the center jump argued that it would de-emphasize the need for height. So Wooden collected data from the nation's top teams to see if they had indeed gotten shorter. What Wooden discovered may seem obvious when viewed through a modern lens, but at the time it was a counterintuitive revelation: size still mattered. Rather than experiencing a decline in height, the top teams had actually gotten taller by an average of around two inches. The findings would seem to undercut the argument against the center jump, but Wooden still believed eliminating it was a great idea. "Men closely associated with the game are almost unanimous in the opinion that there has been tremendous improvement in the game as a result of the rule change, even though it may have failed to accomplish one of its primary aims," he wrote in his conclusion. "The game has been speeded up greatly by the change, and attendance records are continually being established— evidently voicing approval of the basketball fans."

That was the style he taught his new players in Terre Haute. Once again, he busied himself with the smallest details, beginning with the proper way to put on their shoes and socks so they wouldn't get blisters. "I can remember sitting in that little locker room we had, and he showed us how to put Vaseline on our feet, then put on a pair of socks, some powder, and then another pair of socks," Klueh said. Klueh also recalled that Wooden had strict ideas about what they should eat. "He would order roast beef, but it would be four ounces—not eight or six, but four ounces. He was a very easy person to talk to, but he was in charge, no question about that."

Most of all, he made them run. And run and run and run. Each day's practice began with thirty minutes of three-lane running drills mimicking various fast break patterns. That was followed by another fifteen minutes using two defenders in the lane. Practices lasted for three hours or longer, with much of that time spent scrimmaging full court. "Even the night before a game, we'd scrimmage for an hour," Klueh said. "He said games are won in the last two minutes. He wanted us to do well when the other guys were huffing and puffing."

To help him implement his unique style, Wooden hired Ed Powell, his former player at South Bend Central High, to be his assistant. "We had a saying," Powell said. "If we stay with them the first half, we'll beat them the second half." One of their more innovative tactics was an unusual full-court press. Instead of applying the pressure through man-to-man defense, as was customary, Wooden sometimes used a zone, which enabled his players to trap the ball handler with two defenders and still have a third well positioned to intercept the pass and break for a layup. Wooden would use the press in brief spurts if his team got behind.

After losing their opening game by 2 points to a team of servicemen from Fort Sheridan, Illinois, the Sycamores won seven of their next nine, eclipsing the 70-point mark in three of those wins. (One of the losses came in mid-December at Purdue, where 8,500 fans turned out to see the Boilermakers beat their favorite son's team, 54–49.) Sportswriters, having been accustomed to Curtis's stallball over the previous eight seasons, were whiplashed. They dubbed the team the "Scrappin' Sycamores," the "Hurryin' Sycamores," and "the fast-breaking Sycamores of State." This team didn't just win. It was also fun to watch.

Wooden still taught by demonstrating, but he was not the same young buck who barreled through his players as a high school coach. "He'd occasionally play three on three with us, but he had a bad back," said Charlie Foudy, a reserve guard from Terre Haute. One day in practice, Wooden told his players they had to make ten straight free throws before they could leave. Then, according to the *Terre Haute Tribune*, "Wooden took the ball and sank 15 charity tosses in rapid fire succession without missing one—just to prove he hasn't lost his eye for the basket."

Wooden's combative side shone through on game day. He had developed a habit of clutching a rolled-up program in his hands while sitting on the bench, and when he saw something that really displeased him, he would smack that program loudly into an open hand. He also lobbed caustic barbs at officials and opposing players. His own players described him as generally composed, but there was one occasion that first season when Wooden really lost his cool. It happened during a bad stretch in late February after his team suffered a grinding 49–48 loss at Evansville, its third consecutive defeat and the fourth in five games. As the Sycamores readied to leave the arena, they found their bus surrounded by Evansville fans. "Somebody made some kind of remark, and Coach Wooden didn't appreciate it," Klueh recalled. "He fired his coat off. He was ready to take on a guy twice his size. It didn't go to blows or anything like that, but it could have."

There were other moments when Wooden's need for control seemed excessive. In mid-February, he took his team to New York City for a big showdown against St. John's in Madison Square Garden. The game would be Wooden's first real experience with big-time, big-city college basketball. He took command of every aspect of the trip, including the food his players ate along the way. As they made their way east by automobiles, the team stopped for lunch, but some of the players left the meal still feeling hungry. So they pulled over in their car and bought some sandwiches. In Wooden's mind, this was close to mutiny. "He was so upset with what they did, not following his orders, that he didn't play anyone else but the five starters," said Lenny Rzeszewski, another Indiana State player who had played for Wooden in South Bend. "He was just that type of individual. Basically, he was tough."

Once they got to the Garden, the Hurryin' Sycamores performed well. With 16,593 fans looking on, they staged a fabulous tussle with the Redmen of St. John's, who were coached by Wooden's former pugilist from their pro days, Joe Lapchick. St. John's was arguably the most prominent college program in the country, having qualified for six of the nine National Invitation Tournaments that had been played and winning titles in 1943 and 1944. Led by six-foot-nine forward Harry Boykoff and prized guard Dick McGuire, St. John's built a 13-point lead midway through the second half.

At that point, the Sycamores' superior conditioning took hold. They rallied furiously to within 2 points with a minute to play before losing, 62–58. The Associated Press reported that during their second-half surge, Indiana State "literally ran the Red Men off the court." It was a harbinger of things to come.

Indiana State ended the 1946–47 season on a seven-game win streak as Duane Klueh set a school record for points in a season with 337. While that did not earn the Sycamores an invitation to the still-nascent NCAA tournament (the event was in its ninth year and included an eight-team field), they were asked to compete in a thirty-two-team single-elimination tournament hosted at Municipal Auditorium in Kansas City, Missouri, by the National Association of Intercollegiate Basketball (NAIB). (The organization later changed its name to the National Association of Intercollegiate Athletics, or NAIA. The NAIA still exists today separately from the NCAA.) The Sycamores had played in the 1946 championship game, so they benefited from the NAIB's policy of automatically inviting the previous year's finalists.

Indiana State, however, turned down the invitation. At the time, it did not seem like a big deal to the players. "Those things weren't as important then as they are now," Klueh said. "We just knew the season was over." When the school announced it was turning down the NAIB, the *Terre Haute Tribune* reported that the reason was academics. "It was the feeling of the athletic committee that because of several extended road

trips this month no additional school work should be missed by participation in the tournament," the paper wrote. "Coach Johnny Wooden said
that the tournament experience would have been valuable to the team,
but in view of existing conditions it was advisable to pass up the tourney
this season."

In later years, Wooden would offer another explanation for his decision. The NAIB had a policy forbidding the participation of blacks, and
the Sycamores had a black player on its roster named Clarence Walker. A
five-foot-eleven guard from East Chicago, Indiana, Walker was a little-
used reserve whom Wooden had already left behind from the team's trip
to New York City. New York was not a segregated town, but bringing
Walker meant dealing with segregated restaurants and hotels on the way
there. Wooden's decision caused Walker immense pain. Now, according
to Wooden, he did not want to face either the hassle of bringing Walker
or the difficulty of leaving him in Terre Haute. So he passed on going to
Kansas City altogether.

If Wooden truly did not accept the invitation for the reason he later
claimed, it is disappointing that he declined to reveal it and speak out
against the ban, instead of hiding behind a phony explanation about schoolwork. But that was not his way. When he stood up for racial progress,
Wooden did so firmly but quietly. While Wooden's actions in this area
sometimes fell short of his ideals (as with the decision not to take Walker
to New York), the fact that he held those ideals was nonetheless remarkable for a man who grew up where he did, when he did.

Martinsville, Indiana, was not exactly a bastion of racial diversity when
John Wooden was young. There were so few blacks in town that many
decades later, Wooden could specifically recall the two whom he knew.
"One was a track man on our team. The other one worked in the barber-
shop shining shoes and things like that," he said. "I would say both were
very, very well-liked by all the people."

This was hardly unusual. According to the census of 1920, the year
Wooden turned ten, blacks accounted for less than 3 percent of the population in Indiana. During the decade that followed, the state was the
setting for an unprecedented rise to power by the Ku Klux Klan. The Klan
soared through the state like a comet—burning bright and traveling fast,
and flaming out just as quickly—but in Martinsville, the legacy of racial
intolerance has sadly endured like a never-ending tail.

The Indiana Klan's watershed moment arrived during the statewide elections of 1924. Under the leadership of David Curtis Stephenson, the Klan sponsored an array of Republican candidates who won dozens of offices, including governor. Their reign did not last long. The following year, Stephenson was convicted of rape and second-degree murder and was sentenced to life in prison. In 1927, the Klan-sponsored governor, Ed Jackson, was indicted for bribery. Scores of other Klan-backed Republicans were sent to jail as part of the scandal, and though Jackson served out his term, by the time he left office, the Klan in Indiana was a shell of its former self.

To this day, Martinsville is frequently referred to as a former mid-western "headquarters" for the KKK. That is flatly untrue. According to *Citizen Klansmen*, an exhaustive history of the KKK in 1920s Indiana written by the historian Leonard J. Moore, nearly one-third of all white men living in the state were dues-paying members of the Klan, and in some communities the figure approached 50 percent. Martinsville's participation was actually below average. The membership in Morgan County, where Martinsville sits, was 26.8 percent in 1925. That was substantially lower than other counties like White (37.7 percent), Hamilton (35.4), Tipton (34.3), Hendricks (33.2), Madison (33.2), and Rush (32.8). Martinsville was the site of a Klan rally in October 1923 that attracted several thousand followers, but that was dwarfed by the national convention held that same year in Kokomo, where more than a hundred thousand attendees assembled from Indiana and surrounding states. The most notorious lynching in the state's history occurred in 1930 not in Martinsville but Marion, more than a hundred miles away. Asked if he could recall any Klan-related activities in his hometown while he was growing up, Wooden replied, "I'd hear about it, but I never saw it."

Still, there is no denying that compared to most places in America, Martinsville was unwelcoming to blacks during the 1920s. Wooden, however, emerged without a trace of racial hostility, which he attributed to his father, even though Hugh Wooden never couched his teachings in racial terms. "He talked about treating everybody alike, that you're no better than anyone but just as good as anyone, but he never mentioned race," Wooden said. Though the Indiana Klan was committed to the notion of white supremacy, its primary mission at the time was the enforcement of Prohibition. It was also vehemently anti-Catholic; it's likely Wooden witnessed more prejudice directed toward his Irish Catholic girlfriend than the two blacks he knew.

Wooden's experiences playing basketball contributed to his progressive views on race. As evidenced by his adulation for the Harlem Rens, he learned at an early age that a basketball didn't care about the color of the hands that shot it. If the arc was true, the ball went in. Wooden didn't coach any black players during his two years in Dayton, Kentucky, so his racial attitudes were not tested until he arrived in South Bend. The blacks there faced no restrictions on buses or streetcars, but there were plenty of other Jim Crow–like impediments.

For example, black people in South Bend were not permitted to swim in the community pool at Playland Park except for a single day at the end of the summer. They could buy hamburgers at the downtown five-and-ten-cent store, but they couldn't sit in the downstairs dining room. They could go to the movies, but at certain theaters they were required to watch from the balcony. "You knew what you could do and couldn't do," said Mamie Taylor, a black student at South Bend Central who dated and later married one of Wooden's players, Tom Taylor. "There were a lot of places in South Bend we couldn't eat. The black girls couldn't swim at the pool in the school. We couldn't even sing at the glee club." According to Mamie, Wooden stood out among the faculty at Central High. "There were a lot of racist teachers at Central, but Wooden was always nice to me. He would tease me and say, 'If Tom doesn't treat you right, let me know.'"

Central's interracial basketball team was met with some disapproval among the townsfolk. "I'd see people on the street, and they'd say, 'You use the same towels as that black kid?'" Jim Powers said. "That was kind of the environment at the time, but it just was not a factor on the team." As Wooden chaperoned the Bears around the state, he took stand after stand on behalf of his black players. He once led his team out of a local movie theater when the manager insisted that the black players sit separately upstairs. He threatened to do the same thing at a restaurant called Clark's. As Mamie Taylor recalled, "He said the whole team eats here or nobody does. They let them eat there. He broke that barrier." Before a game at Madison, one of Wooden's black players, Pete Donaldson, was momentarily refused entry into the gym. "Wooden came over and said, 'What's going on?'" John Gassensmith recalled. "They said he couldn't come in. Wooden said, 'If he can't come in, nobody can come in.' So they let him in."

When Wooden took the Bears to Martinsville, he was embarrassed when a restaurant refused to serve them. When they played in the state tournament, he wouldn't let the team eat at another restaurant because the manager had asked a black player, Parson Howell, to dine in the kitchen. "I remember him in his polite, beautiful English telling people that it wasn't going to hurt to have his team eat there with one or two or three black kids eating there," said Stan Jacobs, a former South Bend player. Jacobs recalled a separate instance when Wooden took the team to a nearby grocery store to buy lunch meat because a local restaurant had refused to serve the black players. They ate while sitting outside by a park.

"He looked after us," Tom Taylor said. "If we traveled, he'd call ahead and make sure that if we were going to stay at a hotel, everybody was treated equally. I never remember staying at a different hotel or eating separately from the team."

Through it all, Wooden never explained to his players what he was doing and why, even though it might have accelerated their own understanding of the importance of racial equality. As usual, Wooden was all walk and no talk. "He never talked to us about race," Powers said. "I don't think he wanted to get into the political thing. He just took care of number one. There was no difference between a black kid and a white kid on his basketball team."

In this respect, as in so many others, Wooden's wife was a kindred spirit. Having faced discrimination against Catholics while growing up, Nellie shared Wooden's disdain for bigotry. That was especially evident when Wooden brought the family to Georgia while he was serving in the navy. "Mom always butted heads with some of the locals about the way they treated blacks," Nan said. "Mom always said she didn't understand. 'They won't sit and eat with them, yet they allow them to serve food and nurse their babies. It doesn't make sense.'" When Nan went to school on Abraham Lincoln's birthday, her father playfully suggested she ask her teacher what she thought of his favorite president, who was still held in low regard throughout the Deep South for having freed the slaves less than a century before.

Wooden would have been content to continue making his stands through modest, unremarked-upon gestures, but his new job would not allow it. That was never more true than at the end of his second season at Indiana State, when Wooden played an unintentional, unaccustomed role in breaking down a significant barrier. Racial progress was slow in America in the 1940s. It was only fitting that the Sycamores should hurry it up.

9

Clarence

Wooden was on much firmer ground with the locals as his second season at Indiana State got under way in the fall of 1947. The Sycamores lost just one player from the team that had gone 17–8 the year before, and with nine sophomores and a junior comprising the ten returning lettermen, the future was bright. Sure enough, the team hurried its way to eleven wins in its first twelve games.

Up-tempo basketball was becoming more in vogue, especially in the Midwest, but it wasn't being played everywhere. In late January, Indiana State traveled to Chicago to play in a doubleheader that also included Oklahoma A&M, which by then had already won two NCAA championships. (The school would later change its name to Oklahoma State University.) The Cowboys' coach, Henry Iba, had built his powerhouse with a style that couldn't have been more different from Wooden's. His "swinging gate" man-to-man defense was one of the game's foremost innovations, and he buttressed it with a brutally slow pace on offense. Iba's presence in Chicago provided an intriguing contrast with the run-and-gunning upstarts from Terre Haute. "Oklahoma A&M, coached by Henry Iba, is one of the few college basketball teams which still believes in a planned, ball-controlled system of attack," the *Chicago Daily Tribune* wrote on the eve of the doubleheader. "It is likely that the invading Sycamores will go to the other extreme in performance and exhibit the speed and finesse known throughout the Hoosier state as fire department basketball."

Both teams won their games that night, giving each man some validation. That set in motion a long-running narrative pitting Wooden against Iba, both professionally and socially. At the time, Iba was by far the more popular and accomplished coach, whereas Wooden was just getting started. Over the years, Wooden often expressed respect for Iba, but his praise sometimes carried a hint of condescension. "At the beginning of each year, if you were to say that among the top five defensive teams in the country as far as points scored, Oklahoma State's going to be among them," Wooden said. "But it wasn't because of their defense and it wasn't because they didn't play good defense. It's because they held the ball so long on offense."

The Sycamores continued to roll through the 1947–48 season. By the middle of February, they were 13–2, and with nine games remaining they were just 200 points from breaking the season scoring record set by the previous year's team. Duane Klueh had already broken the individual scoring record he had set as a freshman, and on the surface the team appeared not to have a care in the world. But there was one person among them who was enduring a private struggle. That was Clarence Walker, the team's lone black player.

Walker had been a track star in high school before coming to Indiana State, where he won a spot on the basketball team during tryouts his freshman season. He was well liked by his teammates, but he was not very well known. "He was an intelligent, smart kid, and rather quiet," Klueh recalled. Jim Powers described Walker as "very quiet, very distinguished. Kept everything to himself."

Unbeknown to his teammates, Walker suffered intense anxiety from having to deal with the Jim Crow segregation laws that were a normal part of life in Indiana. Walker didn't feel as if he could express his feelings to his coach or his teammates, so he poured them into the only outlet he could find: a typewriter. At the start of the season, he began writing a journal that would chronicle his sophomore season at Indiana State. The Walker who emerges from those pages is confused yet wise, pained yet resilient, chastened yet hopeful.

Walker titled his journal "Mr. J. C."—as in Jim Crow. "I have decided to keep an account of the numerous incidents occuring [sic] in the 1947–1948 basketball season at Indiana State Teachers College," he began. "I am the only Negro on the team. I encountered some very severe setbacks in the 1946–1947 season at the same college. The most severe was my not going to New York . . . because I, among many, was born a Negro."

Walker's reverence for Wooden was palpable from the first page, despite the coach's decision the previous year to leave Walker home for the New York trip. "My opinion of Johnny Wooden, the coach of our basketball team, is that he is a wonderful coach," Walker wrote. "He is brilliant in knowledge of basketball. As far as I know, he is not bias [sic].

I realize the fact that he is obligated to someone else. If all people were in mind as he is in character, I <u>think</u> Mr. J. C. would be trivial."

In the journal, Walker described a litany of slights that occurred as the Sycamores racked up wins. Over Thanksgiving weekend, Walker stayed behind in Terre Haute while the rest of the players went home, and Wooden referred him to the owner of a local restaurant for meals. On Thanksgiving morning, Walker went there to have breakfast, but the restaurant owner asked him to eat in the kitchen. He decided to take his food home instead. "I do not think I am too good to eat in anybody's kitchen," Walker wrote. "I know my presence is not preferred in the proper part of a café, and I figured eating at home would be just as well." Not surprisingly, Walker expressed a low opinion of the town of Terre Haute, which he described as an unsanitary "J. C. place" populated by outdoor toilets.

Whenever Walker traveled with the team outside Terre Haute, Mr. J. C. followed. On one occasion, the players ate at a drugstore during a trip to South Bend to play Notre Dame. The waiter took everybody's order but Walker's, and it was only when the team manager intervened that Walker finally got served. During another trip, to play at Marshall, Walker had to stay apart from the team at a Negro hotel called the Allen. "It was pretty nice," he wrote. "We lost by an upset."

During a tournament that Indiana State hosted in early January, the Sycamores played Southeastern Oklahoma. As Walker battled for a rebound, he heard the opposing coach shout to his player, "Jerk that nigger's head off!" Walker wrote of how his coach rose to his defense: "Mr. Wooden heard him and told him, 'Why don't you go back to Oklahoma.' After the game, Mr. Wooden went into their dressing room and there was a big argument."

Only once did Walker mention witnessing racism from a teammate. It happened in the locker room in mid-February, following a 70–66 win over Valparaiso. As Walker was momentarily hidden behind a dressing rack, one of the Indiana State players, Don McDonald, started singing "eeny-meeny-miny-moe." Not realizing Walker was within earshot, McDonald said, "Catch a nigger by the toe." There was an awkward silence when McDonald realized Walker heard him, but Walker bore him no animus. As he wrote in his journal, "Mac's hometown is known to dislike Negroes. However, Mac is a very congenial and easy to get along with fellow. I find myself not being affected by such [things] as much as I used to."

Walker's teammates were surprised to learn many years later just how torn he was. "We probably should have been more sensitive and known the pain that he was feeling that turned up in his writings," Duane Klueh said. "But we didn't really know. We just went out and played basketball and enjoyed him."

The slurs and slights were minor scrapes compared to the emotional injury Walker sustained after that win over Valparaiso in February. He was standing in the locker room when he noticed a piece of paper being passed around for the players to sign. He later learned it was an entry form for the NAIB tournament in Kansas City. Nobody asked Walker to sign it, and he soon learned why. Wooden and the school had decided this time to accept the invitation, but because of the ban against black players, the team was not taking Walker. "I asked Wooden what the dope is on the Kansas City tournament," Walker wrote. "In his suave but candid way he told me, of which I expected that it was in the charter or in some written rule, that Negroes could not play." It was the second time Wooden had let Walker down in this fashion.

The news of Indiana State's return to the tournament after a one-year hiatus was made public eight days later. "Indiana State's Scrappin' Sycamores return to the thicket in the National Intercollegiate cage championship at Kansas City this year. Coach Johnny Wooden told us about it on Friday," sports editor Bob Nesbit wrote in the *Terre Haute Sunday Tribune* on February 22. "The team drew an invitation last year, but was unable to accept due to a conflict with college final examination." A week after Nesbit's report, the school issued a formal announcement. "Twelve players have been certified to represent Blue and White," the *Tribune* article read. "Ten of these boys will make the trip." The newspaper listed the names of the ten players headed to Kansas City but offered no explanation for why Clarence Walker's was not among them.

On an intellectual level, Walker understood why Wooden had made the decision. As he wrote at the beginning of his journal, he recognized Wooden was "obligated to someone else." But he was deeply wounded. Wooden may have believed that the NAIB's racial ban was wrong, but he didn't believe it strongly enough to stand up for Walker, either in public or in private. Once again, Walker had nowhere to turn but his typewriter. "This is the second big opportunity which hurt me in a peculiar way. The first one rendered me most unstable for almost a week," he wrote. "This one didn't hurt as much because I had made up in my mind that one was enough. Yet when they come, believe me, it is hard to take."

Walker would have been justified in being angry with Wooden, yet he never expressed disappointment in his coach. In his view, Wooden was just another instrument of authority who was on his side until it was inconvenient. He may have liked Wooden personally, but the turn of events left Walker despondent about his prospects as a young black man living in a racist country. "Let's be frank," Walker wrote, "can a boy of age or at any level in life be proud he is a Negro? The thing he aspires to do can be done, I mean the opportunity comes, but cannot be taken, not because I am not capable or my ability is not up to par, but only because I am a NEGRO. God bless this inane world."

Fortunately for Walker, there were some influential people on the East Coast who were willing to fight for him in a way that Wooden was not. When Manhattan College's athletic director learned of the NAIB's rule prohibiting Negroes from competing in the tournament, he requested that it be changed, even though Manhattan did not have any blacks on its roster. After two days of exchanging telegrams, the NAIB informed Manhattan that it was too late to repeal the rule for that year's tournament, so Manhattan withdrew and the athletic director publicly stated the reason. The NAIB then offered its spot to Siena College in Albany, but that school also turned the invitation down because of the racial ban. Long Island University did the same.

The battle might have ended there but for a man named Harry Henshel, who was a member of the U.S. Olympic basketball committee. One of the reasons the NAIB tournament was so prestigious was that the champion was invited to compete at the U.S. Olympic trials in New York City in late March. (The other teams invited were the two NCAA finalists, three teams from the Amateur Athletic Union, the winner of the National Invitation Tournament, and a YMCA team.) After reading about the protests made by the New York schools, Henshel sent a telegram to the Olympic committee's chairman recommending that the NAIB champion be dropped from the Olympic trials unless the ban was rescinded. Suddenly, the members of the NAIB's executive committee had a change of heart. They conducted a quick poll by telegraph, and on Friday, March 6, two days before the tournament was due to tip off, they announced that the prohibition had been removed.

The development did not make a huge splash back in Terre Haute, warranting only a mention deep in Bob Nesbit's Sunday column reporting that the change "enabled Wooden to shift his squad at the last moment and take Clarence Walker, the East Chicago speed merchant, on the trip.

Wooden revealed to Nesbit that he had been told Walker probably would be the only colored boy playing in the meet."

However, the news was a big deal in Kansas City, where the prospect of the tournament losing its connection with the U.S. Olympic trials was cause for much concern. No outlet followed the events with more interest than the *Call*, Kansas City's most prominent black newspaper. Though the paper's sports columnist, John I. Johnson, was pleased by the end of the Negro ban, he was realistic about the reasons behind the decision. "We would like to report that the committee saw the injustice of its racial prejudice bars and voluntarily voted to remove them, thus showing to the world that the motivation came from a spirit of fair play and sportsmanship. But this is not true," Johnson wrote. "We can't shout glory, glory for the rescinding committee as we would like to do, for their act was somewhat forced, and the hallelujahs belong to others."

Those "others," alas, did not include Clarence Walker's coach, but by then Walker didn't much care. In his journal, he announced the reprieve in matter-of-fact language. "At the last minute, I was sought by coaches, friends, etc., and the reason being that I was to go to Kansas City, Mo., to play in the NAIB tournament," he wrote. "Mr. Wooden readily understanding the situation got in contact with me and talked the deal over."

On their way to Columbia, Missouri, where they were going to spend the night before completing the trip to Kansas City, the Sycamores stopped to eat lunch at a local restaurant. Shortly after the players ordered their food, a woman approached Wooden and told him that Walker couldn't eat there. Wooden replied that if Walker couldn't eat there, none of them would. "You can't leave," the woman protested. "You already ordered."

"Watch us," Wooden said. And they left.

"I thought they might get some local policeman or something but they didn't," Wooden said. "To the best of my knowledge that's the only problem we had. I didn't expect any there because we had checked in advance."

The hotel where the team was staying in Columbia was segregated, too, but since there were no Negro hotels or private homes available, the hotel allowed Walker to stay in a storage room next to a bathroom in the basement. This was a demeaning arrangement, but Wooden apparently felt he had no choice but to go along. The hotel staff rolled in a cot and placed it next to some broken furniture. Walker had a fitful night because of the noise emanating from a sorority party upstairs. At around 2:00 a.m., a group of boys used the bathroom next to Walker's space. "About ten minutes later, they all cleared out but believe me they did not take everything with them," Walker wrote in his journal. "The aroma coming from the bathroom through a furnace inlet was unbearable. I had to get up and shut the inlet off. One can guess how much sleep I got."

Once the team arrived in Kansas City, Walker again had to sleep in a separate hotel. Things were not much better for him inside Municipal Auditorium. Before Indiana State's first-round game, he was in the bathroom at the arena with a teammate named Dan Dimich when he heard a member of another team ask, "How did you guys happen to have a nigger on your team?" Making history was no fun.

The NAIB's Negro ban officially ended in the first round when Walker made his entrance during the first half of the Sycamores' 72–40 win over St. Francis, but you'd never know from reading the city's two major newspapers that something significant had occurred. The only evidence came from the box score, which noted that Walker had scored one goal, made one free throw, and committed zero fouls. Even the fans, to their credit, were nonchalant. "I can't remember anybody booing him or anything like that," Klueh said.

The fans were plenty excited, however, about the tournament, which had grown significantly since its inception ten years before. It was so prominent that Brigham Young University, which had won its conference, turned down its automatic invitation to the NCAA tournament to come to Kansas City. (The league's runner up, Utah, went in BYU's place.) This promised to be the most wide-open field the NAIB had ever assembled. Even though Indiana State had gone 23–6 during the regular season and had almost won the tournament two years before, nobody considered the Sycamores a threat to win it. On the eve of the opener, the *Kansas City Star* named twelve teams it considered to be headliners. Indiana State was not among them. Even after the field had been whittled over two days from thirty-two teams to sixteen, a poll of five sportswriters determined that six other schools were the favorites.

The group of teams that came to Kansas City reflected just how prevalent fast break basketball was becoming. Piggy Lambert's vision for the game was finally taking hold. After the first day's action, the *Star* reported that out of the sixteen teams that had played that day, Kirksville (Mo.) Teachers College was the only one that "used defensive basketball in earnest." The sport was getting faster, with scoring inching higher and higher. "One observer went so far as to remark that they'd have to change the name of the game to 'run and shoot,'" the article noted. "The main reliance of modern basketball teaching is on making points and letting the defense be a potent offense." It was assumed that this trend would not sit well with the coach who lorded over the sport. "Hank Iba would have a field day giving pointers to the sixteen teams which played opening day. The old master of the ball control school would have seen nothing familiar in the eight games. Not once did a team honestly freeze the ball to protect a lead."

The Hurryin' Sycamores fit right in. The faster the pace, the more the games played into their hands (not to mention their well-conditioned legs). For the rest of the tournament, Indiana State's games followed the same pattern: the opponents built a big lead, and the Sycamores came storming back late in the second half. The machine was working exactly as its engineer had designed it.

When Indiana State won its first two games with dramatic second-half comebacks, the local writers finally took notice. "The Sycamores uphold the old Indiana basketball tradition that the last half is the most important," read the next day's account in the *Kansas City Star*. "The Sycamores have what might be termed average height for a basketball team. They have plenty of speed and their attack is tricky and hard to stop."

The team saved its most dramatic comeback for its semifinal contest against Hamline University from St. Paul, Minnesota. As a crowd of around eight thousand looked on, Indiana State built a 12-point lead in the first half, but Hamline charged back to claim an 11-point advantage with eight minutes left in the second half. Indiana State slowly carved into the deficit but still trailed by 2 in the final seconds. Klueh's attempt at a game-tying shot fell short, but he was fouled. He sank two clutch free throws to send the game into overtime. "I wasn't a great free throw shooter," Klueh said. "I don't remember if Wooden said anything to me, but he was a very optimistic guy. He'd give you that smile, and when you got there, you were confident that whatever you were doing was going to be okay."

In the extra session, Hamline took a 1-point lead into the closing seconds, and once again Klueh had the ball in his hands. As the clock was winding down, Klueh flung a running, underhanded shot toward the backboard. The gun went off, and then the ball bounced off the board and dropped through the net. Ball game. Klueh's teammates were delirious. They rushed the court, hoisted him onto their shoulders, and carried him to the locker room.

The win vaulted the Sycamores into the championship game against Louisville. There would be no more overlooking this undersized bunch.

"The Indiana team has thrilled fans on successive nights with a second half rally that has all the elements of a horse opry chase," read the story in the next day's *Star*. "The Sycamores—and they should really have a name more fitting their run-for-cover break—have pulled two out of the fire and now stand on the threshold of a title."

The local press was also finally starting to focus on the intense, bespectacled man on Indiana State's sidelines. Wooden was a full sixteen years removed from his senior year at Purdue, and memories of his playing exploits were already fading. In introducing Wooden, the *Star* reminded its readers that when the Sycamores had reached the NAIB finals two years before, they had been coached by Glenn Curtis. "The coach now is John R. Wooden," the paper wrote. "Wooden is a protégé of Curtis and helped Curtis win the Indiana state high school basketball championship for Martinsville High. Wooden later achieved All-American honors at Purdue University under Ward (Piggy) Lambert." The newspaper mistakenly reported that Wooden "is still considered the best dribbler to come out of Illinois high schools," but it paid him the ultimate compliment as a coach: "Whatever else Wooden teaches his team, one thing is certain. The boys don't know when to quit."

This newfound attention was having some unintended consequences. That same day, Bob Nesbit wrote in his column in the *Terre Haute Star* that "a note from Los Angeles claims that U.C.L.A. is trying to sign Johnny Wooden as its basketball coach. We hope the story is wrong."

The championship game against Louisville was broadcast in Terre Haute on WTHI radio, where an announcer offered play-by-play from a transcription that came in via telephone from Kansas City. The station joined the game in progress after the completion of the high school state semifinals. (High school hoops was still king in Indiana.) When Louisville and Indiana State took the floor of Municipal Auditorium on the night of March 13, more than 9,000 paying customers had settled into their seats. They were about to get their money's worth.

Like Wooden, Louisville coach Peck Hickman believed in the fast break, and the two teams raced up and down the court at breakneck speed. This time, the Sycamores would spot their opponents an 18-point lead at halftime. Indiana State came rushing back once more after intermission, but Louisville's free throw shooting down the stretch enabled the Cardinals to claim the title with an 82–70 victory. "We had a difficult time getting inside because we weren't very big," said Klueh, who scored 25 points in the final and was named the tournament's most valuable player despite the loss. "We were disappointed but we weren't tremendously upset because we hadn't really thought about getting that far in the first place. We just played."

Plenty of history was made at the 1948 NAIB tournament. The 9,200 people who watched the final set a new single-game attendance record for the tournament. So did the 53,704 who watched over six days, as well as the total of $65,777.59 they paid for admission. The event had drawn schools from thirty-one states, also a new high. And of course, a black man had competed for the first time.

In the end, Clarence Walker's presence on the court drew little notice—which is exactly what Walker wanted. Though the two major newspapers in town never mentioned the breakthrough, the reaction (or non-reaction) from the fans and players had a profound effect on John Johnson, the sports columnist at the *Call*. "The opposing players regarded Walker as just another basketball player. At no time was there any evidence of difference shown to Walker by players whether they were from the North or the South, the East or the West," Johnson wrote. "The spectators for the most part appeared to savor the participation of the Negro player, for they applauded his play whenever he was recalled to the bench. No expressions of disapproval were heard. Judging by this acceptance of the first Negro to ever play in the NAIB, the inference is that sports fans are not too much concerned with the race of a player; in fact, they seem to welcome the change and came out in larger numbers to see democracy in action on the fields of contest."

Walker had a few more unpleasant experiences on his way back to Terre Haute. When the Sycamores stayed overnight in a hotel outside St. Louis, he again had to sleep in the basement. Wooden met him for breakfast the next morning. As they were leaving the hotel, Walker walked past a woman holding her young daughter. "Look, Mommy, a nigger," the girl said, pointing. The woman hushed her daughter by saying, "Sh! A colored boy."

For all the indignities he suffered, Walker wouldn't have traded that week for anything. He met the Olympic track star Jesse Owens, boxing champion Henry Armstrong, and Floyd Bates, a black professional basketball player. Walker spoke with Bates until five in the morning and was so excited he couldn't sleep. He learned some important lessons, many of them unpleasant, all of them worthwhile. He understood that his presence in Kansas City had resulted because someone confronted an unjust system, not the man he knew and revered, but rather strangers who lived thousands of miles away. This realization presaged the larger struggle to come in America. "An important trait among men is their ability to assert themselves in relation to other men," Walker wrote in his journal. "It is not necessary to win all the little battles, but if and when human issues arise—we must take a stand—and this we must do by assertion."

Because the Sycamores had lost to Louisville, they did not get to compete at the Olympic trials, but their performance in Kansas City was still hailed as a triumph back home. They ended the 1947–48 season with a 27–7 record, the best ever at the school. They also set a new single-season team scoring record, while Klueh shattered his own single-season mark by 260 points. When the team got back to Terre Haute, the whole town turned out to greet them. The players were paraded down Wabash Avenue in a caravan of fire trucks that took them to the gymnasium for a huge pep rally. The day included frequent predictions that the team's success would be the catalyst for the new field house the school had been hoping to build.

Once the celebration subsided, Wooden's assistant, Ed Powell, assumed that his boss would begin preparing for the year ahead. "I thought he was happy at Indiana State," Powell said. What Powell didn't realize was that Wooden was itching to leave.

Wooden confided as much to Louisville coach Peck Hickman shortly after their two teams met in the NAIB finals. Hickman later recalled Wooden saying, "Peck, I've got to get out of here. If you hear of anything, let me know." Wooden never explained why he was looking to leave Indiana State, but it likely stemmed from his awareness that his success would only create more pressure to win. He sensed this dynamic as soon as he took the job, when the town gave him such grief for building his roster with quicker players from South Bend. Wooden confessed his concerns to his former grade school principal, Earl Warriner, who had traveled to Indianapolis to watch Wooden's team play during that first season. "He said, 'Mr. Warriner, I may be in bad down there,'" Warriner said. "I said, 'Oh, John, why?' He says, 'I'll tell you what it is.' He had taken his high school team down there with him, and he kicked off seniors and juniors. He said, 'I'm playing my freshman team this year. I've got to win. I'm gone if I don't win.'" Now, with his entire team returning from its runner-up finish in the NAIB tournament, Wooden would face expectations unlike any he had encountered as a coach.

One of the jobs Hickman mentioned to Wooden was at the University of California, Los Angeles, which had already contacted Hickman about its opening. As Bob Nesbit's item in the *Star* revealed, UCLA had been interested in Wooden for some time, but he was not the school's first choice. The UCLA athletic director, Wilbur Johns, had offered the job twice to Branch McCracken, who by then had coached for eight seasons at Indiana. After turning Johns down the year before, McCracken actually accepted the UCLA job in the spring of 1948. He had gone so far as to find a buyer for his house until Indiana increased his salary and convinced him to stay. When McCracken called Johns to say he was backing out, he recommended Wooden.

It was not the first time someone had made that suggestion. Back in 1941, when Johns was in his second season at UCLA, he was eating dinner with Piggy Lambert and mentioned that he wanted to stop coaching soon. As Johns recalled, "He said, 'Wilbur, when you do and you're looking for a coach, just keep this guy in mind—John Wooden.'" Johns heard the same thing from Bob Kelley, a radio broadcaster who had lived in South Bend when Wooden was coaching there and had since moved to Los Angeles to call professional football games. But it was the word of Wooden's former Purdue teammate, Dutch Fehring, who had become an assistant football coach at UCLA, that weighed heaviest of all. "One man convinced me that John Wooden was the man. It was Dutch Fehring," Johns said. "He told me that if he could choose any man in basketball, any man, 'I couldn't give you a better name than John Wooden.'"

At first blush, it looked like a poor fit. UCLA had enjoyed just three winning seasons in the previous twenty-one years. Wooden had no ties to the West Coast, and he had all of two years' experience coaching in college. But when Johns contacted Wooden and invited him to Los Angeles, Wooden figured he should at least check it out.

He was disappointed to discover that UCLA had poor facilities. The Bruins played their games on the third floor of a small, stuffy gymnasium. Even the gym at Martinsville High put it to shame. Johns told Wooden (without explicitly promising) that UCLA hoped to build a new, first-rate basketball arena in the near future. Johns offered Wooden a two-year contract, but Wooden insisted he wouldn't come for anything less than a three-year deal. When Johns agreed, Wooden said he wanted to go home and think it over.

Ed Powell originally assumed that Wooden had no real interest in the UCLA job, but he noticed a change when his boss returned to Terre Haute. "I met John at the airport upon his return and knew that he was hooked," Powell said. "Because this very conservative gentleman was wearing a loud Hawaiian shirt and argyle socks. I felt that he had made up his mind that he was to take the job at UCLA."

UCLA was not the only college pursuing Wooden, however. Some influential people associated with his alma mater, Purdue, informed Wooden that they wanted him to coach there. The catch was that he would have to remain at Indiana State for one more season, after which he would replace the school's current coach, Mel Taube, who would be fired the next season. Wooden told them no thanks. "I didn't like that way of doing things," he said.

Boston University also called, and a wealthy Indiana businessman named Tony Hulman had promised Wooden (among other things) a summer job at the Indianapolis Motor Speedway if he stayed in Terre Haute. But the place where Wooden really wanted to go was the University of Minnesota. The school's athletic director, Frank McCormick, had just relieved Dave McMillan of his job as the basketball coach, and McCormick wanted Wooden to take the position. There was, however, one condition: Wooden would have to retain McMillan as his assistant. Wooden demurred, not least because McMillan favored a slow, Henry Iba–style of basketball. He also believed the arrangement would be awkward. As Powell recalled, "John always told me, 'Never take a job where your predecessor remains on the premises.'" Wooden told McCormick that he would come to Minnesota, but only if he could bring Powell with him as an assistant. McCormick said he would have to clear Wooden's request through the school's athletics board. "I wanted the Minnesota job," Wooden said. "I wanted to stay in the Big Ten. I was a midwesterner."

By this point, UCLA was pressing Wooden for a decision. It all came to a head on the evening of April 17, 1948. Wooden was due to receive a phone call at 6:00 p.m. from McCormick to learn whether he would be permitted to bring Powell to Minnesota. Johns was supposed to call an hour later. When Wooden didn't hear from McCormick at the appointed time, he assumed Minnesota was no longer an option. So when Johns called to ask whether he was prepared to accept UCLA's offer, Wooden told him yes.

About an hour later, McCormick called. Unbeknown to Wooden, Minnesota had been hit by a major snowstorm, unseasonable even by that state's standards. The storm had knocked down some phone lines, preventing McCormick from getting through. He was now calling to say he had gotten the green light for Wooden to bring Powell. Wooden told McCormick he had already agreed to take the position at UCLA. When McCormick asked if he could call UCLA back to tell them he changed his mind, Wooden said no. Not only had Wooden given Johns his word, but UCLA had already notified the press that Wooden had accepted the position.

Such were the odd circumstances that paved the way for John Wooden to become the fourth coach in the inglorious history of UCLA basketball. Upon announcing his decision to the people of Terre Haute, Wooden sounded almost apologetic. "I deeply regret leaving State at this time, but an opportunity such as the one UCLA offered does not come along every day," his statement read. Johns wanted him to come to Los Angeles immediately, but Wooden said he preferred to wait until July so he could finish coaching the baseball season.

Wooden's basketball players were naturally disappointed, especially since they learned the news by reading the newspapers. But they were happy for their coach. "I hated to see him go. We all did," Klueh said. "It was a real feather in our cap that he could go from a school of about twenty-two hundred students, a little teachers college, to a big place like UCLA. But we definitely had mixed emotions." Clarence Walker echoed that sentiment in his journal entry dated April 26: "A week ago it was publicly announced that John R. Wooden, coach of I.S.T.C. basketball team will not return next year due to his going to U.C.L.A. as head basketball coach. A truly wonderful man is leaving."

It was an illogical career move for many reasons, but John and Nell didn't see this as a permanent change. They figured he could go out to Los Angeles, coach there for a few years, and then come back to the Midwest—probably in the Big Ten, maybe even at Purdue. Little did Wooden realize that he would never return. Strange as it seemed, unplanned though it may have been, a new season was upon him. Johnny Wooden was going west.

PART TWO

Summer

10

Unwelcome

It was another fine spring day at Joe E. Brown Field in Los Angeles, California, where the UCLA baseball team was holding practice. Early in the workout, Ken Proctor, the Bruins' second baseman, noticed a short, trim man standing quietly behind the third base dugout. The stranger was wearing athletic apparel, but Proctor didn't recognize him. "Everybody wondered who he was," Proctor said. "Then one of the guys said that's the new basketball coach."

John Wooden had flown into town in April 1948 to spend a few days meeting the community and conducting basketball practices before heading back to Terre Haute to finish coaching Indiana State's baseball season. The visit lasted only a few days, but it was long enough to alert the locals that he planned to bring a different kind of game to the campus in Westwood. "The fast break is my system," he declared at the UCLA athletic department's semimonthly breakfast with local sportswriters. "We'll win fifty percent of our games by outrunning the other team in the last five minutes."

It would not be easy to whip the hoops program into shape. UCLA had posted a winning record just twice in the previous seventeen seasons and at one point had lost thirty-nine consecutive games to its crosstown rival, the University of Southern California. The previous March, the Bruins finished dead last in the Southern Division of the Pacific Coast Conference (PCC), and they were about to lose their entire starting lineup to graduation. But that did not stop Wooden from laying down an ambitious (and apocryphal) marker. "I've never played for nor coached a losing team in my life," he told the players. "I don't plan on starting now."

After Wooden returned to Indiana, Bill Putnam, a holdover assistant coach at UCLA, presided over the rest of the spring practices. Wooden monitored things from Terre Haute through the mail. Despite his pedigree as an All-American collegian and the coach of a squad that was the runner-up in a prestigious national tournament, his reputation had not preceded him. People who lived on the West Coast barely followed their local basketball teams, much less those all the way out in Indiana. "He was just a coach from the Midwest somewhere. We didn't know anything about him," said Ralph Joeckel, a forward on Wooden's first two UCLA teams.

Two months later, John, Nell, and their two young children enjoyed a lovely long drive to California, pulling over their Mercury to visit the Grand Canyon and Carlsbad Caverns along the way. When they reached their new home, however, they were overcome with despair. "I felt like I was coming to the end of the world," Nell said. "We got on the Pasadena Freeway, and it almost scared us to death. We'd never seen a freeway before. I remember John getting all upset and saying, 'What are we doing here anyway?'"

It was an understandable reaction. To that point, Wooden's idea of a big city was South Bend. "I came from the farm, the country, and Los Angeles was frightening to me," he said. "Nellie, my dear wife, wasn't the happiest she could be. Neither were my children at the very beginning."

Wilbur Johns, the school's athletic director, arranged for Putnam and his wife, Betty, to show John and Nell around town and help them look for a house. The Putnams tried their best to make conversation with the newcomers, but it wasn't easy. "They were very, very quiet. I think UCLA felt too big for them for a while," Betty recalled. "They were used to a smaller town and close friends. They were religious, and they had a hard time finding a group of people they were compatible with." The Woodens decided to rent an apartment in the Culver City neighborhood. It occurred to Betty that by renting instead of buying, they were preserving their freedom to leave on short notice.

As if being transported to this big, uncomfortable new world wasn't hard enough, Wooden soon made a disturbing discovery. UCLA's athletic department was under the purview of the Associated Students, which meant that the president of the student body was technically Wooden's boss. Not only did Wooden receive no pension contribution on his paltry salary of $6,000, but he also had to suffer the ignominy of having his paycheck signed by an undergraduate. While the student body president had his own office, Wooden shared a small space with Ed Powell (whom Wooden had brought with him as an assistant coach) in Kerckhoff Hall, the building that housed the student association, the school store, the student newspaper, and the athletic department. "Had I realized the situation, I'm quite certain I wouldn't have come," he said.

As part of his new gig, Wooden was also required to attend cocktail parties. This was considered necessary to stir up interest in the basketball program, which had never been a problem back in Indiana. Wooden hated public speaking, and his insistence on avoiding alcohol led to awkward moments. During one press luncheon, when Wooden declined a writer's invitation to imbibe, the writer snapped, "You think you're too good to drink with us?"

"In the two years we were at Indiana State, I don't think John gave more than six or seven talks," Powell said. "At UCLA, he was now asked to attend every type of function. He doesn't like to barge into a room full of people, and he doesn't drink. This disturbed him. One of my major jobs when we'd go to a function was for me to go over and say, 'So-and-so, have you had an opportunity to meet our coach, John Wooden? C'mon, let me introduce you.'"

To ease Wooden's burden, Powell often brought a harmonica to parties as a gimmick. When it came time for the coach to speak, Wooden would say to the group, "Have you ever heard Eddie play the harmonica? You can make a request, but all his songs sound like 'Red Wings.'"

"Let me tell you," Powell said, "he was lost."

Wooden's awkwardness was also apparent to his former Purdue teammate, Dutch Fehring. "John is misunderstood by many people," Fehring said. "He is quiet and unassuming and really a little shy. Just because he is up and down on the bench doesn't make him an outgoing fellow."

That native shyness stood in stark contrast to the football coach who would be hired midway through Wooden's first season. Henry "Red" Sanders was a hard-drinking, swashbuckling good ole boy who had previously spent four seasons as the head coach at Vanderbilt. While Sanders would quaff drinks, slap backs, and hold court at these functions, Wooden could be found standing in a corner with his finger to his mouth. "Red had come in and captured the town," said Vic Kelley, the school's sports publicist. "He had great personality, magnetism and charisma. He and Wooden would be together at many social events and the people would gravitate toward Sanders."

At least Wooden had a job that could fulfill him. His wife did not. That left her feeling even more out of place. When people would say to Nell that they heard she was from "back east," she would sharply correct them. Not back east. Indiana. "We came out here and we were made to feel unwelcome," she said.

To commemorate this new chapter in their lives, John presented Nell with an engraved gold charm for her bracelet, just as he had done for previous significant events. The charm was shaped like a four-leaf clover, an homage to her Irish heritage. The year 1948 was engraved on one side. A question mark appeared opposite that number. John and Nell did not know precisely when they would leave California, but they obviously would not be staying for long.

Wooden placed an advertisement in the school's newspaper, the *Daily Bruin*, inviting students to try out for his team. When he held his first team meeting two weeks before the start of practice, just 42 players showed up. In his two years at Indiana State, there were 187 and 178 boys, respectively, at the first day of tryouts. ("I remember those figures because they just transposed the last numbers," he said.) Now fewer than a quarter of that total had come, despite the fact that UCLA had more than five times the number of undergraduates.

Many of the players were World War II veterans who were in their early to midtwenties. After taking their names and information, Wooden let them know that the most important thing they needed to do before practice started in two weeks was to toughen up their feet. "I didn't say anything about their wind because I knew if their feet are going to be toughened up, their wind's going to be alright too," Wooden said. Wooden showed them some drills they should do to accomplish this. No matter what state he was coaching in, Wooden's view of the game always boiled down to basics. He taught the game from the ground up.

Once practice began, Wooden became even more disheartened. The group reminded him of his phys ed classes at Indiana State. It's not that these guys were unskilled. They were just accustomed to the plodding, deliberate style taught by Wilbur Johns. Most every school in the eight-team Pacific Coast Conference played walk-it-up basketball. The pace was dictated by elder statesmen like Nibs Price at California, Everett Dean at Stanford, and especially Sam Barry at USC. Barry was the coach who, during a game against UCLA in 1932, ordered his players to hold the ball for so long that some of them literally sat on the court and read from a newspaper while waiting for the Bruins to come out of their zone defense. That game, which UCLA won, 19–17, was instrumental in convincing the national rules committee to add a provision requiring the offense to bring the ball past half court within ten seconds.

The ability of Wooden's players was not nearly as big a problem as the facility where they played their games. The men's gymnasium had been built in 1932, just sixteen years earlier, but it was woefully inadequate.

The players had a locker room, but there were no private showers and no separate rooms for the coaches. Everybody had to climb three flights of stairs to get to a practice floor that had just two baskets. Moreover, the basketball team often had to share the floor with the gymnastics team, with wrestlers practicing one floor below. The gymnasts would regularly leave the playing surface covered with chalk. Wooden asked the buildings and grounds workers to build him two six-foot-wide brooms and mops, and each day before practice his assistants would have to clean the floor. "I took the easy job, I must say," Wooden said. "I'd take a bucket and go along in front of them, just like I was feeding the chickens, to get the floor a little damp."

It would have been bad enough if these were just the practice conditions, but the men's gym was also where the Bruins played their home games. With the bleachers pulled out, the gym could hold only about 2,500 spectators. If the place was filled on game nights, it was hot as hell. "There were a hundred high school gyms in Indiana that were far, far better than what we were playing in," Wooden said.

As part of his lecture about the importance of tough feet, Wooden showed his players how to put on their footwear. He instructed them to use two pairs of socks that were 50 percent cotton, and then demonstrated how to smooth the wrinkles to avoid blisters. Their shoes were to be black (always black), tightly laced, and a half size too small. He didn't want them to smoke or drink alcohol during the season, but he didn't give them a lot of other rules. "One rule he never had was about when you go to bed," said Eddie Sheldrake, a five-foot-nine point guard from Los Angeles. "He told us, 'I'm gonna work you so hard you'll want to go to sleep.'"

When practice began, Wooden was true to his word. He did not believe in wind sprints or running on an outside track to build his players' condition. They did their running in basketball-oriented drills. Practices lasted up to three hours, and there was nary a wasted moment. If the players weren't participating in a drill, they were practicing free throws—and they were not permitted to drink any water. Wooden gave them salt tablets to prevent cramping, and it wouldn't be long before the corners of their mouths were caked from dehydration. "We had to suck on a wet towel when he wasn't looking," said Art Alper, a sophomore forward that first season. "That first year we didn't realize what we were going through. We'd have training table after practice, and the football players would come around, and half our guys couldn't finish dinner because they were so tired. We had all come from a slower game."

Wooden's demeanor was also a reversal from his predecessor's.

"Wilbur Johns was very laid-back. He wasn't a disciplinarian at all," Ralph Joeckel said. Wooden, on the other hand, was all business. He could be serene and pleasant away from the court, but he did not exude much warmth. "He was always very serious when I saw him. I don't think I ever saw him smile," said Ralph Bauer, who played on Wooden's first freshman team. Alper added, "He wasn't a hail-fellow-well-met. He was stern and he didn't smile a lot. But he was very fair."

The new man commanded an instant respect. His players could see from the start that Wooden knew the game and put a great deal of thought into organizing his practices. To him, it was no different than putting together a lesson plan for a high school English class. It was the teacher's job to show up early and be ready to work. He came to practice in his athletic gear and black shoes, and he constantly referred to his three-by-five-inch index cards as he presided over the workouts.

Wooden's experience as a player was invaluable. He had seen this process from that point of view, and he knew just how hard to push without stretching them past their limits. He kept his drills mostly to five-to-ten-minute increments, alternating between difficult and less difficult to keep the workout from becoming mundane. "He had those drills down to a precise point. Just at the point where you felt like you weren't going to be able to make it another length of the floor, he would change the drill," said Paul Saunders, a sophomore forward on that first team.

His instructions were highly specific. He taught them precisely how to pivot, pass, catch, dribble, shoot. He showed them how to watch the ball into their hands when receiving a pass. A shot was to be taken with a flick off the nose. When they ran through his fast break drill, the dribbler always stopped at the foul line, and the two wing players cut to the basket at a forty-five-degree angle. When the pass was made, the players had the option of finishing a layup or pulling up for a shot, but they were always—always—to use the backboard. Wooden learned many of these details from Piggy Lambert, but the specifics of what he taught weren't important. What mattered was how *well* he taught them.

Wooden was exacting but not inflexible. During those first few weeks, he tried to show his players how to shoot free throws underhanded with two hands, as he did, but they were so inept that he gave up after a few weeks. "He said, 'My high school teams could shoot free throws better than you guys,'" recalled Wayne Boulding, a six-foot-one junior forward.

Wooden was stronger and in better shape than his players, but this was not the same young buck who had dashed his way through high school practices in South Bend. Wooden turned thirty-eight years old as practice began, and the back injury he had suffered at navy flight school flared up frequently. Sometimes he would have to conduct practice from a chair at half court or from the bleachers. As was the case in Dayton, South Bend, and Terre Haute, Wooden's new charges were struck at how this genial, quiet, reserved midwesterner was transformed once he stepped onto a basketball court. "He was a tenacious, tough, hard-nosed, vicious competitor," Eddie Sheldrake said. "He looks like a preacher and acts like a preacher . . . but when you look at those beady eyes and that pointed nose and you get him on you, he's wiry. Let him guard you for a game and you'd wish you never went on the basketball court. That's the truth."

As the first game drew nigh, Wooden started putting his players through full-court scrimmages. This was not just a matter of assessing talent; he wanted to experiment with different combinations to discern who played well with whom. Baseball fan that he was (he was a numbers freak who devoured the *Sporting News* every week), Wooden also kept detailed statistics for every scrimmage. His goal was to decide which six or seven players would make up his rotation for the entire season. Once the games began, Wooden did very little substituting, even when his team held a large lead in the final minutes.

Everyone wanted to play, of course, but Wooden did not hear much complaining from the benchwarmers. Many of the players came from strict homes, and several had recently served in the military. They were raised in a culture that acquiesced to authority. "I never felt neglected," said Boulding, who saw very little court time that season. "Once you were relegated to the second or third team, you kind of found your place and did what you could to support everybody else. That's the way the game is played."

In Wooden's mind, these boys were students first, players second. They saw him at practice, at games, and at team meals. Aside from road trips, he did not spend much time with them away from basketball. If the players had personal or academic problems, they would go to the assistant coaches or the team's trainer, Ducky Drake, who was also UCLA's track coach. "I don't remember ever having a one-on-one with Coach Wooden at any time," Ralph Joeckel said. "To me, he was the guy that blew the whistle and said here's what I want you to do." George Stanich, who played on Wooden's first two teams, added that a player "might get razzed if you were too tiffy with the coach." Asked how much time he spent in Wooden's office just shooting the breeze, Stanich went silent for several seconds. "Gosh," he finally answered. "I don't even remember where his office was."

The 1948–49 season was the first and last that John Wooden opened without having to deal with external pressure. It was a refreshing change from the environment he had left behind in Terre Haute. Shortly before the first game, the *Daily Bruin* predicted that "under Wooden's herd-running, modified fire-house type of basketball, the Bruins ought to pull an occasional surprise, although nobody expects them to nail down the PCC bunting at this stage of the proceedings." Even Wooden's bio in the school's media guide, so often an instrument of propaganda, tried to tamp down expectations: "His prospects here are such that might not instill the greatest of optimism in a man with a new job on his hands."

What everyone, including Wooden, failed to realize was that this ragtag bunch was in many ways uniquely suited to his style. This owed largely to the presence of the "Sacramento whiz kids," a group of transfers from Sacramento Junior College who had won a junior college state title in 1946. The players had been brought in by Bill Putnam, himself a Sacramento JC alum, and they had the requisite skills to play fast-break basketball. "They were the runningest, hardest-working guys I'd ever seen," Joeckel said. "Not much height, but nobody could keep up with them."

George Stanich was the best of the bunch. Besides also serving as a starting pitcher for the UCLA baseball team, Stanich was an elite high jumper who had just won a bronze medal at the 1948 Olympics in London. The school billed Stanich as "UCLA's greatest all-around athlete since Jackie Robinson" and put a photograph of him and Wooden on the cover of the team's media guide.

One of the first adjustments Wooden made was to switch the six-foot-three Stanich from center to guard, even though the kid couldn't dribble a lick. In Wooden's eyes, Stanich's quickness was a far greater asset than his size. Moving him away from the basket would enable him to exploit it. "I didn't like it, and he knew I didn't like it, but as long as I was playing, I was all right," Stanich said. Stanich was also the type of player who would benefit from Wooden's counterintuitive approach to rebounding. Unlike most coaches, Wooden did not teach his players to "box out," which means blocking an opponent with their bodies so they can establish inside position. He derided that tactic as "negative rebounding." Instead, Wooden wanted his guys to pursue the ball.

Wooden didn't deploy his racehorse style purely for tactical reasons. He also knew it would excite the fans. This was especially important in Southern California, where because of the beautiful weather outdoor sports like football and baseball flourished. Even track and field, which produced Olympic heroes like Stanich, was a bigger draw than hoops. "We have an obligation not only to try to win, but to entertain the customers, especially here in Los Angeles where there are so many other attractions," Wooden said. "A coach who plays up-tempo style, as opposed to ball control, is less likely to be fired." The man may have been old-fashioned in many respects, but on this front he was a cutting-edge marketer.

The Bruins surprised everyone by sprinting out of the gate. They opened with six consecutive wins, equaling the school's longest streak in fifteen years. But even though the Bruins were winning, Wooden could see that his players were not in the kind of tip-top shape they would need to be in for conference play. So they spent the next few weeks running their tails off.

This was always Wooden's fallback position: there wasn't a problem in basketball that couldn't be solved with better conditioning. It was right there in the center of his Pyramid of Success, one-third of the belief system instilled by Piggy Lambert: *Condition. Skill. Team Spirit.* Wooden may have understood at some level the importance of defense, but he didn't emphasize it. "He didn't teach too much defense. His theory was to get the most high-percentage shots," said Don Seidel, a six-foot-one guard on that first team. This way of thinking frustrated his assistant, Bill Putnam, who came from the Wilbur Johns school, where teams slowed the pace and guarded their way to victory. "Bill liked defense, so he and John would bump heads once in a while," Betty Putnam said. "Bill never said anything derogatory about John, ever. But Bill would come home and work on these defensive moves, and he'd try to get John to use them. Most of the time John wouldn't pay much attention." As a result, Putnam took on an administrative role with the team while Wooden and Powell, the two transplanted Hoosiers, did the bulk of the teaching.

In mid-December the Bruins got the chance to test their mettle in a pair of doubleheaders featuring visitors from the Midwest, a region that the *Los Angeles Times* described as the "cradle of basketball and spawning ground of the greatest basketball teams the game has ever seen." In the first game, UCLA squeaked by Northwestern, 49–44, to improve to 6–0. The next night they suffered their first loss, to Wisconsin, by a score of 49–46. These games were played before 6,800 spectators at the Pan-Pacific

Auditorium, a venue in downtown Los Angeles that often hosted ice shows and hockey games. However, most of those fans were on hand to watch USC, which was also participating in the doubleheaders. "It was," said Powell, "an SC town."

Wooden's extra conditioning work started to pay off once the conference schedule got under way in January. Over the next two months, the Bruins would play four games against each of the other three teams in the PCC's Southern Division—California, Stanford, and USC. After losing the opener to Stanford, UCLA used an 11–2 run late in the first half to beat Cal by 9. That was followed by Wooden's first two-game series against USC. The specter of the fresh face squaring off against the old guard represented by USC coach Sam Barry provided an irresistible story line. "Wooden brought to Westwood a fast-breaking, lung-searing style of play which demands speed and more speed from his players," the *Los Angeles Times* wrote in advance of the weekend clashes. "Barry has had singular success with the 'slow break' where control of the ball pays off. 'Race-horse' teams here have been forced to slow down when confronted by Barry's pass-and-wait-for-the-breaks performance. So it'll be interesting to see which team has its own way."

In the first game, Barry made the mistake of asking his boys to try to run with the Bruins on their home floor. By the end of the game, the Trojans were spent, which enabled UCLA to overcome a 9-point deficit over the last eight minutes and prevail in overtime, 74–68. That was the most points UCLA had ever scored against its crosstown rival. Barry slammed on the breaks the next night in the Olympic Auditorium, USC's home court. It was an ugly, rugged affair, with forty-three fouls called on the two teams. But the strategy worked as the Trojans won, 59–52.

From there, UCLA won its next eight games, including a nonconference beatdown of Fresno State in which the Bruins scored 57 points in the first half. (Too bad just 1,500 people were in the men's gym to witness it.) Wooden had unleashed a completely different way of playing, and opposing coaches were mystified by it. Many of them made the mistake that Barry did by trying to keep up. The problem was, their players were not physically capable of pulling it off. "We had a saying at halftime. If we stay with them the first half, we'll beat them the second half," Powell said. "Several times during a game it would be five-on-zero. All five of our boys would be nearer the basket than any one of the opposition."

Many of UCLA's wins that first season were secured late in the second half, just as Wooden had promised at the writers' luncheon the previous spring. The Bruins outscored Cal by 11 in the second half of a 3-point win; used a 13–2 run early in the second half to beat Stanford 59–48; and broke open another game against Cal with a 20–3 burst before coasting to a 59–50 victory. "We didn't win games because we had better talent," Joeckel said. "We won by being in better shape."

To the uninformed outsider, it seemed that Wooden was more sorcerer than basketball coach. "Many times this season, Wooden has seen his speed merchants leave the court at halftime on the short end of the score," Jack Geyer wrote in the *Los Angeles Times*. "What he says [at halftime] or what he does, none but his players know, but it works like magic."

One of Wooden's primary advantages was that he cared about the sport more than many of his western rivals. Where he came from, basketball was religion. Here, it was a diversion. For example, when UCLA took a trip north to play a two-game series in Oregon, one of the opposing coaches asked Wooden if he wanted to set up a scrimmage the following morning for players who didn't get into the game. This had been done for many years as a way to make the road trip worthwhile. Wooden balked. "We didn't come up here to scrimmage," he said. "We came up here to play games, and every boy that we have is prepared to get into the action. We don't want to use up our talent in a scrimmage on a Saturday morning."

Wooden also recognized the mental edge in superior conditioning. When his team got behind, the players didn't panic. They simply waited for the pace to exact its toll. This was also why Wooden spent so little time discussing his opponents. It's not that Wooden never scouted; he traveled to Santa Barbara that February to watch Cal play two nights before the Golden Bears were to come to Westwood. But he did not spend much time talking with his players about the other team. "He gave us a tremendous amount of self-confidence," Joeckel said. "We basically got to the point where the other team was nothing to us. He didn't belittle them in any way, but he had us ignore them so much that in my mind, I didn't have any use for the other team."

There was, however, one way in which Wooden became a different coach from the one he had been back in Kentucky and Indiana. There were hardly any outbursts of the kind that pockmarked his years in Dayton, South Bend, and Terre Haute. This was partly because of Wooden's maturity—he was, after all, inching closer to his fortieth birthday—but it also reflected his tenuous standing. In Indiana, Wooden was a legend. In California, he was an unknown commodity. The days of busting down doors, booting players in the rear, and getting into chin-to-chin brouhahas with opposing coaches were gone—for now, anyway. "I've seen him upset, but I felt he was always under control," Stanich said. "I don't ever remember him really losing his temper." Still, he was plenty feisty with officials and opposing players. During the Bruins' win over Wisconsin, Wooden rode the Badgers' best player, center Don Rehfeldt, so mercilessly that at one point Rehfeldt looked right at Wooden and gave him the finger. "Coach had been chewing on him pretty good," Eddie Sheldrake recalled, chuckling.

Remarkably, UCLA entered its season-ending, home-and-away, two-night series against USC in late February tied with the Trojans for first place in the Southern Division with an 8–2 record. Once again the teams staged bitter, physical contests. In the first game, seen by 6,500 at the Olympic Auditorium, UCLA won 51–50. The following night, the Bruins won by 8 points at the men's gym in Westwood despite 28 points from USC's brilliant forward, Bill Sharman. That clinched the Bruins' first-ever PCC Southern Division championship. For all of Wooden's complaints about the conditions of his home court, it was proving to be even more uncomfortable for his team's opponents. The Bruins finished undefeated at home for the first time in school history.

The locals were impressed, to say the least. The *Daily Bruin* published a lengthy story on February 25 under the headline "The Man Who Doesn't Like to Lose." It read: "Wooden's first UCLA basketball team is a fast-breaking, hard-running, driving, aggressive club. One sports writer summed it up by saying that it was the first basketball team he had ever seen that had the fight and team spirit of a football team." The article also mentioned that Wooden had never coached a losing season, repeating the falsehood that was becoming embedded in his biography.

Since the PCC could send only one team to the eight-team NCAA tournament, the conference championship was decided by a best-of-three series between the South and North Division champions. The divisions took turns hosting the championships, and in 1949 it was the North's turn. That sent the Bruins to Corvallis to face Oregon State, which had beaten UCLA by 16 points during the inaugural PCC tournament in San Francisco back in December. (Those games did not count in the league standings.) The Beavers' coach, Slats Gill, was one of the few coaches out west who favored a quicker tempo, but in the championship series, he and Wooden took turns slowing down the action in an effort to win.

After Oregon State won the opener by 12 points, UCLA bounced back with a 46–39 victory in game 2. Wooden liked to say he disapproved of stalling tactics, but in that second game, he ordered his Bruins to hold the ball for the final four minutes to preserve the victory. In the rubber match, the Bruins trailed by 15 points early in the second half before embarking on their trademark late-game rally. Alas, they came up short, allowing Oregon State to escape with a 41–35 victory. That gave the Beavers the PCC crown and a berth in the NCAA tournament's Western Regionals in Kansas City.

Despite that loss, nobody, least of all Wooden, could brand the season a disappointment. In just a few short months, this unassuming, unknown, unwelcome stranger had made history. The 1948 49 Bruins set school records for longest winning streak (twelve) and overall wins (twenty-two) and became the first UCLA team to win a game against a Northern Division opponent in the PCC play-offs. In later years, when Wooden was asked to name his favorite UCLA teams, he would often include this first unit right alongside his championship teams. "I was at a new place, trying to get established. You want to do well," he said. "No championship ever gave me greater pleasure or satisfaction than that."

He may not have left Corvallis with a championship trophy, but John Wooden knew success when he saw it. He flew home with a peaceful mind.

11

The Nonconformist

Two senior starters graduated from Wooden's first team at UCLA. Three more departed from his second. This, of course, was the nature of college sports: the teacher remained the same, but the students turned over each autumn. Gone were the military veterans and the boys who grew up in strict homes. In their stead came a different set of players—younger, looser, more free-spirited. Wooden had to adapt to the changes without abandoning his core principles, a challenge he would face repeatedly during the decades to come.

The ringleader of this new bunch was Eddie Sheldrake, the diminutive, wily guard from Los Angeles. On the court, Sheldrake was an alpha male who could run Wooden's high-post offense and still score in bunches, much as Wooden himself had done in his heyday. Off the court, Sheldrake was a merry prankster who found hilarity in juvenile antics like sneaking up to the window of a classroom and interrupting a lecture by shouting, "That's bullshit!" and then dashing away. On road trips, Sheldrake would sometimes catch pigeons and release them in the lobby of the team's hotel. Once, he knocked on the door of a room where Wooden and Ducky Drake were playing cards. "You guys need another pigeon for bridge?" he asked. When they said yes, Sheldrake let loose one of his feathered friends right in their room.

Then there was Dick Ridgway, a graceful six-foot-four forward who joined the varsity in Wooden's second season. He was fond of dropping water balloons from hotel balconies. When a hotel manager called Wooden to complain during a trip to the Midwest, Wooden went ballistic and benched Ridgway for two games. As he summoned Ridgway for his return against Michigan State, the player sarcastically raised his hand and said "May I?" Then he checked into the game. "That was as much a comeback as I can remember anyone having to the coach," said Barry

Porter, a six-foot-one guard. "Most of us were pretty much under his spell."

Art Alper was another Los Angeles native with an adventurous streak. After the Bruins lost in the 1949 PCC play-offs at Oregon State, Alper decided to hit the town with some football players and ended up going to a local tavern for a few drinks. When the team returned home, Wooden called Alper to his office, told him he had heard what Alper did, and informed the player that he was indefinitely suspended. Wooden made Alper visit his office nearly a dozen times over the summer before reinstating him.

Another player, Paul Saunders, showed up at practice one day with floppy hair. Saunders knew Wooden liked his players to keep their hair short, but when the coach said nothing, Saunders figured he was in the clear. After practice, a trainer asked Saunders to come to a downstairs locker room, where he and several other trainers held Saunders down so they could shear his locks. "I never talked to Wooden about it," Saunders said. "I wasn't mad at him, either. I knew that he didn't like long hair, so therefore he took some steps to see that I had short hair."

Of all the players who tested Wooden's authority on those early teams, none pushed the envelope further than an intense, dark-haired, streetwise guard named Jerry Norman. Norman fit right in with the team's adolescent ethos. He respected Wooden, but he wasn't cowed by him. During practice, Norman would think nothing of attempting a fancy shot without looking at the basket or chucking up jumpers from halfcourt. He could be equally audacious off the court, like the time during a trip to Kansas City when Norman got the brilliant idea to hop a fence during a visit to President Truman's house in nearby Independence, Missouri. He was detained briefly by the Secret Service before rejoining the team with a smile.

It was clear from the start that Norman and Wooden were not simpatico. "Wooden was a little cornballish and had some straitlaced ideas, and Jerry was a little more sophisticated," Ed Powell said. "Jerry continued to do things his own way, and sometimes he found that trying his way was not the best way. But I will say this. Wooden always knew his potential, and he was willing to put up with it."

The two men shared many qualities: talent, pride, intelligence, most of all hardheadedness. Yet they also had some fundamental differences. In the first place, Norman had a desultory attitude toward schoolwork. He would wait until the end of the semester to get serious about studying, but he was so smart that he could keep himself eligible. Like Wooden,

Norman derived his outlook from his father, a son of German immigrants who had dropped out of high school after the ninth grade and worked most of his life for the Southern California Gas Company. "My father reached the highest position in the company for someone who didn't go to college," Norman said. "His parents believed in work, not education." Jerry was the middle of three children, and his father gave them a lot of leeway. "You could go anywhere you wanted as long as you didn't get into trouble," Norman said. For many players, Wooden was an extension of their father, but that was not the case for Norman.

Worst of all, in Wooden's view, Norman did not bring a lot of energy to practice. He preferred to save it for game night. "I probably wasn't the greatest practice player," Norman conceded. "Some guys are practice players and some are game players. It's a whole different atmosphere when you play a game. I'm sure I didn't play hard every day."

Wooden tried to get Norman to exert more effort, but that did little to change Norman's modus operandi. "Jerry had an attitude. He didn't pay attention the way Wooden wanted," Art Alper said. Norman could get a little mouthy with Wooden, but it was what came out of his mouth that rankled the coach the most. "He was very profane," Wooden said. "I just can't stand that and I probably kicked him off the floor more times for profanity than all the rest of the players that I've ever had put together."

Norman called that claim "a total fabrication," adding, "I don't know why he ever came up with that." Regardless, there is no doubt that Norman bridled against Wooden's discipline. The stricter the coach tried to be, the more Norman resisted.

"Jerry was the guy who didn't fit. He was a nonconformist," Ralph Joeckel said. "I don't remember Norman being profane, but there were times during practice when Wooden just told Norman to get off the court because he was fooling around. Wooden didn't like horseplay. The guys that never smiled and worked the hardest got the most attention from Wooden."

Still, Norman loved basketball, and he possessed a mind for the game that surpassed even his considerable physical talents. In December 1949, in Norman's sophomore season, UCLA traveled to New York City to play in Madison Square Garden against City College of New York, a powerhouse program that would end that season as the only team in history to win both the NCAA and NIT championships. (CCNY would have to forfeit those titles the following year after an epic point-shaving scandal that rocked the sport.) Norman had spent the previous summer playing with several CCNY players while working for a hotel in the Catskill Mountains of upstate New York. In those days, the Catskills were a basketball hotbed during the summertime, when prominent college and even some professional players would work as busboys and waiters during the day and then entertain the guests by playing games at night. While sitting in the locker room before the matchup at the Garden, Norman briefed his UCLA teammates on the respective strengths and weaknesses of their opponents. "It was pretty amazing," Alper recalled. "Wooden's whole thing was don't worry about the other guys, but Jerry is saying, 'This guy can't go to his right,' and 'This guy will give you a head fake, but he can't shoot outside.' By the time he was done, we knew those guys cold." Norman's insights helped UCLA emerge with a 60–53 victory.

The big win on the big stage infused the Bruins with great confidence. After they returned home, they steamrolled their way through the Southern Division and won a spot in the two-out-of-three PCC play-off against Washington State. The Northern Division champs were a typical West Coast slow-ball outfit featuring center Gene Conley, who would go on to play for the NBA's Boston Celtics and to pitch for eleven years in the major leagues. At six foot eight, Conley was referred to by newspaper writers as a "giant." Said Wooden, "Our hope is to run Conley so much we cut him down to our size."

The first game ended with the most dramatic moment thus far in UCLA basketball history, when Joeckel banked in a shot from just beyond half-court in the closing seconds to give the Bruins a 60–58 victory. The delirious fans rushed onto the floor of the men's gym and carried Joeckel off. The following night, the Bruins clinched the crown with a 52–49 win as their opponents were visibly gassed down the stretch. "I like to play basketball but not that way," Conley said.

The triumph propelled Wooden to his first-ever NCAA tournament. The field consisted of four teams that would play in an Eastern Regional in New York, and another four that assembled for the Western Regional in Kansas City. The championship game would be played three days later in New York. UCLA's opening game took place before more than ten thousand fans in Municipal Auditorium, the same arena where two years earlier Wooden's Hurryin' Sycamores had broken a racial barrier and nearly won a national championship.

UCLA's first opponent was Bradley, which was ranked No. 1 in the country by the Associated Press. The game was so big that Wooden cast aside his policy of never talking to his players about their opponent. Bradley was a Midwest powerhouse that competed in his former league, the Missouri Valley Conference, so he asked a friend to deliver a detailed presentation on the Braves to Wooden's players. It backfired, badly. "We were in there about an hour. By the time we got out, we thought we were playing the Minneapolis Lakers," Jerry Norman said. "Bradley probably would have finished third or fourth in our conference, but instead of just playing our game, we spent the whole game waiting for them to do something. Because of that, they stayed in it until the end."

Not only did the Bruins lose, they did so in distinctly un-UCLA-like fashion. They led by 7 points with five minutes to play but were outscored by an astonishing 23–2 margin the rest of the way. Jack Geyer noted in the *Los Angeles Times* that the Bruins had "turned deliberate." The team played a consolation game the next day against Brigham Young University, which had lost to Baylor in the other regional semifinal, but Wooden had a low opinion of consolation games. He played his reserves for extended minutes, and UCLA lost by 21. It was a disappointing experience, but it taught Wooden an invaluable lesson. "He never believed in scouting again," Norman said.

Even as Wooden was turning around UCLA's basketball fortunes, he and Nell pined for the chance to return to their home state. A perfect opportunity presented itself in the spring of 1950, when Purdue sent three top administrators to Los Angeles to convince Wooden to come back to his alma mater. This was a classier, more straightforward way of doing business than two years before, when the school tried to use back channels to lure Wooden away from Indiana State. The fruits they bore were plenty tempting. Besides offering a five-year contract that would renew annually and more than double his $6,000 salary, Purdue also dangled perks like membership at a country club, a new car every year, a house at reduced rent, and a fully paid life insurance policy.

Wooden was impressed by the material persuasions, but the clinchers were two basketball assets that UCLA could not match: a full-time assistant coach and a brand-new arena. The Purdue officials showed Wooden designs for the new facility just as Wilbur Johns had done when Wooden interviewed for the UCLA job. Johns hadn't technically promised Wooden he would have a new pavilion by the end of his three-year contract, but he'd led Wooden to believe that would be the case. Two years later, Wooden could see that was far from happening. The lack of enthusiasm for basketball in Los Angeles made it difficult for the school to raise enough money, and every time someone in the athletic department tried to raise undergraduate fees to finance the project, he was voted down by the student association.

The decision was easy. Wooden wanted the job. He told the Purdue officials that he would accept their offer as long as UCLA released him from the final year of his contract.

He asked to meet with Wilbur Johns and Bill Ackerman, the graduate manager of UCLA's student association. Ackerman, whom the students affectionately called "Mr. A," was a revered figure on campus. He was also the varsity tennis coach whose squad would capture UCLA's first-ever NCAA championship later that spring. Wooden considered the meeting a formality, but Johns and Ackerman asked that he bring Nell with him. "They knew what I wanted to talk about," Wooden said.

When Wooden made his request, his bosses didn't quite say no. They did, however, remind Wooden that *he* was the one who had insisted on a three-year contract as a condition for his coming to UCLA. We thought you were an honorable man, they told him. You promised to be here for the full three years. We'll let you out if you want, but it won't be the right thing to do.

We thought you were an honorable man. The words gnawed at Wooden, just as Johns and Ackerman knew they would. "I guess they had learned enough about me in the first two years that they probably had me there," he said. Nell still wanted him to leave—in her mind the failure to build the pavilion justified the breach—but Wooden knew his bosses were right. Besides, Purdue had now come calling twice in a three-year span. Surely they would call again.

Amid much public speculation, UCLA made a formal announcement that the coach was staying put. "For a number of weeks it has been more or less common knowledge that there was some question of Coach Wooden's remaining at UCLA because of other offers," Johns said in a statement. "It pleases me to announce that Coach Wooden has decided to remain at UCLA. We all hope his tenure will be happy and permanent." The *Los Angeles Mirror* reported that UCLA kept Wooden by giving him a ten-year contract and assuring him of "provisions of a new pavilion." That first part was incorrect—the contract was actually a permanent three-year deal that automatically renewed at the end of each season—but the promise of the pavilion was an essential part of Wooden's decision. "I like it here," Wooden said. "My family likes it here and so I chose to stay."

In truth, the Woodens were bitter that UCLA had placed such shackles on them. The episode reinforced their strong desire to move home as soon as possible. "I was irritated to say the least. Though I understood their position at the time, I thought it was unfair," Wooden said. "But I fulfilled my contract. In the back of my mind, I said, 'Yes, I'll fulfill it. Then I'll probably fly the coop.'" The near loss of Wooden prompted the student varsity club to circulate a petition a few weeks later calling for the immediate construction of a new basketball pavilion on campus. "If there is no hope of a new pavilion," the petition read, "there is no hope of keeping Wooden."

The tension between John Wooden and Jerry Norman continued to percolate during the 1950–51 season. It finally boiled over in January as the Bruins were trying to unshackle themselves from a stretch in which they had lost five times in eight games. As Wooden was addressing the team before the start of practice, he spotted Norman lying on the floor with his head on a ball and talking to a teammate, not paying attention. This time, Wooden didn't just boot Norman out of practice. He booted him right off the team.

In reporting Norman's suspension, the *Los Angeles Herald Examiner* wrote that Wooden had dropped Norman from the team "temporarily" because of the player's "attitude." Though the paper indicated Norman probably would be back in a few days, he ended up being gone for two weeks—and it would have been longer if it hadn't been for Eddie Sheldrake, who by that point had grown friendlier with Wooden than any other player. Sheldrake had also become close with Norman's parents, who treated him as one of their own after Sheldrake's father died. Norman needed to be convinced to come back to the team, and Wooden needed to be convinced to take him back. Sheldrake brokered the rapprochement.

From then on, Norman toed the line and emerged as a dependable backcourt starter. Sheldrake, meanwhile, remained the ace of the squad, lighting up Stanford for a school-record 38 points in February. But UCLA's defense was even more porous than before. The Bruins were giving up more than 64 points per game, up from 53.5 the previous season, and they surrendered 90 points during an especially bad loss to Long Island University in December. Yet, despite their suspect defense, the Bruins finished the regular season in a tie with USC for first place in the Southern Division. That set up a one-game play-off between the rivals, which UCLA won by 8 points.

Alas, the season ended in Seattle, where UCLA lost two straight games to Washington in the PCC play-offs. It didn't help that Wooden had to bench the incorrigible Ridgway in the second game for all but the final thirteen minutes. "Ridgway was being disciplined," Wooden explained without revealing specifics. "I played him in the late stages of the game because he saw the light in a talk we had at halftime."

Unfortunately, over the summer of 1951, Ridgway suffered a debilitating head injury while working under a car that fell off its jack. He was unavailable for the 1952–53 season. (Ridgway would return a year later and complete his final two seasons, but he never regained the all-conference form he showed as a sophomore.) That meant the team would need more production from Norman, who was now a senior and the undisputed team leader with Sheldrake having graduated. Norman responded like the gamer he was, spurring UCLA toward yet another division title. After Norman lit up Stanford for 34 points in mid-February, the Indians' coach, Bob Burnett, said, "Stop Norman and you can stop the Bruins." Wooden also recognized that this heretofore frisky colt had finally matured into a thoroughbred. "Norman has been our spark," he said. "We didn't see eye to eye on some things last year, but I believe that Jerry has now whipped himself." Asked by a reporter about his "two-week vacation from the basketball team" the year before, Norman replied, "Mr. Wooden and I just had a few differences, so we had a heart-to-heart talk. I wasn't working too hard in practice, for one thing, and Mr. Wooden didn't like it. So he told me what he thought and I told him what I thought and we reached a compromise. We decided to do things his way."

The Bruins prevailed over Washington in the 1952 PCC play-offs to capture their second conference title in Wooden's four seasons. But they were visited by more bad luck. Because so many college students around the country had left school to serve in the Korean War, the NCAA had temporarily permitted freshmen to play varsity sports. And so Don Bragg, a six-foot-four forward from San Francisco, was able to join Wooden's roster. Even though he was a freshman, Bragg was UCLA's leading scorer during the regular season, but following the PCC clincher over Washington, he broke a toe as he exited the shower. Bragg's mishap left him severely hampered for the Bruins' opener against Santa Clara in the NCAA tournament's Western Regional in Corvallis, Oregon.

The NCAA tournament field had expanded from eight to sixteen teams, but once again, the Bruins' stay was short. With Bragg on the bench, the other Bruins suffered some early foul trouble, and Wooden was forced to insert Bragg into the game midway through the second half, but he was clearly hobbled. UCLA made just twenty of its eighty-five shot attempts and fell, 68–59. Wooden took the loss hard. "It was one of our worst games in quite a while," he said. "I thought our kids were right, but they didn't play like they were." The next day, UCLA lost to Oklahoma City, 55–53, in the Western Regional's consolation game. John Wooden may have accomplished great things during his first four seasons at UCLA, but he was now 0–4 in NCAA tournament play.

The loss to Oklahoma City also marked the end of Jerry Norman's college playing career. It had been a wild ride, but he left school more mature than when he came in, and even he had to admit that Wooden deserved much of the credit. Now it was time for them to go their separate ways; Wooden had another team to teach, while Norman was bound for the navy. Neither would have guessed that this talented, obstinate, profane, keenly intelligent nonconformist would someday be more responsible than anyone besides Wooden for launching a basketball dynasty at UCLA.

12

L.A. Story

A $6,000 annual salary did not go far in a place like Los Angeles. During his first four years at UCLA, Wooden worked mornings as a dispatcher for a dairy company in the San Fernando Valley. "After all the trucks made their deliveries and came back, I would call the next day's orders, sweep out the place, and head over the hill to UCLA," he said. "Why did I do it? Because I needed the money."

That the UCLA basketball coach needed to hold down a second job illustrated just how little the sport mattered on the West Coast. UCLA did not even provide Wooden with a full-time assistant. Ed Powell doubled as an assistant baseball coach alongside his basketball duties. Wooden's other assistant, Bill Putnam, also served as an assistant athletic director. After Powell left in 1952 to become the head coach at Loyola University, his replacement, Doug Sale, assumed his duties with the baseball team.

Moreover, there was scant interest in basketball at the grassroots level. This was a common lament of Wooden's during those early years. "I remember him saying to me, 'You're from Iowa. Did you know this state does not have a high school basketball championship tournament? Can you believe that?'" said Bob Seizer, who was an undergraduate reporter for the *Daily Bruin*. During a media luncheon in 1950, Wooden pointed out that his son, Jimmy, had played organized basketball in Terre Haute beginning in the sixth grade. In Los Angeles, he said, Jimmy could only play in a loosely organized club program until he got to high school. "The better basketball players in the Midwest are no better than our basketball players in the far west," Wooden said. "But there are many more of the better class players in the Midwest than we have out here. Back there you just about must have an indoor game. Basketball is it. Out here fans and boys can be outdoors all the year around. That splits basketball interest with other activities. Basketball suffers."

Such comments fed the impression that the coach was not long for Westwood. As much as Sale enjoyed being Wooden's assistant, he would quit two years later to take a high school coaching job in Northern California because he feared Wooden would soon accept one of the many offers he was getting from midwestern universities. Wooden didn't try to talk Sale out of leaving. The best he could do was promise that if he did take one of those offers, Sale could come along with him. "I told him I don't want to go to the Midwest because it's too far from my family," Sale said. "He said, 'Well, that's your decision.'"

The low salary, the lack of a full-time assistant, a deficient grassroots pipeline—all of these impediments would have been more bearable if Wooden's teams had an adequate place to play. There seemed to be no end to his frustration on this front. Every year brought another futile push to give Wooden the pavilion he had been led to believe was coming. In 1952, a member of the school's faculty committee on finances recommended that the project be financed by raising the annual student fee by four dollars, but the students rejected the idea, as they had rejected similar appeals in the past. Wooden was quoted in the *Daily Bruin* arguing that a pavilion was "feasible, advisable, and possible," but it seemed as elusive as ever.

And yet as uncomfortable as Wooden was in the men's gym, his opponents had it much worse. In the *Los Angeles Times*, Jack Geyer dubbed it the "B.O. barn," and the nickname stuck. Since the Bruins were generally in better physical condition than their opponents, they were virtually unbeatable there. During Wooden's first three years, his teams won forty of the forty-two games they played in the gym. "It was nothing but murder in there. Like walking into an oven," said veteran PCC referee Al Lightner.

Bill Leiser, a columnist at the *San Francisco Chronicle*, called the UCLA gym "an unfair handicap." The Bruins' advantage was so pronounced that a conspiracy theory took hold, accusing Wooden of intentionally turning up the heat. At the very least, opponents suspected that Wooden did nothing to alleviate the sauna-like conditions. "They wouldn't open the windows," said Ken Flower, a forward at USC. "In fact, our alumni would try to get them to open windows, and they wouldn't do it. It was unnaturally hot, but they liked the home-court advantage." Ron Tomsic, who played for Stanford, said that his coach, Bob Burnett, also told his players that Wooden manufactured those conditions. "He heated that place up like you couldn't believe," Tomsic said. "We referred to it as the sweatbox. Our coach claimed he did this on purpose because it was more conducive for his players."

Wooden thought the accusations were ridiculous. "There was no way, as far as I know, that the heat could be turned on in the place. I don't think there was any heat, as a matter of fact. It was just when the crowds got in there, it was warm," he said. Yet he did not go out of his way to dispel the conjecture. "It didn't displease me that other teams felt that it was a sweatbox. We didn't do anything to change their feeling," he said. "I wanted them to dislike coming in to play. The more they felt that they couldn't win there, the less likely they were going to win there."

Each season the Bruins played a few home games outside the men's gymnasium, but those venues weren't much better. The Pan-Pacific Auditorium was built for hockey games and ice shows, with the hockey boards visible around the perimeter. The games occasionally had to be halted so workers could mop up condensation. The Olympic Auditorium was the best facility in town, but that was USC's home floor. Even when the Bruins played a different opponent there, most of the crowd rooted for them to lose.

Each day before practice in the men's gym, Wooden swept the floor to clear the dust left by the gymnasts. One time Wooden tripped over a gymnast while pacing the sidelines during practice. Later in his career, Wooden said he believed he had developed what he called a "persecution complex" during this time. It was hard to blame him. "When I look back on my first years [at UCLA]," he said, "I don't know how I got anything done."

John and Nell might have felt lonely in the big city, but they were far from alone. Unbeknown to them, the Woodens had joined a large migration of midwesterners who flooded into Southern California during the middle of the twentieth century. They reached Los Angeles just as it was undergoing a population explosion that was transforming it from a loosely connected group of burgs into a bona fide metropolis.

It was a propitious time for him to come to UCLA. The school's undergraduate ranks were swelling with the return of World War II veterans, who could afford to attend because of the GI Bill of Rights. In the fall of 1947, a year before Wooden got there, some 6,200 veterans enrolled. They accounted for 43 percent of the student body, which had grown from 5,000 to more than 14,000 in six short years. (The number would climb to 17,000 by 1960.) The increased enrollment and ballooning tax revenue enabled UCLA to expand its campus in rapid fashion. Fifteen new buildings were erected between 1945 and 1950, including a library wing, an engineering building, a law school, and additions to the men's and women's gymnasiums. This reflected the education boom across the city, where the public school system was adding a new building every week.

It took several years, but the Woodens slowly found pockets of friends, which made the place feel more like home. A few months after he and Nell arrived, Wooden walked into a restaurant that was owned by a local man named Hollis Johnson. The place was a cozy neighborhood eatery in the back of the Westwood Drugstore that would have fit right in on Main Street in Martinsville. The two men struck up an immediate friendship, and Wooden started eating there regularly. "I'm just a common person," Johnson said. "I guess maybe he wanted to get hold of somebody who's common."

Wooden craved such small, comfortable routines. When he wasn't dining at Johnson's grill, he would meet a few friends at Pete Lilly's restaurant on Pico Boulevard. He also met some fellow Christians through his role as a deacon at a church in Santa Monica. Little by little, year by year, he and Nell developed something resembling a social life. "There was an old guard that was part of the UCLA community before the Woodens came out here. Those people took them into their bosom," Betty Putnam said. "I really think Los Angeles came to him rather than the other way around. And of course, nothing makes friends better than winning."

Their children adapted as well. Nan was a pretty and popular student at University High School, where she dated a strikingly handsome blond basketball star named Denny Miller, who went on to play for Wooden at UCLA before leaving to star in the title role in one of the *Tarzan* movies. Wooden's son, Jim, also played for University High's basketball team, although it was a struggle for him to compete in the shadow of his famous father. Jim was a decent enough player, but he wasn't good enough to play past high school. "He maybe felt that he had expectations from his father that he should have been an outstanding basketball player," said Ben Rogers, who played for UCLA in the mid-1950s. "I know that caused John some anguish. He felt a little estranged from his son. That's something I recall him sharing on one occasion."

Sadly, Wooden's mother and father were never an integral part of his new life. They drove from Indiana to visit him shortly after he came to UCLA, but they never visited again. "California was a little too fast for them," Wooden said. In 1950, Hugh died of leukemia at the age of sixty-eight. The obituary published in the *Martinsville Daily Reporter* described him as a man with "a genial disposition" who had "made many friends, and had always followed with great interest the athletic and teaching careers of his sons." Roxie passed nine years later. Wooden's parents were buried in Centerton alongside their young daughters.

Fortunately, John did have some family nearby. His oldest brother, Cat, was the principal at West Covina High School, east of Los Angeles. Cat was much more outgoing than his younger brother, and he brought out John's playful side. John would stride into West Covina High and demand to an unsuspecting secretary, "Who's in charge of this school?" When told it was Mr. Wooden, John would insist he see this man immediately. Cat would come into the office to see what the fuss was about and then laugh when he saw it was only his little brother.

John and Nell's social circle was never very wide. For them, a big night on the town meant eating dinner after a game with Bill and Betty Putnam or with Ducky Drake and his wife. "I don't know anybody who was a real close personal friend except the guys who worked and played for him. Coach just wasn't that way," Sheldrake said. By most standards, Nell was pretty reserved, but she was a lively chatterbox compared to her husband. "She was a cute little peanut. She had a lot of sparkle," Betty Putnam said. "It wouldn't bother her to tell a joke with a little sexual innuendo. I think that appealed to John because he was very straight. He would say platitudes and quote people, but I don't remember him ever telling a joke. He was more pleasant than funny."

The Woodens' aversion to alcohol prevented them from expanding their circle. Nell had grown up around too many Irish relatives who drank and was more stridently antialcohol than her husband. She had no compunctions about expressing her disapproval if someone drank in her presence. "She had definite ideas of right and wrong and good and bad, and she expected that of her children as well as her friends," Betty Putnam said. "She would not cozy up to people if they didn't have the same values."

Though John was more abiding of other people's vices, he likewise would not consume alcohol under any circumstances. One time when UCLA was on a road trip to Illinois to play Bradley, he came down with a bad case of hemorrhoids. A doctor offered some medicine, but when Wooden read the label and saw that it contained blackberry brandy, he refused to drink the stuff.

This puritanical lifestyle also kept Wooden from forming close

relationships with his coaching peers. When the Pacific Coast Conference held its annual meetings, John was the only coach who always
brought his wife. He rarely went out to dinner with the guys, much less
hung out with them late at night drinking liquor and chasing skirts.
"When he first came out west he was provincial, a little aloof," said Pete
Newell, who became the head coach at California in 1954. "The coaches
he was closest to were the midwesterners, the Branch McCrackens, the
Tony Hinkles. He may have considered himself an outsider and some
western coaches did, too." Marv Harshman encountered the same reactions after he took over at Washington State in 1958. "A lot of the coaches
said he was stuck up," Harshman said. "In my opinion he was never
stuck up. It's just that his family was more important to him than being
around two or three old coaches who were drinking beer."

Unfortunately, Nell's resistance to alcohol did not extend to cigarettes. John smoked during his first few years at UCLA, but he eventually quit. Nell never could. At one point he got her an appointment with
a hypnotist, but it didn't work. Nell did her best to hide her habit from
her husband. She would keep a couple of packs of cigarettes tucked away
in her closet, or she would stash them in her purse. If she wanted to
smoke, she stepped outside or sneaked off to a neighbor's house. "She
thought she was fooling Daddy, but he knew," Nan said. John was disappointed, but it was not his style to reprimand her. "He didn't make a big
deal of it. He knew she was trying to stop," Betty Putnam said. "He was
so devoted to her. She could have done anything in the world, and he
would have said, 'It's okay, Nellie.'"

One of the reasons Nell smoked was that it calmed her nerves on
game night. She kept smelling salts in her pockets in case she felt faint.
Though John was notorious for refusing to yank his starters until the
final moments of a blowout, Nell was even more paranoid. On a couple
of occasions when John mass substituted, she called out from behind the
bench, "Too soon!" He would eventually ask that she sit a few rows back.

Not surprisingly, Nell harbored an especially low opinion of the officials. "She was worse on the refs than he was. She was something," Art
Alper said. "She sat two rows behind the bench and let 'em have it. The
referees were never right when they called a foul on us." During one taut
contest against USC, Nell tapped on Ed Powell's shoulder after a UCLA
player was whistled for fouling Bill Sharman.

"I didn't think that was a foul, did you?" Nell asked.

Powell told her he thought it was a good call.

"Where's your loyalty?" she snapped.

"Loyalty has nothing to do with it," Powell replied. "You asked me a question."

Indeed, Nell had little tolerance for any slight, perceived or real, that was directed at her husband. She resented the way UCLA had deceived them about the prospects of a new pavilion. If she felt her husband was getting any kind of short shrift, she spoke up. "Nell could be vicious towards someone who was getting more notoriety than John. Red Sanders was one of those," Sheldrake said. And heaven forbid someone should outright disrespect her husband's coaching decisions. That brought on the full force of her Irish temper. "She would not tolerate anything that was negative towards John," Betty Putnam said. "If anyone ever criticized him or said anything bad, that was the end of the friendship."

The rapid growth occurring around Los Angeles began to change Wooden's mind about the possibilities at UCLA. There may not have been a grassroots basketball scene at first, but he could see that the sport was going to get bigger on campus. This was especially important because Wooden disdained recruiting. In his view, students should want to come to a school like UCLA to get a first-rate education. It was not his job to convince them. He often told friends that he missed working in high school, where there was no need for recruiting at all. You simply coached the kids who showed up in your gym, just as you taught the kids who showed up in your English class. "I hoped each year to get two or three of the top-quality players from Southern California," he said. "I probably would have had a rough time at some place where you have to go out and get them."

As the years went on and the wins piled up, the job offers continued to roll in from his native Midwest. Purdue called again. So did Notre Dame and Illinois. Fritz Crisler, the former football coach and longtime athletic director at the University of Michigan, pleaded for Wooden to come to Ann Arbor. Each time John discussed the matter with his family, his children would protest more loudly. They were teenagers now and had made lots of friends. Besides, they loved the California sunshine. Who wouldn't? "You know, this is not a bad place to live," Wooden said. "It takes a while to get accustomed to it, but once you stop and think, within an hour or two I can be at the ocean, I can be at the mountains, I can be in the desert, I can be at Disneyland. I don't have to put chains on my tires. I don't have to put in antifreeze. I don't have to scrape sleet off my windshield." Eventually, the other schools stopped calling. "After a few years," Wooden said, "we were more acclimated to Los Angeles. We became settled."

For John and Nell, the big changes were mostly behind them. They would never again move to a different part of the country. At one point Nell wanted a third child, but she miscarried while they were living in Indiana and never got pregnant again. "We had problems, and the doctor said she should never try anymore. I disagreed," John said. They also had a cocker spaniel, but when he died, it broke Nell's heart. No more dogs for them.

He drew strength from her presence and depended on her in every way. She poured his cereal, picked out his clothes, did all his laundry. She even washed his hair. When the team had a road game, Nell packed suitcases for both of them and came along. The only time they bickered in front of the kids was when he discovered she had again neglected to register checks she had written from their bank account. (He finally learned to keep a few extra bucks in reserve.) That aside, even their closest friends never witnessed a hint of marital strife. "They were," said Betty Putnam, "the strongest couple I've ever known."

In the end, it didn't much matter where they lived. Nothing ever really changed between them. In her mind's eye, he would always be the vigorous young guard who bounced off the floor like rubber. Before each game, John still winked at Nell and flashed the "okay" sign right before tip-off, just as when they were in high school. The only thing that was missing was her cornet. She would forever believe he was beyond reproach and beyond compare. A former UCLA player named Jerry Evans learned that one day when he raved to Nell about a college player he had just watched. When Evans said he had never seen anyone quite as good as this kid, Nell just shook her head and smiled. "You should have seen my Johnny," she said.

Willie the Whale

In the spring of 1950, a six-foot-two forward at Visalia Junior College named Bobby Pounds received a phone call from the head basketball coach at UCLA. John Wooden was calling to tell Pounds that a couple of his players had sung his praises after seeing Pounds play in a recent junior college tournament, and Wooden wanted to know if Pounds would consider playing for UCLA. By coincidence, Pounds was going to be competing in a state championship track meet the following week in Los Angeles, so Wooden invited him to visit UCLA's campus. A few months later, Pounds enrolled in UCLA as a sophomore, and during the 1950–51 season, he scored a total of 40 points in twenty-one games as a reserve.

The story was unremarkable save for one detail: Bobby Pounds was black.

Wooden did not set out to perform a social experiment when he offered Pounds a scholarship. He was not trying to agitate for progress. He was trying to win basketball games. Far from generating fanfare, Wooden rarely spoke about race. Not to his assistants, not to the media, not even to his own players. "He was about actions, not statements," Pounds said. "He integrated basketball quietly, little by little. If you didn't see it, too bad. Maybe he didn't want people to notice."

For Pounds, Jim Crow segregation was a distant notion that he experienced only through the descriptions from his parents, who migrated to California from Louisiana before he was born. When Pounds's grandparents died, his mother refused to take him home to their funerals. "You're a smart aleck," she told him. "You'll get hurt." Pounds was not immune to racism growing up in Fresno, but his childhood was about as idyllic as a black youngster could experience in America during the 1930s and 1940s. His school, Edison High, was 85 percent white, but the community was a melting pot that included blacks, Germans, Russians, and Italians.

Bobby was outgoing and popular. Besides being the star of Edison's undefeated state championship basketball team, he was also the senior class president.

Still, because of his race, Pounds had difficulty eliciting interest from colleges. He wrote letters to many schools, including the University of San Francisco and the University of California, but UCLA was the only one to reply. When Wooden called, Pounds said, "I was shocked. Absolutely." At that point, Pounds knew very little about Wooden, but he knew one important thing about the place where he coached. "Jackie Robinson went to UCLA," Pounds said. "So I said, I'm going there."

Indeed, Jack Roosevelt Robinson, who integrated Major League Baseball in 1947, was the best ambassador to the black community that any school could ask for. Years before he took the field for the Brooklyn Dodgers, Robinson had captivated black people in California while starring as a running back for UCLA's football team. Robinson, who entered UCLA as a junior following a two-year stint at Pasadena Junior College, joined Kenny Washington and Woody Strode, the famed "Goal Dust Twins," to lead UCLA to an undefeated season in 1939. Robinson also became the first athlete in UCLA's young history to letter in four varsity sports during the same academic year. The other three were track (he won the 1940 NCAA title in the long jump), basketball, and baseball. Surprisingly, baseball was Robinson's worst sport in college. He played just one season for UCLA and batted .097.

As a basketball player, Robinson struggled at first in Wilbur Johns's deliberate offense. (The *Daily Bruin* said Jackie looked like a "wasted robot" on the court.) Eventually, he flourished and won the PCC's individual scoring title in each of his two seasons. Still, the league's coaches declined to vote Jackie onto the PCC's all-conference first team, which the sports editor of the *Daily Bruin* dubbed a "flagrant bit of prejudice." California's Nibs Price was the worst offender. He left Robinson off his first, second, and third teams when he cast his ballot.

UCLA's policy of admitting black athletes was rooted in competition, not altruism. The school was a perennial doormat in almost every sport. In the mid-1920s, when it was still known as California State Normal School and housed on Vermont Avenue, a local black student named Ralph Bunche signed up to play football, baseball, and basketball. Bunche was a decent athlete, but he was a stellar performer in the classroom, graduating in 1927 as class valedictorian. As with Robinson, Bunche's real impact on UCLA came years after he had graduated, when he served in prominent positions at the State Department and the United Nations.

Two months after Bobby Pounds enrolled at UCLA, Bunche became the first black man to win the Nobel Peace Prize.

If you were a young black man on the West Coast and you wanted to go to college, UCLA was the place to be. The swift ones wanted to be like Jackie. The smart ones wanted to be like Ralph.

And so when John Wooden made that first phone call to Bobby Pounds, he was not initiating a tradition of tolerance at UCLA. That had already been well established. Wilbur Johns's last team had included Don Barksdale, who was the country's first black All-American and went on to become the first black man to play in an NBA All-Star game. The year before Wooden arrived, UCLA's undergraduates elected as their student body president Sherrill Luke, a black student who grew up crashing the gates at the Coliseum to watch Jackie Robinson gallop alongside the Goal Dust Twins. Luke's election made national news. He even received a letter from Harry S. Truman, addressed "From one President to another."

As the president of the Associated Students of UCLA, Luke served on the search committee that hired Wooden. He also signed the coach's paychecks. Luke's office was located down the hall from Wooden's, which allowed Luke to encounter a softer version of the man than his players did. "I would say *shy* and *reserved* are good descriptive words to apply to him," Luke said. "He was always a consummate gentleman. He respected the dignity of every individual he ever met as far as I could tell. He had almost an evangelical or a ministerial air about him that made you like him and feel like you could trust him."

For a long time, Wooden's Bruins were an anomaly inside the lily-white Pacific Coast Conference. During Bobby Pounds's first season, he was the only black player in the league. Stanford did have one black player on its roster in 1951–52, but USC didn't suit up its first until 1960. Five years would pass before the Trojans added another. Wooden, on the other hand, had at least one black player on his roster every year starting with Pounds's arrival in 1950. From 1954 until he retired in 1975, he never had fewer than three.

UCLA's reputation with blacks was a major boon in recruiting. During the spring of 1951, Wooden's assistant, Ed Powell, was visiting his family in Indiana. When a friend mentioned that there was a terrific black player in Gary named Johnny Moore, Powell figured he'd pay the kid a visit. Moore's parents seemed cool to Powell's entreaties until his mother noticed that Powell's wife was sitting by herself in the car, where she was flipping through some old UCLA yearbooks. Mrs. Moore invited Powell's wife inside and was soon flipping through the yearbooks herself.

At one point, Mrs. Moore spotted a photograph of Sherrill Luke. She stopped flipping and asked Powell, "You mean there are fifteen thousand students at this school, and out of all these people the student body president is black?"

"Oh, yes," Powell replied. "I didn't want to make that an issue."

"Well," Johnny's mother said, "this is where he's going to school."

That's how Johnny Moore became the second black player whom Wooden recruited to UCLA. Moore was not as outgoing as Pounds, which made the distance between Los Angeles and Gary feel even greater. Sherrill Luke, who was still living in town while pursuing his master's degree in political science at UCLA, tried to help by inviting Moore to live with him during his first semester, but it wasn't easy. "Johnny was very quiet, very unassuming. You had to egg him on to engage him in conversation," Luke said. Luke soon came up with a better idea. Five years before, Luke had moved into the Zeta Beta Tau fraternity house, where all the fraternity brothers were Jewish. Luke was the first non-Jewish—not to mention nonwhite—person to live there. So Luke rang up his old fraternity brothers and arranged for Moore to live in the ZBT house as well.

When it came to playing ball, however, Moore was vastly superior to Pounds, not to mention most of the other players in the conference. He was also unfazed by the crowds. When a local sportswriter asked Moore if he was nervous before playing his first game in a packed gym, Moore shook his head and said, "No, sir. My last game in high school was in front of eighteen thousand people."

Wooden did not involve himself in the personal lives of Pounds and Moore any more than he did for his white players. They would have to adjust to college life on their own. "I never talked to him where it was just him and me, but I didn't need to. I was getting along fine," Pounds said. Nor did the presence of blacks stir much notice among the white players, even though during many of their road games Pounds and Moore were the only black people in the gym. For example, Moore became very close with a white teammate, Bill Johnston, who used to take Moore to his parents' house for dinner. The two of them shared their thoughts on every topic under the sun—except race. "We talked about our families and school and classes, but we didn't talk about black and white," Johnston said. "I don't know why. Maybe we should have. It just didn't come up."

Pounds felt no need to discuss the issue. He had come to UCLA for one reason: to get a degree. The only way he was going to accomplish that was by listening to John Wooden. "He was as intense as you could be. There was no screwing around," Pounds said. "I remember he said it *behooves* you to pay attention. That's where I learned that word. When he said *behooves*, something important was coming up."

There was only one occasion when Wooden had no choice but to address the issue of race. It happened during Christmas break in 1951, when UCLA went on a three-game swing through the Midwest. The trip began with a huge game at Kentucky, which was ranked No. 2 in the AP poll. Because the hotels in Lexington were segregated, Pounds and Moore would not have been able to stay with the team. Rather than splitting up his players, Wooden arranged for the Bruins to stay in Cincinnati, ninety miles away. UCLA rode to Lexington by bus, got walloped by 31 points, and then rode back to the hotel after the game. Wooden never explained why they were staying so far away, but he didn't have to. "There was no big announcement or anything, but word filtered out," Jerry Evans said.

As the Bruins rolled into town that night, Pounds noticed a public bus driving alongside. All the black passengers were seated in the back. It was the first time he had come face-to-face with Jim Crow. "It scared the shit out of me," he said. "I thought to myself, Yup, Mom was right. I'm glad I don't live here."

Pounds returned to school in the fall of 1952 for his senior season. The team was less experienced and supposedly less talented than it had been the year before, but as they entered the final week of the season, the Bruins trailed California by just one game in the Southern Division. Wooden's four-year streak of finishing in at least a tie for first was in jeopardy. *Los Angeles Daily News* columnist Ned Cronin sounded the alarm. "Fame is fleeting and Johnny stands on the brink of being a has-been," Cronin wrote. "He's like a batter who hits a homer the first time up. The only way to go from there is down, sooner or later." Forget about how inept the program had been before Wooden got there. He had proved he could win, so he was expected to keep winning. This might not have fit his own definition of success, but the California sportswriters didn't share his view on that any more than did the parents of his high school students in Dayton, Kentucky. It was bound to intrude on Wooden's peace of mind.

The streak did, in fact, end when the Bruins were swept by USC in their last two games, ending the season with a 6–6 league record, good for third place. Wooden gained some solace a few weeks later when his childhood chum Branch McCracken coached Indiana to its second NCAA championship with a 1-point win in the final over Kansas. Wooden attended the game in Kansas City, but he couldn't help but feel bitter-sweet. "Johnny was the first person in my dressing room [after the game]," McCracken said. "He ran straight at me and jumped up and put his arms around my neck. He said, 'It looks like I'll never win an NCAA. We get so far and then something always happens.'"

UCLA's prospects seemed brighter as the Bruins entered the 1953–54 season. Pounds was gone, but four starters were back, including Moore, now a junior. Wooden also added two talented black sophomores from Southern California. The first was Morris Taft, a six-foot-two guard who had won all-city honors at Los Angeles's Polytechnic High School and all-state honors during his one season at Compton Community College.

From the start, Wooden got along well with Taft, but the coach would have a much more complicated relationship with the other black prodigy who joined the team. Willie Naulls was a six-foot-five center with strong hands, an ample waistline, and boundless potential. Because of his physique, Naulls was given the nickname of Willie the Whale, but on the court he moved like a shark. In fact, Naulls was so good in high school that up and down the West Coast, coaches who had been reluctant to recruit blacks offered him scholarships. If they were going to integrate their programs, they were damn sure going to do it with a player of his caliber.

Naulls came close to attending the University of California, but he chose UCLA because several UCLA alumni assured him that they would take care of all his financial needs. One man even gave Willie about $1,500 cash during his recruitment. When Willie's mother, who was a devout Christian, heard about the illicit payments, she marched her son into the man's office and made him return the money. "My mother doesn't think that I should accept this money, and neither do I," Willie said.

His mother made him say those words, but he didn't really believe them. Naulls expected that the other alumni would deliver on their promises once he enrolled in college. He could not begin his freshman year until the second semester for academic reasons, but once he got to Westwood, he learned that those promises would go unfulfilled. When Naulls complained to Wooden, the coach told Naulls he knew nothing about such arrangements. Besides, they were against NCAA rules.

That's not the only disappointment Naulls encountered. He had chosen UCLA without realizing that the school did not offer housing for blacks on campus. Nor did he realize just how segregated most of Westwood was at the time. (Naulls spent his formative years in the mostly white community of San Pedro, thirty miles south of Los Angeles.)

Naulls had had a strained relationship with his father, but he was close with his mother, and he recognized in Wooden the same devotion to Christian ideals. He hoped, even assumed, that once he got to UCLA, Wooden would provide the paternal guidance he had never received from his own dad. On this, too, his expectations were unmet. "When a boy leaves home for the first time, his coach becomes a father figure, a guy you should be able to go to with your problems and your questions," Naulls said. "With Wooden, you don't feel you can do this."

Because he was broke, Naulls decided he would have to hustle to make ends meet. At that time, the athletic department reimbursed athletes for their textbooks. Naulls enrolled in extra classes, got reimbursed for the books, and then he returned them to the bookstore and pocketed the refunds. Eventually, Wooden caught wind of the scheme and called Naulls into his office for a brutal tongue-lashing. "Gracious sakes alive, Willie, what were you thinking?" Wooden said as Wilbur Johns looked on. "I know your parents didn't raise you to be this way." Naulls was sure he was going to be expelled, but when the meeting ended with no such penalty, Naulls realized he was in the clear.

A few months later, Naulls again was called onto the carpet in Wooden's office after he accrued more than a dozen unpaid parking tickets. When Naulls complained that the only reason he got so many tickets was that he couldn't find any place to park, Wooden retorted, "Welcome to student campus life here at UCLA. You do not deserve any special parking privileges."

Class dismissed.

Aside from these confrontations, Naulls did not have much contact with Wooden after he enrolled for that first semester at UCLA in the spring of 1953. He joined the basketball program the following fall. Since Naulls had enrolled as a second-semester freshman, he was allowed to play for UCLA's freshman team for one more semester, but Wooden surprised Naulls by inviting him to join the varsity for the second game of the season, even though Naulls's conditioning was poor because he had not competed for a year. "Our team will be helped and will improve when Naulls gets into shape," Wooden said. "I have high hopes for Willie."

Willie the Whale tipped the scales at a cool 262 pounds when he started his college career by scoring 11 points in a 45-point rout of Arizona. UCLA won three more times before returning to Lexington, Kentucky, for a holiday tournament. They played two games there, losing to

La Salle and defeating Duke. This time, instead of busing back and forth to Cincinnati, the team stayed in Lexington in what was usually a segregated hotel. The hotel's manager wanted Taft, Moore, and Naulls to sleep separately on the basement level, but Wooden insisted that all of his players have the same accommodations. So the entire team slept in the basement. They also sat together that night in a segregated movie theater.

During the Bruins' second game of the tournament, Naulls heard one of the Duke players call out his defensive assignment by pointing to Naulls and shouting, "I got this nigger over here." Naulls was especially furious because the player seemed to have no idea he had uttered a hateful slur. Naulls maintained his composure until late in the second half, when on a drive to the basket, he elbowed the guy in the mouth as hard as he could. As the Duke player stood bleeding and complaining to the referee (who had not seen the elbow), Wooden glared at Naulls but said nothing. Naulls believed he had earned Wooden's respect for retaliating in such a controlled fashion. Wooden, in turn, earned Naulls's affection for refusing to bend to the strictures of Jim Crow.

The warm feelings would not last long. The Bruins began the conference portion of their schedule with a two-game series at California. During the first half of the first game, Wooden surprised Naulls by ripping into him for throwing a behind-the-back pass. "No fancy stuff out there!" he yelled during a time-out. When the players walked onto the court, Naulls asked Johnny Moore what the coach had meant. The soft-spoken Moore shrugged his shoulders and said, "Two hands on the ball will get you more playing time."

Naulls spent nearly the entire second game on the bench. Not coincidentally, UCLA lost. Even Willie's teammates were surprised, teasing him by asking if he had stayed out too late or something.

Naulls was angry and confused. It was bad enough that Wooden had benched him, but the coach didn't even bother to explain the reason why. At that moment, Naulls needed his coach to be a man of statements, not just actions. But that was not John Wooden's way. "I was tremendously insulted because he never even discussed it with me," Naulls said.

When UCLA returned home from Berkeley, Naulls went to the men's gym and cleaned out his locker. On his way out, he found the team's trainer, Ducky Drake. To Naulls, Drake was the anti-Wooden—a warm, compassionate, easygoing fellow who spent many hours talking about life while he taped Naulls's ankles. Naulls briefly explained to Drake what had happened, and he told Drake that he was leaving UCLA for good.

As Naulls sat in his mother's home and stewed, he wondered if

Wooden might be a racist after all. In a memoir written decades later, Naulls described the profound hurt he felt that night. "I mumbled to myself, My own father didn't know what I was thinking. So how could this White man, who never invited me to his home or asked me anything about how I felt, deign to know what I was thinking?" he wrote. "If he thought that little of my character, well, he could play those players with whom he was more comfortable—those who were readily accepted into Westwood housing."

A few days later, Wooden surprised Naulls by calling him at his mother's home to apologize and to ask him to come back to the team. Naulls sensed the gesture had come at Drake's behest, but he agreed to return anyway. He played sparingly in the following game, which the Bruins lost to USC, but the next night against the Trojans he had his best outing as a collegian, scoring 16 points to help the team snap a three-game losing streak. A writer from the *Los Angeles Examiner* reported that "Willie Naulls, the talented Bruin rookie who had shown nothing except size in his early appearances ... for the first time indicated the greatness that is in store for him."

That greatness was on display often during January and February 1954. UCLA reeled off eight more wins heading into the season-ending series at home against USC with the Trojans trailing the Bruins by just one game in the Southern Division standings. The season was headed for a dramatic climax, but the day before the series began, Naulls had yet another unpleasant experience with Wooden.

That day, the *Los Angeles Times* published a lengthy story by Jack Geyer under the headline "Wooden's Threat Builds Sizzling Fire Under Huge Willie Naulls." The article attributed Willie's turnaround not to his own diligence and talent, but rather to the heavy-handed tactics of his coach. The story began by re-creating a discussion that supposedly had taken place between Wooden and Naulls in the locker room before his breakout game against USC the month before. "Tonight's your chance, Willie, your last chance," Wooden had said, according to Geyer (who had obviously been told this account by Wooden). "But the first time I see you getting shoved around or not scrapping you're coming out of there. And you might not get back in the rest of the year." Geyer, who described Naulls as "a shy, soft-spoken Negro lad," reported that the player had been a "new man" since the contentious tête-à-tête.

Naulls found the article deeply offensive. As he recounted in his memoir, he believed it was evidence that "[Wooden] and the media had a field day at the expense of Willie, the Big Black Whale. And they gave Coach the credit for my performance in our winning effort." The episode also fed Naulls's suspicion that the real reason Wooden did not permit his players to talk to the press was so the coach could build up his own image. In that belief, there was a nugget of truth. Wooden was still shaped by having lived through the Depression, always sensing that his career could go belly-up if he didn't live up to the high expectations that he himself had set.

Despite his anger, Naulls pressed on, but the season would end in heartbreaking fashion. After dropping the first game to USC, 79–68, the Bruins lost the second when Trojans guard Chet Carr hit a ten-foot shot in the waning seconds to give USC a 1-point victory and the Southern Division title. Naulls finished the season as the team's leading rebounder. He also averaged 8.5 points per game.

Naulls never forgot how Geyer's article made him feel. And he never forgot the coach's failure to provide the emotional support he craved. "Oh, Wooden is the best college coach of all time. Really, he's a professional college coach," Naulls said in 1972. "But I don't think he does much to make the college experience more beneficial to his players. His Pyramid of Success and things like that imply that he spends a lot of time in the development of men, not just in basketball and fundamentals. But he doesn't. I certainly needed a lot of help in other directions, and I didn't get it."

Naulls may have felt frustrated by Wooden—again—but this time he made no attempt to quit. He had come a long way over the course of the season, and it didn't matter whether that was despite Wooden or because of him. Nor did Wooden reach out before the start of the next season to talk to Naulls about what they had gone through. The coach had much bigger problems by then. A powerful force was emerging in Northern California, and no amount of running would enable Wooden's racehorses to overtake it.

14

The Dons

The word was starting to get out: UCLA had a special player, and potentially a special team. The Bruins had entered the 1954–55 season unranked by the Associated Press, but when they won their first two games by a total of 64 points, they entered the poll at No. 13. They were poised to become the dominant team in the West—until, that is, they hosted the University of San Francisco on December 11, 1954.

The occasion gave the Bruins their first glimpse of the Dons' frighteningly gifted center, a gangly, sprightly, six-foot-nine, left-handed sophomore from Oakland named William Felton Russell. This was not a typical, plodding post player like most centers of the era. Despite his imposing physique, Russell was a competitive distance runner and world-class high jumper, and he possessed the foot speed of a much smaller guard. His ability to quickly and repeatedly bound high above the rim enabled him to deploy methods of defensive basketball that nobody had ever tried. Russell was the first college player who not only dominated the game but actually changed it. And he stood, quite literally, in UCLA's path.

For once, Wooden's willingness to recruit blacks hadn't given him a competitive advantage. Russell was one of three black players in Dons coach Phil Woolpert's starting lineup that day. (The other two were K. C. Jones and Hal Perry.) Woolpert was much less rigid than Wooden, too. He allowed, and sometimes encouraged, his players to dunk, including during warm-ups. As the UCLA players climbed the steps of the men's gym, they could hear the squeals of delight coming from their own fans as Russell and his mates glided in their layup lines for dunk after dunk. When the Bruins reached the court, they, too, stood in awe—so much so that Wooden ordered them back into the locker room, where he upbraided them for being so impressed.

As the centers stepped to the midcourt circle for the opening tap,

Russell looked down at the shorter Willie Naulls, slapped his hand, and said, "I'm gonna whip you, boy, real bad." Russell was not a skilled scorer, but he was such an effective offensive rebounder that he got a lot of points on putbacks. His real impact, of course, came at the defensive end. Russell was the first prolific shot blocker the game had ever seen. At that time, blocks weren't tracked as an official statistic, and there was no rule in the books forbidding a player from swatting a field goal attempt on its way down toward the basket. (The national committee instituted a goaltending rule the following season, along with a decree to widen the lane from six to twelve feet. Both changes were made to contain Russell.) UCLA won that first meeting, 47–40, by slowing the tempo and getting physical, but even in defeat the Dons' big man made a lasting impression.

"Russell was invaluable under the basket," Jack Geyer wrote in the next day's *Los Angeles Times*. "He played a type of one-man volley ball, leaping up and tapping the ball to where he could grab it without interference. He also blocked at least a half-dozen Bruin shots, leaping high in the air and slapping the ball down the marksman's throat." Geyer concluded that "Russell is a cinch to be either a Harlem Globetrotter or a top pro player, whoever bids the higher."

The two teams met again seven days later in San Francisco, where the Dons held UCLA without a field goal for the first ten minutes and coasted to a 56–44 win. The next day's *San Francisco Chronicle* reported that Russell had spun Naulls "like a fat, round top. The speedy Russell was constantly going left while The Whale was still moving right." Russell ended up with 28 points in what Wooden called "the greatest job any one man ever did against UCLA."

Fortunately for Wooden, there was only one Bill Russell. From that point on, the Bruins had their way with most of their other opponents, entering their series with Stanford in the middle of February tied with the Indians for first place in the PCC's Southern Division. The back-to-back games in Westwood would go a long way toward deciding which team would win the conference. UCLA cruised to an 85–63 win in the first contest thanks to 24 points from Morris Taft, who was quickly establishing himself as one of the best perimeter scorers in the country. The next night, the Bruins opened up a 7-point lead late in the first half. That's when Howie Dallmar, Stanford's first-year coach, ordered his players to switch to a zone defense. Wooden countered by instructing his players to hold the ball. Wooden had become increasingly willing to slow down the tempo, but it was unusual for him to deploy a flat-out stall. For three and a half minutes, Bruins guard Don Bragg stood next to the half-court line with the ball under his arm, doing nothing. The fans jeered. The clock ticked. The Indians stayed in their zone. Finally, after a full five minutes of inaction, Stanford pressured Bragg, and UCLA resumed its regular offense.

The same situation occurred over a two-minute span late in the second half. These tactics helped UCLA to a 72–59 win that gave them a commanding two-game lead with just four to go. Needless to say, the strategy did not go over well in the Bay Area, not least because Wooden had so often tweaked other coaches who used those tactics against him. Dallmar's response was measured—he claimed Wooden's decision helped the Indians because it "gave us a chance to rest"—but the *San Francisco Examiner* published a photograph of the entire court that showed Bragg holding the ball under his arm while the other players stood and watched. The caption mocked Stanford's opponent as the "Stall-Wart Bruins."

Wooden defended himself after the game. "I always have felt the responsibility belongs to the team behind to change what they're doing, whether offensively or defensively," he said. "I never would under any circumstances do what Stanford did. I'd go get them. If you're behind, you've got to go after them." At the local writers' luncheon the following week, USC coach Forrest Twogood admonished the two coaches. "I think both of them should give this game of basketball some thought as to what they are doing to it," he said. "However, I consider Wooden more right than Dallmar. The team behind must force the play."

In defending himself against criticism, Wooden was trying to thread an impossibly tight needle. He also revealed why some of his coaching peers were beginning to be turned off by what they saw as his holier-than-thou attitude. According to Wooden, stalling was bad for the game— unless UCLA needed to do it to win. Not only was he trying to have it both ways, he argued that there was no contradiction between his actions and his statements. The idea that Wooden would bend his principles in an effort to win was not earth-shattering in 1955, but in later years, as he burnished a public self-image that rival coaches would derisively refer to as "Saint John," his hypocrisy on relatively small matters like this one would loom large.

The contretemps over the Stanford stall also revived an ongoing debate about whether college basketball should install a shot clock similar to the one the NBA had put in place that season. There was no doubt where Wooden stood: he wanted the clock, though he preferred it to be thirty seconds as opposed to the twenty-four-second clock that the pros had implemented. Wooden argued that a clock would help defenses because it would prevent stalling. When he was once asked about a game in which California had stalled for more than nine minutes before losing a game to San Francisco, Wooden said, "Contrary to a lot of opinions, I'd like to see a lot more games just like that. Then they'd put in the 24-second rule."

UCLA's victories over Stanford were part of an eleven-game winning streak that delivered the Bruins another Southern Division title. It was the fifth time in seven years that Wooden's teams had won or shared the crown. They couldn't have done it without Willie the Whale, who set a new Southern Division rebounding record and ended his junior season by being named to the division's first team. But as well as Naulls was playing, Wooden believed his laid-back approach was preventing him from reaching his potential. "There are times when I don't know what to do with Willie Naulls," Wooden said in March. "He's such a likable kid that it's pretty hard to get sore at him for failing to give it the blood-and-thunder treatment. Exasperated would be more like it."

The season ended once again in Corvallis, where UCLA was unable to collar Oregon State's seven-foot-three center, Swede Halbrook, who helped the Northern Division champs to a sweep and the PCC title. Oregon State went on to lose in the NCAA tournament to San Francisco, and a week later in Kansas City, USF claimed the national championship. It was a great moment for Russell and the Dons, but Wooden had every reason to believe that with Naulls and Taft leading the way as seniors, 1956 might be the year when he finally took his turn at the top.

His first defeat came five months before the season opener, when the state of California's fire marshal office in Sacramento ruled that the men's gym was unsafe to hold more than 1,500 spectators. Wooden could hardly believe it. His shabby, stuffy, subpar facility had been essentially condemned. The Bruins could still practice there, but they would have to find other venues for games. On the eve of the 1955–56 season, Wooden wrote a guest column for the *Long Beach Press-Telegram* that addressed the question of where UCLA would play its home games that winter. "This has not been determined yet," Wooden wrote. "Wilbur Johns, our athletic director, will select the most favorable site after scrutinizing all available locations in the Los Angeles area."

Willie Naulls, meanwhile, entered his senior season in great condition and ready to lead. Unfortunately, the same could not be said for Morris Taft, who was hospitalized the first two weeks because of disc herniations in his lower back. Without him, the Bruins dropped four of their first six games, but Taft was close to full strength for the team's return visit to New York City for the Holiday Festival in Madison Square Garden. Waiting for them in New York, once again, would be the University of San Francisco Dons. He may have been three thousand miles from home, but Wooden could not escape the specter of Bill Russell.

The Bruins were unusually unbalanced for a Wooden-coached team, with Taft and Naulls each averaging more than 20 points per game. The two men could hardly have been more different. Naulls was calm, elegant, introverted. Taft was flamboyant, temperamental, even a little mischievous. Most of the players may have found Wooden to be unapproachable, but Taft had no reservations about penetrating that veneer. Wooden liked him. When Taft came out of games, Wooden asked him to sit next to him on the bench so they could maintain a running dialogue. Taft also served as an intermediary when tension flared up between Wooden and Naulls. More often than not, he took the coach's side. "Willie was a very fine gentleman, but he had his own way of doing things," Taft said. "I told him, I'm not going to be passing you the ball if you're not passing it back."

Unlike Naulls, Taft appreciated Wooden's nonverbal means of communicating. "John was the most different type of coach I had ever seen," Taft said. "A lot of coaches threaten you and call you a fool, but Wooden listened to you. He was very calm and he didn't talk that much." Sitting next to Wooden on the bench, Taft would chuckle as this otherwise laconic gentleman harangued the referees from tap to buzzer. "I'll tell you, for a little man, Wooden had a big mouth," he said.

The relationship between Taft and Wooden helped the coach figure out ways to motivate his star guard. At the Holiday Festival in New York, the Bruins opened the tournament by knocking off the hometown favorite, St. John's, which advanced them into a matchup with Duquesne and its All-American guard, Sihugo Green. Wooden knew that Taft was best suited to guard Green, but he also knew Taft did not like to play defense. So Wooden had to trick him. He approached Taft in the locker room before the game and said, "I don't think Skeeter can guard Green. Can you?" The mind game was designed to appeal to Taft's ego—and it worked. UCLA won, 72–57.

That set up a rematch with the Dons in the final. The game was going to be a really big deal, both for Madison Square Garden and for West Coast basketball. Russell's team still had not lost since the Bruins had defeated them twelve months before, and their thirty-five-game winning streak was just four shy of the NCAA record. The game against UCLA promised to be a study in contrasts, but for once it was Wooden's Bruins who were playing the tortoise. Referring to their win over the Dons the previous season, Wooden said, "We got out ahead of them and slowed down our style of play. If we get a lead again tomorrow night, we'll do the same thing."

However, the night before the game, Naulls and Taft returned to their hotel rooms well past their curfew. They had visited a seedy part of New York City and couldn't get back in time. Wooden was livid. He immediately decided to send the two of them back to Los Angeles while the rest of the team took on the Dons. "Willie was crushed," said Bill Eblen, a player who roomed with Naulls on the road. "He was really upset that he had let the team down like that."

Wooden's decision was not well received by the men who were putting on the event. Foremost among them was Ned Irish, the president of the NBA's New York Knicks and the chief promoter of college basketball at the Garden. He and several other executives met with Wooden in an effort to convince him to let his stars play. "We were on pins and needles waiting for the decision," said Carroll Adams, a six-foot-one junior forward on that team. Wooden had always preached the importance of sticking to principles, but on this occasion his principles were trumped by business. Naulls and Taft played. "The New York guys told him, 'You can't do this. This is the biggest tournament of the year.'" Adams said. "I don't know what compromises were made, but Coach relented."

Wooden had hoped his team would build an early lead so he could implement his deliberate offense, and midway through the first half, it appeared he would get his chance. With the Bruins leading by 1, Naulls faked out Russell, drove by him, and rose to the rim for a two-handed layup. Russell, however, recovered in a flash and blocked the ball. "It stunned us—and it beat us," Wooden said. Naulls spent most of the second half in foul trouble, Russell scored 17 points, and USF cruised to a 70–53 win. The crowd of 16,357 gave Russell a standing ovation when he left the game with over a minute to play. "Russell's defensive play kills you," Wooden said. "They would be a good team without Russell, but with him they're simply great."

Despite the setback in New York, the Bruins returned home with plenty of confidence for the league season. The year before, the Pacific Coast Conference had decided to abandon its two-division format and have each school play every other team in a single two-game series. That meant UCLA's opponents would only have to come to Westwood every other year, prompting one Bay Area sportswriter to declare "an amen is in order."

In the wake of the fire marshal's decision closing down the men's gym, Wilbur Johns could not find a locale suitable for all of UCLA's games. The team therefore had to spend the season shuttling among three different venues: the Pan-Pacific Auditorium, Loyola University, and Venice High School. Despite the lack of a permanent home, the Bruins piled up wins with ease. Naulls was clearly establishing himself as the best player in the conference and arguably the best player in the country next to Russell.

After all the tumult they had been through, Naulls and Wooden had arrived at a subtle, unspoken understanding. During a game at Stanford in February, Taft was fouled as he drove for a layup. He missed the shot, but as the referees momentarily looked away, Naulls reached up and tipped the ball in. The officials thought that Taft had made his shot and awarded him a 3-point opportunity. That brought jeers of protest from the Stanford players, coaches, and fans. After one of the Stanford players told a referee what he had seen, the official then asked Naulls if it really was he, and not Taft, who had put the ball in. Willie looked at Wooden, but the coach said nothing. So Naulls told the referee the truth. The basket was waved off, and UCLA eventually won in overtime as Naulls scored 37 points.

Many years later, Naulls reminded Wooden of that moment and asked the coach if he thought he had done the right thing that night. Wooden carefully laid out all the various considerations before concluding, "A man has to make up his own mind in a situation that affects so many others." Naulls took that as a yes.

UCLA headed into its February series against California with a 12–0 conference record. The games were played at Venice High School. If the Bruins could sweep the Bears, they would clinch the 1956 conference crown. Wooden was none too pleased to have to play such a big game in a high school gym, where the length of the floor was ten feet shorter than regulation. Apparently, he was not alone. "I've heard some protests from the Bay Area regarding Venice High's short floor, and I hope they do protest," Wooden said during that week's press luncheon. "If they do, we'll move it right back to Westwood. There's nothing I'd like better."

UCLA got the sweep it needed. In the first game, Naulls eclipsed Eddie Sheldrake's single-game school record by pouring in 39 points in an 85–80 win. Taft scored 26 the following night to put the Bruins over the top. When the buzzer sounded, the players carried Wooden across the court. The only suspense in an otherwise meaningless final series against USC was whether the Bruins would finish the season with a perfect conference record. They did: 16–0. The same John Wooden who had once boasted of his decision to bench Naulls now lavished a whale of a compliment on him: he actually argued that Naulls was a better all-around player than Russell. In his memoir, Naulls described this as "an out-of-character outburst," but he was gratified that Wooden had finally extolled him in public. "Willie can do so many more things [than Russell]," Wooden said. "Granted that Russell is tremendous in some respects, and in picking a team, you'd have to choose Russell, but . . . I've never had a boy so strong in all offensive departments as Willie." Wooden later told the local sports columnist Sam Balter that Naulls was "the greatest I have ever coached. He is the greatest I have ever seen. And you know I have seen many."

Since there were no longer separate divisions in the PCC, UCLA's regular season title allowed the Bruins, who were ranked No. 10 by the Associated Press, to return to the NCAA tournament for the first time in four years. That was the good news. The bad news was that their first opponent in the West Regional would be top-ranked San Francisco, who still had not lost since UCLA had clipped them in the men's gym fifteen months before.

Since this was the postseason, the Bruins were due for another brush with bad luck. This one came when Taft fell in practice and re-aggravated his back injury. Taft was in such pain that he had a hard time getting in and out of a car. He played in the game, but he was limited, which rendered a difficult task all but impossible. UCLA lost, 81–72. One week later Russell would crown his college career with a second consecutive NCAA title.

Naulls's own brilliant career came to an end the day after the USF loss, when UCLA defeated Seattle University by 24 points in the West Regional's consolation game. It was technically Wooden's first win in the NCAA tournament, but because it did not come in the main bracket, the game was not counted in the record books. Thus, at the age of forty-five and in his eighth season at UCLA, Wooden still had not won an official game in the NCAA tournament.

Naulls had high hopes of playing for the United States in the Summer

Olympics in Melbourne, Australia. Since he was obviously one of the best players in the country, he should have made the team with ease. Imagine his surprise when he was cut despite scoring 42 points in three games during the Olympic trials in New York. Wooden figured that Naulls had been cut because there were too many players on the team from the West, and he was appalled that such a consideration could cause his All-American—the best player he had ever coached—to be left off the team. "I expressed my disappointment. To this day I can't understand how they could have passed up Willie Naulls," Wooden said nearly fifty years later. From that point on, Wooden would keep an icy distance from the American Olympic movement, which would isolate him even further from coaching peers who were deeply involved.

That disappointment aside, Naulls and Taft were the only players to be selected unanimously to the 1956 PCC first team. With their impending graduation, it would be that much harder for Wooden to claim his elusive NCAA tournament win. Bill Russell was also leaving, but while Wooden welcomed that news, he would soon face another imposing obstacle from the Bay Area. This time it arrived in the form of a coach, not a shot-blocking center, but it would be just as effective at preventing the hard-driving Wooden from reaching his goals.

15

Pete

Another off-season, another unforeseen shakeup.

This time, the tremors came from UCLA's football program. In March 1956, the *Oakland Tribune* published an article alleging that UCLA football players were given $40 above the $75 in expenses permitted by the Pacific Coast Conference. The PCC found the charges to be true and responded in heavy-handed fashion, declaring all UCLA football players ineligible unless they could prove that they had not been given illicit cash. In response to that action, the Los Angeles district attorney, who happened to be a UCLA alumnus, called a press conference to claim that he had evidence that USC had paid more than fifty athletes a total of over $71,000. The remaining conference schools jumped in, and the scandal metastasized into a blur of charges and countercharges. When the smoke finally cleared, the PCC imposed on UCLA a three-year suspension from championship and bowl competitions in all sports, plus fines totaling around $93,000. The Los Angeles City Council struck back by passing a resolution recommending that UCLA and USC "seriously consider" withdrawing from the PCC. It was an ugly, destablizing few months for this once proud forty-one-year-old league.

Though Wooden's basketball program had not been accused of breaking any rules, it was swept up in the scandal. The three-year postseason ban was a devastating blow for Wooden. His team had already lost its home court and four starters, including Willie Naulls and Morris Taft. Now it had lost the chance to play for a national championship and was on the brink of losing its league. This was not the way Wooden had hoped to begin the 1956–57 season.

Despite these setbacks, the Bruins were a pleasant surprise in the early going, winning seven of their first eight games, which set up a big test during their midwestern road swing in late December. They were scheduled to play at No. 5 St. Louis, which had an All-American candidate in forward Bob Ferry. Trailing by 4 points with seven minutes to play, the Bruins went on one of their patented late-game bursts, outscoring the Billikens 16–4 to pull off the upset.

The win would have been cause for celebration if Wooden had allowed it. When he heard his players whooping it up afterward in the shower, the coach marched into the locker room and ordered them to knock it off. "He was very strident about it," said Roland Underhill, a six-foot-four sophomore forward. "He always told us to treat defeat the same way you treat victory."

That trip, and that lecture, set the tone for a terrific season. Having vaulted to No. 8 in the AP poll because of the upset, the Bruins justified that standing by winning eleven of their first twelve PCC games. Unlike the previous season, when Taft and Naulls did most of the damage, the Bruins got scoring from several different players. That appealed to the engineer in Wooden. He liked things to be neat, tidy, structured—and most of all, balanced. "I noticed in checking our four conference games that the leading scorer has averaged 12 points, with the lowest 9 points," he said in January. "Our balance again proved true." A 4-point loss to USC dropped the Bruins to 11–2 in the league. That left them one game behind first-place California heading into the two-game series between those teams in Berkeley on the first weekend in March.

Cal's program, which hadn't made it to the NCAA tournament since its lone appearance in 1949, was in the midst of a remarkable resurgence, and it wasn't because the team had a bunch of heralded recruits. It was because Pete Newell had taken over as coach just two years before. A Southern California native who played for Loyola University, Newell had previously coached the University of San Francisco to the NIT championship in 1949. He left the following year for Michigan State and returned to the Bay Area in 1954. Newell's team at Cal won just one conference game in his first season. The next year, it won ten. Now, in year three, Newell had his Bears poised to challenge the titans from the south for the PCC crown.

Newell and Wooden had much in common. They both loved baseball (Newell spent a summer playing for the Brooklyn Dodgers' Single-A affiliate in Pine Bluff, Arkansas), shared an affection for the English language (Newell was also a prolific letter writer), and heeded quirky superstitions (Wooden liked to stick found bobby pins in trees; Newell tucked them into his pocket). Those similarities, however, were dwarfed by their contrasts. Newell was no teetotaling hermit. He was a man's man and a coach's coach. He smoked two packs of cigarettes a day (often lighting up before he even got out of bed in the morning) and was an inveterate night prowler. Newell loved nothing more than to hang with the fellas well past midnight, downing bourbon and talking ball. He could be tough on his players, but he was just as quick to put an arm around them once practice was over. He believed it was his job not just to tell them what to do, but why. He insisted they call him Pete.

Unlike Wooden, Newell never mastered the art of the even keel. Coaching basketball made him such a nervous wreck that he often said that fifteen minutes before each game, he wondered why he had ever gotten into the profession. "When my team went out on the court for warm-ups, I would stay in the dressing room for several minutes, thinking of all the things that might go wrong," he said. "It was a feeling of being alone and no one understanding the dark thoughts I was having."

Most of all, Newell taught a style of basketball that was the exact antithesis of Wooden's. Newell liked his tempo slow and his scores low. He was a devoted defensive tactician who was one of the first coaches to use a full-court man-to-man press. On offense, he ran a system called "reverse action," whereby players passed the ball from side to side over and over again, moving defenders back and forth, until an opportunity to score finally presented itself. "It would drive you up a wall," Bruin center John Berberich said of playing Cal. "They would pass the ball for ten minutes and then finally take a shot that they'd passed up seven minutes ago."

Wooden looked down his nose at this kind of basketball. Sometimes, if one of his own players passed up an open shot in practice, Wooden would chastise him by saying, "If you don't want to shoot, go to Cal." Newell was equally unimpressed with the racehorse attack Wooden had imported from the Midwest. "John didn't like our slowdown style at first," Newell said. "He came from the Piggy Lambert school, which had a lot more imagination and movement in the offense, but Lambert's teams just outscored people. They didn't play defense. The whole state of Indiana was one of the worst areas for defense I'd ever seen."

Wooden frequently quoted Lambert as saying, "The team that makes the most mistakes usually wins." In 1960, Newell told *Sports Illustrated*, "Basketball is a game of mistakes, and the team making the fewer mistakes generally wins." The two men coached the same sport, and yet they taught two completely different games.

They did share at least one fundamental policy: they never wanted to call the first time-out. Both men had started their careers in an era when coaches weren't allowed to huddle with their players on the sidelines. In those days, when time-out was called, the players gathered in a circle by themselves on the court. Newell and Wooden wanted their guys to think for themselves. They were also both fanatical about conditioning, which was even more reason never to call time-out. When Newell said that "a player should be conditioned to play the last five minutes of a game, not just the first five," he was uttering words that often came out of Wooden's mouth.

Their disdain for calling time-out was more than a piece of strategy. It was a point of pride. Earl Schulz, a guard at Cal, recalled: "It was just a mental game, a way of saying, 'We're not a bunch of candy asses. We're not going to roll over.'"

Such was the collision course that brought UCLA and Cal together on the final weekend of the 1956–57 season, with first place in the PCC on the line. The games had been sold out for over a week, and tickets were being scalped for ten dollars and up. "Never before has a Cal cage game so excited this city," the Los Angeles Times reported. The San Francisco Chronicle pronounced the Bruins to be "maybe the best team Johnny Wooden [has] produced at Westwood. Certainly it is the best balanced."

In preparing for UCLA, Newell left no stone unturned. He dispatched his assistant coach, Rene Herrerias, to scout the Bruins during their game against Oregon. Newell himself was on hand when they took on USC a few days before. This was yet another way in which Newell and Wooden were different. Whereas Wooden hardly ever mentioned the opponent to his team, Newell and Herrerias handed their players detailed reports on opponents' tendencies. During practice, Herrerias would coach the reserves as they formed a "scout team" that ran the offense the starters were going to defend. By the time the game arrived, the Bears knew their opponents' plays as well as they did, if not better. "I remember one time we were playing at Oregon, and I said to one of the guys, 'Hey, you're supposed to be over here,'" said Bill McClintock, who played at Cal from 1959 to 1961. "The guy looked at me and said, 'You're right.'"

UCLA drew first blood in game 1, outrebounding the Bears by 11 and overcoming a 15-point halftime deficit to win, 71–66. It was their ninth straight victory over Cal. Game 2 was a different story. This time the referees tightened up the contact under the basket, and as a result, Wooden saw his two centers, Ben Rogers and Conrad Burke, foul out early in the second half. As Cal cranked up the full-court pressure, Newell kept glancing at the opposite bench, wondering if Wooden would turn candy ass and stop play. With the score tied at 55–all with seven minutes remaining, Cal went on a quick 8–0 burst. Wooden finally relented and called time-out.

It was too late. The Bears held on to prevail, 73–68. When the buzzer sounded, the Cal players carried Newell off the court on their shoulders. The 7,200 fans broke out into a cheer of "We want Pete! We want Pete!" which forced the coach to return for a curtain call. The Bears had not technically locked up the conference title, and even if they had lost, they still would have gone to the NCAA tournament because UCLA was ineligible. But the fans in Berkeley had been humiliated so many times by their rivals to the south that they were sent into a delirious celebration by a single win that decided nothing.

Wooden was less than pleased, not just with the outcome but the disparity in fouls: twenty-seven called against UCLA, fourteen against Cal. The next day's *San Francisco Chronicle* reported that when the game ended, Wooden "stalked away from the placating hand of referee John Kolb and stomped off the floor. Wooden was unhappy all night because Kolb and Lou Batmale called a far different game than they had on Friday night." The Bay Area papers enjoyed needling Wooden on the rare occasions when his team lost there. One of the *Chronicle*'s stories the next day appeared under the headline, "Cal Cagers Beat UCLA (and Unhappy Coach Wooden)." The story included a photo of Wooden barking from the bench with his mouth open and head jutting forward. The caption dripped with sarcasm: "UCLA coach John Wooden no doubt is complimenting the refs on their clear vision at Cal."

Despite that setback, UCLA set a new single-season school record when it notched its twenty-second win in the regular season finale against USC, but California finished in first place with a 14–2 record. In the NCAA tournament's Western Regional in Corvallis—a graveyard where many a UCLA season had been buried—the Bears cakewalked to a 27-point win over BYU. The next day, Cal lost by 4 points to Newell's former employer, San Francisco. In just his third year at Berkeley, Newell had accomplished something Wooden hadn't done in nine years at UCLA: win a game in the NCAA tournament.

For Newell, that first triumph over Wooden would be as significant as any he would experience. From where he sat on the bench, the victory did more than catapult his team to a PCC title. It signified a defining shift in a bitter, long-standing rivalry. "I made time[outs] a big issue in that game. I felt the winning and losing was going to somehow be tied to it, and I was right," Newell said. "They never played timeouts again with us. Psychologically, that had so much to do with our confidence every time we played them. Our guys just figured, 'We never called timeout. They did.'"

For the first time since he came out west, Wooden was coaching against a man who cared as much about basketball as he did. If Wooden didn't know better, he might have thought this new rival had been raised in Martinsville, not Los Angeles.

The hostility between California and UCLA stretched back to UCLA's founding in the 1920s, when the Cal faculty objected to its southern counterpart's desire to move its campus from Vermont Avenue for fear it would sap the flagship campus of prestige. The bitterness festered for decades. It did not go unnoticed in Los Angeles that the football scandal that devastated Red Sanders's powerhouse began with a report in a Bay Area newspaper. "It is obvious, and has been for years, that Cal cannot willingly accept UCLA's development and its athletic success," one Los Angeles resident wrote in a letter to the *Times*. "The time for separation from Berkeley has now come." The people in Berkeley harbored similar resentment. "You couldn't talk about UCLA in our house. They were the antichrist," said Tom Newell, Pete's son.

That history helps explain why the Cal fans reacted so lustily when the Bears finally knocked off the Bruins in a basketball game with few real consequences. It also explains why they embraced their handsome, charming coach. Newell may not have been in Berkeley long, but the people could see that he represented their last, best hope at derailing the Johnny Wooden express.

If Wooden couldn't speed Newell up, he figured he should try to slow his racehorses down. His personnel mandated it. "This could be the tallest and also the slowest Bruin team I've had," he said two days before the first game of the 1957–58 season. What's more, he realized that other coaches around the league, especially Newell, were figuring him out. "They caught up with the fast break after a while, so we altered it," Wooden said. "I switched to a safety fast break. We didn't abolish it completely. We just ran it more cautiously."

Ironically, UCLA's roster that season would include the swiftest athlete Wooden would ever coach. He was Rafer Johnson, a six-foot-three junior guard who was best known for having broken the world decathlon record his freshman year as a member of UCLA's track team. Johnson had played four games for UCLA's freshman basketball team, averaging better than 10 points, but he stopped playing so he could focus on track. Now he was back to playing hoops, but his speed on the track did not translate well. "Rafer could run a lot faster than he could dribble," his teammate, Ben Rogers, said. "If he had concentrated on basketball, he would have been a pretty good player."

The other coaches in the PCC were also catching up to Wooden in the recruiting department. This was not hard to do. Wooden could be persuasive with prospects when they were in his company, but he refused to leave Southern California to find them. "I would not do that. I made that clear when I came here," he said. "My family comes first. I would not go away to scout. I would not be away from home. I refused to do that, and I didn't have assistants do that."

The school was still not providing the Bruins with their own home court, but fortunately the city of Los Angeles stepped in to fill the void. The city announced in the fall of 1957 that an architect's designs had been completed for a multipurpose arena that would host home games for USC and UCLA, among other events. The arena's site—commonly referred to as "the hole"—was located next to USC's campus. That made it less than ideal for UCLA, but it was better than Venice High School.

With his program suffering from a dearth of talent, Wooden was forced to mine the junior college ranks. He brought in six such transfers that fall, including a high-scoring, hard-nosed guard named Denny Crum, a six-foot-one San Fernando Valley native who had been the region's leading junior college scorer at Los Angeles Pierce College. Despite that pedigree, Crum did not warrant a hard sell from UCLA's coach. During his campus visit, Crum spent several hours with Wooden and his players, waiting for the coach to deliver his pitch. Finally, during a team meal Wooden looked at him blankly and asked, "So are you coming or not?"

The fall of 1957 also saw the return of that old nonconformist, Jerry Norman. After serving a three-and-a-half-year hitch in the navy, Norman had taken a teaching and coaching position at West Covina High School, where Cat Wooden was the principal. A year later, Jerry was hired to teach in the physical education department at UCLA. Wooden asked if he would moonlight as the freshman basketball coach. Norman and Wooden may have butted heads when Norman was a player, but Wooden was not one for holding grudges, and he knew that Norman had a sharp basketball mind. He also knew Norman was a fierce competitor, just like him. "Jerry was a natural," said Bill Eblen, another former player who joined the freshman staff the same year that Norman did.

"He was very intense, very volatile, but he was technically a very good coach. He was different from Wooden, but he still used the same philosophies."

The 1957–58 season would mark UCLA's next-to-last campaign in the Pacific Coast Conference. In the wake of the scandals and resulting sanctions, the regents and trustees at UCLA, California, and USC formally decided to withdraw from the league effective the summer of 1959. Washington and Stanford followed suit.

The Bruins began their nonconference schedule with four straight wins to climb to No. 13 in the AP poll, but they were undone during their annual midwestern tour, where they lost three consecutive games. From there they returned to Westwood and immediately dropped their fourth game in a row to eighth-ranked Michigan State.

The Bruins fared better in league play, at one point rattling off six straight wins until Newell's Bears beat them, 61–58, at Pan-Pacific Auditorium, a victory that put Cal in a tie with UCLA for first place. As Newell's teams got harder and harder to beat, Wooden continued to pound the drum in favor of adding a shot clock. He even played two nonconference games that season with the clock in place as an experiment. "The rule would eliminate the occasional, farcical game where a team holds the ball or stalls," he said in a thinly veiled reference to Newell, whose team had lost a game to San Francisco, 33–24, the year before.

Cal prevailed again when the teams met on February 28 in Berkeley. It was Newell's third consecutive victory over Wooden. For Jerry Norman, this was his first chance to see Newell's team up close. Norman would coach the freshman game and then stick around to watch the varsity teams square off. Since he had been away from college basketball for several years, Norman did not know the backgrounds of the players, but from where he sat, he did not see a great differential in talent. "Yet we never won," he said.

Norman noticed two things Newell was doing that made a big difference. The first was control the tempo. "He made you play the way he wanted you to play," Norman said. "In most games, if you're able to do that and the talent is equal, you're probably going to prevail."

The other thing that struck Norman was the unusual way the Bears played defense. At that time, most players dribbled almost exclusively with their strong hand. If a player was right-handed, the opposing coach would tell his defender to force that player to go to his left. Newell, however, had taken this practice a step further and had his defenders shift their feet and position their bodies so the dribbler was physically unable to drive with his strong hand. It was subtle, but it worked.

From his perch in the bleachers, Norman had no idea that Newell and Herrerias were devoting so much time scouting opponents. But he could see the result. "You have to remember, there was no strategy in those days," Norman said. "Coaches didn't have clinics. There were no games on national television. It was like living in a vacuum. It was apparent to me from watching in the stands that [Newell] understood how to take away a player's strength. Basketball is a game of mathematics. It's percentages. Newell was forcing teams to play to their weakness. It was a very effective strategy."

After their second loss that season to Cal, the Bruins limped home with a 10–6 record in the PCC—good for third place—and 16–10 overall. Cal, meanwhile, went on to win the league championship for the second consecutive year and advanced to the NCAA's West Regional in Corvallis, where the Bears knocked off Iowa State before falling to Seattle, which featured Elgin Baylor, by 4 points. It was a disappointing loss, but at least the Bears were no longer measuring themselves against their rivals in the south. It was their turn to cast a shadow from on high.

School resumed at UCLA in the fall of 1958 on a somber note. Over the summer, Red Sanders had died from a sudden heart attack at the age of fifty-three. Sanders had become a larger-than-life character, earning the nickname the "Wizard of Westwood" as he rode his innovative single-wing offense to two Rose Bowl victories and a share of the 1954 national championship. Sanders was also quoted as saying "Winning isn't everything, it's the only thing" more than a decade before that phrase was first attributed to Vince Lombardi. The differences between Wooden and Sanders were illustrated by the circumstances of Red's untimely demise: at the moment his heart gave out, he was sharing a motel bed with a prostitute.

Though there was much speculation that Wooden and Sanders were at odds with each other (the *Los Angeles Herald Examiner* once wrote that Wooden "suffered in silence" because he despised Sanders so much), Wooden always insisted that he liked Sanders. While Nell and John no longer had their eyes on returning to their native Midwest, they also never immersed themselves in the Los Angeles social scene. They were in love with each other and content to keep to themselves. "You never heard them arguing. They were a great pair," Eddie Sheldrake said. "After games, we might go get something to eat with Coach's brother and his wife, and maybe Eddie Powell, but beyond that there were very few others that I remember them socializing with. That wasn't their thing."

The squad that Wooden coached during the 1958–59 season was even bigger and slower than the year before. The roster included the tallest player the school had ever recruited, Warnell Jones, a six-foot-nine sophomore center from Conroe, Texas. Jones was black, earnest, and soft-spoken. He was also ill equipped to play up-tempo basketball. Another big sophomore, six-foot-six forward Kent Miller, was much more athletic, but he frustrated Wooden with his lack of effort.

Rafer Johnson was slated to play a bigger role during his senior year, though he would be a bit distracted by his election to student body president during the off-season, marking another proud chapter in UCLA's racial history. Johnson was not the only two-sport athlete who was going to be featured on Wooden's team that season. Bill Kilmer, a six-foot junior transfer from Citrus Junior College, had been one of the top basketball scorers in Los Angeles as a high school player. He was also a starting tailback on UCLA's football team, and he would eventually play seventeen years as an NFL quarterback for the San Francisco 49ers, New Orleans Saints, and Washington Redskins.

The only full-time starter who had returned to UCLA from the previous year was Walt Torrence, a six-foot-three senior forward. By that time, Torrence had become a full-fledged star, twice being named to the All-PCC second team. He was also a distinguished high jumper on the school's track team.

UCLA fought past a stagnant early start to put together five straight wins, including two over USC in Pan-Pacific Auditorium by a combined 6 points. The two games against Cal in early February would once again go a long way toward deciding who would win the final PCC title. Cal entered the first game leading the nation in defense by allowing just 47.8 points per game. The Bruins' offense was averaging 63.1 points. Mal Florence wrote in the *Los Angeles Times* that "something or someone has to give," but he made clear which side he believed would do the giving: "California's style of play, as coached by Pete Newell, has always proved bothersome to John Wooden's Bruins."

The game wasn't decided until the waning seconds, when Cal guard Al Buch sank a ten-foot jumper to deliver the Bears to a 60–58 win, giving Cal sole possession of first place. Two weeks later, in Berkeley, the Bears handled UCLA with far more ease, winning by 13 points to send the Bruins to their fourth consecutive loss.

Newell's streak over Wooden now stood at five and counting. If Wooden found that bothersome, he didn't let it show. "There was not one occasion when John Wooden would not come into the locker room and congratulate each one of us," Bob Dalton said. "He was as gracious in losing as he was in winning."

UCLA managed to complete its final PCC season by winning its last five games, but the Bruins' 10–6 league record (16–9 overall) left them tied for third place for the second straight year. Cal, meanwhile, finished 14–2 to take the league crown. The Bears had a dominant defensive center in six-foot-ten Darrall Imhoff, whom Wooden often compared to Bill Russell. But they were essentially a no-name outfit. As the NCAA tournament got under way, the Bears were ranked eleventh in the country, and *Sports Illustrated* ranked them the fifteenth-best team in the sixteen-team field.

Cal did, however, have the luxury of playing a virtual home game for the NCAA's Western Regionals at the Cow Palace in San Francisco, where the Bears rolled over Utah and Saint Mary's by a combined 38 points. That sent them to Louisville, Kentucky, for a national semifinal showdown against No. 5 Cincinnati and the consensus best player in America, Oscar Robertson, who averaged nearly 33 points per game and was en route to winning the second of his three national scoring titles. Robertson, however, had never gone up against a defensive tactician like Newell. He scored just one field goal in the entire second half and ended up with 19 points as Cal prevailed, 64–58.

The following night, the Bears played in their school's first-ever NCAA championship game. Their opponents were the West Virginia Mountaineers, who were led by yet another transcendent talent, six-foot-two junior Jerry West, a lithe, crafty guard who had averaged 26.6 points and 12.3 rebounds during the regular season. West was coming off a 38-point, 15-rebound performance in the semifinal against Louisville, and in the final he lifted West Virginia to a 10-point halftime lead. Cal, however, came back and clipped the Mountaineers, 71–70, to take the title.

It spoke volumes about the perceived inferiority of Cal's talent that West, who finished with 28 points and 11 rebounds in the final, was named the tournament's Most Outstanding Player, even though his team lost. Newell's Bears also turned out to be the last all-white team to win an NCAA championship. When it was over, the players lifted Newell onto their shoulders and celebrated.

Cal was just the second western team in the past fifteen years to have won the NCAA tournament. But unlike that other western champ, San Francisco, the Bears did not possess a dominant player like Bill Russell.

It was clear that the reason they had won was because Pete Newell was their coach. UCLA fans took notice. Wooden had left Indiana State partly because he wanted to avoid expectant fans, but now, for the first time, he was about to face real scrutiny. While Newell was riding his players' shoulders in Louisville, Wooden was once again back in Los Angeles, where fans and sportswriters were starting to wonder whether their team would ever enjoy such a glorious view.

The good news for John Wooden heading into the 1959–60 season was that his three years in purgatory were finally up: his Bruins were finally eligible again to compete in the NCAA tournament.

The bad news was that it would be even tougher for them to get there.

In the wake of the PCC's demise, Cal, UCLA, USC, Stanford, and Washington formed a conference called the Athletic Association of Western Universities, or AAWU. That meant the Bruins would now have to play the reigning NCAA champs three times during the regular season instead of two. Moreover, for the first time since coming to UCLA eleven years before, Wooden found himself in a rebuilding situation. Eight lettermen had departed from the previous year's third-place team, leaving him to admit before the start of the 1959–60 season that these Bruins would be "the most inexperienced team since I've been at UCLA."

As if that weren't enough, Wooden pulled a muscle in his leg during one of the first practices while demonstrating something to his players. He hobbled on crutches for several weeks. The India Rubber Man, now less than a year from turning fifty, was losing his elasticity in middle age.

Bolstering UCLA's talent would be Jerry Norman's first priority after he was promoted to varsity assistant in the summer of 1959. It would not be an easy task. Norman was shocked to discover that the program's entire recruiting budget was $500. His other task was even more difficult. He was supposed to help UCLA get past Pete Newell. "Maybe you can figure out what he's doing," Wooden told Norman. "I know I can't."

With the local high school well running dry, Wooden once again brought in six junior college transfers. Three had played for Long Beach City College, which had just won the Southern California junior college championship. The trio included Bob Berry, who at five-foot-ten was the smallest player on UCLA's roster. Berry had served three years in the military before enrolling at Long Beach, so by the time he entered UCLA as a junior, he was twenty-five years old. Wooden had personally tried to convince Berry to come to UCLA the year before, but Berry wanted to stay at Long Beach for one more year.

There were also a few former high school players joining the varsity that fall. The most prominent was Gary Cunningham, a fluid six-foot-five sophomore forward who had averaged 20.7 points and 11.5 rebounds for the freshman team. An all-city player at Inglewood High School, Cunningham had originally committed to play for Newell at Cal, but Jerry Norman continued to pursue him. To Newell's chagrin, Cunningham decided to switch to UCLA because it would allow him to remain close to home.

In many ways Cunningham was the model Wooden player—clean-cut, fastidious, mannerly, serious about the game. And he was as pure a shooter as Wooden had seen. Wooden called Cunningham "one of the most dedicated boys to the game of basketball I have ever coached." Cunningham's classmate, Johnny Green, a six-foot-three forward, recalled that Cunningham "did not mess around. He was probably the only one who really worked hard that first half hour of practice."

Like most of his teammates, Cunningham revered Wooden. Unlike most of his teammates, he thought nothing of stopping by Wooden's office unannounced for a chat—about school, basketball, life, whatever. "I always found that if I wanted to talk to Coach, the door was open," Cunningham said. "A lot of guys were afraid of him, but I actually went to him rather than assistants, and we established a relationship. I don't know why. I just felt like he's my coach and I should go talk to him."

Wooden's new varsity assistant, however, did not feel the same way. Norman liked Wooden—the tension that had existed during Norman's playing days was long gone—but he found his boss to be strangely distant. Some of it could be attributed to their age difference, but Norman sensed it was mostly because John and Nell still preferred to socialize with people who shared their tastes, their values, and especially their background. "They just had this distrust of people who were not from the Midwest," Norman said. "They kind of stayed in their own little world."

At least Wooden's team would finally have a decent place to play. The "hole" that had been dug next to USC's campus had become the Los Angeles Sports Arena, the finest indoor facility in a city that was fast becoming a sports haven. The Brooklyn Dodgers had moved to Los Angeles the year before, and the NBA's Minneapolis Lakers would arrive the following summer. The pro franchises competed with UCLA for spectators, but Wooden recognized that there was a lot of upside in having Los Angeles develop into a pro sports town. It meant more people would want to live there, which meant the local high schools would be filled with more potential recruits.

Of course, building an arena and filling it with fans were two different things. When UCLA and USC played the first basketball game at the Sports Arena on December 1, 1959, the city greeted the historic occasion with a yawn. Just 6,880 people showed up to watch UCLA eke out a 47–45 win on two late free throws from Bob Berry. Three days later, a slightly larger crowd saw UCLA take on Adolph Rupp's Kentucky Wildcats. It was a big game, and Wooden looked for every edge. He harangued the referees so mercilessly that he was assessed a technical foul after Kentucky took its first lead with under six minutes to play. Kentucky won, 68–66, but Rupp was unimpressed by the turnout. "This is the first time in three years that Kentucky has played to an empty seat," he huffed.

After a pair of UCLA wins at home over Santa Clara, the Bruins were set to host Oklahoma State, the former Oklahoma A&M. The Cowboys were still coached by Henry Iba, whose teams had won two NCAA championships in the 1940s by playing eye-glazing, slow-it-down basketball. Between Iba and Newell, Wooden seemed to be losing his argument that racehorse basketball was the way to go. After the Bruins lost, 52–48, Wooden lamented, "We allowed Oklahoma State to play its game and you can't do that."

The Bruins' annual late-December midwestern swing began with a visit to Purdue. It was the first time Wooden had taken his UCLA team back to his alma mater in West Lafayette, and it was not a pleasant experience as Purdue beat his Bruins, 75–74. The trip wasn't enjoyable for Bob Berry, either. He had started against Purdue and thought he played well, but the next day he was not in the starting lineup against Butler. Instead, Berry came off the bench to score 4 points as the Bruins lost their third game in a row.

Over the next few weeks, Berry's role continued to diminish until he was barely getting into the game. He was upset, but mostly he was confused. Wooden had expended considerable effort to convince Berry to come to UCLA, but he had demoted him without a word of explanation, just as he had done to Willie Naulls and many others. "Coach Wooden was supposed to be this great communicator, but he didn't even communicate to me why I'm sitting on the bench. It wouldn't have taken much time," Berry said. "I mean, Wooden brought me to UCLA, not one of the assistants. If he had just explained to me that he had a sophomore who he wanted to give more experience to, or whatever, I would have accepted it.

But he never said one thing about why he put me on the bench. Maybe he felt he didn't have to."

Berry was learning what many past and future Bruins would learn. John Wooden was an intelligent coach and a classy sportsman, but he was not the kind of man who went out of his way to help his young players sort through their feelings of rejection. For all they could tell, Wooden had no clue how they felt. It's not that he didn't care. Quite the contrary. In his own mind, his own heart, Wooden loved his "boys," but he had grown up in an environment where love was to be demonstrated, not spoken; felt, not expressed. Now, he was dealing with young men who had grown up in a much different time and place. They had emotional needs he did not, or would not, understand. It was a shame, because Wooden had great command of the English language, yet he vastly underestimated the power of his own words.

Following the loss at Butler, UCLA returned home to play in a four-team tournament at the Sports Arena that was branded the Los Angeles Basketball Classic. That event brought in good crowds, but the fans didn't come to see USC and UCLA. They came to see Pete Newell's Cal Bears take on West Virginia in a rematch of the 1959 NCAA championship game. As a capacity crowd of 13,024 looked on—the most ever to see a college basketball game in the city—Newell delivered yet another defensive clinic. Cal held Jerry West to just 8 points and cruised to a 65–45 victory.

Before that game tipped off, USC and UCLA met in the third-place game. The arena was half-empty as USC won by 10. Even in his own hometown, Wooden was relegated to the undercard, and an uninteresting one at that.

The loss to USC dropped the Bruins to 5–6 heading into their first slate of games in the AAWU. For the remainder of the 1959–60 season, the biggest question was whether Wooden would suffer his first losing record at UCLA. "John Wooden was not a happy camper with his ballplayers that season," Bob Berry said. Though Wooden still professed to be less concerned with winning and losing than with maximizing potential—his own definition of success, right there beside his trusted pyramid—he found it harder to unwind as the losses piled up. "He would get Ducky Drake, and they'd go walk at two or three in the morning because he couldn't sleep," Cunningham said. "I learned about this much later. Coach didn't like to lose, but he tried not to show it to us players."

There were times, however, when he couldn't help himself. Wooden stopped practice cold one day when he unloaded on Kent Miller for his lack of effort. Harkening back to his days in South Bend, Wooden screamed at Miller and booted him in the rear end. "That was about the angriest I've seen him," Johnny Green said.

Wooden found himself in an even more contentious situation during a game at the Air Force Academy in late January. Midway through the first half, referee Ben Dreith, whom Wooden later characterized as "belligerent," told Wooden he didn't want to hear any more yapping from the bench. "Why don't you call a technical foul on me and get it out of your system?" Wooden asked. Dreith complied. Things got more heated late in the second half, when a fight broke out between two players, prompting hundreds of cadets to pour out of the stands. Air Force coach Bob Spear later accused UCLA of "roughhouse tactics," claiming the Bruins "apparently felt they couldn't win it playing straight basketball." After the floor was cleared, UCLA escaped with a 76–75 win.

The Bruins began their conference slate by sweeping Stanford, giving them four straight wins. That mini-streak was snapped by—who else?—California. When the teams squared off on January 8 in Berkeley, the Bears coasted to a 53–45 win. A week later, the Bears beat UCLA again, this time at the Sports Arena by 10 points.

For Jerry Norman, these losses were evidence that Wooden needed a new approach. Norman thought back to his sophomore year in 1950, when Wooden gave such a thorough scouting report before their NCAA tournament game against Bradley that the Bruins lost their composure and lost. Now, Norman believed that Wooden was overcompensating by ignoring opponents completely. "Wooden was a very good fundamental coach. He was very good at planning practices. He was very good at the relationships with the players," Norman said. "But he didn't have much in the way of strategy. His whole attitude was you play the way you practice."

Always the eager learner, Wooden couldn't deny that Newell was getting the better of him. After Cal knocked off the Bruins in the Sports Arena for the third time that season—and eighth straight win overall against UCLA—Wooden waited for Newell to emerge from his locker room. When he did, Wooden asked if he wouldn't mind getting together in the off-season so they could talk about defense. Like Wooden, Newell was a gentleman as well as a competitor. It was the way in which he and Wooden were most alike. Newell told Wooden he thought that was a wonderful idea. He'd be happy to get together.

Once again, UCLA stumbled down the stretch of the season. After that third loss to Cal, the Bruins lost at Washington to drop to 6–4 in the conference and 13–11 overall. They began their season-ending two-game series against USC by getting blown out, 91–71. It was the most points USC had ever scored against UCLA.

With the outcome of the game no longer in doubt, Wooden summoned Bob Berry to the scorer's table. Berry had barely stepped on the floor since January, and he was insulted at being used for mop-up duty. So he refused to go in. Wooden did not suffer that gladly. "Boy, you want to talk about somebody getting red in the face. He really gave it to me," Berry said. "I told him there was no way I was going to play in garbage time."

The following night's finale was marred by a brouhaha that was extreme even by the standards of the USC-UCLA rivalry. With less than a minute to play, two players exchanged shoves as they dove to the floor to wrestle for the ball. Both benches immediately emptied, and dozens more fans joined the fray. As both coaches and the two referees tried to restore order, USC coach Forrest Twogood accidentally elbowed Wooden in the face, knocking his glasses to the floor and leaving a nasty bruise on his nose.

Once the court was cleared, UCLA finished off a 72–70 win. The Bruins' regular season ended with a 14–12 record, allowing Wooden to claim a winning season. When the 1960 NCAA tournament began, he was once again a spectator as Cal began its national title defense by vanquishing Idaho State at the Cow Palace, 71–44. The Bears then coasted through the Western Regional in Seattle, beating Santa Clara and Oregon by a combined 41 points, to reach the national semifinals for the second straight year.

The tournament would culminate back at the Cow Palace, where once again the Bears would be matched up against Oscar Robertson and the Cincinnati Bearcats in the semifinals. For the second straight year, they sent the Big O packing. Robertson managed just 18 points on four field goals, and Cal won, 77–69. This time, however, the Bears fell short in the final against an Ohio State team that included two future Hall of Famers, John Havlicek and Jerry Lucas, and a feisty reserve guard named Bobby Knight. Ohio State pasted the defending champs, 75–55.

It should have been a joyful time in Newell's life, but in truth he was suffering through a private hell. His diet of nothing but coffee and cigarettes had taken a nasty toll. "Pete was a skeleton by the end of the year," said one of his former players, Ned Averbuck. "He was a walking zombie. Pete's eyes were so sunken, guys thought he was going to die." Winning an NCAA championship had created an expectation that Newell believed would be impossible to meet. "A coach is never really secure," he told *Sports Illustrated* that winter. "I'm not going to coach until I'm sixty. I don't feel that I could go through sixteen more years of the tension that goes with each season."

Unbeknown to the public, Newell had decided back in February that he was going to retire, even though he was just forty-four years old. He made the news official shortly after the loss to Ohio State. He and Wooden never did have that tête-à-tête about defense. They were rivals who respected each other, but it would be a long while before they would become friends.

Newell earned many fans in the Bay Area during his brief stint at Cal. He also gained a huge admirer behind enemy lines. Jerry Norman was enamored of Newell's techniques, his philosophies, his understanding of the game's mathematics. He knew that Wooden was a great teacher, but he also sensed that Wooden needed to adapt better to the changing times. Basketball was evolving, and if UCLA was going to keep up, then Wooden would have to evolve as well. He was great at teaching fundamentals, but he needed to understand that there was more to the game than that. He needed to find a place for percentages inside all that engineering.

Most of all, Norman knew, he needed better players.

16

Walt

One day in the spring of 1959, Jerry Norman walked into Wooden's office and noticed a letter sitting on the desk. It was written by Ron Lawson, a six-foot-four high school senior from Nashville, Tennessee. Besides being an excellent student—his father was the head of the physics department at Fisk University—Lawson was a standout guard at Pearl High School. He had already led his team to two championships at a national tournament for black high schools, and he would eventually add a third.

Like many young black athletes in America, Lawson's hero was UCLA's own Rafer Johnson, who had just been named *Sports Illustrated*'s Sportsman of the Year after setting a world record in the decathlon during a stirring competition in Moscow. Lawson was impressed that Johnson was student body president as well. Wooden didn't seem eager to follow up on Lawson's letter, so Norman asked if he could. It was not a hard pitch. Lawson enrolled as a freshman later that fall.

From the start, the young man showed extraordinary promise. He shattered several freshman records while averaging 24.5 points and leading the team in rebounding. The following year, in just his fifth varsity game, Lawson scored a team-high 19 points in a win over Notre Dame that vaulted the Bruins to thirteenth in the national rankings. By late December of Lawson's sophomore year, the *Los Angeles Times* was predicting that he would be "one of the best basketball players UCLA has ever had."

Things were much more unpleasant behind the scenes, however. As a child of the segregated South, Lawson had experienced a different upbringing from most of his teammates. Many of the white players found Lawson to be enigmatic and hostile. "I remember we were having lunch one day, and I made some comment about how blacks are quicker and can jump higher than us white guys," John Green said. "Ron got up from the table and left. I said, 'Ron, I apologize: it was nothing racial.' But Ron had a chip on his shoulder because he dealt with that stuff a lot in Tennessee."

The conflicts were more than skin deep. For all his talents, Lawson could be moody and selfish on the court. Wooden worked hard to instill a culture of selflessness, but Lawson did not want be a part of it. Though UCLA won twelve of its first fifteen games in the 1960–61 season to rise to No. 10 in the rankings, the team fell apart from there. "[Lawson] was a loner. He never quite fit in," John Berberich said. Lawson did not bother to hide his discontent from the public. "[Basketball] is like a job," he told the *Los Angeles Times*. "I once loved to play. I used to sleep with a basketball when I was a kid."

Lawson wasn't the only player on the outs with Wooden at that time. Bob Berry, who had refused to enter the waning minutes of the USC game the year before, was now a senior, but he had been planted on the bench and left there. "I still have the splinters," he quipped many decades later. Berry was resigned to his fate—and understood his responsibility in sealing it—but he experienced a more personal disappointment in Wooden during a trip to Lexington in December to play Kentucky.

Berry was raised in Indiana, and his parents had made the trip from home to watch the game. He was visiting with them inside the arena beforehand. Berry, the tenth of eleven children, was looking forward to introducing his parents to his coach, a fellow Hoosier. When Wooden came out of the locker room, however, he ignored Berry's family and continued walking. "I thought it would have been nice if he had come over to say hello to my parents," he said. "I don't know if it's because he was shy, but to this day it disturbs me."

This was yet another example of Wooden's aloofness sending a bad message. If Wooden set himself apart from his players, that distance was even greater between him and their parents, which was ironic since Wooden was such a family man himself. He viewed parents as potential distractions who could upend his program. When Wooden wanted to learn about his players' families, he had them fill out a questionnaire. "I did not work with the parents that much," Wooden said. "I felt I must be very careful because some parents were going to be nearby, so they could regularly attend the games, and I might find myself socializing with them, while other parents would be far away, and I wouldn't see them that often." Asked whether Wooden interacted with parents, his former assistant, Bill Putnam, replied, "Well, reluctantly."

Gary Cunningham, on the other hand, remained the apple of Wooden's eye. Some players vexed Wooden with their lack of effort. Cunningham tried so hard that Wooden had to convince him to relax and enjoy himself more on the court. The hard work paid off as Cunningham became one of the most lethal outside shooters in America. He scored 22 second-half points in a 24-point win at home over New York University in the team's fourth game of the season.

By that point, college basketball was finally starting to catch on in Los Angeles. That was partly due to the growing popularity of the sport, but mostly it was because the city's population continued to swell. For decades it had been common for more than 80,000 spectators to attend a USC or UCLA football game, but now the schools' basketball teams were drawing hordes to the downtown Sports Arena as well. A record crowd of 14,589, the largest ever to see an indoor basketball game in Los Angeles, watched sixteenth-ranked UCLA lose to Iowa on December 30. More than 13,000 were on hand in early February to see USC beat UCLA by 15 points.

The Bruins, alas, would prove to be a disappointment as the 1960–61 season wound down. Lawson's chemistry problems prevented the team from reaching its potential—which is the worst thing one could say about a John Wooden–coached team. During a game against USC on March 3, the Bruins uncharacteristically blew a 13-point lead in the last five minutes and lost, 86–85, in overtime. That enabled the Trojans to win the AAWU title while UCLA finished second with a 7–5 record (18–8 overall). It was the fifth straight year that UCLA had failed to qualify for the NCAA tournament.

From a statistical standpoint, Lawson had a very good sophomore season, but he had been a cancer in the locker room. That posed a potential problem for Wooden moving forward, but all that changed in May 1961, when Lawson admitted before a New York grand jury that he had been approached by professional gamblers. The revelation was part of a broad gambling probe that involved eighteen colleges and nearly forty players. No evidence was produced to prove that Lawson shaved points, but his failure to report the contact was enough to warrant his expulsion from UCLA.

In the wake of that revelation, Wooden held individual meetings to ask players if they had ever been contacted by gamblers. He said he had studied game films and saw no evidence that Lawson had fixed games. Wooden was also not exactly crestfallen that he'd lost his leading scorer. "In my twenty-six years of coaching, I've never had a boy who resented instruction and correction as much as Lawson did," he said. "He would have preferred to be completely on his own, even practice on his own and not with the team. He's a boy who was always looking for excuses."

When basketball practice began on October 15, 1961, the day after Wooden's fifty-first birthday, the coach delivered a stern lecture to his players, who saw that he was growing less tolerant of problem children. "This year," he warned them, "is not going to be like the last one."

It didn't matter how talented Lawson was. He wasn't worth the trouble. Wooden had honed his engineering skills for more than a quarter of a century, and he well understood how one flawed piece, one bad gear, could throw everything off-kilter. "I would explain to my players that we're like a machine," Wooden said. "The engine is probably the most expensive to replace, and I might mention one player who was a real standout, that he's sort of the engine. I might mention another player that maybe got to play a lot but who was not a star in that sense. I might explain that this player is a wheel. But what can the machine do if we don't have all four wheels? Then I'd say to another player that gets to play even less, now you're kind of like a nut that holds the wheel in place. But where are we going to go if we don't have a wheel? Where are we going to go if we don't have the engine? Some are more difficult to replace, but everyone has a role."

Whenever the story of John Wooden's life gets told, his years at UCLA before he started winning championships are usually characterized as a period of struggle. Wooden didn't view them that way. He was a diligent, persistent man. He enjoyed developing his craft, one small lesson plan at a time. "Little things add up, and they become big things. That's what I tried to teach my players in practice," he said. "You're not going to make a great improvement today. Maybe you'll make a little bit. But tomorrow it's a little more, and the next day a little more."

Wooden did not utilize his Pyramid of Success as a teaching tool the same way he did at Indiana State, where it was part of the curriculum in his coaching class. He might give his players a copy of the pyramid at the beginning of the season, but it was just one of many mimeographed sheets he distributed during the season. "I don't know anybody on our team that ever looked at the Pyramid of Success or even thought about it," said Chuck Darrow, who played from 1961 to 1964. "It might have been taped in our lockers, but it just hung there like a jock strap."

Wooden, however, could glance every day at the pyramid that was framed and hung on a wall in his modest office. It was his lodestar. His industriousness ("There is no substitute for work"), intentness ("Concentrate on your objective and be determined to reach your goal"), alertness ("Be observing constantly"), poise ("Being at ease in any situation"), and confidence ("May come from faith in yourself in knowing that you are prepared") steeled him during those years when success didn't come quite so easily. Though he still very badly wanted to win—there's a reason Competitive Greatness was the block at the top—Wooden was especially well served by the two bits of spackle that he had carved beside that pinnacle: faith (through prayer) and patience (good things take time).

Whenever Wooden's machine encountered big problems, his instinct was to delve into the smallest details. If the pyramid defines the modern-day image of the man, the more indelible picture in the minds of the men who played for him is that of the three-by-five index card. Every morning before practice, Wooden spent two to three hours drafting his practice plan and then transferring it onto those cards. When practice was over, Wooden filed the cards away for safekeeping. His outline on those cards was precise. His penmanship, exquisite.

Each detail had a larger purpose, although it was not always evident. Nor was Wooden one for explaining such things. He taught his players how to put on their shoes and socks because he didn't want them to get blisters. Wooden told his boys how to eat, how to sleep, even how to dry their hair after a shower. (The better to prevent common colds.) There was a basketball reason he wanted their hair short—he didn't want it to fall into their faces or drip perspiration into their eyes—but he also liked his players to look clean-cut. His time in the military taught him that uniformity created cohesion. On road trips the players wore blazers. Their shirttails had to be tucked in. They could not wear hats during meals. When they played, they had to wear the black shoes they had been issued on the first day of the season. One day, Wooden made Dick Banton run hard for fifteen minutes after practice because he had the audacity to wear white shoes after mistakenly leaving his black ones at home. "He would tell you a rule, but he wouldn't tell you what the consequences were if you broke it," Banton said. "His practices were brutal. If we weren't winning, I don't think the guys would have put up with it."

Those index cards may as well have been stone tablets. Once Wooden crafted his master plan, he became its servant. "A lot of coaches have a tendency to stay with one facet of practice too long," said Doug Sale, a former assistant. "His theory was, I'll hit it today, and if we don't get it completed, we'll come back to it tomorrow."

Wooden may have carried a gentlemanly aspect, but he evinced the authoritarian air of a former navy lieutenant. "I can't imagine too many coaches being that organized and that precise," Roland Underhill said. It helped that during those first two decades at UCLA he operated in a culture of conformity. "We never questioned his authority. We never questioned his ability," Gary Cunningham said. Banton added: "This wasn't a rebellious time. I can't imagine a guy getting a bunch of parking tickets or a bunch of players smoking marijuana or something. There wasn't a big drug culture at UCLA." Wooden applied the same laws of learning to his basketball classes that he once applied to his English classes: explanation, demonstration, imitation, correction, and then repetition, repetition, repetition. "I'll never forget hour after hour working on a pivot," said Jerry Evans, who had been a freshman during Wooden's first season in 1948–49.

There was no playbook at UCLA because there were no plays. Wooden's high-post offense allowed players two or three options for each exchange, but it was up to them to make those decisions. In this respect, Wooden remained a disciple of James Naismith, who believed that coaches were unnecessary, perhaps superfluous. Wooden often said a coach only made four or five real decisions during a game. "It disgusts me to see all these cartoons of raving maniac coaches," he said. "There is far more over-coaching than undercoaching in basketball. It's a great game, an intricate game, but we should not make it complicated."

To Wooden, the games were just the final exams, the coach a proctor. Practice was where the real work got done. Everything he did during those workouts was predicated on quickness. If a player did something Wooden liked, he would bark, "Good! Now do it faster." Wooden also preferred to serve up his advice in small, individual portions rather than addressing the team as a whole. He was never one for meetings. They just slowed things down.

On game days, the players would have the same meal precisely four hours before tip-off: steak or roast beef broiled medium, baked potato, three pieces of celery, fruit cocktail. That was to be followed by a ten-minute walk. Afterward, Wooden wanted his players to lie on their hotel beds in the dark and try to sleep. No reading, no television, no telephone calls. He wanted them rested for the game, but most of all he wanted them to believe they were doing the exact right thing to prepare for it. That was the whole point—belief. Wooden told his players every day that they were in better shape than their opponents. Were they really? Maybe, maybe not. But in his mind, if they believed they were, then they were.

If there was a Holy Grail to be seized through all those routines and all those drills during all those hours of practice, it was this: balance. In every sense of the word. "The one word that my players will hear from me more than any other in practice is *balance*," Wooden said. "It can be mental balance. It can be emotional balance. It can be rebound balance. It can be defensive balance. It can be offensive balance, which is most important. So balance entails all things. You don't have a team without balance."

His quest for this grail could be compulsive. Wooden liked the scoring to be evenly distributed throughout his lineup. On defense, he insisted that his players' hands stay close to their bodies and their heads directly above the midpoint between the feet. He wanted their heads in the right place in a broader sense, as well. He lectured that their top priorities should be, in order, family, religion, school. Only then, if there was time left over, were they to concentrate on basketball. His practices were ultraserious—heaven forbid he should catch someone fooling around—but he balanced that by ending with something fun, like a free throw contest.

Wooden even wanted to see symmetry in the jersey numbers. (His own number back in Martinsville was 99. He was quite proud of that.) At UCLA, the guards wore their numbers in the 20s, the centers were in the 30s, the wings were in the 40s, and the forwards were in the 50s. He never issued a number like 31. "A three and one look off-balance, and I like balance," he said. Late in his career, Wooden boasted that he had charted 36,820 shots attempted by his players over a nineteen-year period at UCLA. His lineups generally featured two guards, two forwards, and one center. The guards combined to take 41.4 percent of the shots, the forwards took 39.4 percent, and the centers took 19.2 percent.

His use of language, which many of his players believed was his greatest asset, reflected his emphasis on balance. For example, he wanted passes to be crisp but not hard. His players should have fun but not be foolish; be spirited but not temperamental; be clever but not fancy; and above all else, move quickly without hurrying. He did not deliver inspirational pep talks, Knute Rockne–style. Sometimes he conducted his pregame meeting with the lights dimmed low. "I wanted the business-like approach covering the essentials and not try to get them all fired up," he said. "I wanted them ready when we started play and not to lose their fire warming up or in the dressing room."

The same held true for after games. Wooden did not conduct lengthy postgame meetings. If the Bruins won, he warned the players not to celebrate excessively. If they lost, he encouraged them not to "get their dobbers down." Either way, when they left the locker room, they should betray no indication of whether they had won or lost. "I never want my players to feel that winning a basketball game was any great accomplishment, and losing a basketball game was nothing to be dejected about," he said.

No wonder Ron Lawson said playing for Wooden felt like a job. He was hardly the first and wouldn't be the last. One of Wooden's few close friends in the profession was Stan Watts, who coached at BYU from 1949 to 1972. When asked if he could recall any humorous anecdotes about Wooden, Watts replied, "John's not the flippant type. He's pretty serious. He doesn't see much humor in basketball other than winning." That was why Wooden refused to play tournaments in Hawaii as most western coaches did. "I love to play those teams that just came back from Hawaii. I *love* to play 'em," he said. "That's when I'd like to play them all. I just don't think it's conducive to the development of your basketball team. I've had a lot of pressures put on me to go there. A lot of coaches use it for recruiting devices. I've had many players ask me, 'Are you going to go to Hawaii?' I tell them we're not, but we are going to go back to the Midwest."

Wooden could be brutally inflexible. In the days leading up to a season's first game, he would decide which seven players were going to comprise his rotation. (Sometimes he would choose eight, but most of the time he capped it at seven.) There might some tweaking along the way, but for the most part, once that decision was made, the rotation was set for good. After Wooden retired, a former player asked him what he did if his seventh- and eighth-best players were essentially equal. Wooden responded that he would pick one because either way he couldn't be wrong, even though it surely felt wrong to the player who wasn't chosen.

By the time he reached his fifties, Wooden had left most of his hotheadedness back in South Bend. His players marveled at his even temperament. He was a walking, breathing flat line. Sure, he occasionally lost his composure—an outburst here, a kick in the behind there. But the reason those moments are so memorable is that they were so rare. Not only could Wooden correct a player without screaming; he could sometimes do it without saying anything at all. He always maintained that a coach's best motivator was the bench. "If I see a boy giving up the baseline [on defense], I take him out for the rest of the half," he once said. "They don't like that."

Wooden's consistency amazed his players more than anything else about him. It was as if the man were a machine himself. "I played varsity for three years and observed him every day in practice. He never once disappointed me in terms of his demeanor, his speech," said Bob Archer, who played at UCLA from 1955 to 1959. "He was no-nonsense and strict, but he never humiliated people. There was always a kindness underneath his austere exterior. You can't fake that."

"The day before my last game as a senior, I ran the same drills I did as a freshman," Pete Blackman, another former player, said. "So over and over again, you were forced to do these precise things. He was very intense and uncompromising. He made it clear what he expected of you."

Bobby Pounds said it best: he was a man of actions, not statements. Wooden told his players not to use profanity, so he never used it himself. He asked them to quit smoking, so he did the same. He told them they were never to criticize a teammate—*That's my job, I'm paid to do it, pitifully poorly I might add*—and he wanted them always to be on time. (Time was of the essence. If you're on time, you don't have to hurry.) "There are lots of things I suggest my players do, and a few things I demand they do," he said. "They learn that I stick by my demands."

As long as Wooden stayed focused on the process, the small details, then he had faith that the big picture would come into focus. He never talked about the score, rarely mentioned the word "win." As long as his players reached their potential, well, there was no reason to get their dobbers down. "He was just a master teacher," Archer said. "He could have taught medicine. He could have taught carpentry. He could have taught English, and he would have done it the same way."

It wasn't always evident in the win-loss column, but Wooden learned a great deal during that first decade and a half at UCLA. He got a little better every day, and if his players matched his persistence, they got better, too. There was, however, a price they had to pay. To become a part of his program, a young man had to surrender his individuality, and that's not easy for a college student to do. When a player named Vince Carson decided to transfer, he told the *Los Angeles Times* that he was leaving because Wooden "handled the team like a machine. Everybody had a function, but he decided what each man would do and that was it." Carson intended the remark as criticism. Wooden considered it the ultimate compliment.

As was the case for many of Wooden's players, Willie Naulls's estimation of his former coach grew in the years after Naulls stopped playing for UCLA. Wooden may not have been the sensitive, attentive father figure Naulls had craved as a student, but he later came to appreciate how well

Wooden had taught him the game. After being selected by the St. Louis Hawks in the 1956 NBA draft, Naulls was traded to the New York Knicks, where he flourished as a professional. He would eventually become the first black man to be named captain of a major professional sports team.

One night in 1959, Naulls was with the Knicks in Philadelphia for a game against the Warriors. The preliminary game that night was a high school contest that included Overbrook High School, the legendary powerhouse that once boasted a gifted giant named Wilt Chamberlain. Naulls sat amazed as he watched Overbrook's point guard dart and dash through the defense. It wasn't just the young man's talent that caught Naulls's eye. It was his creativity, a flair that can only come through countless hours spent on an inner-city playground.

When Naulls inquired about the youngster, he grew even more impressed. The kid had terrific grades. He was student body president. His father was a minister. Naulls realized that not only would the youngster be the ideal spearhead for Wooden's fast break; he would fit nicely into the multihued culture at UCLA.

Naulls called Wooden to tell him about this young man. His name is Walt Hazzard, Naulls said. He was so convinced the kid could help that he told Wooden that if he didn't make the team, Naulls would pay for his tuition. Wooden told him that wouldn't be necessary. "If you say he can play here, that's good enough for me," Wooden said.

Hazzard was naturally thrilled that he had made such an impression on the famous Knickerbocker. For a young black basketball player in 1959, Willie Naulls was the ultimate role model. Even when Hazzard later learned that he didn't have enough academic credits to enroll at UCLA as a freshman, he was undeterred. He volunteered to attend junior college for a year instead of playing for a different four-year school.

Hazzard may have been a stranger from the East Coast when he alit in California in the fall of 1960, but he felt right at home—academically, socially, and especially athletically. He spent that first year at Santa Monica City College, and though he didn't play basketball for his school, he did compete in AAU games around the city. "The first time I saw him was during a summer league game. As soon as he began to perform, I realized that whatever I was doing wasn't basketball," said Larry Gower, a black guard from Los Angeles who was a freshman at UCLA that year. "His adjustment to L.A. was almost seamless. Walt was charismatic, and he could be a leader without really being pushy or arrogant."

To Hazzard, spin dribbles and behind-the-back passes were basic fundamentals. Needless to say, he was in for a rude awakening when he entered John Wooden's classroom. Besides being stylistically unpalatable, Hazzard's trickery gummed up the works in Wooden's machine. Balls bounced off his teammates' hands, their chests, even their heads. Oftentimes they flew straight out of bounds. "If you weren't ready, the ball would hit you in the face and you'd be embarrassed, and Walt would tell you he wasn't going to throw it to you anymore," said Dave Waxman, a junior center on that team. Even when Hazzard completed a pass that was fancy (as opposed to clever), it would earn a scolding from his coach. "When we first started scrimmaging, Walt threw a pass behind his back," Johnny Green said. "The guy caught it and laid it in, but Coach blew the whistle. 'Gracious sakes, Walter, come here! I don't approve of those behind-the-back passes!' Coach said that if you throw the ball and the guy's open but he drops it, I'm still going to blame you."

Hazzard respected Wooden, but he held his ground. He believed he knew some things about basketball that Wooden didn't. "Walt could look to his left and pass flawlessly to the right. But Coach Wooden felt that if you were going to pass to the right, you should be looking to the right," Gower said. "In many ways, Coach Wooden had to catch up to Walt, rather than the other way around."

Regardless of how frustrated Wooden was, there was little he could do. He simply did not have anyone else remotely as good. He made Hazzard a starter from day one. There may have been a period of adjustment, but for the most part his teammates enjoyed playing with him. "Walt really should be given a lot of credit for revitalizing the fast break, because he could bring the ball down quickly," Gary Cunningham said. "And if you got open, you got it, man. It was there." Johnny Green added: "I was glad Walt was there because if they made a basket and started pressing, I'd just give the ball to Walt and say, 'See ya down at the other end.'"

It helped that Hazzard was so easy to get along with. He had a buoyant, fun-loving personality. One of his favorite stunts was to throw himself to the ground in the middle of a crowd, lie there while everyone gathered around out of concern, and then pop up with a laugh. (He enjoyed faking people off the court, too.) He became the school's yell leader at football games. Next to playing ball, the one thing that Hazzard loved most was going to parties. "Walt came to L.A. at a time when the African American community was doing a very sedate version of the twist," Gower said. "Walt came in doing the version which had his arms going one way and his hips going another way. Immediately, people started watching him. Parties didn't really become parties until Walt came."

Around his basketball teammates, Hazzard was the same way. He played on their intramural softball team. He needled them and they needled him back. Green nicknamed him "East Coast." He was one of the guys, and he loved every minute of it.

With a new engine in town, every other player had to find his place in the machine. That would be especially challenging for the Bruins' undersized center, Fred Slaughter. A six-foot-five, 230-pound black sophomore from Topeka, Kansas, Slaughter was unusually fast for a man his size. He was the state champion in the 100-yard dash, and he had come to UCLA on a scholarship that was half track, half basketball. As a freshman in 1960–61, Slaughter had developed a fallaway jump shot that enabled him to score over taller defenders. He was the leading scorer and rebounder on a freshman team that compiled a 20–2 record.

Now that he was a sophomore on the varsity, however, Slaughter had to adapt to a different role. Wooden didn't need him to score but rather to defend and rebound, and most of all to pass the ball to Hazzard. Slaughter went along with it because he wanted to play, but he didn't get much explanation from Wooden. "Coach Wooden was interested in the guards. He didn't care about me," Slaughter said. "I didn't feel that Coach didn't like me. I was fine, but my relationship person-to-person wasn't as great with him as it was with Jerry Norman. Jerry used to work out with me and play defense against me. He brought the human, caring kind of things for me."

Slaughter and Hazzard, the two sophomores, rounded out a starting lineup that also included Gary Cunningham, Johnny Green, and Pete Blackman. That meant Wooden could get back to his racehorse ways. "We're a running club," he said before the 1961–62 season began. "Of course, we don't always bring the ball with us."

Expectations for the team were low, and the Bruins soon showed why, opening the season by losing back-to-back games to unranked BYU in Provo, Utah. The team then returned home for three games at the Sports Arena, winning the first two over Kansas and DePauw before falling to Colorado State, 69–68. The fans were unimpressed—just 1,902 showed up for the home opener—but the media was plenty taken with Walt Hazzard. The *Los Angeles Times* noted that after becoming "a bit conservative in recent years," the Bruins were "back in the running game" now that Hazzard was in charge. After the win over Kansas, the *Times* reported that Hazzard had "delighted the fans with his fancy passing and dribbling in the Bob Cousy manner."

(Wooden, incidentally, would not have considered this a compliment. Though he spoke highly of Cousy's gifts, Wooden often said the former Holy Cross star could never have played for him. "He was fancy. I think it's a good thing they didn't keep turnovers at the time he played," he said. "He had all the ability to play for me, but some of those long, behind-the-back passes I wouldn't have permitted at all.")

UCLA took a 2–3 record into its annual late December road trip. That season, Wooden added a wrinkle to the schedule. UCLA would begin with a game in Omaha, Nebraska, at Creighton, but instead of keeping his team in the Midwest, Wooden entered the Bruins in a two-day tournament in Texas called the Houston Holiday Classic.

That decision had ramifications he did not anticipate. The trouble started about a week before the Bruins were to leave California, when a few of the players received phone calls from strangers, some of whom claimed to represent the NAACP, asking them not to go. The callers warned that the city was a bastion of Jim Crow racism. The University of Houston's arena was said to be segregated. The players were warned of picket lines that would be filled with protesters who would not want black athletes in their city. "We got a lot of calls, especially Walt, from newspapers and folks saying, you know they will not allow Negroes to sit in any place in the arena. How do you feel about that?" Larry Gower said. "I lived a very insulated, privileged kind of life. My folks weren't rich, but I didn't really understand racism and discrimination fully."

The situation was just as unsettling for the white guys. "I remember getting a phone call from a student activist on campus asking me not to go on the trip," Dave Waxman said. "I was sympathetic, but I felt that whatever decision Hazzard and Slaughter made, I was going to support. They wanted to go and play the game."

At first, the players made light of the situation. When they boarded the plane to Houston following a 2-point loss at Creighton, Hazzard noticed that Johnny Green, his softball buddy, was wearing a cowboy hat. Hazzard asked why, and Green cracked, "When we get down there, I'm on *their* side." Hazzard thought it was hilarious.

Things were not so funny after they landed. Instead of heading for the hotel where the other teams were staying, the Bruins' bus took them to the University of Houston. They were going to be sleeping in campus dormitories. "I remember thinking, this is weird," Gower said. Wooden never explained why they were staying in a dorm. He didn't have to.

When the team got to the arena on game night, the players were relieved. Contrary to what they had been told, there were no picket lines out front. Nor was the arena segregated, though the black fans mostly sat together, as did the white fans. During warm-ups the black players were not taunted with racial epithets. Everyone assumed that once the opening tap arrived, it would be just another game.

They were wrong. During the first few minutes of UCLA's game against Houston, the officials repeatedly whistled Hazzard and Slaughter for personal fouls. The refs didn't even bother to pretend that the calls were fair. At one point, after yet another foul on Hazzard, Gower heard one of the Houston coaches shout to an official, "You're doing good! Now get the other one!" Pete Blackman said: "I didn't hear the refs say anything, but it was so obvious they weren't going to let Walt and Fred play. We were getting hosed."

It was never a game. Hazzard and Slaughter spent most of the second half on the bench, and UCLA lost, 91–65. Everyone was in too much shock to say much afterward. "I don't remember that Wooden said anything whatsoever," Gower said. "There was no comment after the game about what had gone on. There really wasn't a lot of comment on anybody's part."

The team went back to the dorm and slept. When the players gathered for breakfast the next morning, many of the white players felt trepidation. How would the black guys react? Would they be bitter? Crushed? Would they somehow hold their white teammates responsible? The season was already at a delicate juncture as the Bruins had now lost five of their first seven games, with the first four losses coming by a total 8 points. This trip threatened to tear the machine apart.

When Hazzard, Slaughter, and Gower came to breakfast, however, they showed none of those attitudes. Instead, they joked about what had happened. Their reaction punctured the tension. They made clear that in their minds, all of the players had suffered an injustice, not just the three of them. "They were unbelievable. I was shocked by what I had seen, but they just made a joke out of it," Blackman said. "Everybody knew it wasn't a joke, but they were making damn sure that their buddies on the UCLA team, who came from a different background, were included in the experience. Instead of being bitter or negative or withdrawn or any of the things they could have been, they were eighteen-year-old guys who said, Screw it. We're gonna hang together no matter what. And wasn't that a crazy experience?"

Wooden did not discuss what happened. Nor did he sit down with Hazzard and Slaughter to make sure their feelings weren't hurt. He did, however, make a change to his lineup. Shortly before UCLA took the floor the following evening against Texas A&M, Wooden informed the team that Hazzard and Slaughter would not be playing. "We thought it was a powerful gesture," Blackman said. "And then we went out and played a hell of a game."

Angry and inspired by what had happened to their teammates the night before, the Bruins took their frustration out on the Aggies. The game was still close midway through the second half, but UCLA broke things open over the last six minutes to win, 81–71, behind 22 points each from Green and Cunningham. The players felt enormous gratification. As they exited the locker room, Blackman, who considered himself quite the poet, left behind a few verses that he had etched onto the blackboard. The last one read: "*They laid me out upon the rack/And only half my name is black.*"

The accounts from local newspapers in Houston made no reference to the way UCLA's black players had been treated. They didn't even report Wooden's lineup change. However, the press corps in Los Angeles was more inquisitive. When the Bruins returned home, the local sportswriters noticed that Hazzard and Slaughter were missing from the Texas A&M box score. When asked to explain it at the weekly writers' luncheon three days later, Wooden insisted that there had been "no incidents" in Houston. "My feeling was that we'd be better off not playing them that night," he said. "The boys told me after the game they were pleased I didn't play them." Wooden added that "there was no segregated seating, no picket lines, and no cat calls." Though the *Los Angeles Times* revealed that "prior to the trip, considerable pressure was brought on the Bruins by various groups and individuals, urging Wooden not to play his Negro players in Houston," the coach himself "indicated he didn't care to enter into any racial discussions."

Wooden was doing more than just avoiding a controversial topic. He was lying. It was one thing to sidestep a public discussion on race when he was coaching in Indiana in 1948, but he was now living in a time when the issue of how blacks were being treated in America had become an important topic in the nation's political and cultural discourse. Wooden had been presented with a rare opportunity to advance the cause of justice, but he chose not to do so, ignoring once again the power of his own words. Who, exactly, was he protecting? His black players? The racist referees?

Blackman saw Wooden's evasions as being consistent with his "dedication to non-pretension," but in this instance it was also an abdication of responsibility. If Wooden really wanted to help his black players, he would have spoken out against what happened to them in Houston, but he didn't do so, out of fear that it might disrupt his little machine.

And yet Wooden's black players did not begrudge his decision. In their eyes, he had spoken quite clearly through his actions. "I can't think of any of the African American players who played for him who would do anything less than revere John Wooden for what he tried to do," Gower said. "We understood that with his background, he wouldn't be as tuned in to the African American experience as someone who came from a more mixed community. He wasn't going to know who James Brown was, or the difference between the SCLC and the SNCC. But that was all right. You cut him some slack because you knew he was sincere."

Racial problems aside, UCLA's trip to Houston proved to be invaluable from a basketball perspective. It was an uncomfortable experience, but it was one that the players had gone through together, and it helped break down some of the barriers between them. "It took our group to another planet in terms of how well we played together. He welded us," Blackman said. For his part, Wooden was just glad it was over. When asked at the press luncheon whether he intended to bring his team back to Houston soon, Wooden answered no. But, he added, "that doesn't mean we won't play there eventually."

17

"Don't Be a Homer!"

"Pressure, self-inflicted, is closing in on UCLA basketball coach John Wooden. A monster of his own making, a record of never experiencing a losing season as a college coach, is in jeopardy. . . ."

Those ominous words appeared at the beginning of an article published in the *Los Angeles Times* on January 25, 1962. Under the headline "Wooden's Record Faces Pitfalls," Mal Florence raised the horrifying specter that Wooden might coach a sub-.500 team. At the time, the Bruins owned a 7–7 overall record and were 3–0 in conference play, yet Florence surmised that "eight of UCLA's remaining 11 games are with teams which, on paper, at least, figure to beat the Bruins." That included Texas Tech, the defending Southwest Conference champion, which was coming to town to face UCLA on consecutive nights at Santa Monica City College.

The team had larger issues than a sportswriter's pessimism. Back in December, three days after returning home from Houston, UCLA had played in the third annual Los Angeles Basketball Classic, a three-day, eight-team tournament at the Sports Arena that had drawn its most prestigious field yet. Five of the teams were ranked in the top twelve of the Associated Press poll, including No. 1 Ohio State. Unranked UCLA beat Army in its first game, advancing to play the Buckeyes in the next round.

Walt Hazzard relished the opportunity to go up against the Buckeyes' All-American forward, Jerry Lucas, but the evening did not go as Hazzard hoped. The trouble started earlier in the day, when Hazzard missed the pregame meal. After arriving at the arena, Hazzard tried to explain to Wooden that he had gotten stuck in traffic, but the coach would have none of it. He informed Hazzard that he would not start against Ohio State. Wooden inserted Hazzard into the game midway through the first half, but by then, the Buckeyes were cruising to victory behind Lucas's 30 points and 30 rebounds. The next evening would see the title game between USC and Ohio State, with UCLA relegated to the third-place game against Utah. This time Hazzard started, but Wooden quickly grew displeased with his star player's showboating style and yanked him again. "He was screaming and yelling at me," Hazzard recalled many years later. "I didn't like anyone yelling at me. I was as sensitive as anyone."

UCLA lost, 88–79, to drop to 4–7. The Bruins were scheduled to have a week off for the Christmas holiday before their next game. That gave Hazzard and Wooden some badly needed time apart, but the break also gave Hazzard the chance to go home and stew. After spending a few days in Philadelphia, he decided he did not want to return to Los Angeles.

Hazzard called his mentor and friend, Willie Naulls, to inform him of his decision. Since Naulls was the one who had brokered Hazzard's recruitment to UCLA, he felt obligated to offer to contact other schools on Walt's behalf. But Naulls also told Hazzard of the similar period of adjustment he had gone through with Wooden, and he advised Hazzard to stick it out. Hazzard also told his father he wanted to transfer, but unbeknown to him, Wooden had already called his father before he benched Hazzard for the Ohio State game. When Hazzard told his dad that he wanted to quit, the reverend's advice was firm. Go back to Los Angeles, he told his son. Play ball. Get good grades. And do whatever the man says.

Hazzard did as his father instructed, and the new year began with some promise. UCLA opened conference play with a two-game sweep of Washington at home and then knocked off Cal in Berkeley by 11 points. And yet the local fans had seen this movie many times before. Wooden's Bruins always pulled off delightful wins in January and February, but when they moved to a bigger stage in March, they got outclassed by some other West Coast outfit—USC, Oregon State, Cal, San Francisco, whatever. That was the underlying message of Florence's article. It wasn't just about the possibility Wooden's team might lose more games than it won. It was about the growing sense that too often his teams were good enough to raise expectations but not good enough to meet them. "Wooden has dribbled himself into a corner," Florence concluded. "Maybe that's the price of success, John."

The losing season never happened, primarily because Hazzard breathed new life into Wooden's old fast break. The quicker tempo unleashed Johnny Green and Gary Cunningham as the prolific scorers they were meant to be, and it allowed UCLA to surge during the last two months of the season. The Bruins shocked Texas Tech in Santa Monica, winning both games by 29 points each, and followed those victories with a 73–59 upset of fifth-ranked USC at the Sports Arena behind Green's 28 points. After the Bruins beat Stanford, 82–64, on February 10, they brought their perfect 5–0 record in the AAWU (or the "Big Five," as it was coming to be called) to their two-game series with USC.

It was customary for a USC-UCLA game to be accompanied by some controversy, but this time it came from an unusual source: Wooden himself. During the first half of the Bruins' upset of USC two weeks earlier, some sideline observers had heard USC cocaptain Ken Stanley yelling, "Lay off of me!" at Wooden as he ran past the UCLA bench. According to Florence, "Wooden had been needling Stanley for allegedly overguarding Gary Cunningham." The issue of Wooden's "bench jockeying tactics," as Florence called them, had been quietly smoldering for many years. When it was raised at the weekly writers' luncheon preceding the USC series, Wooden stood his ground. "I've been singled out, and I sort of question the fairness of this," he said. "I definitely feel I've acted within the bounds of decency. I certainly don't demonstrate to the crowd like other coaches."

Wooden's rough treatment of officials may have been familiar to basketball people along the West Coast, but until then it was largely unknown to the public. It grated on his rivals to know that his private behavior was so at odds with his public persona. "Dallmar and Newell used to tell me that Wooden had this purist image that wasn't exactly accurate," said Dan Hruby, who covered the Bay Area schools for the *San Jose Mercury News*. "Wooden would sit there with his rolled-up program, kind of cover his mouth. When an official made a bad call and ran by him, Wooden would yell at him using some pretty choice terms. Then he'd smile and wave and everybody would say, there's good old Saint John."

The truth is, Wooden had been jockeying from the bench ever since he was a high school coach, but it was jarring when other people, especially his own players, first discovered this side of his personality. "I had been practicing for him for almost two months before we had our first game," Johnny Green said. "Then I get out there and I hear him yelling at a referee who was one of his favorite targets. 'Come on, Joe, that was a foul! Start calling 'em at both ends!' I went, Whoa, where did that come from? That's one thing that really surprised me."

That intensity belied the scholarly pose Wooden struck on the sideline. As the players sped back and forth in front of him, he would squirm in his seat, crossing and uncrossing his legs, clutching that rolled-up program in his hand. He often said the program served as a convenient place to jot notes, but it also doubled as a megaphone. His barbs were frequent, precise, and cutting—but never profane. During a typical exchange, a writer sitting courtside heard Wooden bark, "Dadburn it, Joe, you saw him double dribble down there! Goodness gracious sakes alive, everybody in the place saw that!"

Wooden believed this was not only appropriate but an integral part of his job. "I want my players to know I'm behind them," he said. He also insisted his sideline behavior was no worse—and probably much better—than that of a lot of other coaches. "I don't stand up and do anything to excite the crowd. That's one of the worst things coaches can do," he said. "I don't say, 'You're a homer!' I'll say, 'Don't be a homer!' I'll say, 'See 'em the same at both ends!' I'll say, 'Watch the traveling,' or some such." Furthermore, Wooden added, "No official, no player has ever heard me use a word of profanity. . . . Of course, I have told referees that I couldn't tell their tops from their bottoms, which is almost as bad as swearing."

Wooden believed the criticism directed at him on this front was way out of proportion. "I don't say I keep quiet. I needle, in a soft-sell way," he said. "I don't mean to be questioning their integrity. And yet when I say, 'Don't be a homer,' am I questioning their integrity? I don't think so because it's a subconscious thing. And I think if you can get 'em thinking about it, they'll be less likely to be swayed by the home crowd."

Wooden's close friend and former assistant, Ed Powell, witnessed countless moments when Wooden pulled his Jekyll-and-Hyde act in an effort to manipulate the refs. "Usually, some time in the first half, he would choose one incident, a close call, and jump all over the referee," Powell said. "Just chew him out in, if there is such a thing, a gentlemanly manner. But let him know that side of Wooden. Then the half comes. During the half, as they're walking to the lockers, he'll seek out the referee and apologize to him. 'I know it was a close call. Regardless of whether I thought you were right, it's a job, and you're doing the best you can.' And Wooden in a nice meek-like manner would walk away. Now this fellow has a chance during the halftime to give it some thought. He has seen Wooden in a rage, and he has seen him in a very friendly-like manner. This works on him to the extent that the second half, if a similar situation arises where it's a close call, he will say, 'Do I want to meet this Wooden or do I want to meet that one?' And chances are he'll call the play in Wooden's favor."

Wooden's halftime routine became so established that one veteran league official, Bill Bussenius, sometimes loitered by the scorer's table to avoid the confrontation. "Wooden was no saint," Bussenius said. "There were just two doors in the old Westwood gym, and he'd wait for you by one and give it to you when you came out." Another former PCC ref added, "I've seen him so mad that I've been afraid he'd pop that big blood vessel in his forehead. But I've never heard him curse."

Wooden was especially rabid in his early years at UCLA when he was trying to get the program established. "He was sort of a tiger when he came into the league, but that was in the days when he was trying to make his mark," said Al Lightner, another veteran West Coast official. "I would think that any referee who does not command the respect of John Wooden can expect to be tested." During one game, Wooden became so enraged at the officials that he refused to bring his team out of the locker room for the second half. "The athletic director of the other school came in and talked to me," he said. "Eventually, I went on with the game."

Wooden also developed a habit of bringing a stopwatch to the games in hopes of gaining an advantage with the enforcement of the rule requiring teams to bring the ball past half court within ten seconds. He believed that if the referees knew he was keeping track of the time, they might count a little more quickly. "I'll let them see that I have it there, before the game starts. When I'm talking to them, they may see I have the stopwatch in my hand," he said. Not surprisingly, Pete Newell was one of Wooden's more outspoken critics in this area. "I guess John felt that by badgering the officials and really making them conscious of him, he'd have a better chance of winning the game," Newell said. "Heaven knows he was successful, and maybe it helped him, but I don't think from an educational viewpoint it's the way to coach basketball or coach anything."

The exchange with Ken Stanley revealed another habit of Wooden's that was even less sporting: he razzed opposing players. He often confessed that it was "the thing I may be ashamed of more than anything else." But he still found it useful. "I talk to players to try to get them thinking about [me], hoping it would get them off their game," he said.

In his autobiography *They Call Me Coach*, Wooden admitted to calling Stanley a "butcher." Another former USC player, Ken Flower, who played for the Trojans from 1950 to 1953, remembered Wooden as a "constant intimidator" when it came to opposing players. "I was surprised at how vocal he was," Flower said. "I don't remember another coach in high school, junior college, or college who was like that. It was ongoing chatter. He was trying to be bothersome."

To the outside world, this may have been the most arresting discovery of all. After a UCLA victory over Stanford in 1955, the *San Francisco Chronicle* reported that "the Stanfords were at a complete loss about the ethics they say were employed by Wooden from the coaching bench when he allegedly yelled such phrases as 'You butcher!' and 'Go cry to the ref!' at the Stanford cocaptain. That comes as a complete surprise to us because we know the Bruin coach to be a mild mannered, amiable gentleman. It could easily prove a case of mistaken identity, although the Indians say, 'No.'"

Former Cal guard Earl Schulz said that Wooden especially liked to yell at opposing players while they were trying to shoot free throws. "He was just obnoxious," Schulz said. "He'd dig you a bit, and then hopefully you made both foul shots so you could smile at him when you ran down the court." Walt Hazzard, who had done his fair share of trash talking on the Philadelphia playgrounds, described his coach as having an "antiseptic needle. It's clean but biting, and it hurts."

In the years after he retired, this aspect of Wooden's personality was often whitewashed, inconsistent as it was with his "Saint John" image. To those who played for him and coached against him, however, it was very much a part of the man they knew. Late in his life, Wooden conceded that these memories made him uncomfortable. "I'm not always proud when I think about the way I bothered officials," he said in 2006. "I'd say, 'Don't be a homer!' Well, what am I really saying? I'm telling him he *is* being a homer. 'Call it the same at both ends.' Well, that means he isn't. I try and think how I would feel if I was an official and someone said that. I'm sure I wouldn't have liked it."

Wooden's decorum was again a topic after UCLA suffered its first conference loss of the 1961–62 season on February 16, to USC. A technical foul was called on the Bruin bench, but Wooden insisted afterward he was not the offender. "I was on my feet only once while the other side was up twelve times," he said.

Despite that loss, the Bruins were ready to kick into higher gear. Sometimes, if the team fell behind, Wooden deployed a full-court pressure defense, which resurrected the late flourishes that had characterized his early teams in Westwood. During a game at Washington on March 2, the

Bruins found themselves trailing by 14 points midway through the second half. They rallied behind the press and won by 3.

After Hazzard returned from almost quitting the team over Christmas, he and Wooden came to an understanding, but that did not mean Wooden went easy on him. In fact, Wooden figured out that Hazzard responded better to harsh criticism than he did to gentle praise. So Wooden came at Hazzard, again and again and again, and each time Hazzard's play improved.

With the coach and his point guard learning to coexist, the machine was refined. Hazzard was the humming engine, and though he could score almost at will, he understood that his primary function was to distribute the ball to the sharp-shooting wheels, Green and Cunningham. ("His passes off the break are uncanny," Florence wrote. "It's a shame assists don't show up in the box score.") Fred Slaughter rebounded and played defense, while Pete Blackman was the erudite senior wing who provided leadership on and off the court. Even Wooden was surprised at how well things were coming together. "This group comes as close to attaining maximum efficiency as a team as any group I've coached," he said. "They don't attempt to do each other's job. They've meshed together a lot better than I had expected."

By the time UCLA reached the final weekend of the 1961–62 regular season, it had already sewn up its first conference title since Willie Naulls was a senior. After the Bruins clinched the league title by overcoming a 12-point second-half deficit to win at Washington, they were so exuberant in the postgame locker room that a couple of players got the idea to throw Wooden in the shower. "I wouldn't do that, boys," Norman said. They didn't.

UCLA's first opponent in the NCAA tournament's West Regional was Utah State. The Bruins built a commanding first-half lead, but when it was cut to 2 points with five minutes to play, Wooden ordered Hazzard to stall. Wooden wasn't much for showboating, but Hazzard's Globetrotter impression had been an effective weapon throughout the season, much as Wooden's own trickery had been during his playing days. With the crowd whooping its approval, Hazzard managed by himself to play keep-away from the Aggies for a full three minutes, helping UCLA to a 73–62 win. It had taken him fourteen long years, but Wooden had finally secured his first NCAA tournament victory.

Next up was Oregon State. The Beavers had ended several UCLA seasons in the past, but this time they were no match as the Bruins won handily, 88–69. UCLA was heading to the NCAA semifinals for the first time in its history.

The tournament would climax in Louisville, Kentucky, where the Bruins' semifinal opponent was Cincinnati, which had won the NCAA championship the year before under its first-year head coach, Ed Jucker. The Bearcats possessed just as much speed as the Bruins, but they would have a size advantage inside, in the form of six-foot-nine center Paul Hogue. "We won't be able to run on Cincinnati like we did Oregon State," Wooden said the day before.

UCLA had encountered taller teams all season long but never before in such an intimidating environment. With more than 18,000 fans packed into Freedom Hall, the Bruins were rattled as they found themselves trailing 18–4 in the early going. They fought back to earn a 37–37 tie at halftime and stayed within striking distance throughout the second half, despite the fact that Hogue was having his way with Slaughter en route to scoring a game-high 36 points.

With the score knotted at 70-all heading into the final two minutes, Wooden again ordered Hazzard to play keep-away and then try to get the ball to Cunningham for the last shot. This time the strategy backfired when Hazzard was whistled for charging into Cincinnati guard Tom Sizer. "Hazzard faked the guy and the guy fell down, and Hazzard got called for charging. I'll remember that one forever," Wooden said many years later. That gave the Bearcats the ball with 1:34 to play.

Now it was Jucker's turn to stall. Cincinnati held on to the ball until there were ten seconds remaining, whereupon Jucker called time-out to set up a final play. When the game resumed, the Bearcats swung the ball to Tom Thacker, a six-foot-two junior guard. Thacker had not made a basket all game, but with time winding down, he was forced to launch a twenty-foot jump shot. Swish. There was just enough time for a desperate heave from Hazzard, but it was deflected out of bounds, and Cincinnati escaped with a thrilling 72–70 victory.

The UCLA players were devastated by the loss, but in the postgame locker room they heard only encouraging words from their coach. "I remember him saying how very proud he was of the progress the team had made," Pete Blackman said. "We had come together in such an odd way. We were 4–7 and yet we almost won it all."

Indeed, this team had come a long way from the previous November. The Bruins had endured tension between their best player and their coach, had gone through the crucible of Houston, and had hit their stride at just the right time, a finely tuned machine that got more powerful with each passing week. No Wooden-coached team had ever achieved more "success"—by his definition, anyway. "He never liked the word *over-achiever*," Blackman said. "He said you can only achieve."

Once again, Wooden's "boys" had demonstrated the power of that idea. Once again, they had no trophy to show for it. The pressure, self-inflicted, would continue to build.

18

Gail

Having finally tasted success in the NCAA tournament, UCLA's basketball program was well positioned to keep its momentum. Thanks to a series of bond issues from the state of California, as well as matching federal funds and other gifts, UCLA found itself in the fall of 1962 with $150 million to invest in new facilities. That included the on-campus basketball arena that Wooden had been promised when he interviewed for the job in 1948. The unbuilt structure even had a name: the UCLA Memorial Activities Center, which would be dedicated to students who had lost their lives in World War II. This was real progress.

The initiative was part of a citywide construction boom that was undertaken to keep up with population growth. Los Angeles's high schools were teeming with athletes, and while as a general rule Wooden did not like to attend high school games, he usually made an exception for the city play-offs. That's how Wooden came to be watching John H. Francis Polytechnic High School play a tournament game in early 1959.

Wooden was there to check out a few notable players, but there was one guard on the Poly High team who kept catching his eye. His name was Gail Goodrich, a junior. He stood just five-foot-seven, 140 pounds, but he was crafty, a lefty, and Wooden was taken by the way he sliced through the defense and scored at will. "We ought to watch that player," he said to Jerry Norman. "If he grows, I'd love to have him."

Wooden felt a tap on his shoulder. "Did you really mean that?" a woman asked.

When Wooden said yes, the woman told him, "That's my son."

Poly lost the game, but afterward, Wooden introduced himself to Goodrich and invited him to visit a UCLA practice. The kid was stunned. "I couldn't understand why," Goodrich said. "Would I grow? Would I be big enough?"

Having been a small player himself, Wooden understood how grit and guile could overcome physical shortcomings. Those traits were built into Goodrich's DNA. His father, Gail Sr., had been a captain on USC's basketball team in 1939, and Gail spent most of his childhood obsessed with the game. His mother, Jean, complained that "he'd dribble the ball through the house so much that I thought he'd drive me out of my mind."

As it turned out, Goodrich did grow a couple of inches during his senior year of high school, as he led Poly to the city title and was named the city's high school player of the year. His father's alma mater tried to swoop in at the last minute, but by then it was too late. Goodrich was dead set on going to UCLA. He needed to clear a few academic hurdles before he could enroll, so he didn't arrive on campus until February 1961. That was too late for Goodrich to play basketball, but he did suit up that spring for UCLA's baseball team. Thus, it was on the diamond, not the hardwood, that he first encountered Wooden's competitiveness. "He would sit right behind home plate and ride the umpire the whole game," Goodrich said. "'You sure about that call? Looked a bit outside to me. You watching the same game I am?' He thought it was part of the game."

Goodrich joined UCLA's freshman basketball team the following fall. That was the first year the school staged an official contest between the freshmen and the varsity before the regular season began. The freshmen lost by only 6 points that day, and they went on to enjoy an undefeated season. His academic deficiencies aside—"My first two years I was the king of the poor students," he admitted—Goodrich had a grand old time. He would soon discover, however, that playing on the varsity was a lot different, and a lot less fun.

In the first place, he would have to adjust to playing alongside Walt Hazzard. "I was used to having the ball in my hands," Goodrich said. The glut of perimeter players prompted Wooden to assign Goodrich to play forward next to the undersized center, Fred Slaughter. It was a big job for such a little man. Goodrich thought it was a bad fit.

Goodrich also did not handle criticism well. If Wooden chastised him, Goodrich would pout. Wooden recognized this immediately. Though Goodrich later said, "You've never been ripped until he's ripped you," Wooden did his best to soften his words. Sometimes, when he wanted to get a message through to Goodrich, Wooden would address his critique to the entire team. For example, one day after Goodrich had missed a few too many classes, Wooden delivered a stern lecture to the entire team about the importance of academics. When he was through, one of

Goodrich's teammates said to him, "That speech was for you." As Goodrich recalled, "He would say during a time-out, 'We're getting a little away from our offense.' That was his way of telling me, 'You've done enough.'"

This was completely different from how Wooden treated Hazzard. While Wooden would verbally pat Goodrich gently on the back, his barbs at Hazzard would come, in Wooden's words, "a little lower and a little harder." Hazzard noticed the difference, and it bothered him so much that he wondered whether race might be a factor. "I didn't agree with the way he approached me, as opposed to the way he approached Gail," Hazzard said. "There was a difference, a very implicit kind of thing. It has to do with perceptions. I don't think [Wooden] saw color, but I don't think he would be ecstatic if his daughter married a black man."

Hazzard might not have been so suspicious of Wooden's motives had he known the coach better. That was part of the problem. Hazzard knew Wooden, but he didn't really *know* Wooden. Very few people did. Wooden told his players he loved them and called them his "boys," but the contours of his personality did not come gushing forth. Instead, he chose to reveal himself little by little, drip by drip.

For example, Hazzard discovered during his junior season in 1962–63 that his ultraserious coach had a quirky side. Just as the team was about to take the court for a game, Wooden offered Hazzard a piece of gum. The Bruins won, so Wooden did the exact same thing the next game, and the next. As long as the team kept winning, the ritual remained the same. Just before tip-off Wooden would walk over to Hazzard, reach into his pocket, take out a stick of gum, remove the wrapper, hand it to Hazzard, and pat him on the butt. "The man was one of the most superstitious people I ever met," Hazzard said.

Wooden indulged in lots of rituals like that. The pregame routine he had established with Nell at Martinsville High had evolved over the years. Now, just as each game was about to tip off, Wooden went through the same progression: pull up his socks, spit on the floor, rub the spit with his foot, rub his hands together, pat his assistant on the leg. Only then would he turn around and flash the "okay" sign to his bride. "John has been doing it for so many years now that I don't think the referee could get up steam to blow the whistle if John failed to go through with it," Nell said. "Of course, it's all very silly."

Silly? John Wooden? Well, how else would one describe his incessant habit of sticking hairpins into wood? Wooden first got the idea when he read that the old St. Louis Cardinals baseball teams did it. From that day forward, any time he spied a hairpin on the ground, Wooden picked it up and inserted it into the nearest slab of wood, usually a tree. Nell confessed that sometimes on game day she would purposely drop a hairpin in his path. Likewise, whenever Wooden found a coin on the ground, he would place it in his left shoe for the remainder of the day. "You can keep it, but you must never spend it. And that brings you luck. Oh I know it does," he said. He kept in his pocket a smooth rock, which he called his "Indian worry stone." And both he and Nell carried small metal crosses that were given to them by a minister right before John went into the navy. Those crosses had proved their power. He lived through the war, didn't he?

Indeed, Wooden's experience during World War II taught him to appreciate capricious good fortune. After all, if it weren't for that inflamed appendix, it could have been him, not his college buddy, who died on the USS *Franklin*. Wooden survived a similar brush with death many years later. He had been scheduled to attend a coaches' clinic in North Carolina, but he postponed his departure from a Saturday to a Sunday. The connecting flight he was supposed to take crashed between Atlanta and Raleigh. Everybody aboard was killed.

Whenever UCLA got on a winning streak, Wooden kept everything the same. He wore the same suit over and over. The menu for the pre-game meal never changed. "I don't think I ever looked at it as being superstitious," Wooden said. "Subconsciously, certain rituals may give you a little more peace, a little more calmness, a little more serenity. If you have a feeling that doing a certain thing is going to be helpful to you, then it probably will be."

Wooden was full of such odd revelations. The players quickly figured out just how much he loved westerns. Whenever the team was on a road trip, Wooden usually took them to see one in a movie theater. On a bus ride or team plane, he could be found flipping through a paperback from that genre. The players knew that on Tuesday nights, practice would end a little early because the coach wanted to make sure he got home in time to watch *Wyatt Earp* on television. He loved it when the good guys won.

He wasn't funny, but he could be witty. When he cracked wise, it was often at someone else's expense. "He made fun of you in a way that sliced you up and made everybody laugh but didn't kill you," said another former player, Bill Johnston. Wooden was also quick on his feet. As the team was traveling through an airport one day, Wooden was leafing through a magazine and came across a centerfold of a scantily clad woman. He turned and discovered a group of players smirking at him. "Look," he said, pointing to the page. "Blue shoes."

Then there were the many occasions when Wooden surprised his boys with his prowess at the pool table. The players could not believe this teetotaling goody-goody was so proficient at a game that was usually played in dingy bars. "We used to play snooker down at the bowling alley. I thought I was a decent player at it," Denny Crum said. "When he found out, we went over to the student union. It was unbelievable how good he was. You would've never known he played a game like that." Pete Blackman likewise recalled a trip to the Midwest when the players were shooting some stick and Wooden happened by. "Somebody said, 'Here, Coach, give it a try.' He ran the table," Blackman said.

Wooden did not boast of his exploits at billiards any more than he bragged about his accomplishments as a basketball player. The only glimpses the players saw of the India Rubber Man came through an occasional demonstration in practice. When Wooden put on a shooting exhibition, the players laughed at his antiquated form, but darn if that ball didn't keep going in. During a team meal one night, as the players regaled each other with tales of their toughness, Wooden let drip a piece of his past. "You know," he told them, "one time when I was playing pro ball, the referee threw the ball for the center jump, and the two centers punched each other. Didn't even bother going for the ball." That ended the conversation.

Wooden could be just as eloquent in the things he didn't say. He did his best to live by his father's admonition never to speak poorly of someone else. One day, Wooden was talking to a local newspaper columnist about a former UCLA player who had recently fathered a child out of wedlock and been sent to jail. The columnist disparaged the young man for a few minutes and then asked the coach what he knew of him. "I understand he's a good father," Wooden said.

The main reason Wooden's players didn't know him better is that there were so few opportunities to spend time with him away from the court. "They had my home phone number, but for the most part they didn't come to our home," Wooden said. If a player wanted to get to know Wooden better, it helped to have a common interest. Stan Andersen barely got off the bench when he was on Wooden's teams in 1958–59 and 1959–60, but he frequently ran into the coach while he was reading quietly by himself in a Westwood bookstore. "I was an avid reader. I probably talked to him more often in the bookstore than I did on the court," Andersen said. "He recommended to me a book on photography, which I really enjoyed. When we played at the Sports Arena, I'd want to ride in the car with Wooden just to get into conversation. For me, his biggest strength was his intellect."

It was for that reason that Wooden liked to proctor his players' exams on road trips. He could have delegated that task to an assistant, but by doing it himself, he was showing his players how deeply he valued education. He was also interested in what they were studying. After proctoring an English literature exam one night, he asked the players what they had written about. They told him it was a poem that included the word *diadem*, but none of them knew what that word meant. "He told us what it was," Johnston said. "It's a crown, and you couldn't elaborate on the poem unless you knew what the hell it was. So we learned vocabulary from the UCLA basketball coach."

Wooden operated in a jock culture that was addled by cigarettes and liquor, yet he was the straightest of straight arrows. It was not easy to relax around a man who was so rigid. "There were people who didn't like John very much because he was a little bit austere, a little bit removed," said Bob Murphy, a longtime radio broadcaster for Stanford. "He was very polite and somewhat withdrawn, but he was always very thoughtful."

Wooden's program was an extension of that straight arrow. He wanted his players looking clean-cut and clean-shaven. He conducted impromptu spot checks on their lockers because he wanted "to see they're not getting slovenly." (Though first he had to teach them what *slovenly* meant.) He did not want gum wrappers or wads of tape lying around. If the players didn't throw their orange juice cartons in a trash can, he would refuse to give them juice for a couple of days. Wooden loved to brag about how often he received compliments at the way his boys had left their locker room so clean.

By the early 1960s, Wooden had been teaching basketball for nearly thirty years, and he had many former players who were husbands and fathers, lawyers and doctors, businessmen and teachers and ministers. If they wanted to get to know their old college coach better, they found that he was far more emotionally available than he had been during their playing days. This was especially true of the former players who became teachers themselves. When Wooden's first star player at UCLA, George Stanich, told him that he wanted to go into education, Wooden sat next to him on a flight to a road game and filled several sheets on a legal pad with suggestions. After Stanich graduated, Wooden spent an entire day driving him sixty miles each way to interview with the superintendent of schools in Oxnard, California. Stanich didn't get that job, but he later became a basketball coach at a local junior college. Every few years, he would find himself in a bind that would prompt him to call on Wooden. "He never gave me the answer to my questions, but he gave me situations that he had experienced that were similar and told me how he dealt with them," Stanich said. "On my way home, I would know what I had to do."

Another of Wooden's first players at UCLA, Barry Porter, joined his staff briefly as a freshman coach. "If I would ask him something, he would invariably ask me what I thought first, to get my point of view," Porter said. "He was truly interested in me and wanted to learn." Later, when Porter left coaching and started his own carpet cleaning business, Wooden was one of his first customers.

Wooden's memory was incredible. He never forgot a name or a face, and he could spit out details of games that his players had long forgotten. If a former player wrote him a letter, Wooden wrote back. If someone wanted to have lunch, Wooden found the time. If a player asked him to speak somewhere, the answer was always yes. And if one of them happened to show up at a UCLA game, he was treated like royalty. "One day after I graduated, I went to the Sports Arena and walked in on the team at halftime," said Mike Hibler, who played center at UCLA from 1951 to 1954. "I wasn't sure if I should be there, but he welcomed me in when he was giving his speech. That's just how he was. He *loved* his boys."

"We're going to try to get on the break and run like we did in the old days," Wooden said in the fall of 1962. His Bruins were beginning the season with a rare dollop of respect: *Sports Illustrated* ranked UCLA No. 17 in its preseason college basketball issue. The magazine asserted that "if UCLA is going to have problems, it will be up front," but the presence of Walt Hazzard warranted the ranking. "He has the ability to hit men who don't even realize they're open," Wooden said.

Besides the promotion of Gail Goodrich and another heralded guard from Los Angeles, Freddie Goss, from the undefeated freshman team, Wooden received an unexpected gift from George Stanich. Now the coach at El Camino College, a nearby junior college, Stanich had reached out to Jerry Norman to let him know he had a player named Keith Erickson who might be able to help. The kid couldn't shoot a lick, but he was as gifted an athlete as Stanich had ever coached. Since Erickson was also a terrific baseball player, Norman arranged for him to come to UCLA on a half-baseball, half-basketball scholarship. "That way if I didn't make it in either sport, neither would lose a full scholarship," Erickson said. "That's how much confidence they had in me."

Erickson's real passion, however, was volleyball. He grew up by the ocean in the town of El Segundo, and he spent much of his free time at the beach. With all this energy devoted to sports, Erickson had little time— and even less interest—left over for academics. He often joked that he majored in eligibility. Erickson liked to goof around in practice, but while Wooden got mad at him a lot, he rarely stayed that way. "I'm very fond of Keith," Wooden said. "I like spirited basketball players."

Besides, Wooden had another new player who was giving him even bigger headaches. Jack Hirsch was a spindly, Jewish, six-foot-three forward who had spent his childhood on the hardscrabble streets of Brooklyn's Bedford-Stuyvesant neighborhood. When Hirsch was fifteen, his father moved the family to California, where he became wealthy through his ownership of a chain of bowling alleys. By the time Hirsch was a senior at Van Nuys High School, he was an all-city basketball player who planned on attending Cal State University in Northridge, but he was encouraged by his father to visit UCLA. When Norman brought Hirsch into the men's gym in the spring of 1960 to meet the head coach, Hirsch was not impressed. "He was mopping the floors," Hirsch said. "My first thought was, God, he's an old man."

The old man was equally unimpressed. Wooden got one look at Hirsch's wispy frame, took measure of his cocky attitude, and decided on the spot that he wasn't fit for UCLA. "Come back to me when you're ready," Wooden said. Hirsch was livid. "I walked out of there and said, I'm going to show him. He'll see what kind of player I am."

After spending a year at Los Angeles Valley College in Van Nuys, where he played center and averaged 28 points per game, Hirsch was inclined to quit school and go into the family business, but his father cajoled him into going to UCLA by promising to quit smoking cigarettes. (Hirsch enrolled and his dad quit—for a week, anyway.) Once basketball season began, Hirsch wondered if he had made a mistake. "I was totally unprepared for Wooden's work ethic, his morals, all that stuff," he said.

He was also unprepared for Wooden's coldness, which Hirsch witnessed firsthand after he ripped up his ankle during the first month of practice. "I was lying there and Wooden said, 'Can somebody get him off the court? I'm trying to hold a practice here.' I mean the pain went to the top of my head," Hirsch said. "I had the feeling at that point that he didn't give a shit about me."

Hirsch spent most of the 1961–62 season on crutches. He didn't bother going to practice, and Wooden never once called to see how he was doing. After his ankle healed, Hirsch thought about transferring to Cal State, Northridge, but Norman talked him into coming back to practice for the last couple of weeks. He competed well enough that both he and Wooden realized he could make a contribution—that is, if they could learn to coexist. "He was always abrasive, but he was very smart," Wooden said. Hirsch added: "I was probably the first person that challenged Wooden by being obnoxious and arrogant, which comes from Brooklyn. You know, like you can't tell me what to do, you son of a bitch. I was just as tough as he was in some respects."

One of the ways Hirsch tested Wooden was by calling him "John" or "JW." When he was feeling especially cheeky, he might call him "Woody." Hirsch's teammates were stunned by his audacity. They were even more surprised that Wooden abided it. "I never asked the players to call me 'Coach' or 'Mr. Wooden,' but he's the only one who didn't," Wooden said.

The coach was less forgiving of Hirsch's tardiness. One time when Hirsch was barely a minute late to practice, Wooden literally slammed the door on him. After Hirsch complained the next day, Wooden tersely replied, "Jack, you should discipline yourself so others don't have to." The lesson stuck. "With him, there was always deprivation," Hirsch said. "He was depriving me of doing what I enjoyed most, which was playing basketball with my friends."

Such was the combustible mix that took the floor for UCLA during the 1962–63 season. The six-man rotation featured three blacks and three whites (including one Jew) who had little in common except a love for playing ball. They also lacked a true home court—still. Shortly before the season began, UCLA learned that the Los Angeles Coliseum Commission had allocated most of the Sports Arena's Saturday night slots for the winter to the Los Angeles Lakers and to the Los Angeles Blades, who played in the Western Hockey League. Aside from their three games against USC and the Los Angeles Basketball Classic, the Bruins would have to play all but one of their home games at Santa Monica City College, which barely held two thousand fans. The last game would take place at the men's gymnasium, the old B.O. barn. It was not a happy situation.

Once the games got under way, Wooden realized that his team could be devastating when it got the running game going. During the opener against Denver, UCLA sprinted out to a 10–1 lead and won by 29 points.

Two weeks later, the Bruins hung 101 points on Oklahoma, just 7 points shy of the school's scoring record.

On the other hand, Wooden suspected that the Bruins were going to have problems against teams that had a big, scoring center and could slow the tempo and dominate the boards. Their size deficiency was especially glaring when they struggled with their shooting—as Goodrich did in those first three games, when he made just four of his thirty shot attempts. "My guards can't hit anywhere past 15 feet," Wooden lamented. "On the other hand, my forwards can't hit from ten."

Still, the team had a respectable 7–2 record heading into the Los Angeles Basketball Classic in late December. Stanford was the only team in the tournament that was ranked in the top ten of a national poll. But the Indians lost to USC in their first game, allowing UCLA to emerge as the winner by beating Colorado State in the final. "I don't want to schedule them for three years," said St. Louis coach John Benington, whose team lost to the Bruins by 19 points in the semifinals. "They don't have the big man, but they have superior talent and an excellent bench. Come to think of it, I don't think they even need the big man."

They were still awfully young, however, so they were bound to experience growing pains. That was especially true for Goodrich. "There were nights when I'd come home from practice so tired I'd be lucky to get my clothes off," he said. Late in the first half of UCLA's conference opener at Washington, Goodrich dribbled the ball downcourt on a three-on-one fast break and tried to throw a behind-the-back pass, just as he had seen Hazzard do many times. Except Hazzard usually completed his passes. Goodrich's attempt sailed out of bounds. During halftime, Wooden came at Goodrich hard and low. "He let me have it," Goodrich said. "That was the last time I threw it behind my back in college."

Despite Goodrich's struggles, Wooden kept him in the starting lineup, even though Goss was playing much better. When a reporter privately asked him why, Wooden replied, "Freddie has a better attitude. Gail sulks if he doesn't get to start." That may have been true, but it did not solve Wooden's numbers problem in the backcourt, where he had three players for two spots. "That whole year we struggled because Wooden didn't know who to play," Goss said. "If those guys didn't get the proper amount of playing time, they would say something to him, or their parents might say something. Especially Gail's parents. His father was at practice every day."

UCLA lost both of its first two league games at Washington, but the team quickly rounded into form and won the next five. The main reason was Hazzard, whose playmaking was much more under control than it had been as a sophomore the year before. He emerged as the primary scorer. After he torched USC for 27 points in back-to-back games the first weekend of February, Trojans coach Forrest Twogood called Hazzard "the most complete college basketball player in America."

Meanwhile, Wooden's preseason concerns over rebounding were proving to be unfounded. The players were tougher than he'd realized, and their quickness allowed them to benefit from Wooden's rebounding philosophy, which favored pursuing the basketball over boxing out. When UCLA beat Colorado State in the finals of the Los Angeles Basketball Classic, they outrebounded the Rams 58–42, even though Colorado State's front line featured players who were six foot six, six foot eight, and six foot nine.

When it came to this area of the game, the players possessed some extra motivation. Unbeknown to Wooden, an older fan had started doling out money for each rebound. According to Jack Hirsch, every player got five dollars per rebound per game up to ten, and ten dollars per rebound thereafter. Those payments were against NCAA rules, but the players didn't much care. "Except for Jack, we had no money," Keith Erickson said. "So if someone gave me an extra six dollars for getting some rebounds, I was thrilled and I didn't care where it came from."

Goodrich, however, was less than thrilled when he learned what was going on. "I heard things about getting rebound money, so I went to Coach Norman. 'What about assists? What about the guards? This is very unfair,'" he said. "I knew what was legal and not legal from my dad. Next thing you know, it was stopped. No one knew I did that."

(Told five decades later that Goodrich was the one who put a stop to the rebound money, Erickson quipped, "Even if they were giving out money for assists, Gail wouldn't have gotten any.")

UCLA entered the middle of February in a tie with Stanford for first place in the AAWU, which was now being called the "Big Six" because of the off-season addition of Washington State. The Bruins prepared for their February road games at Stanford at a time of growing friction between Wooden and Fred Slaughter. Having proved early in the season that he was capable of scoring in big numbers, Slaughter bridled when Wooden ordered him to revert to his roles as a rebounder and defender. "I saw him run Fred Slaughter out of the gym one day," Goodrich said. "Coach was running with him, jawing nose to nose the whole way."

UCLA's first game against Stanford started badly and never got better. Wooden was whistled for two technical fouls early in the first half for arguing with officials, but that did not warrant an automatic ejection back then. Unfortunately, that meant he had to stick around to watch Slaughter hoist twenty-two shots and make only six as Stanford won, 86–78. When the Bruins lost two of their next three games, their hopes of winning a league title started slipping away.

UCLA trailed Stanford by two games in the league standings with two games remaining, including one against Stanford at Santa Monica City College. The Bruins fell behind early in that game, which prompted Wooden to install his full-court press. Keith Erickson's athleticism was an enormous asset in the back of that defense. Erickson didn't start, but after Wooden subbed him in for Goodrich early on, Erickson played so well that Goodrich never set foot on the court again. Erickson finished with 13 points, Stanford committed twenty-four turnovers, and UCLA prevailed, 64–54. That left them one game back with one to go.

UCLA easily dispatched Cal the following night by 19 points. That put the Bruins in the rare position of having to root for USC, which was playing Stanford across town at Los Angeles State College. Most of the UCLA fans at the Santa Monica gym were listening to the USC-Stanford game on transistor radios. By the time the Bruins finished off the Bears, the other game was midway through the second half. The UCLA players repaired to their locker room and listened to the end of that game on a radio. The suspense was so great that Hazzard asked a manager to take his radio out of the locker room. Messengers kept the players informed as the Trojans seized the upper hand and sent the game into overtime. "We're backing in," Wooden marveled. "I never thought we'd do it."

USC won, 67–61, setting up a one-game play-off for the right to represent the Big Six in the NCAA West Regional in Provo, Utah. Because Stanford had hosted two of the teams' three meetings, the play-off had to be held in Los Angeles. The only question was where. The Coliseum Commission was itching to host it in the Sports Arena, but UCLA, still smarting over being treated as third-class citizens the previous fall, opted to go back to Santa Monica City College. Since UCLA's radio agreement precluded the game from being televised anywhere but via closed circuit on campus, that meant most of its fans would be shut out. "No one likes money anymore," Mal Florence complained in the *Los Angeles Times*. His colleague Paul Zimmerman argued that UCLA "owed it to the public to present the playoff with Stanford in the Sports Arena where all the thousands who wanted to could see."

The tickets sold out in an hour. With fans packing the tiny, hot gym, UCLA, despite using only six players the entire game, once again unleashed its full-court press for long stretches. The Bruins led by 9 points at halftime and by 14 early in the second half. Fred Slaughter snapped out of his funk and played terrific defense on Stanford center Tom Dose. With six minutes remaining and the Bruins holding a 45–40 lead, Wooden did two things he normally didn't like to do: he called time-out, and he ordered his team to stall. Goodrich and Hazzard dribbled around for the next few minutes as Stanford tried vainly to come back by fouling. It was to no avail as UCLA held on for a 51–45 win, giving Wooden his eighth league title, and second in a row.

It was as unexpected a championship as Wooden had ever experienced, but his elation was short-lived. When Wooden tried to bring out his favorite new toy, the full-court press, against Arizona State in the NCAA West Regional, the tactic backfired. Coach Ned Wulk's Sun Devils also loved to get out and go—they had been ranked second in the country in scoring at 91 points per game—and they ran UCLA out of the gym. Right from the tip, ASU built an 11-point lead that swelled to 31 by halftime. Wooden emptied his bench in the second half as the Bruins sputtered to a 93–79 defeat. Given the setting, it was arguably the biggest drubbing one of Wooden's teams had ever suffered. The following night, UCLA lost the regional third-place game by 1 point to San Francisco. The 1962–63 season had been a delirious ride, but it ended with a thud.

Even when Wooden's machine sputtered that season, he could see it had potential. Sure, the guys could be headstrong and immature, but Wooden had to admit he liked their spirit. They were tough. They were competitive. And while they appeared to have little in common, once they hit the floor they shared a real love for playing.

Whenever Wooden felt the need to relieve stress, he invariably turned to his other great passion: poetry. Not just reading it but writing it as well. Wooden's poems were nothing special compared to the classics he studied, but they were clever and crisp, and he could recite many of them by rote. "He would have never said, 'I'm a poet.' He was a versifier, which is different," Pete Blackman said. "He liked writing lines, and he liked taking simple ideas and conveying them. He was drawn to the symmetry. He enjoyed the intellectual exercise."

Blackman was every bit Wooden's equal in this area. After graduating from UCLA the year before, Blackman enlisted in the navy and was stationed in Hawaii. During the fall of 1962, he wrote a letter to Wooden in verse, and Wooden returned the favor in January with a lengthy poem in which he laid out his analysis of his current team. He sent the letter shortly after the Bruins had lost those first two conference games at Washington. It reflected Wooden's sour mood.

The poem was ten verses long. At times it read like something from Dr. Seuss, such as when Wooden wrote of "*boys who work and boys who don't/Of boys who will and boys who won't.*" Wooden complained to Blackman about his team's selfishness, overbearing parents, the players' insubordination, and especially their academic laziness.

In the final stanza, however, Wooden struck a hopeful chord, predicting that despite his misgivings, the team would eventually come together, and if everything fell into place, "*We could be champs in sixty-four.*"

The work to fulfill that premonition would commence with the first practice the following fall. It would take place when it always did, October 15, one day after John Wooden's fifty-third birthday.

19

Perfect

Gail Goodrich figured, to hell with it. Toward the end of his sophomore season, he had spent long stretches on the bench, and it didn't look like his junior year would be much different. He didn't care much for his classes, either. The one thing that had gone well for Goodrich was baseball. So when school ended in the spring of 1963, he contemplated leaving UCLA to pursue a career in pro baseball.

He didn't bother sharing his thoughts with his basketball coach. "Wooden was up here," Goodrich said, lifting his palm above his head. "I liked him and I respected him, but maybe I was intimidated. I always put him on a pedestal." Gail's mother was dead set against the idea of quitting school, but he was still inclined to leave. Until, that is, he started his summer job working at a lumberyard. At the crack of dawn each morning, Goodrich drove from his home in the San Fernando Valley to Glendale, where he spent long days hauling lumber. "I decided I don't want to do this the rest of my life," he said. He figured he would give college at least one more year.

Fred Slaughter faced the opposite circumstance. He wanted to return to UCLA for his senior year, but his coach wasn't sure he wanted him back. Following the loss to Arizona State, Wooden had bragged to reporters about a player in the program named Vaughn Hoffman, a six-foot-seven center who had redshirted that season because of a knee injury. Wooden predicted that Hoffman would "give Fred Slaughter all he wants to handle and more." For Slaughter, this was not a good sign.

Things came to a head a few weeks later when Wooden called Slaughter into his office. The coach wanted to talk about Edgar Lacey, a hotshot six-foot-six, 190-pound senior from Jefferson High School in Los Angeles. Lacey was a two-time all-city player who set a Los Angeles scoring record while averaging 32.2 points per game. Slaughter had met Lacey in passing a couple of months before, and the high school star had told him he expected to score in college at the same prolific rate. In reply, Slaughter warned Lacey that if his goal was to average 30 points per game, then UCLA was not the place for him.

Somehow, Wooden had gotten wind of Slaughter's advice. During their meeting in Wooden's office, the coach accused Slaughter of trying to "de-recruit" Lacey. This was not Slaughter's intent at all. He was simply telling Lacey the truth about what he could expect if he played for UCLA. Wooden told Slaughter in no uncertain terms that if ever tried to do that again with Lacey or any other player, then Wooden would take away Slaughter's scholarship. "To this day I am just shocked and disappointed that that's how he would treat me," Slaughter said decades later. "He hears a rumor, brings me into his office, and tears into me. Think if he had taken my scholarship and I was gone my senior year. I wasn't a troublemaker. It hurt my feelings. It'd be different if I didn't tell the truth. That definitely kept me from being closer to Coach."

Then again, they had never been close to begin with. Slaughter and Wooden rarely talked about matters that did not directly relate to basketball. One of the few exceptions was a conversation Wooden initiated after Slaughter started dating a white girlfriend. Wooden warned Slaughter about the complications that could result from an interracial relationship. Slaughter didn't think Wooden was racist, but he also didn't appreciate the way the coach insinuated himself into his personal life. "He wasn't telling me not to do it, but he was trying to protect me—and protect, therefore, his plan," Slaughter said. "It surprised me. I thought, You stay out of my business. I'll stay out of yours."

After ripping into Slaughter about Lacey that day in his office, the coach went on to tell Slaughter that he had showed a bad attitude for much of his junior season. "He did a lousy job in '63. He was very unhappy that he wasn't getting any credit. I told him if he didn't change, I didn't want him back for the team next year," Wooden said. "I said, 'You were whining and complaining all year long. Nobody likes you. Go up and down the hall here, any of the coaches and secretaries. You've changed completely. If you don't change, next year I just would prefer you not come out. We'll get along without you.'"

A week later, Wooden picked up the *Daily Bruin* and read that Slaughter had been elected UCLA's senior class president. He couldn't help but chuckle. So much for his contention that nobody liked Fred Slaughter.

This is what a coach's off-season was for: meeting with players, taking inventory, mapping out the road ahead. Every year after the last game, Wooden holed himself in his office and spent hour after hour poring over many years' worth of his three-by-five cards, which now occupied several cabinets. In digging through past history, Wooden hoped to excavate a hint for why his teams kept coming up short in the NCAA tournament. Wooden made subtle changes every year, but this time an adjustment emerged that turned out to be hugely significant.

The Big Idea evolved out of a series of conversations between Wooden and Jerry Norman. The two of them liked to get together almost immediately after each season ended, while the details were fresh in their minds. During the 1962–63 season, the Bruins had reversed their fortunes by using a full-court pressure defense. The tactic, however, had proved to be limited. In the first place, Wooden only sicced the press on opponents when the Bruins got behind. Also, even though the purpose of the press was to speed up the tempo, it failed too often because of bad design. A single skilled dribbler could simply weave through the defense, and then his team could run a delay offense once he got past half-court. Even when UCLA got steals out of the press, it didn't usually result in fast-break baskets. Exhibit A was the play-off win over Stanford, when the Bruins forced 20 turnovers but scored just 51 points. "We fooled ourselves into thinking we forced a bunch of turnovers and won the game, therefore we did the right thing," Norman said. "But we didn't do the right thing. We didn't have any size, and every team in our conference walked the ball up the floor." Once the Bruins went up against a team like Arizona State, which had lots of savvy ball handlers, they were exposed.

So Norman had an idea. Not only did he want Wooden to commit to using a full-court press for an entire game; he also wanted to use a different kind of press altogether. Instead of the man-to-man version they had been using, Norman suggested they go with a zone. Because teams can trap in a zone—that is, use two defenders to surround the player with the ball and prevent him from advancing—that meant the only way a team could get the ball over the half-court line was by passing, not dribbling. This, Norman surmised, would result in more steals and more fast breaks. And even if the Bruins didn't get a lot of steals, a zone press would force the game to be played at a quicker pace. Norman had always been enamored of the way Pete Newell's teams at Cal had controlled the tempo. Now he wanted Wooden to do the same thing—only instead of slowing the game down, he wanted Wooden to speed it up. "The idea wasn't to steal the ball, remember. That would be an ancillary benefit," Norman said. "It was to increase tempo."

After four years of working together, Wooden and Norman had forged a productive relationship, although it fell short of a genuine friendship. Wooden may have come across as insecure to Norman at times, but his decision to hire Norman spoke to his self-confidence. He knew Norman was strong-willed and would always speak his mind. Wooden wanted his assistant to challenge him, to give him balance. "Jerry was not reluctant to make suggestions, but he'd be disappointed if you didn't go along with him," Wooden said. "He was impatient. He expected too much too soon. And maybe I did, too, in my early years."

Wooden was familiar with the concept of a zone press. He had used it when he was coaching in high school and at Indiana State, but at UCLA he had never committed to it full bore, even when he had gifted athletes like Rafer Johnson who would have thrived in it. "Somehow I felt, maybe, that I was up another notch [at UCLA], and it wouldn't work as well," he said. "I've always second-guessed myself a little for that."

Not only did the 1963–64 UCLA team have the suitable personnel for a zone press; Norman argued it was the only way the Bruins could beat bigger teams. He suggested a 2-2-1 formation, but instead of putting the point guard on the front line, which was customary, Norman wanted to go with Slaughter up front alongside Goodrich or Freddie Goss. Slaughter was a track star, after all, and his size would be a formidable weapon against opposing point guards. Hazzard would then go on the second line, where he would be in better position either to steal the ball or to accept a pass from the player who did. With the floor sufficiently spread, Hazzard could work his magic in the open court. Finally, Erickson would occupy the all-important back position, where his grace and instincts would enable him to cover the court from sideline to sideline, and then pounce on an errant pass as if he were spiking a volleyball on the beach.

Wooden was a tough audience, peppering Norman with questions and testing his commitment to the idea. "He could be a devil's advocate," Norman said. "He wanted to see how strong your convictions were." Wooden eventually relented. Fine, he said, we'll give it a try. Let's see how well it works.

Goodrich was lucky he stuck around. Shortly before the start of practice, Goss walked into Wooden's office and asked if he could sit out the season and resume playing the following year. It may have seemed like a generous sacrifice, but for Goss it was an easy decision. Unlike Hazzard and Goodrich, he did not come to UCLA harboring visions of a pro career. He did not want a repeat of the previous season, when there was a glut in the backcourt, and nobody was happy. Goss decided he should wait until after Hazzard graduated, and then it would be just him and Goodrich to man the two guard spots. "Wooden knew we had a problem," Goss said. "Without me there, he wouldn't have three guards rotating in and out. I knew the chemistry needed it."

Chemistry would indeed be vital. Just before the first game, Wooden asked the players to rank themselves from the best to the worst. He performed this exercise almost every year—it was a useful weapon against parents who believed their son should be playing more—but when the results came back, Wooden was surprised to see that the players had ranked themselves almost exactly the same. That had to be a good sign.

As it turned out, Slaughter had no trouble beating out Vaughn Hoffman, Wooden's hot prospect, at center. Thus, the starting five was set—Hazzard, Goodrich, Hirsch, Erickson, and Slaughter. Beyond that, two sophomores emerged as substitutes. They were both southern transplants: Doug McIntosh, a six-foot-six forward from Lily, Kentucky, and Kenny Washington, a reed-thin, six-foot-three guard from Beaufort, South Carolina.

Washington, who was black, faced a far more difficult transition than McIntosh, who was white. Washington had come to UCLA thanks to Hazzard, whom he had met on the playgrounds while visiting his sister in Philadelphia in the summer of 1961, before his senior year of high school. Hazzard thought so highly of Washington's skills that he told Jerry Norman to offer the kid a scholarship. To make sure Norman took his advice, Hazzard told the coach that Washington was a sturdy six-foot-five, 205 pounds, and he could shoot better than Gary Cunningham. That was all Norman needed to hear. He signed up Washington sight unseen.

To get from South Carolina to Southern California, Washington spent three days crouched in the back of a Greyhound bus. When the bus reached Los Angeles, Norman waited for the player Hazzard described to step off. That player never appeared. After a while, Norman spotted the quiet, scrawny, scared-looking kid standing in a corner, and he came to the disappointing realization that this was Walt's guy.

Washington could not have been more out of his element. To that point in his life, he had barely spoken to a white person, and he had been taught to look down when he did talk to one. Now, as a freshman at UCLA, he was living with a white roommate. Washington was also confounded by simple technologies like the milk machine in the cafeteria. When he went to a restaurant, he couldn't tell the waiter what he wanted on his salad because he had never tasted salad dressing. As a result, Washington became a loner, so much so that Hazzard warned him people were getting worried that he would turn out to be another Ron Lawson.

If Washington expected sympathy from his head coach, he would be disappointed. In his autobiography *They Call Me Coach*, Wooden described a freshman practice in the fall of 1962, during which he found Washington standing on the side with tears in his eyes. When Wooden asked Washington what was wrong, the youngster replied that he was upset because he wouldn't get back home to Beaufort for several months. "I said to him, 'If you don't shape up, you can ship out tomorrow on the first Greyhound,'" Wooden wrote.

Washington wasn't put off by the tough love. He had experienced much the same treatment from his own father, an ex-marine. Wooden was simply preaching the same small-town values Washington had known back home. "He had structure, a philosophy based on fairness," Washington said. "The same things his father taught him, my father taught me. I felt like a foster child."

Hazzard may have stretched the truth about Washington's size, but he wasn't lying about his ability. After leading the freshman team in scoring and rebounding, Washington moved up to the varsity in 1963. During those six weeks between the start of practice and the season opener, the Bruins worked feverishly on their new defense. "I had never heard of a zone press," Erickson said. "To my knowledge, nobody had ever done it." Each day, they would climb those three staircases in the men's gym and, after helping to mop up the gymnastics team's chalk as Wooden sprinkled his water, they would run themselves ragged.

Despite being the defending AAWU champions, the Bruins would begin the season unranked in both national polls. *Sports Illustrated* declined to include UCLA in its preseason top twenty, noting that the team's "lack of height again makes things tough."

UCLA served notice from the start that it would be better than anticipated. Playing before just 4,700 fans at the Sports Arena in the season opener, the Bruins set a single-game school scoring record by embarrassing BYU, 113–71. Hazzard led the team in scoring with 20 points, but the real star was the defense. "Our kids got rattled by their press," BYU coach Stan Watts said afterward. "UCLA simply threw us out of our patterns and due to our inexperience we didn't adjust."

The Bruins romped over their next five opponents and rose to No. 4

in the AP poll. That set up the most compelling story line in the five-year history of the Los Angeles Basketball Classic. The Michigan Wolverines, who were also undefeated and ranked third in the AP poll, were going to be playing in the tournament. The Wolverines were exactly the kind of team that was supposed to give UCLA problems. Their vaunted front line, nicknamed the "Anvil Chorus," featured the Big Ten's leading rebounder, six-foot-seven junior Bill Buntin, as well as six-foot-eight forward Oliver Dardin. Michigan also boasted a dynamic six-foot-five sophomore guard named Cazzie Russell, whose blend of size and skill was already drawing comparisons to Oscar Robertson's.

If the folks who ran the Classic had some marketing savvy, they would have arranged for UCLA and Michigan to meet in the final. Instead, the pairings were drawn at random, and the big clash took place in the semis. With 14,241 fans packing into the Sports Arena, UCLA rushed out to a 12-point lead and dominated the first twenty minutes. Cazzie Russell was completely flummoxed by the 2-2-1 zone press. He was whistled for four traveling calls, and he accounted for 7 of his team's 12 turnovers in the first half. The Wolverines managed to close to within 3 points at the half, but the Bruins exploded yet again early in the second half, building a 68–54 advantage with about ten minutes to play. By the time the game ended, Michigan had committed 17 turnovers, Russell had scored just 11 points, and UCLA had secured a shockingly easy 98–80 win. Illinois coach Harry Combes, who was watching courtside preparing to meet the winner in the final, would later say that for those forty minutes, the Bruins were "absolutely the best precision team I've ever seen."

Through the season's first eight games, the Bruins averaged an astounding 93 points. They were emotionally hung over against Illinois, but they scrapped to an 83–79 win and their second consecutive Classic title. Goodrich, who had scored 30 points against Michigan, added 21 more and was named the tournament's most outstanding player. The nation already knew the Bruins had an All-American-caliber guard in Hazzard. Now it was learning that he had a running mate who was also worthy of that stature.

In the next week's polls, UCLA rose to No. 2, trailing only Adolph Rupp's Kentucky Wildcats. The Bruins opened league play with a two-game series at Washington State. After squeezing out an 88–83 win in game 1, the Bruins came out in the first half against the Cougars in game 2 and dominated just as they had the previous night.

When the players got into the locker room for halftime, Wooden followed them inside and made an announcement. "Kentucky has been beaten," he said. Everyone understood what that meant. The Bruins polished off Washington State in the second half with ease, setting yet another school scoring record in a 121–77 victory. On Monday, it became official. The men who voted in both the Associated Press and United Press International college basketball polls installed Johnny Wooden's little UCLA Bruins as the No. 1 team in America.

The games were falling into a pattern. Opponents would hang around for a while, but at a certain point they would make a mistake against the press. They would then compound that mistake with a couple more, and before they knew what hit them, the game had broken open. Wooden and Norman liked to call those game-breaking runs "Bruin Blitzes." Sportswriters started referring to the team as the "glue factory" because of what they did to horses who tried to run with them. "When we first hit with [the zone press], it was an innovation that just shocked people," Hazzard said. "It was a surprise element, and it had a tremendous psychological effect on other teams."

Wooden loved watching those other machines go wobbly. "Passes are intercepted and teammates will sometimes say, 'Watch your passing,' and the other will say, 'Why don't you meet the ball?' You've got them cussing at each other and they're not going to function as well as a team," he said. "You can get well behind but you have to keep the pressure on and have faith in [the press] and not give up."

Game after game, week after week, opponents tried their best to slow the Bruins down. On January 10, USC coach Forrest Twogood tried to let his players run with UCLA, only to see his team lose by 20. The next night, the Trojans held the ball for long stretches, but UCLA still won, 78–71. "Every team we face in the conference will try to do the same thing USC did against us tonight," Wooden said.

A week later, the Bruins unspooled their most devastating run yet. Playing their primary league challenger, Stanford, in the Sports Arena, UCLA found itself in a battle for most of the night. The score was tied fifteen times, and there were ten lead changes. UCLA led 63–60 with nine minutes to play when—*wham!*—they blitzed. After hitting a pair of free throws to put UCLA up by 7, Goodrich stole the ball out of the press and fired a pass to Slaughter for a layup. On the ensuing possession, Hazzard stole the ball, pushed up on a three-on-one fast break, and then hit a streaking Hirsch for a score. Stanford tried to bring the ball upcourt again, and once again Hazzard got a steal that led to a 3-point play for

Slaughter. It only took one minute, twenty seconds, but by the time the Bruins were through they had scored 13 unanswered points. They coasted home, 80–61. "Endurance and quickness. That's what's keeping us up there, especially in those close games," Wooden said afterward. "I don't recall ever seeing us break loose the way we did tonight."

Goodrich and Hazzard were now well on their way to becoming one of the finest backcourts the game had ever seen. Goodrich was leading the Big Six in scoring at 22.4 points per game, and Hazzard was on pace to shatter Willie Naulls's UCLA career scoring record. Now 15–0 and still ranked No. 1 in the country, the Bruins were truly in uncharted waters. "Sure, there's some pressure on us," Wooden conceded. "The more we win, the more the boys would like to keep it going."

After UCLA waxed Cal by 20 points to improve to 18–0, Mal Florence noted in the *Los Angeles Times* that UCLA's press "didn't particularly bother the Bears, but they fell into the Bruins' tempo and it has become quite apparent that you don't run with UCLA." Rene Herrerias, who had succeeded his former boss, Pete Newell, as Cal's coach, reverted to the old Newell slowdown style the next night. The game wasn't decided until Hazzard sank three free throws in the final forty-one seconds, allowing UCLA to escape with a 58–56 win.

Wooden was so stressed out after the game that he went into UCLA's locker room and vomited, which he said had never happened to him in nearly forty years of playing and coaching. "I had an orange juice and a sandwich and then went right in and got sick," he said. The old-fashioned war with Cal had brought out the worst in Wooden. At one point, Rene Herrerias saw his senior guard Dan Lufkin barking at the UCLA bench as he ran downcourt. During the next time-out, Herrerias asked him what he was saying. "I'm trying to tell the coach to get off my back," Lufkin replied.

As usual, the Bay Area sportswriters took note of Wooden's sideline behavior. "UCLA's basketball players took the pressure of possible defeat by California far better than their coaches, Wooden and Norman. That was the general privately expressed opinion by those who saw the teams," the *San Francisco Chronicle* reported the next day. "The opinions specifically involved Wooden shrieking at officials Mel Ross and Jim Tunney when UCLA fell behind, his alleged yelling at California players as they went past the Bruin bench and Norman's grabbing his throat twice, the traditional choke gesture when the referees came to the scorer's table." The *Chronicle* further predicted that "the charge that Wooden yelled at Bear players may be aired at the next conference meeting."

Wooden didn't hide his irritation when the topic of his bench conduct was brought up once again at the weekly Southern California writers' luncheon. "I've won a lot of ball games in the Bay Area, but I could never tell it by reading their newspapers the next day," he said.

It had already been a long season, and there were still seven games to go. Increasingly the question was being asked, in Los Angeles and around the country, whether this UCLA squad could go undefeated. Only two teams had compiled a perfect record while winning an NCAA title, San Francisco in 1956 and North Carolina in 1957. Michigan coach Dave Strack was among those who were unconvinced. "They don't look like any superteam," he said. Even Wooden claimed to be skeptical. "As soon as we meet a team with a good big center, we may be in trouble," he said.

Part of the mystery stemmed from the fact that most people had not seen more than a couple of the country's top teams. One of the few who had was Aleksandar Nikolic, the coach of the Yugoslavian national team who was spending three months that winter traveling around America to study basketball in advance of the 1964 Olympics in Tokyo. Nikolic was wrapping up his swing with a trip to the West Coast in early February, and he was invited to the Los Angeles writers' luncheon. When Nikolic told the writers in his broken English that he had seen more than fifty teams during his travels, they naturally wanted to know which he thought was the best. "UCLA," he answered.

Really? Why?

"Is small team," he replied. "No big man, no big score like Nash of Coach Roop team in Kentucky. But ziss—pardon, my English very bad— ziss is best I see. Because is team."

He held up five fingers. "All five. *Team*. You understand?"

The suggestion that his players functioned like fingers on a hand would have seemed laughable to Wooden. These were the same players who griped to him all the time about not getting enough minutes, or shots, or both. They argued nonstop. When practice was over, everybody went his own way. "Our team play was so good on the floor, you'd think they were the happiest, friendliest people in the world," Wooden said. "Yet, off the floor, they were not that close."

The players, however, saw things differently. They may not have socialized much, but that didn't mean they didn't like playing together. The disconnect between their point of view and Wooden's underscored how times had changed. The days when returning servicemen snapped to

attention on Lieutenant Wooden's command were long gone. These players had no qualms about questioning authority. They spoke their minds,
to him and to each other. They fed off friction.

Signs of discord abounded. Keith Erickson complained about not
getting nearly as many shots as Hazzard and Goodrich. When pressed
for the reason, Wooden would tell him flatly, "Because they make them."
Wooden tried to emphasize the positive with Erickson—*If you get the
rebound . . . outstanding! Now give the ball to Gail or Walter*—but it didn't
always work. "Wooden told me that Keith came to him complaining he
wasn't taking enough shots," Goodrich said. "He said, 'Don't worry, I'll
take care of Keith. You keep shooting.'"

The carping occasionally broke out into the open. After *Sports Illustrated* sent a young writer named Frank Deford to cover the Los Angeles
Basketball Classic in December, Deford wrote that "no other players in
the Classic approached UCLA in displays of anguish and dismay at virtually every call against them. Parleys with the referees went on end-
lessly." Deford quoted an anonymous coach who predicted, "Sure, they're
going fine now so everything is rosy. But if they lose a couple, these guys
might fold up on themselves."

That was precisely what Wooden was afraid of. "Hazzard and Goodrich
didn't get along at all. Erickson and Hirsch were at Hazzard and
Goodrich all year long. They felt that they didn't pass to them enough,
that they weren't getting enough shots," Wooden said. "It didn't worsen
as the season wore on, but it didn't lessen, either. . . . If we hadn't been
having a good year it would have been an untenable thing."

Yet once the ball went up, the pieces fit together beautifully. Part of it
was blind luck. Since two of the starters, Goodrich and Hirsch, were left-
handed, that meant that all four of the players in the front of the zone
press could be positioned with their strong hand next to the sideline. The
quintet also possessed complementary skill sets—Erickson's agility,
Hirsch's guile, Slaughter's jumping ability and keen timing—as well as
mind-sets. The prime example, of course, was the backcourt, where
Hazzard's brilliant passing meshed with Goodrich's deadeye shooting.
"Goodrich can do anything better than Hazzard, including pass," Wooden
said. "But Hazzard *will* pass."

It also helped that the starting five had gotten a year older. That meant
another year of understanding Wooden's expectations. During practice
one day, a ball rolled Erickson's way while he was working on his free
throws. Instead of passing it back, the perennially goofy Erickson
chucked up a long-distance shot. When the ball went in, Erickson milked

the moment by laughing loudly and lying down on the court. He looked up to see his grim-faced coach marching in his direction. "You're lucky I had a chance to count to twenty before I got down here," Wooden said. "If I had counted to ten like I usually do, you'd be out of here."

Then there was Hirsch—incorrigible, irredeemable, irrepressible, and in so many ways, invaluable. Since Hirsch had spent most of his basketball life learning to score inside against bigger players, he was able to prevent defenses from focusing solely on Goodrich. Erickson said that Hirsch was "brilliant" in his ability to find the best spot on the floor to get a rebound. Wooden agreed. "He picks up more garbage than anyone I've ever seen," the coach said.

Because Hirsch was already set for life financially, he was not as intimidated by Wooden as the others were. If the coach kicked him out of school, Hirsch could just go work for his dad, which is what he wanted to do in the first place. He reminded Wooden of this often, but Wooden still drew his lines. For example, when Hirsch complained for the umpteenth time about the low quality of the food at team meals—"I'm not gonna eat this slop," he said—Wooden told him that he should leave the training table and not come back. That was fine with Hirsch. He went to his parents' house and enjoyed a nice steak cooked by his family's personal chef. After about two weeks, he decided he wanted to come back, not because he missed the food but because he missed the camaraderie with his teammates. So he went to Wooden's office to ask if he could return. Wooden made Hirsch practically beg before he relented. For weeks afterward, Hirsch's teammates would tease him at team meals by asking, "How's the food, Jack?"

When he was just starting his coaching career, Wooden would have been a lot tougher on a wiseguy like Hirsch, maybe even kicked him off the team. But Wooden was older now, and he recognized the value of a little levity. When Hirsch would throw a crazy layup and shout, "This one's for you, Woody!" Wooden would pretend he didn't hear him. When Hirsch wanted to end a drill by saying, "That's enough, JW," Wooden might listen. And when Hirsch showed up to practice one day wearing a long-haired Beatles wig, Wooden said nothing about it until right before practice was about to begin. He ended his pre-practice talk by saying, "By the way, if certain people around here believe they can improve their appearance, that's just fine with me." Then he made Hirsch wear the wig for the entire practice. That thing was hot as hell.

"I made him be more human, more understanding, more caring. You can't treat people like robots all the time," Hirsch said. "I think I was the first person that broke him down. I taught him there's more to life than just being a serious, stoic individual, that you can laugh at yourself and we're not all perfect."

So it was that in the midst of his finest season yet, the teacher became a student. Thanks to Hirsch's juvenile antics, the players saw that beneath the ultraserious veneer, Wooden was a regular guy who wanted to have fun, just like them. His demeanor was especially important when games got tight late in the second half. Wooden's response in those moments was simply to sit back and wait for the press to work its magic. "A couple of times when we were way down, I remember looking over at him with his legs crossed and program rolled up," Fred Slaughter said. "I'd think hey, if he's not worried, I'm not worried." Goodrich added: "His words were always the same. 'Don't panic. Keep your poise. They'll break.'"

It didn't matter that the players argued on the court or spent little time together off it. They may not have functioned quite like five fingers on a hand, but they were still a team—a really, really good team. "We used to talk about how we were the All-American team, a group of guys from such diverse backgrounds, yet on the court were a perfect mesh," Slaughter said. "Two black, two white, one Jewish, who after games would go in our separate directions. But game time, practice time, ride-the-bus time, we were pretty well matched. We liked to protect each other. We liked to do our jobs. And we just enjoyed playing for the man."

"If you're a hip sports fan, you've been swinging with college basketball this season. It's L.A.'s newest fad."

So proclaimed the *Los Angeles Times* on January 21, 1964. This was the ultimate front-runner's town, and by that point the fast-breaking Bruins were captivating the Hollywood set. Two weeks before, Wooden had participated in a groundbreaking ceremony for the new athletic pavilion that would be built in the heart of the campus. That was able to happen because of a breakthrough the previous fall, when a wealthy financier and member of the University of California Board of Regents named Edwin Pauley pledged to match donations up to $1 million to supplement the $2 million already committed by the state of California. If all went according to plan, the UCLA Memorial Activities Center would be completed in time to host the 1965 spring commencement.

The players were oblivious to it all. They still played their games in small gyms at Santa Monica City College and Long Beach Arena, which didn't even hold 5,000 people, and some of their crowds at the Sports Arena were sparse. (They drew a little over 7,000 fans for their home games against Washington and Cal.) The USC games drew near-sellouts, but the majority of those folks were Trojans fans. Slaughter remembered picking up an out-of-town newspaper in February and reading speculation the Bruins might go undefeated. It was the first he had ever thought about it. "We were too busy having fun and beating the crap out of everyone," he said.

Still, the sports world was taking a closer look, with much of the focus falling on the man who was leading the charge. For local writers who had covered Wooden for many years, he was impressive but ultimately dull—an "unexciting intellectual whose teams play wildly exciting basketball," in the words of Los Angeles Times columnist Sid Ziff. But to the unitiated out-of-towners, he was a fresh and compelling character, a soft-spoken, scholarly English teacher whose desk included non-sporting volumes like As a Man Thinketh, Immortal Poems of the English Language, and Wise Sayings from the Orient. The New York Times noted Wooden's "Grant Wood face." Sports Illustrated said he had "no equal as a pamphleteer," though an anonymous college coach also told the magazine, "Don't let that professorial manner fool you. He can be meaner than two snakes when he wants to be."

It was a fascinating story, but how would it end? After making its great escape in Berkeley, UCLA reeled off four straight wins to clinch the league title, Wooden's ninth in sixteen seasons. The Bruins won their final three games to finish the regular season 26–0. After surpassing Willie Naulls as UCLA's all-time leading scorer, Walt Hazzard was named first team All-American by both the AP and UPI. Wooden, meanwhile, was tapped as UPI's national coach of the year for the first time.

Finally, the Bruins could begin NCAA tournament play in Corvallis, Oregon, where they were to face Seattle in their opening game. The Chieftains were coached by a man who was plenty familiar with Wooden's style of play: Bob Boyd, a former guard at USC from 1950 to 1952. With a television audience watching back in Los Angeles, the Bruins displayed little of the sharpness that they had shown for most of the regular season. Seattle was just as comfortable playing up-tempo, and with five minutes remaining, the Bruins found themselves clinging to an 81–80 lead.

From there, UCLA pulled away thanks to two critical baskets from Kenny Washington, the sophomore reserve. The Bruins won, 95–90, but Wooden was far from triumphant. "We didn't have our usual zip tonight," he said. "I don't know what was wrong."

He was more angry than he let on. When Wooden came into the locker room after the game, he saw the players lounging in front of their lockers, sipping Pepsi and yukking it up as though they had performed well. According to Hazzard, Wooden ripped into them something fierce. "He was screaming, 'You bunch of fat cats! Look at you, just sitting around satisfied as you can be. No way you're going to win tomorrow night with your attitude tonight,'" Hazzard recalled. Hazzard had scored 26 points, so he ignored the diatribe. Wooden noticed this and turned on his point guard. "You're the main one!" he said. "If you ever play like that again, you'll never play for UCLA again."

Hazzard had heard all this before, but this time he believed Wooden was out of line. He stood up to Wooden and gave as good as he got. The confrontation grew so heated that Ducky Drake had to step in and separate them. "Coach was still screaming like a madman, just going nuts," Hazzard said. "I said, 'Hey, I've taken this for three years and I'm not taking it anymore.'"

About ten minutes later, Hazzard went into the bathroom and saw Wooden in there alone. Wooden looked right at Hazzard . . . and smiled. The whole thing had been a ruse. "I said to myself, this man is nuts," Hazzard said. "He was just trying to keep our guard up, keep us sharp, keep us mentally alert, keep us hungry. It was trick psychology."

The only thing now standing between the Bruins and a return to the NCAA semifinals was their old nemesis, the University of San Francisco, which had lost just four games all season and came into the meeting riding a 19-game winning streak. The Dons controlled the tempo from the start and built two separate 13-point leads in the first half, but the Bruins crawled back and won, 76–72. For the second time in three years, they had won the NCAA's West Regional. They would now take their confidence, and their zone press, to Kansas City for the national semifinals. Even though UCLA was 28–0 and ranked No. 1 in the country, it still had plenty of doubters. The church deacon had pulled off quite a trick. Somehow, Wooden managed to be coaching David and Goliath at the same time.

The last weekend of the NCAA tournament also served as the venue for the annual coaches' convention. For most of the hundreds of coaches who descended on Kansas City, this was their first chance to lay eyes on the four semifinalists. The Bruins would meet Kansas State on Friday night, with the winner taking on either Duke or Michigan the following night for the title. After Mal Florence canvassed the convention on Thursday, he reported in the *Los Angeles Times* that the coaches "showed strong support for Duke or Michigan to win the title, only a few votes for UCLA, and two for Kansas State." Jerry Norman was getting much the same reaction. "The coaches had watched the other teams work out, but they hadn't watched us," he said. "They were calling me over and asking, how did you get here? I said we've already beaten two of the other teams here. Just watch us."

UCLA's semifinal opponent, Kansas State, had the advantage of playing a de facto home game. Back in December, when the two teams played in Manhattan, Kansas, the Wildcats were facing the zone press for the first time. Kansas State coach Tex Winter vowed that his players would be better prepared this time around. He was right. Before 10,731 fans in Kansas City's Municipal Auditorium, Kansas State ran step for step with UCLA and held a 75–70 lead with 7:20 left in the game.

The Bruins clawed back to make it 75-all a minute later. During a time-out, the UCLA song leaders, whose connecting flight had been delayed by a snowstorm in Chicago, hurried into the gymnasium and unpacked their pom-poms. Two of the girls were dating UCLA starters. It may have been a coincidence, but when play resumed, the Bruins completed an 11-point run to take an 81–75 lead that they never relinquished. Erickson had the game of his life, scoring a career-high 28 points to go along with 10 rebounds. Hazzard added 19 points and 9 assists, and UCLA emerged with a 90–84 victory. For the first time in school history, the Bruins would be playing for an NCAA championship.

Did the arrival of the cheerleaders really make the difference? Perhaps, but this team was starting to believe in the power of omens. Even Jerry Norman got into the act, wearing a lucky brown road suit for the twelfth straight time. Hirsch would never forget how that 11-point run had been preceded by a Kansas State jump shot that appeared to go in but spun out. Hirsch collected the rebound and pitched a pass ahead to Goodrich for a layup. Instead of being down by 7, the Bruins only trailed by 3. "It's as if God said, this team is going undefeated," Hirsch said.

The rest of the basketball world still had its doubts as the Bruins prepared to face Duke in the championship game. The Blue Devils boasted not one but two six-foot-ten forwards, Jay Buckley and Hack Tison, and also had an All-American guard in six-foot-four senior Jeff Mullins. After defeating Michigan in the first semifinal, the Duke players had watched the second half of the Bruins' narrow win over Kansas State. They were not impressed. "It was a terrible, sloppy game," Buckley said. "I think we got a little cocky. There was not much regard for western basketball at that time. Yeah, UCLA was undefeated, but who were they playing?"

Duke coach Vic Bubas felt the same way. "I think we can beat their press," he told his assistant, Bucky Waters, "and I'm not so sure we can't run with them."

Wooden understood the scale of the challenge better than anyone. Asked by reporters how he looked at Duke, he replied, "Up." On Saturday morning, he sat in the restaurant of his hotel and nibbled on a breakfast of orange wedges, oatmeal (always oatmeal), and a sweet roll. He said he had slept all of three hours the previous evening. "Nell fell asleep about two, and I was on my own until about four, thinking about Duke," he said.

Dick Wade of the *Kansas City Star* summed up the conventional wisdom the morning of the game. "If you are silly enough to apply logic to basketball, there's no way for UCLA to beat Duke," he wrote. "The Blue Devils simply have too much—height, shooting ability, rebounding ability and defense. But UCLA isn't a logical team. It beats the law of averages with the intangible and the unbelievable."

As Wooden was finishing his breakfast, he spotted a familiar face in the hotel. It belonged to Jerry Tarkanian, the thirty-three-year-old head coach of Riverside City College, which was located about sixty miles east of Los Angeles. Tarkanian's team had just won the California junior college championships, but he barely knew Wooden and assumed Wooden didn't know him. Wooden surprised Tarkanian by coming over and congratulating him on his championship. Tarkanian, surprised, thanked Wooden and wished him luck in that night's championship game. Tarkanian never forgot Wooden's reply: "Even if we don't win, I won't be any less proud of my players than I am right now."

Wooden communicated a different kind of message shortly before tip-off. Before sending his team out for warm-ups, he asked his players, "Can anyone tell me who finished second last year?" Nobody could. It was the closest they had ever heard him talk about winning.

The 10,864 fans who were on hand for the 1964 NCAA championship game represented the largest crowd ever gathered at Municipal Auditorium. The Bruins were not intimidated by the crowd—it was more than 4,000 shy of the capacity of the Sports Arena back home—but they were thrown off by the circumstances. UCLA was so badly out of sorts that early in the first half, Wooden broke his policy not to call the first timeout. He wanted to settle his boys down.

Their task was complicated by the fact that Fred Slaughter was suddenly unavailable. As he leaped for the opening tip, the UCLA center had felt a painful twinge in his lower back. This was a big night for Slaughter, who grew up in nearby Topeka and had a lot of friends and family there. But he knew he was hurt and asked to come out. Wooden replaced Slaughter with Doug McIntosh, who performed so well that when Wooden asked Slaughter if he wanted to go back in, Slaughter said no.

During the first thirteen minutes, the score was tied eight times. Neither team led by more than 4 points. "We had been beating their press pretty regularly," Buckley said. "I think we relaxed a little bit."

Then it happened: the blitz. Goodrich started it off with a long jumper. After a Duke miss, Erickson sank two free throws to put the Bruins up by 1. A block by Washington on the next possession led to an assist from Hazzard to Hirsch. Over the next few possessions, Hirsch had two steals, a block, and a rebound, while Goodrich added another jump shot and a pair of free throws. Twice, Bubas called time-out hoping to stop the onslaught, but it didn't work. In a span of 2 minutes, 33 seconds, UCLA scored 16 unanswered points. The run gave them a 43–30 lead with just over four minutes left in the first half. The Bruins were still up 50–38 when the game broke for halftime.

Duke had run straight into the glue factory. "They weren't a frantic pressing team. They were a poised pressing team. They were ready to spring," Mullins said. "And with Walt Hazzard leading the break, they didn't make a whole lot of mistakes in transition. So we were making the mistakes, and they were making the baskets."

McIntosh wasn't UCLA's only surprise contributor off the bench. Kenny Washington, who Wooden said was "so shy that he hardly ever keeps his chin off his chest," started hitting shots from everywhere during the second half. With his marine father watching him play college basketball for the first time, Washington attempted sixteen shots and made eleven to finish with a career-high 26 points. Remarkably, he and McIntosh, the two subs, combined for more rebounds (23) than did Buckley and Tison (10). Goodrich scored a game-high 27 points, including 17 in the first half, and even after Hazzard fouled out with just over six minutes to play, the game was never close. "We actually played pretty even with them, but that one run was just too much to overcome. They could all shoot the eyes out," Buckley said. As the final minutes ticked off, Wooden sat back, crossed his legs, clutched his program, and watched as his students aced their final exam. When the horn sounded, Hazzard shouted joyfully from the bench, "We couldn't beat 'em! We couldn't beat 'em! Did you read the paper today?"

The final score was UCLA 98, Duke 83. The little Bruins had outrebounded their taller opponents, 51–44. The zone press had forced Duke to commit a whopping 29 turnovers. The Bruins were now the third NCAA champion in history to end the season with a perfect record. And it had all happened on Wooden's daughter's thirtieth birthday. When Wooden stepped out of the locker room, the first person to embrace him was Nell. "Isn't that something?" John said to her.

"We ran 'em. We just ran 'em," Hazzard said afterward. "We knew they could run, but we also knew those big boys of theirs couldn't possibly keep up with us."

The India Rubber Man had finally reached his peak, completing a journey that took him from Martinsville to West Lafayette to South Bend to Terre Haute to Westwood. A champion at last, he lavished on his players the highest praise he knew. "This team," he said, "has come as close to reaching maximum potential as any I've coached."

The championship was only a few minutes old when Wooden delivered a stern warning in the locker room. "Don't let this change you," he said. "You are champions and you must act like champions. You met some people going up to the top. You will meet the same people going down."

The players had heard this many times before, so it was unsurprising that Wooden would say it even in the moment of his greatest triumph. The man was nothing if not consistent. It was one of the things they admired most about him. "I don't ever remember going to a practice when Wooden was not putting one hundred percent of himself on the line, every day, goodness-gracious-sakes-aliving everyone, to prepare people to be the best at what they're capable of. Think about how hard that is," Hirsch said. "Wooden wasn't the best coach who ever lived. He was the best teacher who ever lived."

During his early years at UCLA, Wooden had felt persecuted (his word) because he did not have the resources to build a winner. Now he had more than he needed. An NCAA title. A new arena on the way. A strong local recruiting pipeline. When he had taken the job, UCLA was dwarfed by USC's shadow. Now people back home were suggesting it was time to replace Forrest Twogood because he couldn't beat UCLA. It was true that Hazzard, Hirsch, and Slaughter were graduating, but Goodrich and Erickson were coming back as seniors, Freddie Goss would be eligible for his final year, and McIntosh and Washington had proved they could be championship-level performers. The Bruins' freshmen team, led by Edgar Lacey, had gone 19–1. Indeed, the final buzzer against Duke had barely sounded when Goodrich told Jerry Norman that he expected the Bruins to be back in that game for his senior year.

When Wooden delivered that postgame warning to his players, he was also talking to himself. He had seen how winning a championship devoured coaches like Pete Newell at Cal, Phil Woolpert at San Francisco, and Ed Jucker at Cincinnati. All of them had been so worried about meeting expectations that it drove them to an early retirement. When the Bruins returned to Los Angeles, they were feted like champions, because Hollywood loved a happy ending. But when the credits rolled and the house lights came up, all that remained were Wooden and his three-by-five cards. He hunkered down in his little office and began to build his lesson plans for the road ahead.

At one point during their annual spring talks, Wooden looked up at Jerry Norman and said, "Winning that title was the worst thing that could have happened to us." Norman thought he was kidding. Turns out he wasn't.

PART THREE

Autumn

20

J. D.

A few days before the 1964 NCAA tournament began, Wooden was working in his cramped, temporary office space when he heard a knock at the door. In walked J. D. Morgan, who had taken over as athletic director the previous July after Wilbur Johns retired. Wooden was not in a chatty mood. He was busy putting together the basketball team's budget for the upcoming year, which Johns had always required him to submit by April 1.

Noticing the pile of papers on Wooden's desk, Morgan asked the coach what he was doing. When Wooden told him, Morgan walked over to the desk, grabbed the papers, and, without a word of warning, dumped them into the wastebasket. "I'll take care of the budget," he said. "You get your team ready for this tournament. If your spending gets out of line, I'll let you know."

The new boss may have been ten years Wooden's junior, but there was no question who was in command. Wooden was already familiar with Morgan's bluster and bombast, as well as his brilliance. When Wooden first came to UCLA in the fall of 1948, Morgan was the assistant tennis coach under Bill Ackerman, and he and Wooden got to know each other over the years during casual faculty lunches in the student union. "He was a very dominant, aggressive type of person. Very outspoken and very forceful," Wooden said. "I found that J. D. had a tremendous retentive memory in regard to sporting events, scores, and various things of that sort. Of course, he was very certain that he was correct. He was very outspoken in that manner. We found that he was usually right, so there would be no point in arguing with him in regard to a date or a score."

Morgan carried 240 pounds on his five-foot-eleven frame. His imperious manner was the opposite of Wooden's, yet Wooden had to respect his coaching abilities. As UCLA's tennis coach, Morgan had led his teams to seven NCAA championships, making him by far the most successful coach at the school. He had also brought a rare ferocity to an otherwise genteel sport. His team's spring conditioning regimen was so arduous that the *Los Angeles Times* once suggested that UCLA's football players should be glad they played for Red Sanders instead of J. D. Morgan.

Fred Hessler, who broadcast UCLA sporting events on the radio, first noticed Morgan in the early 1950s when J. D. was ejected from a UCLA basketball game for heckling officials. "I was sitting there during a time-out and I said to the guy sitting next to me, 'Who's he throwing out?' He said, 'Oh, that's J. D. Morgan, the assistant tennis coach,'" Hessler recalled. "He didn't enjoy it too much when I used to kid him about this incident later, but he always had a very fierce feeling about UCLA and the officiating. He only saw it one way—his way."

For many years, Morgan also served as the university's business manager. A 1941 graduate of UCLA's College of Business Administration, he developed an intricate understanding of the school's financial operations, and that, even more than his acumen as a coach, made him the ideal candidate to succeed Johns as athletic director. Morgan's hard-charging personality was a tremendous asset in his role as chief fund-raiser for the new campus pavilion. UCLA had just experienced its biggest one-year enrollment increase since World War II, and Morgan wanted the pavilion to match the grandness of the campus and the city surrounding it. The arena was designed to have room for 13,500 spectators, all of whom would have an unobstructed view of the court thanks to a state-of-the-art design that used massive steel frames to support the roof, which negated the need for columns. Wooden requested that the visitors' locker rooms be the same size as UCLA's, but aside from that, the pavilion project was a J. D. Morgan operation, like everything else that was now happening inside UCLA athletics.

Besides assuming control over the budget, Morgan also informed Wooden that from now on, he was going to handle the scheduling. "That was a tremendous load off my shoulders," Wooden said. Morgan's remark that he would let Wooden know if his spending got out of line was laughable. Wooden was a penny-pinching Depression baby who lacked any kind of business sense. There was no way he was going to go over budget. "John was never interested in money," Hessler said. "He would do things like schedule a game at Indiana State, where he had once coached. I don't think they had more than thirty-five hundred people there."

If anything, Morgan wanted Wooden to spend *more*, especially when it came to recruiting. One of Morgan's first decisions was to install Jerry

Norman as a full-time varsity assistant, which allowed Norman to spend much more time scavenging for players. Morgan also dictated that any time Wooden's team traveled by air, the players would sit in first class. Those boys were prized assets. He wanted them to stretch their legs.

Morgan and Wooden had some similarities that helped them get along. They were both raised in the Midwest (Morgan grew up in Cordell, Oklahoma, where he had lettered in four sports), and they had both served in the military (Morgan commanded a navy PT boat during World War II). A devout Presbyterian, Morgan was a moralist who shared Wooden's devotion to faith. Both men also doted on their spouses. Morgan could be in a red-faced rage in his office, but when his wife, Cynthia, called, he would pick up the receiver and speak sweetly into the phone. "Maybe he was a little tougher on the outside to cover up a certain amount of softness he had," Hessler said. Wooden and Morgan shared a love for all sports. Most of all, each man recognized how the other could help him. "To me, he was not arrogant but very confident," Wooden said. "I think he backed it up. It wasn't a false confidence."

Yet their differences were just as stark. During Wooden's first year at UCLA, he refused to let his starting point guard, Eddie Sheldrake, accompany the team to the Bay Area because his wife was having a baby. Morgan, on the other hand, once told Ron Livingston, who also played basketball for Wooden, that he wanted Livingston to stay with the tennis team in a hotel instead of with his new wife the day after their wedding. Whereas Wooden always sought to maintain a balance between work and family, Morgan regularly toiled in his office late into the night. When he took his family on vacation, he spent most of his time on the telephone. And unlike Wooden, Morgan enjoyed the limelight. He attended the weekly writers' luncheons and was much more colorful in his remarks than his coach ever was.

The contrast between their life philosophies was as easy to see as the sign on Morgan's desk. It read: "Winning Solves All Problems." Wooden liked J. D. Morgan, but he never liked that sign. "I'm more inclined toward what Charlie Brown says in the comics," he said. "'Winning ain't everything but losing is nuthin.'"

In the aftermath of his first NCAA championship, Wooden was a man in demand. He received hundreds of inquiries from coaches who wanted to know more about the zone press. He was peppered with invitations to speak at functions, schools, and clinics. He was named "Father of the

Year" by the California Father's Day Council. (Apparently, winning a championship makes you a better dad.) He fulfilled countless requests for autographed copies of his Pyramid of Success.

His players were in demand as well. One week after the win over Duke, the entire starting five was invited to try out for the United States Olympic team that would compete in Tokyo later that summer. At the time, the NCAA and the Amateur Athletic Union were locked in a scorched-earth dispute over who was going to control amateur basketball. Not wanting to be seen as playing favorites, the U.S. Olympic committee, led by head coach Henry Iba, chose six players from each camp to go to the Olympics. As a result, Walt Hazzard made the team, but Gail Goodrich did not. Wooden was apoplectic. "I saw all those games and the preparations," he said, "and there was no more outstanding guard that played than Goodrich." That experience, coupled with Willie Naulls's omission from the Olympic team in 1956, soured Wooden on USA Basketball for good. "He told me they lied to him," Goodrich said. "After that, he wouldn't have anything to do with the Olympics."

At least the Bruins would no longer be treated like second-class citizens in their hometown. Their new athletic director took a strong stance in negotiations with the Los Angeles Coliseum Commission and secured a guarantee that all thirteen home games during the 1964–65 season would be staged at the Sports Arena. No more high school gyms and junior college bungalows for this bunch. Morgan also negotiated increasingly lucrative television contracts with KTLA, and he threatened to pull out of the Los Angeles Basketball Classic unless his USC counterpart, Jess Hill, agreed to alternate the event between the Sports Arena and the soon-to-be-completed Bruin Memorial Activities Center. J. D. was not trying to make friends. He was trying to make money.

This brought a new set of pressures on Wooden, and he knew he would have to adapt. For example, a few weeks after his team won the NCAA championship, Wooden learned that Goodrich had been drinking heavily at a fraternity party in Berkeley. Goodrich had no idea how Wooden found out, but when he returned to campus, he got a call that the coach wanted to see him in his office the next morning. Goodrich braced for the worst, but it never came. "You know that my rule is if I catch someone drinking, that player is gone," Wooden told him. "I'd hate for anything like that to happen to you." It didn't occur to Goodrich until afterward that the coach never asked him point-blank if the rumors were true. "He was smart enough not to put me in that position," Goodrich said.

Keith Erickson committed a much more serious breach when he missed the team's flight to New York for the Olympic trials because he overslept after spending most of the previous night partying with a buddy. When Wooden returned to Los Angeles, he met with Erickson and told him that he was off the team, although Wooden added he would leave the door open for a possible return in the fall. "He was definitely serious," Erickson said. "I walked out of there not knowing whether I was going to come back to UCLA."

As it turned out, Erickson did play for the United States that summer at the Olympics—as a member of the volleyball team. The squad, which was comprised entirely of players from Southern California, was put together at the last minute and barely practiced before finishing ninth in a field of ten. When the Olympics were over, Erickson returned to campus pessimistic about his chances of playing basketball his senior year. When the big meeting with Wooden came, the coach began by saying, "As far as I'm concerned, you're off the team." Erickson's heart sank. "However," Wooden continued, "my wife really likes you, and my daughter and son like you, too. So I'm going to give you another chance." Erickson walked out of Wooden's office a little more straight, a little more narrow.

Wooden was a man of principles, but his world was changing fast. His school had a new athletic director, a new television contract, and it was about to have a new arena. It also had a new standard for its basketball program, which Wooden had set himself. His job now was to maintain that standard. It would take more than a little rule breaking for him to dismiss his two best players.

There would be no more sneaking up on anyone. The Bruins began the 1964–65 season ranked No. 2 in the AP poll behind Michigan. They carried their thirty-game winning streak into the new season, which put them within reach of breaking the record of sixty set by Bill Russell's San Francisco teams. This UCLA team would not include the incandescent Hazzard—he had been selected by the Los Angeles Lakers with the first pick in the NBA draft—but in some ways the Bruins promised to be better. Goodrich would now handle the ball full-time, and he would be joined in the backcourt by Freddie Goss, who returned from his self-imposed one-year sabbatical. Forwards Kenny Washington and Doug McIntosh were ready to be promoted to the starting lineup, and Mike Lynn, a talented six-foot-six sophomore, would join the rotation. Jack Hirsch's and

Fred Slaughter's skills would be missed, but their departures had the potential to improve chemistry. This machine wouldn't require quite so much friction to generate heat.

The start of the season also meant the varsity debut of the much-heralded sophomore, Edgar Lacey, who had proved during his freshman year that he was worth the hype. Yet even though Lacey scored a lot of points, Wooden did not like the way he shot the basketball. Lacey's form was slow and awkward, and he released the ball from behind his head. Ever the devotee to fundamentals, Wooden believed that Lacey would have trouble making long-range baskets against high-caliber teams, so he worked with Lacey before every practice in an effort to break down his form and rebuild it from scratch. "Edgar seemed comfortable with Wooden," said Mike Serafin, a six-foot-three sophomore forward on that team, "but I think it was an uncomfortable process."

With his genial manner and easy smile, Lacey was well liked by his teammates, but he was essentially a loner. Instead of living near campus, he commuted every day in a beat-up Volkswagen from his home in South Central. "It's not that Edgar didn't like white people. He just wasn't comfortable around white people," said Goss, who was the only other black player on the team. "He didn't go out of his way to ingratiate himself to Wooden or the white community or the booster clubs. His ability to accept any kind of discipline from a white man would have been really hard."

Lacey gave the Bruins some added offensive punch, but everything revolved around Goodrich, who had added fifteen pounds of muscle over the summer. Wooden and Norman tweaked the zone press to a 1-2-1-1 alignment, but aside from that, little else was changed.

UCLA opened its title defense in the Midwest, with a game against an unranked team, the University of Illinois. The game was a reality check. Before a feverish crowd at Assembly Hall, the Bruins got knocked on their heels and never recovered. Their press was impotent against an Illini squad that made more than 60 percent of its shots en route to a 52–38 halftime lead. Even when UCLA was able to get a few steals, they did not result in layups because Hazzard was no longer running the point. Goodrich managed to score 25 points, but the Illini ran roughshod and easily won, 110–83. "It was very deflating," Erickson said. "We were ranked number one again, but we hadn't done anything. So we were cocky."

Fortunately, UCLA had a badly overmatched opponent in its next game—Indiana State, Wooden's former employer—which it beat by 26 points. From there, the Bruins righted the ship by winning their next four, including a 16-point triumph at the Sports Arena over Oklahoma

State. When the Bruins beat Utah by 30 points to win the championship of the Los Angeles Classic, and Michigan took its first loss, UCLA was back on top of the AP poll.

The season-opening loss to Illinois turned out to be a blessing in disguise, as the Bruins could play their games without facing the pressure of trying to stay perfect. Now that Goodrich didn't have to share the ball with Hazzard, he was liberated to unleash his full bag of tricks. He became the most lethal offensive weapon in America. "I guarded Gail every day in practice, and I never blocked his goddamn shot once," said Mike Serafin. Lacey, meanwhile, cemented his status as a starter by scoring 20 points in a 9-point win over USC in December. At six-foot-seven, Lacey was the tallest player and best leaper on the team, which is why he was the leading rebounder, but his shooting woes left him as the team's fourth-leading scorer.

UCLA's winning ways continued through conference play. The Bruins survived a couple of close calls, including a 52–50 squeaker against USC, but they finished undefeated in league play for the second straight year. Their only other regular-season loss came at the Milwaukee Classic on January 29, when the Bruins were clipped by unranked Iowa, 87–82, costing them their No. 1 ranking. When the game was over, the Iowa players lifted their coach, Ralph Miller, onto their shoulders and carried him off the floor. Wooden had grown used to such celebrations in Berkeley and Corvallis, but now it had happened in his native Midwest, the area of the country that the *Los Angeles Times* called "the cradle of basketball" during Wooden's first season in Westwood. Things were a lot different now, and they would stay that way.

West Coast basketball was still weak compared to the rest of the country, so Wooden had an advantage in the postseason because the NCAA tournament's regions were arranged by geography, not competitive balance. The Bruins began their title defense in 1965 with a pair of easy wins at the West Regional in Provo, Utah, over BYU and San Francisco. That vaulted UCLA into the NCAA semifinals for the third time in four years. However, a few days before the team left for the championship weekend in Portland, Keith Erickson, who had scored a total of 57 points in the two wins in Provo, was hitting golf balls when he felt a painful twinge. "I was trying to hit the ball as hard as I could, and I pulled the hamstring in one of my legs," Erickson said. "It was just a great opportunity to be an idiot." He was the team's second-leading scorer, but when he got to Portland, it was obvious that he was badly hurt. UCLA would have to rely more heavily on Washington and Lynn if it was going to win two more games.

The Bruins' semifinal opponent was Wichita State. The Shockers had played slow ball to upset Henry Iba's Oklahoma State team in the Midwest regional final, and Wooden assumed they would attempt the same tactic against UCLA. His Bruins, however, had seen every kind of trick by then, and they had more experience than Wichita State at playing on a big stage. Their dominance was so emphatic that Wooden called off the press by halftime with the Bruins owning a 65–38 lead. Erickson's scoring was replaced by Lacey (25 points, 13 rebounds) and Goss (19 points), leading to a 108–89 victory.

That set up a final that had seemed predestined from the beginning of the season: No. 2 UCLA versus No. 1 Michigan. Very little had changed in the fifteen months since UCLA and Michigan had headlined the Los Angeles Classic. That was bad news for the Wolverines. Once again, it took some time for the pace to wear Michigan down, but when it did, Wooden's racehorses blew by. After Michigan staked a 20–13 lead, thanks to Cazzie Russell's ability to drive by the hobbled Erickson, Wooden replaced Erickson with Kenny Washington, who immediately sank two jumpers to ignite an 11–2 run. A few minutes later, the Bruins went on another burst, this time outscoring Michigan 14–2. The Wolverines were in full panic. "The crowd was yelling louder and louder each time we did something," Doug McIntosh said. "One time I wasn't able to really put any pressure on Cazzie. Then I looked, and I saw the ball just dribble off his leg. I just watched that ball dribble off his leg, and all I could think was, 'Isn't this sweet? We're going to win.'"

UCLA led at halftime, 47–34. With Erickson sidelined the rest of the way, Washington turned in another storybook performance off the bench. The year before, he had torched Duke in the final for 26. This time, he scored 17. Early in the second half, Wooden ordered his team to hold the ball in order to force the Wolverines out of their zone defense. When Michigan obliged by going to an aggressive man-to-man, it opened up more driving lanes for Goodrich, who drew fouls again and again. By the time the game was over, he had set a new NCAA championship game-scoring record with 42 points. Goodrich did much of his damage from the foul line, where he converted eighteen of his twenty attempts.

UCLA won, 91–80, to become just the fourth repeat champion in the twenty-six-year history of the NCAA tournament. Yet, despite Goodrich's historic performance, the tournament's Most Outstanding Player award went to Princeton's All-America forward Bill Bradley, who had scored 58 points in a meaningless win over Wichita State in the third-place game. This was the second snub in twelve months for Goodrich, but he still had two championships to show for it. Not even the great Walt Hazzard could say that.

UCLA's twin titles served as an emphatic validation for the unconventional brand of basketball that Wooden had introduced to the American West. The lessons taught by Piggy Lambert, which emphasized quickness over height, had proved enduring. And yet, for all the changes Wooden had navigated during his three decades in coaching, there was another on the horizon that would literally dwarf all the others. From three thousand miles away, an unusually tall and graceful player was getting ready to plop in his lap. For most of his coaching life, Wooden's teams loomed large by playing small, but things were about to change in a big, big way.

21

Lewis

The kid's first thought was: he looks like the guy in the Pepperidge Farm ad. You know, the one with the little old man who drives a buggy. Same exact hair, cropped short and parted in the middle. Long, angular face. Glasses perched on a pointed nose. Unusually plump earlobes. Then there was the voice: quiet but steady, with an unmistakable midwestern twang. With his suit coat hanging from a peg on the wall behind him, the man sat at his desk in a short-sleeved button-down shirt and tie. The kid thought the pose struck a perfect balance: formal but not stuffy; relaxed but not cavalier. The man looked like he should be working in a one-room schoolhouse.

Most recruits would be put off by such spartan conditions and understated mannerisms, but this was no ordinary recruit. This was Lew Alcindor, a seven-foot-one center from New York City who was being hailed as one of the greatest schoolboy talents in basketball history. Ever since Alcindor was a freshman in high school, he had been approached by peddlers and curiosity seekers, sportswriters and college coaches, all of whom wanted to cajole him, charm him, promise him the world. Yet, here was Mr. Pepperidge Farm, sitting in his makeshift office, promising him nothing more than the chance to get a quality education. "He had very humble circumstances around him," Alcindor said. "He never was ostentatious in any way."

Best of all, the man called him Lewis. Not Lew, or Big Lew, or Lewie. Lewis. Alcindor believed it was his way of saying, *We are gentlemen here. I will treat you with respect.* When Alcindor told the coach that he was impressed with UCLA's basketball program, the man replied, "That's all very good, but I am impressed by your grades. You could do very well here as a student, whether you were an athlete or not. That is important."

Alcindor had never been to California before. His visit to UCLA's campus took place over the first weekend of April 1965, a week after UCLA won its second straight NCAA championship. He was such a coveted recruit that even the speculation that he *might* visit UCLA had warranted a story in the *Los Angeles Times* back in mid-March. The visit itself was cloaked in secrecy. Alcindor arrived by plane on Friday night and was met at the airport by Jerry Norman, Edgar Lacey, and a freshman point guard from South Bend, Indiana, named Mike Warren, who, not coincidentally, was also black. The four of them drove in Lacey's car to UCLA's campus, where Alcindor was assigned a two-room guest suite that was usually reserved for visiting professors and other VIPs. After Norman left, the players went to a rock 'n' roll concert in the student union, ate hamburgers at midnight in a Westwood coffee shop, and were treated to double servings of French toast the following morning at Hollis Johnson's drugstore.

On Saturday, Norman took Alcindor on a tour of the offices of the *Daily Bruin*. The previous summer, Alcindor had been the sports editor at a newspaper published by a youth organization in Harlem, and he was considering a major in journalism. From there, Warren and Lacey took Alcindor to watch Arthur Ashe, who was then a UCLA sophomore, play in a tennis match against Stanford. They showed Alcindor the twenty-minute stroll he would take each day across campus to get to class. Then they tooled around town for a while, showing him the beach and the Hollywood Hills. The evening ended at a party in a residence hall, where Alcindor sat quietly in a corner on a stool, chatting up a few other athletes.

Norman knew it was important for Alcindor to meet Ashe, who was an extension of UCLA's racial tradition. A voracious reader, Alcindor knew all about Jackie Robinson and Ralph Bunche, and he had introduced himself to Willie Naulls at a Knicks game. He had been pleasantly surprised to learn while watching Rafer Johnson on *The Ed Sullivan Show* that Johnson had been UCLA's student body president. "That really impressed me, that a black man could earn that position, that he could excel beyond sports," Alcindor said. From where he sat three thousand miles away, UCLA beckoned as a warm and welcoming place for a young black man, in contrast to his native New York City, not to mention the rest of America.

Yet, it was this white, diminutive, middle-aged midwesterner who made the biggest impression of all. It didn't matter if John Wooden was selling cookies or basketball. Alcindor was buying. "I am a great believer in my own snap judgments, and I am quick to find a major fault in minor offenses, particularly in strangers who need me, but I found myself liking Mr. Wooden right away," Alcindor wrote in his autobiography, *Giant Steps*. "People would always tell me that they cared about me, but I felt Mr. Wooden really meant it. I came out of his office knowing I was going to UCLA."

The connection, naturally, originated from their fathers.

Wooden thought that Alcindor had the bearing of an eagle, just like Wooden's father, Hugh. And Alcindor thought that Wooden resembled his own dad. Not physically, of course—Ferdinand Lewis Alcindor, Sr., known as "Big Al," stood a burly six foot three, two hundred pounds—but they were similar in other ways. Lew was an only child who knew that his father loved him, but Big Al did not go out of his way to express it. He was humble and well read, a man of actions, not statements. Alcindor could tell off the bat that Wooden was the same way.

Lewis was fortunate to have a strong and loving father to guide him, because it was not easy being young, black, and male in New York City in the 1950s and 1960s, especially one who was ridiculously tall. Still, all things considered, Lew had a rather idyllic childhood. When he was three, his parents moved into a government-owned, middle-income housing project on Dyckman Street in the Inwood neighborhood of northern Manhattan. This was no ghetto. Lew's early childhood memories include landscapes of expansive grass. There were scarcely any hoodlums or junkies in sight. He got excellent grades. Most of his friends were white.

Like Wooden, Big Al was an educated man, a gifted musician who had studied at the famed Juilliard School in New York City. His specialty was the trombone, and he hoped to be a conductor, but that wasn't easy work for a black man to find. He became a police officer to support his family, but jazz remained his passion. Big Al jammed regularly at the Elks Club on 126th Street with the likes of Dizzy Gillespie and Art Blakey, and he performed with the Senior Musicians Symphony in Carnegie Hall. Lew took a few piano lessons when he was younger, but he gave it up because he didn't like to practice. He would forever claim that everything he ever needed to know about basketball, he learned by listening to jazz. "A jazz band is not a group that just has individuals doing what they want to do," he explained. "They have to pay attention to each other and understand teamwork and timing."

Big Al also gave Lew his first sad, formative lesson about racism. Lew was in the third grade, and he was riding the bus with his dad to Harlem to get their hair cut. When Lew asked why they had to travel so far just to get trimmed, his father told him it was because the white barbers in their neighborhood didn't want to cut their hair. It took a few days for the idea to sink in, but when it did, Lew felt like he had rocks in his stomach.

As a tall-and-growing grade-schooler, Lew was naturally pushed toward basketball. He came under the sway of a genial white coach named Farrell Hopkins, who taught him how to practice layups. "You only give people something to laugh about when you miss a layup," Hopkins told him. Lew was one of only two black students at his private grade school (his parents, who were Catholic, had enrolled him at a parochial school), and his days were pockmarked by racial slurs, fights with white kids, and a strict, unspoken rule that white girls were off-limits.

It got worse after he entered high school as a six-foot-ten ninth grader at Power Memorial Academy, a Catholic high school on West 61st Street. As Alcindor continued to sprout, he became more of a curiosity to the outside world, and he resented being treated like a circus freak. One day while he was walking through a bus terminal with his team, an elderly white woman walked up to him and poked him with her umbrella. "I could see Lewie flush, but like always, he took it," said his high school coach, Jack Donohue. Alcindor later referred to his junior year of high school as "the apex of my white-hating period." It was easy for him to become a loner, because there was no one else like him. "Face it, Lew," Donohue told him. "You're a minority of one."

On balance, Alcindor's relationship with Donohue was positive, but like everything else in his life, it was complicated by race. Their relationship was irreparably breached during a game in Alcindor's junior year. Power had played a torpid first half, and Donohue was blowing his stack in the locker room at halftime, reaming out each player one by one. When he got to Alcindor, Donohue shouted, "And you! You're not hustling. You're not moving. You go out there and you don't hustle. You don't do any of the things you're supposed to do. You're acting just like a nigger!"

Alcindor couldn't believe his ears. The word hurt much more than that old lady's umbrella. He briefly considered going home (and he was encouraged to do so by the two other black players on the team), but he finished the game, which Power won. After the game, Donohue called Alcindor into his office and said cheerfully, "See? It worked. I knew if I used that word, it would shock you into playing a good second half." It was a long time before Alcindor could forgive what Donohue had done.

By the end of his senior season, Alcindor had set a New York City record for career points (2,067) and rebounds (2,002), and he had led

Power Memorial to three Catholic League championships, two mythical national championships, and a seventy-one-game winning streak. He had also distinguished himself in the classroom. He was in the top 10 percent of his class, scored over 1200 on the SAT, and was awarded a New York State Regents' academic scholarship.

Aside from the segregated colleges in the South, Alcindor had his choice of where he wanted to continue his education. He originally leaned toward eastern schools like St. John's, Columbia, and Boston College, and he was also intrigued by Michigan. But there was one school out west that caught his imagination: UCLA. Lew followed college basketball by reading scores in the newspaper, and he couldn't help but notice how frequently the Bruins won by huge margins. Moreover, Alcindor was seduced by the Hollywood-produced image of California, that glorious land of sun, beaches, pretty girls, and racial comity. As Alcindor watched the Bruins capture the 1964 NCAA championship on television, he was taken with their pell-mell style as well as their teamwork. They looked like a jazz band in sneakers.

At Alcindor's behest, Donohue called Wooden in the spring of 1964, shortly after the Bruins had won their first title. Donohue told Wooden that his star center was interested in UCLA and that he wanted to discuss the matter in person at a coaching clinic in Valley Forge, Pennsylvania, where Wooden was an invited speaker. Wooden told Donohue at the clinic that he was willing to host Alcindor for a weekend, but only if he was genuinely interested in UCLA. Donohue assured Wooden that he was.

By the time that weekend rolled around, however, Wooden was becoming less interested in Alcindor. It was not because he was afraid to build his team around a big man (though he had never done it before). It was because he knew UCLA's fans and alumni would expect multiple NCAA titles if Alcindor came. Wooden could already see that winning a championship had pushed expectations out of whack. He didn't want to set the bar any higher.

But Wooden couldn't get cold feet, because J. D. Morgan was too busy holding them to the fire. Morgan wanted Alcindor badly, and he made sure both Wooden and Norman knew it. "Wooden didn't want to have anything to do with Alcindor," Jerry Norman said. "The only reason he recruited him was because J. D. wanted him to. Believe me, he was not going to cross J. D. Morgan."

When Alcindor took his visit to Westwood, Morgan made sure that

Norman showed him where the Memorial Activities Center was being built. Morgan wanted Alcindor to see that it was not just a drawing on a piece of paper but an actual structure that was nearing completion. The only thing missing was the floor. The arena was going to open in the fall of 1965, and because the very first event would be the annual game between the freshmen and the varsity, Wooden could credibly tell Alcindor that he was going to dedicate the new facility. "We'd never have gotten him to come with the old gym," Wooden said. "Climb up three flights. Two baskets, with gymnastics on the side, wrestling on the end. One big locker room. One shower room, no privacy in any way. You think he would have come under those conditions?"

A week after touring UCLA and meeting Wooden, Alcindor took an official visit to Michigan, but since his mind was already made up, he never really gave that school a chance. (He said later that he regretted that.) He also visited Holy Cross, but only because the school had hired Donohue as its new coach, and Donohue said Alcindor owed it to him to at least take a visit. But Alcindor's mind was made up. He wanted to go to UCLA.

Problem was, his parents had met every other coach who was recruiting him, but they had never met Wooden. Los Angeles was awfully far from New York City. How could they send him there without meeting the man who would take care of him? Donohue called Wooden and asked if he would travel to New York so Alcindor's parents could approve his decision. Wooden wasn't crazy about the idea. He rarely conducted home visits in his own backyard, much less a continent away, but he recognized that this was a special case. Besides, Morgan wouldn't let him turn it down even if he tried.

Morgan told Wooden he wanted Norman to accompany him on the trip to see the Alcindors. He said it was because Norman was Catholic, but Norman suspected the real reason was that Morgan was afraid Wooden would blow it. On the day they arrived in New York, Big Al was working the night shift, and he did not get home until after midnight. The meeting took place in the Alcindors' living room at 1:00 a.m. Lew sat in a separate room trying to listen in as Wooden and Norman talked to his parents about UCLA. Lew's mom and dad liked that Wooden emphasized academics, and they appreciated that he did not try to give them a hard sell. If anything, he seemed to suggest that Lew should consider changing his mind. Several times, he said to them, "If Lewis doesn't want to come to UCLA, we will understand." Norman felt like crawling under the couch. "He practically begged him not to come," Norman said, "but the kid wanted to come so bad."

Lewis's parents were still not happy about sending their only child so far away, but they had raised him to make his own choices. And so, on May 4, 1965, Alcindor walked into the gymnasium at Power Memorial to announce his long-awaited decision. Wearing the school's standard coat-and-tie uniform, he entered the gym at 12:33 p.m. to find more than eighty members of the media waiting for him. When he stepped to the podium and spoke, it was, wrote Phil Pepe of the *New York World-Telegram and Sun*, "the first time the press had ever heard the sound of Alcindor's voice."

"I have an announcement to make. This fall I'll be attending UCLA in Los Angeles," he said. "It had the atmosphere I wanted and the people out there were very nice to me." He later added, "I have always been captivated by California."

This was a truly historic basketball moment, one that caused ripples in two major cities on opposite ends of the country. "Rich Get Richer: Alcindor, 7–1 Cage Whiz, Picks UCLA," blared the headline in the next morning's *Los Angeles Times*. Everybody proclaimed that this was the best high school prospect since Wilt Chamberlain—including Wilt Chamberlain. "I've seen the kid play several times in the playgrounds around Manhattan, and I think he's tremendous," he said. "He's bigger than I was in high school and thirty pounds heavier. I moved better, but he shoots much better." Wooden, meanwhile, tried his best to knock down the assumption that Alcindor's mere presence would guarantee three more NCAA titles. "Anybody who believes that is only displaying his ignorance," he said. "Did Kansas win it with Wilt Chamberlain?"

Wooden further insisted that the arrival of this megatalent would not alter his basketball philosophy. "I don't try to make a star out of anybody. He will fit into the framework of our system," he said. In truth, Wooden didn't really know just how he was going to utilize the incoming giant. After all, to that point, he had never seen Alcindor play.

"Is that Lew Alcindor?"

"Yeah, that's him. He's nothing but a big nigger."

The exchange between two white students as Alcindor passed by occurred a few days after he had arrived on campus. Alcindor's first instinct was to spin around and confront them, but he was talked out of it by the black friend with whom he had been walking. It was not the first time Alcindor had heard himself described this way, and he cursed himself for being so naive. Of course there were racists in California. It was still America, wasn't it?

Alcindor quickly figured out that most people in Los Angeles came from someplace else, and their bigotry came with them. If anything, the racists here were worse than the ones back home. In New York, people would call you names to your face. They might even come right up to you and poke you with an umbrella. You had to respect that. People in Los Angeles, on the other hand, had mastered what Alcindor would later refer to as "the art of seeming to like people that you really don't like."

The incident with the white students fed into the intense culture shock that Alcindor experienced during his first few months at UCLA. "I felt like I was in the middle of the ocean on a raft," he later wrote. Everything about him felt out of place. His wardrobe was Greenwich Village cool—tweed jacket, jeans, wire-rim sunglasses. Out here, it was all button-down shirts, chinos, and penny loafers. He also shared a classroom with girls for the first time since the eighth grade, but he had no idea how to talk to them. His luck with the fellas wasn't much better. One night he tried going to a party with a bunch of UCLA football players, but when some USC players showed up, a huge fight broke out. Alcindor beat it out of there.

Life in the dorms was the same. While Alcindor tried to chill by himself in his room in Dykstra Hall, the other students entertained themselves by flooding the hallway with two inches of water and sliding through it buck naked. These kids may have been the same age as he was, but he felt much older. Unlike them, he had a social conscience. He devoured books like *The Autobiography of Malcolm X* and *Autobiography of a Yogi*, as well as the poetry of LeRoi Jones. He also studied the emerging movement of black nationalism. During the Harlem riots, Alcindor had seen firsthand how racial divisions could boil over, and he knew that Los Angeles had experienced a similar trauma the previous summer in the segregated neighborhood of Watts. That went down just twenty miles from UCLA's campus, yet the other students didn't seem to be affected one bit.

So Alcindor did what he always did when he felt out of place: he retreated. Aside from a couple of other black students, he befriended very few people. Even his teammates found it difficult to penetrate his seven-foot-one-inch shell. That included his roommate, Lucius Allen, a black six-foot-two guard from Kansas City, Kansas, who was arguably the best prospect ever to emerge from his home state. While Allen spent hour after hour hanging downstairs in Dykstra Hall and shooting pool, Alcindor was hunkered in his room listening to jazz and reading books. (Alcindor was a speed reader with a photographic memory. Allen couldn't believe how fast he flipped those pages.) The player with whom Alcindor bonded the most was Edgar Lacey. Alcindor wrote in *Giant Steps* that he and Lacey shared the assumption "that whites were hard to read and harder to trust, that all blacks should be brothers, that you could expect trouble before you could expect peace."

But Alcindor did connect with his teammates on the court, the one place where he wanted to be part of a band. During their first week on campus, Alcindor and Allen joined two other freshmen in a full-court game of pickup four-on-four against the varsity. Allen was unstoppable. After the freshmen won the first two games, Lacey said he wanted to guard him. The first time Allen had the ball, he got Lacey to leave his feet on a shot fake and easily glided past him for a layup. Whatever discomfort Alcindor felt about being a student at UCLA, he knew right away that he was going to enjoy playing with Lucius Allen for the next four years.

By the time the 1965–66 basketball season got under way, John Wooden was eager to put an end to seventeen years of delayed gratification. The Bruins' first practice was the first official activity to take place inside the new on-campus arena, which had been named Pauley Pavilion in honor of Edwin Pauley, the regent whose $1 million donation had pushed the project past the finish line. Finally, after all these years, Wooden was coaching in a facility superior to his old high school gym in Martinsville.

In the wake of his back-to-back titles, Wooden was also presented with a most unusual offer. It came from Joe Brown, the general manager of the Pittsburgh Pirates, who happened to be seated next to Wooden at a dinner. Brown was so impressed by Wooden's knowledge of baseball, his favorite sport, that Brown asked the UCLA coach if he would like to manage the Pirates. At first, Wooden thought he was kidding. When Brown said he wasn't, Wooden declined, saying, "They'd run you out of town before they did me." When asked about this by a Pittsburgh reporter many years later, Brown confirmed that he had indeed made the offer. "Yes, I would have hired him," Brown said. "He can handle any job."

The floor in Pauley was so spacious that both the varsity and the freshmen teams could practice there, separated by a partition. Wooden peeked in on the freshmen often, allowing him to study the seven-foot-one prodigy who had caused so much stir. "I was just astounded the first time I saw Lewis," Wooden said. "His agility for that size was just amazing, and the coordination he had. . . . I never had the opportunity to work with someone of that size."

Besides Alcindor and Allen, Wooden and Norman had recruited two other local freshmen who had garnered All-America honors: Kenny Heitz, a six-foot-three forward from Santa Maria, and Lynn Shackelford, a six-foot-five forward from Burbank. Shackelford was such a deadeye left-handed shooter that his teammates were already calling him the "Machine." The four of them comprised by far the most talented class that Wooden had ever recruited. It affirmed his long-held suspicion that if he ever got things rolling at UCLA, the momentum would carry itself forward, success begetting ever more success.

The start of practice brought Alcindor under the auspices of two men who would be responsible for his early development. The first was the newly hired freshman coach, Gary Cunningham. After graduating from UCLA in 1962, Cunningham had played professionally overseas for a couple of years before returning to Westwood to get his master's degree in education. Cunningham found Alcindor compliant during practices but excruciating to be around in a social setting. "During his freshman year, I used to eat breakfast every morning in the student union. I'd see him and sometimes I would sit down with him, but there was absolutely no conversation," Cunningham said. "I tried to engage him by asking questions. How's school? How's this? How's that? And you'd get one- or two-word answers. Of all the players at UCLA that I encountered, he was the most difficult player to communicate with. I don't know why he came to UCLA, because his heart was on the East Coast."

Wooden also brought in a second coach for the sole purpose of working with Alcindor. His name was Jay Carty, a six-foot-eight, 230-pound, self-professed "slow white guy who couldn't jump." Carty was well qualified to coach a big man: he had played center for Oregon State from 1960 to 1962, and during every practice his senior year, he had gone up against Mel Counts, his seven-foot sophomore teammate. Carty's main job was to pound on Alcindor and try to make him mad, but they also spent a lot of time working on Alcindor's post moves.

While he was at Oregon State, Carty had perfected a unique shooting method that enabled him to score over taller defenders. The shot was called a "flat hook." It defied two conventions about the fundamentals of shooting. In the first place, Carty jumped away from his defender, not toward him. And instead of squaring his shoulders to the basket, Carty turned sideways, which allowed him to reach farther away from the defense before letting the ball fly. That enabled him to create the space he needed to keep his shot from getting blocked.

Carty didn't invent the flat hook by any stretch. As a teenager in the 1950s, he had watched it being utilized by players like Washington's Bob Houbregs and Doug Smart, as well as Oregon State's Tony Vlastelica. He had first been taught the move by his high school coach in China Lake, California. Carty told Alcindor that if he learned the hook, it would make him five inches taller. The kid was a quick study. "It was a duck to water," Carty said. "Once he got the mechanics down, that shot became his liquid gold."

Wooden's decision to assign Carty to work with Alcindor was a tremendous boost to Alcindor's adjustment. Wooden's approach to the media yielded more mixed results. Wooden rendered Alcindor completely off-limits to sportswriters for his entire freshman year. That had been the same policy that had been in place while Alcindor was at Power Memorial. Wooden claimed it was implemented at the request of Alcindor's parents, but Alcindor later insisted that the whole thing was Wooden's idea. Regardless of who came up with it, the decision to hold the press at bay only added to Alcindor's feelings of isolation. When he saw adjectives like *eccentric* and *moody* being ascribed to him in print by white men he had never met, it fed into the distrust he already held.

He would have to let his playing speak for him, and he made his opening statement on November 27, 1965. That was the night that UCLA opened its sparkling, 13,000-seat, on-campus arena to the public. Pauley Pavilion was the finest campus facility anywhere on the West Coast, and perhaps in the country. The main event was the annual freshman-varsity game, which was going to be broadcast live on local television for the first time. Before the game tipped off, the school held a "Salute to John Wooden" ceremony, with some seventy-five of Wooden's former players on hand to mark the moment. Wooden received three standing ovations during the fifteen-minute festivities, an appreciation both for what he had accomplished at UCLA and what he was promising to accomplish in the years ahead.

With all the hoopla focused on Alcindor, the varsity Bruins were an afterthought. Gail Goodrich and Keith Erickson had graduated, but five of the top seven players had returned from the 1965 champs, including Freddie Goss and Edgar Lacey. The incoming sophomore class featured Mike Warren, the highly regarded point guard from South Bend, and Bill Sweek, a six-foot-three forward from Pasadena. The Bruins began the season as the No. 1 team in both the AP and UPI national polls.

However, they were going to have to play the freshmen short-handed. Three weeks before the game, Goss had been awakened by an intense pain in his spine that left him feeling paralyzed. An ambulance rushed him to the UCLA Medical Center, where doctors prepared to perform an appendectomy before deciding that wasn't the problem. The pain was so mysterious that Goss thought he might have been poisoned. His doctors kept asking him if he had traveled outside Los Angeles, perhaps to Mexico. (He hadn't.) Goss was feeling better by the time practice started, but because the illness had caused him to lose so much weight, he would have to watch the freshman-varsity game in street clothes.

As the players were introduced, they walked onto the court through a gauntlet of former Bruins. Finally, at long last, the wait was over. Pauley Pavilion was open for business, and Lew Alcindor was wearing a UCLA uniform. The first time he had the ball, Alcindor rewarded the sellout crowd and the thousands watching on live television by shooting an air ball.

He didn't miss much after that. Once he and his freshman teammates settled down, they unsettled the varsity. UCLA had mounted its two championship runs by being smaller and quicker than its opponents. Now, for the first time, the Bruins were facing a player who was much taller than they were, yet who was just as quick as any of their guards. Alcindor shut off the basket at the defensive end, and on offense, his teammates got him the ball where he could score from in close.

Meanwhile, the varsity's vaunted full-court zone press was ineffective. Not only were the freshmen familiar with it—as was Cunningham, the freshman coach—but they had the perfect antidote. All Cunningham had to do was station Alcindor at the free throw line, have a guard toss him the ball, and allow Alcindor to pivot and decide where to throw it. Alcindor had a long way to go to fulfill his physical potential, but he was already thinking like a senior.

The game was close for a while. The varsity built a 29–28 lead but trailed at halftime, 36–31. At the start of the second half, however, the freshmen did to the varsity what the Bruins had done to so many other hapless foes. They blitzed. The freshmen scored 10 unanswered points, with 6 coming from Alcindor, and a short while later, they completed a 22–6 run to build an 18-point lead. "We didn't have any problem with the press all night," Cunningham said. "We were just better than the varsity. That's the bottom line." With five minutes to go, Cunningham mercifully pulled his starters. Alcindor finished with 31 points and 21 rebounds, but he was not the only freshman to shine. Lucius Allen had 16 points, and Lynn Shackelford added 12. Meanwhile, the highest scorer for the varsity was Mike Lynn, who scored all of 12 points.

The final score of 75–60 would have been much worse if Cunningham had not pulled his starters. Alcindor had done the impossible. He had actually exceeded his outlandish expectations. "I was completely impressed. There's no goon in him. He moves smooth," Wooden said. "I like the fact that he seems to be able to rise to the occasion. A boy can perform well in high school, but you don't know how he'll do when he comes up against older, more experienced players." Meanwhile, Wooden had a brand-new problem on his hands. His varsity Bruins had been humiliated for all the world to see, and they now held the dubious distinction of being the No. 1 team in America yet only the second-best team on their own campus. "We're way out of place if we don't get Goss back," Wooden said. "I'm not even sure we can use the press with this group. They don't have the speed or the toughness. Quite frankly, we're not a good ball club right now. We wouldn't belong on the same floor with some of our teams of the past few years."

Cunningham felt far from triumphant. He was so embarrassed at what had happened to Wooden on his big night that he hid in the locker room after the game to avoid talking to the press. "I guess that was not a mature thing to do, but I didn't want to go out there and say anything about Coach," he said. "I mean, he was my coach, and this was my first game on his staff. I didn't know how to handle the win." The embarrassment lingered through the postgame reception for the former players, where Cunningham and his wife sat quietly at a corner table. "I just didn't feel good about mingling with people."

When Cunningham reported for work on Monday morning, Wooden's secretary came by his office and said the coach wanted to see him. "I'm thinking, geez, I'm going to get fired," Cunningham said. "But he never even talked about the game. I was greatly relieved." Instead, Wooden went over the usual business—what was going on with recruiting, how the players were doing academically, what the plan should be for that afternoon's practices. Wooden knew his Bruins had been demoralized, but he also now fully realized just what the future held. This Alcindor kid was going to take Mr. Pepperidge Farm on one heck of a ride.

22

Stallball

The fresh idea that had been hatched in Wooden's office just two years before was becoming a genuine basketball movement. In the fall of 1965, *Sports Illustrated* previewed the coming season with a cover photo showing UCLA's Doug McIntosh standing upright with his arms raised, positioned to block an in-bounds pass from a crouching opponent. The words underneath read: "The UCLA Press: How to Beat It." Old-school John Wooden from Depression-era Indiana was being hailed as some kind of Dr. Frankenstein, and his monster was stumping the basketball cognoscenti from coast to coast.

That was the thrust of the six-page article headlined "A Press That Panics Them All." *Sports Illustrated* interviewed dozens of college coaches around the country, and each one seemed to have a different theory about how to solve this intricate puzzle. Ohio State coach Fred Taylor's solution was to "look for the long pass. If it's a true zone press, we'll try to eliminate a couple of defenders in a hurry." Michigan's Dave Strack believed his players should "run with the ball. Despite what happened to us in the UCLA game last season, I still think the zone press is vulnerable to quick basketball." Notre Dame's Johnny Dee argued for a bounce pass to the first man because "there is less chance for an interception," and Louisville's Pete Hickman pointed out the importance of keeping your poise. "If one of our big men is shut off by two guards, we tell him to take the five-second penalty of a jump ball rather than throw a bad pass. Then he still has a chance to control the jump."

Wooden was pleased that there was so little agreement. "As long as so many coaches feel there are so many ways to beat the zone press," he said, "that means no one is really sure."

For all their theories, those coaches failed to understand the two most important things about the zone press. First, the main reason it worked was the personnel executing it. Wooden rode two All-American guards to those back-to-back NCAA titles, and he had an Olympic-level athlete playing the pivotal rear position. Second, none of the coaches grasped that the true purpose of the press was to force the tempo. Even if all their geometric theories enabled their team to beat the press for layups, that would have been okay with Wooden. As long as the opponent played faster than it wanted to, Wooden believed his better-conditioned players would gain the advantage over the final minutes.

There was something else missing from the story: an acknowledgment from Wooden that the zone press was not originally his idea. In fact, Jerry Norman's name did not appear anywhere in the article, an omission that did not go unnoticed back in Westwood, least of all by Norman.

The world would soon see how much the zone press—or any defense, for that matter—would depend on having quality personnel. Not only did UCLA have to replace Goodrich and Erickson, but the team would also have to begin the season without Freddie Goss, whose back ailment still had not been definitively diagnosed, though doctors suspected he had a blood infection. That forced Wooden to start Mike Warren, and the smooth little point guard from South Bend proved to be a stellar find. Warren had been recruited primarily to be a setup man, but he scored a combined 51 points as UCLA routed Ohio State and Illinois in its first varsity games in Pauley Pavilion.

As would be the case throughout the season, however, the Bruins were a much different team away from home. That became obvious when they hit the road for a much-ballyhooed two-game series with Duke, which was ranked third by the AP and fifth in the UPI poll. The first game took place on Duke's campus in Durham, and the second was held at the Charlotte Coliseum. UCLA was undermanned and overwhelmed, especially without Goss, and the Blue Devils swept the Bruins by 16 and 19 points. It was UCLA's first back-to-back losses in more than three years. The trip also disgusted Wooden for reasons beyond what happened on the court. This was UCLA's first foray to the South since its ill-fated trip to Houston four years before. While the Bruins did not have to deal with segregated hotels or racist referees, they were confronted by a handful of fans who brought Confederate flags to the games and shouted racial taunts at UCLA's black players. "I said I won't go back to this place again, and I never did," Wooden said years later. "Not because of the coach, not because of the players, but because of the fans. Particularly [their behavior] toward the black players."

The losses dropped UCLA to No. 8 in the AP poll. The Bruins beat Kansas in Pauley by 7 points in their next outing, but after losing to Cincinnati by 6 points in Chicago, they dropped out of the rankings altogether. (The national polls only ranked ten teams back then.) They did not look anything like a team destined to win a third straight NCAA title.

Meanwhile, Alcindor and the freshmen were having no trouble with their opponents. Wooden instructed Cunningham to leave his starters in the game until the waning minutes, regardless of the margin. The final scores looked like typos: 119–43, 152–49, 108–74. "He wanted the scholarship guys to play and get experience," Cunningham said. "There were a lot of games that year that I was kind of embarrassed about the lopsided score."

Wooden remained committed to racehorse basketball, but he was also willing to slam on the brakes if he thought it would earn his team a win. After beginning conference play with routs of Oregon State and Oregon at Pauley, the Bruins hit the road and found themselves leading Cal by just 3 points with seven minutes to play. Wooden ordered his players to stall. When Cal coach Rene Herrerias answered by letting his team sit back in its zone defense, Wooden had his guys play keep-away. The boos rained down from the crowd, but Wooden instructed his players to hold the ball for more than two minutes before resuming their regular action. The tactic worked as UCLA won, 75–66, behind Mike Lynn's game-high 25 points.

The Bruins weren't so fortunate the next night as they lost at Stanford, 74–69, ending their thirty-five-game conference winning streak. Bay Area fans savored the chance to kick a little sand in the face of the bullies from down south. Paul Zimmerman wrote in the *Los Angeles Times* that the win over UCLA had made Stanford coach Howie Dallmar a local hero. "Basketball followers have built up something of a hate for coach John Wooden and his Bruins here [in the Bay Area]," Zimmerman wrote. "Not all of it is predicated on the team's outstanding success. They accuse John of making belittling remarks to opposing players during games as they pass the UCLA bench, and also of intimidating the officials."

UCLA lost two of its next three games to fall to 11–6. The team was clearly struggling to carry the mantle of being the two-time defending champs. After UCLA's 1-point loss to Washington State on February 5, Cougars coach Marv Harshman told Wooden that the Cougars had played their finest game of the season. "He said they were fired up—something I'm getting tired of hearing," Wooden said.

Wooden suspected that something else was ailing his club. He con-fessed to one of his freshmen, Lynn Shackelford, that he believed the varsity players had never recovered mentally from the pounding they had suffered in that exhibition. "This team has been one of the most dif-ficult teams I've ever had to coach because we started off the season by losing to the frosh," he told Shackelford. "They're keeping it inside them-selves but you know that just really killed them."

UCLA followed the loss at Washington State by winning its next three games, only to lose back-to-back games at Oregon State and Ore-gon. The Bruins' AAWU record was now 7–4, and even though they would end the regular season with four straight wins (including a two-game sweep of USC), they still finished in second place. Not only did that keep UCLA out of the NCAA tournament for the first time in three years, but it also denied the Bruins an opportunity to play those games in Pauley Pavilion, which was hosting the NCAA's West Regional in its very first year of existence. (Assist, J. D. Morgan.)

As for Lew Alcindor and his fellow freshmen, they did not lose a game all season. The closest they came was against USC, when the Trojans' freshmen held the ball during every offensive possession. UCLA scored a season-low 28 points in the first half, but when USC freshman coach Bill Mulligan abandoned the stall midway through the second half, UCLA pulled away to win, 72–44. Afterward, Mulligan insisted that his team had "played them the only way you can play them." He also confessed that during the first half, an angry fan approached the USC bench and asked Mulligan for his money back.

Wooden knew that he could expect more stalling once Alcindor moved up to the varsity. But Wooden also knew that his team would face more of the bugaboos that were getting under his skin: Expectations. Pressure. Maximum effort from every opponent. Maximum energy from every crowd. All of it was playing out under the gathering assumption that if the Bruins didn't win a championship—indeed, if they didn't win *three* championships—then the whole Alcindor experiment would be labeled a bust. Al Wolf of the *Los Angeles Times* captured the coach's predica-ment in a column that was published under the headline "Pressure's on 'Poor' Wooden." It read: "If you drop a pin in Azusa, John Wooden will jump a foot in Westwood. He's that jittery these days. The UCLA basket-ball coach, instead of basking in the happy thought that long and silent Lew Alcindor will move up from the frosh to the varsity next season, desperately is attempting to fight off the whammy, hex and evil eye." Acknowledging Wooden's reminder that Wilt Chamberlain did not win a title at Kansas, that Oscar Robertson did not win a title at Cincinnati, that Jerry Lucas and John Havlicek only won one title at Ohio State, and that Cazzie Russell couldn't even bring Michigan back to the NCAA semifinals that were taking place that weekend, Wolf countered that Alcindor would be surrounded with much greater talent than any of those players were. The only acceptable outcome, therefore, was perfection.

There was no getting around it. The bar was going to be set impossibly high. "You can't get off the spot, John," Wolf concluded. "And how many other coaches would like to have your problem!"

Since Stretch Murphy, his old Purdue teammate, was Wooden's only frame of reference for how to play with a true center, it was time for the teacher to go back to school. Wooden spent most of the spring and summer of 1966 calling around the country to learn everything he could about a low-post offense. He called his old nemesis Henry Iba, who had won two NCAA titles with seven-foot center Bob Kurland. He called George Mikan, the three-time All-American center at DePaul who went on to star with the Minneapolis Lakers. He called Mikan's college coach, Ray Meyer. He called Adolph Rupp and Wilt Chamberlain. He often told his players that failure to prepare was preparation to fail, so he made sure he was thoroughly prepared for the 1966–67 season.

When Alcindor returned to campus that fall for his sophomore year, his outlook had changed, and not for the better. The previous spring, without basketball to provide structure and force him to interact with other students, Alcindor felt intensely lonely during the two months between the end of the season and the end of the semester. There were no more parties, no more efforts to join the campus social scene. It was just him, a few black friends, and his studies. "He seemed a lot more angry when he came back that summer. He just became remote," Kenny Heitz said. "We spent a lot of time running around during our freshman year, but after that, there was not much of a personal relationship with me and him."

Alcindor's lifestyle made it easy to cloister himself. Over the summer, he had worked in the publishing and recording divisions of Columbia Pictures in the studio's New York offices. He had gotten the job courtesy of an influential UCLA alumnus named Mike Frankovich, and his responsibilities were so minimal that on some days, Alcindor would check in at the front desk to let them know he was there, and then walk directly to a freight elevator and head home. He earned $125 per week, not exactly a king's ransom, but enough to allow him to save up and buy a 1958 Mercedes for $1,100. Now that he had his own wheels, Alcindor was free to live with Edgar Lacey in a small apartment in Santa Monica. But that proved to be too expensive, so the two of them moved to Pacific Palisades and, later, back to Westwood, where they rented a maid's quarters in a condominium. Basketball star or not, Alcindor never seemed to have enough money in his pocket.

Wooden and Alcindor were not particularly close, but Alcindor respected his coach. When Alcindor bragged to Wooden about how good his grades were, Wooden reminded him that he still had three long years remaining to get his degree. "He knew when to stick his finger in the bubble," Alcindor said. "He let some of that hot air out, let some of that pride and arrogance dissipate into the air where it belonged."

That November, Wooden invited Alcindor and Allen to his home for Thanksgiving. Even though they got lost and arrived an hour late, Wooden was a gracious host, chitchatting with the boys about school, their hometowns, current events—anything besides basketball. Those kinds of exchanges, however, were rare. Neither player craved social time with their coach. He was there to teach them to play basketball, nothing more, nothing less.

There was, however, another adult who became Alcindor's mentor beginning that fall. Willie Naulls had finished his ten-year career with the New York Knicks, San Francisco Warriors, and Boston Celtics, and he had returned to UCLA to pursue a degree in economics. Naulls was working his way into the city's business community, and like Jay Carty, he asked Wooden if he could help out in practice. Naulls took an interest in Alcindor where Wooden didn't and couldn't—as a fellow black man who understood the pressures, expectations, and confusion that came with being a star basketball player at UCLA.

With Alcindor's varsity career set to get under way, the school could no longer keep him under wraps. On the first day of practice, UCLA held a press conference to introduce the team. Of course, the only person the press wanted to talk to was Alcindor, partly because they had never been able to interact with him before. The first question, naturally, was about his height. "I'm seven feet one and three-eighth inches tall. I weigh two-thirty," he said quietly.

Needless to say, the expectations for this team were off the charts. The Bruins were tabbed as the No. 1 team in both the AP and UPI polls. Alcindor was on the cover of a plethora of national magazines, including

Sports Illustrated's season preview issue, where he appeared on a foldout cover under the banner, "The New Superstar." Wooden was already fretting his team couldn't possibly live up to all that hype, so imagine his chagrin when he lost not one but two upperclassman starters for the season. The first was Edgar Lacey, who had season-ending surgery to repair a kneecap he had fractured the previous season. (The loss was a double blow for Alcindor, since Lacey was his best friend on the team.) The Bruins would also have to play without Mike Lynn, who was suspended for the season after pleading guilty to a misdemeanor charge of credit card theft.

With two upperclassmen waylaid, Wooden was faced with the frightening specter of a starting lineup that included four sophomores and one junior (Warren). As good as Alcindor was, he would need help from his teammates, especially Lucius Allen, who had been the second-best player on the freshman team the year before, averaging 22.4 points per game. Like Alcindor, Allen considered Wooden a very good basketball coach, but he did not swing by his office to shoot the breeze. "Jerry Norman and Willie Naulls were the guys I confided in, not Coach Wooden," Allen said. "If you were going to talk with Coach Wooden privately in his office, that was not going to be pleasurable."

Like Alcindor, Allen was also coming to terms with issues of race and society. "In those days, we walked around with a chip on our shoulder. We weren't gonna take anything from Whitey," Allen said. Once in a while, when Wooden would refer to Allen as his "boy" (as he did all his players), Allen would bridle. Wooden would only smile and say, "Of course you're my boy, Lucius." Yet, even in his chippiest moments, Allen never once questioned Wooden's intentions. "I never felt anything racist from him—ever—as much as I tried to bring it into the fold."

When Allen heard that Wooden regularly schooled his former players in shooting contests, he grabbed Mike Warren and gave it a try. "He just whipped the crap out of us," Allen recalled. "He talked the whole time he was beating us. 'Now, listen guys, this is how you shoot a jump shot, okay? Watch this release and—oh, that went in, didn't it.'" Wooden also got the better of Allen on the pool table. Allen spent many hours in his dormitory shooting stick when he should have been studying. He even got good at hustling the other students, letting them win a game or two and then trouncing them when real money was on the line. Wooden happened to see Allen and Alcindor shooting pool during a road trip and cracked, "Aww, that's niche-picking." When Lucius dared him to pick up a cue, Wooden virtually ran the table. "When he missed, he never left me in position where I could make a shot," Allen said. "At the end, he winked at me and said, 'Now, Lucius, if I can beat you, you don't have much chance to make a living at this game. I suggest you go to the library.'"

With the core of the team set, it was up to the rest of the squad to find their place within the machine. "You knew Kareem, Lucius, and Mike were going to get minutes," Heitz said, referring to Alcindor by the name he would later adopt, Kareem Abdul-Jabbar. "The rest was like a street fight." Shackelford was a shoo-in at forward. His size and long-range shooting made him an ideal complement to Alcindor's low-post prowess, and his participation in the Fellowship of Christian Athletes didn't hurt him in Wooden's eyes. Heitz started at the other forward spot, but he had to fight off two other sophomores, Jim Nielsen and Bill Sweek, for minutes. Alcindor came to enjoy the comic relief those frat boys provided, especially on the road, although it took some time for him and Sweek to warm up to each other. "We had a total disconnect at first," Sweek said. "I was a West Coaster, free-living surfer, doing crazy pranks in the dorms. He was sophisticated and serious. I remember the first time he told me I was racist or something, I said, 'Man, you don't even know who I am. Until you really know me, I don't think that's fair.'"

The 1966–67 season was shaping up to be unlike any that the school, or the sport, had experienced. As usual, J. D. Morgan was ready to pounce. Since he was assured of a sellout crowd every time UCLA played at Pauley Pavilion, he loaded up on home games. Moreover, he had secured yet another contract with KTLA-TV. The movie actor Gene Autry had purchased the station from Paramount, and he wanted KTLA to emphasize sports. Morgan negotiated a five-year, six-figure contract that would enable KTLA to broadcast a variety of UCLA sporting events. The problem was, Morgan also had an obligation to the school's radio network to keep most of the basketball games off live TV. So he came up with an ingenious solution: on the nights when KTLA was forbidden from showing the basketball games live, it was permitted to air those games on tape delay. That meant that the local news had to refrain from announcing UCLA scores on its evening newscasts, or at least give viewers a warning that the final score was about to be revealed. To call the games, KTLA hired a thirty-year-old health education teacher and assistant baseball coach at San Fernando Valley State College who had done some sports announcing on radio while he was an undergraduate at Central Michigan University and later as a grad student at Indiana University. The young fellow's name was Dick Enberg.

KTLA also committed to producing a weekly half-hour show with Wooden during the season. Wooden was fast becoming a star in a town full of them, especially after he published his first book that fall. He called it *Practical Modern Basketball*, an homage to the groundbreaking *Practical Basketball* text that Piggy Lambert had written back in 1932. Wooden's book laid out all of his teachings in deep detail (and dry prose). He described his overarching philosophies—including an explanation of the tenets that made up his Pyramid of Success—as well as a step-by-step breakdown of how a coach should manage every aspect of his program. He described precisely what kind of socks players should wear, what they should eat before a game, how they should organize their dressing room, and what they should do to avoid colds. ("Instruct the players to rub down briskly after they shower and to dry their hair well.") Yet for all the intricacies contained in his book, the view of the game that Wooden described was surprisingly simple. He did not worry that publishing this book would give an advantage to opposing coaches because, as he wrote, "there are no real secrets to the game, at least not for very long." The book enhanced his image as a humble champion.

Alcindor was much the same way, which is why he and Wooden got along so well. Wooden told Alcindor early on that if he scored as many points as he was capable of, it would destroy the team's chemistry. Alcindor agreed, but they made an exception for the season opener against USC. This was, after all, Alcindor's first real game. Wooden wanted to strike fear into the hearts of the rest of the conference, not to mention the country.

It helped that Bob Boyd, USC's new coach, had never seen Alcindor play before. Boyd tried to defend him with a straight up, man-to-man scheme, rotating six-foot-six Bill Hewitt and seven-foot Ron Taylor on Alcindor without any double coverage. He might as well have been back in high school. Time after time, Alcindor's teammates fed him the ball down low, and he calmly dropped the ball in the basket. With a packed house of 13,800 looking on, Alcindor shot 23 of 32 from the floor and 10 for 14 from the foul line, for a total of 56 points. In his very first outing, he had shattered the school's single-game scoring record of 42 set by Gail Goodrich in the 1965 NCAA championship game. After UCLA won, 105–90, Wooden told the press, "At times, he frightens me. When he gets it all together, he's going to be something."

The two-game homestand the following weekend was even bigger. The opponent for both games was seventh-ranked Duke. Wooden still had a bad taste from his experience in North Carolina the year before. Though he was never one to emphasize winning, he made sure his players knew he expected them to exact full revenge for the way they had been treated by the fans down there. Allen even heard his coach talking trash to some of the Duke players during warm-ups. *Lucius can't wait to get his hands on you. You're in for a long night, son.* "It looked like he was just walking around being John Wooden," Allen said, "but he was baiting their players."

Duke coach Vic Bubas may have overlearned the lesson from the USC game. During the first game, every time Alcindor touched the ball, he was swarmed by three Duke defenders. Rather than forcing a ton of shots, Alcindor kept dishing to his wide-open teammates. He scored just 19 points, but Warren had 26 as UCLA won, 88–54. The next night, Bubas assigned just two defenders at a time to guard Alcindor. He scored 38 points in a 107–87 drubbing. "Wooden wanted us to beat 'em bad—and we did," Heitz said.

The games were so lacking in competitive drama that a reporter asked Wooden afterward if Alcindor might "wreck" college basketball. "There's no such thing as any one player wrecking the game," Wooden scoffed. He pointed out that when Bill Russell was at San Francisco, he played in a three-second lane that was just six feet wide, instead of the current twelve-foot lane. So Alcindor couldn't possibly dominate the way Russell did. Bubas disagreed, surmising that Alcindor might score 80 points one of these days. "I suppose that if I had one game to play against them and my job depended on it, I'd have to slow the pace of the game way down, play a zone defense, hit about fifty percent and hope like the devil you can do some kind of a job on the boards," Bubas said. "But basically I do not believe in that kind of basketball. We like to go up and down the court."

The Bruins faced a much stiffer challenge twelve days later at home against Colorado State. The Rams were a strong, veteran, physical team, and with six minutes to play, they trailed UCLA by just 1 point. Alcindor was mesmerized by the way Wooden took control of the end-of-game strategy. The coach was always precise with his language, but Alcindor noticed that under pressure he spoke even more loudly, enunciated even more clearly. Wooden never said the word *win*, but he sure wanted his team to finish with more points than the other guys. "When it came to winning a game, he went all out. He held back nothing," Alcindor said. "He didn't try and break the rules, but within the rules, he was going to try and crush you."

After UCLA escaped with an 84–74 victory, thanks to Alcindor's 34 points and 20 rebounds, Wooden sounded relieved that his team had been exposed as less than a juggernaut. "This game proved that we're going to be down on certain nights," Wooden said. "Like I've been saying all along, we're a young team and people expect too much."

The Colorado State game was also the first time—but far from the last—that the referees' treatment of Alcindor became an issue. Rams coach Jim Williams said the reason his team got into foul trouble was that "Alcindor was being overprotected." He added, "Alcindor is great. I don't know what more he could do with the ball once he gets it, but he doesn't need all that protection." When Wooden was asked whether Alcindor was overprotected, he replied, "If he was, then I must be blind."

That question would recur throughout Alcindor's career at UCLA, but he would not play in many more close games. There were certainly none to be found over the next few weeks as the Bruins steamrolled their next four opponents by an average of 29 points per game. That included USC, which UCLA beat by 24 points in the finals of the L.A. Classic in late December. Poor Bob Boyd. At the very moment he had returned to coach his alma mater, he was met by an imposing center the likes of which the game had never seen. And the Trojans still had two games remaining against UCLA on their schedule. Unlike the first two meetings, those would count in the league standings. Boyd realized that if he didn't come up with something new, the Bruins would turn his team into a laughingstock, over and over again.

How badly did Bob Boyd want to win? He was once called for a technical foul for arguing with a referee who had been the best man at his wedding. Boyd knew the biggest reason his predecessor, Forrest Twogood, was let go was that he had fallen so far behind Wooden. USC's two December losses to the Bruins made him realize just how big the gap was. Boyd was close friends with Pete Newell, the only coach who consistently got the better of Wooden, so he picked Newell's brain about his deliberate offense. Boyd began teaching that offense to his players on the first day of practice, but he had no intention of revealing it for a game that didn't count in the conference standings. He decided to save it for the game between USC and UCLA that was scheduled to take place at the Sports Arena on February 4.

The Bruins came into that contest still undefeated and on a roll. Their only hint of a struggle after the Colorado State game had been a 76–67 win at Washington State. At the end of January, they had taken what turned out to be a harrowing trip to the Midwest. First, the team's flight was delayed by a major snowstorm. The Bruins reached Chicago in time only because J. D. Morgan had convinced the pilot to land the plane in St. Louis, where a caravan of taxis awaited to whisk them to a train station. Only Morgan could pull off such a feat. Despite the horrible weather, more than nineteen thousand people packed into Chicago Stadium to watch the Bruins blitz Loyola University Chicago and Illinois on back-to-back nights by a total of 53 points.

Then there was the touchy matter of Alcindor's safety. In the days leading up to the much-ballyhooed trip, he had received death threats via two letters that bore Chicago postmarks. UCLA hired a plainclothes officer to protect Alcindor during the trip. Having seldom traveled outside the comfortable bubble of Westwood, the other Bruins finally got a real taste of the bile that Alcindor had been exposed to for most of his life. "The stuff he went through was horrible," Heitz said. "We'd go through the airport and people would walk by and say, 'That's the biggest nigger I've ever seen.' It happened in the arenas, in hotels. It happened all over the place."

Wooden had grown up in Indiana during the heyday of the Ku Klux Klan, yet he had never witnessed such overt racism. He frequently said that his years coaching Alcindor taught him about "man's inhumanity to man." One day, as he and Alcindor were walking through a hotel lobby, a white woman who was passing by exclaimed, "Look at that big black freak!" When Wooden tried to empathize, Alcindor told him, "You can say you understand, but you're an older man, and you're white. You can never truly understand what it's like to be me."

"Perhaps you're right," Wooden replied. "But I can try, can't I?"

"Yes, you can try. But you can never really know."

The treatment made Alcindor's calm temperament on the court all the more impressive in Wooden's eyes. The coach had always lectured his players about the importance of an even keel, but no player had done it as well, and under more duress, than Alcindor. His defenders were always smaller, slower, and less graceful, so their only hope was to be shove him around and hope the refs swallowed their whistles. After UCLA knocked off California in Pauley by 18 points in January, Wooden complained yet again that Alcindor was "not getting enough protection" and that several of his traveling calls came after he got pushed. "I'm still amazed at the way Lew can keep his poise in there and not get rattled," Wooden said.

At this point, Alcindor's numbers were so overwhelming that the only nit to be picked was the lopsided scores he produced. "How about you? I can't get interested in college basketball this season," John Hall wrote in the *Los Angeles Times*. "UCLA is so good there's no more sport to it." In early January, the *Saturday Evening Post* published an article under the headline, "Can Basketball Survive Lew Alcindor?" Of course, ten years earlier the magazine had asked the very same question about Chamberlain.

Boyd was determined to derail this powerful engine. When the Bruins returned from their trip to Chicago with a 16–0 record, Boyd and his Trojans were ready to spring their surprise. After UCLA jumped out to a quick 7–2 lead, Boyd called time-out. When play resumed, the Trojans went into their Newell-esque offense. Back and forth the ball went, around the perimeter, over and over, with the USC players passing up open shots. The Trojans' seven-foot center, Ron Taylor, moved to the high post in an effort to draw Alcindor away from the basket, but Wooden told Lew to stay put. As the Trojans continued to pass it around, Alcindor simply stood under the basket with his hands on his hips, occasionally stretching down to touch his shoes.

According to the rules, the team that was behind on the scoreboard was required to force the action. The refs, however, did not know that rule. As Boyd acknowledged later, had it been properly applied the Trojans would have had to make a move. But it wasn't, so the Trojans were able to go nearly nine minutes without attempting a shot. The home crowd at the Sports Arena booed Boyd mercilessly, but his offense was working. USC led at halftime, 17–14. As Boyd made his way to the locker room, the fans hurled paper cartons at him.

Still, he was committed to the strategy, and the Trojans surrendered their lead just once in the second half. By that time the home fans had become so unruly that Boyd found his athletic director, Jess Hill, and told him to get some more security around his team's bench. The Trojans actually had a chance to win on their final possession, but Bill Hewitt's jump shot from twenty feet was off. The second half ended in a 31–31 tie.

From there, UCLA owned the overtime. Sweek gave the Bruins a boost off the bench by providing two steals and a key late bucket, and UCLA emerged with a 40–35 win. Given how close the Trojans had just come to knocking off their rival, Boyd might have reasonably expected a standing ovation. Instead, he needed seven police officers to escort him across the court so he could do his postgame radio interview. "Even Trojan fans told me it was the worst thing they had ever seen," he said later.

The treatment of the fans, however, was nothing compared to the sharp elbows thrown by his opposing coach a few minutes later. "It was a good game plan and it was executed well, but something like this is bad for the game, and I'll tell Bob that too," Wooden said. "I'm not critical of him for using it from a tactical standpoint, only from the standpoint of how much this can hurt basketball." Asked whether he believed other coaches would attempt the same tactic against his Bruins down the road, Wooden allowed that it was possible. "But I don't think most coaches will try it," he added. "Too many coaches think too much of basketball to do it."

While there was some validity to what Wooden was saying—if every game were played that way, most fans wouldn't bother watching—his remarks were blatantly hypocritical. This was, after all, the same John Wooden who just thirteen months earlier had also ignored boos and slowed down a game in order to preserve a 9-point win at Cal. Wooden, in fact, had frequently used a stall throughout his career, most notably in 1955 when he brought UCLA's game at Stanford to a complete standstill, prompting the *San Francisco Examiner* to publish that photograph of UCLA guard Don Bragg holding the ball under the headline, "Stall-Wart Bruins." Yet now, after facing the same treatment from USC, Wooden was trying to have it both ways. He wasn't saying that it was wrong to stall per se, just that it should be done in the proper manner, under proper circumstances, for an acceptable length of time. And who was the great sage deeming what was proper and acceptable? Why, John Wooden, of course.

For Boyd, it was a devastating accusation. He was a relatively unknown coach in his first year on the job, and he had darn near knocked off mighty UCLA. Yet, the most influential coach in the country had just vilified him. "It was the worst thing that ever happened to me. I got branded a staller," Boyd said many years later. "We ran a deliberate offense with selective shooting and we made seventeen of twenty-four shots, but the L.A. media took John's position. We weren't stalling. We were trying to win the damn game."

The controversy dominated the weekly writers' luncheon that was held two days later at the Sheraton West hotel, where Wooden softened his tone but held to his opinion. "I want to make it very clear that there was no personal criticism intended and I want to apologize to Bob if he took it that way," Wooden said. "However, if you want to hear me say I thought it was good, you're crazy. Is it illegal? No. Is it bad for Bob to use it? No. I don't profess to be right or wrong. I just think it's bad for the game."

As Wooden stepped away from the podium, he was followed by USC's athletic director, Jess Hill. Seeing that Wooden was headed for the exit, Hill said, "I prefer you stay." As Wooden took his seat, Hill pulled a newspaper clip from his pocket and read Wooden's comments aloud. "There is a certain amount of accusation in that remark, and I resent it," Hill said. "I can't see anything that happened the other night that wasn't good for basketball. Bob had my support in everything he did. Any team that attempts to run against UCLA is doomed for devastation. I don't see much difference in stalling in the last four minutes of the game or at the beginning."

Reached at home later that evening, Wooden was asked about Hill's broadside. "I think I'd be belittling myself to comment on his remarks," he said.

A few other coaches also jumped to Boyd's defense. "All Wooden has to do when he beats somebody, which is all the time, is talk about his own team's performance, compliment the efforts of his opponent and drop the subject," Cal coach Rene Herrerias said. "I notice he didn't have much good to say about the coaching job done by Bob Boyd. He just criticized the style of play Boyd used in the game. Wooden can't expect us to lie down and play dead for him." Sportswriter Dan Hruby asserted in the *San Jose Mercury News* that Wooden "has a knack for ungraciousness that is difficult to beat. . . . Wooden is active in the Fellowship of Christian Athletes and presents a powerful image, but opposing coaches underline that he is in a class by himself as an official baiter. He sometimes is referred to as 'St. John' by the coaching fraternity."

Two weeks after the USC game, Wooden made his point in a more direct fashion. The Bruins were playing at Oregon, whose coach, Steve Belko, was one of the few coaches on the West Coast who also preferred up-tempo basketball. Having just been eviscerated by UCLA in a 34-point loss in Pauley Pavilion the week before, Belko decided he needed to try something completely different. As soon as the game got under way, he ordered his players to slam on the brakes. Like Boyd, Belko was booed by his own fans, but at halftime his Ducks trailed the Bruins 18–14.

Now it was Wooden's turn to counter. First, he checked with his boss to make sure it was okay. Morgan gave his blessing. Then, in the locker room at halftime, Wooden told his team, "I want you to hold the ball." The players were surprised, and more than a little confused. "We didn't know exactly what he meant," Shackelford said. "Did he want us to stand with the ball at halfcourt? 'No, I don't want you to just hold it. I want you to pass it around, but don't shoot.' We were a little mixed up there."

At the start of the half, the Bruins got the ball and did as Wooden instructed. They passed it back and forth, never cutting, never shooting, over and over again. The crowd, realizing what was going on, now turned on Wooden. But he kept the stall in place, daring Belko to come out of his zone. Belko wouldn't bite. Two minutes went by, then three, then four. Still no cutting, no driving, no shooting. Finally, after more than nine minutes had passed without either team attempting a field goal, Wooden gave his players the green light to resume their normal game. UCLA won, 34–25, to improve to 19–0.

Wooden believed that Boyd and Belko were making a mockery of the game. Now he had made a mockery of their mockery. "Their fans were so happy when they did it. I wanted to see how they'd react when we did it," he said. "In no way did I do this because of what happened in L.A. All I am saying is that it is bad for basketball if it is used game after game. Did anybody who saw the game really enjoy what Oregon did? And what we were doing?"

Belko praised Wooden for using "fine, sound strategy." As for his own decision to stall from the outset, Belko asked rhetorically, "How else can you possibly play UCLA and expect to beat them?" Meanwhile, Wooden's claim that his maneuvers had nothing to do with the USC game was silly. A sports columnist for the *Oregon Journal* named Ken Wheeler called Wooden out for this falsehood. In reference to the counterculture movement that was blooming on so many college campuses, Wheeler labeled Wooden's move "a sit-in protest of college basketball's rules."

The tit for tat forced everyone to adjust. Before UCLA's next game, one referee quipped that he had been "studying the rule book more this week than I have in the last five years." Wooden wanted to use a stall the next night against Oregon State, but the players, specifically Mike Warren, talked him out of it. From there, the games unfolded in a more normal manner, but opposing coaches continued to try every tactic they could think of. In advance of his team's game at UCLA on February 25, Washington State coach Marv Harshman had his players use tennis rackets, stools, and paddles during practice in an effort to simulate Alcindor's length. It didn't exactly work: Alcindor scored 61 points in a 22-point UCLA victory. Wooden thought the world of Harshman, a fellow Christian whom Wooden would later call "one of the nicest people the Lord ever made." That may have been true, but on that night, at that moment, Harshman was just another poor soul who happened to be standing in John Wooden's way.

The win over Washington State clinched yet another conference title, and so the only remaining question was whether the Bruins would finish the regular season undefeated. They answered by sailing through their final three games by an average of 31 points, including a road sweep at Stanford and Cal that prompted Wooden to tweak his friends up north. "In my 19 years of coaching at UCLA, it was my most enjoyable weekend in the Bay Area, and that includes summers," he said.

While Wooden floated above the fray and dictated how his players should act on the court, it was up to Jerry Norman to do most of the advance scouting as well as help the players manage their academics and work through personal issues. He and Wooden enjoyed a productive relationship, but it was hardly a close one. Norman was especially careful not to get on Nell's bad side. He had seen how she reacted angrily when Fred Hessler interviewed a coach on his radio show who had disparaged Wooden in the past. "You had to be careful around Nell. She could be very reactive to anything she thought might be negative," Norman said. "It goes back to the whole West Coast–Midwest thing. They didn't trust anybody from out here. I don't recall going out after a game with them at any time. He was very close with his family, and he would go home or get a sandwich or something. But there was no social relationship between us."

By the time the Bruins arrived in Corvallis, Oregon, for the NCAA tournament's West Regional, the public was beginning to appreciate that this was not just a one-man team. Alcindor's fellow sophomores, particularly Shackelford and Allen, had complemented him well. The machine was lubricated by Warren, the lone junior starter, whom Boyd called "the equal of any guard ever to play at UCLA." Articles mentioning Warren invariably referred to his good looks and Hollywood aspirations, but it was his midwestern upbringing that made him the ideal UCLA point guard. He and Wooden were connected by their South Bend roots. Like Wooden, Warren was smart, tough, and respectful. Unlike Wooden, he was an extrovert and a first-class communicator, whether it was with doe-eyed coeds, his fellow teammates, or his taskmaster of a coach. Wooden frequently called Warren the smartest player he had ever coached. It figures that Wooden would ascribe this label to a black player, while he would refer to a white one, Keith Erickson, as his most gifted athlete.

In their first tournament game, the Bruins disemboweled Wyoming by 49 points and then elbowed their way past a scrappy University of the Pacific team by 16. The season culminated in Louisville, where UCLA was scheduled to play No. 7 Houston in the national semifinals. Houston coach Guy Lewis had a nine-man rotation that featured a talented six-foot-five guard in Don Chaney plus six more players who were six foot six or taller—including six-foot-nine junior forward Elvin Hayes, one of the few post players in the country who was even remotely of Alcindor's caliber.

During the opening minutes, Hayes found himself streaking to the basket on a fast break while Alcindor backpedaled on defense. Most players in that situation either pulled up for a jump shot or retreated, but Hayes took the ball right at Big Lew and stuffed it. "That kind of startled us, because we had never seen anyone challenge Alcindor that way," Shackelford said. Hayes yapped at Alcindor the entire game. Before he made a move to the basket, he would bark, "Watch this!" Even after Alcindor blocked several of his shots, Hayes kept right on talking.

Guy Lewis had decided beforehand that he was going to do everything he could to limit Alcindor's scoring. If UCLA was going to win, the other players would have to step up. Alcindor was happy to comply, passing off almost every time he was double- or triple-teamed. His teammates rewarded his confidence as they had all season, with Shackelford leading the way by scoring 22 points on eleven-for-nineteen shooting. Alcindor had only 19 points to go along with his 20 rebounds, but in the end, Houston became just another victim. UCLA won, 73–58.

Hayes finished with 25 points and 24 rebounds, so statistically he got the better of the matchup with Alcindor. He was the only one who seemed to think this mattered. "I beat him one-on-one tonight. I was pleased with myself," Hayes said. "He's not what they say he is, either on offense or defense. He's just got a lot of improving to do. It really irritates me, him getting all that publicity, because it's not really true."

UCLA had just one more opponent to vanquish to complete its perfect season. Surprisingly, that opponent was unranked Dayton, which had upset third-ranked North Carolina in the first semifinal. Norman had scouted that game from courtside, and he could tell early on that both teams were inferior to the two that were playing in the nightcap. As usual, Norman was right. Midway through the first half of the championship game, the Bruins led 20–4. They were up by 29 early in the second half. Wooden started clearing his bench with twelve minutes to go, and by the four-minute mark all of his starters were done. The drubbing only bolstered the growing sense that UCLA's dominance was hurting popular interest in college basketball. This was supposed to be the biggest game of the season, but it was never really a game.

UCLA's 79–64 victory made Wooden the first man to coach two perfect seasons and just the second (along with Adolph Rupp) to claim three

NCAA titles. After the game was over, the Bruins' comportment was so measured that Sid Ziff wrote a column in the *Los Angeles Times* that was headlined "Playing for Wooden Is Great, but No Fun." Ziff wasn't far off. The Bruins were national champs once again, but the accomplishment didn't cause them to cry for joy so much as sigh from relief.

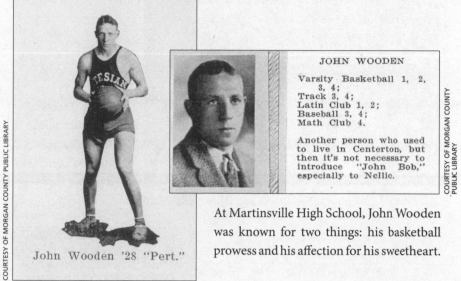

John Wooden '28 "Pert."

JOHN WOODEN

Varsity Basketball 1, 2, 3, 4;
Track 3, 4;
Latin Club 1, 2;
Baseball 3, 4;
Math Club 4.

Another person who used to live in Centerton, but then it's not necessary to introduce "John Bob," especially to Nellie.

At Martinsville High School, John Wooden was known for two things: his basketball prowess and his affection for his sweetheart.

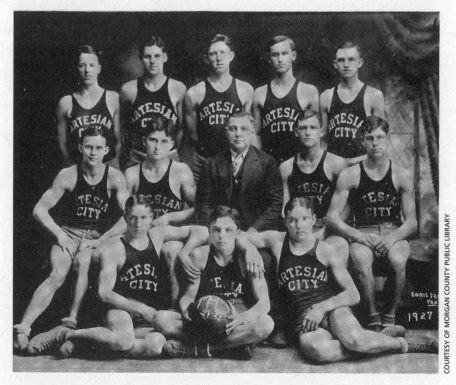

Wooden (front row, far left) was the star of the 1927 Indiana high school champs. But his missed free throw the following year cost Martinsville the title.

Wooden's coach at Purdue, Piggy Lambert (standing), had an enormous influence on young Johnny (center), on and off the court.

Wooden was born too early to have a full-time playing career, but for several years he was one of the biggest draws in professional basketball.

Wooden (back row, second from right) with his first team at Dayton High School in northern Kentucky.

Clarence Walker, a reserve guard for Wooden's 1946–47 and 1947–48 Indiana State teams, made history by becoming the first black man to compete at the NAIB tournament in Kansas City.

Willie (The Whale) Naulls, who played at UCLA from 1953 to 1956, was one of the best to ever suit up for Wooden. But the Bruins could never get past the University of San Francisco and its star center, Bill Russell.

Wooden made few friends among his coaching colleagues because he preferred to spend most of his time with his wife, Nell, and their children, Nan and Jim.

The 1963–64 Bruins did not have a starter above six-foot-five, but these big men on campus gave Wooden his first title: From left, Gail Goodrich, Keith Erickson, Fred Slaughter, Jack Hirsch, and Walt Hazzard.

Lew Alcindor was arguably the best player in the history of college basketball. Sadly, Wooden often said that seeing how other people treated Alcindor taught him a lot about "man's inhumanity to man."

Jerry Norman (left) recruited the players who launched UCLA's championship dynasty, and he convinced Wooden to use the vaunted 2-2-1 full-court press. Yet many former Bruins believe Wooden never gave Norman enough credit.

J. D. Morgan (left) loved to boast that Wooden never won an NCAA title until after Morgan became UCLA's athletic director.

Wooden drew a lot of criticism from opposing coaches and players for his rough verbal treatment of referees.

AP PHOTO/REED SAXON

Sam Gilbert was so close with Wooden's players that many of them called Gilbert "Papa." His actions prompted the NCAA to put UCLA on probation and force the school to disassociate Gilbert from the program—but only after Wooden retired.

Wooden and Sidney Wicks butted heads often, but Wicks came through in a big way against Artis Gilmore and Jacksonville in the 1970 NCAA championship game.

PHOTO BY ASUCLA PHOTOGRAPHY

Whether it was as a clean-cut Bruin or an aging Deadhead, Bill Walton rarely saw eye-to-eye with John Wooden. But they were a great team.

Wooden was all smiles after the Bruins beat Kentucky in 1975 to deliver him his tenth and final NCAA championship.

PHOTO BY ASUCLA PHOTOGRAPHY

Through the years, Wooden was rarely far from Nell, whom he called "the only girl I ever went with." After she died, he visited her gravesite every Sunday and wrote her a letter once a month.

JOHN W. MCDONOUGH/SPORTS ILLUSTRATED/GETTY IMAGES

"He *loved* his boys."

23

Game of the Century

As dominant as the Bruins were during their perfect 1966–67 season, Wooden had every reason to expect them to be even more imposing the following year. After all, the entire starting lineup, including Lew Alcindor, was supposed to return. Unbeknown to the coach, however, the team was in danger of suffering two defections that could have derailed those plans. The events that prevented that from happening set in motion a chain reaction that would slowly but inexorably undermine the very integrity of UCLA basketball.

It started as a typical bitch fest between two college kids. Alcindor had once again been feeling lonely and bitter in the wake of winning the championship. As he vented his feelings to Lucius Allen, he discovered that Allen felt the same way. They railed against the school, the lily-white student body, the unyielding coach who treated them like cogs in a machine. Most of all, they spoke of their loathing for a system that deprived them of the chance to make extra money even as they generated mountains of revenue for their school. Alcindor and Allen complained so much they decided that they had to do something. So they hatched a plan to transfer.

Once Allen started putting the word out that the two of them were thinking of leaving, he was flooded with offers. The most serious conversations took place with people connected to Michigan State, who, according to Allen, were promising to take care of their every financial need. "We were plotting, saying how can we get out of here?" Allen said. "We didn't commit to anything because we were scared to death of John Wooden. We had that much respect for him, even though we talked about him like a dog."

During their lowest moments, Allen and Alcindor sought out Willie Naulls, who they knew could relate to what they were going through. "I had a lot of personal contact with both [Alcindor] and Lucius," Naulls said. "They were unhappy and they came to see me." Naulls empathized, but he also wanted them to remain at UCLA. So he introduced them to a man who Willie thought would be able to alleviate their problems.

The man's name was Sam Gilbert. He was a plump, five-foot-nine, fifty-four-year-old real estate developer who lived in the tony neighborhood of Pacific Palisades and worked out of a penthouse office in Encino. Gilbert had been serving as a mentor to Naulls as he was making his transition from pro basketball to business. He was also charming, cagey, and hardheaded. Naulls said that Gilbert "liked to refer to himself as one of the mules of the world. People who accomplish things."

A self-described "fat little Jewish matzoh ball," Gilbert grew up in Los Angeles as the son of Lithuanian immigrants. He played basketball for Hollywood High School before attending UCLA, but he had to drop out so he could earn money. Gilbert's father had owned a small movie studio in the late 1920s, and for a time Sam worked in his dad's film lab. He later dabbled in inventing before moving into the real estate business, where he oversaw the building of office high-rises and expansive residential communities. Gilbert was one of many entrepreneurs who rode Southern California's postwar construction boom to a life of great privilege.

Gilbert was an intelligent, worldly man who spoke three foreign languages (French, Russian, and German), wore a Bavarian fedora to UCLA basketball games, and loved to tell stories about his brief career as a middleweight boxer. ("I was grossly mediocre," he said.) Gilbert might not have pursued a career inside the ring, but his pugilistic attitude served him well in business. "He's a bundle of dynamite," Naulls said. "Sam is a heavyweight. He can take care of himself in any situation against any opponents. Whoever attacks him better be ready. Sam doesn't fear anybody."

After Naulls had several conversations with Alcindor and Allen about their unhappiness, he asked Gilbert if he could bring the players to his house. Gilbert agreed. Naulls brought them on a Sunday morning, and they bonded over bagels and lox. "I told Lucius, 'Man, you become instant Jewish,'" Gilbert said. "He took me seriously and said, 'No offense, but I've got enough problems without being Jewish.'"

Gilbert was as charming as he was savvy, as generous as he was ruthless. Once his tough-guy veneer was stripped away, he revealed the soft, gentle heart of a *mensch*. Gilbert was already a millionaire, so it didn't seem to Alcindor and Allen that he was looking to make money off of them. They believed he simply wanted to lend advice and ease their anxiety.

"I hadn't met either of them, but they had told the school they were leaving," Gilbert said in 1974. "We didn't even discuss basketball, just people, the world and general feelings. By 2 a.m. they had gotten it all out of their systems." As an immigrant's son, Gilbert found he could relate to these boys, despite the differences in their ages and races. "I was an adult who could rap with them on their own level and who understood the black-white syndrome which most schools want to brush under the carpet," he said. Alcindor concluded that Gilbert "took a genuine liking to me and wanted to see me do well," while Allen called him "probably the most beautiful person I knew. He was a giving person."

After that first meeting, the players were welcome to come to Gilbert's house anytime. They usually went on weekends, when Gilbert laid out a big spread. ("My Jewish soul food buffet," he called it.) Spending time at that house meant spending time with Gilbert's wife, Rose, a highly respected English teacher at Palisades High School. The players thought Rose was just like Sam, only tougher. "I told Lewis he should go to Harvard," Rose said. "He was smart enough."

When Alcindor and Allen came to the Palisades, they didn't have to worry about being treated like stars. In that house, Sam was the star. What they found instead was a sanctuary away from the tumult of their daily lives. "They could sit down on the couch and relax or go swimming and nobody would bother them for a signature," Rose said. "Sam was their father figure, because they didn't have any, frankly. Coach Wooden was a very good coach, but I don't think he ever got into the personal life of the kids."

Gilbert, however, provided Allen and Alcindor with more than just a place to put up their feet. He also helped them with their financial worries. "Sam is everybody's Jewish grandfather," Alcindor said. "He could get it for you wholesale." He started by buying their university-issued game tickets for above face value. Gilbert also squired his young friends around town. They loved how he would drive down the boulevards, point at buildings and say, "That one's mine. . . . That one's mine."

On those forays around town, Gilbert frequently brought the players into stores that were owned by his friends. The boys didn't mind so much getting the star treatment there. "We'd walk into a leather shop and he'd say, 'Lucius, I want you to meet my friend here.' The guy would say, 'Oh man, I love UCLA basketball. Tell you what. Anything in here you like, just take it.' And being a college kid, we found a lot that we wanted," Allen said. "He had somebody that would give me a jacket. He had somebody that would buy me a pair of slacks. So now I'm thinking, this is more like it."

The connections were fruitful even if Sam wasn't around. "I could go to twenty-three different restaurants on the west side, walk in with me and my entourage, Mike Warren, Kareem, and we'd just eat. Didn't have to pay," Allen said. "The guy would say, 'I want you to come here every night. When you come here, it increases my business.'"

Though Allen said that at the time he didn't think anything was improper about all of this—"I was naïve and stupid"—these arrangements were clear violations of the NCAA's policies regarding amateurism. Even so, they were commonplace around the country, as evidenced by Allen's conversations with those people connected to Michigan State, and the NCAA had yet to make it a priority to clamp down on them. In fact, the NCAA had only recently decided to devote its resources to punishing rules violators. For the first forty-five years of its existence, the NCAA did not have any regulatory authority over its schools. It relied on what it called "home rule," which left it up to the schools themselves to maintain honor. That started to change in 1948, when the NCAA formally adopted what it called a "Sanity Code," which laid out a set of rules covering financial aid, recruiting, academics, institutional control, and amateurism.

Three years later, the NCAA hired Walter Byers to be its first executive director, and it assigned him to create a national office in Kansas City that would enforce the Sanity Code. In 1952, Byers filed his first case report, which suspended Kentucky's basketball program for one year because of "pay for participation in athletics," which its players had received in connection with a point-shaving scandal that had originated at CCNY and NYU, effectively ending the basketball programs at those schools.

Still, it wasn't until 1964 that Byers put in place an infrastructure inside the national office that was empowered to investigate schools more thoroughly. Along with establishing a three-member Committee on Infractions, the NCAA for the first time codified a principle mandating that "penalties should be broad if there is a basic institutional pattern of non-deservance, narrow if violations are isolated and institutional dereliction is not involved." It was in this respect that Gilbert's relationship with Allen and Alcindor was so dangerous for UCLA. His favors were clearly not isolated. They were part of a pattern that would continue for several years, with no real effort undertaken by Wooden or anyone else at UCLA to stop it.

Not that any of this mattered to Sam Gilbert. He had a low opinion of the NCAA and its antiquated rulebook. "My dad once said that amateur athletics is administered by amateurs," said Gilbert's son, Michael. Allen and Alcindor were already steeped in black nationalism, the civil rights movement, and the burgeoning counterculture. They did not need to be convinced about the evils of white repression. "I had very little respect for the NCAA. That was one thing that Sam really helped me understand, how we were being exploited," Alcindor said. "His whole thing was, don't hurt yourself but you don't have to worry about the moral fiber of all this, because there is no moral fiber there. It's just a façade."

Besides, Gilbert did not exactly invent the archetype of the overly helpful fan. In many ways, he was a direct descendant of the doctor who came to Piggy Lambert with an offer to pay Wooden's expenses at Purdue, or the owner of the semiprofessional basketball team from South Bend who convinced Wooden to risk his amateur status during his sophomore year of college. And Gilbert was small-time compared to the New York wiseguys who nearly brought down the entire sport during a point-shaving scandal in the early 1950s. Those same kinds of eager fans, who would come to be known as "boosters," were likewise at the heart of the football scandals that tore apart the old Pacific Coast Conference.

At UCLA, the specter of the rogue booster was established long before Gilbert came along. Earl Schulz, the former Cal guard who was named all-city in Los Angeles in 1957, recalled that after he decided he was going to Cal, a UCLA alum picked him up after class, drove him around Beverly Hills, and regaled him with promises of cushy jobs at local movie studios. "He asked me, 'What do we have to do to get you over to this school?'" Schulz said. A few years later, Walt Hazzard and Freddie Goss frequently ate for free at Hollis Johnson's restaurant, which happened to be where Wooden, a man of devout habit, had his own lunch every day. "Any time we were hungry, Walt and I would go there and Hollis would fix it up and bring it to us in the back alley," Goss said. "We didn't see that as big. What's a hamburger and a milk shake?"

The same moneyed crowd that slipped the players five bucks for rebounds during the Hazzard-Goodrich years were still treating players to events around town. "There was always some rich guy that was willing to take you to a game or something," Kenny Heitz said. "I saw Sandy Koufax's perfect game from a second-row seat because some travel agent took us. Was it against the rules? I have no idea." Long before the Bruins were playing in Pauley Pavilion, players were selling their university-issued tickets for face value or more. "It was usually a manager or a trainer, and they'd ask you if you wanted your tickets for the home game," Mike Serafin said. "It was pretty neat to have sixty or eighty bucks, and you could go out. It wasn't until about twenty years later that I thought about that and wondered, was that even legal?"

Freddie Goss found his own Jewish grandfather in a man named Al Levinson, who owned a major steel company based in the Compton neighborhood where Goss grew up. Levinson took such good care of Goss that Goss called him Uncle Al. Levinson, in turn, called Freddie "Preacher" because of his straightlaced Christian upbringing. Any time he wanted, Goss was allowed to walk into Levinson's posh Bel Air home, raid the fridge, turn on the TV, and make himself comfortable.

To help Goss with his money problems, Levinson "hired" Freddie to work at his office. "He gave me ten dollars an hour to study and make straight As. That was big money in 1960," Goss said. "I remember he had a picture of Marilyn Monroe and a stock ticker in his office. I'd go there every day to study after school." Goss said he never discussed this arrangement with any of his coaches, but Wooden knew who Levinson was. When Goss had to spend Thanksgiving in the hospital his senior season while recovering from that mysterious back ailment, Wooden and Levinson visited him together, along with a judge who Goss assumed was in Uncle Al's pocket.

Levinson's association with UCLA ended abruptly when J. D. Morgan accepted the $1 million gift from Edwin Pauley to finance the on-campus pavilion. Levinson had been led to believe that his name would be on the building. Goss did not learn about the rift until the night that the arena was christened with the Salute to John Wooden and freshman-varsity game starring Alcindor. "Al wasn't there. I didn't know there was a falling out," Goss said. "I got upset. I left Pauley Pavilion, drove to Bel Air, went to Al's house. He said, 'What do you want, Preacher?' I asked him why he wasn't at the game, and he told me J. D. Morgan had dogged him around. He never went to a game after that. There was a big void because there was no big booster around until Sam Gilbert came along."

In the years before Willie Naulls brought Alcindor and Allen to Gilbert's house, Sam had been just another benign friend of the program, buying tickets from players and helping them get jobs around town. Keith Erickson remembered him as one of the guys who stood outside the locker room handing out oranges and apples. Mike Serafin had a similar recollection. "When I was a freshman [in 1963–64], the entire freshman team went to his house, played pool, and had dinner," he said. "There wasn't anything more to it than that." Gilbert developed a particularly close friendship with Don Saffer, a six-foot-one Jewish guard from Westchester, California. "He was my angel," Saffer said. Saffer collected tickets from a few of his teammates and gave them to Gilbert, who sold them above face value and gave Saffer the cash.

Still, that was child's play compared to what Gilbert was now doing for Alcindor and Allen. The players knew they had to keep Wooden from finding out, which wasn't hard because he rarely inquired about their personal lives to begin with. "He was on his own little island. The assistant coaches, the alumni, the Willie Naullses, they made things happen. They left Coach out of the loop," Allen said. "I can't think of an alum that would have enough gall to go up to Coach Wooden and tell him there was something illegal about his program. Coach was just too far along on the other side of that."

If anything was going to jeopardize that, it would be Gilbert's audacity. Since he felt no shame about what he was doing, he didn't see any reason to hide it. The radio producer Bob Seizer, the former *Daily Bruin* writer, once found himself in Sam Gilbert's office after meeting someone for lunch in the same building. Gilbert complained that too many other UCLA players were asking for the same kind of help he was giving to Alcindor and Allen. "He said, 'If I buy Lew Alcindor a leather jacket, the whole team wants 'em,'" Seizer recalled. "He said he was going to get twenty guys to chip in. I said to my partner, Is this guy nuts? Does he know what will happen if that gets out?"

Jerry Norman had known Gilbert as one of many UCLA alumni who helped players get jobs, which was allowed under NCAA rules. He grew suspicious when Alcindor called him one day from Gilbert's office. Norman delivered a gentle warning to Lew. "Look, I don't tell you how to live your life, but the little bit I know about this guy Sam Gilbert, if I were you, I'd be very careful," Norman said. "Down the road—maybe not this year, but at some point—he's going to want to extract his pound of flesh."

Alcindor disregarded that advice. For him, Gilbert was a godsend. He didn't just help Alcindor with his money problems; he also taught Alcindor the basics of business and economics, about budgets and investing and tax advantages and long-range planning, concepts that Alcindor's own working-class father could never have imparted. "Sam introduced me to the language of finance," Alcindor said. "He said it was like knowing what the pick and roll is." Alcindor and Allen took such a liking to Gilbert that they started calling him "Papa Sam," or "Papa G," or just plain "Papa." "Sam was like my surrogate father," Alcindor said several years later. "I certainly discussed with him a lot of things I wouldn't discuss with my father."

Would Alcindor and Allen really have transferred to Michigan State if Naulls had not introduced them to Sam Gilbert? Allen thought so. "If not for Sam Gilbert, Kareem and I were going to Michigan State as a package. It was a done deal. Michigan State at that time knew how to take care of their ballplayers and I'll just leave it at that," he said. "We didn't think there was any chance we'd be taken care of like that at UCLA because of who our coach was. . . . My stipend was ninety-two dollars a month, and I was living in Westwood, California. I came from a part of Kansas City that I was very fortunate to get out of. Sam Gilbert and the alumni buying my tickets allowed me to live and buy food and clothes."

In later years, Alcindor contended that all of that talk about transferring was just that—talk. "I feel like that had a lot more to do with being homesick than being a realistic option. Transferring would have really been a setback," he said in 2006. "When you're 19 years old, you think the world is your oyster and they better serve it up quickly. It wasn't being served quickly enough. That's all it was, teenage angst." That was also the story that Alcindor gave to Wooden. "From what Alcindor told me later, no one had any influence, Sam Gilbert or anyone else, about . . . the possibility of leaving," Wooden said years later. "I don't think they discussed it seriously."

In *Giant Steps*, however, Alcindor gave the possibility more credence. As long as their coach and their Papa remained in separate silos, Allen and Alcindor could make Westwood their home. "Sam steered clear of John Wooden, and Mr. Wooden gave him the same wide berth. Both helped the school greatly," Alcindor wrote. "Once the money thing got worked out, I never gave another thought to leaving UCLA."

While Allen and Alcindor were being sucked into Sam Gilbert's orbit, John Wooden was jetting around the country to speak at coaching clinics. New York, Georgia, Alabama, Pennsylvania, North Carolina, out and back, out and back. Wooden had long avoided clinics, not because he didn't want to share information but because he preferred to stay at home with his family. He had also been experiencing intense pain from a ruptured disc in his lower back, a hangover from his days in the navy. Wooden decided to put off surgery, but all those trips in a cramped airplane seat didn't help. Still, he felt obligated. "If you don't go when you're winning, they say you're high hat," he said. "They put a lot of strain on you. Without realizing it, I had worn myself down."

It hit him after he had an anniversary dinner with Nell in August. As he was driving home, Wooden's world suddenly started spinning. "I felt this must be the way you feel if you get drunk," he said. He asked Nell to drive home, where he climbed into bed. At around 3:00 a.m. Wooden woke with a headache so painful that he thought he might be having a brain hemorrhage and told Nell to call an ambulance. Wooden spent the next ten days in the hospital, and he convalesced at home for an additional three weeks. "I walked down to the ocean every day with my little walking stick and talked with the other old people," he said with a chuckle. "I made a lot of friends down there."

Though Wooden's condition was officially (and nebulously) diagnosed as exhaustion, his symptoms indicate a classic case of vertigo, which sometimes strikes middle-aged men even when they are fully rested. Whatever the cause, it was fitting that this episode occurred just as Wooden was about to begin the most dizzying season of his career, one filled with splendid highs, discouraging lows, and lots of vertiginous turns in between.

The first twister had touched down in late March 1967, when the National Basketball Committee of the United States and Canada, which regulated college basketball, passed a rule that made it illegal for a player to touch the ball when it was in "the ring cylinder." In other words, players could no longer dunk. The change was immediately interpreted as a device to limit Alcindor, much as the committee's decision to widen the free throw lane from six to twelve feet a decade earlier had been aimed at Bill Russell. Wooden fed that impression—"There is no question that the rule is designed to curtail the ability of one player," he said at the time—but in actuality that was just a psychological ploy. After he retired, Wooden, who had been a member of the rules committee for five years, revealed that the change was actually made because too many rims had been bent by players who were dunking during warm-ups. "I'm not guessing on this. I know from when I was on the rules committee," Wooden said. Still, this change became known as the "Lew Alcindor Rule," though the man for whom it was named was unfazed. "It appears that people are trying to make it a small man's game," Alcindor said. "It makes no difference to the big man. You can change it to a layup very easily."

Alcindor delivered another tremor in November, when he attended a local meeting of the Black Youth Conference. The conference had been convened by Harry Edwards, a twenty-five-year-old associate professor of sociology at San Jose State College who was trying to organize a boycott of the 1968 Olympics in Mexico City. About 120 other black athletes were present, but Alcindor naturally drew the most attention. As a result, he was deluged with hate mail, and the school was so overwhelmed with phone calls that Wooden arranged a press conference so Alcindor could address the proposed boycott. Alcindor insisted he had not made up his mind about the Olympics, and Wooden, no fan of the Olympics himself, likewise insisted he wouldn't try to make up his star player's mind for him.

Wooden also came closer than he realized to suffering a different kind of loss. Jerry Norman was getting tired of the coaching life—the hours, the stress, the little pay. He had been working part-time with some friends in the finance industry and was ready to move into that business full-time. J. D. Morgan talked Norman into staying, but Norman warned him that it would probably be his last year in Westwood. "Coaching was not a good profession on families, especially in those days," Norman said. "Part of it was because we had won so much. I finally made a decision it wasn't worth it."

As the 1967–68 season got under way, Wooden realized he had yet another complication: too many good players. This was a high-class problem, but it was still a problem. UCLA returned every significant member of the squad that had enjoyed a perfect season and won the NCAA title. To that mix, the Bruins were adding two very talented returnees: Edgar Lacey, who had sat out the previous season while recovering from a fractured kneecap, and Mike Lynn, who was back from his year-long suspension. The team also added six heralded sophomores.

Lacey was especially eager to rejoin the fray. This was his senior year, and he hoped—expected, really—to join his close friend Lew Alcindor to form the best frontcourt in the country. Lacey was so excited that he turned down a chance to sign a contract with the Boston Celtics, who had selected him in the sixth round of the NBA draft, even though Jerry Norman had advised him to consider signing. "Edgar had never played anything but around the basket for us before Lew came up. The pros were taking a big gamble on him," Norman said. Lacey, however, was determined to take the floor for UCLA. "My jump shot is back from the dead," he proclaimed. "I worked on my outside shooting all summer and I've taken a healthier attitude toward playing defense."

The problems, such as they were, manifested from the very first game, a much-publicized contest at Purdue, which had invited its most famous alumnus to christen its brand-new, fourteen-thousand-seat field house. The Boilermakers also unveiled their celebrated sophomore guard Rick Mount, a six-foot-four native of Lebanon, Indiana, who was already being described as one of the best shooters of all time. Mount did not disappoint. After UCLA built a 12-point lead midway through the second half, Mount started drilling shots from all over the court en route to a game-high 28 points.

The Bruins showed an alarming lack of poise. When Lacey missed a few shots and Lynn committed three quick turnovers, Wooden replaced them with Jim Nielsen and Lynn Shackelford. Purdue coach George King used an odd defensive formation called a diamond and one, in which a single defender played Alcindor man-to-man while the other four formed a diamond-shaped zone. Alcindor scored just 17 points, and the Boilermakers kept things close going into the final minute.

Wooden put Lacey back in with three minutes to play, but with twenty-nine seconds on the clock he committed a foul on Mount, and then earned a technical foul for arguing the call. So Wooden put Lacey back on the bench. The extra free throw allowed Mount to tie the game at 71-all. On the ensuing possession, Mount missed a fifteen-foot attempt that could have put the Boilermakers ahead. Alcindor grabbed the rebound and immediately fired a pass ahead to Shackelford, who found Bill Sweek streaking down the wing. Sweek caught the ball and launched a shot from twenty feet. It swished through just as the buzzer sounded, giving UCLA a 73–71 victory. The delirious Bruins piled onto Sweek while the Purdue fans tossed debris onto the court. The game made Wooden feel light-headed all over again. "Well, I'm glad that's over," he said afterward.

Despite the poor performances by Lynn and Lacey, and despite 18 points from Shackelford off the bench, Wooden was intent on keeping his rotation intact. "I don't panic easily," he said. Even so, in the games that followed, he continually shuffled his lineup while also rotating in Heitz and Sweek. For the first time in his career, Wooden was more worried about hurt feelings than what was best for the team. "I made a mistake," he said years later. "You don't make three men happy by having three starters. You make three unhappy. You'd be better to make two happy and one unhappy."

The basic problem Wooden faced was that his most gifted players did not make for the best fit. Lacey and Lynn might have possessed a lot of individual talent, but the player who complemented Alcindor best was Shackelford. He was the best shooter (especially from deep in the corners) and the most willing to play a supporting role. Wooden could see the resentment building. "It was obvious as far as practice was concerned that Lynn and Lacey were buddying up," he said. "They said they each thought they were better ballplayers than Shackelford."

Lacey and Wooden never fought openly, but at close range, the tension was percolating. "I remember one practice when Edgar made a bank shot from the high post. Wooden made a joke and said something like, 'Edgar, you're our best bank shooter from that position.' Kind of sarcastic," Gene Sutherland said. "Edgar looked at him and said, 'You noticed that?' I thought, what's going on with those guys?" Jay Carty added, "You could tell on the floor that something was going on. Lacey wasn't as engaged."

And yet UCLA was so much more talented than its opponents, it was able to roll on without losing a game. In December, the Bruins walloped their only ranked opponent, tenth-ranked Bradley, by 36 points, and then captured the Los Angeles Classic at the Sports Arena. They were 8–0 entering conference play in the Pacific-8 (as the AAWU was now being called), and immediately swept Washington State and Washington in Pauley by a combined 60 points. That was followed by a 30-point win at Cal, where Alcindor set a Harmon Gym record by scoring 44 points.

During the final minutes of that game, however, Cal center Tom Henderson accidentally stuck his finger in Alcindor's left eye. Alcindor asked to be taken out. At first he thought it was a minor scratch, but later that night he awoke in excruciating pain. He called Ducky Drake, who immediately took him to a local hospital. The injury was described as an "extremely superficial abrasion," and the doctor who examined Alcindor said he expected it to heal within forty-eight hours.

That meant Alcindor would be unavailable to play against Stanford the next night. If his teammates were worried, they did a good job hiding it. As the players killed time at their hotel, Nielsen offered his frat buddy Sweek ten bucks if he would jump into the dirty swimming pool with his clothes on. Naturally, Sweek took him up on it. When word got back to Wooden, he called Sweek to his room and ripped into him. He never told Sweek he couldn't play against Stanford, but that was Sweek's assumption.

He assumed right. Without Alcindor or Sweek in the rotation, the Bruins seized the chance to prove to a television audience in five western states that Alcindor's so-called supporting cast could play a little ball, too. Though the game was closer than the others had been, the Bruins led most of the way. Things got dicey late in the second half, when Lucius Allen threw a hard elbow to the back of the head of a Stanford player. A UCLA fan sitting behind the team's bench shouted encouragement at Allen for throwing the elbow, but Wooden thought the remark came from one of his players. He wheeled around and barked at his bench, "Who told him to do that?"

Before the players could speak, Drake said, "Nobody." Sweek, whose ears were still ringing from Wooden's lecture earlier in the day, was irritated. He believed that if a lesser player (such as himself) had thrown an elbow like that, he would have been yanked. "I think [Wooden] was frustrated because he needed Lucius to win the game," Sweek said. "He lost control but he couldn't yell at Lucius. It was maybe one of the few times I saw some hypocrisy there. Which is worse, jumping into a swimming pool or hitting a guy on the back of the head?"

Five players scored in double figures, led by Lynn's 17 points, as UCLA won, 75–63. When they got back to Los Angeles, it became apparent that Alcindor's eye injury was no minor scratch. He was evaluated at UCLA's prestigious Jules Stein Eye Clinic, where he had to spend more than three days in a dark room. Alcindor was out indefinitely. Normally, that wouldn't have been a big deal—it was only January—but there was nothing normal about what was going to happen the following weekend. UCLA was about to play a game unlike any the sport had ever seen. With the eyes of the nation trained upon them, it was imperative that the one man everyone wanted to see would be healthy enough to play.

The seeds for the most significant game in basketball history were planted in 1958 in a dorm room at the Northwestern University School of Law in Chicago. The room served as the "office" for an enterprising young law student named Eddie Einhorn, who had just procured the rights to produce a nationally syndicated radio broadcast of the NCAA basketball championships.

Why would the NCAA give those rights to a law student with virtually no background in broadcasting? Simple: nobody else asked.

Einhorn's network wasn't much of a network, although it did include WOR in New York. He provided play-by-play himself from the championships in Louisville, the first time the games were broadcast nationally over the radio. The next year, Einhorn pulled off the same feat while watching Pete Newell's Cal Bears upset Jerry West and the West Virginia Mountaineers. That convinced him of the sport's potential. Instead of practicing law upon his graduation, Einhorn moved to New Jersey and decided to dive into television.

Einhorn started a company that he called TVS, for Television Sports. Initially, his strategy was to find big games and pipe them back to the teams' home markets. In 1962, TVS broadcast the NCAA final between Cincinnati and Ohio State. (Cincinnati and Columbus were the only places where the game was shown live. The rest of the country saw it on tape delay following ABC's *Wide World of Sports*.) Within a few years, Einhorn was making deals with individual conferences to develop regional television networks. He also signed up some marquee independent schools like Notre Dame, DePaul, Marquette, and Houston. Along the way, he developed contracts with nearly two hundred stations that reached 95 percent of the country. Because college basketball was still considered a regional sport, where fans were said to be interested only in watching their teams, Einhorn had the field to himself as a national producer.

The TVS infrastructure was thus firmly in place by the time J. D. Morgan took over as UCLA's athletic director. Morgan met Einhorn when TVS broadcast some of UCLA's games in Chicago Stadium. It was the first time Einhorn had done business with someone who shared his vision of college basketball's potential as a national product.

As creative and ambitious as those two men were, it took a third person to conjure the spark that set the sport ablaze. Guy Lewis was trying to build a first-rate program as the basketball coach at the University of Houston. Behind Elvin Hayes, a little-known prospect who came to Houston because his home state's school, Louisiana State University, did not accept blacks, Lewis had brought the Cougars to their first NCAA semifinals in 1967, when they lost to UCLA. Like every other coach in the country, Lewis recognized that UCLA was the gold standard. He wanted to grab a few of those nuggets for himself.

Lewis pressed his athletic director, Harry Fouke, on the idea of starting a regular-season series with UCLA. Fouke was lukewarm, largely because Houston didn't have a facility remotely the caliber of Pauley Pavilion. The school's gymnasium was so small that Lewis's teams played their home games at Rice University, where the gym held only around 2,500. So Fouke and Lewis took their idea to Judge Roy Hofheinz, the owner of the Houston Astros, who had just erected a spectacular, futuristic indoor stadium called the Astrodome. It is unclear who first came up with the idea of putting a college basketball game in the Astrodome—Lewis and Morgan have both claimed credit—but Hofheinz was an easy sell. This was, after all, the man who also owned Ringling Bros. and Barnum & Bailey Circus.

The only principal who wasn't sold was Wooden. "I thought it would be making a spectacle out of the game," he said. "I love the game of basketball, and I did not like to see a game turned into a sideshow." Morgan explained to Wooden just how much UCLA's athletes, especially the ones

competing in minor sports, would benefit from all that revenue. He also
told Wooden that the game would be a huge boon to college basketball.
Not that he really needed Wooden's approval. "Morgan scheduled it and
then asked me later if I wanted to play it," Wooden said. "J. D. would do
that."

So it was decided: UCLA would play Houston in the Astrodome, on
Saturday, January 20, 1968, with TVS executing the production. As boffo
as that script was, the reality was turning out to be even better. Like
UCLA, Houston came into the game undefeated, and the Cougars were
ranked No. 2 in both national polls. Hayes, who was averaging 32.5 points
and 16.4 rebounds, was Alcindor's nearest rival. UCLA was the defending
NCAA champ and riding a forty-seven-game winning streak. Houston
had won seventeen straight. Houston's sports information director, Ted
Nance, had dubbed it "The Game of the Century." By the time the game
rolled around, that felt like an understatement. "People were calling and
saying, 'I don't care where I am. Just get me a ticket so I can be in the stadium,'" Nance said.

Now, just a few days before the big event, the entire plot was being
threatened by a microscopic scratch on Lew Alcindor's left eye. As the
UCLA team boarded the flight for Houston, Alcindor's prospects for playing seemed grim. He had emerged from the Jules Stein Institute to practice
on Wednesday, but he wore a thick bandage over his eye and worked out
for only fifteen minutes. "It is my understanding that Lewis can't play
unless he has permission to have the patch removed," Wooden said.

Unlike their last trip to Houston, the Bruins were treated like royalty,
with no shoddy dorm rooms or racist referees in sight. In fact, when
Alcindor walked into his hotel room, he found that a special ten-foot bed
had been made just for his comfort. The words "Big Lew" were painted
on the frame. On the day before the game, Alcindor's patch was removed.
His doctor from Jules Stein, who had flown with the team, cleared Alcindor for practice and told Wooden that while Alcindor still had vertical
double vision, he wouldn't hurt himself any more by playing. Once again,
Alcindor's teammates weren't exactly heartbroken that he might not suit
up. "The whole team wanted to play Houston without him. We were all
psyched up," Heitz said. Wooden himself sensed it might be better for
the team if Alcindor didn't play. But he told Alcindor that he could make
the decision himself, at which point the outcome became obvious. Of
course he wanted to play.

By the time the big night arrived, the anticipation was unprecedented. Einhorn had signed over 150 television stations (including one in

Fairbanks, Alaska) to show the event live. A municipal dispute had prevented Hofheinz from bringing over the wood floor from the Sam Houston Coliseum, and so he had to arrange for the floor from the L.A. Sports
Arena to be disassembled and brought to Houston, piece by piece. That
required a relay of truck drivers taking around-the-clock shifts, but the
court was put in place with three days to spare.

Because the Astrodome was not built for basketball, the setup was
quirky, to say the least. With the court placed in the very center of the
stadium, the nearest seats, which cost five dollars apiece, were more
than one hundred feet away. To give the fans an unobstructed view of
the action, trenches were dug that went eighteen inches deep and four feet
wide for the press, including Dick Enberg, whom J. D. Morgan had insisted
be brought in to call the action. Before sending his players onto the floor
for tip-off, Wooden told them to make sure they went to the bathroom. It
would be too long a walk for them to leave and come back before halftime.

When the game tipped off, there were 52,693 people jammed into the
Astrodome, making it by far the largest crowd ever to watch a live basketball game. (The previous record was 22,822 for a doubleheader at Chicago Stadium in 1946.) That included J. D. Morgan, who sat next to Wooden
on the UCLA bench, as he preferred to do for the biggest games. Unfortunately, Alcindor was a shell of himself. He saw two of everything—two
balls, two rims, and worst of all, two Elvin Hayeses. The time he had
spent lying inert in a dark room had also taken a severe toll on his conditioning. After two or three trips downcourt, Alcindor was completely
winded. He later said he felt as if he was running on a football field. Which,
of course, he was.

Hayes, on the other hand, was in world-class form. He noticed from
the outset that Alcindor was laboring, so he made an extra effort to beat
him downcourt. Wooden had assigned Edgar Lacey to guard Hayes, but
Lacey was ineffective. Hayes was big and strong and a pretty good shooter,
but the one thing he could not do was dribble. Many of the UCLA players
knew that because they had gone up against Houston during the NCAA
semifinals the year before, but Lacey had not played in that game. As a
result, Lacey gave Hayes too much room to shoot, and the Big E found
his stroke early. "You had to get right up next to Elvin and make him put
it on the floor and go by you, but nobody told Lacey that," Heitz said.
"When Elvin hit his first couple of shots, his eyeballs got huge."

Hayes scored 10 quick points to stake Houston to a 9-point lead.
Wooden replaced Lacey with Mike Lynn. According to Wooden, as

Lacey walked to his seat, he shook his head at the coach and said, "I can't do it. I can't do it." That did not bolster Wooden's confidence in him. Meanwhile, Alcindor failed to counter. Not only was he missing shots at an alarming rate (for him, anyway), but his lack of wind slowed down UCLA's fast break. At one point, Mike Warren told Lynn Shackelford that he wanted to ask Wooden to take out Alcindor. Shackelford told him he didn't think that was a good idea.

Mike Lynn couldn't guard Hayes either, so Wooden substituted Jim Nielsen. Nielsen kept Hayes in check the rest of the way, but a lot of damage was done. Hayes scored a remarkable 29 points in the first half, and Houston went into its locker room owning a 46–43 lead.

By the time the second half got under way, the television audience had grown so much that Einhorn was fielding calls from businesses looking to advertise during the second half. He did the deals over the phone and handed scribbled plugs for Enberg to read over the air. Nielsen continued to contain Hayes while the Bruins chipped at the Houston lead. With Alcindor floundering, much of the scoring fell to Lucius Allen, who made a variety of jump shots despite the odd sight lines. "I shot from spots on the floor. I didn't look at the rim. That's why I was able to play the game relatively normally," he said. Meanwhile, Lacey sat anxiously on the Bruins' bench, awaiting his return. At one point, he leaned over and asked Jerry Norman, "Am I going back in?" Norman told him to sit tight.

UCLA finally erased the deficit midway through the second half, knotting the score at 54–all. Houston briefly reclaimed the lead, but with 3 minutes to play, Alcindor tied it again, at 65. Field goals by Hayes and Houston guard Don Chaney pushed the Cougars to a 4-point advantage with 1:53 remaining. Allen made a bucket and two free throws to knot the score once again entering the final minute. By this point, the Astrodome was so loud, Chaney couldn't hear the ball bounce as he dribbled.

With 28 seconds left, Nielsen fouled Hayes on a jump shot. Hayes was only a 60 percent free throw shooter, but he made both attempts to give the Cougars a 71–69 lead. The Bruins followed with a rare mental error. Allen drove the ball and spotted Shackelford in the corner, his favorite spot. Only when he tried to feed Shackelford the pass, Warren thought it was coming for him, and he reached for the ball. It went out of bounds, giving Houston possession. "I don't think I would have made the shot anyway," Shackelford said years later. "I was too tired."

With just a few seconds remaining, the ball went to Hayes on the ensuing inbounds. Displaying his ineptitude at dribbling, Hayes slapped at the ball with just his right hand, but he managed to avoid the defense for several seconds before passing it to a teammate just as the gun went off. The final score was Houston 71, UCLA 69. As the clock expired, the Cougars jubilantly jumped into each other's arms while hundreds of fans sprinted all the way from the stands to the court. A few minutes later, Enberg found Wooden to get his thoughts on the loss. "We've been winning a long time," he said. "The only thing I think is worse than losing too much is winning too much. Maybe we've been winning too much."

The game was a disaster for Alcindor, who finished with 15 points on four-for-eighteen shooting, the only time in his college career that he would shoot under 50 percent. When he was asked afterward if his eye was the reason he played so poorly, Alcindor replied, "No. I can't say what it was. We just lost to a better team." That was far from true, but Alcindor didn't want to be seen as making an excuse. Wooden blamed himself for playing Alcindor in the first place. "During every time out, I asked Lewis if he felt he could keep going, and he always said yes," Wooden said. "I kept him in, but perhaps I was wrong."

For all the buildup, for all the hype, the game had actually exceeded its billing. The eyes of the nation were focused on college basketball as never before, and the sport delivered in dramatic fashion. "For the great majority of the audience, the big attraction of the game was, can anybody beat this John Wooden powerhouse?" Enberg said. "They tuned in looking for the upset, and they got it. That's what made the game so memorable. Had UCLA won, it would have been just another case of the Bruins beating everybody they played." For several weeks, Wooden received mail complimenting him for his postgame interview. For most of the massive audience watching at home, this was the first time they had heard the man's voice, the first time they had witnessed the equipoise that had long become familiar to people in Los Angeles.

The UCLA players knew something that all those millions watching on television didn't. Wooden wasn't just being gracious. He was saying how he genuinely felt. He actually seemed happy that his team had been knocked from its dizzying peak. "He came into the locker room smiling," Shackelford said. "I think he was relieved." Now that the pressure was off, Wooden hoped his world wouldn't spin quite so fast. His bride hoped so, too. "I'll be seeing a pleasant face now," Nell predicted, "instead of a face that's about to explode."

———

Wooden would need his even keel more than ever in the days that followed. Shortly after he returned from Houston, he attended a meeting of the Bruin Hoopsters, an alumni fund-raising group. His team had just ended a forty-seven-game winning streak, yet some of the boosters made Wooden feel as if he had let them down. "It brought me back to earth in a hurry," he said later. To cheer him up, Morgan sent Wooden an article from a 1915 issue of the *Saturday Evening Post*. It was titled "The Penalty of Leadership."

Wooden could handle external pressure. Internally, however, his machine was about to combust. The problem was Edgar Lacey, who never reentered the Houston game after Wooden had yanked him midway through the first half. In the dressing room afterward, Allen could be heard asking aloud, "Why didn't Coach use Lacey?" Lacey felt humiliated. On the bus ride back to the hotel, he sat next to Alcindor and said over and over, "I'm gonna quit."

Lacey stewed over the weekend, but he practiced with the team on Monday. The next morning, he picked up a newspaper and read some comments that Wooden had made the day before during the weekly meeting of the Southern California basketball writers. Asked why he never put Lacey back in the game, Wooden replied, "Edgar got his feelings hurt early. He wasn't effective in our high post and he wasn't effective guarding his man. He didn't especially feel like coming back in anyway, so I didn't feel it was right to use him."

Needless to say, John Wooden was no expert on the feelings of most of his players, least of all a stubborn, taciturn young man like Lacey. It was a foolish remark, and Lacey was offended. "He threw the paper down on the floor," his father, Edgar Sr., said. "He told me he was bouncing up and down on the bench and that he told the coach he wanted to play."

Later that morning, Lacey went to Wooden's office and asked if he really said those words. Wooden replied that he did. "You gave me the impression you didn't want to play," Wooden said. "That's exactly what I told the papers, and I'll tell you that."

"That's all I wanted to know," Lacey said. "I quit."

This was not the first time a player had told Wooden he would quit. Most of the time, they cooled off after a day or two and returned to practice. When Lacey failed to show up later that day or on Wednesday, Wooden asked Mike Warren to see if he could convince Lacey to come back. It didn't work.

At the heart of the dispute was the question of whether Lacey did, in fact, indicate to Wooden that he didn't want to go back in the game. An anonymous player later told *Sports Illustrated* that "Lacey shook off Wooden's motions to re-enter the game," but that was not how Norman and Neville Saner, Lacey's roommate on the road, remembered it. "I was sitting close to Edgar. I remember him saying to Norman, 'Can I get back in?' My impression was he definitely wanted to get back in the ball game," Saner said. Lacey's former teammates also had a hard time believing Wooden's version. "I can't imagine that was true," Lynn said. "Edgar was very proud and competitive. He would do anything for the team. It certainly wasn't Edgar's fault that Elvin had a great game. Somehow, he ended up taking the brunt of that, and it was fairly public. He was a pretty sensitive guy, so he didn't take that very well."

Fourteen years before, when Willie Naulls pulled a similar stunt, Wooden called Naulls at home, apologized, and asked him to come back to the team. If he had done the same with Lacey, he might have come back as well. But Wooden never even tried. "If he kicked you out of practice, you had to ask to come back," Allen said. "Because he was in control."

Alcindor was especially dismayed. Not only was he losing a capable teammate; he was losing his best friend, and his coach wouldn't do anything about it. Alcindor kept waiting for Wooden to explain himself to the team or apologize to Lacey. Instead, he referred to the matter obliquely by saying things like, "We all know that not every player can play every game, but that shouldn't upset them. There are a lot of things involved."

The situation deepened Alcindor's suspicion that Wooden, whom he otherwise regarded as fair and honorable, had a blind spot. He suspected that Wooden favored players who, in Alcindor's words, were "morally right to play." Exhibit A was Lynn Shackelford. He was an active member of the Fellowship of Christian Athletes, a model citizen who always showed up on time and said the right thing. Alcindor believed Lacey and Lynn were more talented than Shackelford, yet because Wooden viewed Shackelford as morally superior to the other two, he was the one who got the most playing time.

By Wednesday, the rift between Wooden and Lacey had spilled out into the public. The Bruins were headed to New York for a high-profile pair of games at Madison Square Garden against Holy Cross and Boston College. This was Alcindor's big homecoming, another marketing ploy by J. D. Morgan that generated $60,000 for the school. When asked why Lacey wasn't making the trip, Wooden explained that Lacey had not practiced in two days. He also conceded that he had not spoken with Lacey since Tuesday morning. "Had he joined us [on Wednesday], he would have made the trip, but he cannot go with us now," Wooden said. "I think it would be ill-advised to dismiss him now because he is hurt enough already. He has to sit down and think it all over. I can understand how he feels. I hope he can think it over and come back."

Lacey was finally reached by a reporter from the *Los Angeles Times* on Wednesday night. "It's his move," he said, referring to Wooden.

Wooden sounded more contrite during a press conference in New York on Friday morning, the day of the Holy Cross game. "He's just very quiet and sensitive, and if I had known he felt this strongly about it, I would have put him back in against Houston," he said. Even with Alcindor still hampered by blurry vision and suboptimal conditioning, UCLA easily dispatched Holy Cross, 90–67, before beating Boston College by a more modest 13 points on Saturday night.

After the Bruins returned home, Lacey remained AWOL and wanted to stay that way. He finally unloaded his feelings about Wooden to Jeff Prugh of the *Los Angeles Times*. "I've never enjoyed playing for that man," Lacey said. "That [Houston game] was the last straw. It all started my sophomore year when he tried to change the mechanics of my shooting. . . . And now, I have no one to blame but myself for staying this long. He has sent people by to persuade me to reconsider, but I have nothing to reconsider. I'm glad I'm getting out now while I still have some of my pride, my sanity and my self-esteem left."

Lacey was still wounded by Wooden's suggestion that he did not want to go back in the game. "That statement is too foul for words. With about eight minutes to go in the game, I asked Coach Norman, 'Am I going to go back in the game?' The answer was negative," Lacey said. "I think a lot of it is because he wanted to play Shack. He is sacrificing my ability and Mike's ability to promote Shack." Lacey added that he felt "misused" in Wooden's offense—"Ever since I've played for him, he has always discouraged me on my shooting"—and he left little doubt that he did not intend to rejoin the squad. "I'm sick and tired of being appeased by the coach. He's on the brink of ruining my confidence. I think I'm better off getting out now."

When Prugh told Wooden what Lacey said, Wooden asked, "You aren't going to print any of this in the paper, are you?" Told that the answer was yes, Wooden indicated that he felt bad about what was happening, but he insisted he would not reach out to Lacey the way he had done for Naulls. "I'm never going to run a boy down," he said. "He should come back because I think he's making a mistake. I have never said anything but that he's the best forward we have. I wish he'd think it over. Regardless of how he feels about me, I do care about him."

And yet how was Lacey supposed to know that? At that moment, he needed Wooden to tell him that he cared, but Wooden was not capable of expressing himself that way. It was simply not how he was raised. Wooden's father was loving, but he was a stoic man not given to gestures of affection, physical or verbal. The most revered adult male of Wooden's youth, Earl Warriner, had once whacked his backside with a paddle in front of the entire school and later denied him the chance to play a game because he had shown a hint of obstreperousness. Piggy Lambert ran Wooden ragged and shamed him into turning down the chance at a more comfortable life. These men—always, they were men—had given John Wooden his primary education. Love was supposed to be shown, not expressed. Life was supposed to be hard, not easy. When the problem arose with Edgar Lacey, Wooden applied what he had learned thirty or forty years earlier. But times had changed, and his players had changed with them. Wooden might have seen that if he hadn't been so stubborn.

Even to those people who had detected friction between Lacey and Wooden, the depth of Lacey's antagonism was shocking. "It seemed out of the blue. I didn't see anything developing," Norman said. Even Neville Saner said he had "no inkling" Lacey was that unhappy. "I was surprised Edgar quit," Saner said. "I thought he would hang in there."

At the next day's writers' luncheon, Wooden was still taken aback by what Lacey had said. "I can't help but believe somebody might be putting words into his mouth," he said. "With some boys, you can tell when they feel this way, but I had no indication of this from Edgar. All I can say is I've never had a cross word with him, and I consider him to be a fine person." As for the comment that set Lacey off, Wooden said, "My remark was correct, and I stood behind what I said, but oftentimes, you can be correct but be better off not having said it."

This was just the latest manifestation of the strain that Wooden had been experiencing ever since Alcindor arrived. "Last year was difficult, my most trying year in coaching, and now there have been a couple of things to happen that I didn't anticipate," he said. "I know a lot of coaches will say they would like to have the problems I have, but it's not all gravy with this kind of record. The only worse thing is when you are losing all the time."

In truth, Wooden suspected that the team would probably be better off without Lacey. As talented as Edgar was, he simply did not complement Alcindor as well as some of the other players, nor would he ever accept that fact. Maybe, with one less player to worry about keeping happy, Wooden's machine could function a little more smoothly. "We lost a *potentially* great player," Wooden said later. "But a potentially great player who isn't playing that well is not a great player."

Still, Edgar Lacey was not some robot or mechanical cog. He was a flesh-and-blood human being, a sensitive, proud young man with hopes for a future in pro basketball. Now those hopes had been dashed. After he quit UCLA, Lacey played a couple of years for an AAU team called the Kitchen Fresh Chippers, and he spent a season with the ABA's Los Angeles Stars. But that was it. This local legend, the best scorer in the history of Los Angeles high schools, a man who had been one stroke of a pen from being a member of the great Boston Celtics, was essentially through with basketball. It wasn't all Wooden's fault, but Lacey certainly felt that it was. And he wasn't alone. "Wooden ruined the boy's life," Walt Hazzard said. "He just destroyed Lacey."

The messy departure left some residual damage in the locker room, especially among the black players who were closest to Lacey. "I didn't like the way Coach Wooden handled it, probably because Edgar was a close friend of mine, so I'm probably biased in my assessment of that," Alcindor said years later. Lucius Allen called it "one of the few times that our master psychologist went too far. Edgar had been there for four years. He was one of the guys who had to be treated gently. You should know your people better than that."

For all their complaints about Wooden's rigid ways—*We talked about him like a dog*—the players had come to depend on his strong, steadying hand. Wooden was their anchor in a world that was falling prey to unrest, disobedience, injustice, violence. Now, for the first time, he had let them down. It made them feel a little dizzy. "It caused us to do a lot of self-checking, because John Wooden personified goodness, piety, integrity, all those things," Allen said. "If you can't trust John Wooden, who can you trust?"

24

Kareem

Despite all the money his team was generating for UCLA, John Wooden's salary remained just $17,000 in 1968. To supplement his income, he ran several youth basketball camps around Los Angeles. Wooden was hands-on and detail-oriented at the camps, just as he was at his regular job. In many ways, he enjoyed working more there than UCLA. "When I have my summer basketball school out at Palisades High School, they're eager to know how to do things," he said one day during an interview in his office. "You don't find that so much in the college players. The college players are more blasé." Getting up from behind his desk, Wooden demonstrated the proper way to fake a pass one way before throwing it another. "If you just tell your youngsters that, the college players will say, 'Aw, why do we do this? I'll just throw him the ball.' They must know *why*." Sitting down again, Wooden added, "If it hadn't been for the war, I don't think I'd have left high school coaching. I enjoyed it very much."

It was understandable why Wooden would want to turn back the clock. Through no fault of his own, he had found himself cast as an avatar of ancient values in a rapidly changing world. That was not a comfortable position for a conservative, fifty-seven-year-old midwesterner who prized his consistency.

The campus culture in which Wooden now operated didn't just encourage students to question authority. It urged them to confront and topple authority wherever it existed. With his gym shorts, zipped-up UCLA jacket, whistle, and old-fashioned strictures, Wooden was the very embodiment of the establishment. He and his players occupied the same space but lived in different worlds. "I really respected him, but I don't know that *like* was in the equation," Kenny Heitz said. "We had a bunch of guys who had really good relationships with our fathers. Wooden became that old guy we couldn't please."

That distance appeared greatest to the players who saw little action in games. "Wooden was running this basketball machine. He was aloof, as far as I was concerned," Neville Saner said. The impression was reinforced during practices, when players like Saner watched Wooden drill his top seven or eight players while the scrubs were left to work with the assistants. "To me, he was like a businessman coach," Gene Sutherland said. "We were like boss and employee. I never really felt close to him."

Wooden faced a Catch-22. If he stuck to his ways, he appeared out of touch. If he bent, he was a hypocrite. Lew Alcindor posed an especially touchy problem. His size alone warranted his own set of standards. From doorways to airplanes to bus rides to hotel rooms, Alcindor needed special accommodations. Plus—and this was more to the point—he was really, really good. If Wooden was going to bend for anyone, it would be for him.

For example, UCLA had a rule that if a player was late for the team airplane, he would have to find his own way to the game. It was one of the reasons why J. D. Morgan had called UCLA athletics "the last great bastion of student discipline that exists on this campus." However, the school's radio announcer, Fred Hessler, recalled that on one occasion when Alcindor failed to show for a flight to the Northwest, Morgan called Vic Kelley, the school's sports publicist, and told him to go to Alcindor's apartment and bring him to the plane. "J. D. realized these places were sold out in the Northwest because of seeing [Alcindor]," Hessler said. "He was going to see that our star attraction got there."

The other players noticed this slippage. Where Wooden saw necessary accommodation, they saw a double standard. "Wooden had this dress code for a team meal, and then one day Lew and Lucius showed up in jeans, and he didn't say anything. It was like, okay," Heitz said. Before Alcindor, the menu had always been precise: steak, potato, melba toast, celery, milk. "Somewhere along the way, out of eleven players, you'd see eight glasses of milk and three Cokes," Don Saffer said. "They were for Lucius, Mike, and Lew. The rest of us didn't want milk, but that's the way it was." Sometimes, Alcindor might not show up for a meal at all, yet nothing happened. These were small things, but Wooden was the one who had said they were big.

When the players complained—and this being the sixties, they felt free to do just that—Wooden conceded their point. Alcindor was a special player. He deserved special treatment. "Two of his teammates made some remarks to a reporter that I gave him special privileges," Wooden said. "Breakfast, for example. He got a couple of glasses of orange juice and they'd get one. True. Then they said I let him room alone while they always had to room with someone else. But you don't find two king-size beds in the same room. . . . I told one of these players, you're lucky he's here. I wouldn't have you if he wasn't here." To Wooden, it all made perfect sense. "If we have only a few good shoes," he said, "I guarantee you Lew's going to have good shoes."

When Lynn Shackelford was asked by a writer from *Sport* magazine what would happen if a player was late for curfew, he replied, "It all depends on how you're playing. It's been a lot looser since the big man came." Bob Marcucci, the team's student manager, said there was a running joke on the team: "If you're going to break a rule, do it with an All-American." Don Saffer followed that rule, and it still almost cost him. During a road trip to Chicago, Saffer and Mike Warren slipped out of the hotel to take some local girls to a movie. ("Everywhere we went, there were taps on the door for Mike," Saffer said.) When Saffer returned by himself to the hotel two hours after curfew, he found Ducky Drake waiting in his room. "Do you want to go home tonight or tomorrow?" Drake asked. Saffer broke down crying, and Drake gave him a pass. Warren, however, didn't face any consequences, even though he didn't return until several hours later. "You have to be realistic," Saffer said. "I knew there was a pecking order."

Nobody was more realistic than the guys at the top of that order. "We black players knew that as a unit we had a lot of power," Warren said. "We did a lot of things that would not have been tolerated otherwise. Before the season, Coach Wooden told Alcindor and me that our hair had grown a little too long last year and suggested that we cut it closer this year. We didn't, and nothing happened."

Part of this was Wooden's nod to progress. "I realize I'm not as strict as I used to be," he conceded, "but society isn't as strict, either." Still, for a man who had always espoused the virtue of standing by one's principles, it was jarring to see him abandon them to accommodate the better players. Wooden had expectations to meet and arenas to fill. He wasn't going to leave his star player at home just because the guy was a few minutes late for the plane. Not anymore, anyway.

The challenge would grow steeper as the culture became more permissive. That included the arrival of a new element in campus social life: drugs. Marijuana had been virtually unheard of just a few years before, but in a flash, it was everywhere. "It happened pretty quick," Mike Lynn said. "You went from having a frat party where everybody was drinking beer, to a couple of years down the road where a lot of guys were smoking pot."

Alcindor was no stranger to this world. In New York City, marijuana had been a staple of teenage black culture, although it was a white student at Power Memorial who first introduced it to him. He didn't feel much effect the first couple of times he tried it, but after church on Easter Sunday 1965, he went to a friend's house, and together they pounded the pipe so hard that Alcindor nearly coughed his lungs out. He felt high, really high, for the first time, and he liked it.

As was the case in New York, marijuana first made its presence known in Los Angeles in black neighborhoods. That's where Edgar Lacey, a Compton native, developed his habit. When Alcindor came to UCLA, the weed bonded them as much as basketball did. "Edgar and Kareem were tight on the smoking thing," Freddie Goss said. "They were the only two guys doing it when I was there."

It wasn't until he got to UCLA that Alcindor first experimented with LSD. He bought two tabs from a friend at $2.50 each, but he didn't take enough the first time to really feel the effects. The next time, he took an entire tab, and he was flying. After a few more acid trips, however, Alcindor decided he didn't like it and pretty much stopped. Still, LSD was all around him. One day, a pair of students who had taken LSD came upon him and thought he was an hallucination. Alcindor found it hilarious, one of the few times he didn't mind strangers becoming fixated on his height.

Alcindor managed to keep his drug use on the down-low, but Lucius Allen was not so lucky. At the end of his sophomore season, he was pulled over for speeding, and the police found a small bag of marijuana in his pocket as well as in his glove compartment. Sam Gilbert bailed Allen out of jail and found him a criminal lawyer, who managed to get the charges dropped a month later because of insufficient evidence. Since it was the off-season, Allen was not suspended from the team, and he never spoke to Wooden about it.

If Wooden had any inkling his players were using illegal drugs, he certainly would not have approved. But as with everything else, he believed their private lives should remain private. The only time he insinuated himself was when their behavior threatened to trip up his machine.

That concern prompted him to call Mike Warren to his office one day for an uncomfortable conversation. A white man had called Wooden to complain that Warren was dating the man's daughter. The man made it clear that if Wooden didn't keep Warren away from the girl, then he would. "He didn't stop me," Warren said of Wooden, "but man, how about telling me my life is in danger? How's that for a hint?"

Wooden had the same talk with Kenny Heitz when he learned that

Heitz was dating an Asian woman, though Heitz believed Wooden only did that so Warren wouldn't think he wasn't being singled out. This was one more way in which Wooden was woefully disconnected from the times. "Interracial dating was just starting," Heitz said. "Wooden was a very cautious man. He would have had no earthly idea that every black guy on his team was banging every white girl on campus. These guys were like candy to them."

Wooden had no objection to interracial dating himself, but he worried about the reactions of those who did, reactions that could disrupt the delicate balance in his program. "I would discourage anybody from interracial dating," Wooden said. "I imagine whites would have trouble dating in an Oriental society, too. It's asking for trouble, but I've never told a player who he could or couldn't date."

Wooden's attitude on this front confirmed his players' belief that his overriding concern was for their welfare as players and nothing more. "His relationships with blacks have no meaning," Warren said shortly after he graduated. "The coaching staff was seriously interested only in us playing, studying and keeping out of trouble. Our individual progress in terms of maturing as black men was of no concern. It's all superficial, the same kind of dialogue every day."

All of those rules, from the dress codes to the requirement to be clean-shaven to the forbidding of phone calls the night before the game, were designed to stave off rebellious influences. In some areas, like interracial dating, Wooden was out of step. In others, his cocoon building was the only thing that allowed his program to survive.

For example, Wooden insisted that players acknowledge each other by pointing when someone made an assist. He believed it created unity. The players bought in. "There was no room at UCLA basketball for racial tension. It was always left in the locker room," Heitz said. "I'm telling you, I passed Kareem a shitload of shots when he was at his angriest-young-black-man period, and I never didn't get acknowledged for it. I never had a black guy refuse to pass me the ball. It was a meritocracy that Wooden created. It was the one thing we never questioned."

With every win, with every championship, Wooden was held ever higher aloft by the silent majority who regarded him as a standard bearer for a forgotten time, when nobody smoked pot or protested a war, when college basketball players wanted to know *how* and not *why*. In a lengthy profile published in the *New Yorker* during Alcindor's senior season, the esteemed sportswriter Herbert Warren Wind described Wooden as an "anachronism." Wooden, he wrote, was "an island of James Whitcomb

Riley in a sea of Ken Kesey, the Grateful Dead, Terry Southern, and Jerry Rubin—and, I would think, the right man in the right place." Wind noted that when he asked Wooden what his favorite poems were, he answered while "smiling with an edge of shyness." Thomas Gray's "Elegy Written in a Country Churchyard," with its balancing reminder that the paths of glory would end at "th'inevitable hour," topped the list.

And yet while the smallest disruptions could still set Wooden off—he blew his top when several of his players showed up for a team photo wearing Adidas shoes instead of their university-issued Converse—he was willing to adapt where necessary. When he spotted the university's chancellor wearing jeans and a turtleneck to work, he dropped his requirement that the players wear blazers and ties on the road. "All I ask is that you be clean and neat," he said. When Wilt Chamberlain, who had just been acquired by the Lakers in a trade, objected to the suggestion that he was hard to handle—"I am not an animal, I'm a man. You don't 'handle' a man"—Wooden called his publisher and asked that in future editions of *Practical Modern Basketball*, the chapter headed "Handling Your Players" be changed to "Working With Your Players." It was a small detail, but it reflected a larger reality. The times they were a-changing. Wooden could either change with them, or he would risk getting left behind.

The divorce from Edgar Lacey was messy, but Wooden was correct that it would streamline his team. After returning from New York at the end of January 1968, UCLA blew through the Pac-8 and completed another perfect conference season. Their one close call came on February 9 at Oregon State, where UCLA won, 55–52.

UCLA entered the NCAA tournament in dominant form, but not as the No. 1–ranked team in America. That honor still belonged to undefeated Houston, and it irked UCLA's players to no end. Yes, they had lost in the Astrodome, but it came by a single bucket, on the road, with their best player obviously hobbled. Alcindor took a copy of the *Sports Illustrated* cover that read "BIG EEEE OVER BIG LEW" and taped it to his locker. He and his teammates hoped they would have the chance to play the Cougars again.

The question of whether Alcindor would boycott the Olympics was cleared up in late February, when the U.S. Olympic Committee announced that no UCLA players would be participating in the trials in Albuquerque. Alcindor insisted he wasn't boycotting for political reasons; he said playing would set him back academically and financially, since he relied on the summer to make enough money to get him through the academic year. Members of the U.S. Olympic Committee asked Wooden to intervene on their behalf, but he refused. "The national championship team always is the bulwark of the United States Olympic basketball squad, and UCLA is providing little or no cooperation whatsoever," an anonymous Olympic administrator was quoted as saying. "It's a disgrace the way they are letting their players run out on this international showcase."

At least the matter was cleared up before the start of the NCAA tournament. By the time the postseason began, the Bruins were playing the best basketball of any team Wooden had coached—and they knew it. *Sports Illustrated* observed that "Edgar Lacey's quitting has not appeared to hurt appreciably. . . . Everybody gets to play more, boosting morale." After defeating New Mexico State and Santa Clara at the West Regional in Salt Lake City, the Bruins got their wish: a rematch with top-ranked Houston, in the semifinals.

Traditionally, Wooden barely scouted opponents, and he had never devised strategies geared to beat one team, much less a single player. But given how Hayes had carved up his team in the Astrodome, he was open to Jerry Norman's suggestion that they design a defense to stop him. They decided to use a diamond-and-one, the same alignment Purdue had used to limit Alcindor in the season opener.

This time, UCLA would have the de facto home-court advantage as the NCAA tournament culminated at the L.A. Sports Arena. Elvin Hayes boasted that UCLA wouldn't "play us as close now as they did then," and Adolph Rupp predicted that "Houston [will go] all the way because UCLA is too complacent and overrated." Wooden, however, refused to indulge in mind games. "Revenge is something I don't harbor," he said. "I believe if I don't harbor it, my boys don't harbor it." In an effort to keep out distractions, Wooden was again the only coach among the four semifinalists who did not allow reporters into his team's dressing room.

The Sports Arena was filled mostly with Bruins fans, who cheered lustily when UCLA won the tip and sprinted to a 12–4 lead. After Houston rallied to within 20–19, the Bruins uncorked one of their patented blitzes, outscoring the Cougars 17–5 over four minutes and fifteen seconds. They never stopped. UCLA led by 22 at halftime, then by 28, then by 39, and finally by 44 with six minutes to play. Only then did Wooden see fit to empty his bench, and the Bruins cruised home to a 101–69 win. Sideline observers suspected, with good reason, that Wooden might have been running up the score. The final margin was redolent of some of Alcindor's old freshman games, only this one had come in the NCAA semifinals, against the undefeated No. 1 team in the country. It was truly a performance for the ages.

"I feel like a dead man," Houston coach Guy Lewis said afterward. "That's the greatest exhibition of basketball I've ever seen." Wooden added his own thinly veiled shot at Rupp. "We knew we were better than some of the Houston players thought we were, and not as complacent as some coaching peers of mine thought we were," he said. The win sent UCLA into an anticlimactic meeting with fourth-ranked North Carolina in the final, where Alcindor had 34 points as UCLA romped to a 78–55 win, prompting Tar Heels coach Dean Smith to call the Bruins "the greatest basketball team of all time."

Unlike the year before, the Bruins felt joy in winning their second straight title, primarily because they had humiliated Houston along the way. "The game against North Carolina counted a whole lot, but the win last night over Houston was the most satisfying victory," Alcindor said. Now that the tournament was over, Alcindor could show his true colors—literally. He emerged from the UCLA locker room wearing a multihued African robe, with red, orange, and yellow stripes and swirls. The giant garment, which Alcindor called his "dignity robe," hung just below his knees. When Wooden saw what Alcindor was wearing, he smiled.

Mike Warren's UCLA career was over, but Alcindor and his fellow juniors were set to return. Lucius Allen was the first to predict an unprecedented third straight title, but Wooden demurred when asked about the possibility. "It's difficult to do, very difficult," he said. "Look back through the history of the NCAA. Isn't it difficult?" Maybe so, but by that point the public had grown accustomed to watching Wooden's teams make the difficult look easy.

When Jerry Norman followed through with his promise to leave UCLA in the spring of 1968, he did so with a sour taste in his mouth. It stemmed from a comment Wooden had made after the win over Houston. When asked about the decision to use the diamond-and-one, Wooden told the press that Norman had originally suggested they use a box-and-one on Hayes, but Wooden changed it to a diamond-and-one. That bothered Norman because he had always preferred the diamond formation to the box. "A box-and-one wouldn't have made sense. It would have taken Alcindor away from the basket," Norman said. "The defense we used was exactly the one that I drew up." He never said anything to Wooden directly, but Wooden later heard that Norman was annoyed, and that his wife, June, was even more ticked off. "She never thought that Jerry got enough credit," Wooden said. "Maybe he didn't, I don't know. It's hard to say. I know I tried personally to always give credit to assistants."

For all they had been through over their two decades in the trenches, Norman liked Wooden, and he respected Wooden's ability to teach the game. But Norman didn't buy into the growing story line that Wooden had transformed into some kind of coaching savant. The way Norman saw it, Wooden won more often now because he was coaching better players—players whom Norman had recruited. "I don't mean to sound derogatory, but if you look at Wooden's record, he was at UCLA fifteen years and never won anything," Norman said. "Then all of a sudden we started to win. Why did we win? Overnight he became a genius? It was pretty much the same stuff over and over, but you're telling it to different players."

Wooden promoted Gary Cunningham to varsity assistant and hired another former UCLA player, Denny Crum, who had been coaching at Pierce College, to fill Cunningham's spot with the freshmen. Before his new staff could get to work, however, the program suffered a second crushing departure when Lucius Allen was arrested a second time on two felony counts of possession of marijuana. This happened in May 1968, exactly one year after his previous arrest. Sam Gilbert again fixed Lucius up with a criminal lawyer, but there was no way UCLA could let Allen back on the team, especially since he was also lagging on his academics. Allen dropped out of school without saying good-bye to Wooden.

With both Allen and Warren gone, UCLA was shorthanded in the backcourt. Bill Sweek was the lone returnee with experience. The team added a six-foot-three junior college transfer named John Vallely, but the dearth of perimeter experience meant Wooden would not be able to deploy his full-court press as extensively as he had in the past.

On the flip side, Wooden was getting ready to coach perhaps the best frontcourt in college basketball history. Alcindor, Shackelford, and Heitz were back, and they were being joined by three elite sophomores: Steve Patterson and Curtis Rowe, who had anchored a UCLA freshman team that had gone undefeated, and Sidney Wicks, a former all-city player at Alexander Hamilton High School in Los Angeles who had spent a year shoring up his academics at Santa Monica City College, where he set a single-season scoring record by averaging 26 points per game. Socially,

Alcindor was entering his own season of adjustment. He had now lost his two best friends on the team in Lacey and Allen, but instead of sulking and withdrawing even further, he broadened his horizons for the first time. Wicks and Rowe were now the only other blacks on the team. Not only were they two years younger; they were also boisterous and flamboyant—very different from himself. So Alcindor spent more time with Mike Lynn and Bill Sweek, as well as with Bob Marcucci, a white student manager who had been close with Alcindor when they had lived in the same freshman dorm but who had not been so during their sophomore and junior years. Alcindor had become an aficionado of martial arts after studying his freshman year with an accomplished instructor-turned-movie actor from Hong Kong named Bruce Lee, and he shared his love of kung fu movies with his white buddies. "The wheel came around the second time for me. It was very satisfying to reconnect with Kareem," Marcucci said. "We spent time going to movies and jazz clubs. It was cool."

Even outsiders noticed this more content, more open-minded Alcindor. "The nonchalance he displays on the court is not new, but his amiable, easy-going manner in public certainly is," Jeff Prugh wrote in the *Los Angeles Times*. "The face lights up in a ready smile. The demeanor is cool, but cordial. The feelings surface more quickly and are expressed sometimes good humoredly." Some of this was the result of natural maturation, but there was another reason Alcindor was evincing a sense of inner peace. Over the summer, he had made a fundamental change in his life. He had converted to Islam.

True to form, Alcindor did not come to this decision lightly. He had first become intrigued by Islam during his freshman year at UCLA, when he read *The Autobiography of Malcolm X*. Like Malcolm, Alcindor eschewed the teachings of Malcolm's original mentor, Elijah Muhammad, whose strain of American-bred Islam included rants about white devils and exhorted violent retribution. Rather, Alcindor was drawn to Islam's more traditional, eastern-based doctrines, what Alcindor referred to as "the real Islam." And he identified with its monotheistic tradition.

While living and working in New York City during the summer of 1968, Alcindor studied at a mosque on 125th Street in Harlem. Having explored the differences between Sunnis and Shiites, Alcindor immersed himself with the Sunnis, mostly because that's what Malcolm was. For two straight weeks, he took instruction each day beginning at 6:00 a.m. He formally converted in late August and was given the new name Kareem Abdul-Jabbar, which means "noble servant of the powerful One."

It was a far more gratifying experience than he would have had if he had competed in the Olympics.

Alcindor did not intend to share the news of his conversion with his teammates or his coaches. That is, until the Bruins took a road swing through the Midwest in December for games against thirteenth-ranked Ohio State and fifth-ranked Notre Dame. (The rankings had expanded that year to twenty teams.) On the long bus ride between Columbus and South Bend, Alcindor started talking religion with Steve Patterson, a born-again Christian who had started a church-based student group. When Patterson argued that the only way for a man to reach Heaven was through Christ, Alcindor challenged him. "What about all those people in Africa who never heard of Jesus?" he asked. "Are they all going to hell?" Patterson answered that they were, and pretty soon the debate got heated.

Yet an amazing thing happened from there. Instead of getting even hotter, the conversation cooled into a thoughtful, civil exchange. Soon, Patterson and Alcindor were joined by Don Saffer, who was Jewish, and Terry Schofield, who was Catholic. Other players shifted to that part of the bus, where they continued to engage in a dialogue about the presence of God, the meaning of life, the shared values of differing religions. When Wooden heard what was happening from his seat up front, he moved closer as well. He didn't say much, adding a few bits of information here and there. Mostly he listened. Finally, Alcindor revealed that he had become a Muslim. Much to his surprise, the players and coaches weren't put off. Instead, they were curious, open-minded, and wholly accepting. "I didn't know who the hell Malcolm X was," Sweek said. "I didn't know anything about Jim Crow. I didn't know about any of this stuff. I learned a lot through him."

If anyone should have been put off by Alcindor's conversion, it was Wooden. He was a white, middle-aged man who served as deacon in his church, never missed a Sunday service, and shared Patterson's devotion to Christ. Yet Wooden had no objection at all to Alcindor's newfound faith. He knew Alcindor would not make such a profound decision without researching it thoroughly. "It could have been a point of contention between me and Coach, but it wasn't," Alcindor said. "He was curious to know what Islam was all about and really showed me the utmost respect in giving me the ability and responsibility of making my own choices."

That bus ride through a cold midwestern night did more to fortify their bonds than any win could. "It's the most memorable moment of the years I spent at UCLA," Heitz said. "It was a bunch of guys really talking,

no barriers. It was just deeply special." For Alcindor—for Abdul-Jabbar—
it was the moment his fellow students finally became his teammates. The
first time they really felt like brothers.

The good vibrations found their way onto the court. UCLA opened the
1968–69 season with its most challenging nonconference slate in years.
The Bruins beat tenth-ranked Purdue at home by 12 points in the opener,
with Curtis Rowe emphatically announcing his arrival to the varsity by
scoring 27 points off the bench. They won both games on that midwestern trip over Ohio State and Notre Dame. The latter game was part of a
new annual nationally televised series brokered by J. D. Morgan and Eddie
Einhorn. The series helped continue to stamp UCLA as a national brand
while also giving Notre Dame visibility to build its basketball profile.

From there, the Bruins steamrolled over nine unranked teams, culminating with a 100–64 laugher over once-mighty Houston at Pauley
Pavilion. As had often been the case in the past, however, those scores
belied rising tensions. Wicks was a primary source. He was playing a lot
of minutes, but he couldn't understand why inferior athletes like Patterson and Shackelford were starting ahead of him. Unlike so many sophomores, Wicks wasn't intimidated by Wooden in the slightest. He had no
compunction about knocking on the coach's office door and asking
point-blank why he wasn't starting. "People say we butted heads," Wicks
said. "I like to say we expressed ourselves."

Wicks also made his displeasure known to Shackelford. "It wasn't a
friendly type competition with Sidney," Shackelford said. "He was very
frustrated. There would even be passing comments about the fact that I
couldn't jump and run and he was so superior. What he didn't realize
was that I was a much smarter player in pressure situations." Now a
senior, Shackelford had been through this before, and it was wearing him
out. All the responsibilities of playing for UCLA, the pressure, the expectations, the grinding, exhausting practices . . . they were all taking a
physical and mental toll. "I was getting very tired of playing basketball at
UCLA," Shackelford said. "It was becoming more of a job. My last year
wasn't as exciting as it should have been."

Little wonder the players embraced every opportunity to blow off
steam, especially on the road. During the trip to Chicago, Bill Sweek
pulled a prank on some of the benchwarmers by stacking a water bucket
on the door of their hotel room. When they opened the door, the bucket

drenched them. That led to a bigger water fight, which prompted the hotel manager to write a letter of complaint to the school. Even though Wicks and Sweek were involved in the water fight, it was the three little-used reserves—Terry Schofield, John Ecker, and Bill Seibert—who bore the brunt of the punishment. They did not play at all the next four games, although they weren't playing that much in the first place.

During a trip to Washington in February, Wicks and a few other play-ers sneaked out of the hotel and went to a party in Seattle. They brought some girls back to their rooms. Wooden found about it. (He always found out.) After the team got back to Los Angeles, he addressed the matter in the locker room. "I understand some of you had girls in your hotel rooms," he said. "If you didn't, you are free to go. If you did, I want you to stay behind." Most of the team got up to leave—including Wicks. Wooden called out to him. "Sidney, are you sure? I will not tolerate a liar."

Chastened, Wicks sat down. "That's the kind of guy Sidney was," Shackelford said. "He wanted to be a big stud guy, but deep down he wanted to be John Wooden's friend."

After delivering a stern lecture, Wooden dismissed the players but asked Marcucci, the student manager, to stay behind. When he started to tell Marcucci that he should hold himself to a higher standard because he was an extension of the coaching staff, Marcucci blew his top. "I kind of got into it with him. 'You have all these double standards,' and all that stuff," he said. "I thought he was going to boot me off the team, but one of the most amazing things about coach was that he did listen to people, even in the heat of battle. We got a chance to air it out. Then he just said, 'Okay, Bob, go to practice.'"

This version of Wooden was far different than the one the public was used to seeing. "He's a genius as a coach, but we all wonder how he got the kindly grandfather image," an anonymous player told *Sport* maga-zine. "To the outside world he's always smiling and very modest, like a nice old man. But we see him as he really is when he plays the role of the coach. He can be tough, uncompromising, totally humorless."

It was only a matter of time before the pressure affected the team's play. It started with a game on January 24 against unranked Northwest-ern in Chicago Stadium. For the first time since the Astrodome, the Bru-ins trailed at halftime, 45–35, but they turned on the motor midway through the second half to win, 81–67. Two weeks later, they found them-selves in another dogfight, this time at home against Washington. The Huskies' coach, Tex Winter, slowed the pace so well that UCLA again found itself trailing at halftime, 33–29, before winning, 62–51. Two weeks later, UCLA nearly lost at Washington, where the Bruins trailed for most of the night before taking their first lead with just over seven minutes to play. UCLA won, 53–44, but this was a team that was trapped in torpor.

It was a sad state of affairs. Here they were, undefeated again, ranked No. 1 in the country, perfectly positioned to mount a run at a third straight NCAA title, and yet everyone was feeling the strain, Wooden most of all. He had an older team now, and those upperclassmen were not as cowed by him as they once were. (After he retired, Wooden was asked who was harder to coach, black players or white players. He replied, "Seniors.") Don Saffer's playing time had dwindled so much that he decided to quit the team. "His feeling was that I wasn't giving him enough of a chance," Wooden said. "I did not try to talk him out of it."

Wooden also had several blistering confrontations with Kenny Heitz. When Wooden received an anonymous letter that aired some of the team's dirty laundry, he assumed that Heitz had written it and confronted him after a pregame meal. Heitz had not, in fact, written the letter, and he resented the accusation. "I just completely lost it. I was like, 'You are out of your mind,'" Heitz said. "I went to my room and I'm thinking, shit, I'm never going to play here again."

Heitz was supremely intelligent—after graduation he would enter Harvard Law School—and he was not shy about offering suggestions. During a game at Oregon State, he suggested to Wooden that he switch offensive roles with John Vallely because Vallely was a much better shooter. It worked so well that Wooden later credited Heitz to the press. But when Heitz offered another idea at halftime a week later, Wooden erupted. "He walks into the locker room and just starts taking me apart in front of everybody," Heitz recalled. "'So you get your name in the paper and you think you're coaching the team, huh?'" Heitz was so fed up that he took off his shoes and socks and resolved not to go back out for the second half. "Then Denny Crum came back in and said, 'Just get dressed and go out out there and be a good teammate,'" Heitz said. "Five minutes later, I was back in the game."

Alcindor was feeling the tension as well. Before a home game against Washington State, he came down with a migraine so intense that the doctor wouldn't allow him to warm up until fifteen minutes before tip-off. "It's got to be the constant pressure he's under right now. He can't even talk to a friend or anybody else and not have to answer questions about what he's going to do about pro basketball," Wooden said. Wooden admitted two days later that he got into his guys during halftime of their home game against Oregon on February 22 because he didn't think they were playing with enough passion, even though they would go on to win by 34 points. "I may have to assume that demeanor a little more often, but it's not good to have to verbally lash a team to keep the pressure on it," he said. "You don't talk natural fight into people. That's inborn." The Bruins may have been on their way to making history, but they weren't having a whole lot of fun doing it.

Wooden hardly recognized what he had wrought. His unparalleled ability to teach the game had coincided with an enormous influx of talent as well as a burgeoning television industry. It was enough to make a guy lose his balance.

One day during Alcindor's senior season, Wooden found himself at the weekly writers' luncheon sitting next to Freddie Goss, who had just been hired as the head basketball coach at the University of California, Riverside. Goss got the job largely on Wooden's recommendation, but at the luncheon Wooden tried to talk Goss out of a career in coaching. "He talked about how J. D. Morgan was putting pressure on him to win. He told me point-blank, 'Freddie, this is no life. You should be like Jerry and get out of it,'" Goss said. "When I went to UCLA to play, the team had just gone 14–12, but he never acted like I gotta win or they're gonna fire me. He looked at coaching basketball as a way to teach ethics. At some point, it became this fast-moving train, and he didn't know how to get off."

Wooden wasn't exactly unhappy; he did like to win, after all. But his program had become a monster, and it was all he could do to keep from being devoured by it. "I can honestly say that I received more criticism after we won a championship than I did before we won one," he said. "That's why I've always said I wish all my really good friends in coaching would win one national championship. And those I don't think highly of, I wish they would win several."

During those unsettling times, Wooden drew stability from Nell. She was the one thing in his life that he could depend on. She always traveled with the team, sat next to her husband on buses and airplanes, and had quiet dinners with him while other coaches and their wives were socializing with each other. He loved their little routines. She washed his hair, packed his suitcase, picked out his clothes.

The pressures of his job took an especially hard toll on her. Nell could never brook criticism the way he could. To her, everything was personal. She resented intrusions into their privacy. She rarely consented to interviews, and if they were out to dinner and a fan came up to the table and said, "Coach, I'm sorry to bother you," Nell would sharply tell the person, "Then don't." Denny Crum said, "Nell demanded respect and you gave it to her. As far as he was concerned, she hung the moon."

None of it helped her to quit smoking. That was a lifelong battle she would never win. "From the time I got there, she looked unhealthy. She always seemed very frail," Goss said. "I took my wife to New York to see them play in Madison Square Garden. Coach and Nell were sitting in the lobby. Nell must have smoked a pack of cigarettes right in front of us while he was holding court."

Wooden tried not to let on that the pressure was bothering him, but people noticed. Joe Jares of *Sports Illustrated* observed that "the impression one gets after spending some time with him is that he has not particularly enjoyed the Alcindor years." Over dinner with Jeff Prugh for a lengthy, three-part series that was published in the *Los Angeles Times* during Alcindor's senior season, Nell confessed, "I sometimes wonder if it's all really worth it." Wooden told her, "Yes, dear. It's like I've told you before. The good far outweighs the bad." But he also confessed that the weight of expectations had been wearing on him. "Once you're number one, people are never satisfied with anything less," he said. "I'm not crying. I'm just saying what it's like."

The games were the worst part. This was the opposite of how it was for Wooden's players, who saw practice as something to survive in order to get to the games. Wooden lived for practice, but when game night came, he could only sit in his seat squirming, clutching his program, barking at the referees, trying to evince a serenity that was at odds with the churning within. "I may appear calm. I strive to be calm. I strive to keep my players calm. But inside, I am not calm," he said. "It does not matter how many games we have won. You always want to win this one, too. And no matter how confident you are, you know you may not win. So you suffer until you have won."

The suffering prompted Wooden to wonder whether it might soon be time to retire. Two months after his team won the 1968 title, Wooden admitted to the *Daily Bruin* that he wasn't sure how much longer he wanted to keep his job. "I have thought a lot about it. Until the last year or two, I planned on coaching until I was sixty-five," he said. "I'm fifty-seven now and I'm thinking that as far as head coaching, I'd like to do it about three more years. . . . The last two years have been tremendous from a winning standpoint, but they have been my most trying years for a number of reasons."

It was all he could do to steal a few quiet moments. Oftentimes, before practice began, Wooden would come to the floor early wearing his standard gym shorts, zipped-up jacket, and sneakers and ask Marcucci to shag for him while he shot underhanded free throws. "We would chitchat a little bit, but I could see he was thinking about a lot of stuff," Marcucci said. "Now that I look back on it, I'm convinced it was a way for him to mentally get away from the pressure. Just be by himself in the middle of Pauley, just him and a manager, shooting free throws."

The less fun a team is having, the worse it usually plays. That was certainly the case for UCLA on the last weekend of February, when they went to the Bay Area with a chance to clinch the Pac-8 title. They did so, but not before needing double overtime to beat California, which had come in having lost seven of its last nine games.

Before they could get to the NCAA tournament, they had to play their annual series with USC, beginning with Friday night's opener at the Sports Arena. USC had lost ten games that season, but the Trojans put up a much bigger fight than UCLA was expecting. Once again, the Trojans executed Bob Boyd's deliberate offense beautifully. USC did not attempt a field goal for the first six and a half minutes, and the game stayed close to the wire. The Trojans appeared to have won when guard Steve Jennings sank a layup to put USC up 47–45 with four seconds remaining, but Shackelford answered with a miraculous thirty-foot buzzer beater— his first shot attempt of the game—to send the game into overtime. It took until the second overtime for UCLA to put USC away, 61–55. Boyd called it "the toughest loss I've ever had."

The Bruins had every reason to expect the Trojans to come into Pauley Pavilion the next night devastated and deflated. Instead, they were ready to finish what they had started. Once again, USC had a chance to win in the final minute. With the score tied at 44–all, Boyd had his players dribble until there were just nineteen seconds left. Then he called time-out and drew up a play for Ernie Powell, his senior guard. The play worked to perfection as Powell drilled a jumper from twenty feet away.

This time, UCLA had no miracle answer. Wicks's last-ditch shot attempt clanged off the rim at the buzzer, and the USC players and fans were soon celebrating wildly on the court. The Trojans had won, 46–44. Alcindor's last regular season game at Pauley turned out to be the first one he had lost there and just his second loss overall since he had come to UCLA. "Our players weren't fired up," Wooden said afterward. "Maybe this loss will help us, put us in good shape for the tournament. At least I hope so."

The loss ended a fifty-one-game winning streak at Pauley, a seventeen-game streak over USC, and a forty-five-game streak in the conference. Most of all, the loss chipped away, if only a little, at the Bruins' aura of invincibility just as they headed into the NCAA tournament.

It had been a long time since Wooden had occasion to visit an opponent's locker room to congratulate them on beating his Bruins. When Wooden got there, he found Boyd standing on a chair and shouting jubilantly to his players, "They're damned lucky we didn't beat them twice!" The players serenaded Boyd with a chorus of "Who's the coach of the year?" Wooden waited patiently for Boyd to notice him, and then he shook Boyd's hand. It was just one more sign of how unbalanced his world had gotten. Recounting the scene a few days later, Wooden groused to a reporter, "When winning becomes that important, I'm getting out."

The loss to USC was not Alcindor's final game in Pauley Pavilion because J. D. Morgan had arranged for UCLA to host the 1969 NCAA tournament's West Regional. The Bruins' first opponent was New Mexico State, which had used a slow pace to hang close with UCLA the year before. This time wasn't so close as UCLA won, 53–38. A 90–52 thrashing of Santa Clara sent the Bruins back to the national semifinals in Louisville, Kentucky.

With each passing year, the NCAA tournament was becoming a bigger deal, and Wooden's Bruins were the main reason. The interest from television had become so high that for the first time, the final weekend games were moved to a Thursday–Saturday schedule because the TV folks believed that not enough people would watch on a Friday night. Wooden, however, still would not allow his players to talk to the press, a decision unpopular with the sportswriters as well as with NCAA officials. "Maybe I am overprotective, but the three years haven't been easy," Wooden said. "I think these boys are taut."

By the time the Bruins got to Louisville, they didn't want to win the title so much as get it over with. That sapped them of their competitive edge, and it nearly cost them in their semifinal against Drake. UCLA immediately ran out to an 11–2 lead, but from there the Bruins seemed to relax. Wooden was particularly annoyed with Bill Sweek, whose playing time had dwindled the last few weeks. When Sweek missed a defensive assignment midway through the first half, Wooden parked him on the bench. Sweek seethed. "I was a senior. This was my eighty-ninth game," he said. "I didn't think I needed a lesson at that point in time."

The old UCLA would have put the game out of reach, but there was no blitz in sight. In fact, the script was being flipped. Now it was the Bruins who were the bigger, slower team, while Drake was the smaller, speedier, more cohesive unit. Sweek sat and watched his senior season teeter on the brink, yet Wooden would not put him back in. The only thing that kept the Bruins in front was John Vallely, the long-range marksman who tossed in a career-high 29 points. But Vallely fouled out with four minutes left, so Wooden had no choice but to send in Sweek.

When the coach summoned Sweek to the scorer's table, Sweek removed his warm-up shirt slowly and sauntered over with a look of disgust on his face. He wanted Wooden to know just how pissed he was. As it turned out, Wooden didn't think he needed any lessons, either. "Sit down," he barked.

Sweek did not sit down. He wheeled around, strutted past everyone on the bench, and headed straight for the locker room. He was through with basketball, through with UCLA, and most all, through with John Wooden. "I thought for a second, 'You know, it's Easter vacation. All my friends are going to Mexico. I'm just going to get in the shower, get my stuff, and hitchhike there. I'm done,'" Sweek said. Wooden put Terry Schofield into the game instead. "I remember thinking, that's weird. Is Bill hurt or something?" Heitz said.

At first, Sweek was unable to open the door to the locker room. It took him several minutes to find someone to unlock it for him. Back on the court, UCLA appeared to stay in control until Drake exploded for 6 quick points in the final twenty seconds, but in the end, the Bulldogs came up just short and lost, 85–82. The close call put the Bruins one win away from an unprecedented third straight NCAA title. Their final opponent would be Wooden's alma mater, Purdue, which had beaten North Carolina by 27 points in the other semifinal. Wooden, however, was not in a celebratory mood. All the pressure, all the conflict, all the mutinous behavior from his senior class had finally pushed him over the edge.

Wooden strode quickly off the court. He was the first member of the team to reach the locker room. There, he found Sweek naked in the shower, and he lit into his fifth-year senior something awful. "It was madder than I had ever seen him. The veins in his head were bulging," Sweek said. When the rest of the team got there, Cunningham and Crum had to restrain Wooden from tackling Sweek in the shower. The players stood with their eyes wide and mouths agape. If they weren't in such shock, they might have burst into hysterics. "It was tragic and hilarious at the time. Mostly hilarious," Heitz said. "Wooden is yelling at Bill like he wants to fight him. Sweek is going, 'You wanna come fight, old man? You've been messing with my mind for five years!' And the whole team is dying laughing."

Sweek gave as good as he got. "You're right, Coach, and I'm wrong," he said sarcastically. "In fact, you're always right. Edgar Lacey quit, but you were right, and he was wrong. Don Saffer quit, but you were right, and he was wrong. All these problems, and you're just never wrong. Did you ever think the problem was you?"

Finally, the assistants pried Wooden away. Since Wooden did not permit reporters in his locker room, nobody in the press got wind of what had happened. Sweek rode with the team back to the hotel, but he was sure he had played his last game for UCLA. Given what he did, he had to admit that he deserved that fate.

When he woke up Friday morning, Sweek had not yet been booted from the squad. So he went to breakfast. As the meal was winding down, Wooden said he wanted to speak to the team. Instead of coming down on Sweek again, Wooden told the team that he had thought about what Sweek had said and conceded his argument had some merit. He went on to tell the players how proud he was of them and how much he enjoyed coaching them. He told them they were a great team. "I remember talking to Kenny about it later, and we were both just stunned that Wooden would be so honest about how he cared for the team," Marcucci said. "Other than his wife and kids, he was not open to talking about his feelings that way. He didn't want to burden other people. It made a real impression on everybody."

At the end of his brief talk, Wooden shook hands with Sweek in front of the team. He never apologized—neither did Sweek, for that matter—but the incident had been put behind them. Sweek was still on the team for the championship game. "It surprised me, because I think most coaches would have thrown me off the team," Sweek said. "We were under all this pressure—I know he felt the pressure—but despite all that, and despite what I had done, the fact that he would try to bring us together and mend this thing and forgive me, I thought was impressive. He forgave me and wanted me to be there and play in the final game."

Maybe it was the catharsis of that confrontation. Maybe it was the presence of Alcindor's father, Big Al, playing first trombone in the UCLA band. Maybe it was the fact that there was only one game left. Or maybe it was simply because they were a great team that had gotten a lousy game out of its system. Whatever the reason, UCLA took the floor with real purpose on Saturday night. Purdue never had a chance. Wooden sicced his best defender, Heitz, on Rick Mount, and he held the Boilermakers star scoreless for more than eighteen consecutive minutes during the first half. During one stretch, Heitz forced Mount to miss fourteen consecutive shots. Wooden also scuttled his full-court press for the first time in seven years; the Drake game had exposed the fact that he did not have the personnel to use it.

As the game wound down, the only suspense was whether Alcindor would go through with his plan to dunk the ball in one last gesture of protest against the basketball rules committee. Wooden removed him with just under two minutes to play, before he had the chance. The final score was UCLA 92, Purdue 72. The only disappointment for Alcindor was that Lucius Allen wasn't there to share the glory with him. "Lucius should be here. I bet he doesn't feel right," he said.

It was an emphatic valedictory for the young giant. He finished with 37 points and 20 rebounds as he completed his college career with an 88–2 record, with both losses coming by a single basket. In becoming the first player to be named the NCAA tournament's Most Oustanding Player three times, Alcindor established himself as arguably the greatest player in the history of college basketball. Wooden did the same as a coach. He was now the first coach to win five NCAA titles as well as the only one to capture three in a row.

After all they had been through, all the pranks and the fights and the parties and the complaints about double standards, the seniors were only just beginning to realize that the important things they learned from Wooden had little to do with basketball. "He came from a conservative environment, yet he was able to understand the feelings of people who were African Americans or downtrodden or weak. He was able to be flexible enough to change his thinking during the craziness of the sixties," Sweek said. "He was such a morally upright person. He could hear and he would listen. Despite his background, he was willing to change. He really was a lifelong learner."

For all that Alcindor had accomplished between the lines, his two most vivid memories from his senior season took place on a bus and over breakfast. He never felt particularly close to Wooden, but he understood that Wooden was a major reason why he was leaving Westwood a better man. "He was the ultimate," Alcindor said years later, well after he became widely known as Kareem Abdul-Jabbar. "He was a teacher above all else. He challenged us without taking away our spirit. He taught me how to instill confidence in others. He made me understand that everything is a learning game. It's all learning about yourself and learning how to be successful."

The teacher learned a great deal from his students as well. It had been a trying three years, but the Alcindor era was officially over. Maybe now life could return to normal. Maybe now Wooden could find a better balance. "I look forward to again coaching to try to win," he said, "rather than trying to avoid being defeated."

25

The Last Banquet

In October 1969, John and Nell spent a glorious weekend with their children in Martinsville, Indiana. Thousands of people welcomed their native son to the annual Morgan County Fall Foliage Festival, where the India Rubber Man served as grand marshal. A street was renamed in Wooden's honor. Even though he had spent more than two decades living two thousand miles from where he grew up, Wooden was still a Hoosier at heart. As one national sportswriter had recently put it, "He goes better with sycamores than palm trees."

His midwestern attitudes were making him feel especially old-fashioned as he watched the game he loved turn into a big business. In the weeks that followed the 1969 NCAA tournament, Wooden watched with disdain as Alcindor became the subject of an unprecedented bidding war between the NBA and its upstart rival, the American Basketball Association. Alcindor had tapped Sam Gilbert to represent him in the negotiations, and Papa Sam told Alcindor he would not charge for his services. The Milwaukee Bucks had won a coin flip to earn the number one pick in the NBA draft, but first they had to ward off ABA commissioner George Mikan, who told Gilbert that Alcindor could choose his team, which would presumably be the New York Nets. Alcindor eventually signed with the Bucks for $1.4 million per year. "I'm glad to see Lewis get all he can get," Wooden said, "but the sort of money being offered to athletes these days is completely out of line."

Given Wooden's paltry salary at UCLA, it was only a matter of time before the pros came calling for him, too. After Lakers coach Butch van Breda Kolff resigned following the 1969 play-offs, the team's owner, Jack Kent Cooke, offered to pay Wooden several times what he was currently making to coach the Lakers. Wooden said he wanted to discuss it with Nell and his children. "I told them I would have had to travel so much more and be away from home," Wooden said. "I said, 'You can have a lot more things that I just simply can't afford now.' But they said, 'No, Dad, you wouldn't be happy with that.'" According to Wooden, Cooke was furious. "I don't think I would have enjoyed working for Jack Kent Cooke," Wooden said years later.

Wooden's off-season was further upended in October, when Alcindor published a lengthy diary in *Sports Illustrated* under his byline that recounted in vivid detail the unhappiness he had felt in college. The second installment was headlined "UCLA Was a Mistake." Wooden admitted he was hurt by the series. "I'm very, very sorry to find out that he seemed to be as unhappy as he has indicated," Wooden said. "I honestly believe that he would have been ten times more miserable at many other places he could have gone."

The articles only deepened Wooden's relief about beginning a new era at UCLA, post-Alcindor. "I am looking forward to this season more than I have the seasons of the last three or four years," he said before the first practice. "We are not on the spot like we were before. The problems are fewer. I don't have to play nursemaid to so many hurt feelings."

The roster lacked a once-in-a-generation talent, but that fit better with Wooden's egalitarian ethos. He was eager to reinstate his full-court pressure and up-tempo attack. He would go back to the high-post offense that he had used in all but three years as a head coach. And while the roster had plenty of talent, there was a significant drop-off between the top seven and the rest of the group. Just the way Wooden liked it.

Naturally, much of the early attention fell on Alcindor's replacement at center, Steve Patterson. A six-foot-nine junior, Patterson had sterling credentials as a former prep All-American at Santa Maria High School. As a sophomore, however, he had mostly been Alcindor's understudy, as well as his foil in practice. "Lew really destroyed my confidence," Patterson said. He couldn't match Alcindor's size, but he was a good passer and a much better long-range shooter. That made him an ideal center for the high-post offense.

Indeed, this was shaping up to be one of Wooden's best-shooting teams in years. Senior guard John Vallely, whose 29 points against Drake had allowed the Bruins to avert disaster in the NCAA semifinals the year before, was as good a shooter as there was in the conference. And there were plenty of possibilities to play alongside him, including Andy Hill, a six-foot-one sophomore guard who had shared the freshman team's MVP award, six-foot-three junior Terry Schofield, and six-foot-three junior Kenny Booker. All of them, however, would quickly be outclassed by

Henry Bibby, a six-foot-one sophomore dynamo from Franklinton, North Carolina. Bibby was the latest to join the conga line of out-of-state black players who came to UCLA because of its prestigious basketball program and progressive racial tradition. Bibby was so good in high school that Wooden sent Jay Carty to scout him. Carty sat next to Bibby's parents during the game, visited their home afterward, and then got chased out of town by white vigilantes who were enforcing a local rule forbidding whites to stay in black neighborhoods late at night.

Bibby had shown great promise as a freshman, averaging 26.8 points per game. He also fit nicely into Wooden's austere culture. "I wasn't a Goody Two-shoes or anything, but I respected him a lot and tried not to go against what he said. I was too scared," Bibby said. Nor was Bibby put off by Wooden's aloofness. "I was seventeen, eighteen years old. I didn't want to get to know him," Bibby said. "It's not like I was looking forward to going over to a white guy's house. I just came out of segregation in North Carolina."

Wooden went into practice believing that the competition for playing time in the backcourt alongside Vallely would be wide open, but it was evident right away that Bibby was ahead of the pack. "I don't believe I've ever had a player with more range," Wooden said. "And Henry not only works hard; he accepts criticism readily."

And yet everyone knew that the heart of this 1969–70 team would be the junior forwards, Sidney Wicks and Curtis Rowe. On the surface, they appeared similar. They were cocky, flamboyant black kids from Los Angeles, and the best of friends. Underneath, however, there were subtle differences. Rowe grew up in all-black Compton, where he broke Edgar Lacey's city scoring record in high school, and he emerged from that environment with a few rough edges. During one game, he got so angry with his defender that he popped him in the mouth with an elbow and knocked a tooth to the floor. As the kid grabbed his face in anguish, Rowe leaned down, picked up the tooth, and handed it back to him.

Wicks, on the other hand, hailed from Santa Monica, a much more well off and diverse community by the Pacific. Wicks could put on a glare when it suited him, but most of the time he was easygoing and fun-loving. He delighted his teammates with his spot-on imitation of the Ratso Rizzo character from the movie *Midnight Cowboy* or his ability to recite lengthy passages from *Butch Cassidy and the Sundance Kid*. Wicks was also a flashy dresser. He loved nothing more than to arrive at Pauley while the freshman game was still going on and strut with Rowe across the court like peacocks, basking in the adoring cheers of the UCLA faithful.

Physically, Wicks had the makings of an All-American. He was a chiseled six-foot-eight, 230 pounds, with stunning quickness and leaping ability—"a real specimen," as Jim Nielsen put it. Problem was, Wicks had gotten by for so long on ability that he never had to learn to play. He was the quintessential wild child. When Wicks was a sophomore, Wooden tried to tame Wicks by planting him on the bench. Without Alcindor on the team, that was no longer an option.

Wicks and Rowe had waited their turn. Now that it had come, they wanted everyone to know it. They showed up for the freshman-varsity game sporting thick Afros and long muttonchop sideburns. Wooden had let Alcindor and Warren get away with that, so they assumed he would do the same for them. They were wrong. Wooden told Wicks and Rowe that if they didn't shave, they would not play. At first they weren't sure he was serious, but Wooden wouldn't budge. So they went to Ducky Drake's training room and cleaned up.

After the game was over, Wicks and Rowe apologized to Wooden. Wooden told the boys to forget it and promised they would have a fine season. Everyone was on the same page, for a little while anyway.

Just as the 1969–70 season was getting under way, UCLA was becoming a center of conflict in the civil rights movement. At the urging of California governor Ronald Reagan, the state's Board of Regents had fired Angela Davis, a visiting UCLA philosophy professor. Davis was an outspoken feminist, a Black Panther, and an avowed member of the Communist Party USA. Her firing set off a wave of student protests, as well as criticism from civil rights leaders that she had been fired on the basis of her race, not her beliefs. Davis was reinstated, but she continued to spout her incendiary rhetoric on campus and around the city throughout the school year.

The Davis contretemps was just one more disruption that Wooden had to shut out of his program. "It was almost schizophrenic going from campus life to this cloistered church of UCLA basketball," Andy Hill said. "There were no people in the stands. All you heard was Coach's whistle, squeaking sneakers, guys talking on defense, the net swishing, dead silence. That was a symphony orchestra compared to what was going on right outside the door."

The players understood the need for Wooden to build a cocoon—they wanted to win just as badly as he did—but unlike him they could not shut out the world. The Vietnam War was not some faraway abstraction for them. Some of their friends from high school had gone to Vietnam and had been killed or badly wounded. This issue was much more important to them than basketball.

As it turned out, the first day of practice in the fall of 1969 coincided with a national campus moratorium that had been called to protest the war. A few days beforehand, Hill and his close friend, junior forward John Ecker, went to Wooden and asked him to cancel the first practice as an expression of solidarity. Wooden wasn't having it. "*You* don't have to come to practice," he told them. "In fact, you don't *ever* have to come to practice. But there is no way that I am going to cancel it."

Wooden never told his players what politics they should have, nor did he ever reveal his own. ("What were his politics? I don't think he had any," Hill said.) Yet, he repeatedly cautioned them against getting too swept up by the tumult, not because he disagreed with the movement's views but because he feared it would penetrate his sacred cocoon. When Wooden heard that Wicks and Rowe had joined UCLA's Black Student Union, he pulled them aside and gave them a gentle warning. As Wicks later recalled, Wooden told them, "I'm not telling you what to believe. You have to follow your hearts, but you can't allow any of this to interfere with your education or playing basketball." Wicks said, "We had to refrain from being too active after that. It was hard, but we understood."

If Wooden hoped that Alcindor's departure would diminish expectations for the coming season, he was disappointed right away. The Bruins were ranked No. 1 in the UPI's preseason poll and No. 4 in the AP poll. It wouldn't take long to find out whether those rankings were reasonable. UCLA's first opponent, Arizona, had been picked to win the Western Athletic Conference. The Bruins beat them by 25 points, with Wicks leading the way with 21 points and 15 rebounds, and all five starters scoring in double figures. "Everybody is doing something now," Arizona coach Bruce Larson said.

Clearly, though, the team was operating with a smaller margin for error. That was evident in the Bruins' next game, at Minnesota. Stymied by the Golden Gophers' zone defense, the Bruins trailed by 7 points with just under five minutes to play. Vallely rescued them with four straight jumpers from the corners to propel them to a 72–71 overtime win.

Over the next three months, UCLA vacillated between easy blowouts and narrow escapes, but they always won. Meanwhile, with J. D. Morgan wielding his magic, vast television audiences followed their exploits. That included a home game against Notre Dame on January 3 that was televised nationally by Eddie Einhorn's TVS Network. (UCLA won, 108–77.) The Bruins ran their record to 21–0, but that included several close shaves.

They needed a ten-foot baseline jumper from Wicks to squeeze by Princeton, 76–75, and they barely squeaked by Oregon State (in Pauley) and
Bradley (in Chicago Stadium) by 1 and 3 points, respectively. Playing at
Washington State on February 9, the Bruins came out flat and found
themselves down by 13 in the first half, yet they still clawed their way to
win 72–70.

At least the games were interesting again. They were also more aes-
thetically pleasing. UCLA had returned to its racehorse ways, with blitzes
and crisp passes and beautiful teamwork. Wooden showed how he had
evolved into a savvy game tactician, toggling between man-to-man and
zone defenses, depending on the circumstances. If teams tried to zone
his club, Wooden ordered his players to stall. When UCLA held the ball
for thirteen minutes without taking a shot during a home win over Washington, even the fans in Pauley Pavilion booed him. These close games
should have caused Wooden more stress, but, like his players, he was gal-
vanized by the challenge of trying to win without Alcindor. "I'm like any
fan, I guess," he said. "I feel like I have something to do. I feel more alive.
It's been a long time."

Wooden especially enjoyed coaching a team that was balanced again.
If one of the players was about to have an Alcindor-esque scoring night,
Wooden would collar him. "He thought that would breed selfishness and
envy," Bibby later said. "There were nights when I was well on my way to
scoring thirty-five, but he would pull me out." The sense of urgency made
for a happier locker room. "The esprit de corps was, frankly, not good last
year," Vallely said. "This year it seems like we're playing real basketball,
the way we grew up playing it. It's a lot more fun now."

In pulling all these great escapes, Wooden knew his team was playing
with fire. With each win, he could see his players were becoming complacent, less engaged. He could also see the usual signs of friction starting to
emerge. One troubling pattern was the way the team was breaking down
along racial lines. The strife was nothing compared to the broader clashes
that were ripping the country apart, but it festered nonetheless. The players generally got along, but outside of basketball, each man socialized
with the guys who looked like him. Wooden tried to break this pattern
by assigning blacks and whites to room with each other in the hotels, but
midway through the season, the players asked if they could resegregate.
"We were right in the middle of the civil rights movement, and it was not
very cool to be white," Terry Schofield said. "There were a lot of racial problems on the team. It wasn't quite reverse racism; it was more subtle than
that. I've never been black, and I'm sure that under the circumstances

that was not an easy thing. But it was one of the least happy experiences I've had."

Meanwhile, Wicks and Rowe continued to test Wooden's authority. When Wooden received a report that they had skipped an early-morning music class, he told them at practice that he didn't want it to happen again. The next morning, Rowe called Wicks to say he had been out late the night before and wanted to skip the class again. Fearing another reproach from Wooden, Wicks convinced him that they should go. When they got to class, they found Wooden waiting for them.

Wooden had returned to his old substitution patterns as well. Even during blowouts, he rarely pulled his starters until the very end, and when he did, he usually didn't play more than one or two other guys. That made life difficult for the players who were not in the top six or seven, many of whom started to feel as if they didn't matter. Andy Hill, for one, noticed that whenever he made a good play in practice, Wooden tended to chastise the starter for having "permitted" the play rather than praising Hill for making it. "I respected him an awful lot, but I didn't feel he liked me very much," John Ecker said. "He wasn't a guy to come out and talk to us a lot personally."

Wooden could be funny when he wanted to be. Once, when Denny Crum was boasting about his prowess at playing cards, Wooden confirmed to the players that Crum was indeed a terrific player. "From here," he said, pointing at his nose, "to here," pointing at his chin. The players retold that story for decades. The joke was memorable because it was so rare.

Still, Wooden had seen really unhappy teams before, and this was not one of them. As long as UCLA kept winning, the team's internal issues would remain insignificant. "We were just so good at every position," Bibby said. "When you're that good, you could have problems and still win."

Their luck finally ran out on February 21 in the twenty-second game of the season. Playing Oregon at McArthur Court in Eugene, UCLA lost, 78–65. Seeing that the frenzied Oregon fans were shuffling to the edges of the court, waiting to celebrate the victory, Wooden walked down the sideline with a minute to play and shook hands with Ducks coach Steve Belko. "It's going to be a little wild at the end," Wooden said. "So I thought I'd say congratulations now."

As usual, Wooden found much to like in losing. He hoped it would restore balance. "Subconsciously, a team that has won as many as we have this season might get a little fat-headed," Wooden said. "This hurts our pride, but it is probably good for us."

The loss to Oregon also forced his players to confront the budding tensions. Later that night, Bibby and Vallely talked into the wee hours of the morning. Bibby promised to speak to Rowe and Wicks, Vallely said he would talk to Patterson, and over the next several days, the players cleared the air. They coalesced for a simple reason: they wanted to prove that they could win a title without the big fella. "We had some underlying problems that we just had to iron out," Vallely said. "When you're winning, you don't do anything to change."

Even after the loss, the Bruins still held a two-game lead for first place in the Pacific Eight, and they would clinch the title the following weekend at home by throttling Stanford and Cal by a combined 44 points. Wooden believed his players were so worn out, physically and mentally, that he gave them two days off for the first time that he could remember. He hoped that this respite would rejuvenate them for the season-ending series with USC as well as the NCAA tournament.

As it turned out, however, the layoff had the opposite effect. In the Friday night game at Pauley Pavilion, the Bruins opened up a 10-point lead, forcing Bob Boyd to switch from his standard zone to a man-to-man defense in the second half. UCLA still led by 12 points with less than seven minutes to play, but the Trojans' defensive pressure started taking its toll, and the Bruins uncharacteristically lost their poise. The Trojans' hero that night was Paul Westphal, a six-foot-four guard from Torrance. Westphal was a rarity, a Southern California native who chose USC over UCLA. "It's more of an achievement to beat Coach Wooden than to win for him," Westphal said. After USC won, 87–86, Wooden conceded, "I thought our loss to Oregon was good for us, but I don't know about this one."

UCLA should have come out blazing the following night at the Sports Arena, but once again, they were desultory as USC built an 18–8 lead out of the gate. Wicks was so bad that Wooden yanked him. As Wicks sat down, Wooden stuck his face right in front of Sidney's and blistered him. Wicks, as usual, answered in kind. Wooden let Wicks marinate on the bench for four minutes, an eternity given the way Wooden had substituted (or rather, not substituted) all season.

The ploy worked. Wicks played angry and inspired in the second half, and the result was his finest effort in a UCLA uniform. By the time the buzzer sounded, he had scored a career-high 31 points, including 18 in the second half. UCLA won going away, 91–78. "He's the best forward in college basketball," Boyd said.

The win was just the momentum boost UCLA needed heading into the 1970 NCAA tournament. The Bruins' first opponent in the West Regional in Seattle was California State College, Long Beach, whose second-year coach, Jerry Tarkanian, had built a 245–19 record in six years as a junior college coach. At thirty-eight years old, Tarkanian was much closer to his players, in both age and temperament, than Wooden was to his. His success at recruiting from inner-city playgrounds also generated an unflattering buzz about his ethics. "As a recruiter, his critics call him devious, ruthless, crooked," Jeff Prugh wrote in the *Los Angeles Times*.

It wasn't easy building a basketball program in UCLA's backyard, but Tarkanian developed a fondness for Wooden. "When we had those sportswriter luncheons, I would try to get there early so I could sit next to him and pump him a little bit about what he would do in practice," Tarkanian said. "He was very gracious." In the days leading up to the game, Wooden heaped praise on Tarkanian, especially for the innovative 1-2-2 zone defense that he used. Wooden had seen Tarkanian lecture on the zone several times at clinics. "He has no superior, to my knowledge, as a zone coach," Wooden said.

Long Beach came into the game unranked but owning a 24–3 record and a nineteen-game winning streak, the nation's longest. Tarkanian believed the game would reveal where his program stood with respect to its crosstown neighbor. The answer did not please him. UCLA forced the 49ers to commit 19 turnovers, built a 22-point lead, and cruised to an 88–65 win. "It just goes to show you how far our program has to go," Tarkanian said. UCLA had an even easier time the next day against No. 16 Utah State, winning 101–79 to earn a trip to the national semifinals in College Park, Maryland.

As always, Wooden ran a closed shop when it came to the press. He was accessible and genial with writers, but his players were off-limits. No other coach was permitted that luxury. "We tell them to go around in twos and not speak to strangers," he quipped. After UCLA defeated No. 5 New Mexico State, 93–77, in the semifinals, Aggies coach Lou Henson admitted that, after losing to UCLA in the tournament for the third consecutive year, "you get a complex after a while. If anybody has a mystique, it's Coach Wooden."

UCLA's opponent in the championship game was fourth-ranked Jacksonville. The contest was instantly cast as a sixties-style culture clash writ small. UCLA was square, old school, establishment; Jacksonville was hip, rebellious, cool. Dolphins coach Joe Williams was the opposite of Wooden, a young and dapper coach who let his players wear the clothes they wanted, grow their hair long, and wander in late for practice. Williams even let them design their own warm-up routine, which they turned into a Harlem Globetrotters–style trick show. Dwight Chapin characterized the match-up in the *Los Angeles Times* as "discipline against devil-may-care, the Establishment against the Age of Aquarius."

The basketball contrasts were just as stark. The Dolphins boasted the closest thing college basketball still had to Alcindor in Artis Gilmore, a seven-foot-two center who was the nation's leading rebounder. He was joined up front by seven-foot Pembrook Burrows and six-foot-ten Rod McIntyre. Wooden had always preferred speed over size, but he recognized that the Dolphins' frontcourt would present a problem. Right before the teams went out for pregame warm-ups, Wooden drew out the starting lineups and defensive assignments as he always did on a chalkboard in the locker room. Wicks was surprised to learn that he would be guarding Gilmore.

In the early going, it looked like a foolish strategy. Wicks stationed himself in front of Gilmore, as Wooden had always taught his players to do, but Gilmore was so big that all his teammates had to do was lob the ball over Wicks's outstretched hand. Gilmore capitalized again and again, scoring 14 of Jacksonville's first 31 points and staking the Dolphins to a 9-point lead midway through the first half. Wicks tried to riposte by attacking the basket on offense. He was called for two quick charging fouls in the first four minutes.

Wicks was frustrated. He was angry. And he believed Wooden was wrong. During a television time-out—this was a new concept; the game was stopped artificially so NBC could air commercials—Wicks told Wooden he wanted to play *behind* Gilmore on defense. All season long, the two of them had told each other exactly what they thought, whether it was in the quiet of Wooden's office or in full view against USC. Now, Wicks was testing his coach again. Wooden passed. He gave Wicks the go-ahead to make the adjustment.

It was an inspired act of trust, and it paid off wonderfully. The next time Jacksonville came down on offense, Wicks allowed Gilmore to receive the pass. When Gilmore turned to lay the ball in, Wicks leapt up and swatted it away. He blocked Gilmore's shot four more times. Wicks admitted later that several of those blocks should have been called as goaltends, but Gilmore was visibly shaken. At the other end, Wicks continued to attack—he even dunked once, conceding the disallowed basket in order to make a statement—but he managed to stay out of foul trouble.

Gilmore never recovered, going more than sixteen minutes without a field goal. Overall, he made just nine of his twenty-nine attempts. UCLA uncorked a miniblitz late in the first half, rattling off 9 straight points to take a 5-point halftime lead it never relinquished. Besides scoring 17 points, Wicks garnered more rebounds than Gilmore, 18 to 16, the first time all season that Gilmore had been outclassed on the boards. When Wooden was questioned afterward why he didn't remove Wicks when he had those two early fouls, Wooden replied, "No matter how good a player is, he doesn't help you sitting on the bench."

True to form, Wooden left his starting five in the game until there were two minutes remaining. The balanced numbers pleased him: Rowe led the way with 19 points, followed by Wicks and Patterson (17 each), Vallely (15), and Bibby (8). As a team, the Bruins garnered 50 rebounds to Jacksonville's 38. (Speed over size, indeed.) The final score was 80–69.

It turned out that UCLA was not much different from "Lew-CLA." Sure, the Bruins had lost twice during the 1969–70 season, and five of their twenty-eight wins had come by 3 points or fewer. Yet at season's end, they still came away with their fourth straight national championship and their sixth in seven years. The establishment had won again. "I don't know about the UCLA mystique," Joe Williams said afterward. "To me, it's more like the Johnny Wooden mystique. He has been here a lot more often than any of his teams."

This was one title that Wooden was not "relieved" to win. This was an achievement to revel in, to savor. "This might be the most gratifying championship ever for John," Nell said. (How nice to have so many championships to sift through and compare.) Wooden was so happy that he agreed to open his locker room to sportswriters. The horde was several times greater than the one that gathered in Kansas City for his first title in 1964. The scene was a fitting testament to the machine that Wooden had built over the previous six months. The Bruins were a true team again. They won because of their balance. "Right now, if Alcindor was on the team, who would the reporters be talking to?" Rowe said. "Look around the room. The reporters are with five people. That's beautiful."

The city of Los Angeles responded to UCLA's latest championship with a smile and a yawn. When the Bruins' plane touched down, there were only about two thousand fans at the airport, a fraction of the throng that had welcomed them in the past. Nor were there any spontaneous bonfires on campus like the ones that had greeted Alcindor's first two titles. "It's better that we're not fawned over," Wooden said. "If they made too much of it when we did well, they might make too much of it when we do poorly." Wooden did, however, get a congratulatory phone call from President Richard Nixon, which Wooden described as a "a great personal thrill." Wooden did not appear to mean that as a political endorsement, but it did not endear him in the eyes of his players.

The school staged its own celebration on May 4, 1970, by holding its annual spring basketball banquet at the Beverly Hilton, with Dick Enberg serving as master of ceremonies. The highlight of this event was the final speeches from the seniors. Each player was given the privilege of stepping to the podium, where he could reflect on his experience and thank the folks who made it happen. There were only two seniors that year, John Vallely and Bill Seibert. Vallely's speech was pleasant and conventional. Seibert's was not. A six-foot-six forward who had played locally for University High School, Seibert was one of those rarely used benchwarmers who should have felt fortunate just to be on the team. But he had always been a contentious sort. When he was a freshman, Seibert was kicked out of practice so often for cursing that the players called him "Early Showers Seibert." Bill Sweek referred to him as "Funky Bill Seibert" because "he'd hurt you with his elbows. He was all over the place." When Seibert came to UCLA, he was not even guaranteed a place on the team, but Wooden eventually awarded him a scholarship.

Seibert had frequently complained to his teammates about Wooden, but that was hardly unusual. Lots of guys complained about Wooden. Still, nobody knew Seibert's intentions when he took his turn at the podium. He began by saying that if the purpose of this exercise was to describe his experiences at UCLA, then he wanted to be honest and say that he had, in his words, "an unhappy experience." The room fell silent. "I was like, wow, Bill, do you really want to say this?" Bibby recalled. "I think that was the consensus of everyone there."

Seibert then laid out all the reasons why he had not enjoyed playing for John Wooden. Much of it was centered on his lack of playing time, but he had broader complaints as well. Seibert spoke about what he perceived as "unequal treatment," as well as "double rules standard" and a general "lack of communication" between the coaches and the players, especially the end-of-the-bench guys. He talked about the hotel water fight the previous season in Chicago, when Sweek and Wicks, the primary culprits, went unpunished while Seibert and the other reserves were suspended. He told of a time when he and another reserve got caught with a television on in their room on game day and were told they couldn't play that night, but a starter who was caught with a girl in his room went unscathed. Seibert claimed that the trainers spent much more time helping the guys who played than the guys who didn't. As Seibert spoke, his mother started to cry. His father stood up and shouted at him to sit down. But he kept right on talking. "It was," said Enberg, "the most uncomfortable I have ever felt in my life."

Sitting at tables right in front of the dais, Seibert's teammates experienced a range of reactions. On the one hand, they were mortified. On the other hand, they agreed with him. "I don't think he showed very much class in that situation, but the things he said were pretty much true," Ecker said. "The players who were sitting on the bench felt like they were unjustly treated."

As Seibert spoke, Terry Schofield was overcome by a kaleidoscope of emotions—shock, amusement, jealousy, awe. He couldn't believe that Seibert had the guts to say those things in such a formal setting— "Everyone's in a coat and tie and they're happy, and this guy just gets up and lays a turd in the punch bowl," he said—but despite the awkwardness of the moment, Schofield found himself rooting on his teammate. "I got the chills. He had the courage to say what he said because there wasn't anything he said that wasn't true," Schofield said several decades later. "I knew how he felt because I was a failure just like him. I didn't play, either. Bill was basically trying to say, 'I'm not a failure. I have some dignity left here, and let me tell you how difficult it has been to maintain my dignity.' It took real balls to do what Bill did. He challenged the king in his court."

Seibert spoke for just under ten minutes, but it seemed a lot longer. When he was through, there was a smattering of boos from the audience, but the other UCLA players, including the freshmen, rose in unison and gave him a standing ovation. This was an even bigger rebuff to Wooden than the one Seibert had just dealt—and Wooden took notice. It was one thing for a lone, little-used reserve to voice his bitterness about not playing. But for all of the players to give him a standing ovation gave Seibert's remarks credibility.

The ovation was largely misconstrued. It was not necessarily an endorsement of what Seibert had done, nor was it planned in advance. Rather, it was simply a spontaneous, poignant gesture of solidarity for a teammate. "Nobody said, 'Let's stand up,'" Ecker said. "It was more the feeling of, oh my God, Bill Seibert has put himself out on a limb. He's going to get creamed if we don't support him." Wicks added, "He spoke from the heart. I felt for him." The freshmen had no understanding of whether Seibert's complaints were justified, but they instinctively followed the lead of their older teammates. "I thought it took a lot of courage to say what he said," recalled Larry Farmer, a freshman forward. "Speaking for myself, that's why I stood up. I didn't stand up to piss Coach off, although I'm sure it did."

Once Seibert and the other players sat down, Wooden came to the microphone. He showed a grace that Seibert had lacked. Wooden said he was sorry that Bill was so unhappy, but he had always encouraged his players to speak their minds. From there, the evening limped to a close.

Seibert briefly spoke to Wooden after his remarks. "He seemed hurt, for reasons you can imagine. He said it was mostly because his wife and family were hurt," Seibert said. A week later, Seibert revealed that he had begun writing the speech four days before the banquet and that he did not consult with anyone before he delivered it. "I just decided to tell my experiences about UCLA basketball. The speech wasn't written in anger," he said. He also conceded that his reference to a lack of communication was the part of his speech he directed most toward Wooden. "I had hoped it would be received as constructive," Seibert said. "I did not want it to be a mean speech toward Coach Wooden, because he has many qualities that I greatly admire. As Kenny Heitz used to say of him, he's the greatest coach in history at working with a team during practice."

That was clearly a backhanded compliment. The implication was that Wooden only cared about his players as players, not people. "I don't think I would have played anyone on the team any differently, except to maybe let the reserves play more in some of the games that were not close," Seibert said. "What I would suggest, however, is that the coaching staff spend more time with each individual and tell him what his role on the team was. The aim of the team was to win, and that was the definition of success."

Wooden was far more angry than his immediate public reaction indicated. He wasn't just furious with Seibert but at the other players as well. He believed some of them had to have known what Seibert was going to do and had probably encouraged him. "I think it really hurt him inside," Ecker said. "It hurt his integrity, his own vision of himself. I don't know how much of what he heard really sank in."

The players would soon find out just how mad the coach was. The following morning, Denny Crum pulled Schofield from his 8:00 a.m. class and brought him to Wooden's office. When Schofield got there, Wooden and Cunningham were waiting. The three coaches grilled Schofield at length. Wooden listed all the ways in which he believed Schofield was undermining the team, calling him a left-wing activist, a bad influence on his teammates, and a malcontent who would probably be better off quitting the team. "Wooden just unloaded on me," Schofield said. "To some degree, what the coaches said was true. I was very unhappy." Schofield started to cry and swore that he had no idea that Seibert was going to give that speech, but he didn't sense that Wooden believed him.

The next day, Hill and Ecker were called to Wooden's office to face the same inquisition. "I was like, wait a minute. Everyone was giving him a standing ovation. Why are you singling us out?" Hill said. Ecker likewise refused to take blame for Seibert's stunt. "I didn't put him up to it, and I could say that with all honesty," Ecker said. "I wanted to stay on the team."

Schofield, Hill, and Ecker were incensed at Wooden's behavior. Their teammates reacted the same way when the three of them shared their stories. All of the returning players met at Sidney Wicks's house to talk about what Wooden had done. They continued to meet among themselves, and when Wooden got wind of those conversations, he started calling in other players as well. His message was the same: if you feel the same way Seibert does, then you should quit the team.

In the midst of all this acrimony, the national crisis over the Vietnam War was reaching critical mass. Just a few days before Seibert's speech, President Nixon had revealed in a nationally televised address that he was escalating the war into Cambodia. That ignited yet another wave of bitter campus protests. And on the day of the basketball banquet, a student protest at Kent State University turned tragic when the Ohio National Guard opened fire on the protesters, killing four students and wounding nine others.

The Kent State massacre, as it came to be called, spurred a rash of violent demonstrations on campuses around the country. UCLA was no exception. Two days after the shootings, a hundred riot-equipped officers from the Los Angeles Police Department moved from an off-campus command post to the old men's gym. Students and faculty members reported seeing officers on a "window-smashing march" through the campus, arresting people indiscriminately. For the first time in school history, UCLA's administration declared a state of emergency and shut down all campus operations. The next day, Chancellor Charles Young called for a convocation to be held inside Pauley Pavilion, where he addressed more than eight thousand listeners. Young conceded that Nixon's decision to push into Cambodia represented a "crisis of authority," but he also sought to defuse the tension on campus. "I cannot see how the problems of Cambodia, Vietnam or Kent State can be solved by turning UCLA into another battlefield," he said.

The basketball players were determined to do their part. They wanted to leverage their celebrity in support of the cause that had consumed their friends and fellow students. So they wrote, signed, and mailed an angry letter to President Nixon in care of his chief of staff, H. R. Haldeman, a UCLA alumnus and fund-raiser (not to mention a friend of Wooden's). The letter began: "We, the undersigned, are 13 UCLA students (12 players and a student manager) who wish to express our grave concern and disapproval over the President's policy of expansion of the immoral, genocidal and imperialistic war the United States is now waging in Southeast Asia." It concluded by demanding immediate withdrawal from Cambodia, rapid de-escalation from Vietnam, a public investigation into the killings at Kent State, and "the end of harassment of youth by the Nixon-Agnew Administration, by those in authority at the federal, state or local level."

Sam Gilbert, who, unlike Wooden, shared the players' political views, tried to get the letter published in the *Los Angeles Times*, but the paper declined. Somehow, Wooden got hold of the letter and again summoned Hill to his office to voice his displeasure. At first, Hill tried to deny that he had written it, but it did him no good. He was not going to fool a former high school English teacher.

In Wooden's mind, all of these dots were connected: long hair, shaggy sideburns, student protests, letters to the president, societal chaos, players wanting to know *why* and not *how*. It had caused a joyful night to be upended by a selfish kid who was bitter that he didn't get to play more. Wooden was growing tired of adapting to all this change. He was tired of being cast as an evil symbol of the establishment. Now, it was his turn to protest.

Hill, Ecker, and Schofield were the targets of Wooden's ire because they, along with Steve Patterson, had been the most passionate adherents of counterculture causes. Unlike Patterson, however, Hill, Ecker, and Schofield did not play a lot. Moreover, Hill and Ecker had gone to the same high school as Seibert. That's why Wooden assumed they were in cahoots. "I felt from the actions of some of the players they seemed to be real pleased that someone was taking a grab at the establishment," Wooden said. "Some of those players had previously done some things that had indicated that they were anti-establishment. . . . Most of the players were embarrassed [by what Seibert did] but the particular ones who were singled out seemed to be smirking. The ones I could see seemed to be delighted."

After weeks of talking among themselves, the players decided to request a meeting with Wooden so they could air their grievances. Sam Gilbert made arrangements to secure a hotel conference room, but when J. D. Morgan got wind of those plans, he decided to host the gathering in his office. The atmosphere was tense. Wooden opened by saying that he wanted to know whether any of the players in the room agreed with what Bill Seibert had said. He set on the table a notebook in which he had written the players' names in alphabetical order. (With Wooden, there was always an order.) He started to go down the list and ask each man to speak.

The first to be called on was Rick Betchley, a soft-spoken sophomore guard. Betchley mumbled that he didn't really have any complaints other than maybe a few double standards. Before Wooden could even get to the next name, the players jumped in. The complaints came rapid-fire from every corner of the room. "He was kind of flabbergasted by it all," Ecker said. "We emphasized over and over, 'We are not here to hurt the UCLA basketball program. We are here to iron out some of the problems. We're after the same thing that you are.'"

The exercise was painful but healthy. Wooden did his best to listen, but he did not change his mind. "Some members of the team felt that I should not have called those men into my office. I still think I was right in doing it," Wooden later told the author Tony Medley. "I don't think they got the straight dope from the players that I called in. I think they inferred to the other players that I asked them to quit, which I did not. I said, 'If you feel that way, I think you'd be better off to quit.'"

The main complaint was that Wooden's actions had been so at odds with the posture he had always assumed. In the players' minds, he was now attempting to control their lives outside of basketball—and they did not welcome it. "I told him we came to UCLA because we wanted him to coach basketball, not coach our private lives," one player described as a "prominent Bruin" later told Sports Illustrated. "He had been trying to divide and harass us. Wooden has always said we were students first and players next, but he never considered what the ramifications of that are, that as a basketball coach he can't control our identities."

Eventually, it was Wicks who salved the wound during the meeting. "You shouldn't feel threatened by this," he told Wooden. "We're here as a team and you taught us that."

In the end, nothing was firmly decided. Wooden still believed he had treated Seibert and the other benchwarmers fairly and respectfully. "A player gets the treatment he earns and deserves," Wooden said. "If I treated them alike, they'd know I was lying to somebody. Seibert felt he had the right to do what he did, but the boy took advantage of the situation. I didn't feel it was in good taste or polite or good manners, either."

In the weeks after the crisis passed, Wooden reflected on all that had happened. He had learned some important things and, as always, would do his best to adapt. Yet, his faith in his core philosophies emerged unshaken. "All I want to know is, have I been fair?" he said. "Not have I been right, because I know I haven't always been. But have I been fair? I think I have. I always remember to do my best, and I have peace of mind."

A few months after Bill Seibert roiled Wooden's world, he asked his now-former coach to write him a recommendation letter for a teaching position in Australia. Wooden agreed. He was, after all, never one to hold a grudge. Seibert got the job, and life inside Wooden's cloistered church went back to the way it was before. That is, with one exception. UCLA never held a spring banquet for one of Wooden's teams again.

26

The Redhead

Denny Crum knew that Wooden did not like to leave Los Angeles to recruit, so he had to take his case to a higher authority. He told Nell one day in the winter of 1970 that John wouldn't be home for dinner. That way, when Wooden tried to object, Crum could tell him that Nell already knew about it, so he had no excuse not to go.

If Crum was going to take such drastic measures, the player had better be good. Really, really good. When Wooden said he was skeptical, Crum told him, "You didn't question me on these other guys we've got. Why would you question me here?"

Crum drove Wooden to the airport, where the two of them hopped on a twenty-minute flight to San Diego. They drove to a basketball game at Helix High School in the suburb of La Mesa. At first, Crum was concerned Wooden couldn't concentrate on the game because he was besieged by people wanting his autograph. Finally, toward the end of the game, Crum asked his boss what he thought of Helix's center. "Well he is pretty good, isn't he," Wooden replied. For the coach, that qualified as overwhelming enthusiasm.

Bill Walton was better than pretty good. He was the best center ever to come out of California. Walton cut quite the colorful figure back then. Bushy red hair, spindly arms, wobbly legs, tender knees, bursting with boundless, infectious, youthful energy. Walton might not have been a nationally known phenom like Lew Alcindor, but the folks out west knew all about him. "He's the best high school player I've ever seen," San Diego State coach Dick Davis said. "He's probably a better shot blocker at this stage than Alcindor was." After watching Walton in action, Wooden said he was "as good a prospect at this stage of development as anyone I have ever seen."

Walton must have been something special to warrant a rare twofer from Wooden: an out-of-town scouting trip *and* a home visit. But by the time Wooden arrived at Ted and Gloria Walton's modest home later during Walton's senior season, the recruitment was essentially over. Walton had been enamored of Wooden ever since he saw the coach speak at a basketball camp in San Diego six years earlier. UCLA's championship win over Michigan in 1965 was the first basketball game Walton had ever watched on television. The Bruins were scrawny and quick, just like him. He loved their teamwork, their ball movement. Walton attended Lew Alcindor's final game in Pauley Pavilion during the 1969 NCAA West Regional, and he wore number 33 at Helix High School in Alcindor's honor. "I was," Walton said, "the easiest recruit UCLA ever had."

Some two hundred colleges had contacted Walton and his family in hopes of landing him. They brandished all kinds of grand promises, many of which strayed well outside the bounds of NCAA rules. "Let your imagination run wild and you still wouldn't come close," Walton said. Only four coaches made it into the Waltons' home: Notre Dame's Johnny Dee, USC's Bob Boyd, San Diego State's Dick Davis, and Wooden. Fittingly, the coach who left the strongest impression was the one who promised the least. "I won't even promise you'll make the team," Wooden told Walton. "First, you'll have to prove you are a fine young man with good personal values. Then you'll have to demonstrate you can do well in the classroom. If you can do that, we'll give you a practice jersey and allow you to try out."

The Waltons were simpatico with Wooden in a very fundamental way: they didn't have much, but they didn't want for anything. Despite living paycheck to paycheck, Ted and Gloria raised their four children in a loving, nurturing environment. Ted wasn't much for sports—"I never shot a single basketball with my dad," Bill said—but he loved music. Many nights after dinner, the family moved into the living room and jammed around Ted's piano. Bill was on the baritone horn, his older brother Bruce played trombone, younger brother Andy blew the sax, and sister Candy pounded the drums. Meanwhile, Gloria, a full-time librarian, taught her children to love reading. Her kids called her "Glo." Bill's parents were hippies long before anyone knew what that was.

Since their father wasn't into sports, the Walton boys had to discover athletics on their own. Bruce played lineman for Helix's football team. Bill played football and excelled at the high jump until he started focusing on basketball in the eighth grade. Bill was so tall for his age that he played against boys who were a year or two older, but since he was the best ball handler, he usually played point guard. While playing a pickup game at Helix as a freshman, however, Bill tore cartilage in his left knee and had to undergo surgery. He was still growing, which prevented his surgically repaired knee from healing properly. And though he had an insatiable appetite, Bill had a hard time putting on weight. When he was a sophomore at Helix High School, he was so tall, skinny, and uncoordinated that he spent most of the season playing for the junior varsity. He was, in his words, "the ectomorph."

Bill moved up to the varsity as a six-foot-seven, 180-pound junior, but he was so frail that he could play only for limited stretches. Though he was a dominant shot blocker and rebounder, he wasn't much of a scorer. This was by his own design. Because of the tenderness in his knees, Bill's preferred contribution to the offense was to crash the defensive boards and fire bullet passes to the streaking guards. Sometimes, he would throw those long outlet passes before his feet even touched the floor. "He averaged thirty a game, but two-thirds of the time he never got across the ten-second line," Crum said. "If he did, he could've scored sixty." Wooden said that he hadn't seen "anyone throw the outlet pass like that since Jerry Lucas."

This habit wasn't just born from the pain in Bill's knees. It also dovetailed with the communal mind-set his parents had fostered in him. He firmly believed that basketball was a team game, and he was much happier watching his teammates score than getting points of his own. "I sort of enjoyed standing back there watching our guys destroying everybody at the other end," he said. His high school coach, Gordon Nash, had to convince him that his teammates needed him to do some destroying, too. "There were a lot of times I had to ask him to shoot more," Nash said. "He was always conscious of his teammates."

Bill grew another two inches by the start of his senior year, and he improved his conditioning through long bike rides. When Nash finally convinced him it was okay to shoot, the results were spectacular. Walton averaged 29 points and 24 rebounds his senior season while leading Helix to a 33–0 record and a state championship. The only downside to all that success was the attention that came with it. Much like Alcindor, Walton felt uncomfortable standing out in a crowd, and he hated it when strangers gazed up at him and asked, "Do you play basketball?" When a local newspaper ran a story that Walton had attended a concert with his girlfriend, he complained to Nash, "I can't do anything without reading about it in the paper."

After arriving as a freshman at UCLA in the fall of 1970, Walton did his best to blend in, pedaling around campus in sandals while his long auburn locks fluttered in the wind. But everyone knew how special he was. Wooden accorded Walton the rare privilege of practicing with the varsity twice a week as a freshman. This did not go over well with the older players. One day, during Wooden's favorite fast break drill, the three-on-two, two-on-one conditioner, Sidney Wicks took a pass from Bibby and soared toward Walton, the lone defender. When Walton shuffled over to block a layup attempt, Wicks reached over Bill's outstretched hand and dunked with authority. The wild child made his point at the golden child's expense. "It was like that dunk came from Santa Monica. Just POW!" Larry Farmer said. "Coach Wooden blew the whistle. *'Sidney! What do you think you're doing!'* Bill is beet-red, because he just got ran. Curtis Rowe is on the other end of the floor, and he just falls on the floor laughing. It was as close as I ever saw to Coach losing control of practice. It was one of the greatest plays in UCLA history, and nobody saw it except that group of guys."

Basketball was the easy part of Walton's transition. Though he did well in school, he suffered from a debilitating speech impediment. If he could avoid talking to someone, especially someone he didn't know, he would. "When you're a stutterer, you don't talk," Walton said. "I was extremely shy, extremely self-conscious. Uncomfortable in the presence of people who I did not know and saddled with an unbelievable speech impediment and the inability to communicate. I just wanted to be a college student. I feel uncomfortable to this day being recognized individually in a team sport."

Alcindor had avoided contact with strangers as well, but there was a difference. Whereas Alcindor chose to withdraw into a bookish loner's world, Walton was by nature a joiner. He immersed himself in every aspect of campus life, especially the raging counterculture. Walton's parents were staunchly liberal, antiwar, antiestablishment, and it didn't take long for folks at UCLA to learn that Bill was a rabble-rouser. He was kicked out of his first freshman dorm because he and another student ran down the hall knocking off lightbulbs. "It was a prank, but also a form of rebellion," Bruce said.

Though he preferred to socialize in small groups, Bill was fun and inclusive, the kind of guy who would buy beer and pizza for everyone if he had a few bucks in his pocket. No one ever said that about Alcindor. "He stuttered so bad that people thought he was antisocial, but he was very gregarious. A lot of fun to be around," said Jamaal Wilkes, a six-foot-six forward from Santa Barbara who was in the same class as Walton. (When Wilkes played for UCLA, his first name was Keith. Like Alcindor, he changed his name when he converted to Islam after graduation.) Walton shared with his new teammates his passion for music, especially the Grateful Dead. Walton loved music, loved reading, loved parties. And he loved to play ball.

It was this joie de vivre that set Walton apart, not just from Alcindor but from most of the human population. He was a large man with voracious appetites. His belly was never full. "College was perfect," he said many years later. "Are you kidding? An all-you-can-eat buffet at five thirty in the morning. Classes start at seven with the most interesting, fascinating speakers. All-you-can-eat buffet at lunch. Basketball all afternoon. All-you-can-eat buffet at dinner. Then you get to go to bed early and do it all over the next day."

He shook his head and smiled at the memory. "I loved UCLA. It was better than perfect."

The start of basketball practice always coincided with Wooden's birthday, but 1970 marked a special occasion. The day before, on October 14, Wooden turned sixty. Just prior to taking the official team photo, the players sang to Wooden and presented him with a cake. The *Los Angeles Times* noted that "a couple of days ago, several of the Bruin players sported beards, moustaches and long hair, but none of those remained Wednesday." Wooden's friends threw him a private party that week at Bel Air Country Club (Lew Alcindor was also in attendance, showing there were no hard feelings over his *Sports Illustrated* series), but on the night of his actual birthday, Wooden preferred to go out for a quiet dinner with his family. "The older I get, the more I feel like Maurice Chevalier," he quipped. "I remember him saying when he became eighty, 'It's just great, when you consider the alternatives.'"

As usual, Wooden's team was bursting with talent. The six weeks between the start of practice and the first game was going to be another Darwinian elimination ritual. Between the veteran players, rising sophomores, former redshirts, and junior college transfers, Wooden had twenty to thirty players who genuinely hoped to make the twelve-man varsity roster. There was such a glut that Swen Nater, a prized six-foot-eleven transfer from Cypress College, decided to redshirt, and sophomore guard Tommy Curtis, a two-time prep All-American from Tallahassee, did not make the cut. "It was traumatic," Curtis said. "I couldn't accept the rationale behind the decision."

That was just the race to make the traveling squad. The fight to get into Wooden's coveted top six or seven was even more intense. With four starters returning from the national championship team, the primary question at the outset was who would replace John Vallely as the starting guard opposite Henry Bibby. Andy Hill and Terry Schofield had not so patiently waited their turn, but Wooden opted to go with Kenny Booker, who wasn't as good a shooter as the other two but was the best perimeter defender on the team. The Bruins were loaded, and everyone knew it. After they blitzed Baylor by 31 points in their opening game, Baylor coach Bill Menefee said that UCLA was not only better than they had been the previous season; they were the best team he had ever coached against. "That includes the Bruin team with Gail Goodrich and Walt Hazzard," Menefee said. "I've never seen big men shoot so well from the outside. It will take a combination of the New York Knicks and the Milwaukee Bucks to dethrone them."

UCLA's next opponent was another unranked team, Rice University. The players knew the game would be a cakewalk, which is why Wicks and Rowe strolled into the pregame meal ten minutes late without a word of explanation. The other players looked at Wooden to see if he would scold them, but he didn't. Same old star system. "I'm thinking, okay, here's the chink in the armor," Farmer said. "Coach would always say, 'Be on time when time is involved.' I was thinking, yeah, unless it's these two guys."

Shortly before sending the team out on the court against Rice, Wooden stood in the locker room and listed the starting lineup. When he got to the forward spots, he wrote the names *Ecker* and *Farmer* on the board. Then he turned to Wicks and Rowe and said, "You guys were late, so you're not starting. I don't know when I'm going to put you in, or if I'm going to put you in." He kept them on the bench for the first ten minutes. At halftime, the Bruins' lead was just 52–43.

J. D. Morgan was not pleased. He scheduled these easy home games so the athletic department could make some money while assuring the fans of a win. The fans came to see the stars, and Morgan wanted Wooden to deliver them. As the team filed into the locker room, Morgan cornered Crum and ordered him to tell Wooden to start Wicks and Rowe in the second half. The team's manager, Steve Aranoff, heard the exchange and later asked Crum what he had told Wooden. "Are you kidding?" Crum replied, chuckling. "I didn't tell him a thing."

As it turned out, Crum didn't need to deliver the message, because Wicks and Rowe started the second half. They finished with 29 and 27 points, respectively, in a 124–78 romp. After the game, Crum told his boss about his conversation with Morgan. Now Wooden was the one who was not pleased.

On Monday morning, Wooden walked into Morgan's office and objected to what Morgan had done. Wooden described the confrontation in 1982 for an oral history of Morgan compiled by UCLA. "I told him I didn't appreciate him trying to tell me who to play or trying to take over the discipline of the team," Wooden said. "If he wanted to do that, then he can get another coach." According to Wooden, Morgan conceded that he was out of line, and he assured the coach it would never happen again.

That kind of confrontation, however, was unusual. For the most part, UCLA's bombastic athletic director and its low-key basketball coach forged a productive, respectful partnership. And when they did butt heads, it was usually Morgan doing the butting. At the core of the relationship lay a mutual understanding: J. D. was the boss. On this, there was never an argument.

Not that Wooden had much choice. Morgan may have been capable, but he could also be overbearing and meddlesome, and Wooden was powerless to stop him. Morgan insisted on meeting personally with Wooden's recruits, often asking the coach to leave Morgan's office so he could speak with the young men alone. J. D. insisted on knowing every detail about every program at UCLA, not just basketball and football, and especially regarding academics. "J. D. was never modest about telling Coach whether he was right or wrong. He'd tell him," said Bill Ackerman, who coached Morgan on UCLA's tennis team before becoming the university's director of Associated Students. "J. D. was very close to Wooden. I think he was probably maybe closer than Wooden would have liked to have him."

The most obvious example was Morgan's habit of sitting on Wooden's bench during major games as well as for the NCAA tournament. This was an affront to Wooden's authority, but the coach never objected. "Coach didn't like J. D. sitting on the bench. He didn't like that at all," Gary Cunningham said. "Coach wasn't a person that wanted to be confrontational, so J. D. sat there. He second-guessed Coach sometimes, too. We'd hear it as assistants." Charles Young, who became UCLA's chancellor in 1968, said that Morgan believed he was "a calming and helpful force" on that bench, which was curious given that Morgan was Wooden's equal, if not superior, when it came to riding the refs. "J. D. used to be on the bench and he was very tough on officials. He'd write reports on them," the broadcaster Fred Hessler said. During a game at Washington, Morgan was actually whistled for a technical foul.

Wooden accepted Morgan's meddling because he knew that in the end, J. D. had his back. When Douglas Hobbs, a prominent political science professor, wrote Wooden a nasty letter complaining about his players' poor sportsmanship, Morgan invited the two of them to his office and brokered a truce. Morgan also ran interference on Wooden's behalf with Sidney Wicks. Over the summer of 1970, Wicks had shown up at an awards dinner for Wooden at the Beverly Hilton sporting a thick beard. When Wooden saw him, he turned to Hessler and said, "Fred, if I had a razor, I'd shave him right here in the lobby." Wicks continued to test Wooden during the season, which prompted Morgan to call Wicks into his office and say, "Whatever you think of Coach Wooden's rules, it would be good for you to play at UCLA this season. A few months from now, you'll turn pro, get a big contract, and you can wear the beard anyway you like. So why not humor him for a few more months?" It was good advice, and Wicks took it.

Morgan and Wooden had few disputes but several disagreements. The primary one was over scheduling. Wooden believed that Morgan's habit of loading up on easy nonconference home games hindered the Bruins' preparation for conference play. "I would talk to him about it sometimes and he'd say, 'Well, you're doing all right, aren't you?' Since we were winning the conference and national championships almost every year, I could not argue," Wooden said. Morgan had scheduled the 1968 "Game of the Century" in the Astrodome against Wooden's wishes, but Morgan turned down a repeat invitation the following year. He told Wooden that the first game was great for basketball, but a second would be exploitative.

The other point of contention between the two men was recruiting. Morgan may have been the first athletic director in history to complain that one of his coaches wasn't spending *more* money. Wooden was adamantly opposed to out-of-state recruiting unless the player made the first contact. (When Wooden declined to pursue Pete Trgovich, a six-foot-four forward from East Chicago, Indiana, Cunningham wrote a phony letter from Trgovich to Wooden to get the ball rolling.) Whenever Morgan tried to prod Wooden into changing his approach, the coach stood his ground. As Wooden put it, "I could tell him like he told me about the scheduling. . . . Well, we're doing all right with the players I'm recruiting."

Morgan's tireless work ethic fueled his ascension to the NCAA's powerful basketball committee, where he worked hand in glove with NCAA president Walter Byers to negotiate multimillion-dollar television contracts. Nobody could match Morgan's contacts within the TV industry, and he was the first to say that his negotiating skills were unsurpassed. Morgan also held a similar position inside the Pac-8 Conference, where he helped the league secure a lucrative contract for the Rose Bowl. "I'm not exaggerating when I say what J. D. wanted, J. D. got," Professor Douglas Hobbs said.

"J. D. was a remarkable guy. He was a real operator," said Pete Newell, who served as Cal's athletic director from 1960 to 1968. "He could break every darn rule in the book, but he was able to get more for UCLA than any athletic director in the history of any school. . . . Look at all the [NCAA tournament] regionals he got for UCLA. They didn't just play there by accident. J. D. somehow convinced the powers that be to do it."

Morgan was smart and powerful, and he wanted everyone to know it. Cunningham recalled several occasions when Morgan would summon him to his office and make him sit there for several minutes while Morgan finished up whatever he was scribbling on his desk. "It was a power deal that he wanted you to know that he's in charge," Cunningham said. Wooden likewise recalled hearing shouting matches in the hallways, with Morgan doing most of the shouting. "I think he was highly respected by all the others in the conference, but not personally liked by many," Wooden said. "I think that was true at UCLA, to be honest with you."

Among the players, the reviews on Morgan were mixed. They liked flying first class (while Morgan volunteered to sit in coach), benefited from his business acumen, respected his influence, and appreciated his interest in their academics. On the other hand, they didn't like his intrusions, and they sure as heck didn't think he belonged on their bench. "He was a bully and a blowhard," Kenny Heitz said. "We wouldn't see him all season until the Final Four, and then he'd be sitting on the bench. One game a ref told him to sit down and shut up, and we all cheered."

The relationship between Wooden and Morgan would never have worked if the men did not share a genuine respect. "He's the greatest fundamental coach ever in the game," said Morgan, who won eight NCAA titles himself as UCLA's tennis coach. That did not mean, however, that they were close friends. Their conversations revolved almost exclusively around business. For example, even though the entire country was talking about the Vietnam War, Wooden had no idea how Morgan felt about it. "I don't think, as a coach under him, it was my responsibility in any way to be concerned about how J. D. Morgan felt about the Vietnam War," Wooden said. Note Wooden's use of the phrase "under him." This was not a partnership between equals. They were a powerful two-man machine, but only one could be the engine. As Gary Cunningham put it, "It was a professional relationship. It wasn't one you'd call a friendship."

Could this be the year?

That titillating question was on the lips of USC basketball fans as the 1970–71 season tipped off. It had taken four years, but Bob Boyd now had enough high-caliber players to dethrone John Wooden's mighty Bruins. Along with All-America candidate Paul Westphal, now a junior, Boyd returned eleven of twelve players from the group that had shared second place in the Pac-8 the year before. "This is the best team I've had since I've been here," the coach said on USC's first day of practice. "It has the best chance of winning the conference title of any team I've had, too."

The Trojans began the season ranked seventh in the Associated Press preseason poll, and by mid-January they were No. 3 and still undefeated. Of course, that still left them two spots below the Bruins, who had also breezed through their early schedule unscathed. The only lingering concern UCLA had as conference play got under way was Henry Bibby, whose shooting, normally so dependable, had been thrown off by his move to point guard. In January, Bibby was averaging 11 points per game (down from 15 as a junior) while converting just 38 percent from the floor. Still, Wooden never wavered. "This guy never gave up on me," Bibby said. "He would talk to me after practice. I remember him telling me, 'We believe in you. You can shoot.' If I was the coach, I probably wouldn't have played me, but he gave me confidence."

UCLA was a perfect 13–0 as it embarked on a two-game trip to Chicago in late January. After they dispatched a weak Loyola team by 25 points, Wooden fretted that "right now we are not as hungry as we need to be." It was a naked motivational ploy for the challenge that lay ahead the following afternoon in South Bend, Indiana, where the Bruins would face ninth-ranked Notre Dame on national television. UCLA's bus didn't roll into town until 3:00 a.m. the night before, but sleep deprivation was a minor problem compared to the one posed by Notre Dame guard Austin Carr, who was leading the nation in scoring at 37.8 points per game. Once the game tipped off, Carr was otherworldly, tossing in jumpers from every angle to fuel Notre Dame's burst to an early 13-point lead. Wooden had hoped Kenny Booker would be able to slow Carr down, but Carr was shredding him so badly that Wooden switched Terry Schofield on him. That worked until Schofield had to leave the game late in the first half because of an injured elbow. Meanwhile, UCLA's full-court press was so impotent that Wooden abandoned it a few minutes into the game.

A couple of jumpers from Bibby helped the Bruins trim the deficit to 5 at halftime, and they managed to tie the game at 47–all with 16:40 to play. In the end, however, Notre Dame just had too much Carr. After he burned Larry Hollyfield, a little-used six-foot-five sophomore, for 15 points in the final 6 minutes, Wooden sent in Sidney Wicks for one more try even though he had four fouls. He immediately got called for his fifth. As Wicks stalked back to the UCLA bench, he barked at Wooden, "I told you, Coach! I told you not to put me on him!"

The final was Notre Dame 89, UCLA 82. The loss snapped UCLA's nineteen-game winning streak, and it was the school's first nonconference loss in forty-nine games. Carr finished with 46 points. "There is no one to compare with him man-to-man," Wooden said. "They outplayed us. They were more spirited. But we are a better team."

The loss dropped UCLA to third in the AP poll, and while it was hardly reason to panic, it did take some of the luster off the much-anticipated first meeting with USC. Instead of pitting the nation's top two teams against each other, the matchup now featured UCLA in the unaccustomed position of being ranked below USC, which was No. 1 in the UPI poll and No. 2 in the AP. (Undefeated Marquette had replaced UCLA as the AP's No. 1.) The excitement on USC's campus was unprecedented. Many students camped out the night before tickets were made available, and the game took less than three hours to sell out. They were primed to see UCLA toppled at last.

For a while, it looked as if UCLA might suffer back-to-back losses for the first time in five years. It was a stark role reversal. Bibby couldn't hit a shot against USC's zone (he would finish three-for-twelve from the floor), the Bruins threw the ball all over the gym, and USC converted those turnovers into layup after layup. Midway through the second half, USC owned a 59–50 lead, its biggest of the game.

After a UCLA bucket cut the lead to 7, Boyd called time-out. Wooden later said he was "very pleased to see" this because it allowed his guys to regroup. Over the next 3½ minutes, the Bruins went on a 9–0 spurt, taking a 61–59 lead on a steal-and-layup by Booker with 5:30 to play. Having watched his team finally seize a lead, Wooden immediately ordered his Bruins to stall. "I knew they wanted to stay in a zone defense to try to prevent fouls, and might not come out to contest us too much," he said. The tactic worked beautifully. The Trojans scored just one point over the final 9½ minutes, and UCLA emerged with a dramatic 64–60 victory.

Wooden's use of the stall provided Boyd with a golden opportunity to rebuke him in the same way that Wooden had criticized Boyd four years before. But Boyd had long ago accepted that he was never going to win a public relations battle with Saint John. "I don't like stall basketball, but it is legal and I'll do it when I believe the status of the game dictates," Wooden said. "I have never said it wasn't good strategy under certain conditions."

Having dodged a bullet in the USC game, UCLA continued to bob and weave its way to victory. Four of the Bruins' next six wins came by 4 points or fewer. The Bruins' proclivity for winning so many close games burnished their coach's mystical aura—so much so that UCLA's publicity department started applying Red Sanders's old sobriquet "The Wizard of Westwood" to Wooden. The nickname made Wooden uneasy. He hoped it wouldn't catch on.

Wooden knew that there was no magic behind what was happening. He simply had the best players, and he taught them well. There was no better example than Wicks, who had evolved into an efficient, disciplined, intelligent player, all without sacrificing his innate creativity. Wicks relished a challenge. Going up against Cal's star forward, Jackie Ridgle, in Berkeley, Wicks scored a career-high 33 points to go with 17 rebounds and 5 assists. Defensively, he made life so miserable for Ridgle that Wooden chided Ridgle from the bench, "Hey Jackie, how are you going to keep your scoring average up if your teammates don't give you the ball?" After another superlative performance by Wicks in a home win over Oregon (28 points, 13 rebounds), Ducks coach Steve Belko called him "one of the greatest college forwards I've ever seen. He has the quickness of an antelope, he's strong as a big cat inside and both his shot selection and his shooting are much better. The only one I can think to compare him with is Elgin Baylor, and Wicks may be better at this stage because he's bigger."

Despite all this winning, Wooden continued to complain about the way college players had changed over the years. "In my opinion, they're not as coachable now," he said in February. "There's a rebellion against supervision of almost any sort. To accept discipline for many of them now is almost a badge of dishonor." At the first sign of trouble—and there weren't many—Wooden was quick to connect those dots again between the rebellious counterculture and poor performance on the court. After UCLA nearly blew a 10-point lead at Washington before winning by 2, Wooden told his players during a time-out that they had "given in to a permissive society."

When Wooden referred to permissiveness, he was invariably talking about sexual promiscuity. Sure, he could bend a little on hair length and dress code, but he could never brook the carnal free-for-all he imagined was taking place around campus. Privately, Wooden cracked that his players would probably "lead the country in V.D."

One of Wooden's most frequent targets on this front was Steve Patterson. He may have been an outspoken, God-fearing Christian, but when the sun set Patterson could be devilish with the ladies. The season was already wearing on Patterson's psyche. He had spent the early part of his career getting dominated by Lew Alcindor. Now he was hearing from his coach that his subpar play happened because he was spending too much time "catting around." Wooden levied this charge so often that Patterson's friends teased him by calling him "The Cat Man" and "El Gato." Midway through the season, Patterson decided he wanted to quit. Fortunately, as he was heading for his car to leave for the airport, he was spotted by his two best friends on the team, Andy Hill and John Ecker, who spent several hours talking him out of leaving. It was an especially noble effort on Ecker's part, since he would have benefited more than any other player if Patterson had bolted.

And yet the UCLA train rolled on. The Bruins had the most talent, the best coach, and they prized winning above all else. This all came together in their rematch with USC on the final day of the regular season. The Trojans had also not lost since falling to UCLA the month before, and so they entered the final weekend trailing the Bruins by just one game in the Pac-8 standings.

The national television audience that watched in record numbers were treated to another UCLA yawner. During one stretch, the Trojans went seven and a half minutes without a point. At halftime, UCLA owned a 19-point lead, which swelled to 24 early in the second half. The Trojans never got closer than 15 until Wooden emptied his bench. The 73–62 final left Boyd dispirited. "The one thing I feared would happen did happen," he said. "When we got behind early, we had to abandon any game plan we may have had."

Boyd was not lying five months before when he said that this could be his best USC team. In fact, it turned out to be the best team in school history, finishing the season with a 24–2 record. Alas, the question everyone had been asking—*Could this be the year?*—yielded the same answer as the year before, and the year before that, and the year before that. Boyd's Trojans had risen to unprecedented heights, yet they ended back where they started, always and forever looking up at UCLA.

If there was one man who could relate to Boyd's predicament, it was Jerry Tarkanian, who had also engineered a rousing revival at Cal State Long Beach. Tarkanian's 49ers finished the regular season with a 22–4 record and claimed their third straight Pacific Coast Athletic Association title. Yet, because teams were still sent to NCAA tournament regions based on geography, not competitive balance, Tarkanian's path to the NCAA championship was always obstructed by Wooden.

Unlike Boyd, Tarkanian developed both a professional and personal admiration for Wooden, even if some of it was begrudging. "I used to watch Wooden's teams win national championships, and they used to come back to L.A. and land at the airport, and the media would ask him, 'Coach, what are you going to do now?' And he'd say, 'I'm going to take my grandkids to get a milkshake, and then on Sunday, I'm going to go to church,'" Tarkanian said with a chuckle. "And I've got to recruit against him."

Both teams breezed through their opening games—UCLA stomped BYU by 18, Long Beach cruised by Weber State University and Pacific—to earn a meeting in the postseason for the second straight year. Like Boyd, Tarkanian believed he had assembled his finest team, which featured an All-American-caliber player in six-foot-six sophomore guard Ed Ratleff. As soon as the game got under way, the Bruins knew they were in for a fight. Tarkanian, master of the zone defense, surprised Wooden by deploying a 2-3 formation instead of his usual 1-2-2 trap. That forced UCLA to beat the 49ers with outside shots, and the Bruins went cold. Three of UCLA's starters—Booker, Bibby, and Patterson—were a combined oh-for-seventeen in the first half, yet UCLA trailed by just 4 points. Things got worse in the second half, as Long Beach built an 11-point lead with fourteen minutes to play. When Wicks went to the bench at that point with his fourth foul, it looked as if the end of UCLA's championship run was nigh.

Wooden was furious. As UCLA huddled during the second half, he appeared to lose composure. He glared at his players and shouted, "You guys are a bunch of cock hounds!" Then he walked away from the huddle.

The players were momentarily stunned. *Did he really just say that?* They had never heard him use profanity before, and they weren't sure how to react. After a few seconds of silence, Denny Crum dove into the huddle, delivered some final pieces of instruction, and sent them back onto the court.

Did Wooden consciously abandon his prohibition against profanity in hopes it would kick-start his team? We'll never know, because Wooden never discussed it. But that was what happened. UCLA scored 9 straight points and eventually clawed back to a 50–50 tie with six minutes to go.

The game's pivotal play occurred when Ratleff fouled out with four minutes left. Tarkanian saw this as more than just a bad break. According to Loel Schrader, the 49ers' beat writer for the *Long Beach Press-Telegram*, as the Bruins were falling behind, J. D. Morgan started yelling at referee Art White. Tarkanian was convinced that Morgan's intimidation had led White to make that call—"Only time Eddie ever fouled out in his career"—but regardless of whether that's true, it put the 49ers in a bind. With the game tied again at 53–all two minutes later, Tarkanian, desperate, went to a delay offense.

To his surprise, Wooden did not adjust. "I was amazed that he let us stall. He never came out and tried to trap us," Tarkanian said many years later. Long Beach could have stalled its way until the final seconds, but one of their guards, Dwight Taylor, took a pair of ill-advised jumpers that gave UCLA extra possessions. ("I swear to God if I had a gun, I would have shot him," Tarkanian said.) That enabled the Bruins to send Wicks to the foul line, where he sank four nerve-rattling free throws to seal the 57–55 win. "Sidney certainly wasn't one of my better free throw shooters," Wooden said years later, "but in a clutch situation, if you had to have the free throw, I never had anyone that I'd rather have on the line than Sidney."

Tarkanian, like Boyd two weeks ago, was disconsolate. "We did everything we wanted to win," he said, "except we lost."

For UCLA, it was just the latest escape in a season full of them. Tarkanian had seen many of those at close range. He did not believe a man could be so lucky unless there were greater forces at work. "I never saw a coach win so many close games," Tarkanian marveled many years later. "So many strange things would happen. I think that Wooden was such a nice man who went to church all the time that the good Lord wanted him to win."

Did he really believe that?

"Yes, I do. I don't think he was lucky. I think the good Lord just said, 'This is a good man.'"

UCLA was back in the Astrodome, not for a spectacle this time but rather for a chance to win a championship—its fifth straight. In an effort to capitalize on the growing popularity of the tournament, the NCAA staged its culminating weekend inside an indoor football stadium for the first time. Wooden tried to display his usual equanimity, but inside he was wound tight. He had a senior-laden team, and he knew the next year he would have to rebuild mostly with sophomores. If this was going to be UCLA's last chance to continue its championship string, Wooden wanted his team to pull it off.

On the afternoon of UCLA's semifinal against No. 4 Kansas, Cunningham and Crum waited in the hotel lobby for Wooden so they could all walk over to the Astrodome. When Wooden was uncharacteristically late, the assistants checked with Nell, who told them that Wooden had left a half hour before. Figuring Wooden had gotten the meeting time mixed up, Crum and Cunningham went to the arena. They looked for Wooden for a while, but when they couldn't find him, they went to an upper-level box so they could scout the first semifinal. When they finally met up with Wooden toward the end of the game, they discovered that their boss was royally pissed. "He really got after both of us," Cunningham said. "He was angry at me, but he thought Denny was the instigator. It was just a screw-up. . . . It shows the tension of the tournament and the pressure and wanting to win. All of those ingredients you put together, it's like a time bomb ready to go off."

When the game got under way, the anger between the coaches was still simmering. Normally, Crum and Cunningham spoke to the team before the game and during time-outs, but Wooden refused to let them. "He didn't let us do what we normally do. We couldn't talk in the locker room or anything," Cunningham said.

Midway through the first half, Crum told Schofield to report into the game. It was not unusual for Wooden to delegate substitutions to his assistants, but on this occasion, he objected and sent Schofield back to the bench. When Crum tried to send Schofield to the scorer's table a second time, Wooden objected again. "He told me to go sit down at the end of the bench because he didn't want to listen to me," Crum said. "I said, 'I'm not going down there, Coach. This is my responsibility. I'm going to sit right here like I always do.'" The two men argued loudly and continued to go at it during a time-out. Bibby stepped in in an effort to calm the two of them down, but it didn't do much good.

For Schofield, the exchange was awkward, to say the least. "I'm standing right there, and Wooden's yelling, 'I'll make sure you never sit on this bench again!'" Schofield recalled. "It was a difficult situation because Crum told me to stay. But I wasn't going into the game until Wooden said so."

The arguing had no palpable effect on the players. UCLA built a huge second-half lead before winning, 68–60, to advance to the championship game. The next morning, Wooden called Crum and Cunningham to apologize. He invited them to join him at the annual Fellowship of Christian Athletes breakfast. "I had been up all night and I wanted to sleep, but I said yes," Cunningham said. "It was an uneasy time for a few weeks after that. I mean, I had never been dealt with like that by Coach in the whole time I knew him. I don't think Denny had, either. He let emotions take over."

UCLA's opponent in the final was a bit of a surprise. Villanova, which was ranked nineteenth in the AP poll, had reached the final game by upsetting undefeated third-ranked Penn in the East Regional final and then squeaking by Western Kentucky in two overtimes in the semis.

It turned out to be a much different contest than any of UCLA's previous six NCAA finals had been. In the first place, the game was close. Villanova coach Jack Kraft came out in a zone defense, which given UCLA's size advantage was a smart strategy. The obvious counter would be for Wooden to hold the ball, just as he had done against USC and several other teams, to force the Wildcats into a man-to-man. But would Wooden really attempt to do that here, in an NCAA championship game with 33,000-plus fans in attendance and millions more watching on television across the country? If that wasn't "bad for the game," what was?

Of course he would. Wooden wanted to win. After UCLA built a 45–37 halftime lead, thanks to 20 points from Patterson, the Bruins began the second half by stalling. Soon, a smattering of boos and chants of "Bruins are bush!" rained from the crowd. The Villanova players taunted the Bruins as well. "You're the national champions! Play ball!" one yelled. Another asked sarcastically, "You guys sick?"

From a strategic standpoint, Wooden's move backfired. When Kraft switched to a pressure man-to-man, it exposed the ball-handling weaknesses that had plagued UCLA all season. Three baskets by Villanova forward Howard Porter closed the deficit to 3 points with under two minutes to play. But Villanova would get no closer as UCLA won, 68–62. It was the first time one of Wooden's teams had won a championship game by fewer than 11 points.

Wooden was again pleased that it was a team effort. On a night when Wicks and Rowe were ineffective (7 and 8 points, respectively), Patterson (29 points) and Bibby (17) had saved the day. The machine worked again. When Wooden substituted for Wicks in the final seconds so he could get his senior ovation, Wicks shook Wooden's hand, leaned down, and said into his ear, "Coach, you're somethin'."

One can only imagine what Wooden would have said if another coach had used a stall against UCLA in an NCAA championship game, but Kraft voiced no objections. "I personally would not have done it, but I can't criticize John Wooden for it because this is the national championship and the idea is to win," he said. "I'm happy and I'm proud that he feared us that much."

Wooden admitted he wasn't crazy about the stall—"Maybe now the rules committee will think a little bit more about putting a shot clock in"—but he was even less crazy about losing the game. "If we had let them stay in their zone, I was afraid we might have hit a cold spot and start missing our shots," he said. "I felt we could beat Villanova man-to-man."

Given the pressure Wooden was under that weekend, it was understandable that he would do whatever it took to win. "If we had lost today, I know our fans would say we had an unsuccessful season, even though our record would have been 29–2," Patterson said. "The pressure on us had been that bad, believe me."

For Patterson and his fellow seniors Rowe and Wicks, it was a gratifying, triumphant moment. Now they, too, could boast that they had won three straight NCAA championships, just like Lew Alcindor and Mike Warren. When the game was over, Wooden was naturally asked whether a sixth straight title was in the offing, even though he was losing seven of his top eight players. "I'm sure you writers will put pressure on us. You'll pick us to win everything again," he said. "Only a lame brain would pick us for national honors with a completely new team."

Needless to say, his admonition fell on deaf ears. As far as the public was concerned, it didn't much matter who was playing for the Bruins anymore. As long as the Wizard of Westwood was casting his spells, you'd have to be a lame brain to pick against them.

27

Sam

As the spring 1971 semester was winding down, Larry Farmer happened to run into Wooden while walking across campus. The two of them were chatting when Farmer heard Sidney Wicks calling to him from across the quad. For a moment, Farmer was unsure if he should answer Wicks or finish his conversation with the coach.

"Are you at his beck and call?" Wooden taunted. "I hope you don't think that next season you're going to try the same stunts he did."

Suffice to say, Farmer didn't go anywhere. "I don't know what was going on between those two guys, but all of a sudden I was coldly in the middle of it," he said. "If I was going to give in to one of them, it was definitely going to be the guy that designed the plays."

The wild child was gone, but the old man stayed behind, unmoved and unbowed. He had coached at UCLA now for nearly a quarter century. Showerless gyms, chalky floors, and meager expectations were figments of the past. As a college coach, Wooden was accustomed to seeing departures followed by arrivals, older players moving on and younger ones moving up. Thus, when Wicks bade farewell to Westwood, it again marked the end of one era and the beginning of another. This one belonged to a player who was even more talented, more colorful, more childlike, more wild.

Bill Walton was some different kind of cat. His unique size and skills forced Wooden to go back to the low-post offense he had used with Lew Alcindor. Unlike Alcindor, however, Walton was also a gifted outlet passer, and Wooden wanted to take advantage of that as well as his team's overall quickness. That meant spreading the floor and reviving the full-court zone press. Wooden relished this kind of intellectual exercise, the lonesome engineer toiling in his workshop. By the time fall arrived, he had filled nearly thirty notebooks with ideas.

Wooden spent much of the summer of 1971 jetting around the country to teach at clinics, but his doctor eventually shut him down. Walton, by contrast, kept a low profile, staying by the beach and spending most of his time reading. In the spring, he had asked Denny Crum to find him a job, but once he had just enough money to see him through the summer, he stopped showing up for work. Walton needed money to live. He didn't live to make money.

As it turned out, Crum would not be at UCLA to coach Walton as a varsity player. In April, he accepted the head coaching position at the University of Louisville. "Coach may have been disappointed because we were doing well and I did a lot of the recruiting, which he didn't like to do, but he would never say anything," Crum said. "I wanted to prove I could be a successful head coach." Wooden replaced Crum with Frank Arnold, who had spent the previous five years as an assistant at Oregon. Crum's departure did nothing to diminish Walton's excitement about playing for his childhood icon. He showed up at Wooden's office every morning to grill the coach on what he was planning for that day's practice. "I knew I had to get in there by nine thirty to get my two cents in. Why are we doing this? Why can't we do that?" Walton said. "I was his worst nightmare."

It was not easy for Walton to control his emotions. His intemperance got the better of him one day when Farmer scored over him in practice. Walton got so angry he fired the ball and hit Farmer, and the two of them had to be separated. On game days, the locker room could barely hold him. "He would just sit there and literally throw the ball around the locker room. He was just in another zone," Jamaal Wilkes said many years later.

Properly channeled, Walton's energy was a great asset. He was an avid communicator on the court, barking out instructions on defense, shouting for joy when a teammate scored, screaming when someone else made a mistake. The only thing that could silence Walton was his speech impediment, which got the better of him during huddles. "In the heat of a game, when he knew he had to hurry because he only had a little bit of time, he wouldn't be able to get it out," said Bob Webb, a six-foot-two guard from Pennsylvania. "It wasn't like he stuttered just a little bit. To say one word could take him five seconds."

His teammates tolerated Walton's antics because they knew he was a great player. They also knew he was his own worst critic. "He's so young, he still tends to get down on himself when things don't go just the way he thinks they should," Wooden said early that season. "He has to have the experience to learn to shrug off things that don't seem to go quite right."

It would have been nice if Walton were surrounded by upperclassmen, but he did not have that luxury. Farmer was the only returning starter, and he had played meager minutes the season before behind Wicks, Rowe, and Patterson. So Wooden had no choice but to fill out his starting lineup with two of Walton's classmates. The first was Greg Lee, a six-foot-four guard from nearby Reseda, just over the hill from Westwood. A two-time city player of the year in Los Angeles, Lee shared many of Walton's interests and passions. Lee was as glib as Walton was laconic, so he often served as Bill's voice. A teammate once likened the pair to Lenny and George from *Of Mice and Men*.

The other sophomore starter was Keith Wilkes. He and Wooden were on the same wavelength from the start. Wilkes grew up the son of a Baptist minister in the picturesque seaside town of Santa Barbara. He was slightly built at six-foot-six, 167 pounds, but he was so smooth on the court that he earned the nickname "Silk." Wilkes was by far the youngest player on the team; his nineteenth birthday wouldn't come until May.

Wilkes got his indoctrination into Wooden's teaching methods when the coach beckoned him after practice one day early in his sophomore season. Wilkes thought he was about to get reamed, but Wooden only wanted to watch him shoot. For the next ten minutes, the coach put Wilkes through the paces. Wilkes ran around the court, fielding Wooden's passes and lobbing jumpers toward the rim. "What I remember most—and I'll never forget this—was that every pass he made to me was a perfect pass. It was the pass that he taught us," Wilkes said. "At that time, I was not real familiar with his playing background, other than he had been an All-American."

As Wilkes attempted shot after shot, Wooden looked closely at his form. While growing up on the playgrounds, Wilkes had taught himself to wind up and release the ball from behind his head. That made it harder to block, but it was also unconventional. Wooden preferred the textbook approach, with the ball cocked from the side. As Wilkes took his shots, Wooden peppered him with questions. *Why do you hold the ball like that? What are you thinking on your release? Where are you aiming?* Wilkes's form looked funny, but it worked.

Five years before, Wooden had put Edgar Lacey through this same exercise and decided to drastically change Lacey's form. This time, Wooden left well enough alone. "Okay," he finally told Wilkes, "you can go."

Class dismissed.

Wooden had many options beyond his starting five heading into the 1971–72 season. There was Tommy Curtis, finally moved up to the varsity, as well as Swen Nater, the six-foot-eleven, 250-pound native of Holland. Wooden told Nater that as long as Walton was in the program, Nater probably wouldn't get much playing time. Nater didn't mind.

Before the season got started, Wooden sat at his desk, pulled out a sheet of paper, and assembled a game-by-game prediction of how the season would unfurl. He decided the Bruins would finish with a 24–2 record, with losses at Oregon State and USC. He had been completing this little ritual the last couple of years. His secretary was the only other person who knew about it.

Once again, J. D. Morgan had lined up a bunch of easy, early home games. First up was The Citadel, which UCLA slaughtered 105–49. After the game, Greg Lee quipped that The Citadel was like a "good junior college team." When Wooden saw that quote in the newspaper, he gave Lee quite an earful. A writer from the *Los Angeles Herald Examiner* named Doug Krikorian took it a step further and wrote that The Citadel couldn't even beat Crenshaw High School's jayvee team.

Krikorian repeated the quip when he introduced Wooden at the writers' luncheon the following Monday. Wooden was not amused. "It's belittling and demeaning the way you try to pull things out of our players, things they don't mean to say," he said to Krikorian in front of everyone. "I suppose I should apologize for J. D. Morgan, who is not here, for okaying our schedules. I guess I should apologize for our record over the past eight years. Nothing seems to please people anymore." Wooden went on to lambaste Krikorian for failing to live up to the tradition set by legendary sportswriters like Grantland Rice, who had used his columns to anoint sporting heroes—in verse, no less. After the gathering broke up, Wooden added, "Yes, I was upset. There are a lot of fellows who are about to die because we've been doing so well. I think we have a tremendously entertaining product, but they've been demeaning and belittling us."

It was unusual for Wooden to lose his composure under any circumstances, much less in public. Even more remarkable was the fact that he used such an open forum to criticize his boss. At practice later that afternoon, Wooden warned his players that they would read some unflattering things about him in the newspapers, and the next day he called Krikorian at work to apologize. "He was thin-skinned in a lot of ways, but we never had a problem after that," Krikorian said. "I mean, it's hard to write bad things about a guy who wins all the time."

Seven easy wins later, the Bruins found themselves facing what was supposed to be their toughest test yet: a clash with No. 6 Ohio State in the final of the Bruin Classic. It ended up being another UCLA waltz, 79–53. Walton spent much of the game in foul trouble, needing just eighteen minutes to amass 14 points and 13 rebounds. He was asked afterward if Luke Witte, the Buckeyes' heralded big man, was the best center he had ever faced. "No," Walton replied. "Swen Nater is."

Aside from a few postgame interviews, Walton kept himself off-limits to the press. No matter. For all his protests about wanting to be considered a part of the team, the sportswriters started calling UCLA the "Walton Gang." As Walton continued to astound opponents with his skills, drive, and court vision, the tributes came pouring forth. "He's better than Bill Russell at their comparative age and development," Stanford coach Howie Dallmar said after watching Walton collect 32 points and 15 rebounds in a 39-point win. "I'm not so sure I'm glad Alcindor graduated. Walton never lets up on you," added Washington State's Marv Harshman, following Walton's 31-point, 15-rebound, six-block performance against the Cougars. Pete Newell, who was working as a scout for the NBA's Houston Rockets, declared himself a believer after just a few games. "He may be the most dominant center ever to play basketball," Newell said.

It was incredible. UCLA once again had a bona fide once-in-a-generation player, just five years removed since another had dropped in Wooden's lap. Even Wooden conceded that the redhead compared favorably to the once-incomparable Lew Alcindor. "Lewis had more of a psychological barrier than Bill does. Lewis was more phlegmatic," Wooden said, in what was surely the first time a college basketball coach ever described a player as *phlegmatic*. "Bill, on the other hand, is more of an extrovert in every respect, and because he is, he will become aroused in a game more often."

Walton made it look easy, but few people outside the program knew just how difficult it was for him to get ready to play. Every day, he arrived early for practice so he could treat his knees with thirty minutes of heat. Then he stayed afterward to ice them for another thirty minutes. Wooden gave Walton the day off for Monday's practices so he could recover from the weekend. During games, Wooden accorded him the unprecedented privilege of calling his own time-out. Wooden trusted that Bill wouldn't abuse that privilege, and he never did. In the past, Wooden's players objected to this kind of star treatment, but Walton's teammates knew he wasn't faking it. "When he took those ice bags off his knees, they were big and red. He had those big knobby kneecaps," Farmer said. "None of us were ever jealous that he got to skip practice."

Because Walton tended to overcompensate for his knees, he developed other maladies. During an early February road trip to Washington, he tore tendons in his feet. He had to get cortisone injections into his toes to stop the pain. "There were times my knees hurt so bad, I honestly thought of quitting," Walton said. "If I hadn't been part of a team that was finishing a schedule and going for a championship, I would have quit."

Walton looked for any remedy he could find to alleviate his pain. That included marijuana. For Walton, smoking pot wasn't just something fun to do while listening to the Grateful Dead. It lessened his pain and helped him wind down after games. Walton even asked Wooden for his permission (or more likely, his blessing) to smoke marijuana for these purposes. "He said that a certain doctor had said that the use of marijuana could help his knees," Wooden said. "I said, 'Bill, I'm no doctor, but I only need to know one thing. That's against the law.'"

Over the years, there have been a few published accounts indicating that Wooden granted Walton permission to smoke pot, provided none of his teammates knew about it. Walton laughed at the suggestion. "That's not true," he said. "Some people also said that Richard Nixon was a great president."

If UCLA held a big lead in the final minutes of a game, Wooden would let Walton go to the locker room to get a start on his postgame icing routine. The situation presented itself often. After opening Pac-8 play with a 78–72 win at Oregon State, the Bruins ramrodded their opponents with margins that exceeded even those in Alcindor's heyday: 118–79 over Stanford; 82–43 over Cal; 81–56 over USC; 109–70 over Washington; 91–72 in the rematch at Pauley with Oregon State. The team's annual trip to Chicago produced similar scores: 92–64 over Loyola and 57–32 over Notre Dame. By the end of February, the Bruins were on pace to shatter the NCAA record for an average margin of victory of 28.1 points, which had been set by North Carolina State in 1947–48.

That the Bruins were eviscerating opponents with a lineup that included three sophomores and a junior made it even more remarkable. For the first time in a long time, Wooden had the chance to mold young, eager minds. It wasn't quite as enjoyable as coaching those high school kids in the Palisades, but it was close. "I'm really having fun with this team," Wooden said in early January while sipping ginger ale at a cocktail party. "Why, this team is exciting even when it makes mistakes. And it makes a lot, being so young."

The huge margins also encouraged Wooden to develop his depth. By March, all twelve of his players had earned their varsity letters, the first time that happened in as long as he could remember. Alas, that still did not mean much playing time for Andy Hill. He was a senior who thought he would finally get a chance to play, just as his good friends, John Ecker and Terry Schofield, got minutes when they became seniors. Unlike them, however, Hill was still stuck on the pine. It bruised his pride. Many years after he graduated, a longtime Bruin basketball fan told Hill that he and his buddies used to refer to him as "the man who launched five thousand cars." Because when Wooden sent Hill into the game, that meant it was time to go home.

Hill did not help himself by continuing to irritate the head coach with his various causes. In an effort to convince Wooden to allow his players to wear their hair a little longer, Hill conducted a scientific sample of the student body and presented his findings to Wooden. If nothing else, Hill thought Wooden might be impressed with his industriousness and enthusiasm, the two cornerstones in Wooden's Pyramid of Success. He wasn't.

Hill did, however, get a rare glimpse at Wooden's sense of humor. Most of the players assumed he had none. "He was your coach. He wasn't your friend. He had a job to do, and he took that job very seriously," Walton said. Yet, one day during a team meal, Hill sat stunned as Wooden regaled Swen Nater with plans of going "snipe hunting" later that evening. For half an hour, Wooden told Nater all about how they were going to go hunting for snipes at 2:00 a.m., what that entailed, and where they should meet. When Wooden got up to leave, he winked at Hill. As Nater eagerly talked about how he needed to get a flashlight and pillowcase as the coach instructed, Hill decided he had better let Swen in on the joke.

UCLA barely broke a sweat as it completed a 26–0 regular season. Wooden tried to keep them on edge by criticizing their effort and concentration, but even he had to concede that was just a motivational ploy. The emergence of Greg Lee as a dependable point guard—his lob passes to Walton were beautifully timed and perfectly placed, the two best buddies always simpatico—allowed Wooden to move Bibby back to the wing, where he was more comfortable. And with all the defensive attention paid to Walton, Wilkes was often left unmolested on the perimeter. He emerged as an All-American in his own right.

There were, of course, a few times when this group could show a little too much youthful vigor. During a long layover on their way back from Chicago, several players got drunk in the airport. When they got back on the plane, they started a water and peanut fight, which lasted until a stray nut pegged Wooden on the head. ("We have this great UCLA image, and nobody suspects we are a bunch of wonderful lawbreaking degenerates," one player said.) All the success went right to the players' heads. Wooden warned them that if they kept that up, by the time they were seniors, they would be "intolerable." As Walton recalled, "He told us that numerous times. I think he moved up that timetable every time. We didn't believe anything he said."

UCLA's first stop in the NCAA tournament was at the West Regional in Provo. They were undefeated, ranked No. 1, and quite obviously the team to beat. They proved that by demolishing Weber State in their first game by 32 points. That sent them into yet another regional final against Cal State Long Beach.

The 49ers were ranked No. 5 in the AP poll, but Jerry Tarkanian knew that his team would be badly outmanned. They had no choice but to get physical with Walton. Throughout the game, Walton complained to the referees. Wooden was plenty ticked, too. During the second half, he marched down the bench and chastised Tarkanian's assistant, Dwight Jones. "He told me it was disgraceful and unethical the way our kids were playing," Jones said.

UCLA prevailed, 73–57, but Walton's comportment was becoming an issue. He was developing a reputation for being a whiner, even though his complaints were often justified.

The semifinals and final would take place once again in the Los Angeles Sports Arena, making it feel like just another Bruin Classic, with UCLA set up for the cakewalk. The Bruins' semifinal opponent was No. 6 Louisville, coached by Wooden's former assistant, Denny Crum. The reunion may have been awkward for Wooden, but not for Crum. "He was like a father. If I was going to lose to someone, I figured it might as well be him," Crum said. That's just what the Cardinals did, 96–77, thanks to Walton's 33 points. While Cardinals center Al Vilcheck said afterward that Walton "cries a lot," Crum had nothing but praise for his alma mater. "This is the best UCLA team I've ever seen," he said.

The final victim was No. 10 Florida State. The Seminoles might have been the third-best team UCLA played in the tournament, at least according to the rankings, but the Bruins came out of the gate flat. Florida State hit seven straight shots in the early going to mount a 21–14 lead, the only time the Bruins had trailed by more than 4 points all season. Eventually,

Florida State started committing too many fouls, and the rout was on. With Wilkes leading the way with 23 points, UCLA opened a 50–39 half-time lead. The Bruins were uncharacteristically sloppy with the ball during the second half, but they still emerged with an 81–76 win, completing Wooden's third undefeated season and bringing him his sixth consecutive national championship.

By any standard, this was a remarkable achievement. And yet Walton, who had 24 points and 20 rebounds in the game despite sitting for long stretches because of foul trouble, acted like a spoiled brat afterward. "We didn't play well. There's no reason for elation. We don't like to back into things," he said in the interview room at the Sports Arena. When someone said that it sounded as if UCLA had lost, Walton replied, "I feel like it." Abruptly ending the questioning, Walton left for the locker room, where he refused to take any more questions.

That brought Walton even more criticism from the media, but he couldn't have cared less. He was done with the season, done with sportswriters, done with John Wooden's tightly controlled machine. Now he could grow his hair as long as he wanted and disappear for a few months. A few weeks later, Wooden called Larry Farmer to his office, where he handed him a trophy for being named the most improved player. In the past, that trophy would have been presented at a lavish banquet, but thanks to Bill Seibert, that was no longer the case.

In the days following the championship, Wooden was asked yet again whether his program's dominance was hurting the sport. "The same thing was said about the Yankees in baseball years ago," he said. "Whenever you reach a plateau of excellence, there are always a lot of people who want to see you knocked down." That aside, Wooden was inundated by hundreds of congratulatory letters. One in particular pleased him so much that he took the letter home, framed it, and hung it on his wall. "And you may be certain," it concluded, "that I am counted among those who think John Wooden is just about the finest coach in the long, exciting history of the game."

The letter was signed: "With warm good wishes, Richard Nixon."

In the late spring, Larry Farmer attended an alumni banquet that was staged at a posh hotel to celebrate the 1972 championship. As he was standing in the lobby talking to Willie Naulls, the former Bruin great introduced Farmer to a wealthy alumnus. "This kid's got a great future,"

Naulls said, and the two men shook hands. "That," said Farmer, "was the first time I met Sam Gilbert."

Farmer knew who Gilbert was, but soon he got to know him much better. When Farmer later told Gilbert that he had spent his previous Thanksgiving eating dinner at a local Hamburger Hamlet because he couldn't get home to Denver, Gilbert was appalled. He told Farmer that if he ever needed someplace to go for Thanksgiving, he was welcome to share in the family feast at Gilbert's house in the Palisades. It was the beginning of a beautiful friendship. "Sam helped everybody. He was that kind of soul," Farmer said. "Sam, Coach, and my dad are probably the three people who had the most impact on my life."

Farmer's relationship with Gilbert became unusually close—he would eventually give Gilbert one of his UCLA championship rings—but the dynamic was a familiar one. Lew Alcindor and Lucius Allen had been gone for several years, but Gilbert was still a strong presence in the UCLA basketball program. If anything, he was more entrenched than ever. Many players regularly spent time with Gilbert, attended his weekend barbecues, visited him at his Encino office, and met him for dinners and other events around town. John Wooden may have been their basketball coach, but Sam Gilbert was their life coach. He gave them empathy, friendship, advice. He talked through personal troubles they would never have thought to bring to Wooden. And he provided plenty of other perks, many of which were in direct violation of NCAA rules because they were not generally available to nonathletes.

It's an understatement to say that Gilbert was not bothered by this rule breaking. If anything, he was proud of it. "He really felt the NCAA was screwing the players [by not allowing them to be paid]. He was really adamant and sincere about that," Bob Marcucci said. "That's how he got going with them. It's pretty clear that he was providing I guess what are called extra benefits." Jamaal Wilkes added, "Sam expressed his opinion. He was not a big fan of the NCAA and the way they did things. He was a cut-through-the-BS kind of guy."

The players of Farmer's era experienced the same revelation that Allen and Alcindor did—namely, a surprising karmic connection with a man who was older, wealthier, and in many cases whiter than they. Gilbert bragged that he actually related better to college students than people of his own generation. Where Wooden was openly disdainful of the counterculture, Gilbert was a full-throated devotee. Wooden obsessed over the players' feet. Gilbert engaged their minds. "There was a feeling that this was a guy who was wealthy and dissed the establishment," Wilkes said. "I remember one time walking somewhere and he said, 'You see the birds? They're not prejudiced. The trees aren't prejudiced. Prejudice is a riddle. Only people are prejudiced.' That kind of thinking at that time was stimulating."

That streetwise sensibility, combined with Gilbert's experience in negotiating NBA contracts for Alcindor and Allen, who was drafted by the Seattle SuperSonics after he dropped out of UCLA, led Sidney Wicks to ask Gilbert to represent him after the Portland Trail Blazers selected him with the second pick in the 1971 NBA draft. Gilbert did not charge Wicks a percentage—his lone compensation was a signed picture—but Wicks had to agree to let Gilbert outline his budget, set up tax shelters, and manage his investments. Gilbert rarely used the players' money to invest in one of his own projects to avoid a conflict of interest. Instead, he steered them into safe vehicles like federally insured public housing. His purpose was to help Wicks reach long-term security. Wicks trusted Gilbert completely. "Sam is the conscience of Sidney Wicks," he said during his rookie year with the Trail Blazers.

Curtis Rowe and Steve Patterson also asked Gilbert to represent them in the pros. Gilbert quickly became the de facto agent for UCLA players, even though he wasn't technically an agent.

The players appreciated the way Gilbert railed against the sports agent business, which he considered to be parasitic. "No one is worth ten percent of a man's earnings," Gilbert said in 1971. "A player's position on the draft list determines his value. This limits his ability to negotiate for dollars. In other words the so-called agent does very little, except put on paper that which is already predetermined."

It's understandable why a young college student would cotton to this wealthy, well-connected, generous man. The players could see that his loyalty would extend well beyond their college days. Willie Naulls, who now owned several restaurants and other businesses in mostly black neighborhoods like Compton and Watts, was a prime example. So was Freddie Goss, who turned to Gilbert for advice and assistance when he was the head coach at UC Riverside. On one occasion, Goss asked Gilbert to help one of his assistants avoid the military draft. Sam invited Goss to bring his assistant to his cabin in the mountains for the weekend. When they got there, he told them simply, "It's done."

That describes Gilbert's modus operandi better than any other: he got stuff done. While it is plausible to assume that Gilbert gave players cash, no one has gone on record to say so. "He may have. I really don't remember," Wilkes said. Rather, Gilbert served as a conduit between the players and businessmen he knew around town, men who gave them special discounts, if they charged the players at all. Gilbert massaged his network by handing out game tickets, which he purchased from the players, often above face value. The help extended from the casual to the deeply personal. When Allen was still playing at UCLA, Gilbert paid for his girlfriend to have an abortion. "It happened often," Allen said. "If a ballplayer impregnated someone, there was always a hospital available. I never paid for it, and it was my case."

There was no formal process by which the players entered Sam Gilbert's orbit. They merely succumbed to the laws of gravity. Wilkes had met Gilbert briefly on his recruiting visit, but it wasn't until he became a sophomore that he developed a deeper relationship. "When I got on the varsity, Henry Bibby said, 'All right, kid, we're going to go out and meet the guy now,'" Wilkes recalled. "I said, 'I met him on my recruiting trip.' He said, 'No, we're going to *really* meet him.' So it was like an initiation. From what I gathered, certain guys really, really leaned on him for stuff."

Soon, Wilkes started leaning on him for stuff, too. Gilbert bought his game tickets and helped him get a discount on clothes. Wilkes also said Gilbert got him a sweet deal on a car. "I'm pretty sure it was a Toyota. I don't remember the model," Wilkes said. Asked if he could have afforded that car without the discount, Wilkes replied, "I don't think so. I would have had to go to my parents and had a discussion."

Wilkes also said that he could walk into several restaurants around town and not have to pay for his meal, though that was just as often due to an overeager restaurant owner who had nothing to do with Gilbert. To the players, this did not seem like a big deal. They were rock stars in the entertainment capital of the world. Of course there were going to be some fringe benefits. "There were places that we could go and not pay, but it had nothing to do with Sam," Farmer added. "A lot of it simply had to do with the fact that we were basketball players at UCLA. Could Sam arrange that? Yeah, but he wasn't the only person that did that."

The difference was that Gilbert was a UCLA alumnus and heavy financial donor—a "booster," in the parlance of the NCAA. His gifts were more direct, his relationships more personal. Asked if Gilbert ever helped him get clothes, Farmer said, "I wouldn't know." Then he smiled and admitted, "I'm being coy."

Taken individually, these favors were hardly alarming. If Gilbert had been forking over mountains of cash or had asked the players to shave points, it would have risen to a much higher degree of severity. But it was the pattern of behavior—helping out multiple players over several years—that made Gilbert's role so problematic. It would have been one thing if Gilbert did this for every type of student, but the vast majority of his favors went to athletes.

Even so, it was not difficult for the players to justify all of this on a moral basis. Gilbert's gifts may have been technically against NCAA rules, but to the players, they didn't feel all that scandalous. They talked to enough guys at other schools, including USC, to recognize that this sort of thing went on nearly everywhere. And what about all that money UCLA was making from their unpaid labor? Didn't that entitle them to a little graft on the side?

It was all quite easy to rationalize. "Sam bought me a coat," Larry Farmer said. "So you say, why would he have to buy you a jacket? Well, maybe my parents couldn't afford that jacket, and I played on a team that was going to be on national TV. We were going to play Notre Dame. It was freezing, and I had no winter coat."

It wasn't just the stars who benefited from Gilbert's friendship. When Bob Marcucci asked Gilbert for a summer job while he was still a student, Gilbert helped him find work on the crew that was building a house for Wilt Chamberlain. "It was supposed to be a union job, but when I showed up and asked about paying dues, the guy said, 'Don't worry. It's taken care of,'" Marcucci said. According to Terry Schofield, Gilbert paid to fly his parents, as well as the parents of other seniors, to attend the 1971 NCAA championships in Houston. Gilbert also arranged for Jim Nielsen to buy a brand-new Datsun that had just come out but was in high demand. "I think he had a good heart, and I think he really was trying to do things to help people out," Nielsen said. "A lot of those lines get really blurred, especially for people who are playing."

John Ecker was originally introduced to Gilbert by Lew Alcindor. He became as close to Gilbert as anyone besides Farmer. He, too, got a premium discount on a car. "I enjoyed being around Sam intellectually. It wasn't like he supported me with anything of real value," Ecker said. "He opened up his home to us. We would have barbecue dinners there. As far as I was concerned, there wasn't anything illegal about it."

"He was a referral service," Steve Patterson said in 1982. "I needed some tires. He'd call up and say, 'This boy needs some new tires. Give him a good deal.' And you'd get a good deal. It was like he knew everybody in anything. And he wouldn't ask them, he'd tell them, and they'd do it. It was astounding."

The locus for all of this activity was Gilbert's lush abode. When the players were there, they mingled as if they were just a part of the family. "Swen Nater stood right on that diving board carrying my grandchild," Rose Gilbert said years later, nodding toward the pool while sitting in her living room. "Swen was a big kid. Are you kidding? Now that I think about it, it was dangerous." Rose was as much of a commanding presence in that house as Sam was. "She was like Wooden, only louder," Kenny Heitz said. She helped the boys with their homework and otherwise graded papers while they made themselves at home. Wilkes said, "I always figured a guy who married someone that sweet can't be all bad."

Sam Gilbert loved to wash players' cars—he was a stickler for cleanliness—and he was a handy craftsman from his days as an inventor. When Wilkes told Gilbert he was having trouble sleeping, Sam helped him build a sturdy, large-framed bed. "It's still my favorite bed," Wilkes said.

Gilbert tried to argue that his relationships were not limited to star basketball players, or even athletes in general. He described himself as a selfless philanthropist just trying to make the world a better place, favor by favor. "At the moment, I'm helping put a couple of Chicano and black kids through law school. Those kids have nothing to do with athletics," he told *Time* magazine in 1974. That posture did not hold water with people who knew him best. "Sam Gilbert wasn't doing it for chemistry majors. He was doing it for basketball players," Greg Lee said. "I wonder if he'd be doing it if UCLA were an average team and getting five thousand people a game."

To call all of this an open secret would not do it justice. It wasn't even a secret. Gilbert's relationships with UCLA basketball players made him one of the most well-known people in Los Angeles. No less an authority than legendary columnist Jim Murray of the *Los Angeles Times* wrote that Gilbert was "almost as important to the program as Pauley Pavilion" for convincing Allen and Alcindor to stay. When the Bruins played in the 1969 NCAA championships in Louisville, Gilbert took the entire team out to dinner. The nickname that Allen bestowed on Gilbert stuck so well that Sam eventually got a license plate for his car that read "PAPA G." Rose's read "MAMA G." On game nights, Gilbert sat in his premium front-row seat in Pauley Pavilion, brandishing his trademark fedora and a broad smile. This was not a man who acted as if he had something to hide.

To be sure, not every prominent former player interviewed for this book acknowledged that Gilbert provided what the NCAA would consider to be improper benefits. "He never did anything illegal with me. We got summer jobs, but everybody got summer jobs. We didn't get anything extra," said Henry Bibby, who used Gilbert as his professional agent after graduation. Sidney Wicks also insisted that Gilbert never gave him financial assistance while he was at UCLA. "I took a loan out while I was going to school, which I was definitely qualified for. I worked different jobs. I didn't need Sam for that," he said. "Everybody tried to smear the guy. He was really cool. He treated us like we were his kids." When Bill Walton was asked about NCAA violations allegedly committed by Gilbert, he replied, "I'm unaware of that."

Still, Walton readily admitted that he held great affection for the man. "Sam was a great fan," he said. "He was smart, intelligent, tough, fierce. He loved UCLA, loved basketball, loved life, loved business, loved people." Walton found Gilbert to be a kindred spirit, while Gilbert found Walton to be a naive megatalent who could help him expand his influence. While Walton was playing for UCLA, he characterized Gilbert as "sixty-one going on twenty-one. He's just a great dude." When Walton told Gilbert he wanted to move off campus, Gilbert arranged for him to stay at a guest house at a wealthy friend's property in Brentwood. Walton later claimed that he didn't need basketball in his life, which prompted Patterson to rejoin, "He's living in the guest house of a $150,000 home in Brentwood for $150 a month. If he wasn't Bill Walton, basketball player, he wouldn't be there."

Walton became a regular visitor at Gilbert's house. Asked if those were fond memories, Walton smiled and said, "I like to eat." Once, after scarfing down a huge Thanksgiving dinner at Gilbert's house, Walton ate an entire pumpkin pie with a quart of ice cream on top, just because someone dared him. Walton slept over often, though as Gilbert explained it, "We have six bedrooms and Bill Walton has yet to sleep inside. He comes up with his bedroll and disappears into the bush. We see him only when he comes in to take a shower and eat."

Walton didn't even wait to graduate from UCLA before he tapped Gilbert to be his "financial advisor." From the moment Walton joined Wooden's varsity, he faced constant entreaties from professional franchises dangling lots of money if he left school early. Before his sophomore year was over, Walton publicly identified Gilbert as his representative. "[Teams have] called my parents and my brother because I don't have a phone and don't want to be bothered," he said. "I've told my family to refer them to Sam Gilbert."

Walton later explained that he used Gilbert for this purpose because "I knew nothing about business. He was the only guy who I knew that did. I had no experience. That was not my parents' world." Walton's parents were similarly grateful for Gilbert's influence. "Sam's friendship has meant a lot to my son," Ted Walton said. "I rate Sam Gilbert an A-plus."

Walton's older brother, Bruce, an offensive lineman on UCLA's football team, was also treated like family. Gilbert's son, Michael, recalled an incident when Bruce was staying with the family at their cabin in the mountains. Michael was awakened at two in the morning by a rowdy party being held across the street, and he marched outside in hopes of quieting it down. At first, the party continued, but to Michael's surprise the people suddenly scattered. "As I turned around, here's Bruce standing behind me in the driveway in his skivvies with a tennis racket in one hand and a baseball bat in the other. He must have weighed about three hundred pounds," Michael said. "I burst out laughing, because I had no clue he was there."

When Sam later requested an autographed photo from Bruce, he signed it, "Maybe it's corny, but I love you."

The players who spent time with Gilbert saw just how visceral he could be when handling his business. "I was in his office and listened to him go down the list of people and let them know they owed him money," Farmer said. "To see that other side of him, where he was very cold, was abrupt." While Gilbert was able to connect with black players who grew up outside Los Angeles, many of the well-to-do whites who grew up locally were less impressed. When Gilbert heard that Kenny Heitz was headed for Harvard Law School, he took Heitz to lunch and offered to help him find a job. Heitz was put off by his aggressiveness. After Gail Goodrich joined the Lakers, he was told by several people that Gilbert had bragged that Goodrich once worked for him during the summer, which was not true. "Sam was a pain in the ass. He had the answer to everything," Goodrich said. Andy Hill was especially turned off. "I'm Jewish. I grew up around guys like this. I saw right through him," Hill said. "I thought he was a two-bit phony. He was a narcissist and a self-aggrandizer. He'd be really happy that you're asking about him, too. This is Sam's dream come true."

Even players who hobnobbed with Gilbert grew weary of his blandishments. After Nielsen graduated, he ran into Gilbert while shopping at an art store in Westwood. When Gilbert offered to buy him the print he had selected, Nielsen declined. "If I could save a few hundred dollars on something I was buying, that was one thing, but I wasn't looking for a handout," Nielsen said. Wilkes suspected that if he needed even more help from Gilbert he could get it, but he also decided not to go there. "I wasn't that stupid. I knew it wasn't just altruism that motivated him," Wilkes said. "I only wanted to go so far with it."

John Wooden had never heard of Sam Gilbert until after UCLA won its first NCAA championship in 1964. Wooden was used to seeing wealthy alumni magically appear at the first sign of success—and vanish at the first sign of failure. He claimed that when Gilbert tried to initiate a friendship, "I just as politely, as courteously as I could, cut it off." After that, the two of them might say hello to each other once in a while, but their interaction was virtually nonexistent.

Like the public, much of what Wooden knew about Gilbert came through what he read in the newspapers during Alcindor's contract negotiations. Now, Gilbert's burgeoning relationship with Walton was thrusting Sam even further into the spotlight. This was a problem for UCLA. The school's string of national championships had brought a great deal of scrutiny. As Wooden mentioned while taking exception to Doug Krikorian's snide remark about the weak schedule, there were a lot of people in and out of basketball who would love nothing more than to knock the program down a few pegs from its "plateau of excellence." Now, Wooden was facing the possibility that some two-bit rogue booster might jeopardize all that he had built.

Wooden was first asked about Gilbert by a *Los Angeles Times* reporter in 1972. He was clearly uncomfortable. "I personally hardly know Sam Gilbert," he said. "I think he's a person who's trying to be helpful in every way that he can. I sometimes feel that in his interest to be helpful it's in direct contrast with what I would like to have him do to be helpful. I think he means very well and, for the most part, he has attached himself to the minority-race players. I really don't want to get involved in saying much about that, to be honest with you."

Wooden quietly voiced his concerns to some of his players. "During my freshman year, Coach made a comment about who we were hanging around with," Farmer said. "He said something like, 'I know a lot of you like to hang out with your uncle, but we just need to be careful.' He said 'uncle' not 'papa,' but we all knew what he meant." Wooden later claimed that he once confronted Wicks and Rowe about their sharp new clothes. "They had jackets, leather jackets," Wooden said. "[I said] where did you get those? Who sent you there? [They said it was] Sam. You didn't get the same price everybody else got if Sam sent you. . . . Of all my years here, he's the only one I really worried about as far as recruiting. The only one."

Still, Wooden never tried outright to forbid his players from associating with Gilbert. Even if he had, it's doubtful they would have listened any more than they listened to his warnings about interracial dating. "You're concerned with the ones who are friendly with your players, but I can't tell Sam Gilbert or anyone else to stay away from my players," Wooden said. "I can't pick their friends for them, but I can tell my players to be careful. You can't accept money or gifts, and if you do, you're putting yourself and all of us in a vulnerable position."

In Wooden's mind, the only thing he could do was take his concerns to the one man who was even more strong-willed and powerful than he: J. D. Morgan. Wooden wasn't telling Morgan anything he didn't know. Morgan was, after all, a former PT boat commander who boasted that he was on top of every detail in his department. He wasn't naive. Byron Atkinson, a former dean of students, said in an interview for Morgan's oral history that J. D. "knew full well" that UCLA athletes were selling their game tickets, but "he turned a blind eye to that." A much bigger problem like Sam Gilbert was not going to escape Morgan's discerning eye.

Morgan asked Gilbert to meet him at his office several times to ask him to dial back his involvement with the players. "J. D. was constantly in trouble with Gilbert. He constantly had him in his office, constantly trying to get him to keep his hands off our kids," Atkinson said. "He tried to twist Gilbert's tail a dozen times because he knew what was happening over there. [But] Gilbert's a pretty crafty character."

Morgan again met with Gilbert in Houston during the final weekend of the 1971 NCAA tournament. The effect of that talk was the same as it ever was—which is to say, no effect at all. "I know J. D. talked to him. I talked to him. We told him to stay away from our youngsters," Wooden said. "Well, we're not going to be able to tell him what to do. He's going to do what he wants to."

Wooden and his acolytes have argued that in the final analysis, it was Morgan's responsibility to shut Gilbert down, and therefore it was Morgan's fault that he didn't. "We did not want Sam Gilbert to be a part of our program. We felt he might do some things that were improper for the players," Gary Cunningham said. "Coach went to J. D. and was concerned about Sam Gilbert's intervention with our players, and J. D. told him that he would take care of it. What happened after that, I don't know, but Coach was a very believing person."

Apparently, Morgan did not want to push too hard. In the first place, Gilbert was a wealthy and influential booster, the kind of man the program depended on for fund-raising. Morgan also likely (and accurately) sensed that Gilbert had damaging information that could hurt the program if it became public.

There was, however, a deeper reason for Morgan's reluctance to lay the hammer down: he believed Gilbert was involved in organized crime, a perception that Gilbert cultivated. When Gilbert got angry with someone, he sometimes suggested that he could push a button on his phone and two men would come through the door and throw the person out the window. When Mario Puzo's best-selling novel *The Godfather* was published in 1969, friends sent Gilbert several copies, which he displayed prominently in his office.

Whether or not Gilbert was actually "connected" did not matter. What mattered was that Morgan was convinced that he was. "J. D. believed that he was a member of the so-called Miami Mafia, and that he either had or was capable of committing physical violence and perhaps murder," former UCLA chancellor Charles Young said. "I remember him saying to me in that deep voice of his, 'Chuck, you don't know about Sam Gilbert. Do you want to end up on a block of concrete at the bottom of the ocean?' J. D.'s view of him was that if you cross Sam, you're likely to be killed, literally. It's the only time I've seen J. D. kind of shaken."

And so the Sam Gilbert Show continued. As word of his activities spread, Wooden's coaching colleagues became annoyed, to say the least. It was bad enough that Wooden was kicking their asses year after year. Now they were hearing that, far from being squeaky clean, his program had the same dirty laundry that theirs did. For many years, these coaches had been told that Wooden wasn't just a great coach but a good man. A teetotaling, church-going, nonswearing, nonsmoking paragon of rectitude. *Saint John*. Now, it turned out that he, too, kept a little devil tucked into his pocket.

Bob Boyd saw much of this happening right before his eyes. "I knew Sam to talk to, but I had no relationship with him," Boyd said. "Sam was belligerent. He didn't care what anybody said. He was going to do what he wanted." Boyd also claimed that Stanford's coach, Howie Dallmar, "couldn't stand John because of Sam. For Howie not to like somebody was very strange." Abe Lemons, the ever-quotable coach at Oklahoma

City, liked to joke that Gilbert was the most important building block in Wooden's Pyramid of Success. Pete Newell also quietly fumed. "I remember Dad talking about Sam Gilbert and how he was getting away with murder down there," Newell's son, Tom, said. "That was the one thing that really bothered Dad."

No coach was more bothered than Jerry Tarkanian. Like Boyd, Tarkanian was forever being compared unfavorably to Wooden, on and off the court. Tarkanian's proclivity for recruiting players off inner-city playgrounds had earned him a reputation for being a shady recruiter, which he believed was grossly unfair. Unfortunately, Tarkanian could be his own worst enemy. When the NCAA launched an investigation into Cal State Long Beach's football and swimming programs, Tarkanian wrote a pair of columns for the *Long Beach Press-Telegram* excoriating the NCAA's policy of selective enforcement. Noting that Western Kentucky's basketball program was under investigation, Tarkanian wrote in the fall of 1972, "The University of Kentucky basketball program breaks more rules in a day than Western Kentucky does in a year. The NCAA just doesn't want to take on the big boys." He voiced the same complaint in another column the following January.

Predictably, Tarkanian's words stirred up a hornet's nest at the NCAA. After his second column was published, Warren Brown, the NCAA's assistant executive director, fired off an acidic letter to Long Beach's athletic director as well as the commissioner of the Pacific Coast Athletic Association. "Enclosed for your leisure-time reading is a copy of a newspaper article which I presume was written by Jerry Tarkanian," Brown wrote. "It always amazes me when successful coaches become instant authorities. As in the case of this article, such instant authorities reflect an obvious unfamiliarity with facts." Three months later, the NCAA expanded its inquiry to include Long Beach's basketball program.

Tarkanian was incensed that the NCAA would train its resources on Cal State Long Beach, when just across town, a school that *Life* magazine had once billed as the "Athens of Athletics" was so blatantly violating rules. During the 1971 NCAA tournament, Tarkanian's team happened to run into Wooden's during a layover at the Las Vegas airport en route to Salt Lake City, where they would eventually meet in the West Regional. "I had this kid, George Trapp. He says, 'Coach, Coach. Look at them gators.' I'm going, what the hell is he talking about?" Tarkanian said. "Then he told me it was alligator shoes. Our guys were in Converse shoes, Long Beach State letterman jackets, and jeans. UCLA looks like they came from Wall Street. They were dressed like you couldn't believe. Our guys look like they came from the Salvation Army. I told the L.A. writers, 'Look at them and look at us and tell me who's cheating.'"

Even if some of the NCAA's gumshoes were inclined to poke around Westwood, Tarkanian suspected that the NCAA's president, Walter Byers, would hold them back as a favor to his good friend J. D. Morgan. Tarkanian said that Morgan was "always wonderful to me," but unbeknown to him, Morgan was working behind Tarkanian's back to get him in trouble. After Tarkanian was quoted in February 1972 in the *Los Angeles Times* talking about Leonard Gray, a guard on his team who was traveling to road games despite being ineligible to play, Morgan wrote a letter to an NCAA official to bring the situation to his attention. "Per our telephone conversation of this date [February 1, 1972], I have enclosed the *Los Angeles Times* article which quotes Tarkanian on Leonard Gray. It is my understanding that Gray has accompanied the team on every trip they have made this year," Morgan wrote. "Right or wrong, we at UCLA have always interpreted that for an institution to pay for travel, room and board and incidentals to take ineligible athletes to athletic trips was against NCAA rules and regulations. . . . If this is now allowed would you please let me know."

After he retired, Wooden claimed numerous times that the NCAA had investigated his program while he was still on the job. While the NCAA may have done a little snooping—Kenny Heitz recalled that someone showed up in his hometown asking whether Kenny's father made enough money to buy Kenny the convertible he was driving—the NCAA never formally launched an investigation the way it did with Long Beach. Nor is there any anecdotal evidence to suggest that investigators spent time on campus. "I was never interviewed by the NCAA," Jamaal Wilkes said. Lucius Allen added: "The NCAA, if they did come around, they did not talk to me."

Tarkanian never blamed Wooden for any of this. "It bothers me when I keep reading about how straight they were at UCLA when I know they weren't, but I don't think Wooden was behind any of that," Tarkanian said. "On at least two or three occasions, he told me about Sam Gilbert and how he went to J. D. Morgan, and J. D. told him, 'You coach the team and let me handle Sam.' I just don't know what more he could have done."

As more information about Sam Gilbert came to light over the years, some people inside the UCLA athletic department were less willing to lay all the blame at Morgan's feet. "A Sam Gilbert gets going because it's tolerated at the player level and at the coach's level," said Norman Miller, a UCLA vice chancellor for student affairs. "Once it kind of gets going, it's difficult for an athletic director to automatically eliminate it or deal with it."

Gilbert had his defenders as well. Chief among them was Willie Naulls, who would not have become such a successful businessman without Gilbert's lifelong friendship. Naulls was also familiar with the stresses, pressures, and inequities that came with being a UCLA basketball player. He thought Gilbert was a huge boon to the program. "These kids are lucky to have Sam because nobody else will help them," Naulls said in 1982. "Who's going to help them? Does the athletic department help them? They should. Does the coach help them? He should. But in my experience, they don't. . . . They should be kissing [Sam's] feet for what he's done."

Inasmuch as these events unfolded in the summer of 1972, it is fitting that they should suggest the question that has formed the bottom line for every so-called scandal since Watergate:

What did John Wooden know, and when did he know it?

There is no question that Wooden knew *something*. He admitted as much himself. To the players, that was only stating the obvious. "My personal opinion," Lucius Allen said, "is that Coach Wooden was a very bright man. He was in control of everything. There's no way that Coach Wooden wouldn't have some type of an idea of what Sam Gilbert was doing with the UCLA players. It's inconceivable to say that he didn't know."

It is, however, equally clear that Wooden did not orchestrate any of this illicit activity. Quite the contrary: he objected to it time and again. There is also no evidence to suggest that he knew the full extent to which Gilbert was violating NCAA rules with his players. For more than two decades, Wooden had stayed out of his players' personal lives. They were his responsibility only during those hours when they were in his gym. If a player wanted to knock on his office door, he was always welcome, but Wooden was not one to insert himself. The lone instance in which he tried to breach that divide was during the fallout from Bill Seibert's speech, and that had blown up in his face.

Moreover, Wooden's players had every incentive to keep him from finding out the seamy details. In the eyes of some, this further removed the coach from culpability. "Coach didn't cheat. I was offered a lot of stuff on my recruiting visits. I was offered nothing to go to UCLA," Farmer said. "No one can control everything. When you do what [Wooden] did in a place like L.A., it would have been impossible for any one person to have managed that whole thing without anybody else interfering from the outside. Because everybody wanted a piece of our program."

"Had he known about it, I'm sure he would have addressed it, but it was a gray area," Wilkes said. "You're not talking about some small college town. You're talking about Los Angeles. You've got a lot going on here. Is Coach responsible to see what cars all his players are driving? I don't believe it was his job to police the program to that extent."

On the other hand, Wooden saw enough to take his concerns to Morgan, to warn his players to stay away from Gilbert, and to confront Wicks and Rowe about their coats. At a certain point, he had to make a choice: he could either keep digging, or he could lay down his shovel. He chose the latter. "I remember we were on a road trip in Chicago, and five guys all got on the bus together wearing matching coats with fur-lined collars," Greg Lee said. "It was pretty conspicuous. It's not like Coach was an ostrich about Sam, but he wouldn't confront the problem."

This view is shared by many of Wooden's former players. "Coach had to look away on certain items in order for this to happen," Saffer said. "If he was here today and you asked him if he was a saint, he'd be the first one to say no."

"Coach never came to me. We never discussed Sam, even up until his death," Jamaal Wilkes said. "You know, Coach wasn't the kind of man who looked for problems. I always sensed the reason Coach never addressed it is that he didn't know how to address it. It never got to a point that he *had* to deal with it. So he let sleeping dogs lie."

Still, even if he is afforded every benefit of the doubt, it is not easy to square the circle between John Wooden, Man of Integrity, and John Wooden, Man Who Tolerated Sam Gilbert. He didn't know everything, but he knew a lot. He knew enough. Wooden always talked to his players about the importance of standing up for their principles regardless of the cost. This was one case where the cost may have been too high. Should he have done more? "I don't know," Farmer replied when he was asked that question. "I'm going to leave that one alone, and I will apologize for that."

For his part, Wooden had no trouble squaring the circle. He always said the softest pillow was a clear conscience, and he insisted he slept soundly. Sam Gilbert was not something he created, or coveted, or encouraged, or wanted. By the time Bill Walton joined Wooden's roster, Gilbert was just one of many distractions that were chipping away at his joy for teaching. As the years went on and more of Gilbert's transgressions came to light, Wooden's critics tried to use Gilbert as a cudgel. They argued that it tainted Wooden's legacy. They may have succeeded in denting the myth, but they never knocked the man off-balance. "I know what the truth of it is," Wooden said in August 2009, ten months before he died. "I never tried to use Sam Gilbert in any way. I never sent a player to him. I tried to keep players away from him. So people can say whatever they want. My conscience is clear."

28

Streaking

Bill Walton despised the limelight and cherished his solitude. That's why he loved the off-season. He could throw on a backpack, hop on his bike, go camping, hitchhike, read, go to Dead shows, smoke weed. Whatever his heart desired.

However, during the spring of 1972, Walton felt compelled to thrust himself into the public eye. In May, President Nixon announced that he was escalating the Vietnam War yet again by ordering the mining of Haiphong harbor. The decision ignited another wave of protests on UCLA's campus that lasted a full week. Just as in basketball, Walton took up the center position. He served himself up as a wild-eyed, long-haired, six-foot-eleven, redheaded poster child of antiwar expression. "I went to demonstrations, but I made sure not to be in front," Jamaal Wilkes said. "Bill was in front. That was the difference."

It was no surprise to anyone who knew him that Walton would dive in with such passion. As Wooden once said of Walton, "He's the type who is either totally committed or totally disinterested—no in-between." Walton could transit from idea to idea, fad to fad, but once he became fixated, he was all in. "I've never seen anybody who could thrust himself into causes as wholeheartedly or as fast as Bill," Greg Lee said. "Boy, could he get excited. He used to come into my room at seven in the morning with his eyes wide open, saying, 'Let's go!'"

In the wake of Nixon's announcement, Walton went everywhere shouting "Let's go!" to his fellow students. He attended a rally in front of the ROTC building where Jane Fonda was one of the speakers. He led a march that was supposed to end at the edge of campus but spontane-ously extended into the San Diego Freeway. Larry Farmer, who had had more than his fair share of ugly exchanges with racist policemen, was in the crowd that day. "We were closing down traffic, so the LAPD showed up in riot gear. They said we had fifteen minutes to disperse," Farmer said. "I said, you can have that, because it's going to take me two minutes to walk back, get in my car, and drive back to the Valley. Because I'm done."

Walton and Lee took part in another march in front of the federal building on Wilshire Boulevard. The throng then veered into the intersection of Westwood and Wilshire, one of the busiest intersections in the city. Several hundred students sat down and brought traffic to a halt, but it was Walton whose picture was published in the *Los Angeles Times* the next morning.

This was precisely the dynamic that bothered Wooden the most. He recognized that Walton genuinely believed in what he was doing, but he also suspected that Walton was allowing himself to be deployed as a tool by the leaders of the antiwar movement. "On the floor, Bill was a leader, but off it he was easily led," Wooden said. "He was always with a group who used him. He never sees that they're using him. He's the one that they want before the cameras. The instigators—were they up there? No, they're back in the crowd. I saw these things. I understood him and yet never understood him." Asked about this observation many years later, Walton shrugged and said, "We all use everybody. That's the way life goes."

It all came to a head when Walton joined an overnight sit-in taking place inside Murphy Hall, UCLA's administrative building. In an effort to prevent university officials from getting to their offices, Walton helped a group of students lift several electric janitor carts and place them in front of the main doorway. When Chancellor Young couldn't convince the students to leave, he called the police. Within minutes, a group of helmet-wearing cops were on the scene. Walton was among those who refused to leave. He was arrested along with fifty-two other protesters. As he was being handcuffed, Walton shouted, "The whole world is watching!" Then he unspooled a river of profanities at Young.

Walton and the others were transported to a nearby police headquarters before being shuffled into a paddy wagon that took them to the Van Nuys police station. Later that night, Walton's brother Bruce bailed him out. As he left the police station, Walton told a radio reporter, "I'm going back to the campus and we're going to close it down. I will do what I can to help close it down." A month later, he pleaded no contest to a misdemeanor charge of disturbing the peace and paid a fifty-dollar fine. Young also put him on one year's probation at the school.

Fortunately for Walton, his coach was out of town that day, or he might still be in jail. Wooden was speaking at a clinic in Portland, where a reporter from the *Independent Press-Telegram* of Long Beach reached him by phone. "I was not surprised Bill was involved in the demonstration," Wooden said. "He is an emotional youngster, and you know where he stands all the time. He is very much against the war." Wooden added that he did not intend to take action against his center. "That is not in my bailiwick. It's out of season and a student's conduct is out of my hands."

Wooden was much more disappointed than he let on, and he told Walton as much during a heart-to-heart conversation after Wooden returned to Los Angeles. Wooden's political views were actually more in line with Walton's than many people realized. Wooden was a registered Democrat, though he often voted for Republican candidates, including Nixon. Wooden shared Walton's views about the war, but he vehemently disagreed with Walton's methods for expressing them.

"I'm not going to say I was opposed to the Vietnam War. I'm going to say I'm opposed to all war," Wooden said. "But I'm also opposed to protests that deny other people their rights. When you do that, I think you're defeating your own purpose. Taking over the administration building when there are people who have jobs in there to do, I think that's not right."

As was the case with so many things, the two of them agreed to disagree. "My friends were coming back in body bags and wheelchairs. His friends were sitting in a mansion on the hill," Walton said. "When everybody thinks alike, nobody thinks."

Wooden's dispassionate attitude toward the antiwar and civil rights movements widened the chasm between him and his players. In their eyes, some actions were so heinous, so unjust, that they demanded a ruckus. Wasn't the United States of America created out of just such a ruckus? Didn't it take protests, unrest, and law breaking to end slavery, earn suffrage for women, enable factory workers to collectively bargain? Wooden agreed with those causes, but he didn't believe in agitating. He believed in conformity. He often counseled his players to see the big picture, but by asking them to curtail their activities to preserve his basketball program, he came off small.

This was one area where the teacher could have learned more from his students. Wooden would have earned an enormous amount of respect from his players if, just once, he had tried to leverage his celebrity to advance a cause that he believed in. Wooden prided himself on being a man of actions, not statements, but he failed to realize that sometimes actions *are* statements. "I would say his biggest flaw was not always voicing how he really felt about things openly," Henry Bibby said. "If he talked about some things, it could have helped society, but he was never the guy to put himself out there to get hit. His thing was, if you don't have something good to say about somebody, don't say it."

Even as they butted heads throughout the spring, Wooden and Walton found themselves on the same side of a different conflict. The United States Olympic Committee wanted Walton to try out for the basketball team that Henry Iba was going to coach at the 1972 Olympic Games in Munich. Walton was concerned about the toll that playing in the Olympics would take on his tender body. He usually played very little basketball during the spring and summer so he could be fresh for the season. If he said yes to the USOC, he would have to leave UCLA for several months, sleep in too-small beds in military barracks, go through a grueling tryout, play a series of barnstorming exhibition games, and then compete in the Olympic tournament.

Still, Walton wanted to play. So he offered a compromise: let me join the team on the eve of training camp, and don't force me to play in any exhibitions. He promised he would show up in shape and ready to represent his country. The USOC told him no. So instead of playing for Iba, Walton spent most of his summer hitchhiking with his buddies across North America.

Wooden had long ago divorced himself from the Olympics, so when the USOC asked him to intervene with Walton, he refused. Ditto for Keith Wilkes, who likewise turned down an invitation to play. "We talked to [Wooden] about it. He kind of said, 'It's your decision,'" Wilkes said. "So I didn't play. Had he pushed it, it probably would have been different."

There was, however, one Bruin who did try out for the team: Swen Nater, who was happy for the chance to play that he would never get as long as Bill Walton was at UCLA. Nater was so impressive in the early going that he displaced Maryland's star center, Tom McMillen, on the preliminary roster. "All the other coaches and players trying out for the team kept coming to me and asking how in the world do you ever stop this guy," said Bob Boyd, a close pal of Iba's who was on the USOC's basketball committee. "I told them all that Swen Nater was at least one UCLA problem that we at USC have never had the pleasure of worrying about."

Nater, however, withered under Iba's exacting ways. Practices at UCLA rarely lasted more than two hours, yet Iba held two three-hour sessions every day. Even worse, he insisted on having team meals just thirty minutes after practice. Nater could not eat so soon after a hard workout, so he asked Iba if he could eat a little later to allow his stomach to settle. Iba refused. By the end of the second week, Nater had lost nearly twenty pounds. He quit and flew back to California. "I'm sorry it happened," he said. "I'm really interested in the team. I hope they do well."

Nater's withdrawal only reinforced the suspicion that Wooden was intentionally keeping his players out of the Olympics. He insisted that wasn't true, but he admitted that "I'm not a very strong, pro-Olympic person to tell you the truth." For starters, Wooden bemoaned that the discussion around the Olympics always boiled down to how the United States was doing compared to the Soviet Union. "Is that what the Olympics are? Are we participating against just one team, or are we participating against all countries?" He also argued that the Americans should send their professional athletes just like the rest of the world did. Most of all, he did not approve of the manner in which the teams were selected— especially when they had been selected in the past without including two of his favorite Bruins, Willie Naulls and Gail Goodrich.

Of course, if the USOC wanted Wooden's players on its team, there was an obvious solution: make him the head coach. This should have been obvious anyway. Wooden was by far the most prominent basketball coach in the country. Yet he was never given the job. Wooden later claimed that he was offered a position as an assistant if he would bring Walton along, "but I wouldn't go on Bill's coattails." He did indicate, however, that if he had been asked to be the head coach, he would have accepted. As to why that never happened, Wooden said, "I really can't answer that. I don't know. There was a time when I would have been delighted to have been considered to be an Olympic coach, but as time went on, it was too late. I liked Mr. Iba very much, but I honestly feel that I'd like to see them change the coach every four years."

Wooden might have had a better chance to coach in the Olympics if he had been part of the good ole boys' network. Iba and Wooden got along fine, but they were never close. One friend of Iba's revealed that he used to make snide comments about Wooden in private. "He called him 'Johnny Two-Faced.' Said he had a Bible in one hand and a knife in the other," this person said.

No doubt this stemmed from professional jealousy, but it was also because Wooden was simply not a social animal. Even Gary Cunningham and his wife rarely shared a meal with John and Nell. Pete Newell recalled a time during the national coaches' convention when he and a couple of buddies came back to their hotel after a night on the town and ran into John and Nell stepping off the elevator in the lobby. "It was pretty funny, but that's the way John was," Newell said. "He was not one of the guys. He kept himself separate." Jerry Tarkanian added, "I remember one time when I was at junior college, all the coaches were pissed off because John brought Nell to the convention, and all the coaches like to go to the convention and chase broads. Nell was sitting with John in the lobby checking out all of this."

An anonymous coach expressed a similar resentment to a *Los Angeles Times* reporter. "Wooden is a completely different person than what he appears," the coach said. "Most of the coaches don't like him because he's never really been one of the guys. He doesn't have to be a bad guy like the rest of us, but he doesn't have to remain apart from us, either."

Wooden loved to sit around with other coaches and talk about the game at length, but he preferred to do it in coffee shops, not bars. If a coach was in the Iba-Newell inner circle, or if he ended up in the Pac-8 conference and saw up close how bitterly competitive Wooden could be, that coach was more likely to form a negative opinion of him. For someone like Tex Winter, who fit both criteria *and* had played at USC, that was triply true. "Johnny Wooden . . . has another side that most people don't know about," Winter said. "Among his colleagues, Wooden wasn't very popular, and he was never voted to the board of directors. That's because he was kind of arrogant. He'd never let his UCLA players participate in the coaches' All-Star game, and he never went out of his way to help anybody."

In retrospect, Iba might have erred by refusing to accept Bill Walton's compromise. In the gold medal game in Munich, the Americans lost for the first time ever at the Olympics. It happened via one of the most controversial endings in the history of sports. The United States appeared to have won the game by a point on two free throws by Illinois State guard Doug Collins, but the secretary-general of the International Basketball Federation intervened to grant the Soviets not one but two additional chances at a game-winning basket. They finally succeeded on a layup that followed a full-court heave. The Americans were so devastated that they refused to accept their silver medals at the postgame ceremonies.

Like everyone else who saw the game, Wooden thought what happened was a travesty. Yet he disagreed with the Americans' stance. "I was disappointed that our players did not accept the silver medals," he said. "There's no disgrace in coming in second, regardless of what happened to us. A lot of things are unfair in athletics, just as they are in business and life. But if the ruling is made against you, you accept it."

The man was nothing if not consistent. A terrible wrong had been committed, but that was no reason to protest.

He was awoken in the middle of the night by a sudden sharp pain in his chest. His first thought was to wait for the pain to subside, but when it wouldn't go away, he went to the hospital. At first, the doctor told him he believed he was having a gastrointestinal issue, but just to be sure, he wanted to perform an angiogram. The results showed that this was no ordinary gas problem. John Wooden was having a heart attack.

As heart attacks go, this one was relatively minor, but it forced Wooden to stay in the hospital for six days in December 1972. For the first time in his coaching career, he would have to miss a game.

Needless to say, this was big news all over Los Angeles. It was also a terrible jolt for his players. For all their bitching, Wooden was the reason they had come to UCLA. Two months before, they had opened practice by celebrating the start of Wooden's twenty-fifth season in Westwood. The Bruins had already won their first three games by comfortable margins. Everything was coming so easily, but now they didn't know how to react.

"I think we were shocked," Walton said. "When you are a great young athlete, you think you're invincible and you're immortal and that nothing bad is ever going to happen to you. Then all of a sudden, we lost our coach. It was a huge blow."

Walton and Wooden had continued to be at odds over politics and the war. During one of Wooden's lectures, he had suggested that a more effective means of agitating would be for Walton to write a letter to an elected official. Walton thought this was a splendid idea. So he went into Wooden's office, grabbed a couple of sheets of stationery with the UCLA Basketball logo, and wrote a petition on behalf of the entire team asking President Nixon to resign. (Walton concluded the letter to the president by writing, "Thanking you in advance for your consideration in this matter.") Walton asked each player to sign the petition and then brought it to Wooden. He could see a pall come over the coach's face. "You're not going to send this, are you?" Wooden asked. Walton assured Wooden that he was. Wooden shook his head in disappointment, but he never told Walton he couldn't mail the letter.

As soon as Walton got the news about Wooden's heart attack, he hopped on his ten-speed bicycle and pedaled down to Saint John's Hospital in Santa Monica. Wooden was touched. "I don't have blind reverence for authority," Walton said. "People I respect earn my respect. Coach Wooden has earned it."

With Wooden temporarily out of action, it was left to Gary Cunningham and Frank Arnold to coach the Bruins during their home game against the University of California Santa Barbara on December 16. The Bruins won by 35 points. Five days later, Wooden returned to practice looking "wan and slow," according to a published report. He said he would have to adjust his lifestyle—no more huge banana splits after games, and his doctor wanted him to exercise more—but otherwise he pronounced himself ready to get back to work. "I've always told my players to be quick but don't hurry," he said, "but my doctors have told me that I can't follow my own advice. I can't be quick *or* hurry."

Wooden's latest health scare revealed just how stressful his life had become. He talked openly about it during several lengthy interviews with two *Los Angeles Times* reporters, Jeff Prugh and Dwight Chapin, who were writing a book about his life. After Wooden was discharged from the hospital, Prugh explained to his readers that life for the Wizard of Westwood was not as magical as it appeared. "He lives a lonely, at times tormenting existence—more so, perhaps, than most realize," Prugh wrote. "The question is not necessarily whether John Wooden is fit for the turbulence surrounding him. That question already has been answered by his doctors, who have allowed him to resume his coaching duties. At issue now, however, is how many of those responsible for that turbulence truly understand how difficult it is for John Wooden."

Wooden always said that he received more criticism after winning his first championship than at any previous point in his career. With each passing title, the volume got turned up another notch. "I don't know whether winning is always good," he said. "It breeds envy and distrust in others, and overconfidence and a lack of appreciation very often in those who enjoy it."

All of this took an especially hard toll on Nell. "I learned to accept things, but she didn't," Wooden said. "We talked about it. She said it's very difficult. I said it's not difficult. That's when we get stronger, when things are difficult." Nell was so bothered by the nitpickers and naysayers that she tried to push Wooden toward an early retirement. "These last few years haven't been the happiest in our lives," she said during the summer of 1972. "Fans are so greedy. They're dissatisfied if we win a championship game by only five points. That's why his children want him to get out. If he loses, a lot of fans are going to say he's too old and has lost his touch. You learn to condition yourself to critics. If he hadn't, he would have broken sometime during the last eight or nine years. But they do have an effect."

Wooden's children noticed this effect as well. "I think the years of the national championships were hard on all of us," Nan said. "Daddy's job wasn't fun for us. It really wasn't."

Their situation might have been more tolerable if UCLA were paying Wooden a sum commensurate with his value, but that was not the case. As the 1972–73 season began, Wooden's salary remained just $31,000. That was a ridiculously low amount, especially since earlier that fall, Wooden had been enshrined in the Basketball Hall of Fame in Springfield, Massachusetts, for his coaching achievements, making him the first man to be inducted as both a player and a coach. By contrast, Jerry Tarkanian had just left Cal State Long Beach to coach at the University of Nevada, Las Vegas for a salary reported to be $70,000. (Taking the Vegas job provided Tarkanian with a convenient exit before the NCAA's hammer came down on Long Beach. Shortly after he left, the NCAA found twenty-six violations in football and basketball recruiting and placed those programs on three years' probation.) In fairness to Morgan, he earned only $35,000 per year himself because of UCLA's policy to keep athletic salaries in line with those of the professors, but that didn't make it more palatable to Wooden's family. Since everyone knew Wooden was too humble to ask for a raise, Nell and their children believed that Morgan should have come to him. "All I can tell you is that Mom especially was really angry about that," Nan said. "She would argue with Daddy about it, but Daddy would always say, 'I'll never ask.' Our question is why wouldn't UCLA have done something about it?"

Moreover, Wooden pursued just a fraction of the opportunities that came his way to earn ancillary income. He gave a few paid speeches and ran his camps, but he was hardly rolling in it. At one point, Wooden was offered a huge sum to endorse the company that made basketball floors out of tartan. He turned it down because he didn't like their courts. "There was a time if my dad had endorsed a shoe it would have made my mom happy," said Wooden's son, Jim. "Mom was in support of that because everybody else was doing it."

In Wooden's first game back following his heart attack, he coached the Bruins to a win over Pittsburgh, their fiftieth straight victory. (During halftime, Wooden was presented with *Sports Illustrated*'s Sportsman of the Year Award, which he shared with Billie Jean King.) UCLA was now just eleven wins away from breaking the NCAA's consecutive wins record, set by the University of San Francisco during the Bill Russell years. If the Bruins kept winning, they would break the record at Notre Dame on January 27, 1973. Wooden tried to downplay the chase for as long as he could, but once the Bruins were just two wins away, he gave up. "There's no sense trying to soft-pedal it," Wooden said on the team's flight to the Midwest following UCLA's fifty-ninth straight victory. "The players are well aware of the record and they'd like to have it."

By this time, Wooden wasn't just an icon. He was an industry. The book written by Prugh and Chapin, called *The Wizard of Westwood*, was due to hit the shelves shortly after the new year. Besides cementing forever the nickname that Wooden despised, the book revealed him to be a gifted, disciplined, but somewhat flawed man—just like the rest of the human race, as it turned out. Jim Murray wrote that the book amounted to "a case against sainthood." Prugh and Chapin revealed for the first time that, contrary to popular belief, the coach actually did suffer a losing season, at Dayton High in Kentucky. (The authors did not discover that Wooden had had a second losing season a few years later, at South Bend Central.) This was no minor detail. Many stories about Wooden had included the claim that he had never had a losing season anywhere. It was part of the Wooden myth, and he had never corrected it. *The Wizard of Westwood* also included lengthy passages about Sam Gilbert, the first time journalists sought to explore his influence in greater depth. The authors never flat out asserted that Gilbert was an NCAA rules violator, but it was not hard to infer from their reporting that he could be.

In the months before publication, after sitting for multiple interviews with Prugh and Chapin, Wooden heard from various friends that they had been contacted by the authors and that the book was taking a negative turn. Another book, Tony Medley's *UCLA Basketball: The Real Story*, had been published earlier that fall. Even though it was written by a former sports editor of the *Daily Bruin*, Wooden was furious at what he regarded as an unfavorable slant, and he told Medley so. With one book in the marketplace and another on the way, Wooden felt the need to rush out his own autobiography in December. The title, *They Call Me Coach*, was a direct riposte to the notion that he was some kind of spellbinding wizard. Wooden's book sold much better than the others, thanks largely to his aggressiveness in promoting it through his television show, store sign-ings, and high-profile interviews. "This may sound crazy," Tommy Curtis said, "but when Coach did that book, that was the first time I ever realized it was a business. Before that, to me, basketball was just a hobby."

Such was the circus surrounding UCLA as it headed for its date with destiny. The Bruins tied the record of sixty straight victories on January 25, with an easy win at Loyola. Wooden was in a good mood during the bus ride to South Bend. As he sat in his customary seat up front next to Nell, the players blasted Rolling Stones music from a boom box. When someone asked Wooden what he thought about Mick Jagger, the coach replied, "I wouldn't turn him on, but he doesn't bug me."

Notre Dame, and the record, loomed. The Fighting Irish were unranked, but they were clearly on the rise under their young, brash coach, Richard Phelps. He went by the nickname "Digger" in homage to his father, who owned a funeral home in upstate New York. Like every other coach in America, Phelps badly wanted to beat Wooden. Unlike every other coach (except for those in the Pac-8), Phelps had the chance to do so twice a year—on national television, no less—thanks to the long-term deal struck between the two schools and TVS.

A graduate of Rider College, the thirty-two-year-old Phelps had been plucked out of the high school ranks to be an assistant at the University of Pennsylvania under Dick Harter, who was now coaching at Oregon. During his first head coaching stop, Phelps engineered a quick turn-around at Fordham, which he coached to a 26–3 record in 1970–71. Now he was trying to do the same at Notre Dame. The Irish had gone 6–20 in his first year, and they were 7–8 entering the UCLA game. Phelps studied Wooden like a student cramming for the biggest exam of his life. He brought a fighter's attitude to the battle. When the Bruins jumped out to an early lead, Phelps shouted at Wooden, "I'm not calling time-out! I read your book! I'm not calling time-out!"

Wooden ignored Phelps's antics, but he could not ignore the Notre Dame players. Phelps told his guys to get as physical with UCLA as the referees would allow. After watching Irish center John Shumate throw one too many elbows at Walton, Wooden marched down to the Notre Dame bench and told Phelps that Shumate better knock it off. "If he doesn't, I'll send in Swen Nater, and then you'll really see something," Wooden barked.

"It's a two-way street," Phelps shot back.

In the end, UCLA won 82–63 for its sixty-first consecutive triumph, a new NCAA record. Phelps was gracious in defeat, handing Wooden the game ball at center court. (Asked afterward what his exchange during the game with Wooden was about, Phelps joked, "He asked me if I had read his book.") Wooden took the microphone and, true to form, soft-pedaled the moment. "This isn't the greatest thing that's happened on this day," he told the crowd. "It is my granddaughter's birthday, but the most important thing is that this was cease-fire day in Vietnam. That's much more important than this."

After the game, Wooden did something truly historic: he opened his locker room to the press. His players were jubilant, not just because they broke the record but because they had done it on the road, in a heated environment, against a good team. They relished their role as dynastic villains. "We like pressure," Walton said. "I know I thrive on it. And I like hostile crowds. They make me want to play better."

In the postgame press conference, Wooden waxed philosophical. "I'm very happy about it, but it doesn't compare with winning your first national championship. It's the continuation thing that makes you proud," he said. "I've had many blessings in this game of basketball. I'm one of the fortunate ones. I think for many years I was a very poor tournament coach. I think I'm better now."

Wooden was glad to get the record behind him, but he felt bad about his exchange with Phelps. He wrote a letter of apology that somehow (wink wink) wound up in the hands of *Philadelphia Inquirer* columnist Frank Dolson, a frequent Wooden critic, who published its contents. "I owe you and John Shumate an apology and hope you will accept it in the spirit it is offered," Wooden wrote to Phelps. "I acted hastily without thinking clearly and taking all things into consideration and, as usual, actions from emotion are seldom with reason." He also added this postscript: "Please convey my feeling to John. He is a fine young man and an outstanding basketball player and I did him an injustice."

Wooden's contrition was no doubt sincere, but it's not hard to imagine a little gamesmanship at play. Just as he had done with referees at the old men's gym, he had shown Phelps both of his faces. By writing the letter, he gave the Notre Dame coach the same implicit choice: Do you want to deal with this John Wooden, or do you want to deal with that one?

Having finally staked yet another place in history, Wooden could go about the business of tinkering with his machine. The 1972–73 Bruins were a wonder to behold. Never before had he had such a splendid combination of talent, depth, and cohesion.

Keith Wilkes, for one, was starting to get his due, not just for being a gifted athlete but a classy, intelligent one as well. A more immature and petulant player would have struggled with having to play in Walton's shadow, but Wilkes never let it bother him. "I've learned to play for my own satisfaction," he said. "I don't place much importance on being recognized."

These Bruins were also high performers in the classroom. Walton, Wilkes, and Lee were all academic All-Americans. "I believe this gives them a certain carryover that enables them to cope with praise off the court," Wooden said. That also explained why Wooden was so flexible when it came to mixing older and younger players to develop his depth. Seasoned thoroughbreds like Larry Farmer and Larry Hollyfield provided steadiness alongside sophomore colts like Dave Meyers and Pete Trgovich. Tommy Curtis, also a sophomore, provided a spark off the bench, although he was starting to cut uncomfortably into Greg Lee's playing time.

And the redhead stood at the center—literally, figuratively, and metaphysically. Wooden's genius lay in his ability to harness Bill Walton's talents without squelching his free spirit. As usual, the coach struck a perfect balance. "There was total structure and complete freedom," Walton said. "He never used the blackboard. We never had a play. There was no number one, no fist, no slash, no come-up-the-court-and-do-this. There was none of that. He never started practice with the words, 'What do you guys want to do today?' But he never held us back. That's the beauty of basketball."

Indeed, the Bruins' offense was so elementary that Bill Bertka, a former coach at Kent State who ran a nationwide scouting service, said that UCLA was among his least-requested reports. "That's because everything they do is so predictable," Bertka said.

For all their differences, Wooden and Walton connected because they both loved the game for the right reasons. And they both really wanted to win. Walton was tickled when Wooden rode referees and opposing players. During one game, as Walton was sitting on the bench while an opposing big man made a basket, he cracked up as he heard Wooden yell, "You think you're really good. Let's see you do that on Walton!" Walton also claimed that during one pregame talk, Wooden told his players that the coach of the opposing team was "bad for the game of basketball" and that he wanted them to win so decisively that the coach would get fired. "John Wooden liked to win," Walton said many years later. "He and Larry Bird were the biggest trash-talkers I ever knew."

Walton was so antsy before games, the last thing he needed was for his coach to fire him up. Wooden's bare-bones pregame speeches were designed to appeal to Walton's mind, not his gut. "He never talked about basketball. He always talked about life, big-picture stuff," Walton said. "When the game came around, he would walk in the locker room and say, 'Men, I've done my job. I've prepared you for this game. When the game starts, don't look over at the bench and look for instructions. If you play to your potential, you will be pleased with the results.'" Knute Rockne, he wasn't.

Away from basketball, they had their conflicts, but once practices and games began, all that washed away. "He worked as hard as any player could possibly work. He was a great player, an unselfish player, and a good student. You never had to worry about his classwork," Wooden said. "The only thing I ever had to worry about him was between practices because he was very active in the anti-establishment era. But as a basketball player, from the time he'd come on the basketball floor until he'd finish, Bill Walton was perfect."

The folks who closely monitored UCLA's streak figured that it was a foregone conclusion that it would at least reach 105 games. That would take the Bruins through the NCAA championship game in Walton's senior year. The only question was whether Walton would stick around that long. Both the NBA and the ABA were positioning themselves to scoop him up if he decided to bolt at the end of his junior season. That included the ABA team in Walton's hometown, the San Diego Conquistadors, whose owner, Leonard Bloom, announced that he would select Walton in the draft just in case.

Meanwhile, the Bruins continued their march through the Pac-8. One of their toughest tests came on February 22 at Oregon. Digger Phelps's former boss, Dick Harter, had come to Oregon precisely because he wanted to take on Wooden, and he imbued his teams with a pugnacious, Philadelphia-bred mentality. The Ducks dove on the floor so often that they were labeled the "Kamikaze Kids."

The game in McArthur Court was an ugly slugfest. After UCLA won, 72–61, Wooden castigated Harter's methods. "I don't remember being in a rougher game," Wooden said. "They ran under us when we went to the basket three times in a row and it was only called once. That just isn't basketball." Harter agreed it was "an exceptionally rough game," but he made no apologies. "The days when they yelled, 'Hey, hey, UCLA, go by and score,' are over," he said. "Our style is aggressive and tough, but it's not rough. I'm amazed that quality coaches can't appreciate good defense."

Aside from a 51–45 home win over Stanford, during which they trailed at halftime by 7, the Bruins breezed through yet another perfect regular season, pushing their streak to seventy-one entering the NCAA tournament. The West Regional was played in Pauley Pavilion, where UCLA's advantage went beyond the partisan crowds. Wooden had arranged for the nets to be woven extra tight. That way, after every basket, the ball would hang an extra second or two before hitting the floor, which would give the Bruins a couple of extra ticks to set up their full-court press.

Not surprisingly, UCLA beat Arizona State and San Francisco by a combined 32 points to advance to the NCAA semifinals in St. Louis. From a competitive standpoint, the championship weekend didn't augur much suspense. The greater intrigue surrounded Walton's plans for the draft. Reports circulated that the Philadelphia 76ers were prepared to offer him a $4 million contract as soon as the tournament was over. (The actual figure was $2 million, still a princely sum.) The Conquistadors were preparing their counteroffer. Rumors were also swirling that the ABA was willing to put a team in the Los Angeles Sports Arena if Walton agreed to play and that the league would sweeten the pot by making Sam Gilbert a part owner. "I'd rather get cancer," Gilbert said. "I want to be Bill's friend, not his owner."

UCLA's semifinal opponent was sixth-ranked Indiana. The Hoosiers were led by another aggressive young coach, a high-octane Ohio State grad named Bob Knight. He had coached for six years at Army before taking the Indiana job the year before. Knight's temper was so volatile that the Indiana press dubbed him "Ragin' Robby." Knight liked to compare himself to George S. Patton, but Wooden often said he was not a big fan of Patton's leadership style. He preferred Omar Bradley, a soft-spoken general who was known to say "please" when giving out orders.

Indiana's offense may have been the only one in the country that was less structured than UCLA's. Instead of drawing specific plays on a blackboard, Knight put his players in position to read the defense and make decisions on the fly. He called this a "motion offense," and he had formulated it with help from Pete Newell, whom Knight had cultivated as a close friend and mentor. Knight's relationship with Newell also led him to become close friends with Henry Iba and Bob Boyd. In other words, he knew all about Johnny Wooden.

Knight insisted that his team would not be intimidated by UCLA, but the Hoosiers were badly outclassed in the early going. UCLA built a 40–22 lead at halftime and owned a 22-point advantage early in the second half, thanks partly to a technical foul on Knight. But then something happened that was rare for a John Wooden–coached team: the Bruins got blitzed. Indiana forced UCLA into a slew of turnovers, many of which ended up in the hands of Hoosiers center Steve Downing, who would finish with a game-high 26 points. By the time they were through, the Hoosiers had scored 17 unanswered points. With 5:51 to play, UCLA led by just 2 points, 57–55. "You bet I was worried," Wooden said afterward.

The game's pivotal play came at the 7:57 mark, when Walton drove to the basket and collided with Downing. Both players had four fouls, so the referee's decision would be decisive. The call was a block on Downing. He left the game with UCLA up by 5 points, and though the Hoosiers later cut the deficit to 2, they could not sustain the momentum with Downing on the bench. UCLA pulled away to win, 70–59. The hero for the Bruins turned out to be Tommy Curtis, who scored 22 points, many of them on long jumpers. After the game, Wooden said he believed his team would have won even if Walton had fouled out instead of Downing. Knight believed Wooden should have been more generous. His team did win, after all.

Toward the end of the game, Walton told Morgan, who was sitting in his customary spot on the Bruins' bench, that he felt worn out. When Morgan asked why, Walton said it was because his room at the team's hotel was way too small. To Walton's delight, Morgan offered to give Walton his room at the Chase Park Plaza, which had a king-sized bed.

When Morgan left the hotel, however, the reception desk assumed he had checked out and assigned his room to someone else. At 2:00 a.m., Walton was awakened by a loud knock but ignored it. A few minutes later, the police were pounding on his door. Walton called down to the front desk to explain the mix-up. The hotel manager spoke to Morgan and then immediately hustled Walton to another room. It was a magnificent penthouse, with a huge bed, multiple rooms, and several baths. Big Red was livin' large.

Walton's hotel switch ignited yet another firestorm of speculation that he was going to sign that contract with the 76ers after the final. Gilbert denied it, but only after a rash of stories had been published. Walton was furious. Wooden was so concerned by the external pressures that he abandoned his protocol and ended the next day's practice with an extended dunk contest. "It was a calculated risk on my part, but I thought we had gotten a little taut," he said. "We showed it when we lost our poise against Indiana."

Their opponent in the final was unranked Memphis State, which surprised the field by upsetting No. 9 Kansas State and No. 4 Providence in its previous two games. The Tigers' coach, Gene Bartow, was similar to Wooden in presentation and style. He was a southerner, not a midwesterner, but he was a homespun churchgoer with a scholarly aspect. He eschewed profanity and alcohol, which is why he was given the nickname "Clean Gene." Bartow also had a pretty good center himself in Larry Kenon, known as "Dr. K," who Bartow thought might be able to defend Walton one-on-one.

He was wrong. Memphis State came out in a straight-up man-to-man defense, with the six-foot-nine Kenon playing directly behind Walton. Big Red shredded him. With Greg Lee floating pinpoint lobs, Walton made every shot imaginable up, over, under, and around the helpless Kenon. Walton missed a short bank shot early in the first half, but every other shot he tried was true. When UCLA built an 11-point lead, Bartow switched to a zone, but he still played Kenon behind Walton with precious little help.

Though he shined on offense, Walton was out of sorts on defense. Kenon made a lot of buckets himself and forced Walton into foul trouble. With the game tied 39–39 at halftime, Bartow fumed as Morgan gave the referees an earful on the way to the locker room.

Early in the second half, Walton had to go to the bench after committing his fourth foul, which allowed Memphis State to briefly take the lead. When Walton returned, he immediately helped the Bruins turn a 45–45 tie into a 57–47 lead with twelve minutes to go. From there, as Walton continued to drop in shots from in close, UCLA pulled away. With under three minutes to play, Walton broke Gail Goodrich's NCAA championship game total by scoring his 44th point. A few seconds later, he injured his ankle and left the game to a huge ovation.

UCLA won, 87–66. The game was Larry Farmer's last at UCLA, ending his college career with an incredible 89–1 record, but the only thing people wanted to talk about afterward was Walton. He had made an astounding twenty-one of his twenty-two shots, giving him by far the highest field goal percentage in the history of the NCAA championship game. "He's super, the best collegiate player I've ever seen," Bartow said. "We played him wrong. We tried three or four things but I guess we didn't try the right one."

Now that the season was over, the national press savored the chance finally to hear directly from the best player in college basketball. Once again, they were disappointed. When several dozen sportswriters entered UCLA's postgame locker room, Walton was already showered, dressed, and itching to leave. "I'm in a hurry to go see some friends. Would you please excuse me?" he said. When someone tried to ask him about the game, Walton snapped, "I don't want to talk about it, man."

Once again, Wooden was left to explain his center's enigmatic behavior. "I'm very surprised he did that, but he was very upset over something that was written about him this week," Wooden said. Though he was usually reluctant to compare his teams, he anointed this as the finest he had ever coached. "Yes, I'd have to say this one is. I don't think I've ever had a greater one," he said. "Except for that one game [against Indiana], this is a team that never lost its poise. What we did was a team accomplishment, built around the tremendous ability of Bill Walton."

Walton's latest Garbo act only intensified the questions about his future plans. "If he has been offered what he has reportedly been offered, with no gimmicks, and he does return to school, I'd take him down to our psychiatric ward," Wooden said. As for Wooden's future, he acknowledged that it had been "a trying season for me, first because of the pressure of the long winning streak, then some books about me have caused me some problems." He said he planned to return, but his wife was not so sure. "I hope this will be his last season," Nell said, "and I intend to try to do all I can to make it his last."

Walton never wavered on his intent to come back to UCLA for his senior season. Still, Sam Gilbert convinced him that he at least owed the 76ers the courtesy of a meeting. So after the game, the two of them returned to Walton's palatial penthouse at the Chase Park Plaza, where they received the pitch from team owner Irving Kosloff, general manager Don DeJardin, and coach Kevin Loughery. Walton listened politely for an hour. Then he told them no thanks.

"I don't need any reasons for coming back," he said later. "I'm here and that's it. Money has never been a factor. I wish people would understand that."

After the 76ers' brass left, Walton called his teammates and invited them over to celebrate. They were college kids, national champs, happy hippies reveling in the last throes of the Age of Aquarius. Now they had their very own penthouse. The UCLA Bruins cut loose something awful that night. Walton would one day joke that the scene should have been labeled "Fear and Loathing in St. Louis."

29

Intolerable

The backlash was in full swing.

To the national press, the message delivered in St. Louis was loud and clear: we're UCLA, and you're not. They blamed John Wooden as much as Bill Walton for the redhead's rudeness. "Far more disturbing than Walton's behavior is that of the UCLA athletic officials," wrote William Gildea in the *Washington Post*. "At the major tournaments over the years, UCLA has treated the interview of an athlete—even after a game—like the security guards at the CIA plant would an approaching stranger. What does UCLA have to hide?"

Gildea also tweaked Wooden for plugging his book during the televised postgame interview following the Memphis State win. "The Wooden sales effort—and gall—reached a rare level," Gildea wrote. Then there was this censure from a columnist at the *San Bernardino Sun*: "UCLA's Bruins, who beat everybody, won't talk to just anybody. . . . Basketball writers usually get an inquisitive crack at just one handpicked Bruin after each game. Coach John Wooden runs an off-limits locker room. Center Bill Walton is practically unapproachable."

Frank Dolson suggested in the *Philadelphia Inquirer* that UCLA's win streak had become "a cancer" and asked: "Isn't there something wrong with a coach who wins his seventh consecutive national championship, his 75th straight game, and then acts as petty, as petulant, as insecure as Wooden acted Monday night?" An editorial in *Long Island Newsday* argued that Wooden was "guilty of self-serving arrogance." Ken Denlinger added in the *Washington Post* that Wooden "often assumes the pompous air of his days as an English teacher at South Bend Central High." The *Sunday News* asserted that Wooden's closed-door policy was a dereliction of his duties as a teacher: "When any college coach abdicates this responsibility, with the result that one of his star players cannot cope with the world outside, then the coach has not developed a star, he has used him."

Those were just the complaints about Walton's silent treatment. The broader indictment contended that UCLA's hegemony was hurting college basketball. Of all the criticisms directed Wooden's way over the years, this was the most misguided. The NCAA tournament had never been more popular, more watched, and more valuable. UCLA wasn't the biggest reason for that. It was the only reason. The Bruins' dominance had compelled NBC to convince the NCAA to move the 1973 NCAA final to Monday night. ABC had enjoyed huge success with *Monday Night Football* the previous few years, and NBC wanted the game played on the biggest viewing night of the week. The previous year's final between UCLA and Florida State had generated a rating of 16, meaning it was watched in approximately ten million homes by thirty million people. The highest rating for an NBA game to that point was 15.5, earned by the Los Angeles Lakers and New York Knicks in their play-off final the previous May. UCLA was the only school in America that could garner consistent national television exposure for regular season games. Everyone in the sport benefited from its popularity.

Yet Wooden had to answer this silly charge once again after winning his seventh straight championship and his ninth overall. "It's a sad thing what has happened to college basketball," Glenn Dickey wrote in the *San Francisco Chronicle*. "UCLA makes everybody play for second place. When you take the suspense out of sport, there's really nothing left.... The shadow of UCLA hangs over the sport like a blight."

No wonder John Wooden had a heart attack. Even when he won, he couldn't win.

The 1972–73 season should have been the most enjoyable of Wooden's career, but he didn't see it that way. In a letter he sent two weeks after the final to Duane Klueh, his former All-American guard at Indiana State, Wooden wrote that it had been "a very 'trying' year for me," because of all the external pressures and the health issues that stemmed from them. "The players were fine," Wooden wrote, "but some of the press and the fans were almost unbearable at times."

Wooden had promised Walton and his classmates that he would coach at UCLA through their senior year, but he was conflicted about how much longer he wanted to continue beyond that. UCLA's mandatory retirement age was sixty-five, which meant he was eligible to coach another three seasons. If he wanted to go beyond that, the school would probably make the allowance, but it seemed unlikely that Wooden would go that long.

As far as his wife was concerned, he couldn't retire soon enough. "If he even loses a game they're going to say that he's too old and he has lost his touch," Nell said. "You learn to prepare yourself for the worst and then hope it doesn't happen. They can stretch the rules and let him stay until he's sixty-seven but I wonder if it would be worth it. What more does my husband have to prove?"

The week after the win over Memphis State, Walton and Wooden flew to Atlanta so Walton could accept the Naismith Trophy at the Atlanta Tipoff Club's annual awards banquet. During the flight, Walton asked the stewardess for a glass of wine. When she brought him juice instead, he looked over and saw a familiar furrowed brow. "As long as you're traveling with me," Wooden said, "you'll not drink wine."

Aside from that, Walton enjoyed a blissful six months away from John Wooden's exacting eyes. That meant being able to grow out his hair and beard, but when the first day of practice came around in October 1973, Walton cleaned himself up. Or so he thought. The start of the practice was open to the press and included the taking of the annual team photo. Wooden told his assistants that he wanted to go to the locker room early because he suspected Walton would try to test him. He was right. Walton came into practice with his hair matted down to look shorter than it was, but Wooden wasn't fooled. They argued back and forth. Walton complained that he had just gotten it cut. Wooden countered that Walton's ears and collar were still covered. Walton argued that it was his right to wear his hair as long as he wanted. Wooden agreed. He then pointed out that it was his right to determine who was permitted to practice.

That settled it. Walton hopped on his bicycle and pedaled as quickly as he could to the nearest barber shop. Thirty minutes later, he returned, freshly shorn, to join his teammates. "I may be an anarchist," Walton said, "but I'm no dummy."

The players teased Walton about what happened, but when the practice was over, he turned serious. After asking Wooden if he could address his teammates, Walton informed them that he had discovered the wonders of transcendental meditation, and he wanted to share it with his teammates. He asked everyone to follow him to the basketball office. "I go back to the office, and there's eight or nine kids sitting on the floor with their legs crossed going, '*Mmmm . . . Mmmmm*,'" Frank Arnold said. "Coach wasn't very happy about that."

Walton also revealed that he had become a vegetarian. Not surprisingly, that idea was planted in his mind by Greg Lee. His teammates were willing to try it. "We were big time, and of course everyone with a cause wanted your attention," Jamaal Wilkes said. "If you weren't at least open to exploring different stuff, you were kind of like an oddball."

All of this was quite an indoctrination for the incoming freshmen. Wooden had once again assembled a stellar recruiting class, which was more significant than ever because the NCAA had just adopted a rule making freshmen eligible for varsity competition. (Wooden had opposed the change.) The gem was Richard Washington, a six-foot-nine center from Portland, Oregon. Washington had committed to UCLA the previous spring after Wooden watched one of Washington's high school games during the Bruins' road trip to Oregon and Oregon State. (Washington later joked that during his campus visit to UCLA, "I took a dip in Sam Gilbert's pool and it cooled me off, and that was the convincer.") Wooden had also recruited Jimmy Spillane, a five-foot-ten guard from nearby Palos Verdes; Ralph Drollinger, a seven-foot sophomore from San Diego; and Marques Johnson, a six-foot-five freshman forward from Crenshaw High School in Los Angeles.

The presence of eligible freshmen created an even bigger glut than usual for Wooden to sort through. Returning at forward would be Dave Meyers, the six-foot junior who Wooden said "made more progress [last season], week by week, than anybody we've had here." The most intriguing battle would come at point guard, where redshirt sophomore Andre McCarter, the six-foot-three blur from Philadelphia's storied Overbrook High School, was poised to challenge two seniors, Tommy Curtis and Greg Lee. The numbers crunch convinced Vince Carson, a once-heralded six-foot-five forward from nearby Altadena, to transfer. "Wooden has his favorites and I'm not one of them, I guess," he said on his way out the door.

Marques Johnson was considered an afterthought among the freshmen, but from the outset, Wooden could see that he had great potential as a rebounder. Not only was Johnson strong for his age; he was also a quick repeat jumper. Johnson was startled at how Wooden's gentle personality transformed during those two hours between the lines. "I just remember this crazy look he had when he conducted practices," Johnson said. "He was this fierce warrior dude, but he was able to use this whole spiritual kind of Christian philosophy. He was a real walking contradiction."

After having not seen Walton all summer, Johnson was delighted when the redhead called out to him while riding his bike across campus one day, because it meant that Walton knew who he was. Johnson and the other freshmen were ready to follow Walton into whatever odd endeavors he suggested. Johnson did as he was asked and brought a handkerchief and two pieces of fruit to Walton's meditation guru in Westwood. The man gave Marques the top-secret mantra he was supposed to recite over and over with his eyes closed, thus empowering him to commune with the universe. "I was caught up in it," Johnson said, "but a certain part of me was thinking, 'If only your homies from Crenshaw could see you now.'"

All of this was Walton's not-so-subtle way of commandeering this team as his own. He was a senior, after all. He had heard Wooden's speeches so many times, he could recite them himself—and he and his fellow seniors often did, to Wooden's annoyance. They knew all of his tricks. For example, before Wooden's annual here's-how-you-put-on-your-shoes-and-socks lecture on the first day of practice, he always had Gary Cunningham plant a penny in a corner of the room. Then Wooden would "find" the penny, tuck it into his left shoe, and tell the boys that it would bring them luck. This time, Walton found the penny beforehand and shoved it into his pocket. When Wooden couldn't find it after several minutes of looking, Walton let Wooden know he had been foiled. "We're a great team," Walton said. "We don't need luck." He might as well have said they didn't need coaching.

So it was that Wooden faced his an annual conundrum: Where should he hold the line, and where should he bend? Walton's and Lee's vegetarianism posed a problem because the team's regular training table served mostly meat. If Walton and Lee were going to get enough nourishment, they would have to eat at the student union. Wooden allowed them to do so, but because he couldn't extend that privilege only to those two, he allowed everyone to eat at the cafeteria as well. Pretty soon, he dropped the training table altogether.

Wooden also let Walton stay at home the night before a home game instead of at the team's hotel, because Walton said he got a better night's sleep there. Remarkably, Wooden disposed of his regular curfew, instead letting the players decide a reasonable time that they should be in bed. "I've changed," Wooden acknowledged. "The times have changed. You can't be rigid and unyielding."

The 1973–74 season marked the arrival of a new broadcaster to fill absences left by Dick Enberg, whose career had taken off to include more national television responsibilities. Enberg's replacement on KTLA's broadcasts was a young California native named Al Michaels, who had left his job calling Cincinnati Reds baseball games to return to his West Coast roots. Having grown up watching Wooden's teams play at the Los Angeles Sports Arena, Michaels was somewhat in awe of the man, but when he met the coach for the first time, Wooden put Michaels at ease by showing a deep curiosity about the inner workings of the Reds. "The Reds had just gotten Joe Morgan, and John was very interested about how Sparky Anderson was folding Morgan into the team," Michaels recalled. "He struck me as a man who enjoyed listening more than talking. He was an absorber of information."

Wooden would have to be especially shrewd about how he managed his own assortment of egos, because for the 1973–74 season J. D. Morgan had put together the toughest schedule the Bruins had ever faced. That included an early-season home game against fourth-ranked Maryland. The Terrapins had a stellar frontcourt duo in Tom McMillen and Len Elmore, as well as a heralded sophomore point guard, John Lucas, who was also a nationally ranked tennis player. The Terrapins' fifth-year coach, Charles "Lefty" Driesell, had been widely mocked when he declared his intention to make Maryland "the UCLA of the east," but now he appeared well on his way. Like most coaches around the country, Dries-ell did not know Wooden well, but he held a deep reverence for him. While they spoke on the phone the week before the game, Driesell picked Wooden's brain about the best way to manage McMillen's and Elmore's transitions to the pros. Wooden recommended that Driesell meet with Sam Gilbert while he was in town. Driesell called Gilbert, who picked up the Maryland coach at the airport and took him to lunch, though he did not end up representing Driesell's players.

The nationally televised game did not lack for drama. UCLA built a 12-point lead shortly after intermission and still led 65–57 late in the second half, but when Driesell switched to a zone, the Bruins' offense went dry. Maryland climbed back to within a point and threatened to take the lead in the closing minute, until Dave Meyers stole the ball from Lucas in the closing seconds to seal the 65–64 win. Curtis was fouled just as time expired, but Driesell argued with the officials that the game was over. He wanted to make sure his margin of defeat remained a single point. Walton finished with 17 points and 27 rebounds, and while Elmore was duly impressed—"Big Red is the baddest dude anywhere," he said—Walton's mother, Gloria, was less elated. "I just think winning all the time is immoral," she said.

Having watched his team barely win its seventy-seventh straight game, Wooden was concerned that it lacked balance. "It's like when we had Kareem Jabbar. We tend to leave things too much to Bill," he said. "Maybe now some of our fans will stop believing we have all the good players."

The best player not in a UCLA uniform also resided in the Atlantic Coast Conference. David Thompson was a six-foot-four prodigious leaper at North Carolina State who was the most exciting player to come into college basketball in a long time. The Wolfpack had finished the previous season 27–0 and ranked No. 2 in the AP poll, but they were ineligible to play in the postseason due to NCAA sanctions for recruiting violations. Thus, they never got the matchup with UCLA that everyone wanted to see. In the spring of 1973, however, the two schools' athletic directors engaged in a protracted negotiation in hopes of getting them together. Since neither man wanted his team to travel to the other's arena, or even a quasi-neutral site in the other's home state, they agreed to meet halfway, in St. Louis, on December 15. ABC gladly forked over $125,000 to each school in order to make it happen, rendering this the most profitable college basketball game ever. Some blight, these Bruins.

Wooden tried to downplay the matchup, emphasizing that it was far less important than the conference games. "I don't even know what kind of defenses North Carolina [State] plays, and I don't care," he said. Still, the game garnered a buildup not seen for a regular-season tilt since the Game of the Century six years earlier. Unlike that game, however, this one was no contest. The Wolfpack hung close for three quarters, partly because Walton got in foul trouble, but once he reentered the contest with nine minutes to play, he led UCLA on a devastating 19–2 run. The final score was 73–56. The star for UCLA was not Walton but Wilkes, who scored a career-high 27 points while on defense limiting Thompson to 17 points on 7-for-20 shooting.

And yet, even after this latest triumph Wooden could not escape sniping from his critics. Frank Dolson of the *Philadelphia Inquirer*, the same columnist who had published Wooden's letter to Digger Phelps and called UCLA a "cancer" on the sport, pronounced himself shocked—shocked!—at Wooden's sideline comportment. Dolson sat close enough to hear most every word Wooden said to the officials. In a column that was carried to newspapers around the country via the Knight News Service, Dolson offered an extensive, near-verbatim accounting of Wooden's caustic remarks.

"I wonder how many college basketball coaches could have verbally abused an official the way Wooden did without receiving a single warning, a single rebuke, a single technical," Dolson wrote. "From a seat in front of your TV set, or a seat in the stands, you'd never suspect what John Wooden is really like while a game is going on. From a seat a few yards away, it's a revelation. 'Watch 'em pushing away. . . . Lookit the elbow. . . . That's an offensive foul. You called that an offensive foul on us. . . . Oh, for crying out loud! Bad call. Bad call." Dolson also reported that he heard Wooden shout at David Thompson after a questionable call awarded him two free throws. "Feeling good? You should be."

When asked about Dolson's column, Wooden conceded, "I have my Achilles' heels like other coaches do. Certainly I am critical of officials, just as I yell at my players, because I expect a great deal from them." The Los Angeles writers were more amused than anything else. If Dolson thought Wooden was bad now, he should have seen Wooden before the old man mellowed.

The streak was now at seventy-nine games and counting. Wooden kept insisting it was only a matter of time before his team lost, but it was hard for people to imagine that happening. At least, not while Bill Walton was there.

Walton was surrounded by more quality players than at any other time of his college career. Dave Meyers was a crafty scorer and dogged defender in the Jack Hirsch mold. He earned the nickname "Spider" because of his long arms. Pete Trgovich was earning more minutes in the backcourt, as was Andre McCarter, whose speed was a terrific asset on the fast break. Marques Johnson was pushing his way onto the court as well. When Walton got frustrated from being double- and triple-teamed, he would yell at Wooden, "Get Marques in here! We need rebounds!" Johnson said, "When I'd hear Bill say that, I'd start unbuttoning my sweatpants. I knew I was coming in."

Wooden was also substituting more liberally than at any point in his career. In the season opener, he played sixteen guys. Against North Carolina State, he played eleven. That made playing for him more fun, but it was not easy for ex-benchwarmers like Andy Hill to see. "I wish he could have changed his mind earlier. It's tough to get in there and look like a player when you're in for only two minutes," said Hill, who had taken a job as an assistant coach at Santa Monica College. While emphasizing that he felt "privileged to have played for him," Hill admitted that "not playing was a painful experience. I had a lot of desire in the past to be resentful, but not now because Wooden is not affecting my everyday life."

The Bruins looked as if they would sail through yet another undefeated season. That is, until January 7, when Walton took a nasty fall
during a 10-point win at Washington State. As he jumped for a
rebound, Walton was undercut—or submarined, to use the common
description—by Cougars center Rich Steele. "It was a despicable act of
intentional violence and a dirty play," Walton said many years later. At
first, Walton hopped up thinking he was okay, but as soon as play
resumed, he called time-out because the pain in his back was so severe.
An X-ray the next day revealed that Walton had suffered two small frac-
tures in his lower vertebrae. The diagnosis was kept secret.

This was a big deal because UCLA was just two weeks from its next
great test, on January 19, at Notre Dame, the school that had last beaten the
Bruins, as well as the team against which UCLA had set the consecutive
wins record. This time, the Irish were undefeated and ranked No. 2 in the
AP poll. The speculation over whether Walton would be available to play
against the Irish mirrored the guessing game that had surrounded Lew
Alcindor's eye before the game against Houston at the Astrodome. After
Walton sat out home wins over Cal and Stanford, Wooden said he didn't
think it was likely Walton would even make the trip to the Midwest. When
Walton did travel with the team but sat out a 24-point win over Iowa,
Wooden said he would leave it up to Bill to decide whether he would play
against Notre Dame. Walton had been practicing while wearing a corset to
get himself ready. To no one's surprise, he chose to play against the Irish.

By this time, UCLA had won eighty-eight games in a row, and even
the great English teacher was at a loss for words. "If I say what I think
about this accomplishment, I know I'll sound immodest, but to me it's
unbelievable, absolutely amazing," he said. "I really can't visualize any
team doing it, especially in this modern day of basketball with so many
outstanding players on other teams everywhere you look."

In advance of the game, Digger Phelps pulled out every motivational
trick he could find. He had the players practice cutting down the nets. He
attended a pregame pep rally for the students. He claimed to know the
Bruins so well that "I could coach them myself." Always eager to promote his program (and especially himself), Phelps invited a small group
of writers into his locker room *before* the game so they could watch him
deliver his twenty-point plan. As he revved up his players, he warned
them to "stay away from [the UCLA] bench during time out in case Coach
Wooden decides to talk to you." He also got a pregame hug from his former boss and current Oregon coach, Dick Harter, who had made the trip
to support his friend and scout the Bruins.

Once again, UCLA took control of the game from the outset. With 6 minutes remaining in the first half, the Bruins led by 17, and they owned a comfortable 43–34 advantage at halftime. The two teams held each other in check for much of the second half, the Irish never quite coming back, the Bruins never quite pulling away. With 3:32 to play, UCLA led, 70–59. The game looked to be over.

Phelps, however, had one last gambit. He called time-out and ordered his team to come out in a full-court, trapping, man-to-man press. He also inserted freshman point guard Ray Martin to give his team more quickness. It worked beautifully. Notre Dame started scoring, and UCLA stopped answering. A hook shot by John Shumate over Walton cut the deficit to 9. Shumate stole the ensuing inbounds pass off the press and scored again. Irish forward Adrian Dantley then stole the ball from Wilkes, drove the length of the court, and converted a layup. After Curtis was called for traveling, Notre Dame guard Gary Brokaw hit a shot from the corner. A Meyers miss was followed by another Brokaw jumper. Remarkably, UCLA's lead was down to a single point, and there was still 1:11 on the clock.

When a team gets bum-rushed like that, the textbook response is for the coach to call time-out, settle his guys down, and make a strategic adjustment. Wooden chose not to do that. Asked about this nondecision after the game, he smiled and said, "Oh, I'm not a time-out caller." Why should he change now? He had seen his teams blow big leads before, and they always found a way to win. Besides, he figured, these guys are seniors. They should know what to do.

Except they didn't. UCLA committed yet another turnover against the press, this time on a charge by Wilkes. On the Irish's next possession, they worked the ball around the perimeter until Brokaw fed junior guard Dwight Clay with a pass to the corner. Clay launched a high-arcing shot with 29 seconds left. Swish. Wooden finally called time-out with his Bruins trailing, 71–70.

On their final possession, the Bruins got not one, not two, but five chances to score, courtesy of multiple offensive rebounds. The last was an attempted tip-in by Meyers. The ball bounced off the rim and into the hands of Clay, who flung it toward the ceiling as the buzzer sounded. The game and the streak were over, and in the most stunning way imaginable. Notre Dame had scored the game's final 12 points to win.

Phelps was breathless when he arrived for the postgame press conference. "Did we win?" he said. Wooden was more even-keeled. He did not try to blame the loss on Walton's back injury, which would have been pointless considering Walton still managed to get 24 points and 9 rebounds, but he did not sound devastated. "Do you want me to say what I really think or what you want to hear?" he said. "I said it once, I have said it a hundred times, that once we broke the record last year, the streak became meaningless. I am fairly certain my players felt this way. I am not mad or glad about the streak, and my players are acting like they should act—like men." Wooden did not open his locker room to reporters, nor did he invite any players to the interview room. "Winners talk. Losers keep quiet," he said.

Wooden also disagreed with Phelps's assertion that the end of the streak was good for college basketball. "If so, then you'd have to say that having such a streak was bad for college basketball," Wooden said. "I think this streak was the most tremendous thing there ever was for college basketball. Look at all the interest it generated, and all the enthusiasm there was at Notre Dame before the game."

The back and forth between Wooden and Phelps was an intriguing table setter for the teams' rematch at Pauley Pavilion one week later. After the loss, Wooden suggested that while Notre Dame deserved to be awarded the No. 1 ranking (which it was), the answer as to which was the better team would be more apparent after the second game. "If they win on the west coast, by golly that will prove they are a better ballclub. If we win, that will prove we will have a better chance on a neutral court," he said. When Phelps joked with Wooden that he'd rather not play the game, Wooden replied with a smile, "You better come."

Wooden said he would not make any wholesale changes because of a single defeat, but he did insert Marques Johnson into the starting lineup for the rematch. That meant shifting Meyers to forward and bringing Trgovich off the bench. Johnson had responded beautifully when Wooden started him in the second half during a midweek win at home over Santa Clara, scoring a career-high 20 points. The coach waited until a few minutes before the tip-off to reveal the change to his players.

The Fighting Irish did not hold their No. 1 ranking for long, as UCLA ran them out of Pauley in a 94–75 rout. Johnson scored 16 points while holding Notre Dame's leading scorer, Adrian Dantley, to just one first-half field goal. "Johnson's starting was the key for them. It gave them added strength on the boards," Phelps said. Walton chipped a season-high 32 points despite fouling out with 5:39 to play. When he came out of the game, Walton headed straight for the locker room to get an early start on icing his knees.

After the game, Phelps reminded everyone that "what we did last week can never be taken away from us. You can't undo history." Still, he acknowledged the obvious: "They're number one. They beat us." The college basketball world had been shaken up for all of seven days. Now, order was restored.

Marques Johnson was pleased to be starting, but he could sense that some guys didn't like it. "It didn't sit well with Pete that I took his place in the lineup," he said of Trgovich. "I could feel that he and Dave Meyers weren't completely happy about it." This was the type of crumbling from within that Wooden had warned about. Johnson noticed that Meyers also bristled whenever Wooden drew offensive formations on a blackboard and assigned the letters *B* and *K* for Walton and Wilkes while everyone else was a simple *X*. "It was like those two guys had just gotten kind of bigger than everybody else," Johnson said. "To this day, if you mention that to Dave, the hair on his neck will rise up."

Wooden predicted all of this two years before, when he told the boys they would be "intolerable" by the time they were seniors. Besides fighting pressure and complacency, Walton and his classmates were becoming increasingly concerned with their pro prospects. "I just think, myself included, we had senioritis. We were starting to look ahead and got a bit distracted," Wilkes said. "It was a combination of the expectations getting so extreme, combined with the fact that we got distracted with the vegetarians and all the different stuff we were into. We had different people pulling at us, and maybe we just lost a bit of our focus."

Walton and Lee weren't helping. Their New Age interests were constantly taking them in strange directions. Wooden even agreed to allow Walton to meditate in his office. One day, Marques Johnson and Richard Washington were meditating when they asked each other to divulge their top-secret mantras. "I'll tell you mine if you tell me yours," Johnson said. When Washington said what his mantra was, Johnson said, "Hey, that's mine, too!"

Lee's minutes had been dwindling throughout the course of the season as Curtis and McCarter improved. He claimed that it didn't bother him that much. "I like to think I'm a well-rounded human being," Lee said in late February. "I still like to play basketball, but it used to constitute a larger percentage of my consciousness than it does now."

"It was almost a team that was too intelligent for its own good," Johnson said. "We used to be a bunch of ballers from the city that just want to go out there and kick some ass. But we'd be sitting in the hotel, and Greg

Lee would hypnotize himself and make himself stiff as a board. He'd give you instructions. 'Give me ten minutes to go into my trance here. You'll see my eyes roll up in my head.' We could lift him and put his head at the end of one bed and his feet at the end of another bed. He'd be just like an ironing board. I mean, that's the kind of shit we were doing."

It had been a long two-plus seasons, and the toughest part was yet to come. Not surprisingly, the player who felt the most worn out was the one who assumed the heaviest burdens. "I get tired carrying my 225 pounds around," Walton said, "but I get doubly tired when I carry some-one else's 225 pounds on my back. Most of the teams we play try to rough me up. Basketball is not always fun. The publicity and the pressure spoil it for me. No one enjoys a game as a game, not the coaches, not the play-ers, not the fans, and not the press. All that matters is whether you win or lose, and I don't feel that way."

That summed up the prevailing emotion on the team. More than anything, these guys were *tired*. Tired of the pressure, tired of taking everyone's best shot, tired of the scrutiny, the nitpicking, the unreason-able expectations. Walton loved playing center, but he could never get used to being the center of attention. "I can't go anywhere without being looked at as a freak," he said. "Nobody knows me and they won't for a long time."

The desire to be better understood led Walton to give lengthy inter-views to a freelance sportswriter named Bill Libby, who published a book called *The Walton Gang* toward the end of Walton's senior season. In the book, Walton aired some of his most radical beliefs. "I don't blame the blacks for hating the whites. If a black man gunned me down right now, I'd figure it was all right because of what whites have done to blacks," he told Libby. "I don't like violence, but violence scares people, and some-times you have to scare people into doing right, into acting. If revolution comes, I'm ready." Those words underscored why coaching the redhead could be such a challenge. "Sometimes with Bill I feel like I'm handling a piece of glass," Wooden said. "At times he is an enigma—inconsistent, changeable, impatient—but his true nature, the one few people see, is extroverted, open and sincere. He definitely ranks up there in the unusual person category."

Walton embarrassed himself in early February, when he was given the Sullivan Award as the nation's top amateur athlete. He was just the second basketball player since 1930 to be given the award. (Bill Bradley was the other.) Wooden had informed Walton that there would be a press conference on campus at which he would be presented with the award.

Wooden explained to him that this was a very big deal, but Walton showed up ten minutes late and woefully underdressed in a blue collared shirt, worn blue jeans, and sandals. His hair was mangled and sweaty from his bike ride. Jim Murray labeled Walton's performance a "a sartorial disaster." ("His socks and tie, in a sense, matched. He didn't have any.") Walton insisted it was an innocent mistake, but Wooden and Morgan were furious.

Then again, Walton and his classmates had long ago stopped listening to John Wooden. "Most of the stuff he said, unless it was related to basketball, you just didn't really hear it," Wilkes said. When Wooden would go into one of his timeworn spiels, the players often mocked him by singing Bob Dylan songs. Wooden finally snapped that he was "tired of all this Bob Dylan crap," prompting the players to double over in laughter. They couldn't believe he said the word *crap*.

Even when it came to basketball, the players were tuning Wooden out. Instead of running a delay offense when they had a big lead, they fired ill-advised jumpers in an effort to impress the pro scouts. On a few occasions, they either missed or deliberately ignored Wooden's specific instructions to put on their full-court press. "They listen," Wooden said, "but do not hear."

As the season headed for the home stretch, Wooden found himself wistful for a simpler time. Six days after his team exacted its revenge over Notre Dame, Wooden was standing in a hallway in Pauley Pavilion, amiably chatting with USC assistant coach Jim Hefner before their teams took the floor. Hefner told Wooden how impressed he was with UCLA's home arena—its size, its design, its environment. Hefner said that Wooden must feel very lucky to have such an asset. Wooden shook his head and smiled. "I liked the old place better," he said.

It was only a matter of time before their play on the court also became intolerable. After struggling at home to beat USC by 11, the Bruins nearly blew a 13-point lead in Pauley against Oregon State before winning by 5. "This team is not as hungry as they were as sophomores and juniors. They seem to lack the killer's instinct," Wooden said afterward. "Too many of our players have been going too individual lately. I don't want them thinking about pro contracts right now."

Beavers coach Ralph Miller agreed. "This group of UCLA players has, more or less, old-timers. They're not as enthusiastic," he said. "They've won so many games and championships that it's easy for them to say, 'What the hell. What else do we have to do?'"

The machine finally came apart during one shocking forty-eight-hour span in late February. It began with a raucous, tense game at Oregon State. The Bruins were clearly the more talented team, but they could not match the intensity of their opponents or their fans. While holding a 9-point lead in the second half, Wooden was barking instructions into his team's huddle when an apple tossed from the stands hit him square on the chest. For a moment, Marques Johnson thought he might have another heart attack. "He turned white," Johnson recalled. "It looked like he could have keeled over right there." As had been the case so often that season, the Bruins couldn't hold on to their lead. The result was a 61–57 defeat. They committed 21 turnovers, 15 of which came courtesy of seniors Walton, Curtis, and Wilkes.

A team of championship mettle would have rebounded with a thrashing the following evening at Oregon. In the days leading up to that game, Wooden and Harter continued to jab at each other through the press. After noting that Harter had scouted UCLA against USC and had also been at the Notre Dame game, Wooden said, "I'm sure he knows all about us, and if there's anything he doesn't know about us I'll be glad to tell him." Harter, in turn, mocked Wooden for skipping a press luncheon in Eugene so he could sign his books at an Oregon State student bookstore. "Is he signing his own book, or the Bible?" Harter cracked. "I respect UCLA's talent but have only distaste for its behavior. Listen to the names Walton calls the man who's playing him. Is it proper for a coach of Wooden's stature to verbally bait opposing players?"

The Kamikaze Kids were primed and ready. The Bruins were not. Harter surprised Wooden with a spread offense, with many of the sets resulting in wide-open shots from the corner by the six-foot-eight sophomore Bruce Coldren. Coldren was doing for Oregon what Lynn Shackelford used to do for UCLA, but Wooden never adjusted. He did, however, tell Coldren to "keep your hands off my players" when Coldren dove for a loose ball and landed on the UCLA bench.

This time, there was no lead to surrender. The Ducks used a 10–0 spurt to give them a 9-point lead with under six minutes to play. From there, Oregon spread its offense, held the ball, and finished off the 56–51 upset, handing UCLA its first back-to-back losses in eight years.

On the very few occasions when Wooden's team was defeated in the past, he claimed to find some benefit. Not so this time. "We're certainly not number one, not the way we're playing," he said. "I wasn't concerned about it last week. I am now." Lee was concerned, too, and openly critical of his coach. "The right people are not playing. I think we were playing better when I was in the lineup, but I don't make those decisions," Lee said. "We're supposed to get the ball to Bill, but we're also supposed to be a five-man offense. The trouble is, the other guys don't know what to do when Bill is double-teamed."

UCLA's greatest asset, its aura of invincibility, had been punctured. Before the game at Oregon State, the public announcer intentionally introduced the Bruins as the "descending national champs . . . er, excuse me, the *defending* national champs." The crowd ate it up. Now, the team was in genuine disarray. "There was the feeling that we were just kind of exposed for what we were," Johnson said, "and that was a good team with a lot of internal stuff going on."

On the plane ride back to Los Angeles, Walton and Wooden sat together and talked about what was going wrong. Walton had long made clear that he preferred having his good buddy Lee on the court over Tommy Curtis. Walton also suggested that Wooden go back to his high-post offense. Normally, Wooden was loath to make wholesale adjustments, especially at this late stage, but he had already shown uncommon flexibility that season. What was one more change?

Now John Wooden was the weary one. "I'll admit it gets tiresome to answer the same questions over and over about what could be wrong," he said. "The other night, I had to get out of bed three times to answer the phone, one from somebody in North Carolina. I'm sorry to say I lost my self-control and got upset with him."

One might think that by now Wooden was past the point of being second-guessed, but that's what happened. "Most coaches I know don't think Wooden is a good X's and O's coach," said Bill Mulligan, the former USC assistant who was now the coach at Riverside City College. "I think his conservative ways are showing. He wasn't really gambling. If Norman and Crum were still assisting Wooden, they might have convinced him to do something different."

Harter was more than happy to pile on as well. "I think it's good for basketball to have UCLA lose. It's bad for any team to dominate the way they've dominated," he said. "[Wooden has] got to be scared now. They don't have the hunger to win." Harter went so far as to predict that USC, which was now tied for first place in the conference, would win the Pac-8.

Soon afterward, Harter received a letter from Wooden. It was the same type of letter Wooden sent to Digger Phelps. Wooden wrote that it did not make sense that they should become such bitter opponents. He also said in the letter that he had done a little research and discovered he and Harter had the same birthday and they were both Betas in college. Harter was appreciative but unmoved. "I am positive he wrote that letter to gain an edge," Harter said. "I'm not saying that's wrong. I've done the same thing. I really think that's how much he competed."

Even though UCLA followed its pair of losses in Oregon with four consecutive wins, the problems festered. The Bruins led by 15 points at Stanford, but the Cardinals came back by sagging their defense around Walton and forcing his teammates to hit from the outside. Wooden had hoped his offensive changes would spark the team, but instead they made things worse. The players were thinking too much, being less instinctive. They barely hung on to win, 62–60.

That set up yet another all-the-marbles finale at USC, which ended in yet another UCLA rout, this time by 30 points. With the regular season finally behind them, the Bruins should have entered the postseason with renewed purpose. Instead, they nearly threw it all away in their first NCAA tournament game against the University of Dayton. It took three overtimes for UCLA to put away the Flyers, 111–100.

The close shave didn't exactly dampen the players' moods. Later that night, they were frolicking in the pool of their hotel when Walton decided to take off his bathing suit and soak naked in the whirlpool. When Gary Cunningham walked by, he told Walton to put his swimsuit on, but Walton blew him off. A few minutes later, the hotel manager spotted Walton and called Wooden. The next thing the players knew, Wooden stormed into the pool area in his nightgown and stocking cap. He ordered them to get to bed immediately.

The next day, the Bruins blew by San Francisco, 83–60, to earn a trip to the 1974 NCAA semifinals in Greensboro. They had every reason to feel confident going into that game. Their opponent would be North Carolina State, the same squad that UCLA had made look like a jayvee squad three months before. "I want North Carolina State to remember we beat them by 18 points on a neutral court," Wooden said after the USF win. "I want them to think about who has the psychological advantage."

Moreover, David Thompson had suffered a frightening head injury during the Wolfpack's win over Pittsburgh in the East Regional final. While soaring for a rebound, Thompson came down on a teammate, and his legs were flipped straight in the air. His head landed with a sickening *thwack!* that was heard throughout the arena. Thompson was taken to the hospital, but X-rays showed no fracture to his skull. Eager to let his teammates and fans know he was all right, Thompson returned to the arena and sat on the team's bench with his head wrapped in a thick white bandage. The Wolfpack won, 100–72, but it was hard to believe Thompson would be at full strength for the rematch with UCLA.

Then again, this was not the same UCLA team that had run the Wolfpack off the court in St. Louis. Since that game, the Bruins had demonstrated they were capable of losing focus, leads, and games, even against inferior opponents.

The semifinal in Greensboro played to an all-too-familiar script. The Bruins controlled the first 29 minutes, twice building 11-point leads. The second of those came with 10:56 to play in the second half. At that point, the Wolfpack missed a shot, and Walton grabbed the rebound. In a flash, NC State's seven-foot-two center, Tom Burleson, who had been so badly outclassed by Walton in St. Louis, ripped the ball out of his hands and laid it in to cut the Bruins' lead to 9. It was a telling exchange. "You never saw anything like that happen with Bill Walton," Marques Johnson said. "Burleson pointed right at Bill, and Bill shouted, 'Fuck you, Burleson!' That was the first sense of feeling I had that maybe we were going to lose the game."

Wooden told his players to spread the floor and run a delay offense. The players listened, but they didn't hear. Three times, the Bruins launched ill-advised shots. Three times they missed. That, plus a few careless turnovers, allowed the Wolfpack to rattle off 10 straight points. The game was nip and tuck the rest of the way. "They were shots we shouldn't have taken," Wooden said later. "If we were trying to catch up, it would have been different."

At the end of regulation, the score was knotted at 65–all. After 5 minutes of extra play, the score was still tied. UCLA took command early in the second overtime, and with 3:27 remaining the Bruins owned a 74–67 lead.

Alas, they came apart one last time. NC State went to a full-court press, and UCLA lost its poise. As the team unraveled, Wooden thought briefly about calling time-out before deciding against it. He would often call that one of the biggest regrets of his coaching career. The Wolfpack rode the uninterrupted momentum to within 1 point with 1:16 on the clock. After Meyers missed the front end of a one-and-one, Thompson, who would finish with 28 points and 10 rebounds, put the Wolfpack in front for good. NC State made all four of its free throw attempts down the stretch to salt away the upset.

And so it all came to an end. The most awesome streak in the history of college sports, maybe of all sports, was snapped. North Carolina State 80, UCLA 77, double overtime. For the first time in eight years, there would be a new NCAA champion in men's basketball.

While he was riding his incredible title wave, Wooden had to dodge all kinds of critics and curmudgeons. Now, in the wake of his most crushing defeat, he elicited mostly adulation. As Wooden walked into the interview room, the writers violated decorum and burst into applause. No one was surprised by his classy response. "I knew it couldn't go on forever," Wooden said. "I'm just happy we had the run we did. It was a great one. A lot of things broke right for us in a lot of ways, but they didn't today."

When he returned to the locker room, a group of writers asked Wooden if they could go inside. Wooden said he would ask the players. About ten minutes later, the school's athletics publicist, Vic Kelley, emerged to tell the press it was okay to enter.

There were not a lot of tears in that hot, cramped room, just blank stares and resigned expressions. Dave Meyers sat on a chair in front of his locker, still wearing his uniform and sweating profusely. Walton sat in a corner with his arm around Andre McCarter. When the writers approached him, Walton waved and said, "Not now, please."

The writers waited for Walton as he brought a chair into the shower and sat for twenty minutes as the water streamed over him. He eventually made his way back to his locker, plopped into a chair, and, without bothering to get dressed, grabbed a banana, peeled it, and chewed. The surrounding scribes tried to prod him, but he gave them only clipped answers.

How do you feel about the loss?

"I don't feel like talking. I'm sure some of the other guys do. I just feel like getting dressed and going home."

Do you not want to talk because it was such a bad moment?

"By saying it's a bad time it would mean that there are good times."

Does that mean you don't remember what your emotions are?

"You know better than that."

As the reporters shifted uncomfortably, Walton said, "You guys are asking me all these questions and I'm not answering any of them, and yet

I know I'll pick up the paper tomorrow and I'll have answered all of them." Then he started whistling.

Later that evening, Walton told Wooden that he did not want to play in the third-place consolation game. Wooden told Walton he hoped he would change his mind, but he did not insist on it. The following afternoon at a press conference for the four head coaches, Wooden revealed Walton's stance but didn't criticize it. "I think consolation games are for the birds," he said. "Several of my players probably won't play and it will be all right with me."

Wooden also for the first time refused to commit to returning to UCLA for a twenty-seventh season. He said he wanted to wait a month, meet with his physicians, and talk it over with his wife. "Yes, this is the first time I've ever undergone this decision process," he said. Though he acknowledged that his players engaged in selective listening against NC State, he still took the blame for the loss. "We haven't been good at protecting leads all year," he said. "That's a coaching mistake."

Sam Gilbert had a long conversation with Walton in hopes he could encourage Bill to play the consolation game. J. D. Morgan hosted a team meeting that night to deliver the same message. When Wooden argued that they should play, Walton, Lee, and the rest of the seniors relented.

Before sending his team onto the floor to take on No. 6 Kansas, Wooden told them they should play like champions. Though they came out flat and trailed by 9 early in the second half, the Bruins finally woke up and laid an old-fashioned blitz on the Jayhawks. With his team comfortably ahead 57–43 en route to a 78–61 win, Wooden emptied his bench. As first Lee, then Wilkes, then Walton left the game for a final time, the crowd at Greensboro Coliseum, which had booed the Bruins so lustily two days before, gave each player a standing ovation. It was an expression of warmth the Bruins had never enjoyed while they were champions.

The postmortems in Los Angeles were surprisingly merciful. In fact, the person who had the harshest words for Wooden was Wooden. "For the first time in my career, I became complacent this season," he said. "I personally lost the Notre Dame game through my own complacency, and after that, Bill Walton's injury softened me on the team as a whole. I eased my discipline in some areas such as dress and promptness, the players being on time. We didn't have a training table this season. I think because I became more lax in some of these areas there was a carryover onto the court. If I'm back, I'll revert to my old style."

In retrospect, it's clear that the Notre Dame loss was the beginning of the end. Wooden did all he could to downplay the importance of the winning streak, but his team's response to the loss demonstrated that he failed. "The streak shouldn't have meant that much," Dave Meyers said. "We should have regrouped and gone undefeated the rest of the way, but we didn't. Suddenly, it was panic time." As Johnson suspected, Meyers did not like the lineup change—"Marques had given us a real lift off the bench. We lost that," he said—and he agreed with Wooden that the team became too reliant on its superstars. "We got away from team play," Meyers said. "In a tight situation, we'd say, 'Well, Bill Walton or Keith Wilkes is there and will pull it out for us.' After the two losses in Oregon, I think Bill felt he had to take us all the way by himself. A lot of people looked to him for other things, things he wasn't equipped to give. That's why he withdrew from people, from the press."

Shortly after the win over Kansas in the third-place game, Nell was taken to the hospital complaining of chest pains. The doctors gave her an EKG but sent her home a few hours later. They said the pain resulted from "emotional and physical exhaustion." A month later, Wooden announced that his doctors had cleared him to return to UCLA for another season. More important, he said, "Mrs. Wooden has given her approval."

One week after Wooden made that announcement, Bill Walton signed a $3 million contract with the NBA's Portland Trail Blazers, a multiyear deal negotiated by Sam Gilbert. Yet, even as Walton began life as a wealthy man, it was dawning on him that for all the burdens he carried at UCLA, life would never again feel so light and joyful. Even more galling was the realization that he had let down the team, the school, the city, and worst of all, the only coach he had ever wanted to play for. Instead of ending his career with a net around his neck, Walton's final pose at UCLA was that of a loser, sitting in a chair and eating a banana in the nude, surrounded by a bunch of men holding notepads. "We should have run the table," he said nearly forty years later. "Playing for UCLA was fun. It was really, really fun, really positive, really upbeat. And I blew it."

Farewell

John Wooden was compulsive about his routines. When he found something he liked, he rarely deviated. This was especially true of restaurants. In a city teeming with fancy and eclectic hot spots, Wooden returned to the same one or two places and ordered the same one or two things. So when Ted Owens, the coach at Kansas, called Wooden during the summer of 1974 and said he would like to meet him for lunch, there was only one place Wooden wanted to go: Hollis Thompson's drugstore.

Wooden ate lunch there most every day. He would slip in through the backdoor, sit with his guests on orange crates, and eat a one-dollar French dip sandwich. Usually, Wooden brought along an assistant or two or maybe a former player like Gail Goodrich. On this day, Wooden and Owens were enjoying a casual meal alone until Wooden grew serious.

"Ted, you can't say anything," Wooden said, "but this is going to be my last season."

Owens was stunned—not only by the news but by Wooden's willingness to share it with him. They were friendly but not close by any means. "I honored that," Owens said years later. "I never said a word to anybody."

Wooden had come closer to retiring at the end of the 1973–74 season than anyone knew. To his surprise, it was Nell who convinced him to return. She didn't want his decision not to call a time-out against NC State to be his final memory in coaching. That wouldn't be good for his peace of mind. When Wooden's doctor gave him clearance to come back, he decided to coach for one more season. But only one.

Everything in Wooden's life was planned to the finest detail. His exit from the game would be no exception. Wooden confided his plan to very few people. Owens was one. The team's broadcaster, Fred Hessler, was another. "He told me earlier in the year that this was going to be his last year, but if I said anything on the air, he would deny it," Hessler said. "I said, 'Well, stick with me, John. Whenever you do, I'll be ready for it.'" And of course, Wooden told J. D. Morgan. He figured his boss would need ample time to find his replacement.

Morgan and Wooden agreed the job should be offered first to Gary Cunningham, but they weren't sure if he would take it. Cunningham still talked of becoming a university administrator. Before practice began, Wooden met privately with Cunningham and told him what he had decided. He told Cunningham that he was Morgan's first choice, but he added a warning: "If you are not fired with enthusiasm, you will *be* fired with enthusiasm." Cunningham said he would think about it. In the meantime, he told no one. "He trusted me," Cunningham said, "and I'm a good secret keeper."

Wooden began each morning with a brisk five-mile walk around UCLA's tartan track. His doctor had ordered him to get more exercise, so he approached this with the same compulsion he applied to all his other routines. Wooden completed his constitutional no matter where he was or what he was doing. If he was on the road and it was raining outside, he paced around the perimeter of his hotel room until he reached the five-mile point.

One morning during the summer of 1974, Wooden allowed Dwight Chapin from the *Los Angeles Times* to join him for his walk. Wooden had supposedly stopped talking to Chapin after *The Wizard of Westwood* was published, but as usual, he didn't hold a grudge. Chapin found the coach in a ruminative mood. "This can get monotonous. I hum and sing and recite poetry—crazy things—to pass the time," Wooden said. "But I'll tell ya, in the fall it's beautiful out here. Each time I come around the track, the sun is a little different. I often wish I were an artist so I could really paint the sunrise. I'd like to know if other people see it the same way I do."

When Chapin asked Wooden if this was going to be his final season, Wooden fibbed. "I'm reasonably certain this [season] won't be my last," he said. He did, however, hedge a little, saying that even if he were going to retire at the end of the season, "I'd be a little reluctant to say so because of recruiting. Each coach in competition with me for a prospect might tell him I'm not coming back."

Wooden was still in a pleasant frame of mind when practice started the day after his sixty-fourth birthday. The craziness of the past three years, usually instigated by a certain six-foot-eleven redhead, was gone. Expectations were only slightly more reasonable: UCLA would start the season ranked No. 2 in the preseason AP poll behind NC State. When Wooden was asked before the season whether UCLA could come back, he replied, "Where have we been?"

Still, it was a welcome change. Everyone agreed that the Bruins could win the national championship. The difference was that nobody thought they *should*.

UCLA still had two of the top forwards in the country in Dave Meyers and Marques Johnson, but the rest of the lineup would be filled with players who had underperformed in the past. That included sophomore Richard Washington, junior Andre McCarter, senior Pete Trgovich, and sophomore Jimmy Spillane. Seven-foot-one center Ralph Drollinger brought a whiff of the Walton eccentricities—he was also from La Mesa, and he was an avid mountain climber who twice attempted to scale the Matterhorn—but he didn't come close to matching Walton's transcendent skills. McCarter was the team's lone vegetarian, and he also had diverse passions like playing the flute and studying kung fu. These were the last vestiges from the Walton Gang, but Wooden made clear he would return to pre-Alcindor discipline. He was bringing back the training table, shorter hair requirements, and a stricter dress code. Without Walton and Lee, said Frank Arnold, "it was a lot more peaceful, let's put it that way."

Wooden always couched his remarks about Walton by saying how much he liked him, but he also acknowledged that, in many ways, life was easier without him. "I'm glad I didn't have Walton another year," Wooden said. "He is a great player, but through no fault of his own, he brought on many problems. He's a very strange person. He was not sheltered here. He sheltered himself. Other players were jealous of him."

The team was dealt a bad blow before practice began. While visiting his sister in Santa Barbara in the fall, Marques Johnson became violently ill with vomiting, chills, and diarrhea. He felt better after a few days, but when he could not regain his appetite or get rid of his fatigue, he checked into the UCLA medical center. A blood test found that Johnson had contracted hepatitis. For weeks, he lay in a hospital bed and watched his weight plummet. At first, he wasn't sure he would ever play competitive basketball again, but he returned to practice in November as an older, wiser sophomore. "Basketball is still very important, but it's not the ultimate thing now," he said. "I just want to enjoy life because I realize as easy as someone snaps his fingers, I could get sick again or hurt and never play another minute."

Johnson's lengthy hospital stay also gave him the chance to spend extended quiet time with his head coach. He was never the type to stop by Wooden's office just to chat—"I was caught up in the whole Wooden mystique. I kind of kept my distance."—but there was no mystique in that hospital room. Just two men, one old and one young, shooting the breeze about basketball, life, family, whatever. When Johnson came back, he saw the coach in a different light. "He was still Coach Wooden with the reverence and all that stuff, but I felt at ease around him," Johnson said.

By the time Johnson rejoined the team, Wooden had done something that he had rarely done in the past: he made Dave Meyers team captain for the entire season. Johnson could have resented that maneuver—this was supposed to be his team, after all—but he didn't. "It was probably better," Johnson said. "Dave became the All-American. He was an incredible leader. He played with so much passion. Now he could restore order and make it about the team again."

For the 1974–75 season, Wooden's salary was $32,500, a laughable sum but still the most he had ever been paid. For the last time in a season of last times, Wooden sat down at his desk and made his game-by-game predictions. He decided his Bruins would go 23–3 but fail to win the national championship. Wooden sealed the paper in an envelope and stowed it in his desk without telling anyone. He was getting good at keeping secrets.

Wooden suspected he might have been overly optimistic after the season opener against unranked Wichita State. The Bruins needed Drollinger to give them 21 points and 14 rebounds, both career highs, to win, 85–74. "Either we're not as good as I thought we had the potential to be, or we played a fine club," Wooden said. It turned out to be the latter. From there, UCLA reeled off five straight home wins by an average margin of 19 points.

The last of those victories came over Notre Dame in a game in which the Bruins had trailed by 19 points in the first half. Digger Phelps had caused quite a stir in the weeks leading up to that game. He had recently authorized a book called *A Coach's World*, a diary of Notre Dame's 1973–74 season written by Larry Keith of *Sports Illustrated*. The book included some incendiary observations about Wooden. "I have tremendous respect for what he has accomplished as a player and as a coach," Phelps was quoted as saying. "Nevertheless, I disagree with many of the things he does. Everyone realizes Wooden has mastered the game; he acts as if he invented it as well."

Phelps went on to call Wooden "sanctimonious" and took him to task for his bench jockeying: "While Wooden sits on the bench clutching that silver cross in his hand, he's also riding officials and players worse than any other coach I have seen. I warned Shumate today not to walk past the UCLA bench during time outs, because I don't want Wooden taking verbal shots at him. That's so bush-league for a man of his stature, yet no referee has the nerve to reprimand him."

Publicly, Wooden shrugged off those comments. "Certain people are always looking to rap someone who's at the top," he said. Privately, he was irate. He called Phelps and asked why he had said those things. According to Wooden, Phelps replied, "Don't worry about that stuff, John. I just did it to sell books."

"I hung up on him," Wooden said.

For a long time, Wooden expressed a mixture of bemusement and pique, seasoned with a dash of condescension, at the way Phelps and the Notre Dame faithful turned a 1-point regular season victory into a cause célèbre. Phelps's former assistant, Dick Kuchen, once bragged to Wooden that Phelps and his staff spent an entire year scouting the Bruins before their historic win. "I said, 'Gosh, Dick, if you'd have spent that time on some of the other games, you would've won all those other games you lost, wouldn't ya? How'd you work out that you were gonna score the last twelve points against us?'" Wooden said. "They made a crusade out of it, but I liked that. I used to tell my players, 'They're making a crusade to beat you. What does that mean? They respect you. They think it'll be great to beat you. Let 'em celebrate if they happen to beat us, like they won the national championship. Then we'll go ahead and win the national championship.'"

After scoring that very satisfying win over Notre Dame in Pauley, the Bruins hit the road to play in the Terrapin Classic at the University of Maryland. Lefty Driesell asked to spend some time with Wooden, so Wooden invited him to his morning exercise. "He walked so fast, the next day I could hardly walk," Driesell said. UCLA defeated St. Bonaventure in the first game to advance to the final against Maryland, and in that contest Wooden made yet another unconventional move: he called time-out to make a strategic adjustment. Driesell had just switched to a three-guard offense, so Wooden responded by inserting Johnson, who was still working his way back into the rotation as a reserve. Johnson scored 11 of UCLA's final 15 points, and the Bruins won, 81–75.

Despite his recovering health, it was not easy for Johnson to deal with not starting. He expressed his anger one day during practice when he dunked over Drollinger during a fast-break drill. To Johnson's surprise, Wooden said nothing. However, when sophomore forward Gavin Smith dunked later in that same practice, Wooden blew his whistle. *Goodness gracious sakes alive, Gavin! Don't ever do that again or you'll never play another minute for UCLA!* When Johnson asked Wooden later why he hadn't said anything to him when he dunked, Wooden said he was just cutting him some slack. "He knew I had been sick and that I was doing it to release my pent-up frustration," Johnson said. "Gavin was just doing it to flaunt his jumping ability."

Wooden was enjoying himself in a way he hadn't for some time. Even a pair of losses in January—by 4 points at Stanford, by 6 at Notre Dame—couldn't sour his mood. "To say I'm pleased with the play of every individual would never be true," he said. "But I am pleased with the *effort* of every individual this season, and that hasn't always been true."

Wooden was less pleased when the NCAA's basketball committee announced a pair of rule changes in early January. The first was a decision to expand the NCAA tournament from twenty-five to thirty-two teams, which meant that for the first time ever, the NCAA would award at-large bids to teams that had failed to win their conference titles. Many coaches and writers had been arguing for this change for several years, but the tipping point was the 1974 Atlantic Coast Conference (ACC) tournament championship game, when No. 1 NC State beat No. 4 Maryland 103–100 in overtime. It was one of the best-played, most exciting games in college basketball history. While NC State went on to win the NCAA championship, Maryland could not play in that tournament at all and had to settle for an invitation to the NIT, which it turned down. Wooden had long argued against adding at-large teams, and he wasn't happy to be overruled. "I thought all along that we play the conference to determine who was going to get in the NCAA tournament," he said. "Teams that don't win the conference, I don't think should be in."

That was a minor annoyance compared to the other rule change. The committee had determined that from now on, every coach was required to open his locker room to the press within ten minutes of the conclusion of all NCAA tournament games. The committee's chairman, Davidson College coach Tom Scott, made clear that the rule had been passed with one man in mind. "Wooden has been a problem, as you know," Scott said. "If he's there this year, we'll have that dressing room open."

Wooden took exception to that remark. "I don't think the press as a whole would say that [I've been a problem], except on this one thing," he said. "I just think that's a poor place to have a great number of the press in, but if they make it a rule, why, it'll be done." After he left coaching, Wooden frequently claimed that Scott's comment was part of the reason he decided to retire, which was unfair considering Wooden had already made his decision before the rule was changed.

After the loss at Notre Dame, the Bruins reeled off six straight conference wins, only one of which came by more than 12 points. Their 89–84 win over USC at Pauley Pavilion marked a historic threshold: the all-time series between the schools was now officially tied. It had taken Wooden a mere twenty-seven years to erase the forty-game advantage the Trojans owned when he came to Westwood.

Wooden remained sanguine even after he suffered the worst loss of his UCLA career, a 103–81 rout at the hands of his good friend, Washington State coach Marv Harshman. "I'm very happy for Marv, and I'm very disappointed for my own team," Wooden said. "I can't say we were jobbed. We weren't out-lucked. It was a good beating."

Wooden was finding that he had the exact opposite problem from a year ago. Now, his players were *too* agreeable. "They're competitors in their own way, but not violent competitors," he said. "It's possible they don't have the fiery spirit that might [make them] better." Still, Wooden was not going to let himself get caught up in whether or not he was satisfying expectations. It had taken him to the age of sixty-four, but he was finally following his father's counsel not to worry about things he couldn't control. "It's human nature, I suppose. Anything short of winning all our games is not enough for some people," Wooden said. "The same is true of the people who used to say we won by such big margins it was boring. Now they're wondering why we don't win by more. At one time, that would have bugged me. I accept it now."

John Wooden had already made a long and compelling case that he was without peer when it came to teaching the game of basketball. The 1974–75 season served as a convincing closing argument.

Yes, he had two of the country's better forwards in Meyers and Johnson, but for most of the season, Johnson was a shell of his former self.

Besides, no one would claim those two belonged in the same class as Alcindor and Walton. They weren't even Hazzard, Goodrich, Wicks, or Wilkes. Yet the Bruins stayed among the college basketball elite because they were better schooled in the fundamentals of the game. They weren't the most talented students. They just had the best teacher.

This was becoming so obvious, even Wooden's most bitter rivals had to acknowledge it. "He put high-profile players together effectively," Bob Boyd said. "It wasn't always easy, but in the end he produced his desired results." Dick Harter added, "The most important thing in basketball is getting players to play unselfishly and play well with each other. I can't remember any UCLA player taking a selfish or a bad shot. When you think about it, John had a lot of very nice guys like Dave Meyers and Marques Johnson, and he had some pain in the asses like Sidney Wicks and Curtis Rowe. Walton could be obnoxious. John got them all to play well together."

Since most sportswriters and opposing coaches were unable to solve this riddle, it was left to a pair of psychology professors to make a clinical study. The two professors—one from the University of Hawaii, the other from UCLA—charted several dozen of Wooden's practices during the 1974–75 season and published their findings in the January 1976 issue of *Psychology Today* magazine. The professors came up with ten different categories of communication (Instructions, Hustles, Praises, Scolds, etc.) and assigned everything Wooden said to one of those. The most frequently cited category by far was Instructions, which the psychologists defined as "verbal statements about what to do or how to do it." That accounted for 50.3 percent of things Wooden said. The professors calculated that overall "at least 75 percent of Wooden's teaching acts carry information."

The researchers were also taken by the qualitative change in Wooden's demeanor once practice began. This was the "walking contradiction" that Marques Johnson and his teammates had come to know so well. "The whistle transforms Wooden," they wrote. "He becomes less the friendly grandfather and more the Marine sergeant . . . [and he] scolds twice as much as he rewards."

What those psychologists witnessed was the result of a lifetime of small, almost unnoticeable advancements. Wooden truly lived the credo that hung on his office wall: *It's what you learn after you know it all that counts.* After all these years, he was still learning, still improving, one three-by-five index card at a time. "You look back at my practice program for the last year or the year before and there wouldn't be much difference," he said. "But go back ten years and you'll find a lot of change. I make small changes regularly almost without realizing it. If you go back twenty to twenty-five years and look at one of my schedules, you'd wonder how I ever got anything done."

One thing that Wooden had learned is that he could relax his ultra-serious demeanor just a little. His friends were well aware that he had a sense of humor, but to his players this was a major revelation. "My sophomore year, he loosened up," Johnson said. "He kind of opened up, and we opened up to him. There was a lot more of back-and-forth joking."

For instance, one day, Raymond Townsend, a freshman guard, was messing around and taking half-court shots after practice. In previous years, Wooden might have ripped into Townsend for horsing around, but on this day he only asked for the ball. Using his patented 1930s-style two-handed set shot, Wooden drilled his first attempt. "Child's play," he said and walked away.

Johnson thought he was going to get an earful when Wooden spotted him shooting pool in the student union one day. Instead, Wooden asked to borrow his stick. Shifting around the toothpick clutched between his teeth, Wooden bent over and started rattling balls into the pockets. "He made five or six in a row, maybe more," Johnson said. "The cue ball would spin and snake up to the next one. *Boom*. Spin and snake up to the next one. *Boom*. *Boom*. *Boom*. *Boom*. Then he handed me the cue and walked out. Didn't say a word. Didn't say one word the whole time."

Wooden also liked to tease Johnson about his hair. Johnson wore a thick Afro, but he matted it down extra tight for practice and games. Every so often, Wooden would walk up to him, pull at a strand, and smirk when it stood straight up. "That was his way of saying, 'I know what you're doing. You're not fooling me,'" Johnson said.

McCarter was a prime target for Wooden's needle. Besides being the team's only vegetarian (though he ate at the training table), McCarter sported the headband-and-dark-glasses look favored by his idol, Jimi Hendrix. McCarter was also a martial arts enthusiast who went through a series of kung fu moves to get ready to play. Once, before a game at Oregon State, McCarter was making his slow-motion hand and leg contortions when Wooden sneaked up behind him and started mimicking his moves. McCarter had no idea why his teammates were laughing so hard until he turned around.

During another trip to the Northwest, Wooden was riding the team bus when he asked Dick Enberg to come sit next to him. Enberg thought he was going to get a lesson on the intricacies of basketball, but instead Wooden asked, "Do you like poetry?" Startled, Enberg said yes. For the rest of the ride, he and Wooden (well, mostly Wooden) spoke about different poets and different eras, with Wooden reciting some of his favorite verses.

There was, however, one person hovering in the background who could disrupt Wooden's serenity. Sam Gilbert remained embedded as ever in the program, despite J. D. Morgan's efforts to pry him away. The two men continued to have heated discussions in Morgan's office. "You could hear J. D. shouting out the door," Frank Arnold said. "J. D. was very strongly telling Sam to stay away, don't get involved. I know that from the inside."

Arnold heard Gilbert's name bandied about when he came to UCLA in the spring of 1971 but didn't know much about him. A few weeks later, Arnold was sitting with Wooden and a few players at a UCLA track meet. When one of the players mentioned he needed some help with a problem, Arnold suggested he go see Sam Gilbert. Wooden nudged Arnold hard with his knee. After the meet, Wooden told Arnold, "Never do that again. And stay away from Sam Gilbert." Arnold did as he was told. "I knew Sam from a distance, and that's all I wanted to know about him," he said. "I had a very low opinion of Sam. Any kind of high-end booster like that isn't good for any program."

That did not stop Gilbert from continuing to befriend Wooden's players. Marques Johnson read about Gilbert in *The Wizard of Westwood* but did not meet him during his recruitment. After Johnson started playing for UCLA, some upperclassmen took him to one of Gilbert's famous weekend barbecues. Johnson soon became a regular visitor. "It wasn't anything crazy. We'd go over and play paddle tennis and just hang out all day. There might be fifteen, twenty people between players and their girlfriends," Johnson said. "You'd have Rose, the kids, and the grandkids swimming, dogs chasing the tennis balls into the pool. It was a real wholesome picture."

Gilbert lavished on Johnson the same less-than-wholesome favors he provided for everyone else. "There was no cash ever. He never paid rent or bought cars or anything, but he would get me discounts on things like tires," Johnson said. "The one thing I got [for free] was buckskin heavy jackets and leather coats from a clothing guy that he knew."

Though Gilbert boasted that he never took a fee for serving as the players' agent, his affiliation with the team obviously enhanced his standing in the business community. There were many times when Gilbert would take Johnson and a friend, usually McCarter or Washington or both, to attend some high-class function in Los Angeles. "That would happen two or three times a month," Johnson said. "We didn't have to pay for the food."

Like the other Bruins, Johnson wasn't the least bit conflicted about what was going on. "It was a different time back then. It wasn't like you were blatantly doing anything wrong," Johnson said. "Being from L.A. and living in the same apartment complex with a couple of USC football players . . . there was a feeling like what we're doing over here is nothing. I hate to say that because I don't want to drag their program though anything, but it's true. I knew guys who were playing at UNLV. L.A. guys. So it was a level playing field for everybody. There were certain things that you were going to try and get, and certain ways you were going to work the system."

As for his coach, well, Johnson may have talked about a lot of personal things with Wooden that season, but this was not one of them. "Coach never talked about what was going on with Sam," Johnson said. Holding his hands apart, he explained, "At that time, he was here, and Sam was here. And never the twain shall meet."

Old habits were hard to break. As February gave way to early March, the usual tensions infiltrated John Wooden's cone of serenity. As the postseason drew nigh, he found it increasingly difficult to sleep. His morning workout at the UCLA track was now starting at 5:00 a.m. The pressure of mounting another run to an NCAA championship was taking an even rougher toll on Nell, which only added to his worries.

Things were also bearing down hard on Gary Cunningham. He had been struggling all season with the question of whether he should be Wooden's successor. Finally, in February Cunningham went to Wooden and told him that he did not want the job. Cunningham told Wooden that when he quit at the end of the season, Cunningham would quit, too. "It's not where my interests were," Cunningham said.

This sent Morgan into scramble mode. At that point, he couldn't be positive that UCLA would even reach the NCAA tournament, much less win another title, and he wanted to have Wooden's replacement locked down. With Cunningham no longer an option, the next obvious choice seemed to be Denny Crum, who was having another fabulous season at Louisville. Morgan, however, was not a huge fan of Crum, considering him a little too rough around the edges. Morgan wanted a coach who could win while maintaining the clean-cut UCLA image that Wooden had promulgated so well.

That also ruled out another winning coach with local ties, Jerry Tarkanian. After leaving Long Beach in a mess, Tarkanian was already attracting the scrutiny of the NCAA at UNLV. "I said to him once, what about [hiring] Tarkanian?" said Byron Atkinson, the UCLA professor and dean of students. "You should have heard the . . . names he called him. They were hot. [Morgan] considered him a scab and a pirate."

Thus, Morgan had no choice but to go outside the UCLA family—and he had someone in mind. Back in the 1973 NCAA final against Memphis State, while everyone else was entranced by Bill Walton's performance, Morgan came away impressed with Gene Bartow, the Tigers' head coach. Not only was Bartow a good coach; Morgan also liked his "Clean Gene" profile. Problem was, Bartow had since left Memphis State and was now in his first year at Illinois. He had just signed a five-year contract.

Bartow was shocked when Morgan called him. "I said, 'J. D., I can't. I'm trying to win games,'" Bartow said. "It was nice of J. D. to do it, but I felt you could win big at Illinois. So at that moment, I didn't give much thought to it." Two weeks later, Morgan called Bartow again and asked him to reconsider. This time, Bartow was more willing to listen. He was a southerner originally, and he had twice recently skidded off the road during a bad snowstorm. Bartow was becoming more enticed by the idea of living in the California sun. More important, he was warming up to the idea of being UCLA's next basketball coach.

On February 8, Illinois lost by 4 points at Northwestern. The next day, Bartow flew to Los Angeles, met with Morgan for two hours over lunch in Santa Monica, and then turned around and flew back home. To that point, Bartow had not told anyone about the situation except for his wife, and he managed to keep word from leaking out about his meeting with Morgan. Among those left in the dark was his athletic director at Illinois, Cecil Coleman. "It probably wasn't real ethical," Bartow said. "I wasn't real proud of it."

Wooden had no idea about Morgan's conversations with Bartow. J. D. figured the coach had enough to worry about as the Bruins entered the final two weeks of the regular season with a one-game lead in the conference standings. Wooden was uncharacteristically emotional down the stretch of the season. After the team scored a dramatic 107–103 victory at Oregon to keep its grip on first place, Wooden had to gather himself before speaking in the locker room. "I've got a frog in my throat," he said. A

12-point win at home over second-place Oregon State pushed that lead to two games. Two weeks later, the Bruins clinched the title by throttling Stanford in Pauley Pavilion by 34 points.

That rendered meaningless the regular season finale at USC, but the game meant a lot to Wooden. Before tip-off, he shared some quiet words with Bob Boyd inside the Sports Arena. Afterward, Boyd went over to his assistant, Jim Hefner, and said, "You won't believe what's happening. Wooden just told me this is the last time he's playing us. He's quitting."

Hefner was surprised Wooden was retiring, but he was not surprised that he would confide in Boyd. "He respected Boyd," Hefner said. "I know that for a fact because his assistants used to say what Wooden thought about him. He knew Bob could coach."

The game was sealed in the final minute when Pete Trgovich, who had so often struggled to find playing time throughout his career, stole a pass meant for Trojans guard Gus Williams and converted a pair of free throws. When the horn sounded, Wooden jumped out of his seat, threw his fist in the air, and shook it several times. "More than anything else, I was elated for Pete," he said. "I know he hasn't done as well here as he probably expected to." Wooden was so thrilled with the win, he opened up his locker room to reporters.

Wooden had done well to keep his impending retirement a secret, but now the news was starting to break, and from a most unlikely source. Washington coach George Raveling first reported the big scoop in his Sunday column for the *Seattle Post-Intelligencer*, which was published on March 8. "The public announcement won't come until mid-April, but John Wooden won't return as head coach at UCLA next year," Raveling wrote. "Several sources up and down the coast have told me of Wooden's pending retirement."

Raveling wasn't totally straight with his readers. He actually had only one source, and it was not from the West Coast, but it was a good one. A few weeks before, Gene Bartow, with whom Raveling had become very good friends over the years, called Raveling to tell him about his meeting with Morgan. "I told him, damn, you know it's going to be tough as hell following a legend. The only expectation they know is a national championship," Raveling said. Once the regular season ended, Raveling called Bartow and asked if he could report the news. Bartow said it was fine with him as long as Raveling didn't reveal his source.

When the column was published, said Raveling, "all hell broke loose." Morgan rang him up and demanded that Raveling tell him his source. "He was livid. He kept saying, 'You can't just say these things. You've got to prove it,'" Raveling said. "He was trying to smoke me out, but I wouldn't tell him where I got it from. I just said, 'Well, let it play its course and we'll see who's right and who's wrong.'" Morgan also got the Pac-8 commissioner to publicly reprimand Raveling.

Raveling's article was just one more piece of conjecture for Wooden to bat down. "I've said it before and I can say it again. I've made no decision about retiring next season yet," he said. "You may put to rest rumors that I have decided not to return."

Wooden, however, was becoming increasingly uncomfortable with having to lie. He knew the questions would only become more frequent during the NCAA tournament. It was going to be hard enough to win the title. Because of the addition of seven at-large slots, a team would have to win five games instead of four to claim the championship. The conference champions were assigned regions by geography, but the at-large teams were drawn out of a hat and placed into the bracket. That's why UCLA's first opponent in the West Regional in Pullman, Washington, was Michigan, which had been the runner-up in the Big Ten to Indiana.

The Bruins' season came very close to ending against the Wolverines, but they pulled out a thrilling 103–91 win in overtime. That sent them to the West Regional semifinals in Portland, where they were nearly upended yet again, this time by a Montana team coached by a hard-nosed Marv Harshman disciple named Jud Heathcote. The Bruins' win in the West Regional final came much easier by way of an 89–75 triumph over Arizona State. After all they had lost, after everything they had been through, the Bruins were headed for the final weekend in San Diego. John Wooden would have the opportunity he wanted, to leave basketball a champion.

Gene Bartow was headed to San Diego, too, but unlike Wooden he was not bringing his team. The Illini had gone 8–18 and failed to make the NCAA tournament. Bartow still was not sure what he was going to tell Morgan, but he felt himself inching closer to taking the job. After he got back from his cloak-and-dagger trip to Los Angeles, Bartow told his boss, Cecil Coleman, what was going on. Coleman was understandably angry, but when Bartow asked him what he would do if he was asked to be UCLA's athletic director, Coleman conceded he had a point.

UCLA arrived for the tournament's final weekend back in its customary perch atop the rankings, courtesy of No. 1 Indiana's loss to Kentucky in the Mideast Regional final. The Bruins' opponent in the NCAA semifinals was No. 4 Louisville. This put Wooden in a tough spot. Not only would he again have to go up against his former player and assistant, Denny Crum, but he still had not told Crum about his plans. That was one more reason why Wooden did not want the news to break, but he was losing the battle. At a party on Friday night, Wooden was cornered by four Los Angeles sportswriters who claimed to have heard from reliable sources that he planned to announce his retirement on Saturday night if UCLA lost or on Monday night if the Bruins reached the final. Wooden was through with the charade. "It might be," he said. "I won't want to lie. I would announce it to my players first and I haven't yet. I wouldn't be surprised if a decision came this weekend. It's been a troubled time. It's not what I'd really want. If I did it, it would be for the best."

In an unbylined story the following morning, the *Los Angeles Times* reported that "a prominent UCLA alumnus said Friday that John Wooden will resign as the Bruins' basketball coach at the NCAA tournament." The *Los Angeles Herald Examiner* published the same claim. When Wooden read those articles during the Kentucky-Syracuse semifinal that preceded his own, he knew the jig was up. The spiraling situation set the stage for one of the most dramatic and wrenching nights of his life.

If anyone could get his team prepared to play UCLA, it was Denny Crum. His Louisville Cardinals built two separate 7-point leads during the first half. Each time, the Bruins managed to hang tight. "It was like playing against ourselves," Marques Johnson said. The game stayed close for the entire second half. Louisville led, 65–61, with 1:06 to go.

After Richard Washington dropped in a pair of free throws to cut Louisville's lead to 2, Wooden went to his zone press for the first time all day. The move baffled the Cardinals, who turned the ball over and allowed Johnson to score on the ensuing possession to tie it at 65–all. When neither team could score during the final minute, the game headed for overtime.

By that time, Drollinger and Trgovich had fouled out, and the Bruins again fell behind by 3 points with 2:20 to go. A Johnson tip-in and two free throws by Meyers sandwiched a Louisville basket, leaving the score at 74–73 in favor of the Cardinals. Crum called time-out and ordered his team into a four-corner stall. For most of the possession, the ball stayed in the hands of Cardinals guard Terry Howard. There was a good reason for this: Howard had not missed a free throw all season. He was a perfect 28 for 28.

With the game slipping away, Washington had no choice but to foul.

It was a one-and-one situation. If Howard made both free throws, it would be a two-possession game, and UCLA would probably be headed for defeat. Howard stepped to the foul line . . . and missed.

If ever there was evidence to support Tarkanian's theory that Wooden was the good Lord's favorite coach, this was it. Howard's miss gave the Bruins new life. Wooden called time-out to set up the final possession. When play resumed, McCarter tried to score on a drive down the lane and missed, but Meyers grabbed the rebound to keep the possession going. The Bruins worked the ball around to Washington, who slipped loose on the baseline and lofted a baseline jumper as the final seconds ticked away.

Swish. Ball game. UCLA 75, Louisville 74.

Wooden and Crum shook hands amid the bedlam. As Wooden walked off the court toward the locker room, he was totally, utterly spent. His players were elated in the locker room. Nobody was trying to avoid peaks and valleys, least of all Wooden. When he came inside, he waited for the whooping and hollering to subside. Once it did, Wooden praised his Bruins for how they played. He said he was proud of them. He said he loved coaching them. He told them he believed they had an excellent chance to beat Kentucky in the final.

Then Wooden dropped the news. Win or lose, Monday was going to be his final game as the UCLA basketball coach. "I'm bowing out," he said. Struggling to push down the frog in his throat, he could only add, "I don't want to. I have to."

At that point, the only player who had known of Wooden's plans was his senior captain, Dave Meyers. The rest were in shock. "There was never a hint that he was going to retire," Johnson said. "I remember feeling a little disappointment, a little sadness that he wasn't going to be there to finish out my career."

Wooden had not told anyone—not Morgan, not Cunningham, not Nell—that he was going to break the news to the players that night. He wasn't even positive himself until he started walking off the court. He dreaded the idea of going into that interview room and facing another round of questions about that morning's reports. He was tired of carrying around his secret, tired of lying to his friends. It was important to him that his players heard the news from him first. Having told them at last, he was ready to reveal his plans to the world.

Wooden was still wrung out when he took his seat in the interview room. "I've always said that my first year in coaching [at UCLA] was my most satisfying. My last year has been equally satisfying, regardless of what happens Monday night," he said. "I've asked J. D. Morgan to release me from my coaching duties at UCLA. I have done that for a number of reasons I'd rather not go into. I just told the players."

The room fell silent. Someone asked Wooden what the players' response was. "Quietness," he said.

Wooden explained, less than truthfully, that he had been considering retirement "for some time" but did not come to a final conclusion until the last week. He said he was making the announcement now instead of after the final "because there has been a lot of conjecture about it recently, most of it reasonably accurate. I certainly don't think I panic when I make decisions." He talked of his recent sleeping troubles—"That had never happened before and I thought, well, maybe it's a sign"—and said he did not make the decision out of his own health concerns but rather "the health of others," presumably Nell, who later confirmed to reporters that her husband had made his decision to retire at the start of the season. Wooden also promised he would not coach anywhere else. "I'll be sixty-five October 14. Practice starts October 15. I made the decision many years ago I'd never coach any place but UCLA.

"But let's don't talk about that," he pleaded. "Let's talk about the game."

Fat chance. Wooden's announcement set off a mad scramble. Frank Arnold was doing an interview with Hessler on the court when Wooden delivered the news to the players. "I had a hunch it might happen, but I didn't know. He didn't tell me," Arnold said. Cunningham was also caught off-guard. He immediately informed the press that he planned to resign as well. "I'm thirty-five years old and things have happened to me that shouldn't be happening to a man my age," he said. "They're directly related to coaching, the hours and pressure."

Now it was Wooden's turn to be caught off-guard. "Did he say for sure he was resigning?" he said to a reporter who relayed what Cunningham had said. Asked if he was surprised, Wooden said, "Yes and no."

Crum may have been the most surprised of anyone. Not only was he unaware that Wooden was going to retire; he had no idea that Morgan had already offered the job to someone else. Crum could barely hold back tears as he talked about his former coach. "There's not much you can say about a man who has done what he has done in his profession," he said as his hands shook. "Basketball will miss him. You'll all miss him. He might miss basketball even more."

When the writers entered the UCLA locker room—Wooden didn't like the rule, but he didn't protest it—the players were still spinning from the night's events. "I felt like I was sitting in on a little bit of sports history," Johnson said of the moment Wooden broke the news. Meyers added, "There was a lot of emotion in the room. Most of our guys are young and maybe don't realize what Wooden has meant to UCLA and the game."

The chance to play in an NCAA championship game was plenty big on its own. Now, Monday night's final wasn't just going to be big. It was going to be historic. The players may have been young, but they weren't naive. As soon as Wooden left the locker room, McCarter brought everyone together and delivered a stern message. "There's no way," he said, "that we are going to let this man lose."

At the traditional Sunday press conference for the semifinal coaches, Wooden sounded like a man unburdened. "When I got wind of the Saturday morning papers in Los Angeles, I made the decision," he said. "I feel much better now that the announcement has been made. I was sort of pent up inside. I wasn't being able to be completely honest with my friends." Wooden answered a few more questions about his retirement before cutting them off. "Isn't it about time that we talk about the important thing—the basketball tournament?"

His opponent in the final, Kentucky coach Joe B. Hall, was happy to oblige. "There's no way we can come up with anything like what's involved in John Wooden's resignation," he said. "Still, it won't dampen our spirits." Hall also joked that he should get the UCLA job because he had already been foolish enough to follow Adolph Rupp. "There's no sense destroying two people," he said.

Kentucky had a major advantage over UCLA in size, experience, and depth. Playing alongside four seniors were three bruising, six-foot-ten freshman centers: Rick Roby, Mike Phillips, and Dan Hall. The Wildcats also featured a rising star in six-foot-five freshman guard Jack Givens. Kentucky posed such a formidable challenge that on Sunday Wooden conducted a walk-through of Kentucky's trapping defense and four-corners offense. "Never before had we done this, but we had to," he said.

When the game began, Wooden was unusually tight. As he feared, his Bruins had all kinds of problems with Kentucky's size. Usually, Marques Johnson could overcome a height disadvantage with strength and quickness, but this was one occasion where he was overmatched. When Kentucky built an early 6-point lead, Wooden replaced him with Drollinger.

From there, UCLA made its move. With Drollinger playing the game of his life, UCLA erased its deficit and fought toe-to-toe with the Wildcats.

There were fifteen lead changes and five ties in the first half alone. Rather than stew on the bench, Johnson found himself cheering Drollinger's every move. "It wasn't like I wanted Ralph to cool off and not play as well so I could get back in there. I was genuinely happy for Ralph," Johnson said. "It's hard to explain. It wasn't about me and my minutes and this and that. It was like, we need to win this game by any means necessary. Ralph's doing the job. I'm glad not to have to battle those big dudes. Go, Ralph, go."

Following the intermission, UCLA slowly started pulling away. With just under twelve minutes to play, Washington scored off an offensive rebound to give the Bruins a 10-point lead, their biggest of the game. Now it was Kentucky's turn to come back. The Wildcats shrank UCLA's lead from 74–67 to 76–75 with under seven minutes to play.

On the ensuing possession, Meyers drove hard to the bucket and crashed into Kevin Grevey, Kentucky's senior captain. When Hank Nichols, a thirty-eight-year-old official who was working his first championship game, called Meyers for a charge, Meyers slammed the ball on the floor in disgust and shouted, "I didn't touch him!" Nichols then slapped Meyers with a technical foul.

Wooden went ballistic. He thought the charge call was wrong, and the technical was atrocious. As he screamed "You crook!" at Nichols, Wooden walked several feet onto the court. Arnold and Cunningham had to restrain him, with help from Meyers. "That's the only time I can remember that happening," Arnold said. Nichols recalled that when Meyers slammed the ball on the floor, "I thought it was going to hit the ceiling." Nichols added that it's probably a good thing in retrospect that Wooden's assistants, as well as the other referee, kept Wooden from walking any closer to him. "I was a cocky rookie," Nichols said. "I don't know what I would have done if he had gotten on the court."

The sequence gave Kentucky a chance to break the game open. But Grevey, a 76 percent foul shooter, missed two free throws—one for the technical, the other a front end of a one-and-one for the foul. Kentucky retained possession because of the technical but turned it over again when James Lee was called for an offensive foul. The Wildcats could have scored 5 unanswered points. Instead they scored none.

The game stayed tense the rest of the way, but UCLA never relinquished its lead. When the horn sounded, John Wooden had his tenth NCAA championship courtesy of a 92–85 victory. He was immediately engulfed by photographers and television cameras. The UCLA band played "Thanks for the Memories." McCarter embraced him and said, "I hope you have a nice life." A Bruin cheerleader cut down one of the nets and hung it around Wooden's neck.

Wooden's final game served as one last affirmation of everything he tried to teach about basketball. He only used six players, yet they outperformed Hall's eleven. Every cog did its part to help the machine fulfill its mission. McCarter had 14 assists. Meyers scored 24 points, grabbed 11 rebounds, and provided his customary emotional leadership. Drollinger fought through Kentucky's burly young centers en route to 13 rebounds and 10 points. Trgovich added 16 points and held Kentucky's star guard Jimmy Dan Conner to 9. Washington finished with 28 points and 12 rebounds and was named the game's Most Outstanding Player. Even Johnson, who only played twenty-three minutes and was just 3-for-9 from the floor, snared several key rebounds down the stretch to keep the Wildcats at bay.

Best of all, the Bruins were champs because they were quicker than Kentucky, but they didn't hurry. "We went out with the idea that the more we ran them, the better we'd be," Drollinger said. "Coach Wooden's basic philosophy is that the best quality a player can have is quickness. It will beat strength every time."

There was no pretense of dispassion when Wooden walked into the postgame interview room. The press gave him a hearty standing ovation. "I guess to say that I thought we would go this far would be stretching the point, but I did think we had a chance," he said. "Yes, I'm sad. Sad that I'm leaving the youngsters and all the wonderful associations I've made. You men, my coaches, other players and coaches. I haven't agreed with you on everything, but we all agree on our love for this game."

As for his future plans, Wooden said he would like to continue working at UCLA in some capacity. He wanted to stick to his daily five-mile walk around the track, "so I'm going to ask J. D. Morgan if I can have a locker." He also said he would do whatever he could to help his successor, whoever it may be. Asked if he would consider returning if the program fell on hard times, Wooden replied, "UCLA basketball is not going to fall on hard times."

It was left to the press to take full measure of the man before them. During the just-completed twelve-year span, Wooden's teams won ten NCAA titles and put together two epic streaks—seven straight national championships and eighty-eight consecutive wins. His records in the sport would forever be unequaled and unsurpassed. "It may be an overexaggeration to call Wooden the best coach in the history of team sports, but not by much," Ken Denlinger wrote in the *Washington Post*. "Keep in mind that Vince Lombardi never had to win an NFL championship without Bart Starr or Paul Hornung, and Red Auerbach was blessed with Bill Russell in the decade he became a genius in the NBA. Wooden has won with dominant guards, dominant forwards and dominant centers, most of whom were coveted by every other major-college coach before they chose UCLA."

Most important, Wooden had accomplished all of that during a period of immense social change. The pressure of being on top eventually got to him, but not nearly as viscerally as it did for so many other great coaches. The ten championships aside, John Wooden's greatest victory may well have been his ability to emerge from all that tumult without losing sense of who he was—not a perfect man but a very good one, a teacher more than a coach, a Christian, a husband, a father, anything but a wizard. He was going out a winner, but what mattered more was that he had been successful, even if he was the only one who understood the difference.

He tried to teach that lesson until the very end. "I'd like to be remembered as a person who tried to do his best, I guess," he said on the night of his grand finale. "A man I've admired for so long, Tony Hinkle of Butler, never got the recognition he deserved because his won-lost record wasn't that great. But no coach ever got more out of his players. It's hard to keep things in perspective sometimes, but we ought to try."

After Wooden left the interview room, he stood in a hallway outside the Bruins' locker room and held court some more with reporters. Denny Crum, whose team had defeated Syracuse in the third-place game, waited for his former coach to finish. Crum was standing next to Wooden when a well-heeled alumnus walked up to offer his good wishes. "Congratulations, Coach," the man said. "You let us down last year, but this made up for it."

You let us down last year. It was all Crum could do to hold himself back. "I could have punched the guy," he said.

The comment summarized the sad irony of John Wooden's career. The very years that produced the greatest coaching record in the history of college sports were in many ways the unhappiest years of his life. Even with his health issues, Wooden could have coached a little while longer. He was still one year short of the mandatory retirement age, and the 1974–75 season proved he was as good as he had ever been. Four of the six players he used in the championship game were returning, and he had signed another top-flight freshman class. Yet, as he put it, he quit not because he wanted to but because he had to. "If it were just coaching, it wouldn't be so bad," Nell said. "But it's all the things together that are getting him uptight. He had to get out from under the pressure. I think that was the biggest thing. When you reach a certain age, it's hard to take those things anymore."

In the decades that followed, Wooden frequently told the story of that booster's remark. He did so with a twinkle in his eye—*It was amusing to me, very funny. Didn't bother me at all*—but that was not the truth. He expressed his real feelings the following morning at breakfast, when he relayed the exchange to Marques Johnson and Richard Washington. As Wooden spoke, Johnson got one last glimpse of the fierce warrior dude. "He was hot," Johnson said. "He was saying, 'I'm just tired of it.' He was real frustrated. We told him, 'Coach, go ahead. Have a good life.'"

In the end, that booster may have done him a favor. If there was any lingering doubt, that man erased it. When John Wooden walked out of San Diego Sports Arena that night, he knew that he had made the right decision. He did his best. He had peace of mind. It was time to bow out.

PART FOUR

Winter

31

Clean Gene

"Coach Bartow's office. Coach Wooden speaking."

The new era of UCLA basketball sounded a lot like the old one. During Gene Bartow's first few months on the job in the spring and summer of 1975, he shared his office with the previous occupant. Neither man was thrilled with the arrangement, which was J. D. Morgan's idea, but it proved to be symbolic. No matter how hard he huffed, no matter how hard he puffed, Bartow could not escape the great man's shadow.

The office, like everything else around UCLA, was a paean to the Wooden dynasty. Dozens of trophies occupied the shelves. Framed magazine covers hung on the walls. Though Wooden was completely surprised by Morgan's decision (he had assumed that his successor would be Denny Crum), he lent his imprimatur to the hire. When Bartow walked into Pauley Pavilion three days after UCLA's championship win over Kentucky to meet the press for the first time, Wooden was right by his side. A photograph published inside UCLA's media guide for the 1975–76 season showed Wooden handing a basketball to Gene Bartow. The message was clear: handle with care.

Wooden's understated ubiquity was of a piece with his declaration that he wasn't really "retired"; he had simply stopped coaching UCLA's basketball team. That allowed him some well-earned rest. He and Nell spent a weekend in Banff, Alberta, between John's appearances at coaching clinics in the Pacific Northwest. "Nobody knew me," he said. "I was doing the daily five-mile walk every morning. It was nice in October and everything was so beautiful. Never had a nicer vacation." Later that month, they took a two-week Caribbean cruise.

Besides that, Wooden remained as active as ever. He was in high demand on the lecture circuit, and for the first time in his life, he had the opportunity to make some real money, although much of what he earned went into trust funds he set up to pay for his grandchildren's education. He and Nell moved out of their modest Santa Monica apartment and purchased an equally modest condominium just over the hill in Encino. The condo had a small den, which Nell decorated herself. She took framed photos of all ten of his championship teams and hung them on the wall in the shape of a pyramid.

Wooden also derived a great deal of income from his basketball camps. This created yet another problem for Bartow. Even though UCLA was supposedly a more prestigious job than the one he left at Illinois, Bartow's salary was roughly the same at $33,000. At Illinois, however, Bartow was able to supplement his earnings through radio and TV shows as well as summer camps. When he got to Los Angeles, however, he discovered that there was not much of a market for him to do those shows. He started his own camp, but there was no way he was going to compete with Wooden's. "I would always get a kick out of when the secretary would take a call and say, 'Do you want your son to be in Coach Wooden's camp or Coach Bartow's camp?'" Bartow said. "The choice was pretty obvious to me."

The start of practice should have provided Bartow with a clean break from the past. Instead, it became just another occasion to celebrate the Wooden mystique as the school feted him with a combination retirement and sixty-fifth birthday party inside Pauley Pavilion. It was a bona fide Hollywood extravaganza. Bob Hope served as emcee. ("Who else would grow alfalfa in his garden so Bill Walton could have a decent lunch?") Frank Sinatra sang a few numbers. Dozens of former players, including Kareem Abdul-Jabbar, Gail Goodrich, and Lucius Allen, were on hand. The school presented Wooden with a pale blue Mercedes-Benz sedan, a gold watch with ten encrusted diamonds (representing his ten NCAA titles), and four lifetime tickets to UCLA home games. The varsity band played the fight song. The glee club sang "Back Home Again in Indiana." Mayor Tom Bradley proclaimed it John Wooden Day. When the night was over, the crowd of nearly seven thousand serenaded the guest of honor with "Happy Birthday" and "Auld Lang Syne."

Wooden was touched. "This is the most memorable evening of my athletic career," he said. "The two great loves of my life are my family and UCLA." After reminiscing about his early years working in the dusty old men's gym, Wooden called his wife to the podium. "You have always been with me since I would see you up there in the high school band holding a trumpet," he said. "Next to my family, I feel closest to my players. I am sorry if I ever hurt any of them. I never meant to. There is no player I haven't loved."

With that, Wooden whisked his bride to yet another coaching clinic, in Atlanta, followed by that cruise through the Caribbean. Bartow was relieved that Wooden would finally be out of sight for a few weeks, but that didn't mean he would soon be out of anyone's mind. "I figure this nostalgia for Coach Wooden will pass in about a year, as long as UCLA keeps winning," Bartow said. "But they love him here, don't they?"

November 11, 1975, was a big day for Gene Bartow: the first time he took the court at Pauley Pavilion for a game as UCLA's coach. His team was only playing an exhibition against a touring team from Australia, but he was still pleased when they delivered a 32-point win.

When the game ended, a reporter approached the man sitting in section 4A, fifteen rows behind the Bruins' bench, and asked him what he thought. "I don't think I left the cupboard bare," John Wooden said.

Wooden did Bartow no favors with that remark. With one turn of a phrase, Wooden solidified the perception that if UCLA won another NCAA championship, it would be because he had stocked the program with great talent. If it didn't, well, it must be because the Bruins were not well coached.

The comment also revealed just how protective Wooden was of his image. For all of his accomplishments, he was still the same insecure kid who grew up poor and lost his savings in the Depression. Wooden had spent a lifetime building up his legacy. Now that he had stopped coaching, it was important to him that he not only maintain his image but continue to burnish it.

For Bartow, there would be no easing into the job. UCLA, which entered the 1975–76 season ranked No. 2 in the AP poll, was going to open with a nationally televised game against No. 1 Indiana in St. Louis. Much of the coverage surrounding Bartow's debut centered on his stylistic similarities with Wooden. Like Wooden, Bartow was a native midwesterner who didn't drink, didn't swear, went to church, and doted on his wife. They were Clean Gene and Saint John. Below the surface, however, there were real differences. For starters, Bartow made it clear he would allow reporters in his team's locker room, so long as it was okay with the players. Bartow's practices were also looser, more fun. They often ended with dunk contests. "He makes you want to play more than Coach

Wooden did," said Gavin Smith, who was a junior guard that season. "There's more encouragement."

Many of Bartow's changes, however, did not go over so well. He told Marques Johnson from the start that he wanted him to shoot twenty to twenty-five times per game, which Johnson feared could hurt the team's spirit. Though Bartow hired Larry Farmer as an assistant to maintain a tether to the program's past, he also brought in Lee Hunt, who had worked as his assistant the previous five years in Memphis and Illinois. Bartow and Hunt put together detailed scouting reports of UCLA's opponents, which represented a cultural shift as much as a tactical one. "The scouting report was worded like this kind of Beverly Hillbillies, homespun language," Johnson said. "'This guy's tougher than a buzz saw, meaner than a junkyard dog,' I remember Gavin Smith being like, 'Buzz saw? What the fuck is that?' Lee Hunt, he was a great guy, but he had this saying, 'If you do that, it's gonna be River City every time. Just think about River City.' It was hard to embrace, put it that way."

Hunt was right about one thing: there was a buzz saw in St. Louis, only the Bruins were the ones who walked into it as the Hoosiers pummeled them, 84–64. Bartow didn't think the loss was so terrible, but he had no concept of the uproar he would face once he and his players returned home. The beat writers were fair, but the columnists were tough. Worst of all were the critical letters from readers that were published daily in the *Los Angeles Times*. Bartow read every one. They cut him to the bone.

"I didn't understand it," he said many years later. "I had been a high school coach for six years, a college coach for fourteen years, and to my knowledge I had never had a negative word written about me."

Bartow's thin-skinned reaction to the criticism made the loss to Indiana even worse. The players were already wondering whether he was up to snuff. Now they were starting to suspect that he was, in the words of Marques Johnson, "in over his head."

"Gene was naive when he took the job," said Gary Cunningham, who watched it all unfold from close range in his new job running the university's alumni association. "When the reaction from the press came, he became very intimidated. He used to call all those people 'kooks.'"

After the opening debacle, UCLA returned to its winning ways, but the vibes around the program never recovered. The Bruins won their next fifteen games, but there were several close shaves along the way. "It used to be that teams were intimidated when they played against us," said Ray Townsend, a six-foot-two sophomore guard. "Now they think we've lost our divinity." Bartow did not handle it well. After UCLA squeaked by

Stanford, 68–67, in Pauley Pavilion on January 16, he stormed into the team's locker room and ripped into his players. Then he left them to talk among themselves well past midnight.

It all took a terrible toll on the coach. He stopped sleeping and dropped fifteen pounds. Bartow's obvious agitation at how he was being treated only spurred the press to agitate him more. A local radio host named Jim Healy entertained his listeners by repeatedly playing tapes of Bartow's high-pitched squeal. At one point, Healy revealed on the air that Bartow's phone number was listed and encouraged his listeners to look it up. After a few too many instances of Bartow's wife, Ruth, picking up the phone to hear heavy breathing, the Bartows changed the number. One time before a game in Pauley, the coaches were told in the locker room that Bartow had been sent a death threat. "Coach Bartow was ashen," Farmer said. "So I said, 'Coach, do you mind if Coach Hunt and I sit next to Ducky, just in case this guy's a bad shot?' That kind of broke the tension."

Throughout all of this, Wooden remained ever-present—in the office, at the games, making speeches to every company and organization in town. Wooden even called a few UCLA games as a television commentator. He was often asked about the Bruins, and he was not shy about offering his thoughts. "I'm going to answer honestly and I don't want this to seem in any way critical. I think the program was slowed by the coaching change," Wooden said in January. "It took the new coach time to get acquainted with his players and it took the players time to get acquainted with him." Wooden added unhelpfully that before he decided to retire, he thought "this year's team would be the strongest I ever had, and that next year's would be even stronger."

Even Bartow's chief coaching rival, Bob Boyd at USC, believed that Bartow was being damaged by this. "I think Coach Wooden was wrong to say this was his best collection of athletes," Boyd said. "Why would he say that? It could only cause heat for the man."

The nadir arrived on February 21, when the Bruins were humiliated in Pauley Pavilion by Oregon, 65–45. The home fans booed as the game reached its late stages. And yet the Bruins still owned a one-game lead in the Pac-8 standings with a 9–1 record. They went on to win their final three games to clinch the title with a 13–1 record (24–3 overall). That sent them back to the NCAA tournament, where they defeated San Diego State, Pepperdine, and Arizona to advance to the 1976 national semifinals in Philadelphia.

Waiting for Bartow was Bob Knight and Indiana. The buzz saw

carved up UCLA once again, this time by a 65–51 margin. The Hoosiers went on to complete a perfect season with a win in the title game over Michigan, while UCLA defeated Rutgers in the third-place game to finish 28–4. All in all, Bartow thought his first season in Westwood had been, to borrow Wooden's favorite word, successful. Sure, there had been a few rough patches, but now that he had made it through, he hoped the fans and the media would go a little easier on him. After all, this nostalgia for Wooden couldn't last forever, could it?

Behind the scenes, Bartow was dealing with a different and growing problem. His name was Sam Gilbert.

Bartow had never heard of Gilbert before he took the job. Shortly after his arrival, he was sitting in his office one day when he received a call from Ralph Shapiro, the local lawyer who partnered with Gilbert on his representation of UCLA players, and was calling to suggest that Bartow meet with him. Over breakfast at the Holiday Inn on Wilshire Boulevard, Gilbert was blunt about his relationships with the players. "He wasn't hiding anything," Bartow said. "He inferred that he was very instrumental in helping the players when they needed help. I told him that I never had an NCAA problem and I didn't want to have an NCAA problem while I was the Bruins coach. He didn't seem too concerned about the NCAA."

When Bartow returned to the office, he asked Wooden about Gilbert. "John said, 'Gene, you knew about Sam Gilbert before you got here,'" Bartow said. "I said I had never heard of him. It just shows how naive I was."

Wooden didn't want to talk about Gilbert, so Bartow took his concerns to J. D. Morgan. Morgan gave Bartow the same reply he had given to Wooden many times. "Don't worry about Sam," he said, according to Bartow. "I'll meet with him. Sam's not breaking rules. He's just a great fan of Bruin basketball." Bartow let the matter rest, but he was not assuaged. "I felt very quickly that he was a person I didn't want to be around much," he said.

Given the increasingly public stance Gilbert had assumed over the previous decade, it was only a matter of time before the NCAA's enforcement office would decide to dig into it. Perhaps it was just a coincidence that it didn't happen until after Wooden retired, but in early 1976, an NCAA investigator finally came to Westwood. His name was Brent Clark, a twenty-three-year-old graduate of the University of Oklahoma law school who had been hired by the NCAA the previous summer. Clark was one of about a half-dozen investigators who had been added to a department that previously had had just one full-time employee. That batch of hires heralded a new era in college sports, but it would take some time before the NCAA committed the proper resources to cracking down on cheaters.

Clark flew to Los Angeles at the behest of David Berst, the NCAA's director of enforcement, who had handed him a batch of newspaper clippings about Gilbert. "The NCAA had file cabinets full of articles about coaches and athletes, most of which were mailed in by competitors," Clark said. "That's how we got our information."

When Clark called Gilbert, he was surprised that Gilbert readily agreed to speak with him. Clark then flew to Los Angeles and drove to the Hamburger Hamlet in Westwood. When Gilbert arrived, Clark was further surprised to see that Gilbert had brought with him a tall, sturdy, young black man. It turned out to be Marques Johnson. "I thought that was kind of brazen," Clark said. "I had never seen that happen before. Generally, people that instinctively think they're in trouble either won't talk to you or they want to talk to you in private. But Sam was very forthcoming. He wasn't the least bit defensive. He was proud of what he had done to be a father figure to UCLA basketball players."

Over the next hour, Gilbert spoke of how he had innocently (and legally) opened his home to give these players a sanctuary from the pressures of playing for UCLA. Clark recalled that Johnson did not say much, except to confirm that the players' relationship with Gilbert was on the up-and-up. Neither revealed that Gilbert had provided the players with gifts and favors that violated NCAA rules, but Clark was justifiably suspicious. "I had enough information from Sam to know that this was an unwholesome situation," he said. "It looked to me like there was a trail leading to extra benefits."

When Clark returned to his hotel room, he called Berst to tell him what he had learned. That's when he encountered still another surprise. "I told David that it had gone well, and I had a lot of information," Clark said. "I said, 'Do you want me to visit with the athletic director and have him arrange a meeting with Coach Wooden?' And Berst said, 'No, that's not really necessary. Just go on to your next stop and come home.' I thought that was kind of peculiar. I had gone all the way to Los Angeles for one interview. That was highly unusual."

Clark was particularly struck by the contrast between the way Berst was approaching Sam Gilbert and the fervor with which the NCAA was prosecuting Jerry Tarkanian, who was building a powerhouse at the

University of Nevada, Las Vegas in just his third season there. Whereas the NCAA had deployed a single newly hired recent law graduate to interview Gilbert, it sent a former FBI agent to Las Vegas to turn up evidence against Tarkanian. In the years since the NCAA brought the hammer down on Cal State Long Beach, Tarkanian's criticisms had become more vocal, both in public and in private. "In those days, he would call me virtually twice a week. Almost every time, he talked about UCLA," Berst said. "He did this when he was at Long Beach State. He'd say, we can barely afford a bus ticket to go to the apartments, and they're driving Rolls-Royces." From Clark's viewpoint, it was obvious the NCAA was a lot more intent on going after Tarkanian than Wooden. "They were on Tarkanian like flies on honey," Clark said. "They were all about getting Tarkanian."

Clark believed that if he had unearthed the favors Gilbert had been lavishing on UCLA players, it is quite possible the NCAA would have concluded that major violations had been committed at UCLA while Wooden had been the coach. The seriousness of the individual favors was less of a concern to him than the overall pattern of behavior, which had obviously gone on for years. "[Gilbert] would have had to demonstrate that his home was open to all UCLA students, that it wasn't just basketball players or athletes. And of course, Sam wouldn't have been able to do that," Clark said. "The NCAA would have been looking for a pattern of behavior. Furthermore, this goes to the heart of the NCAA's philosophy, which is institutional control. . . . When they find a school knew of violations over a period of time and didn't report them, that's when a school is in big trouble."

Clark filed his report on Gilbert and never conducted another interview on the case. He left the NCAA at the end of 1977. Bartow, for one, was relieved that the NCAA did not pursue the matter further. "Gene was a person who I think had concerns about what Sam Gilbert was doing," Berst said. "I don't know that he knew what Sam was doing, but he was concerned." Though he later insisted that he and Gilbert "never had cross words to my knowledge," Bartow revealed his secret fears in a letter he wrote to Berst in 1991 that made reference to the decision to pull Clark off the case. "I want to say 'thank you' for possibly saving my life," Bartow wrote. "I believe Sam Gilbert was Mafia-related and was capable of hurting people. I think, had the NCAA come in hard while I was at UCLA, they would have felt I had reported them, and I would have been in possible danger. Sam was a most unusual person, and he violated many rules knowingly."

As for Marques Johnson, his relationship with Gilbert did not last much beyond that lunch at the Hamburger Hamlet. Shortly after the 1975–76 season ended, Johnson and Richard Washington decided they wanted to turn pro. Gilbert arranged for them to fly to Denver to meet with the ABA's Denver Nuggets and their brash young coach, Larry Brown. The NBA's Detroit Pistons were also interested in Johnson, which drove up the Nuggets' offer. Johnson was ready to sign, but the deal fell apart when the Nuggets got cold feet out of concern that their drafting of an underclassman could jeopardize a possible merger between the ABA and the NBA. Washington kept his name in the draft, but Johnson decided to return to UCLA for his senior season.

Johnson was content with this outcome until later that summer, when a former UCLA player who was working for an agent told him that he might still be able go to the NBA through the league's supplemental draft. Johnson was curious, so he agreed to meet with a local attorney named Jerry Roth. When he got to Roth's office, Johnson said he wanted to get Gilbert on the phone so he could be part of the conversation.

When Gilbert heard where Johnson was, he blew his stack. "He said, 'Fuck you, Marques,'" Johnson said. "I told him, 'Hold on, I'm just calling to let you know what's going on. I haven't signed anything.' I forget the exact words, but he basically said I betrayed him and hung up."

Ten minutes later, the phone in Roth's office rang again. It was a prominent Los Angeles sportscaster calling to ask Johnson about a "rumor" that he was meeting with an agent about signing an NBA contract, which would make him ineligible to play for UCLA. Johnson told the sportscaster that the rumor was not true.

"That's the first time I kind of felt Sam really wielding his power," Johnson said. "It went above and beyond UCLA and the collegiate scene. Now all of a sudden it's into the entertainment area, where a sportscaster is calling me and saying some things. That took it to a whole different level."

That was the end of Marques Johnson's relationship with Sam Gilbert. "At that point, I was going into my senior year," he said, "and Coach Bartow didn't really care too much for him." Even so, Gilbert clearly believed that now that Wooden was no longer the coach at UCLA, he had free rein to expand his influence. This problem was going to get bigger before it got smaller.

While speaking at a clinic in Cincinnati a few weeks after the 1975–76 season ended, Wooden was asked yet again about Bartow's struggles with the media. "I guess I shouldn't be saying this, but I thought the writers were very good to him, for the most part," Wooden said. "I'll say this: It would have been much harder if he hadn't been left with a nucleus of good, extremely talented basketball players."

By now, Bartow was starting to come to terms with reality. "My job here is to preserve a tradition—to live, I guess, with the legend," he said. His second season opened with UCLA ranked No. 4 in the country. The Bruins won their first three games before losing at home to No. 7 Notre Dame, 66–63. Six days after that game, they drew just 9,016 fans against Rice, the smallest crowd that had ever seen a game in Pauley Pavilion. Still, the team played well. Aside from a 1-point loss at home to Oregon at the start of Pac-8 play, the Bruins did not lose another game until February.

The 1976–77 season also featured a visit from another NCAA investigator. This time, he wanted to meet with some of Bartow's players. However, instead of asking them about Sam Gilbert, the investigator wanted to interview two players, David Greenwood and Roy Hamilton, about their experiences being recruited by UNLV. "They were trying to pin something on Tark," Bartow said. The investigator also met with Marques Johnson, but he did not give any help. "We were instructed that whatever he asks you, just look him in the eye and say no," Johnson said. "The guy came out and asked maybe one or two questions. It wasn't a real thorough, intense probing."

Wooden had a brief health scare in early December when he was hospitalized because of a flare-up in his chronic artery condition, but he was able to have it treated without bypass surgery. Aside from that, Wooden maintained his usual posture—not out in front but not completely in the background, either. He sat in his customary seat at home games, signing autographs during time-outs for the many fans who queued up. He inked an agreement with Medalist Industries to do eight to ten clinics per year. He developed a basketball shoe for Beta Inc. He joined a speaking program that sent him to thirty-five colleges a year. And he continued to be in demand as an author. Wooden was working on a book about his Pyramid of Success as well as another that would list his Ten Commandments of basketball.

After completing his walk each morning at the UCLA track, Wooden came into the basketball office four or five times each week. He made some phone calls and caught up on his correspondence, still steadfastly answering every piece of mail with a handwritten reply. "I remember thinking that he looked funny without a tie on," Farmer said. Wooden remained available for interviews, during which he betrayed a tendency to revise history. For example, when he good-naturedly conceded to a reporter that "the officials seem much better to me as a non-coach," he added that over his entire career he was only assessed three technical fouls. This was not true. During another interview, when Wooden was advocating yet again for the installation of a shot clock, he asserted that he had ordered his players to stall during the 1971 NCAA final against Villanova because he wanted "to show how foolish stalling is by holding the ball. Guess it didn't do any good." This claim was laughable. Wooden wasn't trying to make a point that night. He was trying to win a championship.

Wooden also reluctantly agreed to lend his name to a trophy that would be awarded annually to the nation's top college player. The idea was broached to him by the board of directors of the Los Angeles Athletic Club, who conceived it as a parallel to college football's Heisman Trophy. At first, Wooden was opposed. He believed the Heisman was overcommercialized, and he was worried that there were already too many player of the year awards in college basketball (most prominently the Naismith and the Rupp). He said he wanted his award to go to a graduating senior, but the LAAC balked at that idea. They eventually compromised around the idea that the Wooden Award could go to a player from any class as long as he was in good academic standing. The LAAC also agreed to present a $2,000 scholarship each year to the winner's school.

While most people at UCLA liked having Wooden around (and wished he were still coaching), the small pocket of Bartow loyalists believed that his refusal to cede the spotlight was making life difficult for his successor. That view was expressed in a December 1976 article by Skip Bayless in the *Los Angeles Times*, which reported that "some Bartow backers wonder how he can ever establish a strong personal identity as long as Wooden remains in the public eye. The Wizard of Westwood, they believe, cherishes his image and fears it will fade if he isn't on hand to reinforce it."

Wooden rebutted this in his soft-spoken but resolute manner. "Mr. Morgan definitely wanted me to stay around, but if I felt that in a way I was being harmful I wouldn't stay around at all," he said. "If I were following someone who had done well, I would welcome having the individual around to counsel me about the players I had inherited." As for his now-infamous comment about not leaving the "cupboard bare," Wooden said, "I always said that I did not want to leave the cupboard bare for the next man. I'm sure Coach Bartow looked over the material closely before he took the job. Of course, like the Good Book says, to those whom much is given, much is expected."

Several years later, Wooden confessed that it was one of his "greatest mistakes" to share an office with Bartow those first few months. "I think he was uncomfortable with my presence," Wooden said. "Bartow never had any questions to ask about situations. I think I could have helped him if he'd come to me, not in coaching his team but in other areas."

The Bruins could never win big enough to satisfy Bartow's critics. Aside from another home loss to Notre Dame, UCLA hummed along until late February, when it lost at home to Oregon by 20 points. The Bruins were still in first place and poised to return to the NCAA tournament, but once again, the fans and the press were all over Bartow. He stopped reading the newspapers but wanted to know what was in them. "We'd be sitting at the breakfast table, and he would say, 'I don't want to touch the *L.A. Times* as long as I live. Can you read that to me?'" Johnson said. "They were tough on his kid and his dog. It just really rankled him."

UCLA rebounded from the Oregon loss to win its final three regular season games and once again capture the Pac-8 title. For all the tumult, the Bruins entered the 1977 NCAA tournament as the No. 2–ranked team in America. UCLA's first opponent in the West Regional in Pocatello, Idaho, was No. 14 Louisville, coached by Denny Crum. "This was the only time I coached there where I felt that J. D. felt pressure in this game," Bartow said. The Bruins overcame a 6-point deficit in the second half to win, 87–79, but their season ended five days later in a 1-point loss to Big Sky Conference champ Idaho State at the West Regional semifinal in Provo, Utah. It was not a happy flight back to Los Angeles. When someone looked over at Bartow staring out the window and wondered if the coach might not ask for a parachute, Chris Lippert, a sophomore forward, said, "He might jump without it."

Upon arrival back home, Bartow told reporters that he expected to hear from "the kook element." He pointed out that his 52–9 record over his first two years compared favorably to the 55–7 record Wooden had posted during his final two but added, "Yet I don't feel good for some reason, and it's sad. The program hasn't exactly come apart. I mean, I don't think I'm the worst coach in America."

From there, Bartow suffered through a horrible few weeks. Junior center Brett Vroman announced that he was transferring to UNLV because he didn't like Bartow's coaching style. During a speech in front of a group of UCLA boosters, Bartow got into a shouting match with several people who challenged him. The *Los Angeles Times* reported that it had spoken with more than twenty UCLA boosters "and found considerable dissatisfaction with Bartow's performance, both as a coach and as a recruiter."

While Bartow was being interviewed in-studio by a local radio host named Bud Furillo, he bristled constantly as fans called in to question his coaching. "Hogwash, hogwash," he said at one point. "I have better things to do than take that kind of garbage." During a commercial, Bartow took off his headset and walked out of the studio. "I told Bud off the air, 'If this is just a roast Gene Bartow deal, you don't need me sitting here,'" he said.

Other schools took note of Bartow's misery, and a few reached out to see if he would be interested in becoming their coach. Most of the offers did not appeal to him, but there was one that did. The University of Alabama, Birmingham wanted Bartow's advice about its plans to build an athletic department from scratch. To that point, the school only had club and intramural sports, but it had built a 17,500-seat arena and was primed to begin playing basketball for the 1978–79 season. At first, Alabama, Birmingham was only interested in hiring Bartow as a consultant, but the more the two sides talked, the more they considered the possibility of Bartow coming aboard as athletic director and basketball coach. The salary would be three times what Bartow was making at UCLA.

In June, Bartow asked for Morgan's permission to interview for the job. While he was accompanying Marques Johnson to New York City, where Johnson was receiving a player of the year award from *Sport* magazine, two newspapers broke the news of his conversations. That sent Bartow into another paranoid tailspin. He showed up at Johnson's hotel room late that night wearing sunglasses, a fedora pulled low, and an overcoat with the collar turned up. "He kept saying, 'The kooks are after me,'" Johnson said. "He had lost twenty-five pounds, and his stomach was chewed to pieces. His wife was unhappy. My dad told him, 'Hey, Coach, it's a foregone conclusion. It's time to get out.'"

Having suffered under the awesome task of trying to follow a living legend, Bartow was now drawn to a polar opposite circumstance—a school that literally had no athletic history. It was too good to pass up, even though J. D. Morgan made a halfhearted attempt to talk him out of it. "J. D. thought a lot of the people who were so critical were coming from the USC camp," Bartow said. "I told him they were coming from the UCLA camp, and I was going to bail out." On June 13, 1977, Bartow bade farewell to UCLA, leaving Morgan to search for a replacement.

Having been crucified in Los Angeles, Bartow was eventually canonized in Birmingham. He went on to spend eighteen years as UAB's athletic director and basketball coach, at one point taking the Blazers to seven consecutive NCAA tournaments. When he retired in 1996, the school hired his son, Murry, to succeed him and renamed its facility Bartow Arena. In his golden years, Bartow became president of the company that ran the NBA's Memphis Grizzlies, and he was named team president. When he died in January 2012 at the age of eighty-one from stomach cancer, he was celebrated not just as an excellent coach but as one of the finest gentlemen the game has known. He was Clean Gene till the very end.

Still, for all that he accomplished in the last thirty-five years of his life, Bartow's legacy was defined by those two years he spent in Westwood. He will forever be The Man Who Followed John Wooden. Those twenty-six months left many scars but no second thoughts. "I knew it would be difficult following John, but I had no idea of everything it would entail," Bartow said one year before he died. "Some people would portray this story that I was a bitter and unhappy person at UCLA, but I really wasn't. The truth is, I never regretted trying it, and I never regretted walking away."

32

The Shadow

J. D. Morgan was not about to repeat his mistake. This time, his first call went to Denny Crum. Now in his seventh year at Louisville, Crum had recently remarried, so he fit more neatly into the image that Morgan wanted to project. More important, Crum had compiled a 139–37 record and had twice been to the Final Four, as the NCAA tournament's climactic weekend was now being called.

Crum flew to Los Angeles in June 1977 to meet with Morgan. He was ready to take the job until J. D. told him the salary would be around $40,000, barely half of what Crum was making. That was a deal breaker for Crum, who lived lavishly on a 230-acre farm outside Louisville. "When you consider the cost of living, the pay out there is way below par," he said. After Crum turned him down, Morgan spoke with North Carolina's Dean Smith, but he also declined.

Having struck out twice, Morgan considered two current UCLA employees. The first was Larry Farmer, but Morgan judged that the thirty-year-old assistant was not ready. He had no such reservations about Gary Cunningham, who had spent the previous two years as UCLA's director of alumni relations. When Morgan offered Cunningham the job, Cunningham made what he later described as an "emotional decision" and accepted. If anyone could carry on the Wizard's legacy, it would be his favorite former player and assistant. "I don't consider Coach Wooden a shadow because I was a part of what was achieved at this school," Cunningham said. "I want him to feel he can drop by my office or attend practice at any time."

Cunningham reinstituted much of the Wooden culture—the discipline, the team fundamentals, even the 2-2-1 zone press. The Bruins were ranked No. 6 to start the season and played like it, winning every game except the two against their nemesis, Notre Dame, whose coach, Digger

Phelps, was justifiably enjoying his newfound supremacy. Because Cunningham was considered family, however, he didn't face any of the carping that had sliced Bartow to pieces. Mitch Chortkoff reported in the *Los Angeles Herald Examiner* that after speaking with several boosters during a road trip to the Bay Area, Cunningham was benefiting from a deep reservoir of goodwill. "He's just like Wooden," one alumnus said. "He even talks like him."

Unlike Bartow, Cunningham spoke with Wooden often. The same was true for Cunningham's newly hired assistant, Jim Harrick. A native of Charleston, West Virginia, Harrick had come to California in 1960 to try his hand at high school teaching and coaching, and he got to know Wooden and his staff while working as a director at some of Wooden's camps. Harrick was an assistant coach at Utah State when Cunningham brought him back to Los Angeles, and he immediately made himself available to drive Wooden anywhere he needed to go. Harrick loved wandering down the hall to visit with Wooden in his shabby little office. On one occasion, when Harrick was venting about the lack of effort by David Greenwood, a six-foot-nine junior who was a preseason All-American in the fall of 1977, Wooden folded his arms, noted that Greenwood was averaging around 20 points and 10 rebounds, and asked, "Well, would you rather have him or not have him?"

Harrick chuckled at the memory. "That's kind of the way he was," he said. "He'd come up with these pearls of wisdom all the time."

By the time the 1977–78 regular season ended, those two losses to Notre Dame were still the only blemishes on UCLA's record, and the Bruins had completed a perfect season in the Pac-8. Yet Cunningham felt unfulfilled. "I got tired of answering the same questions over and over," he said. "I'm a multidimensional person. I used to pray that I could sit down and talk to somebody about a book or something." Even after the Bruins blew a 13-point lead and lost to Arkansas in the West Regional semifinal of the 1978 NCAA tournament, Cunningham was praised in a way that Bartow would not have been. As a reward, he was given a $3,000 raise.

It soon dawned on Cunningham just how much the profession had changed. When Wooden's seasons were over, he would shut himself in his office, pore over his note cards, take a little vacation, and start preparing for fall practice. Cunningham didn't have that luxury. A burgeoning summertime grassroots circuit had come to dominate the recruiting world, requiring coaches to be away from home for virtually the entire off-season. "I do see a difference—a great difference—in the amount of time that has to be spent on recruiting," Cunningham said. "It's no longer something you do for a period of time. It's a 12-month job. It's a *hard* 12-month job, and the head coach is very involved with it."

Cunningham's disdain for recruiting showed as he brought in three nondescript players that fall, only one of whom, Michael Sanders, would become a contributor. Cunningham realized that his heart was not in coaching. Wooden talked him out of quitting, but Cunningham warned Morgan that he would probably have to find a new coach the following spring.

By any measure UCLA was still an elite program, but it would never be elite enough when compared to the Wooden years. When *Sports Illustrated* ranked the Bruins third in the country before the start of the 1978–79 season, the magazine noted that "its mystique is gone." No matter what the current team achieved, it would never measure up to the past. To wit, the Bruins went 23–4 during the 1978–79 season and earned a No. 1 seed in the West Regional of the NCAA tournament. (This was the first year the NCAA seeded all of its teams.) Yet a few days before their first game, *Sports Illustrated* published a lengthy article by Frank Deford revisiting UCLA's 1964 champs on their fifteenth anniversary. The shadow was long indeed.

The Bruins bowed out in the Regional final with a loss to DePaul. Two days after the season ended, Jim Harrick was hired to be the head coach at Pepperdine University. The following week, Cunningham surprised the public by announcing that he was abdicating Wooden's throne to return to his former job as vice chancellor for alumni affairs. Later that summer, he would leave UCLA altogether to be the athletic director at the Oregon College of Education, a school of 3,100 in tiny Monmouth, Oregon, where Cunningham would be surrounded by professors, go fishing whenever he wanted, and be home for dinner every night. The UCLA basketball coach used to be one of the most prestigious jobs in all of sports, but now, for the third time in four years, the office was vacant. For Cunningham, leaving was a relief. "My time at UCLA was very rewarding, but the job was not always fun," he said. "Coach Wooden's presence was everything. With the master gone, things couldn't be the same."

While the folks hired to replace him were struggling with the big assignment, Wooden was tending to the small details that filled his retirement. That included tweaking the trophy that was to be given to the annual winner of the Wooden Award. The first version included five small statuettes of men in various playing positions, but Wooden didn't like what he saw, so he asked the Los Angeles Athletic Club to come up with a new one. "They were out of balance," Wooden said of the player models. "The shooter's head should be in line with his feet, not in front. The passer was too tight in the arms. Loose, you have to be loose to play basketball." Referring to the defender who was holding his arms waist high, Wooden joked, "He couldn't stop me."

Wooden gave one of his former players, Tommy Curtis, the green light to use his name to start a youth basketball league in Los Angeles and Orange Counties. The league was supposed to go national, but it never took off. UCLA also asked Wooden's permission to lend his name to a new recreation center on campus, and Wooden agreed on the condition that the center would be available for all students to use, not just the athletes. When Wooden accepted invitations to be a guest speaker (his standard fee for a local talk was $1,700), he went out of his way to praise former Bruins who never got much attention while they played for him. "How many of you remember Pete Blackman?" he asked one night while speaking at Orange Coast College. When very few hands went up, Wooden continued, "Isn't that ironic. He's with one of the finest law firms in Los Angeles, but if you didn't play pro ball, you don't get much recognition."

Most of all, Wooden hovered as an interested (if detached) observer of the travails facing UCLA basketball. He continued to balk at assertions that his record would never be duplicated. "Before we did it, people said it couldn't be accomplished," Wooden said. "In some ways it might be easier to accomplish now because coaches have players for four years [because freshmen are eligible] and, if they're successful, they can attract others."

It may have sounded logical to Wooden, but it was hardly realistic. Nobody knew that better than J. D. Morgan. Gary Cunningham's resignation came at a bad time for him. Though he was only sixty years old, his frenetic work schedule had taken a toll on his body. Three months before Cunningham quit, Morgan had open heart surgery, and his recovery was not going well. He had been hospitalized for pneumonia in early March and was recuperating at home. Still, he made it clear that he would be in charge of finding the next basketball coach. And he knew the man he wanted.

His name was Larry Brown, the charming, tempestuous, brilliant, hard-charging, thirty-eight-year-old coach of the NBA's Denver Nuggets. (The Nuggets had moved to the NBA in 1976 when the two professional leagues merged.) Brown had been a standout guard at North Carolina from 1960 to 1963 and was a three-time ABA coach of the year. When Morgan offered Brown the UCLA job, he leapt at the chance, even though he had just signed a five-year, $980,000 contract with the Nuggets.

The chance to work for Morgan was a major reason why Brown said yes. He believed he was working for the best athletic director in history— and Morgan agreed. "It's not an accident that we've won thirty-nine championships since I've been athletic director," Morgan told Brown, referring to all of UCLA's varsity sports. Morgan convinced Brown to retain Larry Farmer as an assistant, and he told Brown that despite the low pay, he would have every chance to win. He also warned Brown about Sam Gilbert. "He told me, 'This is going to be an obstacle. I want you to be aware of it and you're going to have to deal with it,'" Brown said. "I told him I would do my best."

Brown's first exposure to Gilbert came at a function with the Bruin Hoopsters, the organization of alumni boosters who raised money in support of UCLA basketball. When Brown saw his players drinking alcohol with Gilbert and other boosters, he was appalled. "I would have never, ever thought about drinking in front of my coach," he said. Instead of confronting Gilbert, Brown tried to establish a personal connection with his players so they would not need to look outside the program for support. Brown also moved them into on-campus dormitories. Brown said he never told his players not to spend time with Gilbert, but it was clear that he did not approve. Gilbert was none too pleased. He later remarked to a reporter that he could "cut [Brown's] nuts off and he wouldn't know it until he pulled his pants down."

"It got back to me that he was not happy with what was going on," Brown said many years later. "Sam was not a nice man."

Brown faced the same problem that previous UCLA coaches, including Wooden, had faced. He had to weigh the costs of taking on Gilbert against the risk of letting him continue. So he tried to find a middle ground. "I feared this guy would tear down the program if I fought him, so I tried to tolerate him," Brown said. "I was honestly afraid [of] what he would do, and I didn't want to exclude any booster. But it got very ugly and so uncomfortable. . . . He didn't want anyone questioning what he did."

Gilbert's interferences were part of a broader culture of entitlement among UCLA's supporters that Brown found off-putting. "The first thing they say is it will help *you* if you speak at our dinner," he said a few weeks before his first game. "That isn't the way I would ask for a favor." Nor did he realize just how astronomical the cost of living was in Los Angeles. Since he could not afford to buy a home on his meager salary, Brown had to live in a 2,200-square-foot house in Brentwood that had been purchased by a group of UCLA alumni and leased to him. His wife, Barbara, took a job at a travel agency to help make ends meet.

Worst of all, before the season began, Morgan had to retire because of his failing heart. Technically, he would stay on as athletic director until the following June, but his assistant, Bob Fischer, was now calling the shots. When Morgan left, a piece of Brown's enthusiasm for the job went with him.

Brown's first season did not get off to a promising start. The Bruins dropped two straight games in mid-December, a 77–74 decision at Notre Dame and a 99–94 loss to DePaul in Pauley Pavilion. That prompted the publication of a damning *Sports Illustrated* article ("The Bruins Are in Ruins") and further embedded the narrative that nobody would ever accomplish what John Wooden had. Brown asked Wooden for advice from time to time, but they did not socialize. "I don't know if I would call him a friend," Brown said. "He was larger than life to me."

Still, Brown couldn't get enough of hearing about Wooden from Farmer and Ducky Drake. He about fell off his chair when they told him how Wooden really behaved on the bench. "As an outsider, that was the biggest shock of my life to think he would get on referees," Brown said.

UCLA hit its roughest patch in January, losing four out of five games. The main problem was that Brown was still relying on his seniors, even though the freshmen and sophomores were more talented. "I was trying to play all the seniors because I was their third coach," Brown said. "Larry Farmer said that Wooden would never do that." Not only did Brown take Farmer's advice about his rotation; he also went to Wooden to ask for help installing the high-post offense. "His main advice to me was to be myself," Brown said. "He didn't tell me to be like him. He said just value the things that I would trust and I would be all right."

From there, the season turned around in dramatic fashion. The Bruins won seven of their final nine games to finish fourth in the conference, which was now called the Pac-10 because of the additions of Arizona and Arizona State. In Wooden's era, that would have ended the season, but since the NCAA tournament had been expanded to include forty-eight teams (over Wooden's objections), the Bruins were extended an at-large bid. Having been granted the reprieve, they went on a surprising dash through the bracket. They made it all the way to the 1980 national championship game, where they lost to Louisville and Denny Crum, 59–54. Afterward, Sam Gilbert sarcastically congratulated Brown on being the first coach in UCLA history to lose an NCAA final. "I told him I was also the first coach to win five NCAA tournament games at UCLA," Brown said.

In his second season, Brown had to rebuild with a young team that featured a six-foot-five center. When the Bruins beat No. 10 Notre Dame in Pauley Pavilion in their second game, Wooden made another tone-deaf remark saying that the 1980–81 team was better than his 1964 champs. "I don't think he meant anything by it, but I remember thinking, Holy God, how can you duplicate that?" Brown said. That coincided with J. D. Morgan's death on December 16, 1980, a devastating loss for Brown personally and professionally. "J. D. was so strong that he kept people away," Brown said. "When he passed away, I sensed a lot of people were trying to get involved."

After UCLA finished third in the conference, the Bruins were again invited to the 1981 NCAA tournament. This time, however, there was no miracle run. The season ended with a 23-point drubbing at the hands of BYU in the first round. Brown was feeling the two-year itch. The financial pressures, the expectations, and Morgan's death made the job a lot less appealing. When the NBA's New Jersey Nets offered a four-year, $800,000 contract, Brown jumped at the chance to leave.

After needing just four coaches in its first fifty-six years of its existence, UCLA basketball was about to hire its fourth in six years. Many factors had conspired to lay the program low. In 1975, the NCAA set a limit on the number of the maximum allowable scholarships in men's basketball at fifteen, which prevented programs like UCLA from stockpiling talent. Then there was the rise of cable television. In the fall of 1979, an all-sports channel called Entertainment and Sports Programming Network (ESPN) was launched in central Connecticut. The network built much of its early programming around college basketball. Now that there was real money to be made from the sport, schools were investing more and more resources. For example, Oklahoma had unsuccessfully tried to lure coach John Thompson away from Georgetown with a salary of $120,000, but UCLA still believed that $50,000 was sufficient. "I know that I couldn't afford to take the UCLA job," Arkansas coach Eddie Sutton said. "The package they can offer just isn't as attractive as many others."

For someone to agree to become the coach at UCLA, he had to be motivated by something other than money. That's why it made sense when Fischer promoted Larry Farmer to be Brown's replacement. "This is day one of what I hope won't be a two-year stint," Farmer said upon taking the job. Nor did Farmer shy away from the inevitable Wooden questions. "Quite honestly, my background will be with John Wooden's. That's where my roots are," he said. "I am family."

After two years of freewheeling under Brown, Farmer was intent on restoring Wooden's disciplined ways. If anything, he took things too far. "If practice is scheduled for 2:30 and a player shows up at 2:31, he doesn't practice," Farmer said. "Coach [Wooden], he might let you practice." That was quite a jolt for the players, who had grown accustomed to dealing with Farmer in his amiable role as an assistant.

UCLA started the 1981–82 season ranked No. 2 in the country, but the Bruins quickly dropped to seventeenth after losing two of their first three games to BYU and Rutgers. That dispelled any hope that Farmer, or anyone else, for that matter, could return the program to its gloried past. As pessimism set in anew, Wooden lowered his profile. He no longer maintained an office on campus, although he still came to Westwood to do his banking and have lunch. He attended every UCLA home game and did color commentary on some of the Bruins' cable television broadcasts. When he did comment on what was going on, he continued to fight the conventional wisdom that he had ruined the UCLA job for the coaches who followed him. "Every one of those men left for better jobs more suited to their needs, not because of problems at UCLA," he said. "Pressure? I've known coaches who got out when the cupboard was bare. I didn't exactly leave the cupboard bare with Marques Johnson and Richard Washington. Give me talent and I don't give a hoot about outside pressure." Wooden also scoffed at the suggestion that his successors had been treated unfairly by the press. "I don't think any of them got much criticism," he said. "Gracious sakes alive, I had lots of awful letters written about me, too. You just show weakness if you let them get to you."

Farmer did his best to remain upbeat. "I have no fears about comparisons with Coach Wooden," he said. "The tradition doesn't scare me because I always have been a part of it." Yet at the very period when his team was facing its early-season struggles, the program was about to suffer a much bigger defeat, one that would leave a stain on the program, and the sacred Wooden legacy, for a very long time.

Unlike many former UCLA players, Larry Farmer's relationship with Sam Gilbert grew deeper after he was through playing. When Farmer's short-lived effort at a pro career went nowhere and he took a job as UCLA's graduate assistant, he lived for a while at Gilbert's house because he wasn't making much money. Gilbert later lent him rent money to live on his own. Farmer was so grateful, he gave Gilbert one of his NCAA championship rings. He did own three, after all.

Gilbert's relationships with other players varied as the years went on. A few, like Willie Naulls, remained tight. Lucius Allen also stayed in close contact because Gilbert was still helping him in ways that Wooden would not. "I felt like [Wooden] could have done a lot more to enhance players' lives after UCLA," Allen said. "He would help an athlete get a coaching job or a teaching job because for him, those things were in his view the highest you could do in life. But he would not intervene on behalf of any of his other players to get jobs the way someone like Dean Smith would. Wooden had the clout, but money was not important to him."

In a few cases, relationships with Gilbert ended bitterly. After Marques Johnson joined the Milwaukee Bucks, he received a letter from Gilbert claiming that Johnson owed him around $2,000 for "favors" Gilbert had done for him at UCLA. At first, Johnson wasn't going to pay it, but he decided to pony up and wipe the slate clean. Gilbert pulled the same move on Jamaal (formerly Keith) Wilkes. After his first year in the NBA, when he was named rookie of the year and won a league championship with the Golden State Warriors, Wilkes decided to switch agents. Shortly thereafter, Gilbert sent Wilkes's lawyer a copy of a derogatory letter that Gilbert had written about Wilkes and sent to the owner of the Warriors. "I saw a whole other take on him," Wilkes said. "As I would share my story selectively with some of the guys, I started hearing some of their experiences and how he'd keep a little black book on everything he did for you to throw it in your face when he needed to."

Few of Gilbert's relationships with former UCLA players grew more complicated than the one he had once enjoyed with Bill Walton. When Walton first joined the Portland Trail Blazers, Gilbert tried to play the role of handmaiden as much as agent. Larry Weinberg, the owner of the Blazers, recalled spotting Gilbert holding Walton's laundry outside the team's visiting locker room at the Los Angeles Forum. When Walton's situation with the Blazers grew acrimonious in his rookie season, he started castigating Gilbert in public, claiming that Gilbert was "closer to the owners than he is to the players."

Moreover, a human wedge had arisen between the two men. His name was Jack Scott, a left-wing radical who was a former athletic director at Oberlin College and the author of a controversial book called *The Athletic Revolution*. Scott had moved into Walton's home and was writing a book about Walton's first year in the NBA. One day, Scott confronted

Gilbert with a letter that Gilbert had written demanding repayment of $4,500 to a man whom Scott described in his book as a former UCLA player. (After the book was published, Scott revealed that the player was Walton.) According to Scott, Gilbert exclaimed, "Are you going to use that letter [in the book]? UCLA would have to return four NCAA championships. What I did is a total violation of NCAA rules."

When Scott's book, *Bill Walton: On the Road with the Portland Trail Blazers*, was published in June 1978, it included that conversation, that letter, and an incendiary quote from the Big Redhead. "It's hard for me to have a proper perspective on financial matters, since I've always had whatever I wanted since I enrolled at UCLA," Walton told Scott. "I hate to say anything that may hurt UCLA, but I can't be quiet when I see what the NCAA is doing to Jerry Tarkanian only because he has a reputation for giving a second chance to many black athletes other coaches have branded as troublemakers. The NCAA is working day and night trying to get Jerry, but no one from the NCAA ever questioned me during my four years at UCLA."

(Asked many years later about that quote, Walton replied, "I might have said that, I don't know, but I'm a huge Jerry Tarkanian fan.")

The publication of Scott's book caused quite a few ripples in Los Angeles, especially since it happened just four months after Brent Clark, the former NCAA investigator, had testified before the U.S. House Subcommittee on Oversight and Investigations as part of a wider probe into alleged inequities in the NCAA's enforcement actions. Under oath, Clark stated that after he delivered his memorandum on his interview with Sam Gilbert in Los Angeles, one of his superiors in the NCAA's enforcement office, Bill Hunt, "called me aside and said, 'We're just not going after the institution right now.'" Clark told the congressmen that "the conclusion that I draw is that it is an example of a school that is too big, too powerful and too well respected by the public, that the timing was not right to proceed against them." In response, Clark's former boss at the NCAA, David Berst, blasted him. "He lives in a fantasy world," Berst said. "He came up with zip [on Gilbert]."

Now that Walton had essentially corroborated what Clark said, the NCAA could no longer ignore the situation. It finally launched a full-scale investigation into Sam Gilbert's role at UCLA.

The probe lasted several years while Berst's staff interviewed dozens of current and former UCLA players, as well as Gilbert himself. They also talked to several players whom UCLA had unsuccessfully recruited. Three of those recruits—Darryl Mitchell, who went to Minnesota; Greg

Goorjian, who went to UNLV and later transferred to Loyola Mary-mount; and Michael Johnson, who also played for UNLV—told investigators that Gilbert had promised that he would provide them with cars if they chose UCLA. In the case of Goorjian, who grew up in Long Beach, the offer came during a visit to Gilbert's house with other UCLA players while Greg was on an unofficial visit. "It was a Camaro. He said, 'You give me your season tickets, and you get a car,'" Goorjian said. When NCAA investigators came to Las Vegas to interview him and Johnson, Goorjian had no intention of revealing this—until Tarkanian got hold of him. "Jerry hated everything about UCLA," Goorjian said. "He just said, 'Tell 'em everything, Greg. Bury 'em if you get a chance.' I felt very loyal to Jerry at that time, so I did what I was asked."

As the NCAA's investigation picked up steam, word spread through town. The *Los Angeles Times* caught wind and published a report in the summer of 1980 detailing suspicious car acquisitions made by four freshman players. The story was accompanied by a photograph of two sleek sports cars driven by UCLA players that were parked outside Larry Brown's house. By the time Larry Farmer got the job a year later, he and other school officials, along with Gilbert, feared the worst. "The world has become too crass," Gilbert said. "Every move I make is considered insidious, an NCAA violation by innuendo. If they only knew how many of these UCLA players we kept in school, how many problems wound up here [in his house] and not over in the school's athletic department."

The NCAA finally announced its findings on December 10, 1981. None of the violations listed in its report occurred prior to 1977. Taken individually, the violations tied to the unnamed "representative of the university's athletic interests" were relatively minor. They included arranging for two players to live in a home at reduced rent in 1978 and 1979; signing a promissory note to allow a player to buy a car; selling a player's tickets for more than face value; arranging for a recruit to have a used car at no cost; and most damning, giving a recruit "various amounts of cash for his own personal use." The UCLA coaching staff was also found to have committed minor violations such as providing recruits with local car transportation, free meals, and on one occasion, a complimentary T-shirt. However, when the totality of those incidents was coupled with academic-related violations that had recently occurred in both the football and basketball programs, the NCAA concluded that UCLA had committed the cardinal sin of losing "institutional control" over its athletics program.

The NCAA brought down the hammer. UCLA's basketball team was barred from competing in the 1982 postseason; required to vacate its performance in the 1980 NCAA tournament, which ended in the championship game; and placed on two years' probation. The NCAA also ordered that the school "disassociate one representative of its athletic interests from participating in any recruiting activities on behalf of the university in the future." Though Gilbert's name did not appear anywhere in the public report, UCLA did not bother denying that he was the offender in question. "Sam is interested in the program and the kids, but the kind of relationship he had came too close to violation in spirit, if not in fact, of NCAA rules," Chancellor Young conceded.

On the day the NCAA's decision was announced, Larry Farmer vigorously defended Gilbert. "It's a terrible thing, a slap in the face to him. I don't know how he'll take this," Farmer said. "For over a decade, I've seen him do so many good things for student-athletes. I believe to single him out is unfair." As part of the school's reaction to the penalties, Farmer had to drive out to the Palisades and reaffirm that Gilbert could no longer have players over to his house or socialize with recruits. "It broke his heart," Farmer said. "I was a loyal UCLA soldier and the head coach, and I had a conversation with him that they wanted me to have. But it was awful."

Since none of the violations detailed in the NCAA's findings had occurred when Wooden was the coach, it was easy for him to brush the matter aside. "I felt that the things the NCAA came up with were all of an inconsequential nature. I'm pleased they didn't come up with something serious," Wooden said. "To the best of my knowledge, Sam Gilbert was never involved in the recruiting of an athlete. I can't say for sure since I left, but he wasn't when I was coaching."

The notion that Gilbert's illicit activities commenced only after Wooden retired was becoming less and less credible. Since the NCAA saw no need to poke around the past, it would be up to the local press to ferret out the story. The *Los Angeles Times* sent a team of reporters to interview dozens of former players and other associates of the UCLA basketball program. The result was a multipart exposé that was published on January 31 and February 1, 1982. Headlined "Sam Gilbert and UCLA," the stories laid out in devastating detail a wide range of violations and suspicious activity that dated back to the late 1960s. After interviewing more than forty-five people, many of whom were Wooden's former players, the *Times* concluded that "the nine infractions the NCAA listed were insignificant when compared with many others dating back to the Lew Alcindor–led championship teams of the mid-1960's."

"UCLA wouldn't have won any championships without athletes," Lucius Allen told the *Times*. "And without Sam Gilbert, they wouldn't have had the athletes." Keith Erickson said that Gilbert "knows what the rules are and he thinks they're rubbish. So he does what he believes is right, with full knowledge that something was going to come down the pike like this." Allen revealed that Gilbert had paid for a girlfriend's abortion, and Marques Johnson said that Gilbert had paid his airfare to negotiate with the Denver Nuggets following the end of his junior season, a clear and major NCAA violation. When Greg Lee made the remark that "Sam Gilbert wasn't doing this for chemistry majors," he fortified the heart of the NCAA's case—namely, that Gilbert's "favors" were only available to these young men because they were athletes. That's what made them rise to the definition of extra benefits. "The gild is off the lily out there now," Brent Clark crowed to the *Times*. "They are vulnerable to past sins."

In the face of all this evidence, Wooden continued to insist that whatever violations had occurred on his watch were minor. "There's as much crookedness as you want to find," Wooden said. "There was something Abraham Lincoln said—he'd rather trust too much than distrust and be miserable all the time. Maybe I trusted too much."

Wooden later told the *New York Times* that he was not shaken by what had been reported by his hometown paper. "I might be a little disillusioned, but I'm certainly not embarrassed because I know I didn't do anything that I was ashamed of," he said. Wooden also rebutted the suggestion that the NCAA gave the program a pass while he was the coach. "That's ridiculous. We were probably checked more because when the good players came here, other people wanted to know why." Asked how he knew his program was being "checked," Wooden replied, "You know when they're checking you. They don't do it without your knowing it. They don't do it unless they were checking what somebody wanted them to look into."

Wooden's defense centered on his claim that if there were any illicit activities going on with Gilbert while he was coaching, he never orchestrated or sanctioned any of them, and therefore his hands were clean. This ignores his guilt by omission. The fact is that Wooden did nothing to stop what was happening, aside from making a few remarks to his players and then passing the matter up the food chain to J. D. Morgan. Perhaps Wooden would not have succeeded if he had confronted Gilbert directly, but he didn't try very hard. Even his greatest admirers acknowl-edged as much. "I think he knew that things were going on, and he just didn't want to know," Erickson said to the *Los Angeles Times*. Greg Lee added: "On the one hand, he was glad about [Gilbert's] presence. But whatever was happening was going to be out of sight, out of mind."

As the years passed, and as Wooden became a popular author and speaker, Sam Gilbert faded in the mind of the public. Yet Gilbert's mem-ory persisted in basketball circles through private whispers and offhand remarks. Many years later, the NCAA considered naming the champion-ship trophy after Wooden, just as the NFL had renamed its Super Bowl trophy after Vince Lombardi. The idea was quietly shelved, not because people at the NCAA didn't feel Wooden was worthy but because they were concerned that the move would dredge up too many stories about Gilbert. Better to leave that carcass buried.

Pete Newell was among the more prominent coaches who used Gil-bert to denigrate Wooden's record. Though he and Wooden developed a friendship in their later years and appeared on many panels together, Newell made no secret of his belief that Wooden's ten NCAA titles were besmirched in a way that his one championship at California was not. "None of those [UCLA] championship teams meet as teams. Because they operated differently than we did," Newell said in 1994 for an oral history project at Cal. "I think that they may say respect, but there isn't respect, because they know they did it illegally. As great as they were, and as great as those teams were, they still didn't do it within the rules."

Digger Phelps also liked to get in his jabs about Gilbert from time to time. This really ticked off the UCLA faithful, especially since Phelps was never one of their favorite people to begin with. "Digger Phelps couldn't talk about Wooden without mentioning Sam Gilbert. He's obviously an insecure and jealous guy," Kenny Heitz said. "He didn't lose to Wooden because he lacked for good players. He just couldn't fucking coach."

The ties between Gilbert and UCLA were also a major reason why Wooden had a tetchy relationship with Newell's most prestigious acolyte, Bob Knight. Whatever can be said about Knight's own egregious, bully-ing behavior, there was never any hint of impropriety around him with respect to NCAA rules—and that was certainly not the case with many of the men he coached against. Wooden and Knight were inex-tricably linked. Knight won three NCAA titles, establishing himself as the most dominant coach in his era, and he did it in Wooden's native state. As a result, Wooden was often asked about him, and he was gener-ally complimentary—up to a point. "Knight was a great fundamentalist,"

Wooden said in 2003. "Do I agree with his methods? No. But that doesn't make them wrong." Wooden hedged like this so often that Knight's wife privately referred to him as "Mr. However."

Knight and Newell extracted a modicum of revenge through their roles in the 1994 film *Blue Chips*. Newell was a consultant on the movie, and Knight played himself in it. Nick Nolte starred in the lead role as a coach whose integrity was being compromised by a rogue booster. The film was an obvious send-up of UCLA. The fictional school was called "Western University," and its colors were the same shades of blue and gold. Unlike the real-life Wooden, Nolte's character confronts the booster in a press conference, a bold stand for integrity that costs him his job. The coach's first name was Pete. Marques Johnson also worked on the movie, and he saw the obvious parallels. "Pete and Bobby Knight were there. I would overhear them talking at dinner, saying some stuff," Johnson said. "It was a definite UCLA slant showing the booster paying off kids."

Knight tried to refrain from speaking about Wooden in public. He was not one to dole out compliments if he didn't really mean them, and he was smart enough to know that he would never win a public relations war with the Wizard of Westwood. But the undercurrent was apparent in subtle ways. When Knight was asked once about a critical remark that Bill Walton had made about him, he replied, "That would have bothered me more if it came from Pete Newell." Despite Wooden's lifelong disdain for profanity, he delighted visitors by playing an audio recording of Knight's profanity-laced tirade in the Indiana locker room that was widely circulated even before the days of file sharing on the Internet. When Wooden played the R-rated tape, he laughed all the way through.

Once, while being interviewed for a video oral history for the Basketball Hall of Fame, Wooden was asked what he thought of Knight. His one-word answer: "dictator." On another occasion, during an interview with ESPN, Wooden called Knight a "great teacher" but added, "I'm afraid Bobby's going to self-destruct one of these days." (Wooden was right about that. Knight's boorishness finally got him fired from Indiana in 2000.) Then there was the time during a visit to Martinsville when Wooden was asked whether he had ever lost his temper. "I never lost control," Wooden answered, not altogether truthfully. "I never threw anything. I never threw a chair." That was an obvious reference to the infamous 1985 incident where Knight threw a chair during a game in Bloomington to protest a technical foul.

When one of Knight's players at Indiana, Calbert Cheaney, won the Wooden Award in 1993, Cheaney sent in a videotaped acceptance speech instead of attending. Knight also refused to come. The stated reason was that Indiana had classes, but that did not pass the smell test. "It is not an unknown fact that Bobby's not a big fan of John Wooden," said Earl Schulz, the former Cal guard who was a close fishing buddy of Knight's. "A big part of it is because Bobby liked Pete so much."

To be sure, Knight's and Newell's views of Wooden's culpability in the Sam Gilbert saga were not shared by many of Wooden's peers. "We're applying today's norms and standards to something back in the seventies, and I don't think that's fair," George Raveling said. "We didn't sit in judgment back then as quickly as we do today. We've evolved into a society filled with judges. In those days, I think people were more compassionate." Not surprisingly, many of Wooden's former players felt the same way. "I guarantee you there were some alumni at Indiana or Notre Dame who gave something to somebody that they don't know about, or that they did know and looked the other way," Gary Franklin said. "To me, this is just sour grapes and trying to take down a good man."

Even so, there is no denying that the specter of Sam Gilbert still hovers in the rafters of Pauley Pavilion, alongside all those championship banners. The bottom line on this aspect of Wooden's life was best summarized by Mike Littwin and Alan Greenberg, the two *Los Angeles Times* reporters who produced the groundbreaking series on Gilbert. In an editorial written under the headline "Wooden Heard No Evil, Saw No Evil," Littwin and Gilbert delivered their final verdict: "Wooden knew about Gilbert. He knew the players were close to Gilbert. He knew they looked to Gilbert for advice. Maybe he knew more. He should have known much more. If he didn't, it was only because he apparently chose not to look."

As if operating under the great man's shadow wasn't hard enough, Larry Farmer now had to coach a team with no postseason to play for, thanks to the NCAA's penalties. To his credit, the 1981–82 Bruins managed to produce a 21–6 record and finish second in the Pac-10.

During the team's final road trip, the team's best player, Darren Daye, sneaked out of the hotel past curfew. When he returned to his room, Daye found Ducky Drake sleeping in his bed. Farmer decided to make a statement and sit Daye for the entire game, which UCLA won. A few weeks later, Farmer joined Wooden on his morning walk. When he brought up that situation, Wooden agreed he wouldn't have started Daye, either. "But I would have played him," he added. The old man was less strict— and more practical—than Farmer realized.

In Farmer's second year as coach, the Bruins won the Pac-10 regular season title and secured a bid to the 1983 NCAA tournament, only to lose their opening game to unranked Utah, 67–61. The loss was redolent of Wooden's first decade and a half in Westwood, when strong regular seasons were followed by first-round postseason exits. But this was a different coach and a different time. No school was going to wait fourteen years for its coach to win a postseason game anymore. The world had Wooden to thank for that.

After a disastrous 1983–84 campaign, which ended with the Bruins missing out on the NCAA tournament (for competitive reasons) for the first time since 1966, a cloud of uncertainty lingered around Farmer, who was in the final year of his contract. UCLA had hired a new athletic director, Pete Dalis, who refused to extend Farmer's contract before the season was up. Kenny Fields, an all-conference forward, stated the obvious: "The problem we're having is John Wooden. He won too much. Now our fans can't accept anything less." Wooden, however, continued to disagree. "Maybe that was the case at first, but it shouldn't be now. I've been gone for nine years," he said. "You know, as the years go by, I can't believe how so many people have come to believe how I had it easy at UCLA. Believe me, the first seventeen years there were no cakewalk. In retrospect, those were the fun days. The pressure started after we began winning the titles."

Farmer had guided UCLA to its worst record (17–11) in twenty-four years, but Dalis believed Farmer had performed well enough to warrant a contract extension. Farmer, however, was reluctant to sign it. Dalis wanted him to jettison his assistants and replace them with two starters from the glorified 1964 championship team, Walt Hazzard and Jack Hirsch. After a long NBA career, Hazzard was now the head coach at Chapman College, and Hirsch was his unpaid assistant. Sam Gilbert called the three of them into his office in hopes of convincing Farmer to agree to Dalis's condition. He told Farmer it was the only way he could save his job.

Farmer thought he would have a day or two to mull over the decision, but when word leaked out that he had been offered an extension, Dalis hastily called for a press conference and forced his hand. Farmer told the reporters that he was happy with his new contract and committed to UCLA for the long term. He mouthed the right lyrics, but his music was off-key. Two of his friends called to say he did not look happy. "I had to tell them I really wasn't," Farmer said. "That's when I realized that it wasn't fair for me to stay at UCLA. If I really didn't want to do it, I couldn't possibly give a hundred percent."

Three days after the press conference announcing he was staying,

Farmer met with Dalis and Sam Gilbert at a local restaurant. Gilbert may have been technically disassociated from UCLA athletics, but he was still Farmer's close friend and adviser. Farmer confessed to the two men that he was having second thoughts. The following morning, he delivered his resignation letter to Dalis. Within hours, Dalis tapped Walt Hazzard to be the next head basketball coach at UCLA.

The new coach was one of the all-time UCLA greats, a direct link to a storied past that was feeling more distant by the day. The prospect of restoration was reignited—again. "UCLA Hopes It Has Another Wizard," blared the headline in the next day's *Los Angeles Times*. Hazzard said all the right things. He was excited to be the coach. He loved his alma mater. He was prepared to succeed. Most of all, he loved John Wooden and promised to implement all of Wooden's tenets, both on and off the court. He wasn't running from the shadow. He was running toward it. "I want John Wooden up in the seats," Hazzard said. "I'm not afraid of him looking over my shoulder. I think he can be a reminder, a standard, something to live up to,"

Even as he said those words, Hazzard seemed to recognize how ridiculous they sounded. "I'm not saying there's no pressure," he added with a smile. "Hey, it's tough here."

The Hardest Loss

While UCLA basketball spiraled, Wooden floated above the fray, enjoying a contented life. He no longer went into the office, but he stayed plenty busy—traveling, speaking, writing, receiving visitors. He expressed surprise that people still cared so much about what he had to say. "Perhaps one of the reasons people still want to hear me is that I was always known as a teacher as much as a coach," he said. "Of course, winning championships didn't hurt."

Immediately after his retirement, Wooden found work as a television commentator, primarily for NBC. He stopped after a few years. "This is not my cup of tea," he said. "I don't think I provided what the networks or stations wanted because I refused to be extremely critical of coaches or players." Another reason Wooden stepped away is that he could see the destructive influence television was having on the game. "I see coaches who have stopped coaching so they can become actors and get the TV cameras turned on them," he said. "Most of them have forgotten what the game and their responsibilities are all about."

Indeed, Wooden's opinions on the state of the game were widely sought. He became the sport's resident scold. After watching North Carolina win the 1982 ACC tournament championship over Virginia, Wooden chastised Dean Smith for having his team hold the ball for thirteen minutes. "I deplore a game of non-action. I can't see talented teams not playing each other," he said. Wooden believed play was too rough. ("If I want to see something like that, I'll go to a wrestling match.") The refs were too lenient. ("They let them travel, palm the ball, the amount of moving screens are ridiculous.") He opposed expanding the NCAA tournament, but if it was going to be expanded, he wanted every team in the country to be invited—just as Indiana did with its high school tournament. Wooden was pleased when a shot clock was finally added in 1986, but he remained a lone, futile crusader against the offensive rebound basket. Dating back to his days coaching UCLA, Wooden argued that if an offensive player got a rebound, he should have to pass before another shot is taken. He thought it would elevate teamwork. Wooden did acknowledge that bringing back the dunk was good for basketball, but he deplored the way it encouraged showmanship.

Such opinions should have made Wooden seem outdated, but if anything, his voice was resonating even more than when he was coaching. As his grandson, Greg Wooden, put it, "He became much more famous after he retired." In an era of ever-faster changes, Wooden provided a link to a simpler time. "Today's kids are crying out for discipline, and most of the time they're not getting it," he told the *Christian Science Monitor* in 1986. "Until we give them the proper standards to live by, we will continue to be a nation whose young people will be in and out of trouble."

Stepping away from coaching also enabled Wooden to devote more time to his basketball camps. He loved the chance to engage in pure teaching, without alumni and scoreboards determining whether he had "succeeded." He adored children—his schoolmarm's mien softened whenever one of them asked for an autograph or to take a picture—and he enjoyed sitting around for hours talking ball with the staff. "I used to tell the coaches, get your questions ready. That's all he likes to do is hold court," Jim Harrick said. "It was like getting your doctorate degree in basketball."

Many of Wooden's former players worked at the camps or visited him there. They couldn't believe how relaxed, personable, and, yes, funny the man could be. "I saw a totally different side of him," said Jim Nielsen, the former UCLA center, who spent several years as a codirector for Wooden's camps. "He loved to tease me. He'd have me out there demonstrating what foot to pivot on, where your head would be, where your balance would be. He'd always find something that wasn't right and say, 'You didn't listen to me when you were playing for me, and you won't listen to me now.'"

The activity that occupied most of Wooden's time, however, was public speaking. Much of it was unpaid, but Wooden also signed contracts with businesses that committed him to make dozens of appearances per year. He and Nell traveled all over the country as he astounded audiences with his lecture on the Pyramid of Success, which was more relevant to his audiences than it had ever been to his players. Wooden was well into his seventies, but he could deliver the speech without glancing at a single note. He quoted poetry at length (including some poems he had written) and showed off his wit. When he took the stage, he often joked, "I hope the good Lord will forgive my introducer for overpraising, and me for enjoying it so much." Wooden was a spellbinding raconteur. ("So I said to Bill, 'You're right. You don't have to get a haircut. We're gonna miss you.'") When his talk was over, he would stand around signing autographs, posing for pictures, and exchanging words with strangers who would speak of the encounter for the rest of their lives.

Wooden was flooded with countless letters as well as requests for a signed copy of the pyramid. He did his best to answer each one personally, often paying for the postage himself. Each time he dropped something in the mail, he touched another life. "He had a great coaching record, but what he created after coaching was much more than that," said Eddie Sheldrake, the point guard on Wooden's first UCLA team, who remained one of his closest friends. "He developed a following and a mystique. He became like a god."

Wooden bristled at that kind of talk, which only made him seem more impressive. It was as if all of those NCAA championships were a prologue to what Wooden was really meant to be. Or rather, what he had been all along. "I considered myself at UCLA, and prior to being there, just as a teacher. That's all a coach is. You're a teacher," he said during one talk to a group of UCLA alumni. The only difference was that his classroom had gotten a little bigger. "He stopped coaching UCLA a long time ago," Bill Walton said. "Now he just coaches the world."

As he moved into his seventies, Wooden remained in good physical shape for a man his age. He still took his daily five-mile walk around his neighborhood, reciting poetry and Biblical verses to allay his boredom. His active lifestyle and jam-packed calendar kept his body strong and his mind sharp. However, he soon had to dial back his pace for the saddest of reasons. His Nellie was falling ill, and she wasn't getting better.

The cigarettes she had smoked all her life were finally exacting their lethal toll. Among other ailments, Nell's bones were breaking down. In 1982, she went into the hospital for hip surgery, but because of her chronic emphysema, she went into cardiac arrest during the surgery. Her doctors saved her life by massaging her heart for forty-five minutes. Shortly afterward, she suffered a second heart attack and lapsed into a coma. Wooden was told that it was very likely she would never come out of it.

John sat at her bedside every day. His children and grandchildren took turns sitting with him. Bill Walton, who was now a member of the Los Angeles Clippers, came by every day that he was in town. Jim Harrick drove down frequently from Malibu. "My wife and I would just go up there and be with him," he said. "Might sit forty-five minutes without a word being said, but we'd sit there. Trust me, he never forgot stuff like that." Many other former players would drop in as well. "They never called him, never told him they were coming," one of the hospital nurses said. "They just showed up, day after day, to be with him."

Days, weeks, and eventually months went by, and still Nell slept. At one point, a minister was called in to administer last rites. John was convinced she would wake up. "Dad just never gave up hope, even when we were told that if she did come out of the coma, she wouldn't know any of us," Wooden's son, Jim, said. "It was total devotion."

He wasn't nearly as strong as he tried to appear. "I never broke down in front of my family," Wooden said. "I can remember going home some nights and—well, maybe I did there. But I was always up again for the next morning." He followed her doctors' suggestion that he talk to her. "They said that I might not see any signs, but in her subconscious she might be hearing me."

Otherwise, there wasn't much to do except sit next to her bed and squeeze her hand. Finally, ninety-three days after Nell had gone into her coma, she squeezed back.

It was a miraculous comeback, but Nell never regained her full strength. From then on, she was mostly homebound. She and John would watch her favorite soap operas for hours. He had no use for those shows, and the television was extremely loud because she was hard of hearing, but he sat with her and watched nonetheless. He still conducted a few speaking engagements, but he crafted his schedule around her needs. Once, when he was asked to make two appearances on behalf of the Wooden Award on the East Coast a few days apart, he flew back and forth to Los Angeles so he could be with her in the interim. When Nell wasn't in the hospital or at the doctor's office, she was resting at home, greeting his many visitors with her customary smile and peck on the cheek. "I remember a time when eight or nine of us went to have lunch with Coach. We went to the condo," Johnny Green said. "Nell was in a walker, but she came out to greet us all. She just wanted to see her husband's boys."

Nell eventually needed to have her gallbladder removed, and her doctors feared her body could not withstand the trauma. It did, and she recovered well enough to go with John to the 1984 Final Four in Seattle.

John's recall for names and faces was legendary, but Nell would always help him identify people whom he did not know. She was too weak to go to the games, so John pushed her wheelchair around town, allowing her to see people and go out to dinner. At one point, as he wheeled her through a hotel lobby and into an elevator, the dozens of basketball fans milling about the lobby gave them a standing ovation. "It was," John later said, "the last enjoyable thing she did."

On Christmas morning in 1984, Nell fell ill and had to be rushed to the hospital. She was diagnosed with pancreatic cancer. This time, there would be no miracle. The doctors gave Nell only a few months to live. John resumed his sad, lonely vigil. He kept a running ledger of every dose of medication, every meal, all her sleeping and eating patterns. It was as if he were charting rebounds at practice. "He kept copious notes on every single thing that was said and done," said Bill Hicks, who played for Wooden from 1959 to 1962. "I found them in his car one day, and he'd literally written down every word the doctor had said, what TV program she was watching at one o'clock, everything that happened to her. That's the way he kept his mind occupied."

On a few occasions, the doctors performed a Code Blue to bring Nell back from the brink. "I remember we'd try to look hard at the doctor's face as he came out [of her room]," the Woodens' daughter, Nan, said. "You'd try to guess at the expression he had. Your heart would pound." Nell spent most of her time sleeping. She knew her time was short. Once, when she awoke to see her husband leaning over her and weeping, she reached up and brushed his tears away.

In those final days, John was surrounded by family and friends in the daytime. When evening came, however, he preferred to be alone with her. "We respect his wishes," Nan said. "I've known a lot of married people, and I've always said what they had was rare. It's like they were one person." At one point, John was so exhausted that he fainted. He was advised to check himself into the hospital as a patient, but he refused to leave her. "She's slowly slipping, and there's nothing that can be done," he said in February 1985. "What we're trying to do is to relieve as much of her pain as possible. It's impossible to take care of all the things that are bothering her."

"When she's awake, she's very aware, and always thinking of John," Nan said. "The last few weeks, knowing she isn't getting any better, her main concern has been for Dad, my brother and myself. She hasn't thought of herself."

For most of his adult life, Wooden had done everything he could to control the events around him. He was obsessive-compulsive, hyperorganized, forever fixating on the smallest details. Here, finally, was a machine that could not be repaired. Yet he tinkered to the very end. He talked to his wife, told her how much he loved her, tried to coax her through another day. He did his best, but in the end it wasn't good enough. Nell died on the first day of spring.

It was well known that while he was coaching at UCLA, John clutched a silver cross in the palm of his hand during games. It comforted him to know that Nell was sitting in her seat, holding an identical cross in one hand and smelling salts in the other. Before he buried Nell, John took her cross and put it in his pocket. If he couldn't hold her, at least he could hold their talismans.

It was one of the countless ways in which John tried to keep Nell's memory alive. He visited her gravesite every Sunday after church. He wrote her a letter on the twenty-first of every month, because that was the date she died. He listened to the Mills Brothers. He wrote poems for her. When he endorsed checks, he signed her name along with his because "that pleases Nell." He spoke to her in his prayers. He even spread her nightgown on the bed next to him and refused to go under the covers. Her lipstick sat on the dresser. Her license plate reading "MAMA 7" stayed by the foot of the bed. The room looked as if she had just been there the day before. "It was spooky," Jack Hirsch said, "but it was part of the man and his aura."

But he was lost. Badly, badly lost. Nell was the one area of his life where Wooden violated his cardinal rule about avoiding peaks. Their love had brought him to godly heights, given him a glorious view. Without her there to prop him up, he plunged. It sent him on a long, dark walk through the valley.

His children hoped that as painful as Nell's death was at least John would benefit from not having to attend to her manifold illnesses. There would be no more trips to the doctor's office, no more long nights in hospital rooms. "We thought it would make it easier now because of all that he had gone through and all of us had gone through. It affects everybody," Jim said. Instead, Wooden sealed himself in his condo and rarely came out. He received a few visitors and still went to breakfast at Vip's, his favorite local restaurant, but for the most part, he did not want to speak to anyone. When his phone rang, he let his answering machine pick it up so he could listen for who was calling. If it wasn't someone he wanted to speak to—which was most of the time—he wouldn't pick up the phone. It got so bad that his children feared he might take his own life. "He just didn't care whether he lived or not," Jim said.

Many of his friends developed the same concern. "I honestly think he was suicidal. He was that despondent. She was just everything to him," said Betty Putnam, whose husband, Bill, was one of Wooden's first assistants at UCLA. "I tried calling, but most of the time he wouldn't answer the phone. He just didn't want to be with anybody, especially someone who would remind him of Nell."

In the eyes of his former players, Wooden's depression made him seem truly human for the first time. "He was terrible. You really couldn't get to him that first year," Hirsch said. "There's a breaking point to every man. He wasn't the man that everybody perceived him to be. I always perceived him to be a regular Joe. If he didn't go down like that, I would have been disappointed, like what kind of cold son of a bitch are you?"

In an effort to lift the fog, a group of Wooden's closest friends developed a rotation of days on which they were to call or visit. A member of his family stayed with him most every night. Nothing worked. After several months of this, Gary Cunningham decided it was time for some tough love. "You're not doing the things you taught us to do," he told Wooden. "You taught us that when you overcome adversity, you become a stronger person. You're sitting at home and feeling sorry for yourself. I know you lost one of the most important things in your life, if not the most important, but life has to go on. What kind of example are you setting for all of us who played for you and believed in what you taught?"

As Cunningham spoke, Wooden cried on the phone. "I don't know whether it did any good or not, but he needed somebody to say it," Cunningham said. "You can't call and just sympathize, sympathize, sympathize. Sometimes you have to say the truth."

Wooden later confessed that during this period, his faith wavered. This was not surprising since Nell was always the more devout of the two. She decorated their home with Christian-themed pieces, including a plaque she hung on his office wall that read, "God never closes one door without opening another."

It took six months for the new door to swing open. It happened in the fall of 1985 with the birth of Cori Nicholson, the daughter of Nan's daughter Caryn. She was Wooden's first great-grandchild. He had been speaking to a group in downtown Los Angeles the night she was born, but he still got to the hospital before the big moment came. He was so thrilled, he said he wanted to take his family out to dinner to celebrate. On his way home, however, he got into a bad car accident. John and Nan spent four hours that night while he was X-rayed at a hospital in Tarzana. He told Nan that as he saw a big truck getting ready to smack him from behind, he thought to himself, "Well, a new one came in and an old one's going out." He was recovering not only his will to live but also his sense of humor.

"The single biggest factor in his recovery was the birth of Cori," Nan said. Slowly but surely, John began to climb out of the valley. "Picture this seventy-six-year-old man down on the floor with a year-old baby, crawling around and playing with her," Caryn said. "He's an unmerciful tease. I used to get mad at him when Cori was little. He'd tease her to the point where she'd really start to whine." He would eventually have more than a dozen great-grandchildren, all of whom lived within a two hours' drive. Each time another one came into the world, he was lifted a little higher.

Wooden managed to resume something close to a normal life, although the years started to catch up with him. When he reached the age of seventy-eight, he decided to stop doing his camps. "My knees don't handle this very well anymore. I can get through an afternoon, but at night I'm in misery," he said during his final session. Looking down at the great-grandson he was bouncing on his knee, Wooden said, "Little Johnny will replace all of this for me. I don't need much more than him and the rest of my family."

He was content, but he could never be truly happy again, not without Nell. During a trip to Indiana, Wooden was being visited in his hotel room by Jim Powers, his former guard from South Bend Central High and Indiana State, when he was suddenly overcome with emotion. "He was shaving in the bathroom. Tears came to his eyes," Powers recalled. "He said, 'I really miss her. You know, she just did everything for me. I can't even pack my own bag.'" For a while, Jim Wooden hoped that his dad might remarry, but he soon realized there was no chance of that happening. Nor would Wooden entertain the idea of finding a new place to live. "I won't ever leave here, because I see her everywhere," Wooden said four years after Nell died. "I miss her as much now as I ever have. It never gets easier. There are friends who would like to see me find another woman for the companionship. I wouldn't do it. It would never work."

Staying in the home they shared allowed him to keep Nell alive. "I've had people tell me they'd go into the condo and sit on that side of the bed, and he'd get upset and say, 'You can't sit there. That's Nell's side.' And this was fifteen, eighteen years down the road," Marques Johnson said. "Maybe it's psychobabble, but I just didn't know how healthy that was for him. But at the same time, it was endearing because you understood the full extent of his devotion to her."

Wooden also refused to go back to the Final Four and the coaches' convention. There were too many memories, and besides, who would be there to remind him about names and faces? Who would be his buffer to the outside world, shooing away autograph seekers when he was too polite to do it himself? "I couldn't go without her," he said the year after she died. "I have the feeling I'll never go again." He did make brief trips to the Final Four cities to attend a dinner or event, but he never stayed for the games. "I'm having a lot of trouble getting some people to understand," Wooden said in 1988. "I attended the National Association of Basketball Coaches convention, I think it was thirty-five years in succession, always with my wife. I never went to one without her. I lost her. It would be three years ago this month. And I haven't felt like going without her. Maybe next year I'll feel different."

When he finished his morning walks, he was often in what he described as "a somber, almost melancholy mood." In those moments, he turned to poetry. One day he penned an eloquent acknowledgment that he was growing older and would soon die. It began: "*The years have left their imprint on my hands and on my face / Erect no longer is my walk, and slower is my pace . . .*" The poem became a longtime favorite. He would recite it hundreds of times.

This is how it would be for John Wooden the rest of his life. Even when he was cheerful and funny, he carried an elegiac aura. He was an elderly man who spoke freely of his own death. It made him seem even more godly, more ethereal. "I don't think I'm preoccupied with death, but I will say this: The loss of Nellie is responsible for the fact that I have no fear of death, where perhaps at one time I did," he said. "That's the only chance I'll ever have, if my sins are forgiven, to be with her. So why should I fear?"

He assured people that he would not do anything to hurry his death along, but if it wasn't a preoccupation, it was never far away from his consciousness. During a trip back home to Indiana in 1989, Wooden found himself walking through the halls of Martinsville High for the first time in ages. At one point, he stopped to peer at a photo of the Artesians' 1927 state championship team. As he touched all the young faces in the photo, he repeated, "Gone . . . gone . . . gone . . ."

Finally, his finger came to rest on his own visage. "Almost gone," he said.

The only way John Wooden would consent to return to the Final Four would be if UCLA were playing in it. Even then, it took much convincing.

It was not destined to happen under Walt Hazzard. The Bruins failed to reach the NCAA tournament in both of his first two seasons as coach, although they did win the NIT in 1985. Hazzard and Wooden made a good show of having close ties—in his first season, Hazzard even convinced Wooden to come to a practice for the first time since he retired—but behind the scenes there was very little interaction. Much of that was because Wooden was so preoccupied with taking care of Nell, but Jack Hirsch, who was Hazzard's assistant, suspected there were other reasons. "I felt a little slighted by that. He should have given us more input," Hirsch said. "You could talk to him, but he would never really talk about what you should be doing in basketball. Was he afraid of us winning, or was that just him telling us we had to do it ourselves?"

In 1987, Hazzard guided UCLA back to the NCAA tournament, but the Bruins lost to Wyoming in the second round. Six months later, the program once again found itself in hot water because of Sam Gilbert. A second NCAA investigation unearthed another batch of extra benefits, including rent payments that were made on behalf of Carl Pitts, a junior college transfer who signed for UCLA but never enrolled there. In its public report, the NCAA's Committee on Infractions noted that Gilbert was the one who alerted UCLA to his arrangement with Pitts "as if pleased with his actions." Once again, Gilbert was not identified by name; the NCAA described him as "a well-known and highly identifiable representative of the institution's athletics interests . . . who had been involved in serious violations of NCAA rules in a 1981 infractions case involving the institution." The report declared that Gilbert had "ignored repeated warnings from the university to disassociate himself from all recruiting activities." The NCAA also chastised UCLA for continuing to accept money from Gilbert and his family (especially his wife, Rose) for nonathletic purposes. As a result, the infractions committee stated that it "believes it appropriate to require the institution to sever all relations (to the limit of the university's legal authority) between the university's athletics program and this representative."

This time, it was left to Hirsch to deliver the bad news. "I had to betray Sam. I went to his office in Encino and I told him, 'You have to leave the program completely," Hirsch said. "He threatened to kill me."

Hirsch knew that the violations uncovered by the NCAA were penny ante stuff compared to what was really going on. "I'm not going to sit here and tell you I was the most honest coach in the world," he said. "If one of my players came up and said he needed a hundred bucks to take a girl out, what am I going to do, say no?" He finally decided he'd had enough when Hazzard sent him to visit LaPhonso Ellis, a six-foot-eight power forward from East St. Louis, Illinois. According to Hirsch, when he showed up at Ellis's house, he was carrying a bag full of several thousand dollars in cash. "I heard he wanted his mother to be taken care of," Hirsch said. Hirsch never showed the money to Ellis, who ended up going to Notre Dame. "I called Walt and said, 'This is so unethical and so immoral.' But we were tired of being outrecruited."

Based on the evidence it had, the NCAA only levied two minor penalties against UCLA: a public censure and the loss of two scholarships for the 1988–89 season. A few weeks later, Hazzard was given a contract extension. "I think our program has weathered the storm," he said.

The NCAA's report was not the last the world would hear of Sam Gilbert. Those long-held rumors of Mafia ties turned out to have more merit than anyone realized. On November 25, 1987, a federal grand jury in Miami indicted Gilbert and five other men on charges of racketeering and laundering some $36 million in connection with a marijuana smuggling ring dating back to 1975. Gilbert's son, Michael, was among those charged with conspiring to defraud the Internal Revenue Service. The profits from the drug sales were allegedly laundered through the Bicycle Club, a casino in Bell Gardens, California, that had recently been built by Gilbert's construction firm.

There was only one flaw in the government's case: four days before the indictment was handed down, Gilbert died in his home following a long battle with cancer and heart disease. He was seventy-four. The grand jury was unaware of this when it completed its work. So were the federal officials who went to Gilbert's Pacific Palisades home to arrest him. Whatever is said about Sam Gilbert, he must be given his due: the son of a bitch beat the system with four days to spare.

As a result of convictions handed down two and a half years after the indictment, Michael Gilbert would serve five and a half years in federal person. By that time, UCLA basketball had changed coaches yet again. Walt Hazzard was fired on March 30, 1988, after failing to reach the NCAA tournament three times in four seasons.

UCLA athletic director Pete Dalis spoke briefly with Hirsch about replacing Hazzard, but Hirsch had had enough. Once again, Dalis scoured the country for replacements. After being turned down by several prominent coaches, including North Carolina State's Jim Valvano and Larry Brown, who had just won an NCAA title at Kansas, Dalis tapped Jim Harrick, who during his nine years at Pepperdine had compiled a 167–97 record and gone to four NCAA tournaments. Because of his many years coaching high school and college ball in Southern California, Harrick proved to be a savvy recruiter. When he signed Don MacLean, a six-foot-ten All-American from nearby Simi Valley, that summer, it jump-started the program. Though the frustrations of Bruins fans mounted while Harrick's teams compiled sterling regular season records but kept flaming out in the NCAA tournament (sound familiar?), the Bruins finally broke through in 1995, returning to the Final Four for the first time since Brown had taken them there fifteen years before.

Harrick was one of many coaches who had long implored Wooden to come back to the Final Four. "I kept telling him, 'Coach, the young coaches need you. They need to see you, they need to talk to you.' But he wouldn't go." Thus, when Harrick returned from the 1995 West Regional final in Oakland, he drove straight to Wooden's condominium in Encino for an unannounced visit. When Wooden opened the door, he looked at Harrick and said, "I'm not going."

"We sat down for two hours and I just absolutely begged him to go," Harrick said. "I called him every day that week. He was as stubborn as any guy I've known. You couldn't budge him off of what his belief was."

Finally, the old man gave in. Arthur Andersen, the prominent accounting firm, hired him to speak in Seattle and sent a private plane. Wooden didn't arrive until Monday, the day of the final. When he walked into the Kingdome a few minutes before tip-off, the entire arena rose for a standing ovation. "I got cold chills seeing him there," Harrick said. "It was electric."

A few hours later, the Bruins were putting the finishing touches on an 89–78 victory over Arkansas. It would be UCLA's first NCAA title in men's basketball since Wooden's final game twenty years before. With a little over a minute remaining, Wooden got up from his seat and started making his way out of the arena. A fan shouted his congratulations. "Not to me," Wooden replied. "To the team." When the final buzzer sounded, the Bruins players celebrated wildly and jumped into each other's arms, but Wooden never saw it. It was a triumphant moment, but it belonged to someone else.

34

Andy

He lived.

At the end, this was John Wooden's greatest gift to his former players. He was finally available—truly, emotionally available—in a way that he never was when he was coaching. Back then, their interactions were limited to basketball. Now, there was no basketball. There were only moments, memories, and the lessons they shared.

To many of Wooden's players, he didn't start making sense until long after they had left his classroom. Take, for example, Keith Erickson, who played twelve years in the NBA. Toward the end of his career, Erickson was playing in a 1976 play-off game with the Phoenix Suns. The game was close, and as it entered the final minutes, a teammate threw Erickson a pass for a layup. Just as the ball arrived, Erickson reached up to swipe the hair out of his face. The ball went through his hands and sailed out of bounds.

The Suns ended up winning the game, but as Erickson replayed the sequence in his mind later that night, he couldn't believe how boneheaded he had been. "I thought to myself, that's why Coach Wooden told us to keep our hair short," he said. "Before the next game, I went out and got a haircut."

Lucius Allen experienced many such moments during his first few seasons with the Milwaukee Bucks. The team usually had other guards who were more gifted, but Allen still was able to find ways to earn playing time. "I was better equipped than other guys because I had all the fundamentals. I could shoot, I could defend. It gave me longevity," Allen said. "It took me three years to realize what a gift I got from that man. I was using the Pyramid of Success and not even realizing it."

Jack Hirsch spent a lot of time with Wooden in his later years. Since Wooden lived near Hirsch's mother, Hirsch would often ring up his coach and get together for lunch or just drop by to chat in Wooden's den. "At a certain point, you start looking at your parents as people. You start thinking your dad was right," Hirsch said. "That's what happened with every one of Wooden's players. Once you're done with the program and you've been brainwashed by one of the best minds that ever lived, you start saying and doing things that he taught you, and you don't know where those things came from."

Gene Sutherland could relate to that notion. He had never liked the way Wooden was so ultraserious all the time, so when Sutherland became a high school coach and ran his own practices, he tried keeping things loose. It backfired. "I saw the practice deteriorating," he said. "They were having fun, but they weren't learning. So I thought, I can't do that. I have to keep that distance."

Most of the Bruins arrived at these discoveries in small increments over long periods of time. That was not the case, however, with Andy Hill. In the years after he left UCLA, Hill remained bitter about the humiliations he had experienced when Wooden would insert him in the final minute into blowouts. He still got angry when he thought about all those times they butted heads over the Vietnam War protests or the way Wooden subjected Hill to a paranoid (Nixonian?) interrogation in the wake of the Bill Seibert banquet fiasco. In the early 1990s, Hill received a visit from his good buddy and former teammate Terry Schofield, who had become a successful professional basketball coach in Germany. Schofield had his own lingering discontent about Wooden, but he was struck by the level of resentment Hill harbored. "I said to Andy, 'Man, you gotta let this go.' It was ruining his life," Schofield said. "I even suggested he should write some of this stuff down because it might help him come to terms with it. I had the feeling it was sort of consuming him. He had to find another place to be."

Hill had tried his hand briefly at playing professionally in Israel, and when he returned to the States, he spent a few years coaching junior college in Southern California. But he realized that coaching was not for him, so he pivoted to the entertainment industry, where his intellect, charisma, and ambition served him well. Hill became a successful movie and television executive at Columbia Pictures Television, formed his own production company, and went on to become president of CBS Productions. For a while, he maintained ties to UCLA and went to a few games, but when those interactions proved awkward, he broke away from the program altogether. He figured he was done with UCLA—and John Wooden—for good.

Then, one day in 1998, Hill was playing golf with some buddies. As he took a practice swing in the fairway, one of his playing partners chastised him. "Stop hurrying," he said. "You're losing your balance." Hill laughed to himself. For an instant, he felt like he was back inside the symphony of a UCLA practice. When he striped his approach shot and tapped in for birdie, he had to acknowledge that something significant had just happened.

The moment set Hill to thinking. Despite falling short of his basketball ambitions, he had done extremely well for himself in the business world. He began to ponder the qualities that had enabled him to become successful and where he had gotten them from. He realized—conceded, perhaps—that he had learned most of them in John Wooden's classroom. The epiphany was exhilarating and humbling at the same time. He felt the need to share it.

The problem was, Hill had not spoken to Wooden in more than a decade. The idea of just calling him out of the blue filled him with trepidation. Still, he went for it. With his heart pounding in his chest, Hill dialed Wooden's home number. The answering machine picked up— *Please speak slowly and distinctly, and leave your name and number after the tone*—and Hill started rambling. After a few seconds, Wooden came on the line.

"Andy!" he said cheerfully. "How are you? Where are you?"

Hill made small talk and indicated that he would like to visit whenever Wooden could carve out some free time. "Now would be fine," Wooden said. The comment sent Hill's heart racing anew. He asked if he could come the next day, and Wooden agreed. When the time came, Hill climbed into his car and headed north. He had an appointment with his teacher as well as his past.

The first conversation was less awkward than Hill had expected. He was a little taken aback at how Wooden's eighty-seven years had worn him down physically, but the coach's mind was sharp and his ears were open. Hill talked to Wooden about what he had been doing since graduation. He told Wooden what had happened to him on the golf course and what it had made him realize. The teacher was pleased. "So you did learn something after all," Wooden said.

When they were through talking, Hill asked Wooden if it would be all right to call on him again. Wooden said sure. The visits continued regularly for months. Hill described it as "tippy-toeing back into a relationship. It's awkward because you're not sure it's real." But the conversations were intellectually stimulating. As an executive, Hill had long been fascinated by the subject of leadership, so he prodded Wooden at length about it.

At one point, Wooden reached into a cubbyhole and pulled out a card that listed some of his favorite leadership principles. One of them was the importance of making people who aren't in the spotlight feel appreciated. For a moment, Hill figured he should leave well enough alone. Then he reconsidered. "I thought to myself, nah, that's not fair. If we're going to have a really adult relationship, it should based on being truthful," Hill said. "So I said, 'You know, Coach. I think I have come to a point where I understand that in your heart, that's what you meant to do. But I think you need to know that you didn't really do it.'"

As Wooden digested the remark, Hill wondered if he should have just kept his mouth shut. But Wooden surprised him by saying, "If that's what you remember I'm sure you're right, and I'm sorry about that." It was a pivotal moment in their renewed relationship. "My dad was an alcoholic," Hill said. "I waited for 'I'm sorry' my whole life, and I never heard it."

Hill's creative instincts (and clever marketing skills) convinced him that the story of his experiences with Wooden, tracing the arc from frustrated college student to successful entertainment executive to middle-aged man who returned to the classroom, would make for a compelling story. He broached the idea that they should write a book together. Once again, Wooden assented. From that point on, their sessions became more interviews than conversations.

When word spread about the collaboration, some mutual friends were skeptical. "Everybody was terrified when Andy said he was going to write a book," Schofield said. "John Ecker told me that he had talked to Denny Crum, and Crum was worried that the thing was going to be an exposé. Because there is enough material there for an exposé."

Hill's book was no exposé. (Wooden would not have cooperated if it were.) But it was no free pass, either. The warm photograph of Hill and Wooden on the cover, combined with the title, *Be Quick—but Don't Hurry!*, gave the impression that it was yet another gauzy, sterilized tribute, but the story inside was more complicated, more layered. Hill wrote in detail about his discontent as a player, his conflicts with Wooden over protesting the war, even the whole Bill Seibert episode. (There was, however, no mention of Sam Gilbert. "For crying out loud, give me a break!" Hill laughed. "I was worried enough.") Hinting at that underlying discord was a smaller photo tucked into the corner of the book's cover. It shows

Hill and Wooden together cropped from a black-and-white team photo. "Look at his face in that team picture," Hill said. "He ain't smiling."

The book was published in 2001. In the ensuing months, Wooden and Hill embarked on a lengthy promotional tour. Wooden was nervous about how the public would react to these hints of imperfection. As he signed the books, he would often say to people, "Get past the first thirty pages. He ends up liking me."

Be Quick—but Don't Hurry! didn't set any records, but it sold well enough. Then again, all of Wooden's books sold well. He also published a series of inspirational books, and with the help of his most trusted coauthor, Steve Jamison, he dabbled in children's books. Wooden came up with the characters Inch (a worm) and Miles (a mouse) and set them on a course to learn the true meaning of the word "success" from their teacher, Mr. Wooden.

This was one of Wooden's more enjoyable projects because it earned him invitations to do readings at elementary schools. One day during one of these appearances, a little girl asked him if he was afraid of dying. There was a murmur of discomfort in the room until Wooden broke the tension by saying, "Now that's a rather odd question to ask of a ninety-three-year-old man." He then gave his stock answer, which is that while he wasn't doing anything to accelerate his demise, he also did not fear it, because that would be the only way he could be reunited "out yonder" with his dear Nellie. Wooden used that phrase so many times, it inspired Swen Nater to write a poem called "Yonder." Wooden loved to recite it during his talks:

Once I was afraid of dying
Terrified of ever-lying
Petrified of leaving family, home and friends.

Thoughts of absence from my dear ones
Brought a melancholy tear once,
And a dreadful fear of when life ends.

But those days are long behind me
Fear of leaving does not bind me
And departure does not hold a single care.

Peace does comfort as I ponder
A reunion in the yonder
With my dearest one who is waiting for me there.

For Andy Hill, the chance to travel with Wooden to speeches and book signings did wonders for his peace of mind. It also enabled him to see a softer version of the hard-edged man he had played for. One day as Hill was driving Wooden home, Wooden turned to him and said, "Have I ever told you how much I love you and how much I appreciate doing this book with you?" On another occasion after they had breakfast, Hill drove Wooden back to his apartment. When the doors opened, Hill extended his hand as he always did, but this time Wooden ignored it, moved toward Hill, and gave him a hug.

Even after all this time together, Wooden still had the capacity to surprise. His speaking engagements usually ended with a question-and-answer session, and though Hill got used to hearing the same questions over and over, one day someone asked a question that Hill had never heard before: What would Wooden have done if Bill Walton had refused to get that haircut? Was he really going to put him off the team? Hill perked up. He wanted to know the answer himself.

"Well," Wooden said. "Bill sure thought so."

Hill chuckled. "I thought, he's ninety-five years old," he said, "but if you're sitting at the table playing poker with John Wooden, you still don't get to see the hole card."

Even well into his nineties, Wooden managed to feed the public's insatiable demand for his stories and ideas, feeding the image that he was a wise and near-perfect man even as he expressed discomfort that people were making so much of a fuss. He coauthored books with Swen Nater and Jay Carty. He was the subject of numerous television specials and a critically acclaimed HBO documentary. There was even a doctoral thesis written about him by Marv Dunphy, who was working toward a physical education degree at BYU. Dunphy spent dozens of hours interviewing Wooden, his former players, and his former assistants. When he showed Wooden the manuscript, Wooden returned it with numerous markings that corrected spelling and punctuation errors. Dunphy was mortified that the coach had spent so much time doing that. "That's okay," Wooden told him. "I enjoyed it."

Like many compelling storytellers, especially the ones who tell stories about themselves, Wooden sometimes had trouble separating fact from fiction. For example, he frequently claimed that he called time-out in the late stages of NCAA championship games specifically so he could remind his players not to celebrate excessively. Yet not one player who was interviewed for this book could recall him ever doing that.

Wooden also repeated his false claim that he had only been called for two technical fouls in his entire career. Actually, the story varied. Sometimes it was one, sometimes it was two. Sometimes it was two except on one of them, "the official thought that I said something that somebody behind me said. But I kept it." Wooden also liked to describe himself as a lot more even-keeled than he really was. "I can say honestly, and I'm very sincere about it, the pressure didn't bother me. If you are affected by outside pressures, that's a weakness."

The story of Walton's arrest also improved over the years. During many interviews, including the ones for the HBO documentary, both Wooden and Walton described in vivid detail how Wooden had bailed Walton out of jail and then spent the whole car ride back to Westwood arguing with Walton about what he had done. It was a great story, except Wooden was actually in Portland at the time.

If anyone challenged Wooden on Sam Gilbert, he would counter by saying that he was "pleased that years after I retired, the NCAA came in and checked and found nothing that took place during my years." Not true. He also insisted that he had made himself available to talk to his players about sensitive, non-basketball issues. "I tried to ask the players anything that was personal in their family," he said. "I wanted my players definitely to know that I was very interested in them as a person, not just a basketball player." Lucius Allen shook his head when he heard that Wooden had made this claim. "It's interesting that he deluded himself into thinking he was that way, but he wasn't," Allen said. "All the humor came out after we left. When we were there, I did not like that man very much."

These were small fibs compared to the revisionist history Wooden performed on two key episodes in his life. The first concerned the 1948 NAIB tournament, where Wooden's player from Indiana State, Clarence Walker, became the first black man to participate. Because that episode occurred sixteen years before Wooden won his first title at UCLA, many people, including his closest friends, never knew about it until he started mentioning it in books and interviews. While it is clear that Wooden behaved admirably in scores of situations where he was confronted with racial injustice, and while there is no doubt that Walker had great affection for him, it is equally clear that Wooden exaggerated his role in desegregating the tournament.

For example, in an autobiography called *My Personal Best*, which was published in 2004, Wooden wrote, correctly, that Indiana State turned down an invitation to play in the tournament in 1947. He also correctly stated that when the Sycamores qualified to play the following year, the team was asked to leave Walker in Terre Haute because of the racial ban. From there, Wooden's narrative deviates from reality: "I informed the committee that the Sycamores would not attend [in 1948] and gave my reason. They offered a compromise: 'Walker can play in the games, but he must not be seen publicly with the team. He must stay in a private home away from the other players. He must not attend publicity functions with the Sycamores.' I felt this humiliation was worse than leaving Clarence behind in Terre Haute. The answer was easy: No." Wooden went on to write that he changed his mind after the NAIB rescinded its racial ban, and only then because the NAACP implored him to go.

He told this version often. "I refused because they wouldn't let him [play]. Then they broke the rule, so he could come," he said on *Charlie Rose* in 2000. In a videotaped interview for the Basketball Hall of Fame in Springfield, Massachusetts, in 2001, Wooden repeated that "we were invited again [in 1948] and I refused. Finally they said I could bring him but he couldn't stay in the hotel with us, and I refused again. I was approached by the NAACP and Clarence's parents, and they wanted me to go. He stayed with a minister and his wife in Kansas City." In 2002, Wooden told Joe Posnanski of the *Kansas City Star* that he had "refused to go to the [1948] tournament if Clarence couldn't go. He was part of the team, and that was that."

However, the official record, including Walker's diary, makes clear that while Indiana State did decline an invitation to play in the 1947 NAIB tournament, the school accepted its invitation the following year *before* the racial ban was rescinded. Moreover, the NAIB's decision to lift the ban had nothing to do with Wooden. Rather, it was because the eastern universities had protested to the U.S. Olympic Committee, which in turn threatened to take away the NAIB's invitation to the Olympic trials. Only then was the rule changed, and only then did Wooden decide to take Walker.

Then there's the yarn Wooden spun about his decision to retire. He began embellishing this story almost as soon as it happened. In the new and improved version, Wooden claimed that he had not even considered stepping down until after the Bruins had secured their overtime win over Louisville in the 1975 NCAA semifinals. He said the idea struck him like a lightning bolt in the moments after the game was over. Here's how Wooden described it in his 1997 book *Wooden: A Lifetime of Observations and Reflections on and off the Court*:

> As I headed across the court through the thousands of well-wishers and fans, I found myself for the first time ever after a game not wanting to go in and face the hundreds of lights and mikes and reporters asking the same questions over and over. I could predict what they would ask. Suddenly I dreaded the thought of doing it again. I had never experienced that before.
>
> While I was walking to the dressing room, I thought, "If this is bothering me now, after a beautiful game like this, well, it's time to get out." I just knew it at that instant.

After describing the scene where he broke the news to his players, Wooden wrote: "Nobody knew I was going to say it. My assistants didn't know. My trainer didn't know. Nellie didn't know. I didn't know it myself until just before I said it. But I knew it was time."

That was pure fiction, but Wooden stuck to this story the rest of his life. He described it the same way for the HBO documentary. In 2000, he told ESPN, "Two minutes before, I had no intention of retiring for two more years. Gary Cunningham about fainted. Mr. Morgan, my [athletic] director, spent most of the night trying to talk me out of it, but it came that quickly. No one had any idea, even my wife. There were tears of joy from her."

Wooden was a compulsive planner. The idea that he would make such a momentous decision on the spur of the moment stretched credulity past its limit. The record is clear that he had discussed his decision with J. D. Morgan, Gary Cunningham, Nell, Fred Hessler, and others at various points during the 1974–75 season. And Morgan had offered the job to Gene Bartow in February. Unlike the Clarence Walker episode at Indiana State, Wooden couldn't claim that the years had fogged his memory. He just preferred to tell a better story than the one that actually happened.

There was one last example of this pattern that was especially hurtful to the UCLA family, and that was the way Wooden whitewashed Jerry Norman from the historical record. This really bothered the men who played in that era, for they knew that without Norman, Wooden's championship dynasty might never have gotten rolling. "Jerry never got any credit. Most people don't even know who Jerry Norman is," Jack Hirsch said. "The reason nobody gives him credit was because Wooden didn't give him enough credit."

Initially, Wooden did cite Norman as the person who came up with the zone press. While interviewing with Jeff Prugh for a three-part series for the *Los Angeles Times* in 1969, Wooden acknowledged that he only implemented the press after "much prodding" from Norman. "One of my greatest strengths is the fact that I've had good assistant coaches. Jerry wasn't a 'yes man,' by any means," Wooden said. "We haggled for a long time over whether we should use the press. Frankly, I didn't think it would work. I felt that because college guards are so much better ball-handlers than high-school guards, it was difficult to believe that college teams could not handle it."

It appears that Wooden did not realize how remarkable that revelation would seem to the public, because he rarely made it again. "I spent forty hours interviewing Wooden and he never mentioned Jerry," said Tony Medley, the former *Daily Bruin* sports editor and author of *UCLA Basketball: The Real Story*. "Jerry got the players, he did most of the strategy, but he's the forgotten man. The fact that Wooden won't give him any credit upset me and upset a lot of people who know what happened."

Wooden maintained this pose for the remainder of his life. In one of his many authorized biographies, *The John Wooden Pyramid of Success*, he said, "As far as the pressing defense was concerned, if [Norman] says he suggested that, I don't remember it. I think he suggested that I stick to it." Wooden later said in his oral history for the Basketball Hall of Fame that the 2-2-1 press was solely his idea: "I decided to stick with something that had been very successful for me at Indiana State and high school. That was a pressing defense. I looked at the personnel that I had and said I'm going to stick with it."

Norman watched all of this unfold with a mixture of frustration and bemusement. He didn't read Wooden's books, but he would see interviews Wooden gave over the years where he shaded the truth. "He said a couple of things after I left where he tried to take credit for some things that he had nothing to do with, which I didn't feel was right," Norman said. "Like, I read one time where Wooden talked about recruiting, and he said we used to get five letters on every player that we would recruit. We didn't get any letters on anybody. I don't know why he'd say things like that. His main focus in life became creating and enhancing his image."

Still, Norman is not a bitter man. He made a lot of money in the world of finance and set himself up with a beautiful house in Brentwood. He

cherishes his UCLA relationships and has worked hard with Eddie Sheldrake to organize large-scale annual reunions. He insisted there were no
hard feelings, but when he called Wooden "the greatest P.R. person in
history," it did not sound like a compliment.

"I've never been critical of him in this regard," Norman said. "My
only answer is that some coaches will give credit to whoever they want to
give credit to. Some coaches are more secure and don't mind doing it,
and other coaches are less secure. That's my take on it."

No one was more upset about all of this than Sheldrake. Jerry Norman was like a brother to him. Sheldrake tried to address the matter
with Wooden, at one point suggesting that Wooden write a book specifically to thank all the people who helped him—Norman most of all. Wooden
balked. Sheldrake and Wooden were such good friends that Wooden
asked him to be a pallbearer at Nell's funeral, but Sheldrake's crusade on
behalf of Norman damaged his relationship with Wooden's children.
In advance of a ceremony at UCLA to recognize one of their championship teams, Sheldrake wrote a tribute to Norman that included a list of
all the players Norman recruited. Sheldrake wanted it to be included in
the UCLA program, but he said that idea was scuttled because Nan
Wooden objected.

"I was always hurt because I was there when Jerry really turned the
thing around. I was hurt that Jerry couldn't get more of the credit, because
it was deserved," Sheldrake said. "Wooden didn't give much credit to
Jerry in his books. That part I can never really understand."

The lingering rift was a sore spot with a lot of their mutual friends.
"There was adversity between the two of them, but I'm not going to touch
that. I know too much about it," Gary Cunningham said. Fred Slaughter
added, "Jerry Norman has not gotten the credit he deserves. He recruited
me. He's the one who brought the human, caring side of things for me."
Freddie Goss agreed that "Jerry Norman has never been given the credit
he deserves," but he believed that Wooden would have promoted Norman more if Norman had beseeched him. "Jerry never asked," Goss said.
"Maybe Jerry felt like he shouldn't have to ask."

Asked in 2009 whether he and Norman parted on good terms, Wooden
acknowledged, "Yes and no. I don't know how to answer it, really. . . . All
I know is that his wife never thought that Jerry got enough credit in the
days when he was an assistant. Maybe he didn't, I don't know. It's hard
to say." Yet when it came to writing the story of his own life, the English
teacher was never at a loss for words. In Wooden's final book, *A Game
Plan for Life: The Power of Mentoring*, he described an assistant coach

who sounded a lot like Jerry Norman. But in describing himself, Wooden once again strayed into fiction. "One assistant suggested that we bring back a zone press," he wrote. "We'd used it a few years previously but had phased it out. When we resurrected it at the assistant's suggestion, it ended up taking us to our first National Championship, in 1964. I really tried to make a point of praising him to the press after that event because he'd had the courage to suggest something outside the status quo."

No one who knew John Wooden well would claim that last part was true, but in the end that didn't matter. The man owned ten NCAA championships, and history is written by the winners.

The fact that Wooden lived so long was of particular benefit to the players who left UCLA feeling ambivalent, even bitter, about their time there. Fortunately for them, even into his nineties Wooden remained alive, sharp, and always just a phone call away. He was generous with his time because he loved hearing from them. He never made them feel that they were imposing. "If I was in the area, I'd call him from a pay phone and ask if I could come by," Johnny Green said. "He'd say, 'You'd be in trouble if you didn't.'"

Don Saffer was one of the many who traveled a circuitous route back to Wooden's classroom. He had quit the team toward the end of the 1968–69 season ("I did not try to talk him out of it," Wooden told the press), so Saffer was understandably nervous when he approached Wooden to apologize at a reunion ten years later. "I didn't make a fuss about it. I just wanted to be part of the group," he said. Saffer had recently become the headmaster of a private boarding school, so he and Wooden were able to share their common experience as educators. After that awkward first meeting, Saffer and Wooden corresponded regularly. "It was a godsend that I patched it up with him long before he died," Saffer said.

Gary Franklin also left UCLA with hurt feelings because of his lack of playing time. "I had a feeling of resentment over that, like I wasn't really part of the team," he said. That is, until the day Franklin picked up one of Wooden's books and found his name listed as one of the players who Wooden said was more valuable than the public understood. At Wooden's ninetieth birthday celebration in 2000, when UCLA dedicated the floor in Pauley Pavilion in his and Nell's honor, Franklin chatted with Wooden and decided he wanted a more meaningful relationship. From that point forward, he called Wooden, had breakfast with him, went to church with Wooden and Kenny Washington, and visited the condo often. "I can't tell you how thankful I am that he lived so long," Franklin said. "I tried to make up for lost time."

There was nothing ambivalent about Neville Saner's attitude toward Wooden. He flat-out didn't like the man. Like Andy Hill, Gary Franklin, and so many others, Saner was disappointed that he didn't play more, but what hurt him most was the way Wooden allowed him to leave UCLA without so much as a good-bye. "All he had to do was invite me into his office after the season was over, say a few nice words and wish me well, and I would have gone off with a whole different attitude," Saner said. "That was an enigma to me. He liked to finish practices on a positive note. Why not finish your career that way?"

Right before he graduated, Saner offered an unvarnished opinion of Wooden to Jeff Prugh of the *Los Angeles Times*. "He's just a tough, cold guy, and he should just come out and admit that he is," Saner said. After graduation, Saner asked Jerry Norman to help him find work as a teacher and coach. When Norman suggested he go to Wooden for help, Saner said he didn't feel comfortable. "I'm sure he would have helped me, but I never asked him," he said.

Saner applied for a position at Poway High School near San Diego. During the job interview, the principal told Saner that he had spoken to Wooden and the coach had given Saner a glowing recommendation. As Saner started coaching, he implemented many of Wooden's philosophies and won multiple state championships his first few years. His team was on its way to winning another title during the 1985–86 season when he received a handwritten letter from his former coach. In the letter, Wooden congratulated Saner on his success, then struck a balance by reminding Saner of Cervantes's admonition that "The road is better than the inn."

Saner wrote Wooden back to thank him. The exchange sparked a lengthy friendship, with the same rotation of phone calls, letters, meals, and talks in Wooden's den that numerous former players enjoyed. "No matter what happened at UCLA, you were one of his boys, and you were always welcome," Saner said.

To be sure, many of Wooden's former players never developed a close relationship with him in their later years. Some were busy or lived too far away. Others felt resentment that could not be overcome. The most conspicuous of those was Edgar Lacey. After quitting school in the dispute following the Game of the Century, Lacey never reentered the UCLA family, never showed up at a reunion or championship celebration, never reached out to Wooden to try to mend the fence. Once in a while, Lucius Allen would see if he could bring his friend back into the fold, but it never worked. "Edgar felt that Coach Wooden ruined his life," Allen said. "Coach would never call Edgar. I don't think it was in his personality. He was a loving man, but he had an ego."

Wooden may have felt bad about what happened with Lacey, but he remained unapologetic. "Edgar was a nice person, but I wouldn't change one thing of the way that went," Wooden said less than a year before he died. "You don't know in advance how things will turn out, but you do what you think is right. If that didn't turn out to be right, it was not wrong. It was still right."

The most unfortunate part is the way Lacey's hurt feelings prevented him from having meaningful relationships with his former teammates. When he died in the spring of 2011, most of the other Bruins didn't even know where he had been living. (Sacramento, it turned out.) Keith Erickson read in the newspaper that Lacey's funeral was going to be held in Downey, California, so he went to the service, as much out of curiosity as anything else. "He was always very secretive to me. I didn't know much about Edgar," Erickson said. "I didn't even know if he had a wife or children." Mike Warren and Don Saffer were at the funeral, too, but there were not many others. As Erickson listened to the service, he grew melancholy knowing that Lacey was going to his grave without having repaired the breach with Wooden. "The whole situation was very sad," Erickson said.

Andy Hill's good friend and former teammate Terry Schofield read *Be Quick—but Don't Hurry!* with great interest, but he had a more complicated time processing his feelings than Hill did. Schofield became a professional coach in Germany and adopted some of Wooden's teachings, but when it came to dealing with his players, he was determined to be different. "I'd look down at the guys on the bench, and I'd see myself," Schofield said. "I tried to make it fun, because when I was at UCLA, that word was never mentioned. There were much greater things at stake than fun."

Schofield was pleasantly surprised that Wooden wrote some complimentary things about him in his books, but aside from a brief period as Wooden's graduate assistant, he had very little contact with the coach over the years. Then, one day he received an envelope from Wooden out of the blue. It was a signed photograph of the 1971 championship team.

Wooden wrote: "For Terry—with best wishes and thanks for helping us to excel on the court. You will always be one of 'my boys.' John Wooden." The gesture led to a rapprochement of sorts. Schofield called Wooden every year on his birthday, and he tried to see Wooden when he was in the States. When he introduced Wooden to his wife at the reunion celebrating the coach's ninetieth birthday, Wooden said, "Terry, you always had the most attractive women."

Still, while Schofield may have made his peace with Wooden personally, he did not apply that word to his entire UCLA experience. "Peace? I don't know. I've just learned to live with it. Some things still bother me," he said. "I don't think I'd say I've let it go. What happens is you learn to live with stuff."

A happier ending awaited John Ecker, who had brought Schofield to play professionally in Germany, and like Schofield, had stayed there to coach and marry a German woman. When Andy Hill held a fiftieth birthday party for himself in 2000 with Wooden as the guest of honor, Ecker surprised Hill by flying into town. When Ecker arrived at Hill's house for the party, he found Wooden sitting in the corner of the living room, yukking it up with the guys. Hill guided Ecker over to him. It was the first time Ecker had seen Wooden in nearly thirty years. Wooden surprised him by standing up and giving him a hug. "It really moved me," Ecker said. It was Wooden, not Ecker, who brought up the past. "Andy tells me you think I didn't like you. Now why would you say such a thing?" he asked.

Ecker stammered his way through an answer, but he quickly realized how wrong he had been. "He showed me how concerned he was. I really felt that he regretted some things and realized he had made some mistakes," Ecker said. "We sat and talked all evening. He was actually very funny, just poking fun at everyone."

As was the case with so many of Wooden's former players, that first encounter sparked a beautiful friendship. Ecker introduced Wooden to his family. He called from Germany every few months. When he came to California, he rang up Wooden and met him for breakfast or visited him in his den. "He was always a joy to talk to. He was very lucid and very sharp. Always made jokes, those little pin pricks," Ecker said. "I really came to not just respect him but to love him in a sense, too."

Yet it was not until Ecker's son, Danny, read *Be Quick—but Don't Hurry!* that Ecker experienced his own moment of clarity. Danny started asking his dad about his playing days at UCLA, a subject they had barely discussed before. Danny said that he recognized many of the principles that Hill described in the book because he had heard them all from his dad. That had never occurred to Ecker, but the more he thought about it, the more Ecker realized Danny was right.

He had learned something after all.

35

Yonder

The years had left their imprint on all of them. They were men now, fathers and grandfathers themselves, yet still they wrote and called and dropped by the condo. In doing so, his former players didn't just keep him happy; they kept him alive. At a time in life when so many people become lonely and depressed, John Wooden remained a man in full. "Hardly a day goes by that I don't get a call or a letter from someone who was under my supervision in the past . . . some even going back when I taught in high school," Wooden said. "They become almost like your children. Next to your own flesh and blood, you get very close to them. Their joys are your joys, their sorrows are your sorrows, and that goes on forever."

Lucius Allen went more than ten years without speaking to his college coach. Allen had nothing against the man, but he washed his hands of the UCLA basketball program after the school fired his good friend Walt Hazzard. Then one day, Mike Warren suggested that Allen go with him to meet Wooden for breakfast. Allen agreed. Though he and Wooden never spoke about the marijuana arrests that had led to Allen's premature departure from UCLA, Allen felt compelled to apologize for giving the coach so many gray hairs. "Oh, you were no trouble at all," Wooden assured him. "Now Bill Walton on the other hand . . ."

Allen never let the relationship wither again. "I went out there once a month for breakfast. There was always somebody else showing up," Allen said. "We took plane trips together. We were buddies again. Even then he could ask me questions that made the hair stand up on my head. He still had that effect on me."

As Henry Bibby's coaching career blossomed—he would eventually become the head coach at USC, of all places—he leaned on Wooden often, coming by his condo with a pad and pen so he could pepper his old coach with questions. Bibby once rang up Wooden while he was driving through central Indiana. For the next few hours, Bibby kept calling back to ask for suggestions on what he should see in Martinsville—Wooden's high school, his childhood home, and especially his favorite candy store. "He told me where his parents were buried. I saw their names on the grave," Bibby said. "That's the thing about him. He had time for you. It was like this guy was so big and he was doing all these things, but he still had time for you. I never heard anybody say you had to get an appointment to go to his house. You had an open invitation. 'Hey Coach, I'm coming over.' You'd ring the doorbell, and he would come to the door."

Wooden remained an expert needler. When Larry Farmer joined a group of players for breakfast with Wooden one morning, Wooden glanced down at Farmer's bright-colored shoes and cracked, "They used to wear those in the fifties." When Marques Johnson flew on a private jet with Wooden and some other former players to New York City for an awards banquet, they started reminiscing about the 1975 NCAA final. When Wooden told Johnson he played twenty-seven minutes in that game, Johnson said he was sure he had played a lot less. "The way you played," Wooden said, "you weren't the only one who didn't realize you were out there." The whole plane burst out laughing. "It became a lot easier to talk with him, to joke with him, just to be around him," Johnson said. "It was kind of like, take him off the cross, we need the wood. Appreciate him for what he was—a great coach, a great person, but not a god."

Bill Walton was Wooden's favorite foil. When he was in his late twenties, Walton overcame his stutter so well that he went into broadcasting after he was through playing. It was the ultimate irony that he would develop a reputation for rambling interminably. Walton was the foremost Wooden devotee, calling his former coach nearly every day, including when Walton was out of the country—although Wooden liked to quip that he didn't speak with Walton so much as listen to him. "He was just a wonderful person who was happy," Walton said. "He was very, very much like Jerry Garcia in that he could create beauty in a sad, hard, cruel world."

Wooden was still their teacher. He ministered Marques Johnson through his grief after his son drowned, and he counseled Sidney Wicks after Wicks was involved in a severe car accident that killed a close friend. When Walt Hazzard suffered a debilitating stroke in 1996, Wooden came to the hospital and assured Hazzard's wife that Walter was going to be okay. (Wooden still called him Walter.) Shortly after Kareem Abdul-Jabbar's mother died in 1997, he told Wooden about the anger he still felt toward his former high school coach, Jack Donohue, from the time when Donohue used that racial epithet in a clumsy effort to motivate him. "Let me ask you something," Wooden said. "Have you ever made a mistake?" Abdul-Jabbar laughed and said, "More than I can count." That exchange prompted Abdul-Jabbar to reconcile with Donohue before he died.

When Larry Farmer was at the 2003 Final Four in New Orleans, he ran into Nan Wooden in a hotel lobby and asked if he could bring his family to Coach Wooden's room to say hello. When they got there, Farmer could tell that Wooden had just woken up from a nap. No matter. He sat next to Farmer's son, plopped Farmer's daughter on his lap, and said, "Did your dad ever tell you he was a good shooter? Ah, don't ever buy that." Wooden spent the next half hour teasing them, reciting poetry, asking about their lives. "He treated them like they were his kids," Farmer said, choking up at the memory. "It was then I knew how much he really loved me. He could have told me in a hundred different ways, but what he did for my kids that day, that was it."

In the fall of 2007, Andy Hill threw a party in honor of Wooden's ninety-seventh birthday. Some fifty former players showed up, including Abdul-Jabbar, who looked more relaxed that night than anyone had ever seen him. Wooden was the life of the party. "It was like Coach shape-shifted that night. He was on fire," Hill said. "I think everybody was sufficiently aware that the dude's ninety-seven. This could be the last time."

Mike Lynn, the power forward on those Lew Alcindor championship teams, had flown in from his home in Vermont to attend that party. Lynn had been raised in a religious household—his grandfather was a Presbyterian minister—but he lost his enthusiasm when he discovered Charles Darwin in the seventh grade. Yet when Kenny Washington asked Lynn if he wanted to join him and Wooden at church the following morning, Lynn said yes. "It just seemed like something I couldn't pass up," he said. "Maybe it was me trying to say to him that I was willing to meet him at least halfway."

Going to church with Wooden was Lynn's way of acknowledging what all the others could now see. Their coach had stood the test of time, for a long time, living out the credo that had been posted on his office wall: *It's what you learn after you know it all that counts.* After all these years, he was still a student of life, still improving a little bit each day. A man of actions, not statements. "I remember sitting in his den thinking that he always said the most important things in life were faith and family," Sidney Wicks said. "So I'm looking around and I'm thinking, it's all here. Not much to the place, pretty small. He lived simply. He was living what he always said."

When his former players weren't around, Wooden relied on the kindness, and company, of strangers. Doug Erickson was one of them. After graduating from San Jose State University in 1992, Erickson landed an administrative job in the UCLA basketball office. He was naturally curious about Wooden, so he wrote Wooden a letter introducing himself and asking if they could get together sometime. Two days later, Wooden called and invited Erickson over. "It just didn't seem like he was that busy," Erickson said. "He had more time back then."

Wooden told Erickson he could come back anytime. He did, often. When Steve Lavin succeeded Jim Harrick as UCLA's head coach in 1996, he kept Erickson on staff and asked him to check in on Wooden several days a week. Wooden became so comfortable around Erickson that he thought nothing of opening his door to him while wearing his Mickey Mouse pajamas. Erickson estimated that over the years, he brought some five hundred people to Wooden's condo. "He had more energy than we did," Erickson said. "We'd keep him up until ten at night. He got stronger as the night went on."

In all their time together, Wooden got cross with Erickson just once. They were watching *Monday Night Football* when Wooden made some predictions about what was going to happen next. "Coach," Erickson said, "if you're right, you really will be the Wizard of Westwood."

"Don't ever call me that," Wooden snapped. "That's a moniker I've never liked."

Erickson was crushed. "I went to the bathroom so I could get myself together," he said. "I was like, man, Coach just lit me up."

Sometimes, the strangers who spent time with Wooden were just that—strangers. Jeff Weiss was among the countless outsiders who earned an audience with Wooden through sheer persistence. A basketball coach at Lawrence Woodmere Academy on Long Island, Weiss read several of Wooden's books, and in 2004, he wrote a letter to the UCLA athletics office asking if someone could forward his information to Wooden. It took several more letters and phone calls, but Weiss finally received a handwritten note from Wooden that included his phone number and an invitation to visit.

Over the next few weeks, Weiss dialed the number several times. Each time, he left a message on Wooden's answering machine. (He kept assuring Wooden that he wasn't some psycho stalker.) Finally, as Weiss was leaving yet another message, Wooden picked up. He asked Weiss when he wanted to visit. "As soon as you tell me I can," Weiss replied. They made an appointment for the following week.

In advance of the visit, Weiss assembled a notebook filled with information and photographs from Wooden's early days, including some of the high school teams he coached and played for. When he showed up at Wooden's condominium, he was surprised to find Wooden alone. It seemed risky for a ninety-six-year-old man to invite a stranger into his apartment. "I couldn't believe he was allowing me to do this," Weiss said. "I thought it was insane."

Wooden invited Weiss to sit with him in his den. After about a half hour of small talk, Weiss pulled out the notebook. "He loved it," Weiss said. "He knew everything about every guy in the pictures. For the next three or four hours, he would point to a guy and say, 'Oh, I remember this guy. He was a great player. He couldn't go left, couldn't rebound.' His memory was off the charts." After about five hours, Weiss suggested that he should go, but Wooden invited him to stay for dinner so they could watch a Yankees–Red Sox game together. After he got home, Weiss sent Wooden a thank-you note and a picture for him to sign, along with a self-addressed stamped envelope. Wooden obliged the request and dropped it in the mail.

For Jeff Weiss, it was the experience of a lifetime. For John Wooden, it was another day in the life. He was so gentlemanly, so avuncular, that people whom he had never met felt as if they knew him. Once, when Wooden was sitting in his usual seat at a UCLA game, his granddaughter Cathleen got up to go to the bathroom. She returned to see a man sitting in her seat and talking to Wooden, so she shifted one seat down. Wooden chatted with the man for the rest of the game. Afterward, Cathleen asked Wooden who the man was. He said he had no idea.

Wooden prided himself on never turning down a request for an autograph. "I wouldn't say he loved it," Erickson said. "He just didn't want to disappoint anyone." That was especially problematic at UCLA games, where Wooden signed and posed for pictures during time-outs and halftimes. "I won't say that I'm not flattered by things of that sort, but I'm not comfortable with it," Wooden said. Nan was his primary protector, just as her mother had been. If they were eating somewhere and a stranger approached by saying, "I'm sorry to bother you," Nan, like Nell, would interject with a sharp, "Then don't." When Nan learned that Erickson was bringing Wooden mail by the cartload so he could sign and return each item personally, she put a stop to it. "You can't believe all the people who want to make money off his name," she said. "I get so mad at all the mail he gets. He gets big boxes of basketballs people expect him to sign. I can't believe people are that stupid."

The network of UCLA employees that supported Wooden stretched well beyond the former players. There was Marc Dellins, the sports information director who once interviewed Wooden alone in his hotel room during the 1975 Final Four, back when Dellins was a student reporter at the *Daily Bruin*. One day in 2009, Dellins called Wooden because he had heard a rumor that Wooden had died. "Not yet, but I'm well on my way," Wooden said. Dellins called back one more time just to make sure.

Dellins's longtime assistant, Bill Bennett, was the primary point of contact for Wooden in the UCLA athletics office, the designated keeper of the flame. Bennett was a gentle soul who was renowned for wearing canvas high-tops with his suits. He and Wooden shared the same birthday. Wooden was smitten with Bennett's wife, Joanne.

Then there was Tony Spino, the mercurial, emotional, opinionated, hardheaded athletics trainer who became as devoted to the old man as any of his blood kin. Spino first got to know Wooden when he was a trainer for the UCLA freshman teams in the 1970s. After Wooden retired, Spino worked briefly for the NBA's Milwaukee Bucks before returning to Westwood in 1981. For years, Spino would drive to Wooden's condo a few mornings a week to massage him and help him exercise before taking him to breakfast. Wooden once compared Spino to Sam Gilbert because "you can't tell him anything. He's going to do what he wants to do." The two of them had a wonderful rapport. "Tony's a New York Italian. They enjoyed going back and forth at each other," Doug Erickson said. "After being together so long, Tony was not afraid to tell him what he needed to do."

One day in February 2008, Spino opened Wooden's front door and found the coach facedown on the hallway floor, shivering from shock. He had fallen at around 10:00 p.m. the night before and had broken his left wrist and collarbone. Because no one was staying with him that night, and because he was too stubborn to wear a wireless device that could be activated in just such an emergency, Wooden had no choice but to lie on the floor all night long and wait for Spino to show up. Asked later how he spent those eight hours, Wooden replied, "Sometimes I'm crying. Sometimes I'm laughing."

Spino scooped Wooden into his arms and carried him to bed. He called for an ambulance, wrapped Wooden in a blanket, and hugged him in an effort to warm him up. After Wooden finished recuperating, his family and close friends devised a schedule so that someone would be sleeping in the condominium every night. Wooden fought them at first, but for once, he had to let his stubbornness give way.

After that incident, UCLA athletic director Dan Guerrero assigned Spino to be Wooden's full-time caretaker. Spino spent more time with the coach than with his own wife and children. He put a baby monitor beside Wooden's bed, talked to Wooden as he fell asleep, and then slept in a separate bedroom.

Ironically, with all of these men bidding for Wooden's time, the person with whom Wooden became closest was a female gymnastics coach. Her name was Valorie Kondos Field, a 1987 UCLA graduate and former ballet dancer who took over UCLA's gymnastics program in 1991. Valorie grew curious about Wooden after marrying Bob Field, an associate athletic director who had gotten to know Wooden while Bob was a UCLA assistant football coach. She suggested that they invite Wooden over for dinner, but Bob didn't want to because he feared too many people were already bugging him. "The worst he can do is say no," she said. Wooden accepted the invitation, and from that day forward, he dined at the Fields' house several times a year.

Bob and Valorie regularly drove Wooden and Nan to UCLA football games. If they had trouble finding a parking space, Valorie would drive up to a security guard, tell Wooden to sit up straight and smile, and roll down the window so the guard could see who her passenger was. "I could have parked on the field if I wanted to," she said. Valorie frequently brought her gymnasts to visit Wooden at his condo. "He just loved being with all those pretty young girls. They would sit around him and ask questions and he would tell stories," Keith Erickson said. "Valorie was his favorite person on the entire campus."

Wooden, in turn, became a regular at UCLA gymnastics meets. He rarely missed a competition, although he did come close one time when Nan and Kenny Washington showed up ten minutes late to pick him up. He was ninety-five years old, but he was tired of waiting. So he drove himself. Nan was so furious that when she and Washington arrived, she walked right by her dad in a huff and sat on the other side of the bleachers. When it was over, she huddled up with the Fields to figure out how Wooden was getting back. "Never mind," he told them. "I got myself here, I can get myself home."

Valorie and Wooden became so close that she was occasionally invited to take part in forums alongside the likes of Keith Erickson, Rafer Johnson, and Andy Hill. She loved hearing stories about how tough and cold he used to be. "I knew him as the sweet, kind, older man with the twinkling eyes. I didn't know him as a feisty coach," she said. "Mike Warren said to me, 'You've experienced a side of him we rarely got to see.'"

Their more poignant interactions occurred when they were alone. On a day when the UCLA football team was playing on the road, Valorie invited herself over to watch the game with Wooden at his place. During halftime, he looked at her and said, "You know, Nellie and I made love every day." Valorie said, "I stopped and thought, am I gonna get the sex talk from Coach Wooden?" Wooden explained that not a day went by when he and Nell didn't kiss, or hold hands, or say they loved each other. "That was his definition of making love," Valorie said. "I told him I understand." Later, Wooden fixed her a sandwich and handed her a bottle of Ensure. "Drink this," he said. "They tell me it's good for me."

He had stayed alive and sharp for so long, it appeared he was defying science. Eventually, alas, he started losing the battle. In July 2009, the *Sporting News* assembled an expert panel to vote on the top fifty coaches in the history of American sports. Wooden finished first, ahead of Vince Lombardi, Bear Bryant, Phil Jackson, and Don Shula. The magazine honored Wooden with a luncheon at one of his favorite restaurants in Sherman Oaks. He was ninety-eight years old, and as he addressed the room, the listeners strained to hear him, and at one point, they sat through an extended, uncomfortable silence while he tried to gather his thoughts. After Wooden followed that by stumbling through a one-on-one interview with ESPN, Nan made clear that there were to be no more public appearances. "Most of the time, he's not who he was," Nan said. "As a family, we want people to remember him how he has always been."

Andy Hill wanted to throw Wooden a ninety-ninth birthday party at his house that October, but Nan said it would be too much for him. "Wouldn't it be great," Hill told her, "if he blew out the candles in front of everyone and just dropped dead right into the cake. Wouldn't that be amazing?" Nan did not think it would be amazing. So instead, Wooden spent his birthday having dinner with his family at a local restaurant. In early 2010, Wooden went to Pauley Pavilion to help the school celebrate the fortieth anniversary of the 1970 championship team, though he was unable to leave his seat during the halftime ceremony. After the game, the school held a party where each member of the team was invited to speak—including Bill Seibert, who had single-handedly killed the postseason banquet. "I didn't think I'd ever get to speak at this place again," Seibert cracked when he came to the microphone. The room broke up.

Over the next few months, Wooden continued to have periodic hospitalizations. A do-not-resuscitate order was posted on the refrigerator. "I thought the guy was going to die a dozen times," Hill said. "He was just so damn tough." As Wooden's friends and family steeled themselves for what they all knew was coming, UCLA did the same. Dan Guerrero, who had been hired as athletic director in 2002, asked Bob Field to talk to Wooden about the public memorial the school would hold after he died. It was a delicate conversation, but Field picked his moment one night when he was staying over at the condo. "Coach, there's going to be a time where you're going to be with your Nellie," he said. "I know there's going to be a private family service, but there will also be a memorial service at UCLA, and I'd like to talk to you about what you'd like that to be." At first, Wooden demurred that he didn't need a public memorial. Field responded that he might not need it, but his friends and former players would want to come together and celebrate his life. "He looked at me for about fifteen seconds and got misty-eyed," Field said. "Then he said, okay, let's talk about it."

The parade of visitors continued throughout the spring. Johnny Green came by with his granddaughter and a camcorder. Dick Enberg sat with some friends in Wooden's living room. (As he got up to leave, Wooden pointed to his own forehead, and Enberg planted a soft kiss on that spot.) In April, Pete Blackman, Jamaal Wilkes, and Mike Warren visited the condo together. "Wooden had all three of us to poke fun at. He was very much himself," Blackman said. "He remembered all kinds of things that each one of us had done. He was sharp and completely together, but you could see the handwriting. The mind was as clear as could be, but his body was gradually checking out."

Marques Johnson stopped in the Friday before Mother's Day. Wooden slept for an hour, and when he woke up, Johnson mentioned that he was going to conduct a coaching clinic out of the country. Suddenly, Wooden came to life, rattling off details about his favorite drills. Johnson asked him to pause so he could get a pen and paper.

Larry Farmer continued to call Wooden several times a week, even though he usually ended up just talking to Spino. One day in May, Spino told Wooden who was calling, and the coach came to the phone. "He had just gotten back from a doctor's appointment, and his speech was a little bit muffled," Farmer said. "Before I could ask him how he was doing, he said to me, 'How's your family?' I said, 'Coach, they're fine, but I'm calling to find out about you.' He said something to the effect that he was struggling but doing well for a man his age. When Tony came back on the phone, he said Coach had not been that clear in his speech for quite some time."

Doug Erickson and Bill Bennett visited every few weeks. Jim Harrick, who had lost his wife in 2009, tried to do the same. "He was in pretty good shape until about the last three or four months," Harrick said. "Then he got to a point where he didn't want anybody to see him in that condition." Gary Cunningham also brought his wife that May. "I saw an incredible decline," he said. "He was in his recliner. When my wife would talk, he just kept looking at me. I didn't sense an alertness, honestly, and I couldn't understand most of the things he said."

As Wooden continued to deteriorate, there was some hope that he would live long enough to see two landmarks—his one hundredth birthday on October 14, 2010, and the birth of his first great-great-grandchild that fall. Alas, his body could not hold up. He was so uncomfortable at home that his doctors suggested that his family check him back into UCLA's medical center the last week of May. The official reason for his admission was dehydration. Nan and Jim made clear that they did not want anyone taking extreme measures to prolong their father's life.

Wooden was heavily medicated while lying in his hospital bed, but his mind remained lucid, defying science to the end. His face was uncharacteristically shaggy when Ben Howland, the current UCLA basketball coach, came to see him. Looking up at Howland from his bed, Wooden caressed his whiskers and said weakly, "I feel like Bill Walton."

On Wednesday, June 2, news broke of Wooden's condition. A group of UCLA students gathered to hold a vigil outside the hospital. Wooden's favorite local pastor, Dudley Rutherford, was a constant presence in his room. At one point, Rutherford asked Wooden if he loved the Lord. "I'm working on it," Wooden replied. Valorie Kondos Field was also there a lot. During one of the rare moments when Wooden was awake, she asked if there was anything she could do for him. "Move my leg," he said. She moved it twice, and both times he winced in agony.

"I'm hurting you," Kondos Field complained.

"I told you to move my leg," Wooden replied. "I never said it wouldn't hurt."

When Gary Cunningham learned of Wooden's condition, he cut short a vacation and visited the hospital room on the evening of June 3. "We got there about six o'clock. He was drifting in and out of consciousness," Cunningham said. "I went up to him and said, 'Coach, I love you. Thank you for all you've done for me.'" Another former assistant, Ed Powell, an old man himself at eighty-nine, also made it that day. So did Jim Harrick, Lucius Allen, Henry Bibby, Kenny Washington, and Andy Hill. Bill Walton was having back issues that were so severe he could barely get out of bed, so he never saw Wooden in the hospital. But he didn't have to. "He knew that I knew, and I knew that he knew," Walton said. "We had said our good-byes."

On the morning of Friday, June 4, 2010, Doug Erickson went to see Wooden along with Bill and Joanne Bennett, just as they had done every morning that week. Wooden was unconscious. As they were leaving, Joanne asked Jim Wooden if she could give his dad a kiss. "Give him two," Jim said. Keith Erickson also stopped by for about a half hour that morning. "He had lost a lot of weight," Erickson said. "He was weak, his head was back, and his mouth was open. His hair was disheveled. Jim was there. Coach Val was there. Tony was there. They were all fine. They knew he didn't want to be like that."

Marques Johnson had been reluctant to visit Wooden in the hospital because he didn't want to see his coach in that state. On Friday afternoon, however, he was overcome by a strong urge to see him. Johnson got dressed quickly and called Nan as he was riding up the 405 freeway. "There's no need to come now," Nan said. "It's pretty much over." So he turned around and went home.

When th'inevitable hour arrived in the early evening, the circle of people around Wooden was small, just a few immediate family members, Pastor Rutherford, and Spino. As Wooden's family, friends, and former players learned the news, they felt sadness, of course, maybe even a little surprise that he had actually died. But there was also joy because they knew he was no longer in pain, that he was finally where he wanted to be. There was even some relief that he had, in fact, not made it to his hundredth birthday. "It would have been a spectacle," Hill said. "He would have hated it." Better to avoid that peak.

After nearly a century on Earth, John Wooden died much as he had lived. His pillow was softened by a clear conscience. He had scant money but a peaceful mind. Most of all, he was prepared for his death—physically, mentally, emotionally, and spiritually. He was not a perfect man and he did not live a perfect life, but he left this world in perfect balance, a success by any definition of the word.

When the ordeal was finally over, Nan called Bill Bennett and gave permission for UCLA to put out the official word. Bennett dialed a sportswriter friend and delivered the news the only way he knew how.

"Coach is with Nell," he said.

The Poet

I can't be certain that John Wooden was reciting poetry at the moment he died, but I have reason to believe he was. On September 5, 2006, I was sitting alone with Wooden in his den when he told me that he liked to recite poems in order to help him fall asleep. He had a rotation of a half dozen or so that he used. When I asked Wooden if he spoke them aloud, he replied, "Sometimes out loud and sometimes in my head. But I'll never know. I may go to sleep in the second or third, or maybe the fourth. When I wake, I think, 'I wonder which one I fell asleep to.'"

So I like to think that Wooden was whispering rhymes when he left this world on the evening of June 4, 2010. Like many sports fans of my generation, I have no recollection of Wooden as a basketball coach; I was not quite five years old when he claimed his last NCAA title. I didn't know the fiery guy who ran his players ragged and rode referees until their ears burned. I only knew the sweet old fella who liked to read poetry in his den.

I had three lengthy visits with Wooden in that den between 2003 and 2009, the last of which occurred ten months before he died. Our sessions were memorable, but hardly unusual. During the last decade of his life, Wooden loved sitting for interviews. He enjoyed telling all the old stories, even the ones he had repeated more times than he could count. The appointments also allowed Wooden to keep his calendar full and his mind engaged.

Like many writers who cover college basketball, I had always carried a natural curiosity about Wooden, so I finally came up with an excuse to fulfill it. In the spring of 2003, when UCLA fired yet another basketball coach, Steve Lavin, and replaced him with Ben Howland, I hatched an idea for a column: I knew that Wooden ate breakfast at the same restaurant each morning, so I decided to invite Wooden and Howland to breakfast and write about what they talked about. My angle would show that when a man gets the UCLA coaching job, he also gets John Wooden, for better and worse. Yes, he has to deal with the shadow of the Wooden legacy, but he also gains access to one of the greatest coaching minds in the history of American sports.

I called Bill Bennett, UCLA's sports information director for basketball, and asked him to set up the interview. When the appointed day arrived, I walked into Vip's cafe in Tarzana, just a mile or so from where Wooden lived in Encino. Wooden and Howland were already seated when I arrived, but they hadn't ordered yet. When the waitress came over, Wooden asked for the No. 2 special without looking at the menu. That's what you do when you eat breakfast every morning at the same restaurant for over ten years.

"Usually, I sit at a booth on the other side of the room," Wooden told me. He then rattled off the names of the other regular customers, most of whom were elderly like him. "Ed and Margaret sit over there. Next to them will be Millie. Louis will be at the end, next to Barbara, Gene, and Scottie. Jackie used to sit there, too, but not anymore for some reason." Not for nothing did Wooden's son, Jim, refer to Vip's as "Cheers without beer."

Howland was just as happy to be there as I was. He talked about how he used to stay up late as a boy so he could watch the replays of Wooden's games on KTLA. Lots of people in Los Angeles had those memories—which was part of Howland's new problem. "I think, after twenty-eight years, people around here are finally realizing that there will never be another one like Coach Wooden, so let's get past it." Wooden, however, interjected. "I say he's completely wrong," he said. "Someone else always comes along. I never thought someone would break Lou Gehrig's consecutive games record, least of all a shortstop. So never say never."

Wooden then leaned toward me and added with a smile, "Of course, some things are a little more difficult than others."

His wit was disarming. It was easy to be in his presence. Wooden may have been ninety-two years old, but he still had every marble, not to mention a full head of hair. (Even Howland couldn't say that, and he was just forty-six.) Wooden told us that when he wanted to go somewhere, he usually got a ride from his son-in-law or from Tony Spino. When he couldn't find a chauffeur, he simply drove himself. "I get upset because my children don't want me to drive," he said. "But I can drive better than they can."

Howland asked Wooden about some of his methods, and he also talked about his current players. When Howland told Wooden that his six-foot-six junior forward Cedric Bozeman had the potential to be an excellent defender, Wooden replied, "Absolutely. One of the things I used to say is there is absolutely no excuse for a good offensive man to not be a good defensive man. You have to be committed to it."

Howland also told Wooden that he had recently seen Paul Westphal, the former USC guard and NBA coach who was now the head coach at Pepperdine. "I told him, 'Coach Wooden still says you're the only guy he wanted but didn't get,'" Howland said. Wooden smiled and nodded. "That's true," he said. "He'd have been competing with Bibby and those guys. We had good guards, but he would have been the best."

Breakfast lasted about an hour. When the check came, I figured that was the end of the interview. To my surprise, Wooden invited us back to his apartment to continue the conversation. He told Howland he would ride with me so he could show me the way. It was pretty cool to drive in a car with John Wooden, but it was also nerve-racking. God forbid anything happened to him on my watch, I thought. The world would never forgive me.

Fortunately, the drive was short. After guiding me through a few turns on a winding route out of the parking lot behind Vip's, Wooden said, "Now I want you to go as far as you can from here. Those will be your only instructions. Let's see how you do."

"So I'm being coached by John Wooden?" I asked.

"Oh, I love to teach," he said. "I would have been happy being an English teacher my whole life." Thankfully, Wooden had set me up to succeed, because the road we were on led straight to his condominium. As I pulled into the parking space, he told me, "You've done well."

The apartment was comfortable but modest. It hosted an impressive array of memorabilia, including several trophies, framed magazine covers, and letters from numerous U.S. presidents. Wooden showed me his signed Derek Jeter baseball cap and pulled the rusted, dark 1932 Big Ten Academic medal from a box. "This," he said, "is what I'm most proud of."

Wooden, Howland, and I sat in his den and talked for another couple of hours. We talked about everything and nothing, but mostly we talked about basketball. I asked Wooden what trend bothered him the most in recent years. "Showmanship," he answered, without hesitation.

"Players or coaches?"

"Go right down the line. I think television is mostly responsible. It's made actors out of everyone."

At one point, Howland stared at the framed photographs of Wooden's ten NCAA championship teams while Wooden relaxed in his easy chair. It struck me that Howland was standing, quite literally, in the lion's den, but if it intimidated him, he did a good job hiding it. Howland asked Wooden if he would come to one of his practices, and though Wooden responded that he did not like to be a distraction, he didn't rule it out, either. "You won't be overwhelmed by our talent, but hopefully the effort will be there," Howland said. "Our players have no idea about defensive fundamentals. They don't even know how to jump to the ball. We're going to have to do a lot of teaching in a short period of time."

Wooden sat forward and narrowed his eyes. "Well, you know we UCLA alumni are very critical," he said darkly. "So you'd better get it done."

Wooden leaned back in his chair and laughed. He was kidding. I think.

Three years later, I was back in Southern California, and Bill Bennett arranged another breakfast with Coach Wooden at Vip's.

This time we were joined by Tony Spino, and we set off on a wide-ranging conversation, beginning with Wooden's thoughts on the upcoming 2006–07 college basketball season. The previous March, Howland had taken the Bruins to their first Final Four since they won the 1995 NCAA championship. I asked Wooden if he thought this Bruins team would be as good as the last one. "They could be as good," he answered, "and not do as well."

What did that mean?

"You can win when you're outscored. You can lose when you outscore someone. I must admit, the alumni don't look at it that way, but I truly believe that. Of the championships we won, I got more pleasure out of the ones we weren't expected to win."

Wooden was chatty and playful, as usual, and he was surprisingly up to speed on the news of the day—particularly the sports news. He was still a huge baseball fan, having struck up friendships with Angels manager Mike Scioscia and Yankees skipper Joe Torre. In 2002, Wooden was asked to throw out the first pitch at a World Series game between the Anaheim Angels and the San Francisco Giants. "It was a slider," he told me. "I threw it halfway and it slid the rest."

The conversation turned to Giants outfielder Barry Bonds, whose career was winding down amid evidence that he had used performance-enhancing drugs. Did Wooden think Bonds should be voted into the Hall of Fame? "Statistically, yes, but I'm not sure I'd vote for him," he said. "When his buddy would rather go to jail than [testify], it makes you wonder." He also had some critiques for the U.S. national basketball team, which four days earlier had been shocked by Greece in the semifinals of the 2006 FIBA World Championship. "We not only have all NBA players; we have the stars. When you have far superior talent, you should keep pressure on all the time. You're going to give up some easy ones, but you're going to wear them down. Those other teams have been together longer, so they have better team play."

I was also curious to hear Wooden's take on Tiger Woods. Over the weekend, Woods had survived a riveting duel with Vijay Singh to win his fifth straight tournament, a streak that included the British Open. Woods was a once-in-a-generation talent at the peak of his abilities. So I asked Wooden the kind of question that would come up on a sports talk show: Is Tiger Woods the most dominant athlete ever?

Unlike most radio hosts, Wooden had actually lived history. His soliloquy reflected that experience. "I would say Byron Nelson dominated the sport more in his era," he said. "Check the number of tournaments. Eleven in a row, and seventeen of eighteen that year. Tiger plays in a lot more tournaments. In his particular era, I think Byron Nelson was the most dominant in his sport. Just like Sandy Koufax for two or three years had the most dominant stats. I've always said, when trying to pick the best, you need to say best of the era. Remember, Jesse Owens in one afternoon broke four world records. That's rather amazing.

"I think Tiger will be the most dominant over time," he continued. "Wasn't Nicklaus second eighteen times? Let's see if Tiger at the end can match his total. But I don't focus so much on majors. That's like saying someone isn't a good baseball player if he didn't win the World Series."

Wooden ended by paying Woods a major compliment. "What I like about Tiger is his demeanor. He's handled all this so well, particularly after the death of his father. Demeanor is so important to me."

Wooden was in excellent health for a ninety-five-year-old man. Six months earlier, he had been hospitalized with a nasty bout of diverticulitis that required four days of blood transfusions, but there had been no further setbacks. He told me he didn't travel much—and then he talked about all the trips he'd be making in the coming months. "I leave tomorrow for North Dakota. I'm speaking there. The governor is going to be there. Later to Indianapolis for the Wooden Tradition [basketball doubleheader]. I'll be in Ohio for the McDonald's All-America game. I'll be in Kansas City. The NABC is creating something new. In each case, they arrange a private plane. I feel a little embarrassed by it, but I really don't think I could make it through airports."

"He keeps his own schedule on that calendar," Spino said. "He's always busy. I'm surprised he has time to fit me in, actually."

It was mesmerizing to listen to the workings of such a sharp mind in an old man. Except for his appearance, his slight stoop, and his cane, there was nothing old about Wooden at all. I asked him why he thought he had lived so long. "I'm often asked that," he replied. "I say it's not because I never used alcohol, because George Burns drank and smoked every day. Churchill drank. So it's not that. I feel it's just a question in my case of practicing moderation. I've had peace with myself. That's a pure guess.

"Of course," he added, "I'm realistic. You know you don't have too much time left, but that doesn't bother me. I've been blessed in so many ways."

Breakfast was over, but Wooden again invited me back to his apartment, just as I had hoped he would. As we were about to get up from the table, he scooped up the check. "Please, Coach," I said. "Let me pay for breakfast."

"Are you on an expense account?" he asked.

"Yes."

He slid the check toward me just as quickly as he had grabbed it.

As we made our way out of the restaurant, Wooden said hello to strangers who recognized him and good-bye to regulars who knew him. Leaning gently on his cane, moving quickly without hurrying, Wooden reached the front door, turned around to give one last wave, and stepped into the California sunshine, another splendid morning in the long winter of a wonderful life.

Spino had to go to work, so it was just the two of us in his den. This time, the conversation wasn't quite so centered on basketball. Wooden talked about his life, he talked about his family, and most of all, he talked about his love of poetry. "I taught it in high school, and I studied it in college and wrote a paper on it," he said. "Poetry is beautiful. It paints a picture. A lot of people don't like it, but I can't understand that."

Wooden did not strike me as someone who was given to deep self-evaluation. When I asked him what his greatest flaw was, he replied, "Oh, I have many flaws." Okay, I said, name one. "Well, organization was one of my strengths for a long time, but just look at that right there, that table with all that stuff on it. You'd see the same if you looked at my bedroom." This was not exactly the stuff of Dr. Phil.

I prodded Wooden about his treatment of referees, and he admitted that he was not always polite with them. He told me about his odd habit of sticking hairpins into trees and his challenges in remaining consistent during the turbulence of the sixties. "All change isn't progress, but there is no progress without change. We have to keep that in mind." But inevitably, he kept bringing the conversation back to poetry. He pulled out a file full of poems, many of which had been written by Swen Nater. He read a dozen or so to me and recited another half dozen by memory. Poetry wasn't just a passion for Wooden: it was his catharsis.

I reminded Wooden that when I visited him three years earlier, my wife was pregnant with our first child. Now, I was returning as the father of two young boys. Wooden congratulated me and told me that the most important aspect of parenthood was to set a good example. That nugget was followed, naturally, by another poem, called "A Little Fellow Follows Me." Wooden spoke it by rote.

At the end of our visit, Wooden told me he wanted to give me something. He ambled over to his small desk, opened a drawer, and pulled out an eight-by-eleven slab of cardboard. "A Little Fellow Follows Me" was printed on that board alongside a photograph of a man walking on a beach wearing a navy blazer, slacks, and a white sailor's hat. A small boy walks a few paces behind him.

I asked Wooden to autograph the photo for my sons. He sat at the desk, turned on the lamp, and in his meticulous, cursive handwriting he wrote, "To Zachary and Noah. Love, John Wooden." Today, it hangs framed on a wall in the bedroom Zachary and Noah share. I like to think of it as Wooden's voice speaking to them from the grave, in rhyme.

When the *Sporting News* named John Wooden the top coach in the history of American sports in July 2009, I saw a clip of him being interviewed on ESPN. It was the exchange that led his daughter, Nan, to decide not to let him do any more on-camera interviews. I could see why. I was taken aback at how much Wooden had aged in the three years since I had last seen him. When he was asked what winning the award meant to him, he deflected its significance and meandered into another rendition of one of his favorite poems. *The years have left their imprint on my hand and on my face. . . .* It took him so long to get through it that the interview cut off after just one line.

For the first time, it occurred to me that John Wooden might actually die, just like every other mortal. I realized that if I were going to see him again, I had better do it soon.

When I called Bill Bennett to arrange for a visit, he told me in confidence that Wooden was not doing well. The coach had gone through several hospitalizations, yet he was still hanging on. When Bennett called me back to say he had gotten me an appointment, he warned me that I might get a phone call that morning saying that Coach was not up to it. There was no way to know for sure.

On the morning of August 15, 2009, I met Bill in the parking lot outside of Vip's. Wooden was late, which was very unlike him. Just when I started to think he might cancel, Jim Wooden rolled up in his van, with his father sitting in the passenger seat. Jim pulled a wheelchair out of the back, placed it next to the car, and asked me and Bill to help the coach into it. Wooden was dressed in a light blue V-necked sweater, and his hair was neatly combed. "Hello, Coach. You're looking handsome and spry," I said. Wooden did a double take and said with a gusto that surprised me, "You have a great sense of exaggeration."

As Jim wheeled his dad through the front door of Vip's, Lucy Na, who owned the restaurant with her husband, Paul, came over to greet him. Wooden took her hand and kissed it. Lucy and Jim helped Wooden out of his chair and lifted him into his booth. A waitress came over, poured him some coffee, and asked how he was doing.

"Well," Wooden said, "I'm here."

That was no small accomplishment, considering he was just two months shy of his ninety-ninth birthday. "Hope I make it, but if I don't, I've had a long run," he said of the big day. "My eyesight is not nearly as good. My hearing is probably going away. My memory is slipping, too. But I'm still around."

His voice was deep and quiet, and his speech was a little slurred. At times, I had to strain to hear him over the clatter of the restaurant, but all things considered he was pretty clear, and he still had the old Wooden wit. When I asked him if he still ate at Vip's often, he replied, "Conservatively speaking, seven days a week."

What was his typical day like? "It starts off in the morning here. Then I go back. I listen to the news, watch some television. Then I lie back in the den and snooze. Maybe read something during the day. I've always been an avid reader, but my eyes aren't very good. I can honestly say with all the problems, I don't have a lot of pain."

As the four of us ate, we talked about what his one hundredth birthday would be like. I told him the city of Los Angeles might throw him a parade, but he laughed it off. That prompted Jim to say, "In either case, we'll celebrate it with or without you? Is that what you're saying?"

"You'll celebrate the death," Wooden replied.

We talked about whether he could be a successful coach in today's era. I pointed out that I didn't think he would like modern-day recruiting. It was too time-consuming and unethical. Maybe he wouldn't even want to be a college basketball coach at all. "I'd be satisfied in high school," he said. "I honestly believe if I hadn't enlisted in the service, I would never have left high school teaching. I'm sure I would never have left. I turned down several colleges because I was happy with what I was doing."

As it turned out, I was extremely lucky. I had caught Wooden on a very good day. After breakfast, he invited me back to his apartment. Bill Bennett and I drove behind Jim's van and pulled into the garage alongside them. On the way over, Wooden heard on the radio that Michael Vick, the NFL quarterback who had recently been released from prison after serving a nineteen-month sentence for setting up an illicit dogfighting ring, had found a new team.

"Did you hear Vick signed?" Wooden asked me.

"Yes," I replied.

"With who?"

"The Eagles."

He smiled. "As Mother Teresa said, forgiveness will set you free."

When we got into Wooden's apartment, Jim wheeled him into the den. I helped Jim lift his father out of his wheelchair and lower him into his easy chair. I could feel the bones in Wooden's back. There was very little meat on his frame, but he was alert and eager to talk. I asked him about the confrontation with Bill Sweek, the falling out with Edgar Lacey, the awkwardness between him and Jerry Norman. I even asked him about Sam Gilbert. He didn't flinch in the slightest. ("My conscience is clear.") Since nobody seemed to know what his political views were, I asked if he minded if I pried him on it. "Go right ahead," he said. He told me he had voted for Democrats and Republicans for president over the years, and he revealed that he had voted for Barack Obama in the 2008 election. "I didn't vote for Barack Obama because I thought he was outstanding," he said. "I just liked him better than the others. That's all." (Spino later told me that Wooden believed "only a fool" would want to be president of the United States.)

Remarkably, Wooden only lost his train of thought a couple of times, at one point growling, "Oh, gracious, I'm so bad about remembering names." He recited his "years have left their imprint" poem yet again, but when he was through he said he had meant to recite something else. "I have trouble starting 'em. But I started the wrong one." He giggled as he said it.

I also asked him about his more temperamental days as a high school coach in South Bend. Jim reminded him of the time when Wooden was driving with baby Nan in the backseat and a car rammed into them. "What did you tell the guy?" Jim asked.

"I said, if you hurt my wife or baby, I'll kill ya," Wooden replied. "His father was going to have me arrested for threatening his son."

When Wooden asked if I had any children, I reminded him that my wife and I had two young boys and that our third child was due in December. "Nellie wanted three," he told me. "The third one miscarried. We had problems, and the doctor said she should never try anymore. I disagreed."

I was surprised to hear Wooden say he still made about thirty speeches a year—when he felt up to it, that is. He was having a difficult time recovering from a recent month-long bout with pneumonia. "He went into rehab at the end of March. We literally had to force him," Jim told me. Wooden added, "I have a doctor that I like, but every time you get near the hospital, he puts you in."

He said that a big reason he didn't like hospitals was that the nurses had to sponge-bathe him there. I told him that didn't sound like such a bad deal.

"No, I get very embarrassed. Very embarrassed," he replied. "One of the nurses who was bathing me saw I was embarrassed. She said, 'Mr. Wooden, don't be embarrassed. I've been working in this hospital for thirty years. I've seen every kind of penis there is.'"

I told him that so many people his age were depressed, yet he had done well to maintain his positive attitude. He agreed but added, "I'm ready to go."

"Where are you ready to go?" Jim said.

"With you."

"You want to go somewhere?"

After about two hours of conversation, I could tell he was tired. I got the idea that he would have let me prod him for a while longer, but only because he was too polite to ask me to leave. Finally, I stood up, shook his hand, and thanked him for his time. I did the same with Jim and Bill Bennett. As I stepped out of the den, I heard the gravelly voice say from the chair, "Good luck on the coming one."

Somehow I knew those would be the last words John Wooden would ever speak to me. I left the condo thinking they were a fitting coda to our final visit, his way of nodding toward a gracious God who never closes one door without opening another.

JOHN WOODEN'S COACHING RECORD, 1946–1975

SEASON	SCHOOL	W	L	PCT.	NOTES
1946–47	Indiana State	17	8	.680	
1947–48	Indiana State	27	7	.794	runner-up in NAIB finals
1948–49	UCLA	22	7	.759	
1949–50	UCLA	24	7	.774	conference champions
1950–51	UCLA	19	10	.655	
1951–52	UCLA	19	12	.613	conference champions
1952–53	UCLA	16	8	.667	
1953–54	UCLA	18	7	.720	
1954–55	UCLA	21	5	.808	
1955–56	UCLA	22	6	.786	conference champions
1956–57	UCLA	22	4	.846	
1957–58	UCLA	16	10	.615	
1958–59	UCLA	16	9	.640	
1959–60	UCLA	14	12	.538	
1960–61	UCLA	18	8	.692	
1961–62	UCLA	18	11	.621	NCAA West Regional champions
1962–63	UCLA	20	9	.690	conference champions
1963–64	**UCLA**	**30**	**0**	**1.000**	**NCAA CHAMPIONS**
1964–65	**UCLA**	**28**	**2**	**.933**	**NCAA CHAMPIONS**
1965–66	UCLA	18	8	.692	
1966–67	**UCLA**	**30**	**0**	**1.000**	**NCAA CHAMPIONS**
1967–68	**UCLA**	**29**	**1**	**.967**	**NCAA CHAMPIONS**
1968–69	**UCLA**	**29**	**1**	**.967**	**NCAA CHAMPIONS**
1969–70	**UCLA**	**28**	**2**	**.933**	**NCAA CHAMPIONS**
1970–71	**UCLA**	**29**	**1**	**.967**	**NCAA CHAMPIONS**
1971–72	**UCLA**	**30**	**0**	**1.000**	**NCAA CHAMPIONS**
1972–73	**UCLA**	**30**	**0**	**1.000**	**NCAA CHAMPIONS**
1973–74	UCLA	26	4	.867	NCAA West Regional champions
1974–75	**UCLA**	**28**	**3**	**.903**	**NCAA CHAMPIONS**
	Career	664	162	.804	

John Wooden was enshrined in the Basketball Hall of Fame
in 1960 (as a player) and in 1973 (as a coach)

Notes

PROLOGUE: THE DEN

Interview: John Wooden

2   "For instance, he'd do it in a spiral form": Neville L. Johnson, *The John Wooden Pyramid of Success* (Los Angeles: Cool Titles, 2000), p. 250.

2   he dove into the *Leatherstocking* tales and Tom Swift series: Ibid., p. 14.

2   he became close with Martha Miller, an elderly librarian: John Wooden interview with Purdue University, March 1989, courtesy of Purdue Sports Information Department (hereafter cited as Purdue interview).

2   Though his all-time favorite book was *The Robe*: Wooden interview with Academy of Achievement, Washington, D.C., Feb. 27, 1996 (hereafter cited as Academy of Achievement interview).

3   he wrote poems about how those events made him feel: Purdue interview.

1. HUGH

Interviews: Andy Hill, John Wooden

7   "We didn't have much money": Reporter's file for *Sports Illustrated* from Dick Denny of the *Indianapolis News*, Aug. 10, 1960.

8   "Through it all, Dad never winced": John Wooden with Steve Jamison, *My Personal Best: Life Lessons from an All-American Journey* (New York: McGraw-Hill, 2004), p. 8.

8   Wooden's parents were not physically affectionate with each other in front of their children: John Wooden and Don Yeager, *A Game Plan for Life: The Power of Mentoring* (New York: Bloomsbury USA, 2009), p. 15.

8   shortly before he died, a group of local researchers discovered he had been mistaken: "Wooden Birthplace Information Clarified," *Martinsville Reporter-Times*, June 5, 2010.

8   Some of Johnny's favorite childhood memories involved riding with his dad on his horse-drawn carriage: John Wooden with Jack Tobin, *They Call Me Coach* (New York: McGraw-Hill, 1988), p. 23.

9   "particularly my father": Purdue interview.

9   feet that were deformed: Johnson, *John Wooden Pyramid of Success*, p. 251.

9   "Daddy said her heart was broken": Ibid., p. 240.

9   "John did not have an active social life as a kid": Ibid., p. 256.

10   "Dogs that would scare me, he'd pet 'em and they would wag their tails": Steve

Bisheff, *John Wooden: An American Treasure* (Nashville, Tenn.: Cumberland House, 2004), p. 14.

10 "Dad tried to get across to us never try to be better than someone else": Indiana Basketball Hall of Fame, *Indiana Basketball History*, Winter 1996.

11 The town was prospering due to bountiful artesian wells: Joanne Raetz Stuttgen and Curtis Tomak, *Postcard History Series: Martinsville* (Charleston, S.C.: Arcadia Publishing, 2008), p. 7.

11 "I think that's why Daddy always has been such a generous tipper": Bisheff, *John Wooden*, p. 16.

11 "He said there's always time for play": Purdue interview.

11 Roxie made a ball by stuffing an old sock with rags: Johnson, *John Wooden Pyramid of Success*, p. 27.

11 it was made of sand and clay: Ibid., p. 273.

12 He even carved a diamond, *Field of Dreams*–like: Dwight Chapin and Jeff Prugh, *The Wizard of Westwood* (Boston: Houghton Mifflin, 1973), p. 49.

12 "Johnny says what helped him the most was the desire to play": Johnson, *John Wooden Pyramid of Success*, p. 273.

12 "They were lucky if they had shoes": Ibid.

12 "That little rat John": Reporter's file for *Sports Illustrated*, Aug. 10, 1960.

12 "I turned off the furnace. Guess who?": Ibid.

13 So they pretended to sing it: Wooden and Yeager, *Game Plan for Life*, p. 29.

13 "I guess John wanted me to beg him to play": Reporter's file for *Sports Illustrated*, Aug. 10, 1960.

13 "Johnny Wooden learned early in life he was not a necessary article": "Warriner-Wooden," *Indianapolis News*, Mar. 22, 1972.

2. THE ARTESIANS

Interview: John Wooden

15 "Good Lord, man, why didn't you say so long ago?": James Naismith, *Basketball: Its Origin and Development* (New York: Association Press, 1941), p. 127.

16 a movement called "muscular Christianity": Ibid., p. ix.

16 a Presbyterian minister named Nicolas McKay: A. H. Williams, *Big Bang of Basketball: Birth of a Celestial Star* (A. H. Williams, n.d.), p. 8; Herb Schwomeyer, *Hoosier Hysteria: A History of Indiana High School Basketball* (Greenfield, Ind.: Mitchell-Fleming Printing, 1970), p. 11.

17 "it is bound to be popular": Schwomeyer, *History of Indiana High School Basketball*, p. 14; "Why Do Hoops and Hoosiers Go Together?" *Indianapolis Star*, Apr. 3, 2006.

17 Martinsville unveiled its grandiose landmark in time for its first game against Shelbyville: "Memories Remain," *Martinsville Daily Reporter*, May 13, 1982.

17 a popular, nationally syndicated column by Robert Ripley: "The Two Faces of the Rubber Man," *Sports Illustrated*, Jan. 6, 1969.

18 "We Martinsville fellows were city slickers and he was a country boy": Reporter's file for *Sports Illustrated*, Aug. 10, 1960.

19 "You're not going to do to me what you did to my brother!": Wooden with Tobin, *They Call Me Coach*, p. 36.

19 "no one has yet attempted to teach basketball through this medium": *Artesian Herald*, 1936.

20 which was called the "cow barn": Todd Gould, *Pioneers of the Hardwood: Indiana and the Birth of Professional Basketball* (Bloomington: Indiana University Press, 1998), p. 35.

20 "I didn't have as much size as many": Academy of Achievement interview.

20   "He could dribble with either hand": Reporter's file for *Sports Illustrated*, Aug. 10, 1960.

20   "John could palm a basketball. I never could": Johnson, *John Wooden Pyramid of Success*, p. 246.

21   "They'd have these 'Shoot the free throw' contests": Ibid.

21   "It really could have been dangerous, but he always had a toothpick": Reporter's file for *Sports Illustrated*, Aug. 10, 1960.

21   "When he'd get hold of an expression, he'd use it all the time": Ibid.

21   "Pretty pert": Ibid.

22   "Lord, no": Ibid.

22   He told Wooden that he would never win important games because he wasn't mean enough: Chapin and Prugh, *Wizard of Westwood*, p. 59.

22   a flashlight-wielding usher saying it was time to go home: Ed Powell interview with Joe Jares, Aug. 1968.

23   "I've never seen another player give everything, regardless of what might happen to him": Reporter's file for *Sports Illustrated*, Aug. 10, 1968.

3. NELL

Interview: John Wooden

24   she told him he looked like he was dribbling a basketball: Johnson, *John Wooden Pyramid of Success*, p. 237.

25   playing songs like "Ramona" and "In a Little Spanish Town": Wooden and Yeager, *Game Plan for Life*, p. 99.

25   "He was always polite and my parents liked him": Ibid., p. 15.

25   She encouraged him to take a public speaking class: "The Coach and His Champion," *Sports Illustrated*, Apr. 3, 1989.

26   "Mother thought to herself, if he ever makes twenty-five dollars a week, I'll be surprised": Johnson, *John Wooden Pyramid of Success*, p. 15.

27   The arena had cost the school $1 million to build and had a capacity of fifteen thousand: *Indianapolis Star*, Apr. 3, 2006.

27   "the tumbling artist from Martinsville": "John Wooden Lost Last Game Once," *Easton Star-Democrat*, Apr. 4, 1975.

27   It was just the second time a sporting event was being recorded by the station: "The 1928 Game Broadcast Was Recorded," *Martinsville Daily Reporter*, Jan. 27, 1989.

27   "a spectacular defensive battle": "Coach Jolly's Five Tops Martinsville in Final Tilt," *Indianapolis Star*, Mar. 18, 1928.

28   Charlie Secrist, the Muncie center, realized that Martinsville could win by stalling: Dave Krider, *Indiana High School Basketball's 20 Most Dominant Players* (Bloomington, Ind.: Rooftop Publishing, 2007), p. 246.

28   "It was the highest-arching shot I have ever seen": Wooden with Tobin, *They Call Me Coach*, p. 39.

28   "almost without disturbing the net": "Secrist Scores Winning Goal," *Indianapolis Star*, Mar. 17, 1928.

29   "an explosion of gaiety rivaling the Armistice signing": *Martinsville Daily Reporter*, Jan. 27, 1989.

29   "We just sat on the floor and cried": Reporter's file for *Sports Illustrated*, Aug. 10, 1960.

29   "I have never felt badly about that missed free throw": *Indianapolis News*, Jan. 23, 1963.

29   caught the eye of Donnie Bush: Wooden with Tobin, *They Call Me Coach*, p. 42.

4. PIGGY

31      $70-per-semester tuition costs: Purdue interview.

31   Wooden made ends meet by waiting on tables: Wooden with Tobin, *They Call Me Coach*, p. 44.

31   "I'm not a good fraternity man": Purdue interview.

31   Wooden did imbibe some home brew on one occasion: Johnson, *John Wooden Pyramid of Success*, p. 131.

31   "I would have gone to Indiana": Purdue interview.

32   "When you don't have much, you do": John Wooden interview with Joe Jares, Aug. 13, 1968.

32   "That could easily have been my Alamo": "1929 Incident Almost Ruined Wooden's Career," *Hillsdale Daily News*, Mar. 18, 1976.

32   "There was no problem hitchhiking in those days": Purdue interview.

33   "Everybody knew he was going with his high school girlfriend": Johnson, *John Wooden Pyramid of Success*, p. 16.

33   Lambert found out and ordered Wooden to stop: Bisheff, *John Wooden*, p. 19.

33   he turned into a pitch that struck him hard in his right shoulder: Ibid., p. 11.

34   That's how he got the nickname "Piggy": Kenneth L. "Tug" Wilson and Jerry Brondfield, *The Big Ten* (Englewood Cliffs, N.J.: Prentice-Hall, 1967), p. 102; Alan Karpick, *Boilermaker Basketball* (Chicago: Bonus Books, 1989), p. 19.

34   "Our practices were hellish": Charlie Caress interview with Alan Karpick.

34   Lambert insisted that they remain on campus: Karpick, *Boilermaker Basketball*, p. 30.

35   "He was way ahead of his time in fast break basketball": Purdue interview.

35   a solution of benzoin and tannic acid: Ward L. Lambert, *Practical Basketball* (Chicago: Athletic Journal Publishing, 1932), p. 229.

35   Lambert himself was a smoker and inveterate poker player: Karpick, *Boilermaker Basketball*, p. 60.

36   "He taught me the value of a controlled offense": Bisheff, *John Wooden*, p. 18.

36   "I've seen Piggy getting up, leading cheers, coaching, and officiating all at the same time": Clyde Lyle interview with Alan Karpick.

36   "it's an uncomfortable feeling to be calling them as you see 'em": Wilson and Brondfield, *Big Ten*, p. 105.

37   "anxious to be relieved of the nervous strain and mental punishment": Karpick, *Boilermaker Basketball*, p. 60.

37   the place was so jammed that some fans sat on steel trusses above the floor: Ibid., p. 23.

37   his habit of flinging his elbows when cradling the ball could be a menace to his teammates during practice: Ibid., p. 28.

37   "He was a beanpole": Lyle interview with Karpick.

38   Gordon Graham, reported that Wooden "had proven himself capable": "Boilermaker Quintet Looks Good in Opener Against Don White's Bears," *Lafayette Journal and Courier*, Dec. 16, 1929.

38   "I saw them at the hospital instead of at the game": Wooden interview with Jares.

38   Wooden's absence was "keenly felt": "Butler Downs Purdue's Cage Quintet, 36–29," *Lafayette Journal and Courier*, Dec. 23, 1929.

39   "The Boilermakers, without a doubt, turned in one of the most disgusting exhibitions of basketball": "Boilermakers Are Beaten by Montana State Outfield, 38–35," *Lafayette Journal and Courier*, Jan. 2, 1930.

39   Wooden "lacked the stamina": "Coach Piggy Lambert Must Whip Five Into Shape for Conference," *Lafayette Journal and Courier*, Jan. 4, 1930.

39   "the Bob Cousy of our day": Reporter's file for *Sports Illustrated* by Red Marston
         of the *St. Petersburg Times*.

39   "he often flew five or six rows into the stands": Reporter's file for *Sports Illus-
         trated* by Jack Tobin, Aug. 9, 1968.

39   "You need to put two men on Murphy and two men on Wooden": "Boilermaker
         Quintet Grabs 2nd Conference Triumph by Downing Purple Five, 39–22,"
         Lafayette Journal and Courier, Jan. 14, 1930.

39   "Lambert gave us considerable freedom in our play": Reporter's file for *Sports
         Illustrated* by Red Marston of the *St. Petersburg Times*.

40   "India Rubberman": *Lafayette Journal and Courier*, Jan. 14, 1930.

40   "He never held a grudge and you simply couldn't rattle the guy": Reporter's file
         for *Sports Illustrated* by Art Rosenbaum, Aug. 1, 1968.

41   "a sophomore who promises to become an immortal in this league": "A.P. Places
         Murphy and Wooden on All Star Conference Team," *Lafayette Journal and Cou-
         rier*, Mar. 12, 1930.

41   Lambert called Wooden into his office to report that a well-to-do doctor in town
         had offered to take care of Wooden's living expenses: Wooden with Tobin, *They
         Call Me Coach*, p. 45; Bisheff, *John Wooden*, p. 17.

41   "When you walk out of here, your head will be up": John Wooden interview with
         Alan Karpick.

5. JOHNNY WOODEN, ALL-AMERICAN

Interview: John Wooden

43   "comparative midgets": "Lead Purdue Net Champions Against Notre Dame's
         Quintet," *Lafayette Journal and Courier*, Dec. 15, 1930.

43   "The thing I remember the most is that he was so fast": Krider, *Indiana High
         School Basketball's 20 Most Dominant Players*, p. 247.

44   "It took a hunk of meat": Wooden interview with Jares.

44   Wooden missed a chance to tie the score: "Free Throws Win for Easterners;
         Wooden Injured," *Lafayette Journal and Courier*, Dec. 31, 1930.

44   she actually fainted in the stands: Johnson, *John Wooden Pyramid of Success*, p.
         14.

44   "He was always moving": Ibid., p. 290.

45   Wooden was again offered the chance to play professional baseball: Wooden
         with Tobin, *They Call Me Coach*, p. 47.

45   "You can't play in the dirt without getting dirty": Bisheff, *John Wooden*, p. 17.

45   She told Wooden that if he accepted, she would call off the marriage and join a
         convent: Johnson, *John Wooden Pyramid of Success*, p. 16.

45   "We could make a lot more sandwiches that way": Wooden interview with Kar-
         pick.

46   "a squad that depends more on speed and cleverness than physical power": "Pur-
         due Basketball Squad Will Play Tough Schedule," *Lafayette Journal and Courier*,
         Dec. 3, 1931.

46   George Keogan went so far as to devise a "Wooden defense": Reporter's file for
         Sports Illustrated by Jack Tobin, Aug. 9, 1968.

46   his tonsils did flare up: Wooden interview with Karpick; Johnson, *John Wooden
         Pyramid of Success*, p. 26.

47   " 'Fire department basketball,' they call it in Indiana": Associated Press, "Purdue
         Cage Team Looms as Big Ten's Strongest Following Great Showing in Early Sea-
         son Games," *Lafayette Journal and Courier*, Jan. 6, 1932.

47   he sliced the ring finger on his shooting hand: Wooden interview with Karpick.

47   "He had a way of stalling the game out by fantastic dribbling": Reporter's file for *Sports Illustrated* by Art Rosenbaum, Aug. 1, 1968.

47   "Wooden's going to play tomorrow. All you're going to do is sit": Chapin and Prugh, *Wizard of Westwood*, p. 57.

48   "He had a very unusual thing he did": Johnson, *John Wooden Pyramid of Success*, p. 25.

48   "Wooden was somewhat of a folk hero here in Indiana": Ibid., p. 277.

48   "the name of John Wooden outshines all others": "Johnny Wooden Called Best Amateur Player in America," *Lafayette Journal and Courier*, Mar. 21, 1932.

49   "probably the greatest all-around guard of them all": Krider, *Indiana High School Basketball's 20 Most Dominant Players*, p. 243.

49   "because people remembered him thirty years prior as one of the greatest basketball players": Johnson, *John Wooden Pyramid of Success*, p. 209.

49   "Wooden to the kids of my era was what Bill Russell, Wilt Chamberlain, or Lew Alcindor is today": Reporter's file for *Sports Illustrated* by Jack Tobin, Aug. 9, 1968.

49   Halas paid Wooden $100 a game: Wooden with Tobin, *They Call Me Coach*, p. 247.

50   The Celtics were willing to pay Wooden $5,000: Purdue interview.

50   "He told me without telling me": Ibid.

50   First Bank and Trust had gone under: Wooden with Tobin, *They Call Me Coach*, p. 48; Wooden interview with Jares.

51   "You guys sang so long, I thought you would never stop": Purdue interview.

6. AN ENGLISH TEACHER

Interviews: Bob Dunbar, Eddie Ehlers, John Gassensmith, Ed Powell, Jim Powers, Jim Rudasics, Ben Stull, Tom Taylor, John Wooden

52   "We went down there with nothing": Wooden interview with Jares.

52   the regular varsity coach, Willard Bass, was demoted to the girls' team: Chapin and Prugh, *Wizard of Westwood*, p. 46.

52   he spent some time picking the brain of Noble Kizer: Wooden interview with Jares.

53   "You're not man enough to do it": Wooden with Jamison, *My Personal Best*, p. 53.

53   "We had some real loafers on our team": Chapin and Prugh, *Wizard of Westwood*, p. 44.

53   "If you missed an easy layup, he'd be right there to crack you": Ibid., p. 45.

54   "Having been a player of outstanding reputation, perhaps I expected too much": Wooden interview with Jares.

54   Lou Foster, accused Wooden of teaching "dirty basketball": Bisheff, *John Wooden*, p. 27; Chapin and Prugh, *Wizard of Westwood*, p. 44.

54   Dayton finished the season with just 6 wins to 11 losses: Chapin and Prugh, *Wizard of Westwood*, p. 45.

54   "He was such a good Christian man": Ibid., p. 47.

54   "He laid down a set of rules and expected the guys to follow it": Reporter's file for *Sports Illustrated* from Jim Schottelkotte, Aug. 9, 1968.

54   "He'd invite us for supper and we stayed the rest of the evening": Ibid.

55   The teacher had asked his students to come up with their own personal definition of *success*: Wooden with Jamison, *My Personal Best*, p. 86.

55   the "ladder of success" that Glenn Curtis had presented to him: "Glenn Curtis Dies in Hospital," *Martinsville Daily Reporter*, May 13, 1982.

56   a 15–3 record: Chapin and Prugh, *Wizard of Westwood*, p. 46.

56   At South Bend's Central High School, Wooden was again wearing many hats: Bisheff, *John Wooden*, p. 27.

56   In addition, he was the school's comptroller: Wooden with Jamison, *My Personal Best*, p. 60.

57   "I don't think South Bend knew whether I'd be a good English teacher or not": Purdue interview.

57   The players found their own way to the game, but Wooden left them on the bench: Bisheff, *John Wooden*, p. 5.

57   The next day, Nell was looking through a newspaper and came upon a picture of the players at the dance: Johnson, *John Wooden Pyramid of Success*, p. 279.

58   "That made Wooden in South Bend": Reporter's file for *Sports Illustrated* from Jack Tobin, Aug. 9, 1968.

58   he sat his whole team down for fifteen minutes to express his displeasure: "Wooden Files Objection on Umpire Ruling," *South Bend Tribune*, Apr. 30, 1939.

58   Wooden was a "stickler for good penmanship": Bisheff, *John Wooden*, p. 5.

59   "I think he ended up a common laborer": Johnson, *John Wooden Pyramid of Success*, p. 129.

59   "He used this as an example to show that he could quit when he wanted to": Mark Heisler, *They Shoot Coaches, Don't They?: UCLA and the NCAA Since John Wooden* (New York: Macmillan, 1996), p. 21.

60   "You no-good little bulldog!": Johnson, *John Wooden Pyramid of Success*, p. 280.

60   "You have to walk it": Academy of Achievement interview.

61   "Johnny Wooden, South Bend Central's basketball coach, will be the featured speaker at Elkhart High's sports banquet": Chapin and Prugh, *Wizard of Westwood*, p. 17.

61   "Not everybody came out of their exposure to John Wooden and made the grade": Johnson, *John Wooden Pyramid of Success*, p. 285.

62   "You just never had the ball in your hands": Ibid., p. 293.

62   he was floored by how efficient Leahy's workouts were: John Wooden interview with ESPN, Mar. 12, 1998.

63   "I noticed that most players wear shoes that are too large": Academy of Achievement interview.

63   "He was very concerned about nutrition": Johnson, *John Wooden Pyramid of Success*, p. 284.

63   "There is no pass that is lower than a roll": Ibid., p. 291.

63   "When I tell them it was done shooting two-handed, they really don't believe it": "Wooden Hero to Many," *Indianapolis News*, Dec. 11, 1975.

64   "We couldn't stop him": Johnson, *John Wooden Pyramid of Success*, p. 290.

64   "Back then, we used to think Wooden wasn't flexible enough": Bisheff, *John Wooden*, p. 27.

65   "It was not a healthy situation": Purdue interview.

65   Wooden rushed at Shake and swung his fist: Peter J. DeKever, *On the Brink: Shelby Shake and Johnny Wooden* (South Bend, Ind.: South Bend Public Library, 1999), p. 6; Johnson, *John Wooden Pyramid of Success*, p. 294.

65   "I've never seen [Wooden] as upset as I did that night": Powell interview with Jares.

67   "Those kids never quit": "Bears Couldn't Hit; Wooden Praises Rally," *South Bend Tribune*, Mar. 8, 1943.

7. THE KAUTSKYS

Interviews: Ed Orme, Ed Powell, John Wooden

68   "I tell you, he was phenomenal": Bisheff, *John Wooden*, p. 4.

68   Kautsky was a bundle of energy who fancied cigars and three-piece suits: Gould, *Pioneers of the Hardwood*, p. 49.

69   "He was a very wonderful person": Wooden interview with Jares.

69   "My dad always said [Wooden] could stop on a dime and give you five cents change": "A Top Talent in His Day," *Indianapolis Star*, Apr. 2, 2006.

69   "The first thing they asked us when we entered the court was, 'Which one was John Wooden?'" Murry R. Nelson, *The National Basketball League: A History, 1935–1949* (Jefferson, N.C.: McFarland, 2009), p. 49.

69   "I often worked on my lesson plans as I traveled": Wooden interview with Jares.

70   The NBL disbanded after just one year: Gould, *Pioneers of the Hardwood*, p. 57.

70   "I'd have to be careful I didn't stop playing and start watching them": Ibid., p. 59.

70   "Even Johnny Wooden's clever dribbling was lost as [Rens guard] Clarence Jenkins policed the Kautsky star throughout the contest": Ibid.

71   "I went down hard and I came up fightin' mad": Wooden interview with the Naismith Basketball Hall of Fame, July 2001 (hereafter cited as Hall of Fame interview).

71   "Wooden used to be gone two or three days a week": Johnson, *John Wooden Pyramid of Success*, p. 217.

71   Kautsky reached out to his erstwhile partner from Akron to form yet another new league, the Midwest Basketball Conference: Nelson, *National Basketball League*, p. 14.

72   "She came down out of the stands and grabbed that $100 rather quickly": Gould, *Pioneers of the Hardwood*, p. 83.

72   In an effort to speed things up, the NCAA's rules committee added a center line in 1932: Schwomeyer, *Hoosier Hysteria*, p. 99.

72   it decided to give the home team the option of eliminating the center jump after made free throws: Nelson, *National Basketball League*, p. 17.

72   "One of the reasons I am sorry to see the center jump relegated to a subordinate place": Rob Rains, *James Naismith: The Man Who Invented Basketball* (Philadelphia: Temple University Press, 2009), p. 166.

73   "I'd have loved to play [more years] without the center jump": Wooden interview with Jares.

73   "It was a brief meeting—a moment in time": Hall of Fame interview.

73   an estimated 20 million people around the world were playing his game: Rains, *James Naismith*, p. 169.

73   "We finally got the idea, so we went back to the center jump": Wooden interview with Jares.

73   Ciesar got Wooden to agree to a one-year contract: Gould, *Pioneers of the Hardwood*, p. 92.

74   "He was very upset": Ibid., p. 96.

75   "It was probably the major disagreement that my dear wife and I had in all our years": Purdue interview.

75   On April 22, 1943: *South Bend Tribune*, Mar. 8, 1943.

75   When he arrived, he went straight to a doctor, who diagnosed appendicitis: Bisheff, *John Wooden*, p. 28.

75   Freddy Stalcup, a former Purdue football player: "Twists of Fate in Wooden's Life," *Indianapolis Star*, Apr. 2, 2006.

75   "When Dad had to go into the service, I was very unsettled": Bisheff, *John Wooden*, p. 180.

76   he did not want them living in Chicago, so they returned to South Bend: Johnson, *John Wooden Pyramid of Success*, p. 257.

76   It also caused him to walk with a slight stoop that grew more pronounced as he got older: Bill Libby, *The Walton Gang* (New York: Coward, McCann & Geoghegan, 1974), p. 186.

76   "I loved to teach English": Academy of Achievement interview.

77   "I don't know how we ever won the war": Hall of Fame interview.
77   The bank that held his mortgage wanted to charge Wooden for the past-due amount: Wooden interview with Jares.
77   "It was a bitter experience": Powell interview with Jares.
78   "I talked it over with Nellie, and I said, 'Why not?'": Purdue interview.

8. THE HURRYIN' SYCAMORES

Interviews: Charlie Foudy, John Gassensmith, Duane Klueh, Jim Powers, Lenny Rzeszewski, Mamie Taylor, Tom Taylor, John Wooden, Nan Wooden

79   With his teammates looking on, Royer took off dribbling: *Indiana State Alumni Magazine*, Spring 1973.
79   "that's the fastest way to get the ball down the court": Wooden with Jamison, *My Personal Best*, p. 75.
79   "one of the most difficult things I had to do was cutting the squad": Academy of Achievement interview.
80   Wooden's team included fourteen freshmen and one sophomore: Wooden interview with Jares.
80   "A lot of the locals were really disturbed": Reporter's file for *Sports Illustrated* by Jack Tobin, Aug. 9, 1968; Chapin and Prugh, *Wizard of Westwood*, p. 68.
80   "It's amazing to me the thesis would be accepted": Ibid.
82   "We had a saying": Powell interview with Jares.
83   they found their bus surrounded by Evansville fans: Chapin and Prugh, *Wizard of Westwood*, p. 7; author interview with Duane Klueh.
84   "He was just that type of individual": "Living Legend: 'Good Teacher' Is All Wooden Wanted to Be," *Chicago Tribune*, Mar. 5, 1995.
85   Wooden's decision caused Walker immense pain: Clarence Walker's diary, courtesy of Kevin Walker.
85   blacks accounted for less than 3 percent of the population in Indiana: Leonard J. Moore, *Citizen Klansmen: The Ku Klux Klan in Indiana, 1921–1928* (Chapel Hill: University of North Carolina Press, 1991), p. 81.
86   Stephenson was convicted of rape and second-degree murder: "Who Killed Carol Jenkins?" *New Yorker*, Jan. 7, 2002.
86   It was also vehemently anti-Catholic: David M. Chalmers, *Hooded Americanism: The History of the Ku Klux Klan* (Durham, N.C.: Duke University Press, 1987), p. 172.
87   "I remember him in his polite, beautiful English": Johnson, *John Wooden Pyramid of Success*, p. 284.
88   "Mom always butted heads with some of the locals about the way they treated blacks": Bisheff, *John Wooden*, p. 180.

9. CLARENCE

Interviews: Duane Klueh, Jim Powers, John Wooden

90   "It's because they held the ball so long on offense": Purdue interview.
93   Manhattan withdrew and the athletic director publicly stated the reason: "Balk at N.A.I.B. Ruling," *Kansas City Times*, Mar. 5, 1948.
93   Henshel sent a telegram to the Olympic committee's chairman recommending that the NAIB champion be dropped: "Olympic Committeeman Suggests U.S. Trials Drop N.A.I.B. Winner," *New York Times*, Mar. 5, 1948.
93   on Friday, March 6, two days before the tournament was due to tip off, they

announced that the prohibition had been removed: "Lift Negro Ban," *Kansas City Times*, Mar. 6, 1948.

93 The development did not make a huge splash back in Terre Haute: "Indiana State Heads for K.C.," *Terre Haute Star*, Mar. 6, 1948. The story ended with: "Yesterday in Kansas City tourney officials made a ruling that Negro players would be eligible to compete in the tourney. This will permit Clarence Walker, speedy State guard, to play and Coach Wooden immediately placed him on the squad."

95 you'd never know from reading the city's two major newspapers that something significant had occurred: "Sixteen Survivors Face Stern Competition in NAIB Cage Games Today," *Kansas City Times*, Mar. 10, 1948.

95 a poll of five sportswriters: "Rate the Teams," *Kansas City Star*, Mar. 10, 1948.

96 hoisted him onto their shoulders, and carried him to the locker room: "Indiana State Rallies to Edge Hamline, 66–65, in Overtime Sizzler," *Terre Haute Star*, Mar. 13, 1948.

97 "a note from Los Angeles": "Bob Nesbit's News Bits," *Terre Haute Star*, Mar. 15, 1948.

97 The station joined the game in progress after the completion of the high school state semifinals: *Terre Haute Star*, Mar. 13, 1948.

98 So did the 53,704 who watched over six days, as well as the total of $65,777.59 they paid for admission: "Louisville Wins," *Kansas City Star*, Mar. 14, 1948.

99 The players were paraded down Wabash Avenue: "Indiana State Cagers Will Receive Noisy Welcome on Return Home Today," *Terre Haute Tribune*, Mar. 15, 1948.

99 "I thought he was happy at Indiana State": Powell interview with Jares.

99 "He said, 'Mr. Warriner, I may be in bad down there'": Johnson, *John Wooden Pyramid of Success*, p. 275.

100 He had gone so far as to find a buyer for his house until Indiana increased his salary: Reporter's file for *Sports Illustrated* by Dick Denny of the *Indianapolis News*, Aug. 10, 1968.

100 "One man convinced me that John Wooden was the man. It was Dutch Fehring": Reporter's file for *Sports Illustrated* by Jack Tobin, Aug. 9, 1968.

100 "I met John at the airport upon his return and knew that he was hooked": Powell interview with Jares.

101 "I didn't like that way of doing things": Wooden interview with Jares.

101 "John always told me, 'Never take a job where your predecessor remains on the premises'": Bisheff, *John Wooden*, p. 4.

101 "I wanted the Minnesota job": Hall of Fame interview.

101 Wooden told McCormick he had already agreed to take the position at UCLA: Ibid.; Wooden with Jamison, *My Personal Best*, p. 80; Wooden with Tobin, *They Call Me Coach*, p. 32; Chapin and Prugh, *Wizard of Westwood*, p. 71.

102 "I deeply regret leaving State at this time": "Johnny Wooden Resigns," *Indiana Statesman*, Apr. 22, 1948.

10. UNWELCOME

Interviews: Art Alper, Ralph Bauer, Wayne Boulding, Ralph Joeckel, Ken Proctor, Betty Putnam, Paul Saunders, Don Seidel, Eddie Sheldrake, George Stanich

105 "The fast break is my system": "Wooden Arrives for Spring Cage Drills," *Daily Bruin*, April 26, 1948.

105 "I've never played for nor coached a losing team in my life": "Ned Cronin: Wooden Never Was on a Losing Team," *Los Angeles Daily News*, Feb. 27, 1953.

106   "I felt like I was coming to the end of the world": Chapin and Prugh, *Wizard of Westwood*, p. 83.

106   "I came from the farm, the country, and Los Angeles was frightening to me": Academy of Achievement interview.

106   The Woodens decided to rent an apartment in the Culver City neighborhood: Chapin and Prugh, *Wizard of Westwood*, p. 80.

106   "Had I realized the situation, I'm quite certain I wouldn't have come": Heisler, *They Shoot Coaches, Don't They?*, p. 17.

107   "You think you're too good to drink with us?" Chapin and Prugh, *Wizard of Westwood*, p. 82.

107   "At UCLA he was now asked to attend every type of function": Ibid.

107   "he was lost": Bisheff, *John Wooden*, p. 7.

107   "John is misunderstood by many people": Reporter's file for *Sports Illustrated* by Art Rosenbaum, Aug. 1, 1968.

107   "Red had come in and captured the town": Chapin and Prugh, *Wizard of Westwood*, p. 82.

107   "We came out here and we were made to feel unwelcome": Ibid., p. 83.

108   A question mark appeared opposite that number: Ibid., p. 84.

108   "I remember those figures because they just transposed the last numbers": Marv Dunphy, *John R. Wooden: The Coaching Process* (Thesis, Brigham Young University, 1981), p. 55.

108   "I didn't say anything about their wind": Ibid.

108   The men's gymnasium had been built in 1932: Andrew Hamilton and John B. Jackson, *UCLA on the Move: During the Fifty Golden Years, 1919–1969* (Los Angeles: Ward Ritchie Press, 1969), p. 70.

109   "I took the easy job, I must say": Heisler, *They Shoot Coaches, Don't They?*, p. 18.

109   "There were a hundred high school gyms in Indiana that were far, far better": Wooden interview with ESPN, Mar. 12, 1998.

111   "He was a tenacious, tough, hard-nosed, vicious competitor": Johnson, *John Wooden Pyramid of Success*, p. 421.

112   He derided that tactic as "negative rebounding": "UCLA: Simple, Awesomely Simple," *Sports Illustrated*, Nov. 30, 1970.

113   "A coach who plays up-tempo style, as opposed to ball control, is less likely to be fired": Chapin and Prugh, *Wizard of Westwood*, p. 230.

114   "We had a saying": Powell interview with Jares.

115   one of the opposing coaches asked Wooden if he wanted to set up a scrimmage the following morning for players who didn't get into the game: Ibid.

117   "I was at a new place, trying to get established. You want to do well": Wooden interview with ESPN, Mar. 12, 1998.

11. THE NONCONFORMIST

Interviews: Art Alper, Ralph Joeckel, Jerry Norman, Barry Porter, Paul Saunders, Eddie Sheldrake

118   "You guys need another pigeon for bridge?": Reporter file for *Sports Illustrated* by Jack Tobin, Aug. 9, 1968.

119   "Wooden was a little cornballish and had some straitlaced ideas, and Jerry was a little more sophisticated": Powell interview with Jares.

120   "He was very profane": Johnson, *John Wooden Pyramid of Success*, p. 42.

121   "Our hope is to run Conley so much we cut him down to our size": "Midwest Boasts More Top Cagers," *Los Angeles Times*, Mar. 6, 1950.

121   Joeckel banked in a shot from just beyond half-court in the closing seconds: Hamilton and Jackson, *UCLA on the Move*, p. 177.

122   Purdue sent three top administrators to Los Angeles: "How Purdue Failed to Snatch Wooden," *Los Angeles Daily Mirror*, Mar. 3, 1950.

122   Purdue also dangled perks: Wooden with Jamison, *My Personal Best*, p. 98.

123   "They knew what I wanted to talk about": Johnson, *John Wooden Pyramid of Success*, p. 35.

123   "I guess they had learned enough about me": Academy of Achievement interview.

123   "My family likes it here and so I chose to stay": "How Purdue Failed to Snatch Wooden," *Los Angeles Daily Mirror*, Mar. 3, 1950.

124   "I was irritated to say the least": Johnson, *John Wooden Pyramid of Success*, p. 35.

124   "If there was no hope of a new pavilion, there is no hope of keeping Wooden": "OK Pavilion Plans," *Daily Bruin*, Mar. 3, 1950.

125   "Ridgway was being disciplined": "Ridgway 'Saw Light,' Says UCLA Cage Coach," *Los Angeles Times*, Mar. 12, 1951.

125   "Stop Norman and you can stop the Bruins": "Bruins May Sew Up Title Tonight," *Los Angeles Times*, Feb. 29, 1952.

125   "Norman has been our spark": "Huskies to Collide with 'New' UCLA," *Los Angeles Times*, Mar. 4, 1952.

125   "Mr. Wooden and I just had a few differences": "Jerry Norman Transformed, Now Bruin Cage Team's Spark Plug," *Los Angeles Times*, Mar. 20, 1952.

126   "It was one of our worst games in quite a while": "Wooden Sad, Feerick Glad Over Outcome," *Los Angeles Times*, Mar. 22, 1952.

12. L.A. STORY

Interviews: Art Alper, Jerry Evans, Ken Flower, Marv Harshman, Denny Miller, Ed Powell, Betty Putnam, Doug Sale, Bob Seizer, Eddie Sheldrake, Ron Tomsic, John Wooden

127   "After all the trucks made their deliveries and came back, I would call the next day's orders, sweep out the place, and head over the hill to UCLA": Johnson, *John Wooden Pyramid of Success*, p. 36.

127   "The better basketball players in the Midwest are no better than our basketball players in the far west": "Midwest Boasts More Top Cagers," *Los Angeles Times*, Mar. 6, 1950.

128   a member of the school's faculty committee on finances recommended that the project be financed by raising the annual student fee by four dollars: "Pavilion Called Feasible by Rep Meet Speakers," *Daily Bruin*, Apr. 24, 1952.

128   "It was nothing but murder in there. Like walking into an oven": Chapin and Prugh, *Wizard of Westwood*, p. 89.

129   "It didn't displease me that other teams felt that it was a sweatbox": Wooden interview with Jares.

129   "persecution complex": Johnson, *John Wooden Pyramid of Success*, p. 38.

129   "I don't know how I got anything done": Wooden interview with ESPN, Mar. 12, 1998.

129   some 6,200 veterans enrolled: Hamilton and Jackson, *UCLA on the Move*, p. 107.

130   "I'm just a common person": Chapin and Prugh, *Wizard of Westwood*, p. 75.

130   "He felt a little estranged from his son": Johnson, *John Wooden Pyramid of Success*, p. 409.

131   "Who's in charge of this school?": Bisheff, *John Wooden*, p. 251.

131   when Wooden read the label and saw that it contained blackberry brandy, he refused to drink the stuff: Johnson, *John Wooden Pyramid of Success*, p. 407.

132   "When he first came out west he was provincial, a little aloof": Chapin and
        Prugh, *Wizard of Westwood*, p. 241.

132   At one point he got her an appointment with a hypnotist, but it didn't work:
        Bisheff, *John Wooden*, p. 40.

132   "Too soon!": "John Thinks His Pre-Game Bruin Ritual Needs Repairs," *Los
        Angeles Times*, Mar. 13, 1960.

133   "I probably would have had a rough time at some place where you have to go out
        and get them": Wooden interview with ESPN, Mar. 12, 1998.

133   "You know, this is not a bad place to live": Purdue interview.

133   "We became settled": Academy of Achievement interview.

134   The only time they bickered in front of the kids was when he discovered she had
        again neglected to register checks she had written from their bank account:
        Bisheff, *John Wooden*, p. 40.

13. WILLIE THE WHALE

Interviews: Jerry Evans, Bill Johnston, Sherrill Luke, Bobby Pounds, Ed Powell, Morris Taft

136   The *Daily Bruin* said Jackie looked like a "wasted robot": Arnold Rampersad,
        Jackie Robinson: A Biography (New York: Ballantine Books, 1997), p. 73.

138   "My last game in high school was in front of eighteen thousand people": Chapin
        and Prugh, *Wizard of Westwood*, p. 91.

140   "Johnny was the first person in my dressing room": Reporter's file for *Sports
        Illustrated* by Dick Denny, Aug. 10, 1968.

140   "My mother doesn't think that I should accept this money, and neither do I":
        Willie Naulls, *Levitation's View: Lessons Voiced from an Extraordinary Journey*
        (Laguna Niguel, Calif.: Willie Naulls Ministries, 2005), p. 29.

140   When Naulls complained to Wooden, the coach told Naulls he knew nothing
        about such arrangements: Ibid., p. 127.

141   "With Wooden, you don't feel you can do this": Chapin and Prugh, *Wizard of
        Westwood*, p. 300.

141   Naulls enrolled in extra classes, got reimbursed for the books, and then he
        returned them to the bookstore and pocketed the refunds: Naulls, *Levitation's
        View*, p. 74.

141   "You do not deserve any special parking privileges": Ibid., p. 73.

141   "Our team will be helped and will improve when Naulls gets into shape":
        "'Loaded' Bruin Hoopmen Rate as Powerful Title Contenders," *Los Angeles
        Times*, Dec. 10, 1953.

142   They also sat together that night in a segregated movie theater: Naulls, *Levita-
        tion's View*, p. 160.

142   on a drive to the basket, he elbowed the guy in the mouth as hard as he could:
        Ibid., p. 163.

142   "Two hands on the ball will get you more playing time": Ibid., p. 274.

142   "I was tremendously insulted because he never even discussed it with me":
        Chapin and Prugh, *Wizard of Westwood*, p. 299.

144   "Oh, Wooden is the best college coach of all time": Ibid., p. 274.

14. THE DONS

Interviews: Carroll Adams, Bill Eblin, Morris Taft

145   Wooden ordered them back into the locker room, where he upbraided them for
        being so impressed: Naulls, *Levitation's View*, p. 207.

146   "I'm gonna whip you, boy, real bad": Ibid.

146   "the greatest job any one man ever did against UCLA": "Utah Tops Tough Card for Diablos," *Los Angeles Times*, Dec. 22, 1954.

147   "I always have felt the responsibility belongs to the team behind to change what they're doing": "Trojans Expected to Improve This Week," *Los Angeles Times*, Feb. 15, 1955.

147   "I think both of them should give this game of basketball some thought as to what they are doing to it": "Twogood Raps Bruin, Tribe Stalling Tactics," *Los Angeles Times*, Feb. 17, 1955.

148   "Contrary to a lot of opinions, I'd like to see a lot more games just like that": "John Wooden Speaks Up for 24-Second Rule," *Los Angeles Times*, Jan. 31, 1956.

150   "We got out ahead of them and slowed down our style of play": "Dons Favored by Eight over UCLA," *San Francisco Chronicle*, Dec. 30, 1955.

150   "It stunned us—and it beat us": John Wooden interview with Charlie Rose, Dec. 15, 2000.

150   "Russell's defensive play kills you": "Dons Triumph over UCLA," *San Francisco Chronicle*," Dec. 31, 1955.

151   "A man has to make up his own mind in a situation that affects so many others": Naulls, *Levitation's View*, p. 348.

151   "I've heard some protests from the Bay Area regarding Venice High's short floor": "Cal Gets Its Chance to Halt Bruin Quintet," *Los Angeles Times*, Feb. 28, 1956.

152   "Willie can do so many more things": "Wooden Rates Naulls Better All-Around Cager Than Russell," *Los Angeles Times*, Mar. 1, 1956.

153   "To this day I can't understand how they could have passed up Willie Naulls": John Wooden interview with ESPN, Aug. 13, 2002.

15. PETE

Interviews: Ned Averbuck, Bob Berry, Denny Crum, Gary Cunningham, Bob Dalton, Bill Eblen, John Green, Bill Kilmer, Bill McClintock, Tom Newell, Jerry Norman, Ben Rogers, Earl Schulz, Eddie Sheldrake, Roland Underhill

154   the *Oakland Tribune* published an article alleging that UCLA football players were given $40 above the $75 in expenses permitted: "Report Says Bruins Got Secret Grid Pay," *Los Angeles Times*, Mar. 2, 1956.

154   The PCC found the charges to be true and responded in heavy-handed fashion: "Entire UCLA Grid Team Faces Ban," *Los Angeles Times*, May 22, 1956.

154   more than fifty athletes a total of over $71,000: "SC Accused of Paying Athletes $71,235," *Los Angeles Times*, May 24, 1956.

154   the PCC imposed on UCLA a three-year suspension from championship and bowl competitions in all sports, plus fines totaling around $93,000: "Ban Against UCLA Blamed on Rivals," *Los Angeles Times*, July 24, 1956; Hamilton and Jackson, *UCLA on the Move*, pp. 130–31.

154   The Los Angeles City Council struck back by passing a resolution: "City Council Urges SC, UCLA to Bolt," *Los Angeles Times*, July 14, 1956; "Will Bruins Bolt PCC?" *Los Angeles Times*, Nov. 30, 1956.

155   "Our balance again proved true": "Balance Makes Bruin Cagers Click," *Los Angeles Times*, Jan. 15, 1957.

156   "It was a feeling of being alone and no one understanding the dark thoughts I was having": Bruce Jenkins, *A Good Man: The Pete Newell Story* (Berkeley, Calif.: Frog, 1999), p. 182.

156   "It would drive you up a wall": Johnson, *John Wooden Pyramid of Success*, p. 326.
156   "If you don't want to shoot, go to Cal": Jenkins, *Good Man*, p. 121; Joe Jares notes.
156   "John didn't like our slowdown style at first": Jenkins, *Good Man*, p. 120.
156   "the team making the fewer mistakes generally wins": "We Don't Concede Anything," *Sports Illustrated*, Jan. 18, 1960.
157   "a player should be conditioned to play the last five minutes of a game": Ibid.
157   Newell himself was on hand when they took on USC a few days before: "SC Upsets UCLA In 84–80 Cage Thriller," *Los Angeles Times*, Feb. 27, 1957.
158   "They never played timeouts again with us": Jenkins, *Good Man*, p. 119.
159   the Cal faculty objected to its southern counterpart's desire to move its campus: Hamilton and Jenkins, *UCLA on the Move*, p. 7.
159   "This could be the tallest and also the slowest Bruin team I've had": "Optimism Abounds at Cage Lunch," *Los Angeles Times*, Dec. 3, 1957.
159   "They caught up with the fast break after a while": H. Anthony Medley, *UCLA Basketball: The Real Story* (Los Angeles: Galant Press, 1972), p. 11.
160   "I would not do that": Heisler, *They Shoot Coaches, Don't They?*, p. 19.
160   The city announced in the fall of 1957 that an architect's designs had been completed for a multipurpose arena: "Cage Scribes Given Latest Word on 'the Hole' at Weekly Meet," *Los Angeles Times*, Dec. 17, 1957.
161   the regents and trustees at UCLA, California, and USC formally decided to withdraw from the league effective the summer of 1959: "UCLA and Cal Can Withdraw from PCC In '58," *Los Angeles Times*, June 22, 1957.
161   "The rule would eliminate the occasional, farcical game": "Wooden for 30-Second Cage Rule," *Los Angeles Times*, Feb. 4, 1958.
162   earning the nickname the "Wizard of Westwood": "Senior Cagers Falter, Bruins, Waves Roll On," *Los Angeles Times*, Feb. 26, 1962.
162   he was sharing a motel bed with a prostitute: "Red Sanders and a Paradise Lost," *Bruin Report*, July 26, 2010.
162   Wooden "suffered in silence": Chapin and Prugh, *Wizard of Westwood*, p. 81.
165   "the most inexperienced team since I've been at UCLA": "SC-Bruin Cagers Christen Arena," *Los Angeles Times*, Nov. 26, 1959.
165   He hobbled on crutches for several weeks: "First Casualty of Cage Season Is Bruin Coach," *Los Angeles Times*, Oct. 24, 1959.
167   "We allowed Oklahoma State to play its game and you can't do that": "Twogood Praises Kemp," *Los Angeles Times*, Dec. 15, 1959.
169   "Why don't you call a technical foul on me and get it out of your system?": "Ref Let Game Get out of Control, Says Wooden," *Los Angeles Times*, Feb. 1, 1960.
169   Wooden asked if he wouldn't mind getting together in the off-season so they could talk about defense: Johnson, *John Wooden Pyramid of Success*, p. 401.
170   Forrest Twogood accidentally elbowed Wooden in the face: "Players, Fans Riot at SC-UCLA Game," *Los Angeles Times*, Mar. 6, 1960.

16. WALT

Interviews: Bob Archer, Dick Banton, John Berberich, Bob Berry, Pete Blackman, Gary Cunningham, Chuck Darrow, Jerry Evans, Gail Goodrich, Larry Gower, John Green, Jerry Norman, Doug Sale, Fred Slaughter, Roland Underhill, Dave Waxman

172   he would be "one of the best basketball players UCLA has ever had": "Lawson Destined for Cage Stardom," *Los Angeles Times*, Dec. 24, 1960.
173   "He never quite fit in": Johnson, *John Wooden Pyramid of Success*, p. 326.
173   "I once loved to play": *Los Angeles Times*, Dec. 24, 1960.

173 "I did not work with the parents that much": Dunphy, *John R. Wooden*, p. 144.

173 "Well, reluctantly": Ibid.

174 Lawson admitted before a New York grand jury that he had been approached by professional gamblers: "UCLA Cager Lawson Admits Bribe Offer, Quits School," *Los Angeles Times*, May 30, 1961.

174 "I've never had a boy who resented instruction and correction as much as Lawson did": Chapin and Prugh, *Wizard of Westwood*, p. 98.

175 "I would explain to my players that we're like a machine": Dunphy, *John R. Wooden*, p. 69.

175 "Little things add up, and they become big things": Wooden interview with ESPN, Mar. 12, 1998.

177 "It disgusts me to see all these cartoons of raving maniac coaches": Joe Jares notes of Wooden lecture at Kutsher's Country Club, June 26, 1967.

178 "The one word that my players will hear from me more than any other in practice is *balance*": Wooden interview with Jares.

178 "A three and one look off-balance, and I like balance": Joe Jares notes.

178 "I wanted the business-like approach": Dunphy, *John R. Wooden*, p. 123.

179 "I never want my players to feel that winning a basketball game was any great accomplishment": Ibid., p. 128.

179 "John's not the flippant type": Reporter's file for *Sports Illustrated* by George Ferguson, Aug. 1, 1968.

179 "I love to play those teams that just came back from Hawaii": Wooden interview with Jares.

179 "If I see a boy giving up the baseline [on defense], I take him out for the rest of the half": Joe Jares notes of Wooden lecture at Kutsher's Country Club, June 26, 1967.

180 "They learn that I stick by my demands": *Sports Illustrated*, Mar. 19, 1962.

180 "handled the team like a machine": "UCLA Cager Raps Wooden, Quits to Play for San Diego St.," *Los Angeles Times*, July 27, 1973.

181 Naulls called Wooden to tell him about this young man: Naulls, *Levitation's View*, p. 270.

183 "We're a running club": "Wizards in the Land of Oz," *Sports Illustrated*, Mar. 19, 1962.

184 "He was fancy": Hall of Fame interview.

186 "My feeling was that we'd be better off not playing them that night": "UCLA's Negro Stars Benched for Aggie Tilt," *Los Angeles Times*, Dec. 27, 1961.

187 "that doesn't mean we won't play there eventually": Ibid.

17. "DON'T BE A HOMER!"

Interviews: Pete Blackman, Ken Flower, John Green, Dan Hruby, Earl Schulz, John Wooden

189 "He was screaming and yelling at me": Heisler, *They Shoot Coaches, Don't They?*, p. 22.

189 Hazzard called his mentor and friend, Willie Naulls, to inform him of his decision: Naulls, *Levitation's View*, p. 273.

189 unbeknown to him, Wooden had already called his father before he benched Hazzard for the Ohio State game: Wooden with Jamison, *My Personal Best*, p. 132.

190 "I sort of question the fairness of this": *Los Angeles Times*, Feb. 12, 1962.

191 "Dadburn it, Joe, you saw him double dribble down there!": *Sports Illustrated*, Jan. 6, 1969.

191 "I don't stand up and do anything to excite the crowd": Wooden interview with Jares.

191   "I needle, in a soft-sell way": Ibid.

191   "he will say, 'Do I want to meet this Wooden or do I want to meet that one?'":
       Powell interview with Jares.

192   "Wooden was no saint": Chapin and Prugh, *Wizard of Westwood*, p. 311.

192   "I've seen him so mad that I've been afraid he'd pop that big blood vessel in his
       forehead": *Sports Illustrated*, Jan. 6, 1969.

192   "The athletic director of the other school came in and talked to me": Wooden
       interview with ESPN, Mar. 12, 1998.

192   Wooden also developed a habit of bringing a stopwatch to the games: Wooden
       interview with Joe Jares.

192   "I don't think from an educational viewpoint it's the way to coach basketball or
       coach anything": Jenkins, *Good Man*, p. 123.

193   an "antiseptic needle": Reporter's file for *Sports Illustrated* by Phil Taylor, July
       24, 1968.

194   "I wouldn't do that, boys": "Wizards in the Land of Oz," *Sports Illustrated*, Mar.
       19, 1962.

195   "Hazzard faked the guy and the guy fell down": Wooden interview with John
       Akers, *Basketball Times*, Jan. 28, 2005.

18. GAIL

Interviews: Stan Andersen, Pete Blackman, Denny Crum, Keith Erickson, Gail
Goodrich, Mike Hibler, Jack Hirsch, Bill Johnston, Bob Murphy, Jerry Norman, Barry
Porter, Paul Saunders, George Stanich, John Wooden

197    $150 million to invest in new facilities: Hamilton and Jackson, *UCLA on the
       Move*, p. 144.

197   "Would I grow? Would I be big enough?" Reporter's file for *Sports Illustrated* by
       Jack Tobin, Oct. 20, 1970.

198   "I thought he'd drive me out of my mind": "New Kingpin of Go-Go Bruins,"
       Sporting News, Jan. 28, 1965.

198   "My first two years I was the king of the poor students": Reporter's file for *Sports
       Illustrated* by Jack Tobin, Oct. 20, 1970.

198   "You've never been ripped until he's ripped you": Ibid.

199   "I don't think he would be ecstatic if his daughter married a black man": John-
       son, *John Wooden Pyramid of Success*, p. 358.

199   "The man was one of the most superstitious people I ever met": Ibid., p. 361.

199   "Of course, it's all very silly": "John Thinks His Pre-Game Bruin Ritual Needs
       Repairs," *Los Angeles Times*, Mar. 13, 1960.

200   Wooden first got the idea when he read that the old St. Louis Cardinals baseball
       teams did it: Wooden interview with ESPN, Mar. 12, 1998.

200   He kept in his pocket a smooth rock, which he called his "Indian worry stone":
       Joe Jares notes.

200   The connecting flight he was supposed to take crashed between Atlanta and
       Raleigh: Krider, *Indiana High School Basketball's 20 Most Dominant Players*, p.
       249; Chapin and Prugh, *Wizard of Westwood*, p. 6.

200   "I don't think I ever looked at it as being superstitious": Wooden interview with
       ESPN, Mar. 12, 1998.

201   "Look," he said, pointing to the page. "Blue shoes": Dunphy, *John R. Wooden*, p.
       243.

201   "They had my home phone number": Ibid., p. 141.

202   "to see they're not getting slovenly": Johnson, *John Wooden Pyramid of Success*,
       p. 123.

204   "I'm very fond of Keith": Wooden interview with Jares.

205   "He was always abrasive": "Day One of a Dynasty," *Los Angeles Times*, Mar. 29, 1989.

205   "I never asked the players to call me 'Coach'": Ibid.

205   the Los Angeles Coliseum Commission had allocated most of the Sports Arena's Saturday night slots: "West Side Will See Hoopsters," *Los Angeles Times*, Sept. 30, 1962.

206   "My guards can't hit from anywhere past 15 feet": "A Storm Blows In on Sunshine Square," *Sports Illustrated*, Mar. 18, 1963.

206   "I don't want to schedule them for three years": "UCLA, USC Begin Big Six Cage Play," *Los Angeles Times*, Dec. 31, 1962.

206   "There were nights when I'd come home from practice so tired": Reporter's file for *Sports Illustrated* by Jack Tobin, Oct. 20, 1970.

206   "Freddie has a better attitude": Medley, *UCLA Basketball*, p. 33.

208   "We're backing in": *Sports Illustrated*, Mar. 18, 1963.

208   "No one likes money anymore": "No TV, Only 2,000 Seats," *Los Angeles Times*, Mar. 11, 1963.

210   The poem was ten verses long: Wooden with Tobin, *They Call Me Coach*, p. 13.

19: PERFECT

Interviews: Jay Buckley, Keith Erickson, Gail Goodrich, Fred Goss, Walt Hazzard, Jack Hirsch, Rene Herrerias, Jeff Mullins, Jerry Norman, Fred Slaughter, Jerry Tarkanian, Kenny Washington, John Wooden

211   "give Fred Slaughter all he wants to handle and more": "Provo Post-Mortems," *Los Angeles Times*, Mar. 19, 1963.

212   "He did a lousy job in '63": Hall of Fame interview.

214   "Jerry was not reluctant to make suggestions": Ibid.

214   "I've always second-guessed myself a little for that": Bisheff, *John Wooden*, p. 52.

215   To that point in his life, he had barely spoken to a white person: Medley, *UCLA Basketball*, p. 17; "The Team of '64," *Sports Illustrated*, Mar. 26, 1979.

216   "He had structure, a philosophy built on fairness": "Birth of a Dynasty," *Sports Illustrated*, Mar. 19, 2007.

216   "Our kids got rattled by their press": Medley, *UCLA Basketball*, p. 30.

217   the Bruins were "absolutely the best precision team I've ever seen": "UCLA Climbed Hoop Pinnacle in Topping Michigan," *Sporting News*, Jan. 11, 1964.

218   "it was an innovation that just shocked people": Heisler, *They Shoot Coaches, Don't They?*, p. 23.

218   "Passes are intercepted and teammates will sometimes say, 'Watch your passing'": Medley, *UCLA Basketball*, p. 28.

218   "Every team we face in the conference will try to do the same thing": "Sputtering Bruins Catch Fire, 79-59," *Los Angeles Times*, Jan. 11, 1964.

219   "I don't recall ever seeing us break loose the way we did tonight": "Whew! Bruins Gun Down Injuns, 84-71," *Los Angeles Times*, Jan. 18, 1964.

219   "Sure, there's some pressure on us": "Pressure Grows for Streaking Bruins; Huskies Next in Path," *Los Angeles Times*, Feb. 10, 1964.

219   "I had an orange juice and a sandwich and then went right in and got sick": "The Real Bruins," *Los Angeles Times*, Feb. 12, 1964.

220   "I've won a lot of ball games in the Bay Area": "Bruins to Face Bad 'Press' at Stanford," *Los Angeles Times*, Feb. 17, 1964.

220   "They don't look like any superteam": "Five Midgets and a Wink at Nell," *Sports Illustrated*, Feb. 24, 1964.

220   "As soon as we meet a team with a good big center, we may be in trouble":

"U.C.L.A. Five Makes It to Top on Clean Living and Fast Break," *New York Times*, Jan. 22, 1964.

220 "All five. *Team*. You understand?": *Sports Illustrated*, Feb. 24, 1964.

220 "Yet, off the floor, they were not that close": John Wooden interview with ESPN, Apr. 19, 2000.

221 "Hazzard and Goodrich didn't get along at all": Medley, *UCLA Basketball*, p. 36.

221 "But Hazzard *will* pass": Joe Jares notes on Wooden lecture at Kutsher's Country Club, June 26, 1967.

222 "He picks up more garbage than anyone I've ever seen": Ibid.

223 "I remember looking over at him with his legs crossed and program rolled up": *Sports Illustrated*, Mar. 19, 2007.

223 "And we just enjoyed playing for the man": Ibid.

224 "We were too busy having fun and beating the crap out of everyone": Ibid.

225 "I said to myself, this man is nuts": Johnson, *John Wooden Pyramid of Success*, p. 358.

226 "It's as if God said, this team is going undefeated": *Sports Illustrated*, Mar. 19, 2007.

227 "I think we can beat their press": "The Two-Minute Explosion," *Sports Illustrated*, Mar. 30, 1964.

227 "Up": Ibid.

227 Wooden broke his policy not to call the first time-out: Wooden with Tobin, *They Call Me Coach*, p. 132.

228 "We couldn't beat 'em!": Medley, *UCLA Basketball*, p. 39.

229 "You are champions and you must act like champions": *Sports Illustrated*, Mar. 30, 1964.

20. J. D.

Interviews: Keith Erickson, Gail Goodrich, Fred Goss, Ron Livingston, Mike Serafin

233 "I'll take care of the budget": Wooden with Jamison, *My Personal Best*, p. 142; Johnson, *John Wooden Pyramid of Success*, p. 111.

233 "He was a very dominant, aggressive type of person": J. D. Morgan Oral History, UCLA Archives.

234 "I was sitting there during a time-out": Ibid.

234 "That was a tremendous load off my shoulders": Ibid.

234 "John was never interested in money": Ibid.

235 "I'm more inclined toward what Charlie Brown says": Chapin and Prugh, *Wizard of Westwood*, p. 308.

236 "I saw all those games and the preparations": Hall of Fame interview.

239 the Iowa players lifted their coach, Ralph Miller: *Los Angeles Times*, Feb. 8, 1965.

240 "The crowd was yelling louder and louder": "The Power of the Press," *Sports Illustrated*, Mar. 29, 1965.

21. LEWIS

Interviews: Kareem Abdul-Jabbar (including for College Sports Television), Lucius Allen, Jay Carty, Gary Cunningham, Fred Goss, Jerry Norman

242 the man called him Lewis: Kareem Abdul-Jabbar and Peter Knobler, *Giant Steps: The Autobiography of Kareem Abdul-Jabbar* (Toronto: Bantam Books, 1983), p. 108.

242 "I am impressed by your grades": Ibid., p. 109.

243   even the speculation that he *might* visit: "Ace Schoolboy Cage Prospect to Visit UCLA." *Los Angeles Times*, Mar. 17, 1965.

243   Alcindor arrived by plane on Friday night (and many other details of Alcindor's visit): Reporter's file for *Sports Illustrated*, May 5, 1965.

243   "That really impressed me": Bisheff, *John Wooden*, p. 126.

244   jammed regularly at the Elks Club: "My Story," *Sports Illustrated*, Oct. 27, 1969.

245   white barbers in their neighborhood: Ibid.

245   "You only give people something to laugh about": Ibid.

245   "I could see Lewie flush": "Lewie Is a Minority of One," *Sports Illustrated*, Dec. 5, 1966.

245   "You're acting just like a nigger!": Abdul-Jabbar and Knobler, *Giant Steps*, p. 66; *Sports Illustrated*, Oct. 27, 1969.

246   a coaching clinic in Valley Forge, Pennsylvania: Wooden interview with Akers.

247   "We'd never have gotten him to come with the old gym": Ibid.

247   He said it was because Norman was Catholic: J. D. Morgan Oral History, UCLA Library.

248   "the first time the press had ever heard the sound of Alcindor's voice": "The Big Decision," *New York World-Telegram and Sun*, May 5, 1965.

248   "I have an announcement to make": "Schoolboy Star Explains Choice," *New York Times*, May 5, 1965.

248   "I've seen the kid play several times": "Big A Guarded," *New York Journal-American*, Jan. 16, 1965.

248   "Anybody who believes that is only displaying his ignorance": "Alcindor Mature, Modest Young Man," *Christian Science Monitor*, May 6, 1965.

248   "I don't try to make a star out of anybody": Ibid.

248   "*Is that Lew Alcindor?*": "My Story."

249   "ocean on a raft": Ibid.

250   "Yes, I would have hired him": Bisheff, *John Wooden*, p. 11.

251   "I was just astounded": Wooden interview with ESPN, Mar. 12, 1998.

254   "I was completely impressed": "UCLA's Alcindor Rises to Occasion," *Christian Science Monitor*, Dec. 1, 1965.

254   "We're way out of place": Reporter's file by Bill McWhirter, *Time*, Dec. 1, 1965.

22. STALLBALL

Interviews: Kareem Abdul-Jabbar, Lucius Allen, Bob Boyd, Gary Cunningham, Dick Enberg, Fred Goss, Ken Heitz, Mike Lynn, Jerry Norman, Bill Sweek, Mike Warren

256   In the fall of 1965, *Sports Illustrated* previewed the coming season: "A Press That Panics Them All," *Sports Illustrated*, Dec. 6, 1965.

257   "I said I won't go back to this place again": Hall of Fame interview.

258   "Basketball followers have built up something of a hate for coach John Wooden": "Dallmar Hero in Bay Area," *Los Angeles Times*, Jan. 31, 1966. The writer is not the same Paul Zimmerman, also known as "Dr. Z," who spent several decades writing about the National Football League for *Sports Illustrated*.

259   "This team has been one of the most difficult teams": Medley, *UCLA Basketball*, p. 71.

259   "played them the only way you can play them": "Alcindor and Co. Will See More of Stall—Mulligan," *Los Angeles Times*, Mar. 6, 1966.

259   "If you drop a pin in Azusa": "Pressure's on 'Poor' Wooden": *Los Angeles Times*, May 17, 1966.

260   he had worked in the publishing and recording divisions of Columbia Pic-

tures . . . courtesy of an influential UCLA alumnus named Mike Francovich: Abdul-Jabbar and Knobler, *Giant Steps*, p. 118.

261 1958 Mercedes: Ibid., p. 144.

261 Wooden invited Alcindor and Allen to his home for Thanksgiving: Ibid., p. 153.

261 he asked Wooden if he could help out in practice: "Naulls Works to Smooth out Lew's Rough Edges": *Los Angeles Times*, Nov. 16, 1966.

261 "I'm seven feet one and three-eighth inches tall": *Sports Illustrated* reporter's file by Jack Tobin, Oct. 15, 1966.

262 "He just whipped the crap out of us": Medley, *UCLA Basketball*, p. 319.

264 "At times, he frightens me": *New York Times*, Dec. 5, 1966.

265 "There's no such thing": *New York Times*, Dec. 12, 1966.

265 "I suppose that if I had one game to play against them": "He'll Score 80 Points One of These Nights," *Christian Science Monitor*, Dec. 14, 1966.

266 "This game proved that we're going to be down on certain nights": "Alcindor Gets 34, Bruins Get Scare," *Los Angeles Times*, Dec. 23, 1966.

266 "I must be blind": Ibid.

266 a referee who had been the best man at his wedding: "Hello, Drip, Drip! Goodbye, UCLA," *Sports Illustrated*, Dec. 15, 1969.

267 J. D. Morgan had convinced the pilot to land the plane in St. Louis: J. D. Morgan Oral History, UCLA Library.

267 he had received death threats: "Alcindor Threatened, Had Police Bodyguard," *Los Angeles Times*, Feb. 1, 1967.

267 "Look at that big black freak!": Wooden with Jamison, *My Personal Best*, p. 154; Wooden interview with ESPN, Mar. 12, 1998.

267 "I'm still amazed at the way Lew can keep his poise": "Bears Arouse Alcindor," *Los Angeles Times*, Jan. 14, 1967.

268 Instead, he needed seven police officers to escort him: "Bruins Survive Trojans' Stall to Win in Overtime, 40–35," *Los Angeles Times*, Feb. 5, 1967.

269 "I don't think most coaches will try it": "USC Almost Put Bruins in Freezer," *Los Angeles Times*, Feb. 5, 1967.

269 "there was no personal criticism intended": Medley, *UCLA Basketball*, p. 105.

270 "Bob had my support in everything he did": "Trojans' Hill Reprimands Wooden," *Los Angeles Times*, Feb. 7, 1967.

270 "All Wooden has to do": "They Don't Love UCLA's Wooden in the Bay Area," *Los Angeles Herald Examiner*, Feb. 16, 1967.

270 "We didn't know exactly what he meant": Bisheff, *John Wooden*, p. 107.

271 "Their fans were so happy when they did it": Medley, *UCLA Basketball*, p. 108.

271 "studying the rule book": "Bruins Figure to Wrap Up AAWU Title over Weekend," *Los Angeles Times*, Feb. 20, 1967.

271 "one of the nicest people the Lord ever made": Hall of Fame interview.

272 "it was my most enjoyable weekend in the Bay Area": "Must Have Ball to Defeat UCLA," *Los Angeles Times*, Mar. 7, 1967.

273 "I beat him one-on-one tonight": Bisheff, *John Wooden*, p. 112.

23. GAME OF THE CENTURY

Interviews: Kareem Abdul-Jabbar, Lucius Allen, Jay Carty, Keith Erickson, Michael Gilbert, Rose Gilbert, Fred Goss, Ken Heitz, Mike Lynn, Jerry Norman, Don Saffer, Neville Saner, Earl Schulz, Bob Seitzer, Mike Serafin, Gene Sutherland, Bill Sweek

275 "I had a lot of personal contact with both [Alcindor] and Lucius": Chapin and Prugh, *Wizard of Westwood*, p. 298.

276 "one of the mules of the world": "To Those Who Know Him, Gilbert Is the Godfather," *Los Angeles Times*, Feb. 1, 1982.

276 "He's a bundle of dynamite": Ibid.

276 "I told Lucius, 'Man, you become instant Jewish'": Reporter's file for *Time*, Feb. 11, 1974.

277 "I hadn't met either of them": "UCLA's Good Sam," *Los Angeles Times*, Mar. 20, 1974.

277 "took a genuine liking to me": Heisler, *They Shoot Coaches, Don't They?*, p. 55.

277 "Sam is everybody's Jewish grandfather": *Los Angeles Times*, Feb. 1, 1982.

279 "I had very little respect for the NCAA": Heisler, *They Shoot Coaches, Don't They?*, p. 55.

281 "Sam introduced me to the language of finance": *Los Angeles Times*, Feb. 1, 1982.

282 "From what Alcindor told me later, no one had any influence": J. D. Morgan Oral History, UCLA Library.

282 "Sam steered clear of John Wooden": Abdul-Jabbar and Knobler, *Giant Steps*, p. 158.

282 "they say you're high hat": "Wooden Concedes UCLA Stronger," *Los Angeles Times*, Nov. 8, 1967.

283 "the rule is designed to curtail the ability of one player": Chapin and Prugh, *Wizard of Westwood*, p. 157.

283 "I'm not guessing on this": Wooden interview with Rose.

283 "people are trying to make it a small man's game": Reporter's file for *Sports Illustrated*, Apr. 5, 1967.

284 "My jump shot is back from the dead": "Lynn, Lacey Return Welcomed": *Los Angeles Times*, Oct. 27, 1967.

285 "Well, I'm glad that's over": "Whew! Last-Second Basket by Sweek Edges Purdue," *Los Angeles Times*, Dec. 3, 1967.

285 "I made a mistake": Medley, *UCLA Basketball*, p. 115.

285 "Lynn and Lacey were buddying up": Ibid., p. 117.

287 The seeds for the most significant game in basketball history: Many details about Eddie Einhorn and TVS come from Eddie Einhorn with Ron Rapoport, *How March Became Madness* (Chicago: Triumph Books, 2006).

288 "I thought it would be making a spectacle out of the game": J. D. Morgan Oral History, UCLA Library.

289 "People were calling and saying, 'I don't care where I am'": Einhorn with Rapoport, *How March Became Madness*, p. 57.

289 "It is my understanding that Lewis can't play": "Alcindor Still Doubtful for Game with Houston," *Los Angeles Times*, Jan. 19, 1968.

291 "I can't do it. I can't do it": Medley, *UCLA Basketball*, p. 122.

291 Warren told Lynn Shackelford that he wanted to ask Wooden to take out Alcindor: Einhorn with Rapoport, *How March Became Madness*, p. 73.

291 "I don't think I would have made the shot anyway": Ibid.

292 "Maybe we've been winning too much": Johnson, *John Wooden Pyramid of Success*, p. 51.

292 "For the great majority of the audience": Einhorn with Rapoport, *How March Became Madness*, p. 51.

292 "I think he was relieved": Johnson, *John Wooden Pyramid of Success*, p. 419.

292 "I'll be seeing a pleasant face now": "Probably Erred Playing Lew Entire Game, Wooden Admits," *Los Angeles Times*, Jan. 22, 1968.

293 "It brought me back to earth in a hurry": Libby, *Walton Gang*, p. 185.

293 Morgan sent Wooden an article: Ibid.

293 "Why didn't Coach use Lacey?": Chapin and Prugh, *Wizard of Westwood*, p. 167.

293   "Edgar got his feelings hurt early": "Differs with Poll," *Los Angeles Times*, Jan. 23, 1968.

293   "He threw the paper down on the floor": "Lacey May Quit UCLA Cage Team in Dispute," *Los Angeles Times*, Jan. 25, 1968.

294   Wooden favored players who...were "morally right to play": Lew Alcindor, "A Year of Turmoil and Decision," *Sports Illustrated*, Nov. 10, 1969.

295   "he cannot go with us now": *Los Angeles Times*, Jan. 25, 1968.

295   "He's just very quiet and sensitive": "Lacey Quits UCLA Team, Fires Blast at Wooden," *Los Angeles Times*, Jan. 29, 1968.

295   "I've never enjoyed playing for that man": Ibid.

295   "You aren't going to print any of this": Chapin and Prugh, *Wizard of Westwood*, p. 265.

296   "I can't help but believe somebody might be putting words into his mouth": "Wooden Baffled, Remorseful over Sudden Move by Lacey," *Los Angeles Times*, Jan. 30, 1968.

296   "my most trying year in coaching": Ibid.

296   "We lost a *potentially* great player": Medley, *UCLA Basketball*, p. 129.

297   "Wooden ruined the boy's life": Johnson, *John Wooden Pyramid of Success*, p. 362.

24. KAREEM

Interviews: Kareem Abdul-Jabbar, Lucius Allen, Denny Crum, John Ecker, Fred Goss, Ken Heitz, Mike Lynn, Bob Marcucci, Jerry Norman, Don Saffer, Neville Saner, Terry Schofield, Gene Sutherland, Bill Sweek, Sidney Wicks, John Wooden

298   "they're eager to know how to do things": Wooden interview with Jares.

299   "J. D. realized these places were sold out": J. D. Morgan Oral History, UCLA Library.

299   "Two of his teammates made some remarks": Wooden interview with ESPN, Mar. 12, 1998.

300   "I guarantee you Lew's going to have good shoes": Joe Jares notes on clinic at Kutsher's Country Club, June 26, 1967.

300   "It all depends on how you're playing": "The UCLA Dynasty: Behind the Scenes with Lew Alcindor and Company," *Sport*, Apr. 1969.

300   "We black players knew that as a unit we had a lot of power": "Pride and Prejudice," *Sports Illustrated*, July 8, 1968.

301   they pounded the pipe so hard: Abdul-Jabbar and Knobler, *Giant Steps*, p. 113.

301   He bought two tabs: Ibid., p. 138.

301   a pair of students who had taken LSD came upon him and thought he was an hallucination: Lew Alcindor, "UCLA Was a Mistake," *Sports Illustrated*, Nov. 3, 1969.

301   Sam Gilbert bailed Allen out of jail: *Los Angeles Times*, Feb. 1, 1982.

301   "How's that for a hint?": *Sports Illustrated*, Nov. 30, 1970.

302   "I would discourage anybody from interracial dating": Ibid.

302   "His relationships with blacks have no meaning": Ibid.

303   "the right man in the right place": "West of the Wabash," *New Yorker*, Mar. 22, 1969.

303   taped it to his locker: Heisler, *They Shoot Coaches, Don't They?*, p. 30.

304   "It's a disgrace": "Tourney Tongues Drip Poison over Bruins' Olympic Dropout," *Sports Illustrated*, Apr. 6, 1968.

304   "Lacey's quitting has not appeared to hurt appreciably": "Rematch for Elvin and Big Lew," *Sports Illustrated*, Mar. 18, 1968.

304   "Revenge is something I don't harbor": Ibid.

305   "I feel like a dead man": *New York Times*, Apr. 6, 1968.

305   "the win last night over Houston was the more satisfying victory": "Yawn! Bruins Take Win in Stride," *Los Angeles Times*, Mar. 24, 1968.

305   "It's difficult to do, very difficult": "Two Routs to a Title," *Sports Illustrated*, Apr. 1, 1968.

306   "I don't mean to sound derogatory": Johnson, *John Wooden Pyramid of Success*, p. 404.

306   two felony counts of possession of marijuana: "Lucius Allen out on Bail; UCLA Cage Career at End?" *Los Angeles Times*, May 25, 1968.

307   He had converted to Islam (and subsequent details): Abdul-Jabbar and Knobler, *Giant Steps*, pp. 140–41, 166–70; *Sports Illustrated*, Nov. 3, 1969.

309   "It wasn't a friendly type competition with Sidney": Medley, *UCLA Basketball*, p. 416.

309   "I was getting very tired": Ibid., p. 151.

310   "That's the kind of guy Sidney was": Ibid., p. 418.

310   "He's a genius as a coach": *Sport*, Apr. 1969.

311   Wooden erupted: Andrew Hill with John Wooden, *Be Quick—but Don't Hurry!* (New York: Simon & Schuster, 2001), p. 133.

311   "It's got to be the constant pressure": Medley, *UCLA Basketball*, p. 148.

312   "I can honestly say that I received more criticism after we won": Johnson, *John Wooden Pyramid of Success*, p. 128.

313   "Then don't": Bisheff, *John Wooden*, p. 40.

313   "I may appear calm": Libby, *Walton Gang*, p. 184.

315   "When winning becomes that important, I'm getting out": Chapin and Prugh, *Wizard of Westwood*, p. 177.

315   "I think these boys are taut": "The Week He Finally Got Rid of the Yoke," *Sports Illustrated*, Mar. 31, 1969.

318   "Lucius should be here": Ibid.

319   "I look forward to again coaching to try to win": "UCLA," *Sports Illustrated*, Dec. 1, 1969.

25. THE LAST BANQUET

Interviews: Henry Bibby, Kenny Booker, Jay Carty, John Ecker, Dick Enberg, Larry Farmer, Andy Hill, Jim Nielsen, Terry Schofield, Bill Sweek, Jerry Tarkanian, Sidney Wicks, John Wooden

320   "He goes better with sycamores": *Sports Illustrated*, Jan. 6, 1969.

320   "I'm glad to see Lewis get all he can get": "Offer to Lew Is 'Nonsense,' Says Wooden," *Los Angeles Times*, Apr. 1, 1969.

321   "I don't think I would have enjoyed working for Jack Kent Cooke": Bisheff, *John Wooden*, p. 232.

321   "I'm very, very sorry to find out": Chapin and Prugh, *Wizard of Westwood*, p. 182.

321   "We are not on the spot like we were before": "Bruins Will Run and Press Again with Lew Gone," *Los Angeles Times*, Oct. 15, 1969.

321   "Lew really destroyed my confidence": "Patterson: Nobody Can Replace Lew," *Los Angeles Times*, Nov. 30, 1969.

323   Wicks and Rowe apologized to Wooden: Wooden interview with Akers.

324   "*You* don't have to come to practice": Hill with Wooden, *Be Quick—but Don't Hurry!*, p. 26.

324   "We had to refrain from being too active after that": Bisheff, *John Wooden*, p. 155.

324   "Everybody is doing something now": "Lew, Who? Bruins Sharp in Debut," *Los Angeles Times*, Dec. 2, 1969.

325   "I'm like any fan, I guess": "It's More Fun Without Lew," *Sports Illustrated*, Feb. 2, 1970.

325   "The esprit de corps was, frankly, not good last year": Ibid.

327   "might get a little fat-headed": Chapin and Prugh, *Wizard of Westwood*, p. 186.

327   "It's more of an achievement to beat Coach Wooden": *Sports Illustrated*, Nov. 30, 1970.

328   "He has no superior": "Champion Bruins Face Upstart 49ers," *Los Angeles Times*, Mar. 12, 1970.

328   "If anybody has a mystique, it's Coach Wooden": "Victory by Mystique," *Sports Illustrated*, Mar. 30, 1970.

329   "discipline against devil-may-care": "Bruins Turn Aggie Dream into Nightmare," *Los Angeles Times*, Mar. 20, 1970.

330   "That's beautiful": *Sports Illustrated*, Mar. 30, 1970.

331   "It's better that we're not fawned over": *Sports Illustrated*, Nov. 30, 1970.

331   "unequal treatment . . . double rules standard . . . lack of communication": "'Farewell' Address by Bruin Sub Upsets Basketball Fete," *Los Angeles Times*, May 11, 1970.

333   "He seemed hurt, for reasons you can imagine": Ibid.

334   "crisis of authority": "Calm Returns to UCLA After Violent Eruption," *Los Angeles Times*, May 7, 1970.

335   "We, the undersigned": Chapin and Prugh, *Wizard of Westwood*, p. 191.

335   "some of the players they seemed to be real pleased": Medley, *UCLA Basketball*, p. 179.

336   he had written the players' names in alphabetical order: Ibid., p. 178.

336   "I still think I was right in doing it": Ibid., p. 179.

336   "He had been trying to divide and harass us": *Sports Illustrated*, Nov. 30, 1970.

337   "A player gets the treatment he earns and deserves": Ibid.

337   "have I been fair?": Ibid.

26. THE REDHEAD

Interviews: Henry Bibby, Bob Boyd, Denny Crum, Gary Cunningham, Tommy Curtis, Larry Farmer, Ken Heitz, Terry Schofield, Jerry Tarkanian, Bill Walton, Sidney Wicks, Jamaal Wilkes, Charles Young

338   "as good a prospect": Libby, *Walton Gang*, p. 101.

339   "Let your imagination run wild": Bisheff, *John Wooden*, p. 137.

340   "the ectomorph": Bill Walton with Gene Wojciechowski, *Bill Walton: Nothing but Net* (New York: Hyperion, 1994), p. 66.

340   "I sort of enjoyed standing back there watching": "Court Trial for UCLA's New Gang," *Sports Illustrated*, Jan. 10, 1972.

340   attended a concert with his girlfriend: Libby, *Walton Gang*, p. 100.

341   "It was a prank, but also a form of rebellion": Reporter's file for *Time*, Feb. 4, 1974.

342   "The older I get": "Bruin Cagers 'Tuning' Up: 'Happy Birthday' to Coach," *Los Angeles Times*, Oct. 15, 1970.

343   "That includes the Bruin team with Gail Goodrich and Walt Hazzard": "Bruins Breeze Past Baylor in Opening Game, 108–77," *Los Angeles Times*, Dec. 5, 1970.

343   "You guys were late, so you're not starting": Johnson, *John Wooden Pyramid of Success*, pp. 115–16.

343   "Are you kidding?": Bisheff, *John Wooden*, p. 76.

344   "J. D. was never modest about telling Coach whether he was right or wrong": J. D. Morgan Oral History, UCLA Library.

344   "He'd write reports on them": Ibid.

345   Morgan invited the two of them to his office: Ibid.

345   "I could not argue": Ibid.

345   "I could tell him like he told me about the scheduling": Ibid.

346   "J. D. was a remarkable guy": Bisheff, *John Wooden*, p. 75.

346   "I think that was true at UCLA, to be honest with you": J. D. Morgan Oral History, UCLA Library.

348   "I told you, Coach!": "An Irish Carr Moves into High Gear," *Sports Illustrated*, Feb 1, 1971.

349   "I don't like stall basketball, but it is legal": Medley, *UCLA Basketball*, p. 197.

349   Wooden chided Ridgle from the bench: Bisheff, *John Wooden*, p. 41.

350   Patterson decided he wanted to quit: Hill with Wooden, *Be Quick—but Don't Hurry!*, p. 106.

352   J. D. Morgan started yelling at referee Art White: Bisheff, *John Wooden*, p. 218.

352   "Sidney certainly wasn't one of my better free throw shooters": Wooden interview with ESPN, Apr. 19, 2000.

353   "He told me to go sit down": "A Close One at Last," *Sports Illustrated*, Apr. 5, 1971.

354   "You guys sick?": "UCLA Stalls Way to 5th Cage Crown," *Sporting News*, Apr. 10, 1971.

355   "I personally would not have done it": Medley, *UCLA Basketball*, p. 205.

355   "I'm sure you writers will put pressure on us": Libby, *Walton Gang*, p. 107.

27. SAM

Interviews: Lucius Allen, Henry Bibby, Bob Boyd, Denny Crum, Gary Cunningham, John Ecker, Larry Farmer, Michael Gilbert, Rose Gilbert, Gail Goodrich, Fred Goss, Ken Heitz, Andy Hill, Doug Krikorian, Bob Marcucci, Tom Newell, Jim Nielsen, Don Saffer, Terry Schofield, Jerry Tarkanian, Bill Walton, Bruce Walton, Bob Webb, Sidney Wicks, Jamaal Wilkes, John Wooden, Charles Young

357   he had filled nearly thirty notebooks: "Court Trial for UCLA's New Gang," *Sports Illustrated*, Jan. 10, 1972.

357   "He's so young": Libby, *Walton Gang*, p. 112.

359   assembled a game-by-game prediction: Wooden with Tobin, *They Call Me Coach*, p. 171.

359   "It's belittling and demeaning": Libby, *Walton Gang*, p. 250; Medley, *UCLA Basketball*, p. 212.

360   "No," Walton replied: "Walton Stirs Another Bruin Avalanche," *Los Angeles Times*, Dec. 31, 1971.

360   "He may be the most dominant center ever to play basketball": *Sports Illustrated*, Jan. 10, 1972.

360   "Lewis was more phlegmatic": *Los Angeles Times*, Dec. 31, 1971.

360   Wooden accorded him the unprecedented privilege of calling his own time-out: Wooden with Tobin, *They Call Me Coach*, p. 183.

361   "I honestly thought of quitting": Libby, *Walton Gang*, p. 37.

361   "That's against the law": Wooden interview with Akers; *Sports Illustrated*, Apr. 3, 1989.

361   "I'm really having fun with this team": *Sports Illustrated*, Jan. 10, 1972.

362   Hill conducted a scientific sample of the student body: Hill with Wooden, *Be Quick—but Don't Hurry!*, p. 39.

362   Wooden regaled Swen Nater with plans of going "snipe hunting": Ibid., p. 44.

363   "We have this great UCLA image": "Who Are These Guys?," *Sports Illustrated*, Feb. 5, 1973.

363   "He told me it was disgraceful and unethical": "Battered Ratleff Accuses Refs of Protecting UCLA," *Los Angeles Times*, Mar. 19, 1972.

363   Walton "cries a lot": "Oh, Johnny, Oh, Johnny Oh!" *Sports Illustrated*, Apr. 3, 1972.

364   "We didn't play well. There's no reason for elation": "Fla. State Loses," *New York Times*, Mar. 26, 1972.

364   "The same thing was said about the Yankees": "Wooden Defends UCLA's Domination," *Los Angeles Times*, Mar. 28, 1972.

366   "Sam is the conscience of Sidney Wicks": "Who Needs an Agent? Bruins Call on Sam," *Los Angeles Times*, June 9, 1971.

366   "No one is worth ten percent of a man's earnings": Ibid.

367   "If a ballplayer impregnated someone, there was always a hospital available. I never paid for it, and it was my case": "NCAA Missed the Iceberg in Westwood," *Los Angeles Times*, Jan. 31, 1982.

368   "He was a referral service": Ibid.

369   "I'm helping put a couple of Chicano and black kids through law school": Reporter's file for *Time*, Feb. 11, 1974.

369   "Sam Gilbert wasn't doing it for chemistry majors": *Los Angeles Times*, Feb. 1, 1982.

369   "almost as important to the program as Pauley Pavilion": "Saga of Papa Sam and the One That Got Away," *Los Angeles Times*, Jan. 22, 1975.

370   "He's just a great dude": Reporter's file for *Time*, Feb. 11, 1974.

370   "He's living in the guest house of a $150,000 home in Brentwood for $150 a month": "Is Walton Parroting Gilbert?," *Los Angeles Times*, Mar. 12, 1974.

370   "Bill Walton has yet to sleep inside": Reporter's file for *Time*, Feb. 11, 1974.

370   "I've told my family to refer them to Sam Gilbert": "College Player of the Year," *Sporting News*, Mar. 18, 1972.

371   "Sam's friendship has meant a lot to my son": Reporter's file for *Time*, Feb. 11, 1974.

371   "Maybe it's corny, but I love you": Ibid.

372   "I just as politely, as courteously as I could, cut it off": Johnson, *John Wooden Pyramid of Success*, p. 93.

372   "I personally hardly know Sam Gilbert": Chapin and Prugh, *Wizard of Westwood*, p. 282.

372   "You didn't get the same price everybody else got if Sam sent you": Wooden interview with Akers.

373   "I can't tell Sam Gilbert or anyone else to stay away from my players": "Wooden: UCLA's Violations Minor," *Los Angeles Times*, Dec. 27, 1981.

373   "he turned a blind eye to that": J. D. Morgan Oral History, UCLA Library.

373   "J. D. was constantly in trouble with Gilbert": Ibid.

376   "If this is now allowed would you please let me know": J. D. Morgan papers, UCLA Archives.

376   "A Sam Gilbert gets going because it's tolerated at the player level and at the coach's level": J. D. Morgan Oral History, UCLA Library.

377   "These kids are lucky to have Sam because nobody else will help them": *Los Angeles Times*, Jan. 31, 1982.

378   "It's not like Coach was an ostrich about Sam, but he wouldn't confront the problem": *Sports Illustrated*, Apr. 3, 1989.

28. STREAKING

Interviews: Gene Bartow, Henry Bibby, Tommy Curtis, Larry Farmer, Bill Walton, Bruce Walton, Jamaal Wilkes, John Wooden

380   "He's the type who is either totally committed or totally disinterested": Reporter's file for *Time*, Feb. 4, 1974.

380   "Boy, could he get excited": "Bill Walton Won't You Please Play Ball?" *Sports Illustrated*, Jan. 27, 1975.

381   "On the floor, Bill was a leader": "Winning or Waiting, John Wooden Knows Meaning of Pressure," *Los Angeles Times*, Mar. 4, 1984.

381   "I'm going back to the campus" and other details on Walton's arrest: "Walton Arrested in Sitdown," *Los Angeles Times*, May 12, 1972; "Walton Fined, Gets Probation for Protesting," *Los Angeles Times*, June 9, 1972; Reporter's file for *Time*, May 14, 1972; Reporter's file for *Time*, Feb. 4, 1974; "Tall Stories," *Sports Illustrated*, May 22, 1972; Chapin and Prugh, *Wizard of Westwood*, p. 277; Walton with Wojciechowski, *Bill Walton*, p. 22.

382   "That is not in my bailiwick": *Sports Illustrated*, May 22, 1972.

384   "I'm sorry it happened": "'Sorry It Happened,' Says UCLA's Nater," *Los Angeles Times*, July 22, 1972.

384   "I'm not a very strong, pro-Olympic person": Wooden interview with ESPN, Aug. 13, 2002.

384   "I really can't answer that": Ibid.

385   "Johnny Wooden . . . has another side that most people don't know about": Phil Jackson and Charley Rosen, *More Than a Game* (New York: Simon & Schuster, 2002), p. 128.

385   "I was disappointed that our players did not accept the silver medals": Wooden interview with ESPN, Aug. 13, 2002.

386   "Thanking you in advance for your consideration in this matter": "Walton: Basketball's Vegetarian Tiger," *Time*, Feb. 25, 1974.

387   "I don't have blind reverence for authority": Ibid.

387   "I've always told my players to be quick but don't hurry": "Deliberate, Wan Wooden Returns to Coaching Duties," *Los Angeles Times*, Dec. 22, 1972.

387   "He lives a lonely, at times tormenting existence": "Wooden's Job Tougher Than People Think": *Los Angeles Times*, Dec. 25, 1972.

387   "I don't know whether winning is always good": Johnson, *John Wooden Pyramid of Success*, p. 88.

387   "These last few years haven't been the happiest in our lives": Chapin and Prugh, *Wizard of Westwood*, p. 316.

388   "Daddy's job wasn't fun for us": *Sports Illustrated*, Apr. 3, 1989.

388   he earned only $35,000 per year: "Morgan: Bruin Power," *Los Angeles Times*, July 23, 1972.

388   "All I can tell you is that Mom especially was really angry about that": Bisheff, *John Wooden*, p. 102.

388   "There was a time if my dad had endorsed a shoe": Johnson, *John Wooden Pyramid of Success*, p. 262.

389   "There's no sense trying to soft-pedal it": "Streak Can't Last Forever—Wooden," *Los Angeles Times*, Jan. 25, 1973.

390   "I wouldn't turn him on, but he doesn't bug me": *Sports Illustrated*, Feb. 5, 1973.

390   "It's a two-way street": "Wooden Apologizes to Phelps, Shumate," *Los Angeles Times*, Feb. 25, 1973.

391   "He asked me if I had read his book": "It's 61 and All-Time No. 1 for UCLA," *Los Angeles Times*, Jan. 28, 1973.

391   "This isn't the greatest thing": Ibid.

391   "We like pressure": Ibid.

391   He wrote a letter of apology: "Wooden Apologizes to Phelps, Shumate," *Los Angeles Times*, Feb. 25, 1973.

392   "I've learned to play for my own satisfaction": "Walton's Leaping Has UCLA Hopping," *Los Angeles Times*, Jan. 24, 1973.

392   "That's because everything they do is so predictable": Chapin and Prugh, *Wizard of Westwood*, p. 229.

392   "Let's see you do that on Walton": Einhorn with Rapoport, *How March Became Madness*, p. 29.

392   Wooden told his players that the coach of the opposing team was "bad for the game of basketball": Walton with Wojciechowski, *Bill Walton*, p. 42.

393   "Bill Walton was perfect": Hall of Fame interview.

393   "I don't remember being in a rougher game": "Pugnacious Ducks Can't Stop UCLA," *Los Angeles Times*, Feb. 23, 1973.

394   Wooden had arranged for the nets to be woven extra tight: Bisheff, *John Wooden*, p. 109.

394   "I'd rather get cancer": Reporter's file for *Time*, Feb. 11, 1974.

395   "You bet I was worried": "Dynasty Totters, but UCLA Wins," *Los Angeles Times*, Mar. 25, 1973.

395   It was a magnificent penthouse: Walton with Wojciechowski, *Bill Walton*, p. 36.

396   "It was a calculated risk on my part": "Wonderful World of Walton," *Los Angeles Times*, Mar. 27, 1973.

397   "the best collegiate player I've ever seen": Ibid.

397   "I'm in a hurry to go see some friends": "W is for Walton, Wooden and WOW," *Sporting News*, Apr. 7, 1973.

397   "I hope this will be his last season": *Los Angeles Times*, Mar. 27, 1973.

397   "I don't need any reasons for coming back": "A Slight Case of Being Superhuman," *Sports Illustrated*, Apr. 2, 1973.

398   "Fear and Loathing in St. Louis": Jack Scott, *Bill Walton: On the Road with the Portland Trail Blazers* (New York: Thomas Y. Crowell, 1976), p. 271.

29. INTOLERABLE

Interviews: Frank Arnold, Bruce Coldren, Lefty Driesell, Larry Farmer, Dick Harter, Jim Hefner, Marques Johnson, Bill Walton, Jamaal Wilkes, John Wooden

399   "Far more disturbing than Walton's behavior": "Man of Few Words Draws Many Barbs," *Washington Post*, Mar. 30, 1973.

399   "The Wooden sales effort—and gall—reached a rare level": "Wooden Also Intends to Be No. 1 in Nation's Bookstalls," *Washington Post*, Apr. 1, 1973.

399   "UCLA's Bruins, who beat everybody, won't talk to just anybody": "UCLA's Champs as Others See Them: A Blight," *Los Angeles Times*, Apr. 24, 1973.

399   "a cancer": Ibid.

399   Wooden "often assumes the pompous air of his days as an English teacher": "Phelps' Players Dig Him," *Washington Post*, Jan. 21, 1974.

400   "It's a sad thing what has happened to college basketball," Bisheff, *John Wooden*, p. 84.

400   it had been "a very 'trying' year for me": Letter courtesy of Duane Klueh.

401   "If he even loses a game they're going to say that he's too old": Johnson, *John Wooden Pyramid of Success*, p. 88.

401   "you'll not drink wine": Chapin and Prugh, *Wizard of Westwood*, p. 274.

401   He then pointed out that it was his right to determine who was permitted to

practice: "Walton Reports Sans Long Locks; Gives Pep Talk," *Los Angeles Times*, Oct. 17, 1973.

401   "I may be an anarchist, . . . but I'm no dummy": "The Top Twenty," *Sports Illustrated*, Nov. 26, 1973.

402   "I took a dip in Sam Gilbert's pool": *Los Angeles Times*, July 22, 1973.

402   "made more progress [last season], week by week": "Wooden Opens 26th UCLA Season and Hopes to Remain Indefinitely," *Los Angeles Times*, Oct. 17, 1973.

402   "Wooden has his favorites and I'm not one of them": "UCLA Cager Raps Wooden, Quits to Play for San Diego State," *Los Angeles Times*, July 27, 1973.

403   "We don't need luck": Bisheff, *John Wooden*, p. 140; Johnson, *John Wooden Pyramid of Success*, p. 450.

403   "You can't be rigid and unyielding": *Time*, Feb. 25, 1974.

404   "I just think winning all the time is immoral": Ibid.

405   "It's like when we had Kareem Jabbar": "UCLA Leaves Maryland a Shot Short, 65–64": *Los Angeles Times*, Dec. 2, 1973.

405   ABC gladly forked over $125,000 to each school: "Half of Big Red Is Too Much," *Sports Illustrated*, Dec. 24, 1973.

405   "I don't even know what kind of defenses North Carolina [State] plays, and I don't care": "Wolves and Bears," *Time*, Dec. 24, 1973.

406   "I have my Achilles' heels like other coaches do": "Wooden Says He Omits !/*# When He Zings Referees": *Los Angeles Times*, Dec. 21, 1973.

406   "I wish he could have changed his mind earlier": "Bench Warmer: Wooden Frustrated as Well as Taught, Corsair Coach Says," *Los Angeles Times*, Jan. 3, 1974.

407   "If I say what I think about this accomplishment, I know I'll sound immodest": "Even Wooden Admits He Is Dazzled," *Los Angeles Times*, Jan. 17, 1974.

407   "I could coach them myself": "The End of a Week That Never Was," *Sports Illustrated*, Feb. 4, 1974.

408   "Oh, I'm not a time-out caller": "The Streak Ends on Feat of Clay": *Los Angeles Times*, Jan. 20, 1974.

409   "I think this streak was the most tremendous thing there ever was for college basketball": "Did Digger Outcoach the Wizard? A Tale of Two Presses," *Los Angeles Times*, Jan. 21, 1974.

410   "They're number one. They beat us": "UCLA Regains the Poll Position, 94-75," *Los Angeles Times*, Jan. 27, 1974.

410   "I like to think I'm a well-rounded human being": "Greg Lee's Philosophy: Basketball Is Still Just a Game," *Los Angeles Times*, Mar. 1, 1974.

411   "I get tired carrying my 225 pounds around": Libby, *Walton Gang*, p. 34.

411   "Sometimes with Bill I feel like I'm handling a piece of glass": "The Enigma of Westwood," *Los Angeles Times*, Feb. 11, 1974.

412   They couldn't believe he said the word *crap*: Einhorn with Rapoport, *How March Became Madness*, p. 26; Walton with Wojciechowski, *Bill Walton*, p. 26.

412   "They listen . . . but do not hear": "Wooden Says Impatient Bruins Not as Coachable as in the Past," *Los Angeles Times*, Feb. 4, 1974.

412   "This team is not as hungry": "Oregon State Makes It Sticky," *Los Angeles Times*, Feb. 10, 1974.

412   "This group of UCLA players has, more or less, old-timers": "Bruins Lack Killer Instinct—Wooden," *Los Angeles Times*, Feb. 14, 1974.

413   "I'm sure he knows all about us": *Los Angeles Times*, Feb. 4, 1974.

413   "I respect UCLA's talent but have only distaste for its behavior": "Ambushed on the Oregon Trail," *Sports Illustrated*, Feb. 25, 1974.

413   "We're certainly not number one": Ibid.

414   "The right people are not playing": Ibid.

414   "I'll admit it gets tiresome to answer the same questions over and over about what could be wrong": "New Look, New Attitude," *Los Angeles Times*, Feb. 22, 1974.

414   "Most coaches I know don't think Wooden is a good X's and O's coach": "Three Views: UCLA Has Been Caught with Its Guard Down," *Los Angeles Times*, Feb. 20, 1974.

414   "I think it's good for basketball to have UCLA lose": "Dick Harter: USC Has Best Team In College Basketball," *Los Angeles Times*, Feb. 19, 1974.

415   Wooden stormed into the pool area in his nightgown and stocking cap: Einhorn with Rapoport, *How March Became Madness*, p. 26; Walton with Wojciechowski, *Bill Walton*, p. 26.

415   "I want North Carolina State to remember we beat them by 18 points": "Down and Out, Back Up and Ready," *Sports Illustrated*, Mar. 25, 1974.

416   "They were shots we shouldn't have taken": "Wolfpack Rallies for 80–77 Win," *Washington Post*, Mar. 24, 1974.

417   "I knew it couldn't go on forever": "UCLA Loses Poise, Lead, Streak, Title," *Los Angeles Times*, Mar. 24, 1974.

417   "I don't feel like talking": "Walton, Other Bruins May Sit Out Last Game," *Los Angeles Times*, Mar. 24, 1974.

418   "I think consolation games are for the birds": Ibid.

418   "Yes, this is the first time I've ever undergone this decision process": "Walton out of Consolation," *Washington Post*, Mar. 25, 1974.

418   "For the first time in my career, I became complacent this season": "Blame Me— Wooden," *Los Angeles Times*, Mar. 27, 1974.

419   "The streak shouldn't have meant that much": "Suddenly It Was Panic Time," *Los Angeles Times*, Jan. 9, 1975.

419   "emotional and physical exhaustion": "Mrs. Wooden Taken to Hospital After Win," *Los Angeles Times*, Mar. 26, 1974.

30. FAREWELL

Interviews: Frank Arnold, Gene Bartow, Bob Boyd, Gary Cunningham, Lefty Driesell, Dick Enberg, Dick Harter, Jim Hefner, Marques Johnson, Hank Nichols, Ted Owens, George Raveling, John Wooden

420   "He told me earlier in the year that this was going to be his last year": J. D. Morgan Oral History, UCLA Library.

421   "This can get monotonous": "Walk with Wooden," *Los Angeles Times*, July 16, 1974.

422   "Where have we been?": "Scouting Reports," *Sports Illustrated*, Dec. 2, 1974.

422   "I'm glad I didn't have Walton another year": "Wooden Cleans Up on Court," *San Bernardino Sun-Telegram*, Jan. 19, 1975.

422   "Basketball is still very important": "Illness Changed Life of Marques Johnson," *Los Angeles Times*, Mar. 5, 1975.

423   "Either we're not as good as I thought": "For Openers, Bruins, Trojans Show Their Stuff," *Los Angeles Times*, Nov. 30, 1974.

423   "I have tremendous respect for what he has accomplished as a player and as a coach": Richard "Digger" Phelps and Larry Keith, *A Coach's World* (New York: Warner Books, 1975), p. 138.

424   "Certain people are always looking to rap someone who's at the top": "Wooden's Not Saint John," *Los Angeles Times*, Dec. 19, 1974.

424   "They made a crusade out of it, but I liked that": Hall of Fame interview.

425   "To say I'm pleased with the play of every individual would never be true": "Bruins-Trojans: Just Me and My Friends," *Los Angeles Times*, Jan. 30, 1975.

425   "Teams that don't win the conference, I don't think should be in": "Wooden Unhappy with NCAA Format," *Washington Post*, Feb. 12, 1975.

426   "Wooden has been a problem": "NCAA Slaps at Wooden," *Chicago Tribune*, Jan. 6, 1975.

426   "I don't think the press as a whole would say that": Ibid.

426   "I'm very happy for Marv": "Huskies' Fans Linger to Savor Rout of UCLA," *Chicago Tribune*, Feb. 24, 1975.

426   "They're competitors in their own way": "Bruins Need Some Bounce," *Los Angeles Times*, Feb. 28, 1975.

426   "I accept it now": "The Wooden-Boyd Matchup," *Los Angeles Times*, Jan. 31, 1975.

427   The professors came up with ten different categories: "What a Coach Can Teach a Teacher," *Psychology Today*, Jan. 9, 1976.

427   "You look back at my practice program": "Walk with Wooden," *Los Angeles Times*, July 16, 1974.

430   His morning workout at the UCLA track was now starting at 5 a.m.: "Winning or Waiting, John Wooden Knows Meaning of Pressure," *Los Angeles Times*, Mar. 4, 1984.

431   "I said to him once, what about [hiring] Tarkanian?": J. D. Morgan Oral History, UCLA Library.

431   "I've got a frog in my throat": "Caught in a Spider's Web," *Sports Illustrated*, Feb. 17, 1975.

432   "I was elated for Pete": "Elated for Trgovich: Wooden Gets Emotional," *Los Angeles Times*, Mar. 9, 1975.

432   "The public announcement won't come until mid-April": "Raveling Reports Wooden to Retire," *Washington Post*, Mar. 9, 1975.

433   "I've said it before and I can say it again": "Wooden Reported Set to Retire," *Chicago Tribune*, Mar. 10, 1975.

434   "I won't want to lie": "Wooden's Retirement Reported Imminent," *Los Angeles Times*, Mar. 29, 1975.

434   The *Los Angeles Herald Examiner* published the same claim: "What a Wiz of a Win It Was," *Sports Illustrated*, Apr. 7, 1975.

435   "I don't want to. I have to": Ibid.

435   "I've asked J. D. Morgan to release me from my coaching duties at UCLA": "UCLA Gives Wooden a Last Hurray," *Los Angeles Times*, Mar. 30, 1975.

436   "the health of others": "UCLA, Kentucky Advance," *Washington Post*, Mar. 30, 1975.

436   "I'm thirty-five years old": "Wooden's Successor Still a Mystery Man," *Los Angeles Times*, Mar. 31, 1975.

436   "There's not much you can say about a man who has done what he has done in his profession": "Wooden's Swan Song," *Sporting News*, Apr. 19, 1975.

437   "There was a lot of emotion in the room": "The Man Gives the Word," *Los Angeles Times*, Mar. 30, 1975.

437   "I feel much better now that the announcement has been made": *Los Angeles Times*, Mar. 31, 1975.

437   "Still, it won't dampen our spirits": "Retirement Party Success Depends on Kentucky," *Los Angeles Times*, Mar. 31, 1975.

437   "Never before had we done this, but we had to": "Last NCAA Crown for the Wizard of Westwood," *Sporting News*, Apr. 19, 1975.

438   As he screamed "You crook!" at Nichols: *Sports Illustrated*, Apr. 7, 1975.

438   "I hope you have a nice life": Ibid.

439   "We went out with the idea that the more we ran them, the better we'd be": "Wooden Bows Out a Winner as UCLA Whips Kentucky," *Washington Post*, Apr. 1, 1975.

439   "Yes, I'm sad": "Title a Retirement Gift," *Los Angeles Times*, Apr. 1, 1975.

440   "I'd like to be remembered as a person who tried to do his best": "Hall Stays in Shadow of Legend in His Final Hour," *Washington Post*, Mar. 31, 1975.

440   "You let us down last year": Wooden with Jamison, *My Personal Best*, p. 197; Wooden with Tobin, *They Call Me Coach*, p. 199.

441   "If it were just coaching, it wouldn't be so bad": "Wooden's Successor Still a Mystery Man," *Los Angeles Times*, Mar. 31, 1975.

31. CLEAN GENE

Interviews: Gene Bartow, David Berst, Brent Clark, Gary Cunningham, Larry Farmer, Marques Johnson, John Wooden

445   "Nobody knew me": Hall of Fame interview.

446   "This is the most memorable evening of my athletic career": "Wooden Honored on 65th Birthday," *Los Angeles Times*, Oct. 16, 1975.

447   "But they love him here, don't they?": "Pursued by a Very Long Shadow," *Sports Illustrated*, Nov. 17, 1975.

447   "I don't think I left the cupboard bare": "Bartow and UCLA Never Look Back in 88–56 Win," *Los Angeles Times*, Nov. 22, 1975.

447   "He makes you want to play more than Coach Wooden did": *Sports Illustrated*, Nov. 17, 1975.

448   "It used to be that teams were intimidated when they played against us": "Grim, but They're Bearing It," *Sports Illustrated*, Feb. 16, 1976.

449   "I'm going to answer honestly": "Wooden Sees It as a Problem of Adjustment," *Los Angeles Times*, Jan. 20, 1976.

449   "Why would he say that?": "Boyd Says Wooden Put Heat on Bartow," *Los Angeles Times*, Jan. 27, 1976.

452   "I want to say 'thank you' for possibly saving my life": "Bartow Was in Fear of UCLA Booster," *Los Angeles Times*, Aug. 4, 1993.

454   "I thought the writers were very good to him": "Wooden Still Uses the Press in Some Advice to Bartow," *Los Angeles Times*, Apr. 25, 1976.

454   "My job here is to preserve a tradition": "Bartow Still Has That 'Problem,'" *Chicago Tribune*, Nov. 27, 1976.

454   Wooden had a brief health scare: "John Wooden Hospitalized," *Los Angeles Times*, Dec. 3, 1976.

455   he added that over his entire career he was only assessed three technical fouls: "A Year Later, Wooden Likes the Refs Better," *Los Angeles Times*, Mar. 26, 1976.

455   he wanted "to show how foolish stalling is by holding the ball": "Wooden: Let's Help the Defense," *Washington Post*, Mar. 15, 1977.

455   Wooden also reluctantly agreed to lend his name to a trophy: "Wooden One," *Los Angeles Times*, Mar. 8, 1977.

455   "some Bartow backers wonder how he can ever establish a . . . identity": "A Legend Leaves Big Footsteps," *Los Angeles Times*, Dec. 2, 1976.

456   "I think he was uncomfortable with my presence": Johnson, *John Wooden Pyramid of Success*, p. 133.

457   Bartow was being interviewed in-studio by a local radio host named Bud Furillo: Heisler, *They Shoot Coaches, Don't They?*, p. 81.

32. THE SHADOW

Interviews: Lucius Allen, Larry Brown, Brent Clark, Denny Crum, Gary Cunningham, Larry Farmer, Gary Franklin, Greg Goorjian, Jim Harrick, Walt Hazzard, Ken Heitz, Marques Johnson, George Raveling, Earl Schulz, Bill Walton

459   "When you consider the cost of living, the pay out there is way below par": "The Garden of Eden Isn't in Westwood," *Los Angeles Times*, Mar. 22, 1981.

459   "I don't consider Coach Wooden a shadow": "Cunningham: Wooden Will Be a Big Help," *Long Beach Press-Telegram*, July 12, 1977.

460   "I do see a difference—a great difference—in the amount of time that has to be spent on recruiting": "Cunningham: 33⅓ Coach in a Profession of 78s," *Los Angeles Times*, Jan. 16, 1979.

461   "My time at UCLA was very rewarding, but the job was not always fun": "Wise in the Ways of the Wizard," *Sports Illustrated*, Nov. 30, 1981.

462   "They were out of balance": "Anybody's Game," *Washington Post*, Feb. 28, 1978.

462   a youth basketball league in Los Angeles and Orange Counties: "Wooden's Youth Cage Loop Set," *Los Angeles Times*, Apr. 6, 1978.

462   "How many of you remember Pete Blackman?": "John Wooden: A Man Who Has Stories to Tell," *Los Angeles Times*, Dec. 1, 1978.

462   "Before we did it, people said it couldn't be accomplished": "Wooden Likes What He Is Seeing in Westwood These Days," *Los Angeles Times*, Dec. 14, 1979.

462   He had been hospitalized for pneumonia: "Morgan Retires as UCLA Athletic Director," *Los Angeles Times*, Oct. 30, 1979.

463   He later remarked to a reporter that he could "cut [Brown's] nuts off and he wouldn't know it until he pulled his pants down": *Sports Illustrated*, Nov. 30, 1981.

463   "I feared this guy would tear down the program if I fought him": "Call Him Irreplaceable," *Sports Illustrated*, Apr. 11, 1988.

465   "I know that I couldn't afford to take the UCLA job": "The March of the Wooden Soldiers," *Sports Illustrated*, Apr. 16, 1984.

465   "This is day one of what I hope won't be a two-year stint": "Farmer: Move for Country," *Los Angeles Times*, Mar. 18, 1981.

466   "Coach [Wooden], he might let you practice": Heisler, *They Shoot Coaches, Don't They?*, p. 133.

466   "Every one of those men left for better jobs more suited to their needs": *Sports Illustrated*, Nov. 30, 1981.

466   "I have no fears about comparisons with Coach Wooden": Ibid.

467   he gave Gilbert one of his NCAA championship rings: "NCAA Missed the Iceberg in Westwood," *Los Angeles Times*, Jan. 31, 1982.

467   After Marques Johnson joined the Milwaukee Bucks, he received a letter from Gilbert claiming that Johnson owed him around $2,000: "Wilkes Says Gilbert Sold Him Down River," *Los Angeles Times*, Feb. 1, 1982.

467   Gilbert was "closer to the owners than he is to the players": Scott, *Bill Walton*, p. 168.

468   "Are you going to use that letter [in the book]?": Ibid., p. 215.

468   "called me aside and said, 'We're just not going after the institution right now'": "Sam Gilbert and UCLA," *Los Angeles Times*, Jan. 31, 1982.

468   "He came up with zip": "NCAA Unable to Spot a Pattern," *Los Angeles Times*, Feb. 2, 1982.

468   Three of those recruits . . . told investigators that Gilbert had promised that he would provide them with cars: *Los Angeles Times*, Jan. 31, 1982.

469   The *Los Angeles Times* caught wind and published a report: "Car Buying by 4 UCLA Players Spurs Questions," *Los Angeles Times*, July 27, 1980.

469   "The world has become too crass": *Sports Illustrated*, Nov. 30, 1981.

469   The NCAA finally announced its findings on December 10, 1981: NCAA Infractions Report.

470   "Sam is interested in the program and the kids": "Who Got UCLA in Trouble? Sam Gilbert's Role Is Cited," *Los Angeles Times*, Dec. 10, 1981.

470   "It's a terrible thing, a slap in the face to him": Ibid.

470   "I felt that the things the NCAA came up with were of an inconsequential nature": "Wooden: UCLA's Violations Minor," *Los Angeles Times*, Dec. 27, 1981.

471   "I might be a little disillusioned, but I'm certainly not embarrassed": "Wooden Remembers Booster," *New York Times*, Feb. 4, 1982.

472   "he just didn't want to know": *Los Angeles Times*, Jan. 31, 1982.

472   "Knight was a great fundamentalist": John Wooden interview with ESPN, Sept. 29, 2003.

473   "dictator": Hall of Fame interview.

473   "I never threw anything. I never threw a chair": *Sports Illustrated*, Apr. 3, 1989.

473   Cheaney sent in a videotaped acceptance speech instead of attending: "John Wooden Was the King of a Different (and Not Pristine) Era in College Basketball," *Cleveland Plain Dealer*, June 10, 2010.

474   "But I would have played him": Hill with Wooden, *Be Quick—but Don't Hurry!*, p. 121.

475   "The problem we're having is John Wooden": *Los Angeles Times*, Mar. 4, 1984.

475   "Maybe that was the case at first, but it shouldn't be now": "Wooden: Bruins Seem to Be Playing Scared," *Los Angeles Herald Examiner*, Feb. 16, 1984.

475   "I had to tell them I really wasn't": "Farmer: It Wasn't Fair for Me to Stay at UCLA," *Los Angeles Times*, Apr. 2, 1984.

476   "Hey, it's tough here": *Sports Illustrated*, Apr. 16, 1984.

33. THE HARDEST LOSS

Interviews: Gary Cunningham, Michael Gilbert, John Green, Jim Harrick, Jack Hirsch, Marques Johnson, Jim Nielsen, Betty Putnam, Eddie Sheldrake

477   "Perhaps one of the reasons people still want to hear me": "Wooden's Deep Faith Nets Success," *Miami Herald*, July 5, 1986.

477   "This is not my cup of tea": Johnson, *John Wooden Pyramid of Success*, p. 133.

477   "I see coaches who have stopped coaching": "John Wooden's View from Retirement on Basketball, Discipline," *Christian Science Monitor*, Mar. 12, 1986.

477   "I deplore a game of non-action": "We Aren't Going to Change, Says Tar Heels' Smith," *Los Angeles Times*, Mar. 11, 1982.

478   "He became much more famous after he retired": Bisheff, *John Wooden*, p. 185.

478   "Today's kids are crying out for discipline": *Christian Science Monitor*, Mar. 12, 1986.

479   "I hope the good Lord will forgive my introducer": Johnson, *John Wooden Pyramid of Success*, p. 148.

479   "That's all a coach is. You're a teacher": *Chicago Tribune*, Mar. 5, 1995.

479   "Now he just coaches the world": Johnson, *John Wooden Pyramid of Success*, p. 159.

479   Her doctors saved her life by massaging her heart for forty-five minutes: *Los Angeles Times*, Mar. 4, 1984.

480   "They never called him, never told him they were coming": *Miami Herald*, July 5, 1986.

480   "Dad just never gave up hope": Johnson, *John Wooden Pyramid of Success*, p. 261.

480   "I never broke down in front of my family": *Los Angeles Times*, Mar. 4, 1984.

481   "It was . . . the last enjoyable thing she did": *Sports Illustrated*, Apr. 3, 1989.

481   "He kept copious notes": Johnson, *John Wooden Pyramid of Success*, p. 371.

481   "Your heart would pound": *Los Angeles Times*, Mar. 4, 1984.

481   "She's slowly slipping": *Los Angeles Herald Examiner*, Feb. 28, 1985.

481   "When she's awake, she's very aware, and always thinking of John": Ibid.

482   John took her cross and put it in his pocket: *Miami Herald*, July 5, 1986.

482   When he endorsed checks, he signed her name along with his: *Sports Illustrated*, Apr. 3, 1989.

482   "We thought it would make it easier now": Johnson, *John Wooden Pyramid of Success*, p. 262.

484   "Well, a new one came in and an old one's going out": Ibid., p. 239.

484   "He's an unmerciful tease": Ibid., p. 223.

484   "My knees don't handle this very well anymore": "Wooden Holds Court for Last Time," *Los Angeles Times*, Aug. 20, 1988.

484   "He was shaving in the bathroom. Tears came to his eyes": Johnson, *John Wooden Pyramid of Success*, p. 135.

484   "I won't ever leave here, because I see her everywhere": *Sports Illustrated*, Apr. 3, 1989.

485   "I couldn't go without her": *Miami Herald*, July 5, 1986.

485   "somber, almost melancholy mood": "A Wizard on Life," *Long Beach Telegram*, June 29, 1986.

485   "I don't think I'm preoccupied with death": "The Wizard of Willpower," *Los Angeles Times*, Oct. 14, 1990.

485   "Almost gone": *Sports Illustrated*, Apr. 3, 1989.

486   "as if pleased with his actions": NCAA Infractions Report.

487   "I think our program has weathered the storm": "Minor Penalties to UCLA; Gilbert Implicated," *Los Angeles Times*, Sept. 15, 1987.

487   a federal grand jury in Miami indicted Gilbert and five other men: "Sports Figure Is Indicted—4 Days After Death," *Los Angeles Times*, Nov. 26, 1987.

487   Michael Gilbert would serve five and a half years in federal prison: "Miami Trial Gives Startling New Portrait of Sam Gilbert," *Los Angeles Times*, Apr. 23, 1990.

34. ANDY

Interviews: Lucius Allen, Gary Cunningham, John Ecker, Keith Erickson, Gary Franklin, Fred Goss, John Green, Andy Hill, Jack Hirsch, Tony Medley, Jerry Norman, Don Saffer, Neville Saner, Terry Schofield, Eddie Sheldrake, Fred Slaughter, Gene Sutherland, John Wooden

491   "Stop hurrying," he said. "You're losing your balance": Hill with Wooden, *Be Quick—but Don't Hurry!*, p. 49.

494   "Have I ever told you how much I love you": Bisheff, *John Wooden*, p. 165.

494   "I enjoyed it": Johnson, *John Wooden Pyramid of Success*, p. 200.

494   he frequently claimed that he called time-out in the late stages of NCAA championship games: *Sports Illustrated*, Apr. 3, 1989.

495   "the official thought that I said something that somebody behind me said. But I kept it": *Wooden: Basketball and Beyond, The Official UCLA Retrospective* (San Diego: Skybox Press, 2011), p. 7.

495   "the pressure didn't bother me": Academy of Achievement interview.

495   "the NCAA came in and checked and found nothing that took place during my years": Wooden interview with Karpick.

496   "I refused because they wouldn't let him": Wooden interview with Rose,

496 "we were invited again [in 1948] and I refused": Hall of Fame interview.

496 "refused to go to the [1948] tournament if Clarence couldn't go": "Color Wall Came Down Here in '48," *Kansas City Star*, Mar. 13, 2002.

497 "As I headed across the court through the thousands of well-wishers and fans": John Wooden with Steve Jamison, *Wooden: A Lifetime of Observations and Reflections on and off the Court* (New York: McGraw-Hill, 1997), p. 162.

497 "Two minutes before, I had no intention of retiring for two more years": Wooden interview with ESPN, Apr. 19, 2000.

498 "Jerry wasn't a 'yes man,' by any means": "Bruins' Wooden Fought Against Installing Press," *Los Angeles Times*, Feb. 5, 1969.

498 "As far as the pressing defense was concerned": Johnson, *John Wooden Pyramid of Success*, p. 42.

498 "I decided to stick with something that had been very successful for me at Indiana State and high school": Hall of Fame interview.

500 "One assistant suggested that we bring back a zone press": Wooden and Yaeger, *Game Plan for Life*, p. 84.

501 "He's just a tough, cold guy": Chapin and Prugh, *Wizard of Westwood*, p. 307.

35. YONDER

Interviews: Kareem Abdul-Jabbar, Lucius Allen, Bill Bennett, Henry Bibby, Pete Blackman, Dick Enberg, Doug Erickson, Keith Erickson, Larry Farmer, Bob Field, Valorie Kondos Field, John Green, Jim Harrick, Walt Hazzard, Andy Hill, Ben Howland, Marques Johnson, Mike Lynn, Bill Walton, Mike Warren, Jeff Weiss, Jamaal Wilkes, Sidney Wicks

505 "Hardly a day goes by that I don't get a call or a letter": Academy of Achievement interview.

509 Afterward, Cathleen asked Wooden who the man was. He said he had no idea: Johnson, *John Wooden Pyramid of Success*, p. 242.

509 "I won't say that I'm not flattered by things of that sort": Hall of Fame interview.

509 Nan, like Nell, would interject with a sharp, "Then don't": Ibid.

510 "I can't believe people are that stupid": Bisheff, *John Wooden*, p. 183.

510 Dellins called Wooden because he had heard a rumor that Wooden had died: "Wooden Has Too Much Life Left in Him to Call It Quits," *Los Angeles Times*, May 1, 2009.

511 He put a baby monitor beside Wooden's bed: "No One Cared for John Wooden Like Tony Spino," *Los Angeles Times*, Aug. 20, 2011.

512 "Most of the time he's not who he was": "UCLA Coaching Legend John Wooden Celebrates His Birthday Today," *Daily News of Los Angeles*, Oct. 14, 2009.

514 "I'm working on it": Nan Wooden, "Faith, Love and Basketball," *Guideposts*, May 2012.

Acknowledgments

Having spent more than four years deeply embedded in the life of John Wooden, I have developed a profound appreciation for teamwork. So let me begin by acknowledging my most important teammate, Paul Golob, editor extraordinaire at Times Books. It is a part of the writer's DNA to harbor a healthy suspicion (if not outright disdain) for that mercurial species known as "editor," but Paul, who also edited my previous book, *When March Went Mad*, was once again an indispensable asset. His diligence, thoughtfulness, fairness, and impeccable judgment are reflected on every page. I thank him for his strong guidance, his gentle touch, and most of all, his enduring friendship.

The other member of my team's inner circle is my literary agent, David Black. Once again, David went above and beyond the duties laid out in the agent's handbook to serve as an invaluable reader and editor. David's client list includes many authors who are far more talented and successful than I am, but I always know that David will take my call and have my back. Like Paul, he's not just my teammate: he's my very good friend, and I wouldn't have it any other way.

The other critical voice in the editorial process belonged to Rob Fleder. Besides being one of the founding fathers of fantasy sports (how many of you are old enough to remember Rotisserie Baseball?), Rob is a gifted editor who provided some terrific notes that helped us pare down the first draft.

Managing the material for a research-intensive book like this can be tedious and cumbersome, so I took care to utilize (some might say "exploit") the industriousness and enthusiasm proffered by my team of interns. These youngsters stand as a powerful counter against the suspicion that the future of journalism will be less substantive than its past. I heartily endorse them for any jobs they seek. They are: Matt Bloom, Steve Brauntuch, Paul

"Bulldog" Brown, Elliot Cook, Ryan Eshoff, Ryan Feldman, Derek Johnson, Patricia Lee, Matt Norlander, Tessa Rabinowitz, Theo Rabinowitz, Steve Silver, and Kurt Wagner. Special thanks to Chris Taylor, director of Ball State University's Sports Link program, for connecting me with Paul, Derek, and the rest of his fabulous students. Thanks also to my CBS colleague Wayne Fidelman for helping to compile the endnotes.

I benefited from the generosity of several sportswriting colleagues who provided recollections as well as transcripts and/or notes from their interactions with Wooden. The transcripts provided by Alan Karpick, John Akers, and ESPN's Josh Krulewitz were very helpful, but I owe a special debt of gratitude to Joe Jares, formerly of *Sports Illustrated*. I could never have imagined when I walked into Joe's Los Angeles home in the summer of 2010 that he would hand me a thick folder teeming with papers on Wooden that had been sitting in his file cabinet, just waiting for me to come and claim it. Many of those files included long quotes from key people in Wooden's life who long ago passed away. Joe was also kind enough to provide me with copies of his handwritten notes from his own visits with Wooden.

As I went about my travels, I met with gracious hosts who showed me the sights and put me in touch with people I needed to see. That includes Jim Powers in South Bend and Joanne Stuttgen in Martinsville. Not only did Joanne share her wealth of knowledge about the history of Morgan County, she took me on a driving tour of Martinsville and then brought me to Centerton, where we paid our respects at the Wooden family cemetery. Seeing that headstone with the word "INFANT" engraved on it where Wooden's sister was buried was my most moving experience while working on this project.

John Kovach, who works at the St. Joseph County Public Library in South Bend, did yeoman's work assembling many years' worth of newspaper clips on Wooden's coaching days at South Bend. Without his thoroughness, I never would have discovered that Wooden had a losing season there, which had never been reported. Thanks as well to Charlotte Brown in the archives office at the Charles Young Research Library at UCLA.

Clarence Walker's children, Kevin Walker and Adrienne Garrett, cooked me dinner in East Chicago, Indiana, and shared memories of their father. They also provided me with a copy of Clarence's diary from his playing days at Indiana State.

As for the extended UCLA basketball family, I am of course grateful to all of the people I interviewed for this book. Their contributions are recognized in my endnotes, but I would like to give an extra thanks to

Jerry Norman, who provided me with a list of contact information and sat with me as we watched old black-and-white films from Wooden's early years, and Eddie Sheldrake, who invited me to several reunion lunches at his Polly's Pies restaurant in Carson, California. (I loved those lunches even though Eddie always introduced me as "that goddamn liberal from New York.") Lucius Allen, Keith Erickson, Gail Goodrich, and Andy Hill indulged me during multiple interviews so I could properly flesh out this story.

At UCLA, I am thankful for the help extended by athletic director Dan Guerrero, former basketball coach Ben Howland, and director of executive relations Marc Dellins. I also cannot say enough good things about Bill Bennett, the school's former sports information director for men's basketball. As I wrote in the text, Bill was UCLA's steward for all things Wooden during the last decade of the coach's life, and he continues to serve as keeper of the Wooden flame for the university. Bill and Coach shared a birthday, so it makes sense that they should possess the same gentle qualities. That is, if you believe in that sort of thing, which I suppose I do.

In the Wooden tradition, allow me to point a finger to acknowledge two critical assists. One came from Howard Deneroff, the executive producer for Westwood One radio and a longtime friend, who helped me score a key interview that had been eluding me for some time. The other assist came from Bill Boyd, who convinced his reluctant father, Bob, to meet with me.

I would be remiss if I did not call special attention to Ken Heitz, UCLA Class of '69, who succumbed to cancer at the far-too-young age of sixty-five. The three-hour conversation I had with Ken in his law office was the most enjoyable, productive interview I conducted for this book. I had several subsequent conversations with Ken, and he stayed in constant touch through e-mail to help me chase down his fellow Bruins. Ken was also kind enough to invite me to his gorgeous house for a UCLA reunion. I miss him, but not nearly as much as his teammates do.

I am blessed to be a part of two of the most prestigious brands in sports journalism in CBS Sports and *Sports Illustrated*. I've got a lot of bosses who are great at what they do, and I appreciate that they take a genuine interest in my career. (Not that I'm sucking up or anything.) So thanks to the powers that be at CBS (Sean McManus, David Berson, Harold Bryant, Steve Karasik, and Dan Weinberg) and *SI* (Paul Fichtenbaum, Terry McDonell, Chris Stone, Jon Wertheim, Matt Bean, and B. J. Schecter). I also want to give a shout-out to my superlative management team at IMG: Sandy Montag, Ira Stahlberger, and Aimee Leone. I'm not really *that* high maintenance, am I? (Don't answer that.) And at Times Books and Henry Holt, I would like to thank Stephen Rubin, Maggie Richards, Patricia Eisemann, Katie Kurtzman, and Emi Ikkanda.

Thank you, Sons of Equinunk.

Finally, and most important, I want to acknowledge my loving and supportive family, who fill my world with all the *naches* and *mishegoss* that make life worth living. Thanks to Lanny, Carolyn, Josh, and Jeremy Davis; Nevin and Elaine Gibson; David, Marlo, Jake, Sydney, and Devon Sims; Harvey and Gail Cohen; Ian, Allison, Samantha, and Benjamin Cohen; and the most beautiful of them all, my grandmother-in-law, Miriam Cohen.

This book is dedicated to my three sons—Zachary Charney Davis, Noah Michael Davis, and Gabriel Frances Davis—who drive me crazy and keep me sane at the same time. I realize it will be some time before you guys are old enough to read this book, but when you do, I hope it helps you understand why I was such a stickler about making sure you put on your shoes and socks properly before soccer practice. As for Melissa Beth Cohen Davis, aka "The Big Boss," I can only say that I have never felt more grateful, humbled, and blessed that you decided to marry me, of all people. Thank you for being my best friend. Now what say we move to California?

Ridgefield, Connecticut
May 2013

INDEX

About the Author

SETH DAVIS is the author of the *New York Times* bestseller *When March Went Mad: The Game That Transformed Basketball* and the memoir *Equinunk, Tell Your Story: My Return to Summer Camp*. In 1995, he joined the staff of *Sports Illustrated*, where he is currently a senior writer. He is also an on-air studio analyst for CBS Sports and CBS Sports Network during coverage of college basketball and the NCAA tournament. A graduate of Duke University, he lives with his family in Los Angeles.